Time Out
Los Angeles

Penguin Books

PENGUIN BOOKS

Published by the Penguin Group
Penguin Books Ltd, 27 Wrights Lane, London W8 5TZ, England
Penguin Books USA Inc., 375 Hudson Street, New York, New York 10014, USA
Penguin Books Australia Ltd, Ringwood, Victoria, Australia
Penguin Books Canada Ltd, 10 Alcorn Avenue, Toronto, Ontario, Canada M4V 3B2
Penguin Books (NZ) Ltd, 182-190 Wairau Road, Auckland 10, New Zealand

Penguin Books Ltd, Registered Offices: Harmondsworth, Middlesex, England

First published 1997
Second edition 1999
10 9 8 7 6 5 4 3 2 1

Copyright © Time Out Group Ltd, 1997, 1999
All rights reserved

Colour reprographics by Precise Litho, 34-35 Great Sutton Street, London EC1
Printed and bound by William Clowes Ltd, Beccles, Suffolk NR34 9QE

Edited and designed by

Time Out Magazine Limited
Universal House
251 Tottenham Court Road
London W1P 0AB
Tel +44 (0) 171 813 3000
Fax +44 (0) 171 813 6001
E-mail guides@timeout.co.uk
http://www.timeout.com

Editorial

Editoral Director Peter Fiennes
Editor Cath Phillips
Deputy Editor Julian Richards
Consultant Editor Frances Anderton
Listings Editor/Staff Writer Matthew Duersten
Proofreader Tamsin Shelton
Indexer Jacqueline Brind

Design

Art Director John Oakey
Art Editor Mandy Martin
Designers Benjamin de Lotz, Thomas Ludewig, Lucy Grant, Scott Moore
Scanner Operator Chris Quinn
Picture Editor Kerri Miles
Assistant Picture Editor Rupert Nightingale
Picture Researcher Kit Burnet

Advertising

Group Advertisement Director Lesley Gill
Sales Director Mark Phillips
Advertising Director North American Guides Liz Howell (1-800 920 1974, access code ext 11)
Advertising Assistant Ingrid Sigerson

Administration

Publisher Tony Elliott
Managing Director Mike Hardwick
Financial Director Kevin Ellis
Marketing Director Gillian Auld
General Manager Nichola Coulthard
Production Manager Mark Lamond
Production Controller Matthew Forrester
Accountant Catherine Bowen

Features in this guide were written and researched by:

Introduction Frances Anderton. **History** William Fulton. **LA Today** Mick Farren (*Let's get spiritual* Frances Anderton).
Geography & Climate William Fulton. **Celebrity LA** Lesley O'Toole. **Car City** Frances Anderton. **Architecture** Frances
Anderton, Michael Webb. **Ethnic LA** Frances Anderton. **Sightseeing** Frances Anderton, Laura Connolly, Cary Darling,
David Eimer, Dan Epstein, Mary Forgione (*Take a hike*), William Fulton, Martin Hernàndez, Rochelle Mills, Peter Relic.
Los Angeles by Season Matthew Duersten, Katie Klapper. **Accommodation** Erika Lenkert. **Restaurants** Kathryn
Harris. **Coffeehouses** Lesley O'Toole, Victoria Tilney. **Bars** Dan Epstein. **Shops & Services** Kathryn Harris. **Children**
Melissa Payton, Dian Phillips. **Film** Robin E Rauzi, David Eimer. **Gay** John D'Amico. **Lesbian** Jennifer C Swiatek,
Kimberly Wallace. **Media** Dan Epstein (*'Zine scene* Matthew Duersten). **Museums & Galleries** Peter Frank, Lisa
Auerbach (*The Getty Center* Frances Anderton). **Music** Dan Epstein, Martin Fleischmann. **Nightlife** Peter Relic, Dan
O'Connor. **Sport & Fitness** Peter Relic, David Eimer, Kathryn Harris, Nick Karno, Katie Klapper. **Theatre** Dee Dokus,
Victoria Tilney. **Dance** David Gere, Joanne Parkes. **Trips Out of Town** Frances Anderton, Mary Forgione (*Skiing & snow-boarding*), Gus Funnell. **Directory** Matthew Duersten, David Eimer, Rebecca Epstein, Lesley O'Toole, Julian Richards.

The editors would like to thank the following:

Jonathan Liebhold, Lisa Sichi, Chris Rhodes, Tatiana Alvarez, Metropolitan Transit Authority, Caro Taverne, Ruth
Jarvis, Zoë Sanders, David Oshinski & Ramada West Hollywood.

Maps by JS Graphics, Hill View Cottage, 17 Beadles Lane, Old Oxted, Surrey RH8 9JG.

Photography by Laurence Cottrell except: p4, p11, p240 Corbis; p7 Hamish Hamilton; p7 Geff Hinds; p8 Archive
Photos; p12 Neal Preston/Corbis; p13, p19 Associated Press; p16 California Department of Health Services; p21,
p89 Popperfoto; p28, p196, p199, p241 Cath Phillips; p33 Joshua White; p1, p39, p49, p79 Los Angeles
CVB/Michele & Tom Grimm; p85 Elizabeth Annas; p185 Press Association; piii, p1, p3, p25, p44, p45, p48 p175,
p220, p229 p252 Martin Salter; p208 Jesse Chornesky; p233 Holly Stein; p234 Daniel Scott; p241, p244, p250
Robert Harding; p235, p242 Charlie Varley; p245 Image Bank; p246 World Pictures; p247 Jon Perugia; p249, p251
Colorific. The following photographs were supplied by the featured establishments: p30, p99, p135, p184.

Cath Phillips flew to Los Angeles with Virgin Atlantic (reservations: UK 01293 747747; US 1-800 862 8621).

Contents

About the Guide

This is the second edition of the *Time Out Los Angeles* guide, one in an ever-expanding series of city guides produced by the people behind London and New York's successful listings magazines: we now cover more than 20 cities around the world. All the contributors to the guide are resident in Los Angeles and specialists in the subjects on which they have written.

We offer advice on how to orientate yourself in the city sprawl and find within it not only the recognised tourist sites and Hollywood shrines, but access to a city life the way Angelenos know it. And because getting to know Los Angeles is as much about experiencing a state of mind as seeing specific sights, we've included a section called In Context, which includes information on such subjects as LA's particular geographical features and natural disasters, its multi-ethnic communities, the cult of celebrity and the significance of the automobile in the city's psyche.

DETAILS, DETAILS, DETAILS

Above all, we've tried to make this book as useful as possible. Addresses, telephone numbers, transport details, opening times, admission times and credit card details are all included in our listings. We've also given details of facilities, services and events and included fully indexed maps to the most frequented areas of the city, as well as a map of Metro routes.

Many of our chapters are subdivided into areas, so your choice of restaurant, for example, doesn't have to be a schlep away from where you are. We've provided detailed driving directions, giving not only the address and cross street for places listed but instructions on how to reach them from the most convenient freeway or major road. (The exit given might not always be the nearest, but it should result in the fastest and most straightforward journey.)

TELEPHONE NUMBERS

All phone numbers in the guide are prefaced by a 1 and an area code; for example 1-310 923 1361. If you are dialling from within that area, you can drop the 1 and the area code. If you're calling from abroad, you still need to put a 1 before the area code: it's the code for the USA. At the time of writing, Los Angeles's area codes are changing; for details on the changes (and more on telephones in general), *see page 264* **Directory**. You can dial most (but not all) 1-800 numbers from the UK, but they are not toll-free: you must pay for the call at the usual transatlantic rate.

CREDIT CARDS

The following abbreviations have been used for credit cards: **AmEX** American Express; **DC** Diners' Club; **Disc** Discover; **JCB** Japanese credit cards; **MC** Mastercard; and **V** Visa. Virtually all shops, restaurants, hotels and attractions will accept dollar travellers' cheques issued by a major financial institution (such as American Express).

PRICES

The prices we've supplied should be treated as guidelines, not gospel. Fluctuating exchange rates and inflation can cause prices to change rapidly, particularly in shops and restaurants. Note that prices marked in shops do not include sales tax, currently 8.25 per cent in LA County. If prices vary wildly from those we've quoted, ask whether there's a good reason. If not, go elsewhere. Then please write and let us know. We aim to give the best and most up-to-date advice, so we want to know if you've been badly treated or overcharged.

CHECKED AND CORRECT

All listings information and other factual details are thoroughly checked during production of the guide. Inevitably, however, businesses open and close, change their hours or alter their service in some other way. Therefore we recommend you always phone ahead before going out of your way. While every effort and care has been made to ensure the accuracy of the information contained in this guide, the publishers cannot accept responsibility for any errors it may contain.

RIGHT TO REPLY

It should be stressed that the information we give is impartial. No organisation has been included in this guide because its owner or manager has advertised in our publications. We hope you enjoy the *Time Out Los Angeles Guide*, but we'd also like to know if you don't. We welcome tips for places that you think we should include in future editions and take notice of your criticism of our choices. There's a reader's reply card for your comments at the back of the book.

> There is an online version of this guide, as well as weekly events listings for several international cities, at http://www.timeout.com.

Introduction

Everyone is on the move in Los Angeles. Go to the beach at the weekend and see – speeding past on rollerblades and bicycles – Lycra-clad grannies, pony-tailed dads, over-fed, wobbly visitors and underfed, impossibly gorgeous Angelenos of every ethnicity. Hit the roads on a weekday and join the thousands of drivers, tuned to the radio or car phone, navigating their lives via the streets and freeways. Take to the mountains and locals will be hiking and mountain-biking, or, when the snows come, skiing.

The essence of Los Angeles is mobility: literal, metaphorical, upward, downward. LA is about freedom from social and physical restrictions, the pursuit of which has generated a place without a centre, defined by the car and symbolised by its freeways. It is inhabited by a pan-national citizenry loosely united by a sense of possibility that's inflated by Hollywood's self-mythologising. With success, however, has come a flipside; Los Angeles is beset by urban unrest, smog and environmental disasters – ingredients for LA's popular apocalyptic image.

But this concrete jungle is a place of fascinating complexity, and one that does not reveal its secrets instantly. It's a high-tech city in a stupendous and volatile natural environment. Depending on where you are, it feels: Anglo, Latino, Jewish, gay, super-rich, third world. While known for its theme parks, malls, movies and junk food, LA is now a world player in the arts thanks to its new Getty Center, its superlative orchestra, and numerous museums, galleries and theatres. Los Angeles draws readers to its many bookstores and gourmets to its unbeatable selection of ethnic and eclectic cuisines.

While it appears to be overwhelmingly vast and characterless, LA is, like older cities, a collection of small neighbourhoods and municipalities, each with their own distinct identity, charms, pedestrian areas (yes, you can walk in LA) as well as geography and micro-climate. Choose from, for starters: bohemian, beachside Venice; exclusive, lush Beverly Hills; hilly and hip West Hollywood or Silver Lake; the suburban, scorching Valley; gritty Downtown or the surfing cities of the South Bay.

When in LA, don't go looking for a New York-style urban experience. Do as Angelenos do: get a car and take to the road. Forget standard notions about time and space – expect to travel huge distances in a short time, and enjoy the view while you're at it. Ringed by mountains and the shimmering Pacific Ocean, usually drenched in bright blue skies, LA is unbeatable for sheer natural splendour.

Los Angeles is about mobility, and liberation. Savour the expansiveness of a place where the palm trees are taller than many buildings, where every house is different, where complete strangers, who may be short on irony but long on good will, not only greet you but are soon sharing their dreams, their personal problems and, best of all, their hot tips for what you should do in their LA.
Frances Anderton

In Context

History

For two centuries, LA has hoodwinked its way through boom and bust. Speculation, fantasy and sleaze have fuelled its growth from dusty cow town to the mega-metropolis of today.

1883 woodcut: 'Founders of Los Angeles'.

PRE-1888: MISSIONS & COW TOWNS

Perhaps it shouldn't be surprising, given Los Angeles's more recent history, that human settlement here began with a series of Native American single-family suburbs scattered across the landscape in seemingly haphazard fashion. Prior to the arrival of Spanish colonists in the latter part of the eighteenth century, what is now metropolitan LA was populated by some 30,000 Native Americans. But they were not farmers – they relied on hunting and native plants for food – and, unlike the Iroquois and other tribes in North America, they had not organised into strong political confederations. Instead, they lived in small settlements surrounding the area's few rivers, each group adopting a separate identity (the names most of them are known by today – Gabrieleno, Juaneno, Luisenos and so on – were given them by the Spanish).

The Spanish arrived in 1769 and established a string of Franciscan missions along the Californian coast (the first at San Diego), backed by military muscle. The San Gabriel mission was founded in 1771, marking the first Spanish foray into the Los Angeles area. The supposed purpose of the missions was to spread the Christian faith and the early Franciscan missionaries, especially their leader Father Junipéro Serra, have been glorified over the centuries. In fact, mission life was feudal and even brutal, especially for the reluctant Native American converts. They were rounded up from their small settlements and virtually enslaved by the Franciscans, and thousands died – a problem that forced the missions to expand deep into the countryside in search of more converts.

The history of Los Angeles as a city dates back to 1781 – the same year that the British surrendered to George Washington in Virginia, ending the American War of Independence – when the Spaniards decided they needed a settlement, or pueblo, in Southern California to serve as a way-station for the military. A site was selected nine miles east of the San Gabriel mission, where the Los Angeles River widened from a narrows. California's military governor, Felipe De Neve, laid out a plaza 275 by 180 feet (84 by 55 metres), with lots around it, each with a 55-foot (17-metre) wide frontage on the plaza. He commissioned his aides to recruit 24 settlers and their families from Sonora, over 300 miles (480 kilometres) away, and on 18 August 1781, after a forced march of 100 days through desert heat, what remained of this group arrived at the plaza: 12 men, 11 women and 21 children. They were immediately quarantined because of smallpox. What is left of the plaza can be viewed at El Pueblo de Los Angeles Historical Monument (more commonly known as Olvera Street), a 44-acre (18-hectare) historical area in downtown LA, bounded by Alameda, Arcadia, Spring and Macy Streets. As many writers have observed, El Pueblo de Nuestra Señora la Reina de Los Angeles began as it has always grown – not with a hardy band of motivated settlers, but with a real estate agent looking for customers.

The new settlement remained a dusty cow town for decades – in 1800 the population was 315 people and 12,500 cows. But other missions were added in what would become the Los Angeles area,

including San Buenaventura, San Fernando and
San Juan Capistrano (for more information on the
Spanish missions and how to visit them, *see page
246* **Trips Out of Town**).

After Mexico declared itself independent and
annexed California in 1822, Spanish-born priests
were ordered out of California, the mission system
broke down and powerful local families – eager to
exploit mission land – received dozens of large
land grants from the Mexican government. Most
of these 'ranchos', typically several thousand acres
in size, were recognised as valid claims of title
when California entered the United States in 1850.
Many remained intact into the twentieth century
– one of many factors that allowed large-scale,
mass-production land development to occur in LA.

The Americans had been informally colonising
LA throughout the era of Mexican rule, as oppor-
tunists arrived in town, married into prominent
'Spanish' families, and called themselves 'Don Otto'
or 'Don Bill'. The actual transfer of the cow town
into US hands occurred during the forcible annex-
ation of California that triggered the Mexican-
American war of June 1846. Two months later, on
13 August, Commodore RF Stockton landed at San
Pedro with 500 marines and started his march to
the pueblo. With political support from the 'Dons',
he captured the settlement without firing a shot.
The US-Mexican treaty of 1848 confirmed US
dominion over California and in 1850 it officially
became the 31st state of the Union.

Los Angeles grew steadily but unspectacularly
for the next 20 years, becoming a centre of
California's 'hide-and-tallow' trade – raising cattle
and selling the hides for coats and the fat for
candle tallow to trading companies from the East
Coast and Europe. California's first literary masterpiece, Richard Henry Dana's *Two Years Before
the Mast*, features memorable scenes of Dana himself trudging through the shallow water of San
Pedro harbour with cowhides on his back. When
the Gold Rush hit Northern California in 1848,
however, the cattle barons of Los Angeles discovered they could sell the cows for beef at $30 a head
to the goldfields, rather than $3 a head to the
traders. The 1872 publication of Helen Hunt
Jackson's novel *Ramona*, which romanticised
rancho life at the expense of historical accuracy,
sparked a period of national publicity and interest
in Southern California.

In 1886, the transcontinental railroad from St
Louis to Los Angeles was completed, bringing
with it the long-expected – but short-lived – boom.
A price war broke out among the railroads, and
the cost of a one-way ticket to LA dropped from
$125 to $1. In 1887, Southern Pacific Railroad
transported 120,000 people to Los Angeles, then a
city of about 10,000 residents. The result was LA's
first real-estate boom, with more than 100 communities subdivided in a four-year period.

Key events

1771 Spanish mission established at San Gabriel.
1781 Pueblo of Los Angeles founded on present
site of the Olvera Street Plaza.
1822 Mexico declares independence from Spain
and annexes California, freeing Los Angeles from
Spanish rule.
1846 US marines land at San Pedro and take
Los Angeles pueblo from the Mexican army
without a fight.
1848 US-Mexican treaty confirms US dominion
over California.
1850 California becomes the 31st state of
the Union.
1851 California recognises most large Spanish
land grants in the Los Angeles area.
1868 Transcontinental railroad reaches San
Franciso, opening up California to the East.
1886 Transcontinental railroad reaches
Los Angeles.
1887 Fare war cuts cost of one-way trip from
St Louis to Los Angeles from $125 to $1.
1888 City experiences first real-estate boom.
Chamber of Commerce is set up and begins
promoting LA in the Midwest.
1889 City experiences first real-estate bust.
1902 Rose Parade is founded.
1906 Los Angeles announces plans to build
aqueduct from Owens Valley.
1913 Owens Valley aqueduct opens.
1917 US enters World War 1.
1923 Biltmore Hotel opens in Downtown
Los Angeles.
1928 District attorney Asa Keyes is indicted on
bribery charge after losing case against oil-stock
swindlers.
1929 Stock market crashes; Depression begins.
1932 Los Angeles hosts the Olympics for the
first time.
1933 Long Beach earthquake.
1934 Upton Sinclair nearly elected Governor of
California.
1937 Auto Club of Southern California proposes
freeway system.
1939 The Arroyo Seco Parkway (Pasadena
Freeway) opens.
1941 US enters World War II.
1943 Zoot Suit riots.
1955 Disneyland opens in Anaheim.
1958 Brooklyn Dodgers baseball team moves to
Los Angeles.
1965 Watts riots erupt.
1966 Ronald Reagan elected Governor of
California.
1969 Charles Manson and followers murder
Sharon Tate.
1971 Sylmar earthquake hits.
1973 Tom Bradley elected mayor of Los Angeles.
1984 Los Angeles hosts the Olympics for the
second time.
1990 Cutbacks in defence budget hits LA.
1991 Rodney King arrested.
1992 King verdict sparks widespread rioting.
1994 Northridge earthquake hits.
1995 OJ Simpson acquitted of murdering his wife.
1998 Rupert Murdoch buys the LA Dodgers
baseball team. Former mayor Tom Bradley dies.

Paper fortunes were made overnight – and then lost when the boom shrivelled in 1889. 'I had half a million dollars wiped out in the crash,' one fictional character reported in a novel. 'And what's worse, $500 of it was cash.' The population had grown dramatically, in part because many immigrants could not afford to leave. But, despite the crash, the boom of the 1880s had permanently transformed Los Angeles from a cow town into a fast-growing hustlers' paradise.

1888-1929: BOOMS AND BUSTS

After the boom of the 1880s, the land barons and real-estate operators who came to dominate Los Angeles's growth were determined to build a more solid basis for expansion. Forming the Los Angeles Chamber of Commerce in 1888, they took the unprecedented step of embarking on a nation-wide campaign, focused on the Midwest, to attract new immigrants. It was this campaign that led the journalist Morrow Mayo, writing in the 1930s, to conclude that Los Angeles was not a city but 'a commodity; something to be advertised and sold to the people of the United States like automobiles, cigarettes and mouth washes'.

The Chamber of Commerce began sending speakers, advertisements and brochures to the Midwest; 1902 saw the launch of the Rose Bowl (a college football game held on New Year's Day) and the preceding Rose Parade (in which flower-covered floats parade through Pasadena), as a promotion for LA's sunny climate. It was not long before the advertisements had the desired effect and, as commodity prices rose in the first decade of the new century, thousands of Midwestern farmers sold out and a new boom ensued.

Encouraged by the boom, the city's land barons pulled off one of the most audacious and duplicitous schemes ever devised to ensure a city's future greatness. In 1904, a former mayor of Los Angeles named Fred Eaton went to the Owens Valley – a high-desert region 230 miles (370 kilometres) north of Los Angeles – claiming that he was working on a dam project for the federal government, and began buying land along the Owens River. Once the land was purchased, Eaton said the federal project was dead and revealed his true purpose: to divert the Owens River through an aqueduct to LA.

Whipped into a frenzy by trumped-up fears of a drought, LA voters approved a bond issue in 1905 to build an aqueduct from the Owens Valley to the city. LA had enough water to serve the population at the time, but not enough to grow. As William Mulholland, the city's water engineer, put it at the time: 'If we don't get it, we won't need it.' Mulholland, a self-taught Irish immigrant, then accomplished one of the great engineering feats in US history. Eighty years after its completion, his 230-mile (370km) aqueduct still operates, without electrical power, entirely on a gravity system. 'There

it is,' Mulholland told the people of Los Angeles when the floodway opened in 1913. 'Take it.'

The aqueduct didn't come to Los Angeles proper, however. Instead, it went only as far as the San Fernando Valley, an adjacent farming region. In the last – and most masterful – part of the scam, Los Angeles's land barons had secretly bought the valley cheaply, annexed it to the city and then splashed Owens Valley water on to it for irrigation, greatly increasing its value. Today, the San Fernando Valley, population 1.3 million, is the prototypical US suburb, and its people regularly chafe under the LA City controls that brought water to their valley in the first place. The past few years have seen a renewed attempt by Valley 'secessionists' to break off from Los Angeles and form their own city.

With the water in place, Los Angeles boomed in the 1910s and 1920s as did no other US city – partly on the strength of real-estate speculation, and partly on the rise of three new industries: petroleum, aircraft and movies.

With little natural wood and almost no coal, isolated Los Angeles had always had a fuel crisis almost as severe as its water crisis. The discovery of oil throughout metropolitan Los Angeles between 1900 and 1925 changed all that. Oil fields were discovered around the La Brea Tar Pits and in Huntington Beach and Santa Fe Springs. The result was a plentiful supply of oil that enriched the region and helped to fuel the city's growing love affair with the car.

More dispersed than any other US city, Los Angeles took to the car more readily than anywhere except Detroit. Soon the city had its own thriving oil, automobile and tyre industries, each with their own monuments. In 1928, Adolph Schleicher, president of Samson Tire & Rubber Co, constructed an $8 million tyre plant modelled after a royal palace once built by the king of Assyria. The plant (at 5675 Telegraph Road, City of Commerce) has recently been reborn as a retailing mecca known as the Citadel.

Movies and aircraft came to LA during the 1910s, and for the same reasons: the area's temperate weather, low rainfall and cheap land provided the wide open spaces that both needed to operate. Donald Douglas founded his aircraft company (a predecessor to McDonnell-Douglas) at Clover Field in Santa Monica – now the Santa Monica Municipal Airport – in 1921, while the Lockheed brothers started their company in Santa Barbara in 1914 before moving it to LA. Jack Northrop, who had worked with both Douglas and the Lockheeds, started his own company in Burbank in 1928. All three firms later formed the foundation of the US's 'military-industrial' complex.

Filming began in Los Angeles around 1910, and moved to Hollywood when the Blondeau Tavern at Gower Street and Sunset Boulevard was turned

The Chandler legacy

From the beginning, the clash of pure ideals and the seamy realities of urban life have given Los Angeles an edge unlike any other city. The founders of Hollywood were determined to create a teetotalling, moralistic alternative to sordid urbanity – and they stuck to it until they sold out the whole town to the entertainment industry. Ever since, the tension between LA the dream and LA the reality has fuelled a 'noir' culture, exploring the unpleasant reality against a sun-splashed backdrop.

No writer has captured this dichotomy better than Raymond Chandler (*see* **photo** *above*), who wrote several Philip Marlowe detective novels between 1939 and 1958. Born in Nebraska, Chandler grew up in Ireland and Britain and was a contemporary of PG Wodehouse at Dulwich public school. He bounced around the United States and served in the Canadian armed forces during World War I before settling in Los Angeles permanently in 1919.

Chandler's timing was perfect. Los Angeles was about to embark upon a decade of growth unprecedented in American history. And he was lucky enough to get a job in the city's sleaziest and most exciting business – oil. The tarry liquid had recently been discovered on the outskirts of the city, and even residential subdivisions were being torn out to make way for gushing derricks. In a region that had almost no coal or wood, oil was crucial.

As a vice-president of Dabney Oil Co, Chandler quickly came to understand the relationship between LA's snooty new wealth and its sordid dark corners. His novels are filled with men and women of modest beginnings who are trying to hide or eradicate – always unsuccessfully – their past behind the conspicuous consumption characteristic of the 1920s. Chandler couldn't handle his success any better. Like one of the broken-down characters in his books, he lapsed into alcoholism and womanising, lost his job and was broke for almost a decade before publishing his first novel, the classic *The Big Sleep*, at the age of 50.

In the 1940s, Chandler and Billy Wilder adapted James M Cain's classic LA noir novel *Double Indemnity* for the screen – breaking new ground for wickedness and treachery in the movies. Soon the highest-paid screenwriter in Hollywood, Chandler became famous for his ability to write while drunk and even persuaded producer John Houseman to provide him with a car and a driver so he could drink continuously and therefore finish a screenwriting assignment more quickly.

Since then, Chandler's heirs have returned again and again to LA for noir inspiration – from Roman Polanski's classic film *Chinatown* to the screaming, horrific novels of James Ellroy (*see* **photo** *right*), who is still haunted by his mother's unsolved 1958 murder in El Monte (as described in his searingly brilliant book *My Dark Places*). Ellroy was at the forefront of the LA 'noir revival' of the 1990s: police corruption and the city's seamy underside ooze out of his quartet of novels set in LA in the 1940s and 1950s – the most famous of which, *LA Confidential*, was turned into a hit film. Angelenos don't know quite what to make of their noir masters because they don't want to admit that life in LA has a downside.

into a movie studio overnight in 1911. At the time, Hollywood was being marketed as a pious and sedate suburb of large homes, and the intrusion of the film industry was resented. The movie business was never really centred there, however; Culver City and Burbank, which also have studios, have equally strong claims as the capital of film land. Nevertheless, Hollywood became the financial and social centre of the industry, growing from a population of 4,000 in 1910 to 30,000 in 1920 to 235,000 in 1930, and the wealth of the period is still visible today in the magnificent commercial architecture along Hollywood Boulevard between Cahuenga and Highland Avenues. The early movie palaces (some still in operation today) were built not in Hollywood but downtown on Broadway, adjacent to Spring Street. For more on the history of the film industry, *see chapter* **Film**.

LA's first freeway was built in 1939. City Hall was the tallest building until 1957.

In the 1920s, when the population of Los Angeles doubled, the city was a kind of 'national suburb' where the middle class sought refuge from the teeming immigrant classes evident in other large cities. During this period, civic leaders worked hard to build the edifices and institutions they thought a big city should have, including the Biltmore Hotel and the adjacent Los Angeles Central Library, Los Angeles City Hall, the University of Southern California and adjacent Exposition Park, and Los Angeles Coliseum. LA also became the financial capital of the West Coast during this decade with the creation of the Los Angeles (now Pacific) Stock Exchange. The 'Wall Street of the West' was centred on Spring Street, between Third and Eighth Streets, where many of the original buildings remain today.

However, this same process of making LA the great 'white' city marginalised the minority groups that had always been a part of life here. The Mexican and Mexican-American population, which was growing rapidly to provide labourers for the expanding city, was pushed out of downtown into what is now the East LA barrio. African-Americans, who had previously lived all over the city, became confined to an area south of downtown straddling Central Avenue, which became known as South Central. Both these developments laid the foundation for later social unrest.

Still, Los Angeles in the 1920s had an irrepressible energy that even its critics loved. The boom and the arrival of so many newcomers created a rootlessness that manifested itself in a thousand different ways, many of which provided the seeds for the city's later kooky reputation. Those in need of companionship were drawn to the city's many cafeterias (invented in LA), which served as incubators of random social activity. Those in need of a restored faith had (and still have) their choice of any number of high-profile faith healers. And those with a little cash searching for a quick profit were drawn to the tantalising claims of local oil companies in search of investors.

Indeed, nothing captures a sense of the primal energy of Los Angeles during the 1920s as well as stories from the oil business. With a steady supply of gushers spouting in the suburbs (often in residential neighbourhoods), oil promoters had a ready-made promotional device with which to attract investors. With a stream of equity-rich farm refugees from the Midwest, they also had a ready-made pool of gullible investors. The promoters took out newspaper ads, held weekend barbecues at the gushers and used other strong-arm tactics to attract investment.

The most skilled oil promoter was a Canadian immigrant named CC Julian, who attracted millions of dollars to his oil company with a string of daily newspaper ads that had the narrative drive of a continuing soap opera. When it became clear that Julian couldn't deliver on his investment promises, he was elbowed out of his own firm by an array of other swindlers who continued the scam and turned it into the longest-running scandal of the 1920s. By the time it was all over, Julian Petroleum had issued millions of bogus shares and the district attorney had been indicted on a bribery charge. The end came in 1931, when a defrauded investor opened fire in a LA courtroom on a banker who had been involved in the scam. The failed investor had ten cents in his pocket when he was arrested; the crooked banker had $63,000 in his pocket when he died. The murder epitomised the disreputable state that Los Angeles was in by the time the 1920s boom ended.

1929-1965: GROWING UP

The 1930s was a more sober period for LA, as elsewhere in the US. With the boom over and the Depression settling in, the city grew more slowly, and the new arrivals were very different from their predecessors. Instead of wooing wealthy Midwestern farmers, LA now attracted poor white refugees from the so-called 'Dust Bowl' of Oklahoma and Texas – the 'Okies' made famous in John Steinbeck's novel *The Grapes of Wrath*. These unskilled workers wound up as farm labourers and hangers-on in the margins of society.

Dealing with these newcomers proved difficult for Los Angeles, and was intertwined with another problem – how to handle the equally poor and unskilled Mexican and Mexican-American population. Since farm owners chose to hire the Okies over the Mexicans, LA County was overwhelmed with the cost of public relief and resorted to forcibly 'repatriating' even those Mexicans who were born and raised in Los Angeles.

Meanwhile, the continual arrival of Okies and other 'hobos' caused a nasty public backlash. But it also built a liberal political mood among the have-nots, which culminated in the near-election of reformer and novelist Upton Sinclair as governor of California in 1934. Having moved to Pasadena in the 1910s, Sinclair wrote a diatribe called *I, Governor of California, and How I Ended Poverty*. As a result, he founded the End Poverty In California (EPIC) movement and won the Democratic gubernatorial nomination. Only a concerted effort by reactionary political forces (aided by movie-house propaganda from the film industry) defeated Sinclair's bid. Afterwards, he wrote another book, this one called *I, Governor of California, and How I Got Licked*.

The region had other problems, such as the 1933 Long Beach earthquake, the first major quake to hit the city since it became populous. But in the mid-1930s, optimism returned, heralded by the 1932 Olympic Games, which were held at the city's Coliseum. To celebrate the games, Tenth Street was expanded, spruced up, renamed Olympic Boulevard and lined with palm trees – thus setting the fashion for palms in LA. In 1939, the first local freeway was built: the Arroyo Seco Parkway, now the Pasadena Freeway. A new aqueduct bringing water from the Hoover Dam along the Colorado River opened in 1941. And then the coming of World War II caused the biggest upheaval Los Angeles had seen to that point, and set the stage for the modern metropolis.

Already at the forefront of aviation, LA industrialised rapidly as it became a major military manufacturing centre and staging ground for the United States fight against Japan in the Pacific Ocean. More than 5,000 new manufacturing plants were built in LA during the war, mostly in outlying locations. New dormitory communities sprang up to accommodate the workers. Many were 'model' towns sponsored by industrialists or the military, and they helped to establish the sprawling pattern of city development that came to characterise LA in the post-war period.

Los Angeles's population quickly diversified, laying more groundwork for the racial unrest that would later characterise the city. During the war, more than 200,000 African-Americans moved to the city, mostly from Texas and Louisiana, to take advantage of job opportunities. But the South Central ghetto wasn't allowed to expand geographically to accommodate them, resulting in the creation of an overcrowded district (in 1948 the Supreme Court threw out restrictive convenants, paving the way for an exodus of middle-class blacks west into the Crenshaw district). In need of labourers, Los Angeles again welcomed the return of the Mexicans and Mexican-Americans who had been pushed out a decade before. However, a backlash once again ensued.

After a murder at the Sleepy Lagoon swimming hole in East LA in 1942, the authorities arrested more than 300 Latino youths, putting 23 on trial for first-degree murder. Most were minors. In a trial thick with racial epithets, 17 of the defendants were convicted. The convictions were later overturned by an appeal court, but several months later, a mob, including many servicemen, attacked Latinos and others in what became known as the 'Zoot Suit' riots after the baggy suits the men often wore. Thereafter, local newspapers, stoking the fires of prejudice, stopped referring to Latinos as Mexicans and, instead, called them 'zoot suits' or *pachucos*.

Discrimination against LA's growing Japanese community was even more pronounced. Most Japanese-Americans on the West Coast were interned in camps by the federal government during World War II, no matter how patriotic they were (in a supreme irony, some young men were permitted to leave the internment camps to join the US armed forces). Most Japanese lost their property, then concentrated in the Little Tokyo area of LA just east of City Hall. It took decades for Little

The reluctant metropolis

New York, the old saying goes, is a nice place to visit but you wouldn't want to live there. Los Angeles, in many ways, is the opposite: a city of neighbourhoods and out-of-the-way places that natives enjoy living in, but are nearly impossible for visitors to find. In other words, LA is the world's largest small town – an enormous collection of communities that people think of as small and intimate, even as they putter at ten miles an hour on the freeway to get to work.

The reason Angelenos see themselves this way derives from the city's peculiar history. With little but the climate to recommend it, LA became a metropolis not through typical economic forces but through marketing. More than a century ago, Southern California's real-estate barons peddled LA's virtues throughout the US as an alternative to the grimy industrial cities of the North-east and the Midwest. As LA urban planner William Fulton pointed out in his recent bestseller *The Reluctant Metropolis* (Solano Press Books), Los Angeles grew to be an enormous city by promoting an essentially anti-urban way of life.

People came to Southern California hoping to build a subsistence agricultural lifestyle on five or ten acres of irrigated land. Others sought to use LA as a transition between a rural past and an urban, industrial present: they worked in urban jobs, but revelled in the decentralised small-town life LA had deliberately created. Some continued to consider themselves rural folk and eagerly bought up the hobby farms being created all over Southern California. In LA, even the factories were in suburbs – and, until the 1940s, the factories and their adjacent residential neighbourhoods were surrounded by truck farms, so the place truly had a small-town feel even as it was becoming a big city.

This belief in 'the reluctant metropolis' was a fraud, of course; since the 1920s, Los Angeles has been one of the US's largest cities. But Angelenos do not part very willingly with their small-town fantasies. Since the 1970s, many residents have been discontented with the way the city has grown. No wonder they voted overwhelmingly to limit taxation with the famous Proposition 13 – a 1978 state initiative that froze property taxes and hence slashed funds for public services and schools. They saw no reason to help pay for continued growth. No wonder LA is America's capital of gated communities. No wonder LA residents are always petitioning the US Postal Service to allow them to have any postal address other than LA – even if they really live there.

This reluctance to accept the realities of urban living is likely to cause more explosive social problems in the future – especially as new immigrants from Latin America and Asia arrive every day. The new immigrants don't have the same rural viewpoint. But many of the long-term residents still cling to the idea that Los Angeles is a small town whose problems can somehow be ignored if they are kept outside the gate of their clean little subdivision.

Tokyo to return to prosperity, but an infusion of Japanese capital in the 1970s and 1980s has now created a thriving district.

Many African-Americans, Latinos and Japanese from LA fought for the United States during World War II. When they returned to suffer continued housing discrimination, police brutality and the general LA attitude that they were not 'real Americans', their sense of alienation grew further. But, because LA was a highly segregated city, most whites could ignore the race problem – especially after the war, when the city reaped the benefits of industrialisation and a new suburban boom began.

The post-war era in LA is often recalled as an idyllic period of prosperity and harmony. In fact, it was an unsettled period in which the city struggled to keep up with the demands of massive growth. Taxes rose in order to build new facilities and heavily oversubscribed schools went on 'double-sessions', teaching two classes in the same classroom at different times of the day.

Most of all, the entire LA region devoted itself to building things. Freeway construction, which was stymied by the war, exploded in 1947, when California imposed an additional gas tax to pay for it. Virtually the entire freeway system – truly a marvel of modern engineering – was built between 1950 and 1970. Perhaps its most important long-term effect was to open up vast tracts in outlying areas for urban development, especially in the San Fernando Valley and Orange County, which was linked to Los Angeles by the I-5 (Golden State Freeway). A seminal event in this suburbanisation was the opening, in 1955, of Disneyland. It was the first theme park ever built and helped to popularise Orange County.

Other leisure attractions also helped to establish LA as a major city during this period. In 1958, the city achieved 'major-league' status by luring New York's Brooklyn Dodgers baseball team. But, as has so often been the case in LA's history, even this event was marred by the tense relationship

Interracial tensions and poverty fuelled the Watts riots in 1965.

between the races. To obtain the team, the city gave the Dodgers a spectacular site in Chavez Ravine, overlooking downtown Los Angeles. Located in a low-income Latino neighbourhood, the site had been earmarked for use as a public housing project, which was never built. However, Dodger Stadium remains one of the finest sports facilities in the US.

As suburbanisation continued in the 1950s and 1960s, more and more neglected areas were left behind as LA prospered. On a hot summer night in 1965, the pent-up frustrations of the black ghetto exploded into one of the first and most destructive of the US's urban riots. The Watts riots began when an African-American man was pulled over on a drink-driving charge; by the time they were over, dozens of people had been killed and hundreds of buildings had been destroyed. For many Angelenos living in their comfortable suburbs, the Watts riots were the first indication that all was not well in their metropolis.

1965-1998: THE METROPOLIS

After the Watts riots, Los Angeles began to suffer from an image problem for the first time, and the city struggled with it for the better part of a decade. National newspapers and magazines proclaimed the end of the California Dream. The Los Angeles Police Department, under a series of hard-line chiefs, continued to treat minority neighbourhoods as if they were occupied territory. As in other US cities, the breakdown of African-American families left black teenagers with few male role models, and they began to form gangs.

In 1966, LA actor Ronald Reagan, with no previous experience in politics, was elected state governor on a law-and-order platform. Three years later, the Charles Manson cult killed actress Sharon Tate and others at a home in Benedict Canyon, disturbing the sense of tranquility even in that high-end Beverly Hills suburb. In 1971, the city suffered its worst earthquake in 38 years. It escaped enormous damage only because the quake struck at 6am.

Out of this troubled situation, however, emerged a towering political figure capable of healing the city. Tom Bradley was an African-American police captain who had grown up in the segregated world of Central Avenue and later held his own in such white-dominated enclaves as UCLA and the LAPD. In the 1950s, Bradley was assigned to improve relations with beleaguered Jewish shopkeepers in black neighbourhoods, a task he used to create the foundation for a cross-racial political alliance that sustained him for 30 years.

After retiring from the police force, Bradley was elected to the City Council and, with strong support in South Central and the largely Jewish Westside, ran for mayor. He lost in 1969 but ran again in 1973 and won, becoming the first African-American mayor of a predominantly white city (according to the 1990 census, the black population of the City of LA is only 13 per cent and that of LA County even less, 10.5 per cent). By moving into the mayor's mansion, he helped desegregate the Hancock Park neighbourhood, which had violently resisted the arrival of Nat 'King' Cole some years before.

LA mayor Tom Bradley with Stevie Wonder.

A low-key man with a calming personality, Bradley successfully ruled the city for 20 years through the power of persuasion. During the 1970s, he sought to heal racial wounds, while in the early 1980s, he turned his attention to business development, reviving Downtown and courting international business; the 1984 Olympics were his greatest triumph. Bradley's efforts also benefited from a huge flow of Japanese capital into Los Angeles real estate in the 1980s. He died in 1998.

However, this period proved to be a mere respite from LA's chronic social and racial tensions. The area became more polarised in the 1970s, as affluent whites grew more conservative and found little in common with the immigrants who were turning LA into the new US melting pot. Los Angeles had traditionally drawn its immigrants from the rest of the US. From the 1960s, however, most of its newcomers came from abroad.

The decline of agriculture in Latin America made LA a magnet for immigrants – legal and illegal – from rural Mexico and elsewhere, while political strife in Central America also brought in hundreds of thousands. The city's position on the edge of the burgeoning Pacific Rim also attracted people (and capital) from Korea, the Philippines, Taiwan and Hong Kong.

The vast central areas of Los Angeles were re-energised by these newcomers. Tourism, trade and the garment industry boomed, as did the rapidly expanding Koreatown. But, as the neighbourhoods changed, friction grew. Latin American immigrants began crowding into historically black South Central, creating a culture clash with middle- and working-class homeowners. African-Americans, in particular, felt more alienated than ever.

These tensions, fuelled by a declining economy shattered by the Pentagon cutbacks at the end of the Cold War, turned Los Angeles into a social tinderbox at the beginning of the 1990s. The arrest of black motorist Rodney King by four LAPD officers in 1991 (captured on tape by a home-video enthusiast) proved to be the turning point. When a jury acquitted the officers in 1992, it touched off a riot far more widespread and destructive than the Watts riots of 1965. It lasted three days, during which 50 people died and over 1,000 buildings were destroyed by fire and looting. More than 1,000 people were arrested, more of them Latino than black. It was the worst urban riot in US history.

Things got worse in LA before they got better. The arrest and trial of football and TV star OJ Simpson in 1995 gripped the city as it did the nation. Simpson, an African-American divorced from a white woman, was accused of killing his ex-wife and another man; his acquittal stunned white residents and reassured black residents that the legal system could be on their side, but did not lead to more violence.

Yet an economic renaissance beginning in the mid-1990s has brought the city back. As the aerospace industry declined, the entertainment industry expanded rapidly. Asian immigrants are helping with the current economic recovery. And in 1997, home prices started to skyrocket again, just as they did in the 1970s and 1980s.

Meanwhile, the Latino community has grown dramatically. Latinos are now the dominant racial group in LA County, and are starting to gain representation in the political and business leadership. Many older shopping areas have been revived with Latino commerce, including Broadway in downtown LA and Pacific Boulevard in Huntington Park. During the 1998 World Cup, Anglo LA paid little attention, but near-riots rocked Pacific Boulevard in celebration of Mexico's performance.

As LA ponders the twenty-first century, the city faces the challenge of casting aside its history as the national suburb once and for all, and finding ways to harness its multicultural strength in order to remain one of the world's great cities.

LA Today

Cops strut like gangstas, movie stars are low-life, children gasp for breath and it could all end tomorrow; this is the fantastic, deluded city of Los Angeles.

It's around 1.15am and last call for alcohol is under an hour away. A half-dozen cops have gathered in the brightly unflattering, aquarium light of the Seven-Eleven just down the block from the Tom Kat porno theatre and are fuelling up on doughnuts and hazelnut mocha before climbing into their black-and-whites to bust departing bar patrons and roust the speed freaks and drag queens plying their trade a few blocks further east on Santa Monica Boulevard. Even after Rodney King and the riots, their body language is bully-boy hostile and their guns are worn high on the hip, a strange cop version of gangsta chic. The drag queens who will soon be their targets have been experiencing a hard time lately, since their turf was declared a 'prostitution abatement zone'. Outside, the neon air is shirt-sleeve warm, velvet dark and smells of gasoline and night-blooming jasmine. The atmosphere is sufficiently neo-Chandler for any literary tourist in a town famous – but probably unjustly so – for its cultural illiteracy.

Now add the celebrity connection that is mandatory in the City of Angels. Eddie Murphy was busted in one of these closing-time sweeps for picking up a drag queen while driving home from the set of *Dr Dolittle*. He later claimed that he was only giving the young man a lift to a safer part of town. A few months later, the same young man died, wearing only a towel, after falling from a fifth-floor window of his apartment. According to the police report, he had managed to lock himself out while taking a shower and then attempted to regain entry by swinging, Tarzan-style, into the open window.

Many of the signs on this particular West Hollywood strip of Santa Monica Boulevard are now in Russian. Drugstores are identified by the word *anteka*, often in Cyrillic script, which, in the context of the USA's geopolitical history of the last half-century, verges on the strange. The area is in a state of flux. The entrepreneurial and highly motivated Russian immigrant community is making its mark on streets that once belonged to gays, hippies and the blue-collar end of the movie industry. Now the Russians command the day, while gay men – either Latino or from the Axl Rose heartland of trailer parks and child abuse – own the night, though only on the meagre sufferance of the police department and deputy sheriffs.

The ever-controversial LAPD: major players in the LA story.

A half-mile north and 800 feet (240 metres) higher up stands the home that *Melrose Place* TV mogul Aaron Spelling built in the early 1990s. (The joke has always been that, to find the bathroom, you turn left at the Matisse.) Initially, local residents expressed dismay at the project. Architecturally, it was an eyesore hybrid of a concrete UFO and a gun emplacement on the Maginot Line. The top of a small mountain was literally sawn off to provide its foundations, a move that some considered less than wise in a terrain of mudslides and earthquakes. Today, however, the Spelling monster is surrounded by masking foliage and has all but ceased to be noticeable.

The reason for these vignettes? First, LA tends to come at one in such fragments. The easy pedestrian pace of Paris or New York only happens in LA's malls or on a few localised shopping strips. The majority of the time, its sprawl has to be viewed from a moving vehicle: the reality equivalent of a jump-cut movie sequence, with the car radio providing the soundtrack of choice.

A second reason is to demonstrate that LA can absorb much more punishment than one might expect. Some might say this is merely a symptom of the famous vapid passivity of the population. A

Let's get spiritual

From early evangelist Aimee Semple McPherson to the transgalactic Heaven's Gate sect, Southern California, and the City of Angels in particular, have always been synonymous with kooky religion and cults. Evelyn Waugh immortalised LA-style death in *The Loved One*, while Nathaniel West mocked LA spirituality in *The Day of the Locust* through his character Tod Hackett, who worshipped at different churches each night.

Pentecostalist McPherson personified LA's religious zeal – she used radio and theatricals to attract thousands to her Foursquare Gospel Church, and then faked her own drowning in 1926. (Founded in 1923, the Angelus Temple that she built at 1100 Glendale Boulevard is still the headquarters of the Church, which claims 17 million followers worldwide.) Later came Reverend Robert Schuller, who began preaching from the roof of a refreshment stand at a drive-in cinema and now broadcasts his tele-evangelical services from the all-glass **Crystal Cathedral** (*see page 32* **Architecture**) on what he terms his '22-acre shopping center for Christ' in Orange County. For sheer nuttiness, however, no one beats the 39 members of the Heaven's Gate sect, who in 1997 committed mass suicide in a suburban house north of San Diego, so as to speed themselves to a rendezvous with a spaceship that they believed was following the Hale-Bopp comet.

Religion and Hollywood have also gone together – at their most macabre in Charles Manson and his followers in the 1960s, and more recently in the hugely successful **Church of Scientology**, which boasts John Travolta, Tom Cruise and Nicole Kidman among its many celebrity members. Its headquarters are housed in a former movie mogul's house (5930 Franklin Avenue, Hollywood; 1-323 960 3100); the Celebrity Center is open to the public 9am-10pm

Find calm at **Self-Realization Lake Shrine.**

daily. Richard Gere uses his star status to promote Buddhism, while Madonna, the original Material Girl, has for the time being traded Catholicism for the **Kabbalah**, a brand of Jewish mysticism currently much in vogue in Hollywood – other celeb followers include Courtney Love, Roseanne Barr and Jeff Goldblum. The Kabbalah Learning Center in Beverly Hills (1062 S Robertson Boulevard; 1-310 657 5404) is so popular that it is currently looking for larger premises.

But while unconventional sects attract the most attention, the real boom in religious devotion in LA is in the world's oldest religions.

more charitable theory might be that, with its incredible ethnic mix, its hard-to-grasp urban sprawl and constant sense of living on the edge – sometimes the edge of the world and sometimes the edge of complete disaster – LA has discovered that it is a great deal more resilient than it ever imagined; though perhaps the Romans believed in the resilience of their empire, too, until it fell.

As everyone almost certainly knows, the early 1990s were hardly kind to Los Angeles. A cycle of fires and flooding, one earthquake of fairly apocalyptic proportions and an underclass uprising all contributed to the feeling that the Four Horsemen

were under starter's orders. The Michael Jackson scandal, the Menendez brothers trial and then the Great OJ Simpson Three-Ring Circus made the city ground zero in three world-class media frenzies. We gave thanks that Louise Woodward wasn't babysitting in our town, and breathed a sigh of relief when Brynn Hartman had the decency to shoot herself after murdering her husband Phil, sparing us yet another 'trial of the century' downtown on Temple Street.

The big trials may have temporarily abated but small celebrity court hearings abound – and some of our most talented young actors are

---

Catholicism, Judaism, Buddhism, Islam and evangelical **Protestantism** are all on the rise in LA, thanks in part to the huge influx of immigrants from all over the world who've brought their belief systems with them, and in part to the tendency of baby-boomers to experiment with religions other than those they grew up with, or to return to a stricter version of their own religion. Among Jews, for example, you'll find growing numbers of both 'Bu-Jews' (Buddhist-Jews) and Orthodox Jews. The latter attribute their success to the need for discipline and structure in a decadent society, while Buddhists believe people are searching for a common-sense code and path to happiness that suits real life in modern California.

Catholicism is far and away the largest religion in LA, with more than three million members, due to the huge Mexican and Central American population, although a significant number of Hispanic Catholics are converting to Protestant evangelism (preached in modest shopfront churches all over Latino LA). The numbers of Baptists, Presbyterians, Episcopalians and other brands of Protestantism are kept up by Asians, especially Koreans, who have taken over the traditionally WASP churches in Midtown and made them their own.

The lesser-known religions are also attracting converts – **Santoria**, the animist Afro-Caribbean faith, is said to be practised in private living rooms by 100,000 believers; the relatively new **Church of Religious Science**, or 'Agape', is an amalgam of different beliefs with an upbeat spirit and inter-ethnic congregation that appeals to increasing numbers (for service times and locations, call 1-310 348 1260); while **Mormonism** claims to be doubling in size thanks to its emphasis on family values. Its huge Los Angeles Temple of the Church of Jesus

Christ of Latter-day Saints is unmissable, looming over Santa Monica Boulevard at Overland Avenue in West LA; the visitor centre (1-310 474 1549) is open 9am-9pm daily.

This new-found zeal has prompted a building boom in religious institutions, from private day-schools to church-related youth centres to places of worship. A new Catholic cathedral, the Cathedral of Our Lady of Angels, is currently under construction on Grand Avenue in Downtown and is due to be consecrated on 4 September 2000. Meanwhile, a new cathedral for the largest black Pentecostal church, the West Angeles Church of God in Christ, has just broken ground at the corner of Crenshaw and Exposition Boulevards in the Crenshaw district.

WHERE TO WORSHIP

Pick up a copy of the *LA Times* on Saturday for a full listing of services plus articles on religion (*see also page 262* **Directory**). Otherwise, highly recommended for atmosphere are: Our Lady, Queen of the Angels, known as **La Placita** (535 N Main Street, Downtown; 1-213 629 3101), the oldest Catholic church in Los Angeles, particularly festive on Sunday mornings; the **West Angeles Church of God in Christ** (3045 Crenshaw Boulevard; 1-213 733 8300), which has more than 16,000 members, an incredible choir and holds five services on Sundays; **Wat Thai Temple** (8225 Coldwater Canyon Avenue, North Hollywood; 1-818 780 4200), where you can eat Thai vegetarian food as well as join Buddhist devotees; and the Self-Realization Fellowship Church's **Lake Shrine** (*see page 56* **Sightseeing**), an enchanting retreat for meditation with a spring-fed lake, lush gardens, swans and picturesque pathways, where anyone is welcome to quietly wander.

currently in detox, rehab or the county jail. As though the movie industry has commenced to eat its young, Charlie Sheen, Christian Slater and the unfortunate Robert Downey Jr are all enmeshed in various circles of judicial hell for antics that would hardly have given pause to late legends like Errol Flynn, Robert Mitchum, John Belushi or Elvis. In the past few years, Hollywood has adopted a smug neo-morality, primarily enforced by the corporations that insure films whose

Mind if I smoke?

"Your scent is intoxicating..."

"Yours is carcinogenic."

On 1 January 1998, the State of California started enforcing a law that prohibits smoking in bars and nightclubs. Legislation had already been enacted banning cigarettes and cigars from public buildings and restaurants, and for many smokers this was the last straw.

The only place that one can now legally light up, apart from private homes and the open air, is in small designated areas of hotel lobbies, and the smoking ban in bars has become a major bone of contention. To sit hunched at the bar, cigarette in one hand, Scotch in the other, with Sinatra singing *One For My Baby* on the jukebox (or would you prefer Patsy Cline's *Walking After Midnight*?) is such a time-honoured cliché that it seems scarcely credible that it could be legislated out of existence – at least, until a possible repeal comes to a vote. The situation is particularly ironic in Hollywood, when so many of us learned to smoke at the movies, from such role models as Humphrey Bogart, James Dean and Bette Davis.

Needless to say, the smoking drinkers are mad as hell and only grudgingly prepared to take it. The law is supposedly designed to protect bar employees from long hours in a smoke-filled environment. But many bar workers find that it costs them tips and, since the law makes them the enforcers, they have now to deal with surly customers, including tourists who don't know the score and immediately resent it. Some bar owners are so opposed to the ban that they militantly ignore it.

The medical fulcrum of the argument is the true danger of second-hand smoke. On the one hand, the American Lung Association uncompromisingly states that cigarette smoke is a Class A carcinogen with no acceptable levels of tolerance. On the other, we have the World Health Organisation's under-publicised report that the dangers are negligible. Culturally, smokers see the ban as creeping prohibition and part of the current Californian misapprehension that narcissistic good health is a holy virtue. The anti-smoking lobby tends to treat smokers as infectious drug addicts and are supported in this by Board of Health advertising using images like this exchange between a sophisticated cocktail couple – Him: 'Mind if I smoke?' Her: 'Mind if I die?'

To counter this gallows humour, smokers frequently repeat the famous line of *Absolutely Fabulous*'s Patsy Stone when asked if she knows second-hand smoke can kill: 'Yes, darling, but unfortunately not fast enough.'

budgets now routinely run close to $100 million, and executives who firmly believe that the motion picture industry could plunge to its doom if Leonardo DiCaprio ever started messing around with whores and dope, or got himself shot to death behind mindless gangsta-ismo like the brilliantly promising Tupac Shakur.

Where, a few years ago, LA seemed to dread the coming millennium, the current attitude is that we are not only ready for it, but gearing up to market it to the rest of the world. The new cycle of disaster epics is proving infinitely bankable. Ocean liners sink, volcanoes erupt, aliens attack, comets and asteroids smash into the Earth, Godzilla eats Manhattan – and the profits pile up at the box offices all across the planet. The former flirtation with independent film has shrivelled and withered. Tales of costumed Brits and New York junkies are no longer courted, let alone committed to celluloid with studio finance. Hollywood embraces Armageddon, confident that all the global audience requires is a bigger bang for its buck.

Part of this new upbeat mood is a sense that we have already seen the unfriendly face of the millennium and survived it. Both seismic and urban pressures have attempted to bring the city down, but, although bruised, it's still standing and still able to pull off a passable imitation of paradise when the sun is shining and the ocean's blue. When the 30 or so members of the Heaven's Gate cult stopped building web pages in their desirable suburban residence, swallowed the vodka and Vicodan and pulled the plastic bags over their heads to discorporate up to the starship lurking in the tail of the Hale-Bopp comet, a sobering sense of absurdity took hold. That people should commit mass suicide for a religion that appeared to be concocted from equal parts *Star Trek* and New Age paranoia dramatically underscored the futility of obsession with the latest popular foolishness.

That said, Los Angeles still clings to its illusions and maintains quite implausible levels of denial. It's probably quite natural, in a location where the very ground shakes and nothing is quite what it first appears. Even the city itself is deceptive. Unlike New York or Chicago, it's a pure twentieth-century city with none of the Victorian legacies of tenements, soot-caked Gothic cathedrals or dark satanic mills that popularly define a metropolis uncomfortably close to losing control. The verdant plant life makes even murderous neighbourhoods funkily attractive. LA's industry is mostly high-tech manufacturing enterprises housed in low-slung industrial facilities, making consumer gadgets or nameless components for the Pentagon. The pollution comes from the failed car culture experiment (foisted on the city, many believe, by General Motors half a century ago), which remains unchallenged even though the incidence of asthma and other respiratory problems among children is at epidemic levels.

The population continues to grow, stressing many of the poorer neighbourhoods to near breaking point. The city administration, corrupt as ever, will be as incapable of solving the pressing problems of the next century as it was through the last. The education system collapses and mass transit continues to be little more than a few miles of operational track and a series of large holes in Hollywood Boulevard. The Bay is so polluted by the garbage from the storm drains that an uncomfortable number of veteran surfers are showing symptoms of a mysterious immune disorder. Efforts by the LAPD to pry gangstas loose from their turf result in little but traffic screw-ups in which one finds oneself rerouted into poorly lit and unfamiliar streets to become hopelessly lost and possibly victimised. The post-riot lip service paid to the need for improved schools and something better than minimum-wage jobs remains nothing but election rhetoric; and the fire of Glocks and AK47s can still be heard in the East LA night.

Maybe the worst that can really be said about the city of Los Angeles is that it seems incapable of learning from its mistakes. Ever since the city was founded in its desert river basin, water has been the primary, but rarely discussed, problem. Currently, much of LA's water comes from man-made Lake Mead in Nevada. However, as Las Vegas prospers and expands while LA simply grows, Vegas may decide that it needs that water for itself, and then LA is in big trouble. The given intelligence is that market forces will ultimately take care of everything. By the time Nevada water becomes too expensive, desalination plants will be economically feasible. What the pro-market pundits tend to forget is that history has repeatedly proved it often takes a disaster such as a massive drought or catastrophic city-sized conflagration before the market rolls over and acts. It was, after all, a five-year drought in the nineteenth century that enabled the Anglos to first wrest title to the LA basin from the Mexican cattle barons.

Even on a more prosaic level, Angelenos have a hard time learning the lesson. The current vogue in spectator sports is for live-on-TV car chases. Scarcely a week goes by without at least one clown who's been pulled over for erratic driving or a broken tail light deciding to take it on the lam and lead the cops a 100-mile-an-hour dance from freeway to freeway until his gas tank runs dry. The various TV stations' choppers jockey for position with their rivals and the helicopters of the Highway Patrol, and we all settle back in the couch to see if the poor sap is going to get out alive. The one thing that's for sure is he's not going to escape. Whether these people really believe they'll beat the heat is debatable. Maybe they're just desperately claiming their promised Warholian 15 minutes. Fame and how to acquire it is, of course, something else that Los Angeles is all about.

Geography & Climate

If Hollywood is a modern Babylon, LA provides biblical plagues to match. Fires, floods and earthquakes are the price Angelenos pay for their Promised Land of endless summer.

In many ways, there is very little reason for Los Angeles to exist. It has none of the natural features so common to big cities elsewhere in the world. It is not located along a great river, has no natural deep-water harbour and is far from any of the raw materials necessary for urban life – especially water (an exception is oil, which has always been abundant). It is also the largest city in the world located so near to a geographically unstable mountain range. And even before the Europeans came, the natives complained about the smog.

The city also seems unconnected to the land on which it has been built: so many landscapes have been levelled, deserts paved and rivers turned into channels, the argument goes, that Los Angeles – like New York – has become nothing more than an alienating concrete island. And Angelenos often seem to inhabit a wholly artificial environment of air-conditioning and cars, freeways and airports, with their biggest river little more than a storm drain.

But, in fact, LA's natural environment makes itself felt far more strongly than in, say, the big cities of Northern Europe. Earthquakes threaten lives and fortunes, as do unstoppable wildfires, floods and mudslides. And LA also owes much of its wealth to nature: to the oil fields that lie under the city and, overhead, the bright, clear sunshine of its fabulously benign climate, which drew the infant movie business here – and now draws tourists in great numbers every year.

Los Angeles has often been described as an 'island on the land' – sealed off from the rest of the world by mountains to the north and south, desert to the east and the ocean to the west. Because of this isolation, Southern California, like Australia, contains numerous plant and animal species found nowhere else in the world, such as the many endangered birds that roost in the low-lying shrubs along the coast.

Likewise, the shape of Los Angeles has been determined by natural topography. Southern California, like most of the American West, is a series of rugged and dramatic mountain ranges interspersed by valleys of all sizes, and it is the few passes between the mountains that have set the terms for urban growth.

For example, Los Angeles is often considered a city created by the automobile, but today's freeway system simply follows the same logical routes that were used by Native Americans, pioneers' horses and early commuter railroads. British architectural historian Reyner Banham, writing almost 30 years ago in his definitive study *Los Angeles: The Architecture of Four Ecologies*, identified a 'transportation palimpsest' – a natural tablet of five transportation routes written upon by each generation. Today, these most beaten of tracks form the basis of the Hollywood (Highway 170), Santa Monica (I-10), San Bernardino (I-10), Santa Ana (I-5) and Harbor (I-110) Freeways.

Average temperatures

Month	Max (°F/°C)	Min (°F/°C)	Rainfall (in/cm)	Dry days
Jan	65/18	46/8	2.9/7.3	25
Feb	66/19	48/9	3.1/7.8	22
Mar	67/19	50/10	2.6/6.6	25
Apr	70/21	52/11	1/2.5	26
May	72/22	55/13	0.2/0.5	29
June	76/24	58/14	0	29
July	81/27	61/16	0	31
Aug	82/28	60/15	0	31
Sept	81/27	58/14	0.5/1.3	29
Oct	76/24	54/12	0.3/0.7	29
Nov	73/23	50/10	2/5	27
Dec	67/19	47/8	2/5	25

Humidity averages 65-77%, except on extremely foggy days or sometimes when the wind is southerly, pushing tropical air north.
Rainfall source: National Climatic Data Center

CLIMATE IS CRUCIAL

Mountains and valleys have played an important role in moulding the city, but the greatest natural influence on Los Angeles is its weather. Without the city's Mediterranean-like climate – quite possibly the most temperate in the world – there would be no LA. Standing at the confluence of the desert and the ocean, the Los Angeles basin basks in the mild commingling of gentle, cool ocean breezes and warm desert sun. Winters are so mild that Angelenos often forget to pack an overcoat when they fly east in February. Summer comes in April at the latest and lingers at least until October. And although temperatures can reach 100°F (38°C), it's a dry, desert-like heat: to a dripping tourist from Atlanta or Baltimore, the most humid summer day in LA will seem like an airy heaven.

Snow is out of the question – a dusting will hit the mountain tops every decade or two – and, in Mediterranean style, rain is seasonal. The first storm will typically hit during November, and a rainy day beyond the end of March is an anomaly. At about 14 inches (36 centimetres), the city's average annual rainfall is a third of New York's and a quarter of Tokyo's.

Yet alongside the sameness and mildness that characterise Los Angeles's climate are the more subtle and often frightening habits of the natural environment. The seasons do change – just not very dramatically. Spring is often cool and overcast.

Wildfires are common in the dry season.

In June and July, the coastal cities are swathed for most of the day in sea mist, known as 'June gloom'. The hot, dry summer can turn sour in September and October, when the typical wind pattern is reversed and the hot, dry 'Santa Ana' winds come roaring out of the desert toward the ocean (writers as varied as Raymond Chandler and Joan Didion have relayed tales of how people get spooky and weird at Santa Ana time).

This is also prime smog time – during hot, dry periods, Los Angeles's ring of mountains creates a kind of pressure cooker in which car pollutants 'bake' into photochemical haze. Once that's over, autumn and winter can feature torrential rains when Southern California gets pounded by one El Niño-like storm after another. And driving in LA rainstorms is nightmarish: unaccustomed to wet weather, drivers treat every drizzle as if it were a blizzard.

Just as important, the climate changes dramatically from place to place. Cut off from the ocean breezes by the mountains, the San Gabriel and San Fernando Valleys can be 20-30°F (11-17°C) warmer than the beachfront communities. The foothills of Hollywood and West Hollywood, above Sunset Strip, trap heat so well they can be 10°F (6°C) hotter than the flatlands only a few blocks away. A February drive from Venice to Mount Baldy – only 40 miles (65 kilometres) away inland – can mean a tour of several such microclimates: starting with a mild 60°F (15°C) at the beach, you pass through valleys steaming at 90°F (32°C) to find the mountain top still snowy at 30°F (-1°C).

DROUGHTS, FIRES AND FLOODS

Probably 95 per cent of the time, LA's mild weather is harmless, even with the dramatic temperature variations. But the other five per cent of the time, you'd better get out of the way. Southern California is geographically 'young' and therefore unstable, with a fragile natural environment that's easily thrown out of whack. The weather and precipitation patterns can also vary dramatically from year to year. Earthquakes (*see opposite* **The Big One**) are the least of it. Just as frequently, Los Angeles suffers a deadly cycle of drought, fires and floods.

If you look on the mountains and hillsides around Los Angeles, you'll see a mixture of native 'chaparral' (thick scrub) and European annual grasses that turn brown in the summer. Come summer these plants are pure kindling. The annual dry season, often stretching into October or November, provides ample opportunity for them to burn, as they often do – in fact, the local ecosystems rely on regular incineration for refreshment and rebalancing. And Californian wildfires move rapidly. Once they get moving, they often skip over whole streets and blocks: firefighters prefer to contain them and let them burn out rather than try to extinguish them.

But as the city has pushed up against these grassy hillsides, Angelenos have put themselves in harm's way. Hence the almost annual television footage of bomber planes dumping loads of water and chemicals on some burning hillside in Malibu, trying to pummel the fire into submission before it sweeps away a whole neighbourhood.

The pattern of incineration is bad enough by itself, but it gets even worse during the periodic droughts. In the late 1980s and early 1990s, for example, Southern California's annual rainfall dropped to as little as two inches (five centimetres) a year in some places. The result, not surprisingly, was that the entire region became a tinderbox. Devastating fires swept Santa Barbara in 1991 and Malibu and Laguna Beach two years later.

Destructive as they are, the fires themselves are not the worst of it. These conflagrations typically set off a vicious cycle of flooding as well. The fires burn the plants that bind the soil of hillsides. When the winter rains come, the hillsides turn into a muddy, unstable goo that is politely known in local circles as a 'debris flow', which barrels down the mountains into the riverbeds below, washing away everything in its path. This phenomenon is reported to most of the world as 'flooding', but this does not do it justice. A debris flow is a kind of rolling mud mountain that gathers momentum as it heads downhill, collecting trees, cars and houses as it goes.

It has taken all that modern engineering can offer to keep this phenomenon from wiping out Los Angeles completely. The LA County Flood Control District has spent millions of dollars building 'debris basins' – essentially, large pits in the ground at the bottom of the San Gabriel Mountains – to catch the slurry and keep it from moving downstream. With the help of the federal government, the Flood Control District has also converted virtually all the rivers in LA into concrete culverts to minimise the chance of flooding – though, recently, environmental advocates have sought to restore the natural flood flow in some areas, especially along the LA River.

THE EL NINO EFFECT

To make matters worse, the rains that create this 'flooding' do not come in a predictable pattern. Scientists can calculate figures for average yearly rainfall – but there is no such thing as an average year in Southern California. Once the drought cycle passed in 1992, rainfall moved progressively upward until the El Niño winter of 1997-98, when the region was battered by about 40 inches (100 centimetres) of rain. Some areas got up to eight inches (20 centimetres) – over half the 'average' annual rainfall – in a single day.

The El Niño effect has hit Los Angeles twice in the past 15 years, and each time the result has been a series of devastating storms that have wiped out ocean piers, houses and freeway bridges. In a typical year, Southern California doesn't really get any rainstorms of its own: the rainfall that arrives is just the dregs of harder storms that pound the Pacific Northwest and Northern California. But with the El Niño cycle, which warms the water in the Pacific, the typical storm pattern drops much further south, so that for a few months LA feels like Seattle: gloomy, saturated, reeling from the last storm and skittish about the next one.

The most recent El Niño has been so severe that it has limited LA's famous mobility. The spectacular Pacific Coast Highway was wiped out for almost the whole winter in 1998 due to El Niño-driven mudslides, and other road closures cut off Santa Barbara and some remote areas. Even after El Niño vanished, however, a peculiar trailing set of weather patterns brought more storms, heatwaves and other climatic extremes. El Niño has simply reminded the world that, while the weather is great most of the time in LA, sunny days can sometimes be deceptive.

The big unknown about Los Angeles's climate is just how stable it really is. Recent history shows a pattern of about six or seven wet years followed by six or seven dry ones. But deeper historical evidence suggests that much longer 'mood swings' have occurred in the past.

Still, the fire-and-flood cycle yields one ironic bonus: it tends to hit the rich hardest. They're the only ones who can afford to live high up on those treacherous hills.

The Big One

With slo-mo violence that puts Sam Peckinpah to shame, the vast slab of rock – or tectonic plate – that is the bed of the Pacific Ocean is crashing into another plate that we know as North America. As the plates grind against each other, they slip and judder. Which is where earthquakes come from.

Sitting on top of this geological crumple zone, Los Angeles is regularly rocked by groundshaking events large and small. In fact, tiny tremors hit the city thousands of times each day, but only rarely is an earthquake large enough for people to actually notice it. The big ones, however, are hard to miss – and in recent years they seem to have been growing in frequency.

California's most important geological fault line, the San Andreas Fault, runs in a north-west/south-east direction through the Mojave desert east of Los Angeles. Dozens – or maybe even hundreds – of other, smaller faults criss-cross the region. Most are classified as 'inactive', meaning they have not erupted in the past 10,000 years. But the thing about earthquakes is that you never know when or where one will hit. Unlike a blizzard or a hurricane, a big earthquake could happen anytime, anywhere, without warning.

Los Angeles lives in fear of the 'Big One' – a San Andreas quake measuring 8 or 8.5 on the Richter scale, which would undoubtedly destroy large parts of the city. Such a quake has not rocked LA since it began getting big a century ago. But the most recent 'Little One' was scary enough. The Northridge earthquake, measuring 6.8 on the Richter scale when it hit in January 1994, caused apartment buildings and stores to collapse, killed more than 20 people and left thousands homeless. As in most earthquakes, the problems were compounded by fires created by broken fuel lines. Aftershocks measuring above 5 on the Richter scale rocked the city even as President Clinton held a special meeting on the crisis. Many people lost their homes altogether, or were forced to wait a year or more until repairs could be done.

Angelenos respond to the risk of earthquakes with equal parts fear, preparation and laconic humour. A century of small quakes has led to strong building standards that lessen the likelihood of complete disaster: in comparison with the 20 deaths of the Northridge quake, the recent quake in Armenia – about the same violence on the Richter scale – killed 25,000.

Most Southern Californians have water and food stashed in the garage and some cash hidden

under the mattress in case the Big One hits and knocks out supermarkets and automated teller machines. As a visitor, you can't go to such survivalist extremes, but all the same, it's smart to carry a small torch to cope with the inevitable power failures after a big quake. And if you feel a shaking underfoot, you can participate in LA's favourite parlour game: guessing the Richter intensity of the earthquake even as it's going on. Old-timers insist they can tell the difference between a 'four' and a 'five', and they'll argue with each other as if they were trained seismologists.

What to do in an earthquake

● Get away from anything that may collapse, indoors or out: notably trees, bridges or power lines.
● If you're inside, stand under a solid door frame or sturdy piece of furniture such as a large table or desk. Hold on to it firmly until all movement has subsided.
● If you're in a car, pull over and stop where it's safe. Keep away from flyovers and power lines.
● After the quake, think twice before you do anything. Don't light a cigarette, a candle or anything else, and don't turn on lights or use any electrical appliance (not even a telephone): chances are you'll be near a gas or water leak or power line break, and you could spark an explosion or cause a shock.

American Red Cross LA

2700 Wilshire Boulevard, Los Angeles, CA 90057 (1-213 739 5200).
The Red Cross helps co-ordinate disaster relief operations and sends out information packs on earthquake readiness. In the event of a quake, it recommends non-US citizens phone a friend or relative at home as soon as they can, to prevent the phonelines getting clogged up with enquiries from abroad (outgoing calls are more likely to get through than incoming ones).

Quake info

California Institute of Technology (CalTech): earthquake information hotline 1-626 395 6977; website www.gps.caltech.edu/seismo/earthquakes/
Map of recent earthquakes in LA: www.scecdc.scec.org/recenteqs/Maps/Los_Angeles.html
The three biggest LA earthquakes since 1932: www.scecdc.scec.org/labasin.html

Celebrity LA

The cult of celebrity is all-pervasive in LA. Whether you want to spot some stars or try to grab your own 15 minutes of fame, this is the place to do it.

Los Angeles has more celebrities per capita than any other city in the world. Period. And whatever they may claim to the contrary, Angelenos are inveterate star-worshippers. Every dry cleaner, car repair shop or shoe mender has a wall emblazoned with personally signed, faded black and white head-shots of the stars. It doesn't, of course, mean that the stars frequent said establishment. In fact, many are fakes designed to attract business: you can buy a glossy headshot of your favourite celebrity at any of the tourist shops on Hollywood Boulevard.

The famous people themselves collude in this obsession. For instance, there is an unwritten law in Los Angeles that celebrities may only interact with other celebrities. If Jeff Goldblum and Fabio are dining separately in a restaurant they will necessarily gravitate towards each other. Angelenos see this all the time and can only marvel at the subject of conversation between two people who clearly have absolutely nothing in common but their fame. And, of course, true celebs only marry other celebs (unless they're Elizabeth Taylor), although they may do so as frequently as they like.

These days, another quirk expected of celebs is that they will be devoted to a religion – the less conventional, the better (*see page 14* **LA Today** for a roll-call of spiritually inclined stars) – as long as it doesn't ban seven-figure fees for movie appearances, of course. This is understandable in a city where so many cultures rub shoulders, though the cynical might see it as an aspect of faddish consumerism: an elevated version of giving the patio a makeover with white paint, gravel and a few Japanese characters in the belief that this delivers the wisdom of Zen Buddhism without all that tedious meditation and self-denial.

Oddly, many a common man and woman living in Los Angeles seems to prize celebritydom for his- or herself above money, health and sometimes even a place to live. Some people even advertise their own desperation. One such is the infamous Dennis Woodruff, a struggling actor who owns several cars, all emblazoned with his headshot, plastic Oscars and begging slogans.

One bizarre by-product of the cult of celebrity is **Angelyne**. You don't have to spend long in LA before you start to notice her huge billboards, paintings of a big-eyed blonde thrusting exuberant

breasts forward while fixing the passer-by with a centrefold's pout. The only word on the billboard is 'Angelyne' (sometimes with her website, www.angelyne.com). Who is she? Is she real? What's she selling? Who's paying for all this? You can find out plenty of things about her on her website or on her answerphone message (1-310 289 4469): the trouble is that none of it is believable. Some say she's the wife of the boss of the billboard company; others, an aspiring starlet. The only thing that's certain is that someone has expended a lot of effort and money to create a patently and perfectly artificial character. Thanks to them, the public has an object for its own curiosity, musings, fantasies and desires. In fact, Angelyne is the perfect celebrity.

Celebrity-spotting

The best place to find a celebrity is on a studio lot: it's where they do what passes for work in their world, after all. Unfortunately, even when studio tours are offered (*see page 182* **Film**), tourists are kept as far away from the sound stages as possible and much closer to facilities where money can be spent. You'll need to try harder than that.

AT HOME

Celebrities spend most of their time in their homes or in their cars. If you want to home-spot, you can buy a star map on the main touristy thoroughfares of Sunset and Hollywood Boulevards, between La Brea Avenue and Doheny Drive. Don't expect them to be accurate, though. And don't expect to see anything: the more famous the celeb, the taller the hedge, the larger the front yard and the bigger the security system separating you from the house.

Brad Pitt has bought the home of Elvira, a US TV personality, so if you see her name on a star map, you know where to find Chez Pitt. Jack Nicholson has lived in the same place for years so he's pretty much a sure thing. You can save your shoe leather by visiting a quintessentially LA website, the self-explanatory Driveways of the Rich & Famous (www.driveways.com).

If you can infiltrate Malibu Colony (a housing estate for the super-rich) you'll hit paydirt – but without a resident's pass or your name on the guest list at the gate, you won't stand a chance.

*Famous for being famous: the mysterious **Angelyne** hovers over Hollywood Boulevard.*

Broad Beach is a better bet. Just north of Zuma Beach, Broad Beach Road houses Sting, Steven Spielberg and Richard Gere for starters, so an amble on the beach is a reasonably good bet. Take the Pacific Coast Highway north, go through Malibu and continue to Broad Beach Road. Turn left, drive a little way along the street and walk to the beach – there are a number of narrow paths down to it. Look for the dark wooden house with the lawn: that's Chez Spielberg.

SHOPPING WITH THE STARS

To track down celebs at large, you'll need to learn the peculiar habits of these secretive creatures. For the most part, they won't want to be seen by you unless you're their lover, hairstylist, manicurist or personal trainer. But swanky hair salons such as **Privé**, Christophe and **Juan Juan** (*see chapter* **Shops & Services**) will take care of your follicles, too, and there's always someone of interest waiting their turn for an appointment – because the top stylists and colourists are themselves celebrities who are far too busy to make house calls.

But there are only so many times you can have your hair cut in one week. Where else do celebs have to go? Unfortunately, one of the perks of being a celebrity is that you don't have to go shopping. Many don't even carry cash: it does spoil the cut of one's clothes, and what are personal assistants for, anyway? Fortunately, the sort of celebs you'd actually want to meet – people such as Steven Spielberg and Tom Hanks – are the ones who have no trouble shopping personally at the quaint **Brentwood Country Mart** (225 26th Street, at San Vicente Boulevard, Brentwood; 1-310 395 6714). An odd collection of shops and the splendid English Penny Lane diner will keep you occupied as you check under the baseball cap of every single passer-by.

Gelsons, the Harrods of supermarkets, has a branch at 15424 Sunset Boulevard (at Temescal Canyon Road, Pacific Palisades; 1-310 459 4483): prime Spielberg territory. **Hughes** (23841 W Malibu Road, at Malibu Colony Plaza, Malibu; 1-310 456 2917) is the supermarket that serves Malibu Colony and therefore plenty of big stars who simply have to live in a gated, heavily secured community.

A measure of any establishment's popularity with the chosen few is whether they show up at weekends. Pitiably timid, most stars avoid going out at times when the public is free to walk the streets, making exception only for their very favouritest spots. And come Sunday, the highest concentration of cool celebs will be at **Barneys of New York** (*see page 152* **Shops & Services**). Don't be intimidated by the staff: they're actually pretty friendly underneath, and they've seen so many stars they're just as happy to serve you as them.

Melrose News (647 N Martel Avenue; 1-323 655 2866) adds to its wide selection of periodicals the added experience of seeing many cover stories pop in to buy a mag or a cigar. Ironically, Eddie Murphy allegedly stopped here the night of his notorious transvestite encounter (*see page 13*). Other prime retail locations are the **Beverly Center, Century City Shopping Center** and **Fred Segal** (for all, *see chapter* **Shops & Services**).

The best place to spot someone famous at any given time is the complex known as **8000 Sunset Boulevard**, on the site of Schwab's Drugstore, where Lana Turner was, reportedly, spotted and plucked from obscurity. The mall houses the movie house Julia Roberts and Winona Ryder call a favourite, the **Laemmle's Sunset 5**, which at any given time screens the best of the independent films playing in Los Angeles.

The **Virgin Megastore**, also in 8000 Sunset, is a good place to catch Quentin Tarantino. He, however, wouldn't be spotted dead next door at **Crunch**, LA's gym of the moment, which gives free membership to all the people who don't need free anything: Nicolas Cage, Salma Hayek, Elisabeth Shue and a whole host of others have been spotted pounding the hyperbaric treadmill.

When they've finished their oxygen deprivation treatment, such celebs like to fuel up on a chopped vegetable salad at the **Wolfgang Puck Café** (a favourite of Matt Damon's at the time of going to press) or a non-fat latte at **Buzz Coffee**. Seriously, this spot is a celebrity goldmine.

FEEDING TIME
Celebs love to eat out and you could spend thousands weekly looking for them in the top-end restaurants. Hot eating places come and go faster than LA winters, but there are a few enduring staples. **Drai's** (*see page 121* **Restaurants**) is a serious power spot on Monday nights – the only time worth visiting for celeb-spotting, but also the time you really need a reservation (which will probably not buy you a prime table). If you don't have celebrity-depth pockets, many pricey restaurants have bars where a cat may look at a king.

Unassuming celebrities enjoy **Orso** (*see page 124* **Restaurants**), which not only despises but actively discourages any publicity. Besides being super low-key, Orso also serves excellent, not overpriced food with unpretentious service.

Celebrity tours

Celebs are a flighty breed. Dead ones, however, don't change their homes as often as the rest, and so may be the most rewarding for the star-hunter. If you're thinking of beating the cemetery trail, there's no better way than in the customised Cadillac hearse of **Grave Line** tours, run by a former undertaker. Forty-four bucks guarantees you a close encounter (as close as six feet) with at least 70 celebrities. The information line alone is worth two minutes of anyone's time (1-323 469 4149; reservations 1-816 333 2577).

For the less morbid, there's the **Movie Stars' Homes Tour**, which costs $29 and takes you to a slew of celeb homes; the particular itinerary depends on the driver. There are four departures a day; call 1-800 286 8752 or 1-323 937 3361 for information and reservations.

Death sites
Bugsy Siegel *810 Linden Drive, between Lomitas Avenue & Whittier Drive, Beverly Hills.* **Map 3 B2**
Mafia bigwig – the Warren Beatty film *Bugsy* is based on his life – who was shot a billion times here.
John Belushi *Chateau Marmont: for listings, see p99* **Accommodation. Map 4 B1**
Belushi overdosed here on a speedball, the same lethal combination of cocaine and heroin that killed River Phoenix.
Marilyn Monroe *12305 Fifth Helena Street, at Carmilina Avenue, Brentwood.*
This is the house where Monroe breathed her last.

River Phoenix *The Viper Room: for listings, see p217* **Nightlife. Map 4 A1**
Phoenix died right on the pavement of Sunset Boulevard, by the Viper Club's back door (the main entrance is on Larrabee Street).
Robert F Kennedy *Ambassador Hotel, 3400 Wilshire Boulevard, between Alexandria & Mariposa Avenues, Mid Wilshire (1-213 387 7011).* **Map 5 C4**
Kennedy was assassinated in the kitchen of the Ambassador by Sirhan Sirhan.

Award shows

Celebs have no choice but to brave the horror that is the public come award show season. You might have to arrive early, but you'll never find more stars in one spot at the same time, and watching the congestion of ludicrously long limos is a surreal joy in itself.

The Academy Awards
On Oscar Day, the whole city – the sections you'll probably want to visit, anyway – closes down. Streets are empty apart from scores of limos picking up makeup artists and outfits and then later delivering the finished product Downtown to the **Dorothy Chandler Pavilion** (*see p205* **Music**). If you don't go to the actual show, you watch it at home since everyone must appear to have actually attended. Then, when the time is right to facilitate that impression, one begins the party circuit. The two A-list party perennials are *Vanity Fair*'s at **Mortons** and Elton John's AIDS benefit at the new **Spago** (for both, *see chapter* **Restaurants**). Assured A-list celeb success.

The Oscars have been held on the last or second-last Monday in March for pretty much time immemorial. From 1999 onwards, they will be held on a Sunday. In 2001, the Oscars should be moving to a new, permanent and more appropriate home on Hollywood Boulevard. *See also p88* **Los Angeles by Season**.

The Emmys
Prime-time TV's Oscars equivalent, and second only to them in celeb quotient. Held on a mid-September evening every year. Check local press for details.

The Golden Globes
The Hollywood Foreign Press Association's award show would be small feed were it not the only serious precursor to the Oscars. Held mid-January on a Sunday, normally at the Beverly Hills Hilton. Check local press for specific dates.

Independent Spirit Awards
Not so independent in star power: they are held every year on the Saturday in March immediately before the Oscars, so countless celebs are in town and looking to party. The ceremony is held in a tent on Santa Monica beach and is therefore extra-cool and very relaxed.

The Razzies
Possibly the most fun awards show, unfortunately this is a very poor celebrity prospect. The Razzies celebrate the worst of Hollywood: hence past winners include Demi Moore and Kevin Costner, who, failing to show any semblance of a sense of humour, did not collect their awards in person.

Car City

Driving a car in LA is like wearing shoes in other cities: no one says you have to do it, but you'll suffer if you don't.

A rare glimpse of a pedestrian in LA.

'I drive, therefore I am' should be the motto of Los Angeles, a city whose culture, urban form and image is predicated on ownership of an automobile.

Not that this was always so. The vast agglomeration that is contemporary LA was in its early years a collection of small, distinct cities, such as Pasadena, Santa Monica, Venice and Los Angeles (now Downtown), that were connected first by carriage and horse tracks, then by steam, and subsequently by the Redline electric railroad.

Downtown emerged as the commercial and transit centre, with Union Station as the hub of an efficient network of trams and rail. But by the 1940s the area had become highly congested and, in order to avoid it altogether, a burgeoning car-driving populace voted for the development of the boulevard system. The boulevards, traversing LA from west to east and criss-crossing the north-to-south avenues, were the first step towards the decentralisation of Los Angeles and the amalgamation of the separate cities into Greater Los Angeles (*see also page 42* **Sightseeing**).

BUILDING THE FREEWAYS

In 1939, the Pasadena Freeway (US 110), the first of its kind and now considered a classic, was built. Designed for cars travelling at 45 miles (70 kilometres) an hour, it is a charming byway that weaves its way under stone bridges and through rolling landscapes from Downtown LA to Pasadena.

In the 1950s, major freeway construction began. The planning of the routes was a highly politicised process. Avoiding the wealthier districts of the Westside, the freeways gouged their way through poor, disenfranchised neighbourhoods, leaving in their wake broken communities and a network of concrete and tarmac viaducts that have become the chief arteries and defining forms of the city.

Freeway construction more or less stopped in the 1970s (though a painful 30-year battle to prevent the extension of the Pasadena Freeway into picturesque South Pasadena still rages). The last freeway to be completed, after a lengthy construction process, was US 105 (aka Century or Glenn Anderson Freeway) in 1995. This dramatic feat of engineering (immortalised in the movie *Speed* while still under construction, when an as yet incomplete stretch of overpass was jumped during the bus chase) supposedly heralds the freeway of the future. It comes complete with high-tech sensors and a rail system along the centre.

The latter reflects a new stage in the evolution of Los Angeles. To cater to an expanding population, a vast, federally funded public transit project, comprising overground train and subway systems and intended to wean the populace from car dependency, is under way. Administered by the Metropolitan Transit Authority (MTA), this, too, is a highly politicised undertaking, which has not only been riddled with scandal and construction problems from its inception but also ill serves the poorer neighbourhoods that need it most and neglects to improve the existing bus system.

The result is that locals have little hope of Los Angeles becoming a public transit-based city and, despite the many measures conceived to mitigate pollution (including catalytic converters, emission-free petrol and incentives to car-pool), automobile use continues to rise.

THE DRIVING EXPERIENCE

Driving in LA delivers agony and ecstacy in equal measure. The ecstacy of whizzing along a freeway towards infinity, music playing, is countered by the pain of being stuck on that same freeway in rush hour – or worse, breaking down on it, ending up huddled in a locked car on the hard shoulder, praying for the arrival of the **Automobile Club of Southern California** (around $50 a year for roadside assistance and four free pick-ups, it's the club for sensible Angelenos; *see page 256* **Directory**).

Delight in acquiring the vehicle of one's choice – be it classic, wrecked, customised or hot off the production line – and the availability of ridiculously cheap petrol is tempered by the direct and hidden costs of car use. Quite apart from the obvious expenses of insurance (the highest in the US), maintenance, registration, smog tests, parking tickets and so on, a good half of California tax revenue goes towards the construction and maintenance of the highways system and the California Highway Patrol that protects it. Driving in LA also evokes the conflicting feelings of joy at being on the open road in one of the most spectacular terrains on the planet, and guilt that such liberation is achieved at the expense of that self-same natural environment.

A CITY BUILT FOR THE CAR

Car dependence has left its mark on the city not only in the network of freeways but in the form of the city itself. Car use encouraged the characteristic suburban LA lifestyle, emphasising private over public. Acres of land are covered by tracts of one- and two-storey single-family housing, with wide streets and driveways, two-car garages and large front and back yards, complete with pool and barbecue. The portable barbecue, incidentally, was invented by Henry Ford, who promoted the idea of 'picnicking' as one of the joys of leisure driving.

Car use also spawned a city zoned into residential neighbourhoods, some of which do not even have pavements, and commercial boulevards – 'strips' lined with buildings designed to cater to the driver. If not actually the originator, Los Angeles popularised stores with entrances on the rear parking lot (the historic Bullocks building on Wilshire Boulevard was the first of this type), corner mini-malls and drive-in motels (take Sunset Boulevard between Fairfax and La Brea Avenues to see some classics).

Drive-through fast-food restaurants and diners flourished on the strips. McDonald's, Jack in The Box, Taco Bell and In-n-Out Burger (the undisputed best of the burger chains) are ubiquitous and largely anonymous – though must-see fast-food outlets include a great new retro-style In-n-Out in Westwood Village, a sculptural Kentucky Fried Chicken on Western Avenue and one of the earliest McDonald's, in Pomona. Some classic diners, built in the 1950s and 1960s 'Googie' era of LA architecture, such as Bob's Big Boy in Burbank, still exist. Catch them before they disappear.

Most noticeable of all, however, are the signs. Since business owners realised they needed to catch the eye of a motorist skating by at 40 or more miles an hour, commercial art – huge advertising billboards, ads painted on the sides of buildings and buildings as signs in themselves – have emerged as the vernacular artform of Los Angeles.

Drive along Sunset Strip between Doheny Drive and La Cienega Boulevard for the most sensational, eye-popping sequence of huge signs. Take in the Cabazon Monster (a life-size model of a dinosaur) on the I-10 east of Los Angeles, and visit the Tail-o'-the-Pup on San Vicente Boulevard in West Hollywood or the Big Donut on Manchester Boulevard in Inglewood to experience the few remaining iconic incarnations of buildings as signs. There are also the 'Giant Triplets': huge, menacing advertising icons comprising 'Golf Man' (off the I-405 in Carson), 'Lumberjack Man' (outside a hardware store on Long Beach Boulevard) and 'Gas Station Man' (on Third Street in East LA).

Los Angeles is also the city of car lots, lube shops, 'body shops', car showrooms, carwashes and, most of all, parking lots, which cover huge amounts of land. To get the full flavour of all this, visit Heritage Classics (Santa Monica Boulevard at La Peer Drive; 1-310 657 9699) or Sunset Carwash (7955 Sunset Boulevard, opposite the Screen Actors Guild; 1-323 656 2777) for a classic carwash experience and the chance of seeing a star in a car.

YOU ARE WHAT YOU DRIVE

Car culture has bred a weird sense of time and space – locals measure the length of a journey by the time it takes rather than the distance covered. It has also generated a mindset where other forms of locomotion are confined to leisure activities, such as walking or cycling – you drive to the gym to use the step machine – and a dependence on technology that spawns yet more technology; hence the ubiquitous car phone/fax/stereo and the 'intelligent' freeway, with in-built sensors supposed to alert drivers to traffic problems ahead.

Car culture has also created snobbery based on the car you drive, with those thousands who do not drive or own a car at the bottom of the social ladder, a condition reinforced by the fact that the California driving licence is the most commonly used form of ID in the state. It is used instead of a bank card to authorise a cheque, get access to clubs and to prove you're old enough to buy alcohol.

Angelenos go to absurd extremes to keep up automobile appearances. Many cars on the road in LA are not actually owned but leased, for a night or for as long as you can keep up the monthly payments. Among many urban myths is the belief that certain Beverly Hills divorcees down on their uppers live in their cars, and, in so doing, maintain some semblance of their former glory.

Some people define themselves by their car, as they define their location by the freeway exit to which it is closest. Within the hierarchy of car ownership are numerous automobile subcultures: tribes include Latino lowriders, Valley Boy hot-rodders, media trendies in Jeep Wranglers, executive Lexus owners, proud custodians of classic American cars (still going strong because the desert dryness means that cars do not rust), wannabe macho dudes on pumped-up pick-up trucks and urban survivalist Westside mothers battling the streets in four-wheel Ford Explorers.

The cult of the car has bred a whole battery of gimmicks and services for car users, from bizarre personalised number plates – BRAK NEK, FAT LADY, SSTA GRL, SHRINK and ALI CAT are some we've spotted (check out more at www.plates.ca.gov) – to valet parking. Legions of besuited valet parkers mark the entrances to restaurants, clubs and, sometimes, car parks: the answer to parking in a city that has run out of space. (Don't forget to tip your valet.)

You can probably rent any type of car in LA, but for a *California Dreamin'* experience, try the infamous car-wreck supplier to the studios, Rent-A-Wreck in West LA (12333 Pico Boulevard, at Centinela Boulevard; 1-310 478 0676). Depending on your budget, at R-A-W you can hire anything from a beat-up old Ford to a pink convertible Caddy. And if you want to do the movie star thang, the car rental of choice has to be a stretch limousine. Limos, used to transport people in style to prom nights, the Oscars and the Grammies, or as mobile party rooms for stag nights, are available for hire any time, in numerous different makes and lengths. At Mercedes Limousines (9641 Sunset Boulevard, Beverly Hills; 1-310 271 8559) you can hog the road in a stretch Lincoln for $60 an hour (plus tip); for $110 you can command a stretch Merc and, for $110-$130, a Roller. For more hire companies, *see page 255* **Directory**.

Car culture has also bred some terrific radio. Tune into KCRW (89.9 FM), a favourite on the Westside for eclectic music and great news programming; KPWR (106.3 FM) for hip-hop and rap; KROQ (106.7 FM) for rock; KPFK (90.7 FM) for earnest radicalism; or KXEZ (100 FM) for the easy listening playing in the white BMW on Hugh Grant's fateful night. If you want to experience contemporary American culture at its most shrill, sample the talk radio shows on several AM stations, especially KFI (640 AM). For other radio choices, *see chapter* **Media**.

On the downside, car dependence has given rise to drive-by shootings, car-jacking, impossible building codes (demanding unachievable levels of parking space to accompany a new building), acquisitiveness, smog and traffic school. This last is an only-in-LA institution dreamed up by insurance companies, whereby you pay to attend a day of traffic school instead of getting an endorsement on your driving licence. It's a total con, but has given rise to all sorts of creative variations, such as Comedy Traffic School and Chocoholics and Ice-cream Lovers' School.

But, surprisingly, reliance on cars has also bred a generosity of sorts. With a collective sense of 'there but for the grace of God, go I – and my car', Angelenos will drive miles out of their way to give acquaintances a ride home, porter friends to and from the airport and often freely lend out cars (insurance permitting), exhibiting a casualness that results from taking the car for granted.

If you want to find out more about the evolution of automobile culture in LA as well as see some fabulous historic cars, visit the **Petersen Automotive Museum** on Wilshire Boulevard. Founded by the owner of Petersen Publishing Company, a producer of numerous car magazines, it offers a largely uncritical view of the automobile, but is great fun nonetheless (*see page 201* **Museums & Galleries**). For more information on driving in Los Angeles, including car hire, *see page 255* **Directory**.

Architecture

It may lack New York's dramatic skyscrapers, but amid the sprawl of low-rise strip malls stand examples of LA's delight in originality, excess and fantasy.

Los Angeles was founded and repeatedly reinvented by adventurers and fortune-seekers, some of whom came laden with cultural baggage, others with 'nothing to declare but their genius', as Oscar Wilde told a US customs officer. This helps to explain why most of Los Angeles and its 170 contiguous communities are a chaotic mishmash of borrowed styles, often executed with little finesse or imagination. But originality has also flourished here, ever since the arrival of intercontinental railroad in 1887 and the rapid transformation of a dusty cow town into a metropolis.

There are few major public buildings or landmark corporate structures. Like Tokyo, Los Angeles appears bewilderingly vast, featureless and horizontal from the freeways; one needs to explore the neighbourhoods to discover its extraordinary diversity and well-concealed treasures. Topography offers a clue: much of the best work is tucked away in the hills, clinging to 'unbuildable' sites that appeal to clients whose ambitions are matched by their budgets.

For organised tours that feature architecture, art and design, contact **Architours** (1-323 294 5825). Occasional house tours are also offered by the Los Angeles chapter of the **American Institute of Architects** (1-310 785 1809), the **Los Angeles Conservancy** (1-213 623 2489) and the **Society for Architectural Historians** (1-800 972 4722). For addresses and more information on many of the buildings mentioned here, see chapters **Sightseeing**, **Accommodation**, **Film**, **Museums & Galleries**, and **Theatre and Dance**.

*Double vision: Claes Oldenburg's binoculars for the **Chiat/Day** ad agency. See page 33.*

A CITY IS BORN

Only a few fragments remain of the early settlement with the long-winded name, El Pueblo de Nuestra Señora la Reina de Los Angeles. Misty-eyed preservationists blather on about the city's roots and the adobe tradition, but the evidence is unconvincing: dull provincial buildings, rebuilt or prettified, are best forgotten.

There is, however, a rich legacy of buildings from the land boom of the late 1880s, notably the houses built in the Queen Anne and Eastlake styles on the 1300 block of **Carroll Avenue**, between Douglas Street and Edgeware Road, in Echo Park, just north-west of Downtown. One of the Victorian offices that Angelenos commuted to by streetcar was the **Bradbury Building**. Behind its century-old brick façade is a stunning skylit atrium surrounded by tiled galleries with polished wood balustrades and open-cage lifts. It was inspired by a science fiction novel and, fittingly, appeared in the film *Blade Runner*.

Ten miles (16 kilometres) north-east, at the foot of the San Gabriel Mountains, lies Pasadena, which flourished as a winter resort for rich Easterners around the turn of the century. Remnants of the flamboyant resort hotels survive, as do many handsome 'bungalows' in the 'Craftsman' style – an offshoot of the Victorian Arts and Crafts movement. The standout is the **Gamble House**, built by Charles and Henry Greene in 1908, a marvel of polished mahogany and Tiffany glass.

Bradbury Building

304 S Broadway, at Third Street, Downtown (1-213 626 1893). Metro Civic Center/Tom Bradley or Pershing Square/bus 1, 2, 3, 4, 10/I-10, exit Fourth Street east. **Open** *ground floor only* 9am-6pm Mon-Fri; 9am-5pm Sat, Sun. **Admission** free. **Map 7 B2**

Gamble House

4 Westmoreland Place, at Walnut Street, Pasadena (1-626 793 3334). Bus 177, 267/I-10, exit Orange Grove Boulevard north. **Open** noon-3pm Thur-Sun (tours every 20 mins). **Admission** $5; $4 seniors; $3 under-12s.

INTERWAR BOOM

During the growth years of the 1920s, Southern California embraced the Mediterranean tradition, building thousands of pocket haciendas, 'Churrigueresque' car showrooms and abstracted Andalusian farmhouses. The city developed an indiscriminate appetite for all things foreign and exotic: Wallace Neff and George Washington Smith set the pace, but all Beaux Arts-trained architects were masters of period style, and every builder could run up a mosque, a medieval castle or an Egyptian tomb to satisfy a devotee of romantic fiction. Hollywood legitimised this exuberant eclecticism, but the impulse came from newcomers who flocked to LA from around the world, dreaming of fortune or an easy life in the sun.

The greatest personal fantasy to survive, however, was not a rich man's folly. **Watts Towers** (1921-54) were built over three decades by a poor Italian immigrant, Simon Rodia. Every day he hoisted himself up one of the slender iron frameworks, implanting scraps of broken china and glass in wet cement. The towers – nearly 100 feet (30 metres) tall – are currently covered in scaffolding for restoration; they are scheduled to reopen in 2000. For more information, *see page 76* **Sightseeing**.

Spadena House (Walden Drive, at Carmelita Avenue, Beverly Hills), also known as the Witch's House, was built as a movie set in Culver City in 1921 and was later moved to its present site.

Mass fantasies found their outlet in exotic movie palaces. Still flourishing is **Mann's Chinese Theater** (6925 Hollywood Boulevard, at Highland Avenue); newly reborn is **El Capitan Theater** (No.6838). Other palaces are now used for the performing arts: art deco fans should catch a show at the **Pantages Theater** (6233 Hollywood Boulevard) or the **Wiltern Theater** (Wilshire Boulevard, at Western Avenue). There is a cluster of decaying vintage movie palaces on South Broadway.

Recently restored and expanded by US firm Hardy Holzman Pfeiffer, Bertram Goodhue's **Central Library** embodies the civic pride and Beaux Arts scholarship of the 1920s in its Egyptian massing, lofty inscriptions and spirited murals. Likewise, the vast, pyramid-capped 1928 **City Hall** (200 N Spring Street, between First and Temple Streets), designed by Austin, Parkinson, Martin, Whittlesey, was intended to impress, to the point of pomposity: until 1957, it was the only exception that had been permitted to the city's 13-storey height limit. The commercial counterpart was **Bullocks Wilshire** (3050 Wilshire Boulevard), the grandest of department stores and the first to be designed so that motorists could unload beneath a *porte cochère* – a drive-through canopy attached to the entrance – and park in the rear. It has recently been transformed into a law school, with its art deco façades and ornament preserved.

Frank Lloyd Wright and his Austrian-born protégés, Rudolph Schindler and Richard Neutra, pioneered modern architecture in Southern California from 1920 onwards. Highlights include Wright's **Hollyhock House** and **Ennis-Brown House** (both of which are open to the public) and the **Schindler House** (now known as the MAK Center) in West Hollywood. Built as the architect's live-work space, the latter is a dazzling combination of tilt-up concrete walls, redwood partitions, rooftop 'sleeping baskets' and outdoor living rooms. Another major work by Schindler is the concrete-frame **Lovell Beach House** (13th Street, at Beach Walk, Balboa Island, Orange County).

Neutra had a 40-year career in Los Angeles: among his finest 'International Modern' residences are the **Lovell Health House** (4616 Dundee Drive, at the southern end of Griffith Park), which featured recently in *LA Confidential*, and the **Strathmore Apartments**, stacked up a hillside in Westwood (11005 Strathmore Drive, off Gayley Avenue).

Another influential Los Angeles architect born out of Frank Lloyd Wright's organic modern tradition was John Lautner, designer of structurally dynamic futuristic buildings, such as the 1960 **Chemosphere** (7776 Torreyson Drive, north of Mount Olympus), most familiar as the exotic setting of choice in James Bond films. Lautner first came to Los Angeles in 1939 to supervise construction of Frank Lloyd Wright's Sturges House and was sickened by the ugliness of what he found in the city. But he realised, as Wright had in the 1920s, that he could realise his vision here, in the soft clay of a burgeoning community, as he never could in the tradition-bound East or Midwest. He settled and built a succession of daring, highly original houses – although he did no more than scrape a living and achieved widespread fame only in the last few years before his death in 1994.

The Los Angeles region fared better than most during the Depression, but the old extravagance was gone and New World 'streamline moderne' replaced European models for many public buildings and a few homes. You can drive by the **Coca-Cola Bottling Plant** (1334 Central Avenue, at 14th Street), which resembles an ocean liner moored amid the warehouses of Downtown, and take a train from **Union Station** (800 N Alameda Street), last of the great US passenger terminals.

Broadway movie palaces
Million Dollar, Los Angeles, Orpheum, United Artists: S Broadway, between Third Street & Olympic Boulevard, Downtown. Metro Pershing Square or Seventh Street/ Metro Center/bus 10, 11, 40, 45/I-110 north, exit Sixth Street east. **Open** Orpheum for films; others for church services, special events and on Los Angeles Conservancy tours. **Information** Orpheum 1-213 239 0939; others 1-213 623 2489. **Map 7 B2-B4**

Central Library
630 W Fifth Street, between Flower Street & Grand Avenue, Downtown (1-213 228 7000). Metro Pershing Square or Seventh Street/Metro Center/bus DASH E/ I-110 north, exit Sixth Street east. **Open** 10am-5.30pm Mon, Thur-Sat; noon-8pm Tue, Wed; 1-5pm Sun. **Map 7 B3**

Hollyhock House
Barnsdall Art Park, 4800 Hollywood Boulevard, at Vermont Avenue, Los Feliz (1-213 228 7000). Bus 1, 180, 181, 204, 217/US 101, exit Vermont Avenue north. **Open** noon-3pm (tours on the hour) Wed-Sun. **Admission** $2; $1 seniors; free under-12s. **Map 6 A2**

*Labour of love: the fabulous **Watts Towers** in South Central. See page 29.*

Ennis-Brown House

2655 Glendower Avenue, at Vermont Avenue & Los Feliz
Boulevard, Los Feliz (1-213 660 0607). Bus 180, 181/
US 101, exit Vermont Avenue north. **Open** *tours* second
Sat Jan, Mar, May, July, Sept, Nov; at other times by
reservation. **Tours** $10; $5 students, seniors.
Map 6 A1

MAK Center for Art & Architecture at the Schindler House

835 N Kings Road, between Santa Monica Boulevard &
Melrose Avenue, West Hollywood (1-213 651 1510).
Bus 4, 105, 304/I-10, exit La Cienega Boulevard north.
Open 11am-6pm Wed-Sun. **Admission** $5. **Map 4 B2**

THE GOOGIE LEGACY

When America emerged from Depression and war,
there was a mood of optimism and of faith in
technology. Cars were designed to look like jet
fighters and the coffeeshops (like car washes) also
strove to look as though they were moving at warp
speed. Lloyd Wright (Frank's son) and John
Lautner led the charge; in 1949, Lautner designed
an angular, wood and glass coffeeshop called
Googie's, next door to the legendary Schwab's
drugstore on Sunset Strip. Both landmarks have
now vanished, replaced by a pastel shopping/
movie theatre complex, but the name Googie lives
on as shorthand for the post-war generation of
coffeeshops that epitomises 1950s and 1960s futuristic drive-by design. Flashing neon signs towered
over these single-storey boxes, and within, the
furnishings were a mix of cosy and gee-whizz:
Naugahyde booths and space-age lamps.

Of the survivors, the best may be **Pann's** (at the
intersection of La Tijera, La Cienega and Centinela
Boulevards, Inglewood) and **Ship's Culver City**
(Overland Avenue, at Washington Boulevard).
The earliest surviving **McDonald's** (10807
Lakewood Boulevard, at Florence Avenue,
Downey), built in 1953, shares the aesthetic.

These designs also drew on the tradition of the
building as sign: the overscaled doughnuts, wind-
mills and hot dogs that had lured passing
motorists from the 1930s onward. The **Tail-o'-
the-Pup** in West Hollywood (329 N San Vicente
Boulevard, at Beverly Boulevard), built in 1946,
and **Randy's Donut** in Inglewood (805 W
Manchester Boulevard, at La Cienega Boulevard),
built in 1954, are surviving examples of this once
ubiquitous building-type.

POST-WAR GROWTH

The population of Southern California exploded in
the 1950s and new suburbs obliterated fields and
citrus orchards, extending, with the freeways, over
the mountains and into the desert. Business interests spurred the renewal of Downtown, razing the
decaying Victorian mansions atop Bunker Hill and
creating, from the early 1960s onwards, a corridor
of office towers. But, as freeways clogged and public transportation lagged, Century City and other
commercial hubs grew to serve an increasingly

fragmented and suburban metropolis. This period
also saw the construction of the landmark **Theme
Building** (Paul Williams, 1961) at LAX, a space-
age fantasy that has now slipped into a kitsch-clas-
sic middle age. It has recently been revived by the
opening of the lovingly retro transgalactic
Encounter restaurant inside.

From 1945 to 1962, the influential magazine
Arts + Architecture sponsored the Case Study
House programme, a visionary project fuelled by
post-war optimism whose mission was to create
prototypical low-cost houses using new prefabri-
cated materials and building methods. Although
they never achieved the anticipated mass popularity, the Case Study Houses stand as icons of
Southern Californian modern design, characterised
by the use of glass walls and doors – to make the
exterior landscape flow into the interior, and vice
versa – and open-plan glass and steel volumes.
One of the best was the steel-framed **Eames
House**, a fusion of poetry and technology by
Charles and Ray Eames, the US's most talented
husband and wife design team, built in 1949 from
off-the-shelf components.

Just as Frank Lloyd Wright inspired the first
generation of modernists in Southern California,
so has Toronto-born Frank Gehry served as
mentor to several generations of free-spirited
architects. There are several must-see buildings
by architects influenced by Gehry's idiosyncratic
forms and inventive use of materials – often low-
cost industrial stuff. The UCLA campus in
Westwood has one striking example: the **'Towell'
(Temporary Powell) Library**, a sizzling temporary structure designed by Hodgetts and Fung.
And, in Culver City, Eric Owen Moss has remodelled a succession of drab warehouses, creating
cutting-edge workspaces for innovative companies, including the **Box** (8520 National Boulevard)
and **Samitaur** (3457 S La Cienega Boulevard).

Outstanding examples of contemporary architecture in Downtown include the **Museum of
Contemporary Art** (250 S Grand Avenue) – a
powerful complex of geometric solids and skylit
galleries designed by Japanese architect Arata
Isozaki – and Pei Cobb Freed's soaring extension
to the **Convention Center** (at S Figueroa Street
and W Pico Boulevard). For relaxation, there's
Pershing Square (at S Olive and Fifth Streets),
LA's second-oldest public space. The square was
dramatically re-landscaped in 1994 by Laurie Olin,
with colourful architectural features added by
Ricardo Legorreta.

Neither Gehry nor his acolytes got to build LA's
largest civic project this decade: the newly opened
Getty Center (*see page 198* **Museums &
Galleries**). That choice commission went to East
Coast architect Richard Meier, who reintroduced
cool International Modernism to LA in his hilltop
complex. Meier also designed the crisp **Museum**

of Television & Radio in Beverly Hills. The original Getty Museum, a replica Roman villa in Malibu, is being remodelled by Machado & Silvetti Associates, also from the East Coast, and will reopen in 2001 as a centre for classical antiquities and comparative archeology.

In Burbank, Robert Stern brings smiles to motorists crawling home on the Ventura Freeway with his cartoon-like **Disney Animation Building** (at Alameda Avenue and Buena Vista Street). To the south, in Orange County, Philip Johnson and John Burgee created the aptly named **Crystal Cathedral** for one of California's leading pop preachers.

Eames House

203 Chautauqua Boulevard, off Pacific Coast Highway, Pacific Palisades. Bus 9, 434/I-10, exit PCH north. **Open** *office* 10am-5pm Mon-Fri. Exterior tours only; information 1-310 396 5991.

Crystal Cathedral

12141 Lewis Street, at Chapman Avenue, Garden Grove, Orange County (1-714 971 4000). I-5 south, exit The Center Drive to Chapman Avenue west. **Open** 9am-3.30pm Mon-Sat (except during weddings and funerals); tours every 20 mins. **Admission** free.

THE 1990S

The architecture scene in Los Angeles changed dramatically in the early 1990s, when architects were hit first by the recession, then by the 1992 riots, 1994 earthquake and floods. These cataclysms jolted many architects into a sense of responsibility for the city. With a zeal comparable only to the early modernists, architects organised seminars, community workshops and master-planning sessions out of which came numerous, well-intentioned plans for LA. In reality, the devastated parts of the city were largely rebuilt by developers and politicians in the most expedient way possible.

However, that brief period of reflection did produce some legacies, such as **Inner City Arts**, an arts school for poor kids in Downtown public schools. With a post-riot rush of donations, they were able to move into a new home, an imaginatively converted car repair shop in Skid Row (720 S Kohler Street), designed by Michael Maltzan Architecture. Maltzan, a protégé of Frank Gehry's and one of LA's up-and-coming young architects, also designed a strong, sculptural arts complex at **Harvard-Westlake School** (3700 Coldwater Canyon, at Hacienda Drive, North Hollywood; call ahead for opening times on 1-818 980 6692).

While the 1980s produced a recognisable architectural aesthetic, the 1990s have been less distinctive. The recession produced an aesthetic shift away from the deconstructivist contortions that characterised much of the prominent late 1980s design towards simpler and stylistically varied buildings. On one hand, you can see Googie

Frank Gehry

One of LA's most famous sons is Frank Gehry: his voluptuous, titanium-clad Guggenheim Museum in Bilbao, Spain, opened last year, firmly establishing him as one of the world's most extraordinary architects.

Gehry's family moved to LA from Toronto in his youth, and he studied at the University of Southern California before spending several years working for corporate architecture firm Victor Gruen & Associates and then establishing his own firm, Frank O Gehry & Associates, in his early 30s in 1962. With commercial work for bread and butter, he proceeded to design a string of low-budget studios and residences; an early (1964) notable project is the **Danziger Studio/ Residence**, two simple, bold, cubic structures buffered from the busy street by a high surrounding wall (7001 Melrose Avenue, at Sycamore Avenue, Hollywood).

Gehry drew inspiration from LA artists, not architects, and became increasingly experimental, creating collages of cheap materials and banal building elements. He catapulted himself on to the world stage with the 1978 remodelling of his own house in a polite residential neighbourhood in Santa Monica (1002 22nd Street, at Washington Avenue), a seemingly chaotic collage of chainlink fencing, plywood and exposed structure.

Although Gehry likes to claim that he is only appreciated outside Los Angeles, he has built many buildings here. Must-see examples from the 1980s and early 1990s are the **Geffen Contemporary Museum** (formerly the Temporary Contemporary, 152 N Central Avenue, at First Street, Downtown), a subtle and very effective warehouse

revisited – for example, in Stephen Ehrlich's **Robertson Library** (1719 S Robertson Boulevard, at Airdrome Street, Midtown; 1-310 840 2147) and Kanner Architects' vibrant **In-N-Out Burger** in Westwood (Gayley Avenue, at Le Conte Avenue). On the other is a starker minimalism, as in buildings by David Hertz Work, whose spare **McKinley Residence** (2420 McKinley Avenue in Venice) and **Lehrer Residence** (2238 Stradella Road, Bel Air) are laboratories for environmental sustainability, in the use of solar panels, underfloor heating and a recycled concrete product called 'syndecrete' for surfaces and furnishings.

Arguably one of the most interesting examples

conversion; **Loyola Law School** (1441 W Olympic Boulevard, between Albany and Valencia Streets, Downtown), a complex of different forms; the **Edgemar Development** (2433 Main Street between Ocean Park Boulevard and Hollister Avenue, Santa Monica; 1-310 450 0222); **Santa Monica Place Shopping Center** (between Broadway and Colorado Avenue, at Second and Fourth Streets, Santa Monica), famous for its layered chainlink façade on the parking garage, visible from Second Street to the south; the West Coast headquarters for the **Chiat/Day** advertising agency (340 Main Street, at Rose Avenue, Venice), with its eye-catching portico in the form of a huge pair of upturned binoculars designed by Claes Oldenburg and Coosje van Bruggen. Also in Venice are several residential projects by Gehry.

With increased stature, up went Gehry's budgets, and in the 1990s his work moved from raw, makeshift construction to complex, sensuous structures clad in rich materials, designed with the aid of sophisticated computer programmes. Buildings from this era include the **Team Disney** administration building (800 W Ball Road, Anaheim) with its fabulous undulating yellow façade; the muscular **Disney Ice** arena (300 W Lincoln Avenue, also in Anaheim), with its wavy roof; and, of course, the yet-to-be-built **Disney Concert Hall** (*see photo*), an exploding flower of curving forms, which will be the new Downtown home for the Los Angeles Philharmonic.

The concert hall, heralded as the culmination of Gehry's career, has been held up for cost reasons (and its thunder has arguably been stolen by the Guggenheim Museum, which has a similar aesthetic), but it is now being modified and is due to start construction in late 1998, with opening set for 2002. It will be the first major civic building designed by Gehry for Los Angeles and should further enhance his – and the city's – reputation.

of recent design in LA was by a Frenchman: Philippe Starck's brilliantly effective, surreal remodelling of the **Mondrian Hotel** (8440 Sunset Boulevard, West Hollywood).

Since the economy picked up in the mid-1990s, the biggest source of work for architects has been the entertainment industry. All the studios have embarked on massive expansion plans, and many are developing restaurants, leisure centres and themed entertainment/retail destinations, exemplified by **Universal CityWalk**, an amalgam of LA buildings distilled into an artificial street of exploding noise and colour at Universal City. CityWalk's designers, the Jerde Partnership International – also responsible for the Fremont Street Experience in Las Vegas and Mall of America, the world's largest shopping centre, in Bloomington, Minneapolis – is among Los Angeles's most successful and influential architects, exporting huge, controversial but very popular commercial complexes throughout the US and the rest of the world.

An antidote to such excessive architecture is the serene, spacious and elegant **Form Zero**, an architectural bookshop with an interior designed by the store's owner, Andrew Liang, in the Gehry-designed **Edgemar Development**. This shop is also a goldmine of information about architecture in Los Angeles. For guidebooks to LA's buildings, *see page 267* **Further Reading**.

Ethnic LA

Immigration has transformed Los Angeles into the most multiracial city in the US, where the world's different peoples meet, collide and create new cultures.

When the Beach Boys eulogised 'California Girls' in the early 1960s, the image that came to mind was of athletic, tall, blue-eyed blondes who played volleyball and tanned themselves on the beach. Not in that picture were the dark-skinned, brown-eyed beauties that people Los Angeles today. In the past 30 years LA has undergone a huge transformation – from Iowa-on-the-Pacific to the US capital of foreign immigration; from whitebread city to one where Mexicans are fast becoming the majority population and where inter-ethnic relations are the primary social and political concern.

In large part, this change is thanks to a 1965 immigration act that transformed patterns of immigration to the US. The Hart-Celler Act abolished the old country-of-origin quotas, which had favoured Europeans, particularly Irish. Instead, family ties to US citizens or possession of scarce skills became the criteria for entry.

Designed to contain immigration, the act in fact released a flood of migrants from Latin America, the Caribbean, the Middle East and – where the reformers least expected – Asia. Well-educated Chinese, Filipinos, Koreans and East Asians (from India) poured in, followed by their less skilled relatives, making Asians today the third largest group in Los Angeles, more numerous than African-Americans. Mexicans, already established in Southern California (*see page 37* **Mexican LA**) jumped from a population of just over one million in 1970 to almost four million in 1990, of whom almost half were immigrants.

Many thousands of people came to US shores simply seeking a better life and chose Los Angeles for the traditional reasons – sun, sea and opportunity. But political upheavals overseas in the 1970s and early 1980s also injected a sudden rush of new arrivals. LA became home to exiles from the 1973 Arab-Israeli wars, the Lebanese civil war that began in 1975, the Iranian revolution of 1978-79; from the collapse of the US-supported regime in South Vietnam and the Communist takeovers in Cambodia and Laos; from the conflicts in El Salvador and Guatamala; and, in the late 1980s, the fall of the Iron Curtain and the dissolution of Russia.

The result has been the transformation of the 33,210 square miles (86,010 square kilometres) of

A newsstand in Chinatown.

the five-county Los Angeles region into a mosaic of communities speaking more than 80 languages. If you drive through LA, you'll see its endless miles of tract housing and strip mall development overlaid with the markings of different cultures: vividly painted walls and murals in heavily Hispanic areas from Pacoima in the north Valley down to Compton in South Los Angeles; Chinese and Vietnamese sculptures and signs in Little Saigon in Orange County; and Armenian schools and churches in Glendale. Recently, the Los Angeles Convention and

Visitors Bureau has recognised the marketing potential of these concentrated ethnicities (*see below* **The multicultural tourist**).

THE ETHNIC DISTRICTS

Central Americans – 300,000 Salvadorans and 150,000 Guatamalans – are dispersed throughout the city, though concentrated in South Central LA. Many start their US life in the Pico-Union and MacArthur Park area just west of Downtown. Don't be surprised if people tell you to avoid this notoriously dangerous neighbourhood – poverty and gang trouble are common – but, really, it's fine for outsiders and has its share of interesting shops and eateries. For cheap Salvadoran food and plenty of atmosphere, try **El Izalqueno** restaurant (1830 Pico Boulevard, between Union Avenue and Alvarado Street; 1-213 387 2467)

Chinese, hailing from Hong Kong, Taiwan and the mainland, have transformed Monterey Park in the eastern San Gabriel Valley into a thriving enclave, thanks to the efforts of a creative Chinese developer who sold the neighbourhood to his compatriots as the 'Chinese Beverly Hills'. Go there for full immersion in Chinese culture – and, reputedly, the best Chinese food in the US. The rest of LA's more than 300,000 Chinese mostly live in old Chinatown, north of Downtown.

Many Middle Easterners, now numbering over 300,000 in LA, have settled in the 'three Bs': Beverly Hills, Brentwood and Bel Air. California's Vietnamese also number around 300,000: airlifted from Vietnam by US planes and deposited at Camp Pendleton north of San Diego, they have remained in the region. They have concentrated in Orange County, where the white community tends to be conservative and therefore supported these exiles from a Communist regime. In LA, they have created a capital in Little Saigon, three square miles of strip malls and industrial buildings centered on Bolsa Avenue in Westminster – a must if you want an authentic flavour of Vietnam, especially its superb French-Vietnamese food, best exemplified at **Song Long** restaurant (9361 Bolsa Avenue, suite 108, between Brookhurst and Magnolia Streets; 1-714 775 3724).

Koreatown is both home and workplace to many of the city's 200,000 Koreans. Located north and south of Wilshire Boulevard around Western Avenue, just east of Miracle Mile (in the Mid Wilshire district), Koreatown features such outposts of Korean culture as the fabulous **Beverly Hot Springs** (*see page 170* **Shops & Services**), a natural mineral water baths that is also a shiatsu massage and treatment centre.

Indians have dispersed across the basin but there are small concentrations in Artesia, in the South Bay and in the Valley. **Indian Sweets & Spices** is a wonderful chain of Indian groceries, where you can also get very cheap platefuls of

The multicultural tourist

In 1984, community activists in East LA and South Central expressed their outrage that tourists, in town for the Olympics, were discouraged from visiting their neighbourhoods. In 1992, shortly after the riots, they complained again, rightly, that the Los Angeles Convention and Visitors Bureau sold Los Angeles as five distinct neighbourhoods: Downtown, Hollywood, the Westside, Coastal and the Valleys. The bureau's publication, *Destination Los Angeles*, completely ignored – did not even highlight on a map – South and South Central LA, East LA, Pico-Union, Koreatown and virtually all working-class and/or ethnic neighbourhoods.

Well, six years later, that same tourist office is attempting to redress the balance. Coerced by activists, as well as slowly waking up to the idea that there's gold in them thar ethnic enclaves – 'if Harlem can do it, we can too' – the bureau, on the advice of 100 or so people from different communities in LA, is trying to attract people to many of those areas previously off the map.

The office's website – **www.californias edge.com** – contains a series of self-guided itineraries to the cultural and culinary artefacts of ethnic neighbourhoods in Los Angeles, San Diego and San Francisco. Collected under such themed categories as 'African-American Heritage', 'Pride' (gay and lesbian culture), 'Jewish Heritage', 'Fiesta' (Latin culture) and 'East is West' are listings of restaurants, shops, galleries, theatres and festivals in Leimert Park, East LA, Little Tokyo, Chinatown and so on.

Admittedly, it's all a bit cute, but it is useful, and makes an advance towards increasing the visibility and hence economic strength of ethnic neighbourhoods. However, some complain that the tourist office is selling a sanitised version of such areas, excluding, for example, historical sites that might present a bad image – such as the site of the Watts riots or the intersection of Florence and Normandie Avenues, the notorious spot in South Central Los Angeles where the 1992 riots began.

curry. Scattered through the suburbs, the most central branch is at 9409 Venice Boulevard, at Bagley Avenue, in Culver City (1-310 837 5286).

One nucleus of African LA is Fairfax, south of Wilshire Boulevard, where you can find an Ethiopian restaurant row. Armenians, 115,000 in total, concentrate in suburban Glendale. Older Russians, many of them Jewish (and so with no great reason to love their country of origin) have settled in the social-service-heavy city of West Hollywood. Some 400,000 Britons currently live in LA and many of those strange creatures populate the beach – mainly Santa Monica (also known as Santa Margate) – and the Hollywood area, making their presence felt in such pubs as **Ye Olde King's Head** and the **Coach & Horses** (for both, *see chapter* **Bars**).

INTERRACIAL TENSIONS

Just because many new immigrants arrived in Los Angeles at the same time did not mean they arrived at the same level. LA is tussling not only with interracial conflicts but race-class conflict, demonstrated most shockingly in the 1992 riots. The rage of blacks following the Rodney King beating was vented not, as expected, on whites but on Koreans – perceived by blacks as economically better off and exploiters of their neighbourhoods. Two thousand Korean businesses were looted, damaged or destroyed in the three days of trouble; of those, 200 liquor stores were destroyed in South Central LA alone.

Many Middle Easterners were successful entrepreneurs and professionals in their home countries – Iranians, for example, chose to come to LA, says one Iranian journalist, because their children were already there, studying at UCLA and other good California schools. They were able to transfer large sums of money and settle in traditionally affluent white neighbourhoods, and have a reputation for flamboyant wealth.

Africans, too, from Ethiopia and Ghana, tend to be well educated and affluent. In a cruel irony, they seem to move more easily in white professional classes than their distant African-American cousins. Many Africans consider themselves very different from African-Americans – they tend not to feel as strongly the racial preoccupations that are the legacy of slavery – and this gives rise to tensions between the two groups.

Indians (called East Asians in LA) are often entrepreneurial and very well educated – often better educated than their white US counterparts. They feature prominently in computer and high technology: Bill Gates has upset immigration-control advocates by going to bat for Asian computer experts, without whom, he says, his company would be short-handed. They have also created a niche market for themselves – motel ownership. Speaking English on arrival has given Indian immigrants a strong advantage. In West Hollywood, the Russian newcomers' lack of English and seemingly unfriendly manners have given rise to tensions with the gay population that also considers WeHo home.

Central Americans have not been made welcome for other reasons. Salvadorans have arrived fleeing a US-supported right-wing regime, unlike the Indo-Chinese, and arrive ill-educated and very poor. Having entered at the bottom of the heap, Central Americans and Mexicans are the backbone of LA's economy, working in disproportionately high numbers in the garment and service industries. Because labour is so cheap and supply so high, an astounding number of middle-class whites in Los Angeles have nannies, gardeners, cleaners, sometimes even cooks, giving rise to the charge that LA is a third-world economy.

And, in addition to helping grease the wheels of double-income white Westside family life, many Latin Americans are also sending a portion of their paltry incomes home, to support relatives there. 'Envios' – small businesses that arrange money transfers to Central America and Mexico – can be found throughout Latino neighbourhoods.

ETHNIC ACTION

In the past decade, ethnic Los Angeles has become a subject of academic study, material for novels, grist for politicians' mills and scourge of those who hate political correctness. The *Los Angeles Times*, once a bastion of the conservative white establishment, has hired a race relations correspondent, while news programmes bend over backwards to put an 'ethnic' anchor on screen – the preferred type being an indefinable hybrid, clearly not Anglo, but not identifiably another individual race.

The reason for this ethnic appeasement is that over the past ten years or so the tensions have turned into a series of social and political events. In Monterey Park, inter-ethnic murmurings began in the late 1980s, after the area had gone from being predominantly white then heavily Latino to majority Chinese in the space of 15 years, and triggered a series of ugly racial fights and political battles that have only now settled down. The riots in 1992 were the most brutal but arguably most cathartic expression of the stresses. The civil unrest (as the riots are more politically-correctly termed) wiped complacency off the face of LA and provoked an unprecedented surge of community and corporate efforts to stimulate economic development and mutual understanding.

One unexpected consequence was that Koreans found a voice, transforming themselves overnight from a silent to a relatively vocal minority. One of LA's most prominent Korean spokeswomen during the riots and their aftermath, Angela Oh, is now a member of President Clinton's Race Commission.

Mexican LA

For most of the twentieth century, Los Angeles's Mexican roots were either 'ignored by Anglo Angelenos or turned into a mythical "Spanish" past,' says sociologist Vilma Ortiz. But the past 25 years of immigration have reconnected LA with its roots and made people of Mexican ancestry the largest ethnic block in the region – 40 per cent of LA County residents, or four million people, are either Mexican-born or trace their origins to Mexico. LA has become the capital of Mexican America, the largest single Mexican concentration outside Mexico City, and Mexicans are predicted to overtake all other ethnic groups combined by 2020 at the latest.

The number of Mexicans has soared since 1970, but they have lived in Southern California since its inception. When Mexico gained its independence from Spain in 1822, large tracts of land were deeded to local Mexican families, many of whom grew prosperous as ranchers and merchants, until the Mexican-American war in 1848 brought an end to Mexican supremacy. But they left their mark on the region, in the naming of places (Santa Monica, Pasadena, Ventura) and boulevards (La Cienega, La Brea, Figueroa and Sepulveda), in adobes and Spanish mission-style architecture, and in festivals, such as Cinco de Mayo (5 May), celebrating a military victory over French invaders in 1862, and Diez y Seis de Septiembre (16 September), commemorating Mexico's Independence Day.

Under white dominance, Mexicans were reduced to an inferior status, labouring in menial jobs and in the fields of the Central Valley agricultural belt – as a disproportionate number still do. Now, however, a rising number are moving into the middle class, and so great is the Mexican population that an entire economy has arisen around it. Spanish-speaking radio dominates the airwaves, there are publications, sporting events, countless shops and restaurants, real estate and insurance companies and so on, all

catering to Mexicans and Central Americans (many of the latter, incidentally, complain of being treated as inferior by Mexicans). Many municipal signs and much official literature are printed in English and Spanish. And the Catholic Church has taken over from Protestantism to become the dominant religion, with the churches introducing Spanish masses and crying out for Spanish-speaking priests.

The emergence of Mexican economic and political power appears threatening to many in the fast-diminishing black and white communities, so much so that the past decade has seen bitter fights over political seats and legislative attempts to slow immigration and stop bilingual education in schools. And, worryingly, tax cuts passed during the past two decades mean that public education and services, now catering increasingly to Mexicans, are far inferior to those enjoyed by previous, white generations, spawning hysterical visions of an uneducated, angry, brown mob.

Short of the Mexican birth rate freezing (LA's population is projected to reach 22 million by 2020, due in large part to Mexican population growth) and immigration stopping, the trend will continue, thoroughly transforming LA from majority white to majority Latino. But, if the trend toward economic self-improvement also continues, Mexicans will, like all other past immigrants to the United States, assimilate into the home-owning, gas-guzzling, Coke-drinking, cheerleading, channel-surfing, God-fearing Americans that many already are.

To really get a sense of Mexican LA, take a walk down Broadway or Olvera Street in Downtown. Or drive into East LA, the heart of the Mexican community. Or take Sunset Boulevard through Silver Lake, or head south into South Central on Vermont or Normandie Avenues. Or take Van Nuys Boulevard north in the Valley. What you'll find is, LA is Mexican LA.

선물세트 $15.00 　 FRESH BAKERY 　 우유식빵 $3.00

따근따끈한 식빵 · 호박빵 · 맘모스 · 애플 · 야채빵　2 For $5.0

More than 200,000 Koreans live, work – and eat – in Koreatown.

She has often said: 'Korean-Americans were born on 29 April 1992.'

Similarly, Hispanic-Americans were arguably born, or reborn, after the 1994 passage of Proposition 187, a state-wide initiative passed convincingly by California voters, which cut off social services and public education to the children of immigrants. It was later deemed unconstitutional by the Supreme Court, and rather than stop the flow of immigrants, as its authors intended, it galvanised the Latino community. Notoriously indifferent to politics, Mexicans and Central Americans rushed to become citizens and activate the voters in their communities, with the result being a sudden, large increase in the number of Latino politicians at local and state level, ousting long-held seats in traditionally white, black and Jewish strongholds.

FUSION CITY

But the counterpart to ethnic tension in Los Angeles is fusion. LA is, after all, the home of the teriyaki hamburger and the kosher burrito. And even though some parts of the city are relatively segregated, many are increasingly mixed. Mike Davis, author of the bestseller *City of Quartz*, once said that the stretch of Vermont Avenue between the I-10 and Hollywood Boulevard has the highest number of different cultures represented on one street in LA, and probably in the world. Koreatown actually shares its neighbourhood with Latinos and blacks, and to the east overlaps with posh, Anglo Hancock Park; the unoffical jokey term for Hancock Park, where 300 Korean families reportedly now live, is Han Kook, the native term for Korea.

Much of South Central is both Latino and black, while in the Baldwin Hills area of the predominantly black Crenshaw district – south of the I-10, surrounding Crenshaw Boulevard – you will find the manicured gardens and pagoda-style roofs bequeathed by a former Japanese community (which relocated there after returning from internment camps), some of whom still live there.

Los Angeles is also home to wonderful fusion music groups, such as Ozomatli (a large, multiethnic band that mixes Cuban, Brazilian, African, Jamaican, Mexican and jazz influences to perfection), and boasts one of the highest rates of interracial marriage in America. For a taste of inter-ethnic harmony, you need only walk down the Boardwalk in Venice, Third Street Promenade in Santa Monica or CityWalk in Universal City.

Rodney King's poignant plea to the public during the riots – 'Can't we all get along?' – was and is heeded by vast numbers in the city. The sense that LA is a microcosm of the world, a multiracial template for the future, is another reason why this city is such an exciting place to be.

For more sources of information on ethnic Los Angeles, *see page 267* **Further Reading**.

Sightseeing

Sightseeing

Generations of movie-makers have exploited LA's landmarks, vistas and distinctive neighbourhoods – experience them for yourself to find out why.

It will take a while to get your bearings in Los Angeles. The one sign you will not see when you arrive is the one directing you to the city centre – because there isn't one. Greater LA is an amorphous, sprawling agglomeration spread over a huge geographical flood basin, subdivided by freeways and bounded by ocean and mountains: on its western edge by 160 miles (257 kilometres) of Pacific Rim coastline, and then, clockwise, by the Santa Monica, San Gabriel, San Bernadino, San Jacinto and Santa Ana Mountains. Laid over this geography is a dizzying variety of cityscapes and neighbourhoods.

As you drive around what you think is Los Angeles, you may be confused by signs pointing to 'Los Angeles'. This is because the City of Los Angeles is a distinct city within the County of Los Angeles. LA County contains 88 incorporated cities, each with their own downtowns and jurisdictions, including Malibu, Santa Monica, Beverly Hills, West Hollywood, Culver City, Inglewood, Pasadena and Los Angeles itself. Together, they add up to the LA of popular imagination. On the other hand, Hollywood, which seems to be a distinct place, is not an official city but just one of many neighbourhoods in the amorphous City of LA (which also includes Downtown).

There are also broad, unofficial districts that people use to talk about the different parts of LA County: the **Westside**, **East LA** (largely Latino), **Hollywood and Midtown**, **the Valleys** and **South Central** (comprising many black and Latino neighbourhoods). These areas are in turn made up of smaller neighbourhoods.

The **Westside** is considered by many to extend beyond the I-405 to the more easterly La Cienega Boulevard, taking in **Beverly Hills** and **West Hollywood**. You will also see some guidebooks refer to the Westside as only the inland neighbourhoods, rather than including the beach towns of **Malibu**, **Santa Monica**, **Venice** and **Marina del Rey**, as we have done. The truth is, the Westside is an attitude as well as a place: it is synonymous with affluence and white culture. Westsiders are mocked for never venturing east of La Cienega Boulevard or south of the I-10. Within the Westside is an area called, confusingly, **West LA**. This refers to a western portion of Los Angeles that encompasses those areas between the distinct cities of Santa Monica, Beverly Hills and Culver City.

The Valleys – San Fernando to the north-west and San Gabriel to the north-east – are separated, physically and spiritually, from the rest of LA by the Santa Monica Mountains. The San Fernando Valley is Quentin Tarantino land: flat, hot and post-war, while the San Gabriel Valley contains older, prettier cities such as Pasadena and new 'eth-noburbs' such as heavily Chinese Monterey Park.

LA County is one of the counties in the Los Angeles Five County Area. Together with Riverside, Ventura, Orange and San Bernadino Counties, the Five County Area constitutes a colossal area of about 34,000 square miles (88,083 square kilometres) and 14.5 million people.

To make exploring this mega-metropolis a little easier, we have split the Los Angeles region into ten areas: **Westside: beach towns; Westside: inland; Hollywood and Midtown; Downtown; East of Hollywood; the Valleys; South Bay & Long Beach; East LA; South Central;** and **Orange County.**

WESTSIDE: BEACH TOWNS

There's more to the Westside beach towns than just sun, sea and sand. **Santa Monica**, **Venice**, **Marina del Rey**, **Pacific Palisades** and **Malibu** are all home to feisty communities who have created neighbourhoods with distinct character and plenty to do. Just remember that the beach cities are not at their best in June, during which they are swathed in morning cloud known as June Gloom. For information on the beaches themselves, *see page 52* **Life's a beach**. Also note that this includes areas of West LA.

WESTSIDE: INLAND

Palm-lined streets, movie stars' houses, astronomically pricey shopping; Sunset Strip, UCLA and the Getty Center; if the name 'Los Angeles' puts you in mind of these things, you're thinking about the mostly wealthy, mostly white area that lies east of the beach towns of Venice and Santa Monica, south of the Santa Monica Mountains, north of LAX and west of Fairfax Avenue. It contains the rock music and gay heartland of **West Hollywood**, the seriously monied enclaves of **Beverly Hills** and **Bel Air**, the UCLA campus and studenty **Westwood Village**, wealthy, rustic **Brentwood**, workaday **Culver City** and the

Streets & freeways

LA is subdivided by numerous freeways and by a loose grid of large arteries – the boulevards and avenues. These non-freeway streets are referred to as 'surface streets'. Boulevards typically (but not exclusively) go east to west – with street numbers starting at zero in Downtown and ascending westwards – while avenues usually run north to south. Sometimes the boulevards and avenues are divided into 'North' and 'South' and 'East' and 'West' and the numbering will restart at a city boundary (North Robertson Boulevard, for example, changes numbers three times as it passes through three cities), so check which stretch of road you want and watch the numbers carefully.

In the central portion of LA County, the geographical basin where you are likely to spend most of your time, the **I-10** freeway traverses Los Angeles from west to east and separates Hollywood and Midtown from south and South Central LA. The **I-405** goes north to south on the west side of the City of Los Angeles, separating the affluent coastal and inland cities from the rest of LA. The **I-110** also goes north to south, on the east side, separating Downtown and East LA from west and central LA. The **US 101** and the **I-5** head north-west from Downtown into the Valleys.

The freeways have names (often more than one) as well as numbers, so it helps to know both. Here are the ones you're most likely to use:

I-5 Golden State Freeway/Santa Ana Freeway
I-10 Santa Monica Freeway/San Bernadino Freeway
US 101 Hollywood Freeway/Ventura Freeway
I-110 Harbor Freeway/Pasadena Freeway
Hwy 134 Ventura Freeway
I-405 San Diego Freeway
I-210 Foothill Freeway
I-710 Long Beach Freeway

When planning a journey in Los Angeles make sure you find out not only the address but the nearest cross-street – for example, La Cienega and Third. If you're taking the freeway, find out the exit nearest to your destination. Unless you are sure of the district you are heading for, also get the city and the zip code (Highland Avenue, Santa Monica, CA 90405, for example). Remember that the same street name will occur in different cities.

Most importantly, if you are intending to do any driving in LA, get hold of the *Thomas Guide* to LA County (available from Thomas Brothers Maps & Travel Bookstore; *see page 154* **Shops & Services**). Although it will set you back $30 or so, this is LA's indispensable street directory.

Westside's own high-rise business district, **Century City**. In-between districts fall into the West LA category.

HOLLYWOOD & MIDTOWN

If you want Los Angeles's contrasts in a nutshell, look no further than the disparate patch known – for want of a better name – as Midtown. Bounded by **Hollywood** (unique icons at odds with a mostly threadbare reality) to the north, Downtown to the east, Beverly Hills to the west and the I-10 freeway and South Central to the south, Midtown encompasses both wealthy, residential **Hancock Park**, where you'll be ignoring the suspicious stares of security guards, and the very different MacArthur Park, where the stares will come from the drug dealers, addicts, homeless people and working-class families who populate the district.

In between is **Koreatown**, while back west along Wilshire Boulevard is faded **Miracle Mile** – now miraculous only for its profusion of museums – sandwiched between the monied blocs of Hancock Park and Beverly Hills. The **Fairfax District** also falls into this area.

DOWNTOWN

Stretching south from the eastern end of Sunset Boulevard, Downtown is the site of the original city and home to most of LA's political and financial institutions, many of its major historical landmarks and the Museum of Contemporary Art (MOCA). As the oldest part of the city, it's an area of contrasts: nowhere else in LA will you find such an intriguing array of comparatively old buildings (many of them dating from the turn of the century), but nor can any other part of the city match Downtown for soulless 1980s skyscrapers and bank plazas. Compared to the downtowns of Chicago, San Francisco or New York, LA's is a little pathetic – small, lacking buzz and pretty much lifeless out of office hours – but it does boast some impressive architecture, the Latin enclaves of **Olvera Street** and bustling **Broadway**, **Chinatown** and, less than a mile away, **Little Tokyo**, the heart of LA's Japanese community.

EAST OF HOLLYWOOD

While a tourist's preconception of a visit to Los Angeles might centre on Hollywood and the beaches, it would be an omission not to venture

Palisades Park *in Santa Monica, overlooking the Pacific Ocean.*

any further east into a part of LA both relatively safe and manageable to the casual visitor and with a homey charm that's lacking in the slicker parts of town. Here are the bohemian enclaves of **Silver Lake** and **Los Feliz**, **Echo Park**, home of the Dodgers stadium, and **Griffith Park**, a vast hilly open space with the famous Griffith Observatory and open-air sports from golf to horse-riding.

EAST LA

One of the most distinctive neighbourhoods of Los Angeles is also the least visited by outsiders: East LA, an unincorporated area of eight square miles (20 square kilometres) east of Downtown and the heartland of LA's Mexican community. 'El Este' (the East Side) has traditionally been the gateway for migrant communities: pre-war East LA and neighbouring Boyle Heights housed a large Jewish population. It has now crystallised into a Mexican hub, and almost 90 per cent of its population is Latino and predominantly Mexican. In fact, East LA is deemed the most homogeneous area in the entire Southern California region.

SOUTH CENTRAL

Everyone's heard of South Central. It's the part of Los Angeles you are told to avoid, the part that is synonymous with gangs, drugs, poverty, violence – in other words, black LA. But very few people can actually tell you where it is. That's because South Central is as generic and loose a term as the Westside.

Essentially, it includes the areas of the City of Los Angeles that extend south of the I-10 freeway as far as the I-105, bound on the west by the cities of Culver City and **Inglewood** (the latter, because

it is predominantly black, is often lumped in with South Central) and on the east, the heavily Latino cities of Vernon, Huntington Park and South Gate. And while it does contain many poor and sometimes troubled neighbourhoods, it also, on its outer west edge, can include (depending on who you talk to) the **Crenshaw District**, LA's most affluent black neighbourhood. Furthermore, while South Central used to be majority black, much of it has lately been occupied by Central Americans and Mexicans – now equal in number to blacks – which has caused tremendous political and social tensions.

THE VALLEYS

These two interior valleys – the **San Fernando Valley** to the north of LA and the **San Gabriel Valley** to the east – are usually, at best, ridiculed and, at worst, condemned for embodying the horrors of American suburbia: they are hot, often smoggy and covered with unrelenting low-rise sprawl. Cut off from ocean breezes by the mountains, they can be 10-20°F (11-17°C) hotter than LA proper in summer – and 10-20°F cooler in winter.

Yet they are not without charm. Hidden within are communities and attractions well worth a visit. In particular, they have many small 'suburban downtowns' – business and shopping districts, both old and new, where you can get out of your car and stroll for a few blocks enjoying a small-town atmosphere. Westsiders mock the Valleys, but natives wouldn't live anywhere else.

THE SOUTH BAY & LONG BEACH

The living is easy in much of the South Bay; but defining exactly what makes up the region is not. Some definitions include everything from condo-

crazy Marina del Rey in the north to such hard-bit-
ten, inland communities as Compton, Gardena,
Lawndale, Hawthorne and Lomita to the south-
east. But when Los Angeles residents speak of the
South Bay, they're usually referring to the coast-
hugging cities just south of LAX: **El Segundo**,
Manhattan Beach, **Hermosa Beach** and
Redondo Beach, with the landlocked suburb of
Torrance just to the east thrown in for good measure. For a detailed description of LA's beaches,
including these, *see page 52*.

Drive over the majestic Vincent Thomas Bridge
from **San Pedro** and there is **Long Beach**, the
old US Navy port that's now a city of nearly
500,000 and a cosmopolitan mix of yuppies,
artists, harbour workers, gays and students as
well as a rainbow of races, including the largest
Cambodian community outside Cambodia.

ORANGE COUNTY

Bordering Los Angeles County to the south-east,
Orange County is best known as the home of
Disneyland. With the additional blessing of a
copious coastline, it lures 40 million visitors a year.
Angelenos look down on it as a conservative white-
collar suburb, with some justification. But if you're
making the trip to Disney, it's worth straying off
the freeway to have a look around.

Westside: beach towns

See Map 2

Santa Monica

With the Santa Monica Mountains to the north, the
glistening Pacific Ocean to the west, palm tree-
lined cliffs and almost year-round sun tempered
by ocean breezes, affluent Santa Monica is indis-
putably the jewel of LA's Westside. Known locally
as 'the people's republic of Santa Monica', it is also
the heartland of bourgeois liberalism, noted for its
espousal of environmental causes, rent control
and tolerance of the homeless. The hipper
denizens of Hollywood and Silver Lake see Santa
Monica as totally un-cool – because it is short on
nightclubs and long on Starbucks coffeehouses.
Well, Santa Monica may not be cool, but it is comfortable and casual – shorts, healthy bodies and
rollerblades are the uniform. Get yours on and
take to the beach (town).

The Santa Monica area was inhabited for centuries by the Gabrieleno Native Americans, then

by Spanish settlers who named the city and many of its major streets. It was acquired by Anglo pioneers in the late nineteenth century and snowballed from a small vacation town into today's city of about 87,000. Brits abound in Santa Monica (aka Santa Margate) as do Iranians (since the fall of the Shah), many other immigrant groups, retirees (septuagenarians on wheels are the biggest danger on the city's streets), health fanatics, beach bums and entertainment industry titans. One famous Santa Monican, Arnold Schwarzenegger, also owns a chunk of commercial property in Santa Monica and a mediocre restaurant, **Schatzi on Main** (3110 Main Street; 1-310 399 4800).

As well as the tourist-oriented beaches, pier and shops, Santa Monica also boasts some of the best restaurants in the LA basin, a burgeoning creative business centre and a thriving art, coffeehouse and literary scene (there's one bookshop per quarter of a square mile). It has some great modern architecture: much of **Frank Gehry**'s work is here, including his own house (*see page 32* **Architecture**), as well as some art deco landmarks, such as the **Shangri-La** hotel (*see page 97* **Accommodation**) and good 1950s 'modern' architecture, such as the **Santa Monica Civic Auditorium** (1855 Main Street, at Pico Boulevard).

From pumped-up posers to wandering minstrels, the people parade never stops in **Venice Beach**. *See page 49.*

Santa Monica has three main shopping and entertainment areas: Montana Avenue, Third Street Promenade and Main Street.

Montana Avenue

Montana Avenue runs parallel to Wilshire Boulevard, the city's main east-west artery, towards the northern, affluent end of town bordering on the Santa Monica Canyons. Montana Avenue metamorphosed in the 1970s from a bland commercial strip into the Rodeo Drive of the coast, and is very popular with wealthy liberals in north Santa Monica and Brentwood. Locals get a workout with a spiritual dimension at **Yoga Works** (No.1426); buy their wheatgrass juice and wholesome groceries at **Wild Oats Market** opposite (No.1425); drink microbrews at **Father's Office** (No.1018), LA's first smoke-free bar; and tuck into pizzas at the ever-popular **Louise's Trattoria** (No.1008). North of Montana Avenue, at Fourth Street and Adelaide Drive, are the infamous **Fourth Street Steps**: 189 concrete steps that

*Fun and games on **Santa Monica Pier**.*

serve as a cliffside Stairmaster and, reputedly, a pick-up place for fit singles.

Running parallel to Montana Avenue a few blocks north is **San Vicente Boulevard**, a wide street lined with grass verges that is very popular with joggers. The east end of San Vicente, around Bundy Drive, also features some eating haunts popular with the Brentwood set (Mezzaluna restaurant, made notorious because Nicole Brown Simpson ate her last meal there, finally closed down in 1997).

Third Street Promenade

South of Montana Avenue, below Wilshire Boulevard at Third Street, is the wildly popular Third Street Promenade. Anchored by three cineplexes, the Frank Gehry-designed **Santa Monica Place** shopping mall at the southern end (approach from Main Street to the south for a surprising façade) and adjacent parking structures, these four blocks of pedestrianised streets are by day and night a hugely popular shopping, eating and entertainment zone. At the north end is the **Radisson Huntley Hotel** (*see below*), offering the best views in town from its top-floor Mexican restaurant and cocktail bar.

Third Street Promenade is constantly active with street performers, farmers' markets on Wednesday and Saturday mornings, seasonal festivals and numerous shops and hangouts. These include two popular bookshops – the ubiquitous

Barnes & Noble branch and café (1201 Third Street Promenade) and the independent **Midnight Special Bookstore** (*see page 154* **Shops & Services**), both of which offer regular readings – **Urban Outfitters** clothes shop (No.1440) and **Gotham Hall** club and pool house (*see page 225* **Sport & Fitness**). Third Street proves that people really do walk in Los Angeles.

Main Street

Even further south is Main Street, an upmarket commercial strip two blocks west of the Santa Monica Boardwalk. A popular breakfast-time haunt for early-morning joggers, Main Street offers an eclectic mix of fashion and knick-knack stores, as well as numerous coffee bars and eateries. Highlights include the **Novel Café**, an extremely laid-back bookstore/coffee bar at Pier Avenue (*see page 141* **Coffeehouses**), Wolfgang Puck's **Chinois on Main** (*see page 115* **Restaurants**) and the Frank Gehry-designed **Edgemar Complex** (No.2437), a sculptural mall that houses the MOCA Store, a great place for presents, and the high-class **Röckenwagner** restaurant (*see page 117* **Restaurants**). Main Street runs through **Ocean Park**, a hilly, bohemian neighbourhood at the south end of Santa Monica, whose intense light and tranquillity were celebrated on canvas by late resident Richard Diebenkorn in a celebrated series of paintings.

Worth visiting inland is the new **Bergamot Station**, a complex of art galleries created at a former Red Trolley terminus (accessible from Michigan Avenue, off Cloverfield Boulevard), and Santa Monica Airport. Built before much of the rest of Santa Monica, the airport is the hip hangout for plane enthusiasts. Top gun Tom Cruise keeps his Pitts Special biplane here; mere mortals (with a licence) can rent a plane for only $60 an hour or take a simulated flight at the **Museum of Flying** (*see page 178* **Children**). Large parties are held at the airport, architects and designers have offices in hangars and there are two good restaurants there, **DC-3** (*see page 177* **Children**) and **Typhoon** (*see page 118* **Restaurants**), both serving very good food in full view of the planes.

Radisson Huntley Hotel

1111 Second Street, between Wilshire Boulevard & California Avenue, Santa Monica (1-310 394 5454/ Toppers restaurant 1-310 393 8080). Bus 1, 2, 3, 4/I-10, exit Lincoln Boulevard north. **Meals served** 5.30am-10.30pm daily. **Credit** AmEx, DC, Disc, MC, V.

Toppers, the Mexican restaurant and cantina on the top floor of the Radisson Huntley, offers one of the most beautiful and sweeping views of the coast. On a clear day, you can see all the way to Catalina Island and the endless roll of the San Bernardino Mountains. Take the outside glass elevator to the top. Since the city has ruled against the erection of buildings over eight storeys, the Huntley (which featured memorably in John Boorman's movie *Point Blank*) is in no danger of losing its exquisite view. The bar closes at 1.30am daily. *Parking $8.50 overnight; $2.75 day.*

Experience life on the ocean wave at **Marina del Rey** *harbour (p55).*

Santa Monica Visitor Center

1400 Ocean Avenue, Santa Monica, CA 90401 (1-310 393 7593). **Open** *10am-4pm daily. Website: www.santamonica.com*

Venice

Santa Monica is so perfect that it can, in some areas, seem a bit precious, something that could never be said of its southerly neighbour, Venice. Despite gentrification during the 1980s, Venice remains the bohemian quarter of Los Angeles, populated by ageing hippies, artists, students and young professionals in creative industries who can't yet afford a place in Santa Monica. It is also home to transients and a poor black – and increasingly Latino – community beset by drug dealing and periodic gang fights that make the Oakwood area (circumscribed by Lincoln and Venice Boulevards and Sunset and Electric Avenues) a no-go zone after dark.

Formerly a beach resort, the section of Venice west of Lincoln Boulevard has rows of tumbledown clapboard beach houses, 'walk-streets' (pedestrian-only alleyways leading to the beach) and, in the more affluent southern end, canals. Venice owes its existence to entrepreneur Abbot Kinney, who founded it in 1900, envisaging it as the hub of a cultural renaissance in America. He oversaw the construction of canals, a lagoon and buildings in the Venetian style, even importing two dozen genuine gondoliers to complete the effect (one of whom apparently got so homesick that he tried to sail back to Italy; he made it as far as San Pedro). Venice's canals, south of Venice Boulevard, are an idyllic enclave of bridges, waterways and eclectic architecture.

Although Kinney failed to achieve the cultural rebirth – visitors were far more interested in amusing themselves – he did succeed in creating a successful resort known in its heyday as the 'Playland of the Pacific'. Venice's main commercial street, **Abbot Kinney Boulevard**, is named in his honour and well worth visiting for its collection of art galleries, accessories, bric-a-brac and design stores and good eateries – including **Hal's Bar & Grill** (*see page 119* **Restaurants**), the eternally hip hangout for local meedja folk (the atmosphere compensates for the overpriced food). Also try **Joe's** (*see page 119* **Restaurants**) for excellent food in simple surroundings, **Mobay** (No.1031; 1-310 450 1933) for Caribbean cuisine on a delightful patio, and the **Abbot's Habit** (*see page 142* **Coffeehouses**) for coffee and snacks.

In the 1980s, Venice became a hotbed of architectural activity. You can see several buildings by acclaimed contemporary local architects, such as Frank Gehry's Norton and Spiller houses and a still popular bar and restaurant, **Rebecca's** (*see page 119* **Restaurants**); the Bergren, Sedlak and 2-4-6-8 houses by Morphosis; Dennis Hopper's residence by Brian Murphy; as well as Frank Israel's renovation of the former Charles and Ray Eames studio, now Bright and Associates, and Frank Gehry's Chiat/Day Building.

You can't miss the latter as its entrance is marked by an enormous pair of Claes Oldenburg-designed binoculars and, currently, by a huge poster for Apple computers featuring Gehry's face, which fills one wall of the building. The binoculars are one of the better examples of public art that can be found in Venice. A more controversial art piece is Jonathan Borofsky's unmissable Dancing Clown perched on the corner of Main

Farmers markets

In a city that often seems fuelled by junk food alone, farmers markets are an under-publicised joy. All over the city there are weekly markets where you can buy fresh, seasonal produce, some of it organic, from small local farmers.

California was always America's Garden of Eden, exploiting the perpetual sunny weather, cheap migrant labour and ever-stronger pesticides to become the country's leading producer of bland, cheap vegetables. But thanks to a change in consciousness – the cult of fresh produce, inspired in the 1970s by Alice Waters's famous Chez Panisse restaurant in Berkeley – and a new law that permitted farmers to sell directly to the public, farmers markets have grown to become the hottest new shopping phenomenon in Los Angeles.

With typical American zest, farmers markets (not to be confused with the Farmers Market, a former farmers market, now tourist haven, at Fairfax Avenue and Third Street; *see page 64*) do not sell only veggies. Many have stalls peddling flowers, fresh juices, coffee, hot food and handmade knick-knacks. Some offer live music, donkey rides, pottery classes for children and massage services. Angelenos develop fierce loyalties to their favourite market and favourite farmers. And so will you.

Below we've listed the best markets, but you should be able to find a market going on somewhere in the city on any given day of the week. For more information, call the **Southland Farmers Market Association** (1-213 244 9190) or visit the website run by farmers market expert **Mark Thompson** (www.market report.com).

Santa Monica

Information 1-310 458 8712.
Pico Boulevard, at Cloverfield Boulevard.
Open 8am-1pm Sat. **Map 2 C3**
Arizona Avenue, at Second Street. **Open** 9am-2pm Wed; 8.30am-1pm Sat (organic market). **Map 2 A2**
Heritage Museum, Ocean Park Boulevard & Main Street. **Open** 9.30am-1pm Sun. **Map 2 A3**
There are four weekly markets in Santa Monica: the main ones are held on Wednesday and Saturday mornings, where local restaurateurs go to hand-pick their daily vegetables; a smaller, but delightful one is held in the parking lot of the Heritage Museum on Sundays. There's also an organic market on Saturdays.

Hollywood

Ivar Avenue, between Hollywood Boulevard & Sunset Boulevard (1-213 463 3171). **Open** 8.30am-1pm Sun. **Map 5 B1**

West Hollywood

Plummer Park, Santa Monica Boulevard, at Fuller Avenue (1-213 848 6502). **Open** 9am-2pm Mon. **Map 4 C3**

Life's a beach

The come-on of Southern California's coastline, with its gorgeous interface of sea and sky against a chiselled mountain backdrop, is irresistible, and the 30 miles (48 kilometres) of beaches along Los Angeles County's 72-mile (116-kilometre) coastline – from Malibu south through Santa Monica and Venice to the South Bay – are well worth exploring.

Despite the palm trees (imported, incidentally), the Pacific Ocean in Southern California is inhumanly chilly a full two-thirds of the year. By July, however, the insulation of a wetsuit is no longer required, and in August the water temperature can reach a warm and refreshing 70°F (21°C). The smog is at its worst in late summer and early autumn and, like cloud cover, offers deceptively little protection against the sun's rays, so don't be foolish – use proper sunblock. As for pollution, the general rule is that the further you are from Santa Monica Bay (where waste is pumped into the ocean), the cleaner the water – although the bay has been cleaned up in recent years. The worst time to go swimming is immediately after a rainfall, when the flood channels empty into the sea. Luckily, it doesn't rain much.

Beaches usually open at sunrise and close at sunset, but staying late to enjoy one of LA's breathtaking sunsets is worth it. Most beaches welcome children, and have space and rental gear for rollerblading, roller-hockey, bicycling, surfing and volleyball, as well as refreshment stands, showers and toilets. On LA County beaches, lifeguards are on duty daily, all year round, and alcohol, pets and nudity are prohibited. Bonfires are permitted (in designated cement fire rings) only at Dockweiler State Beach (in Vista del Mar) and Cabrillo Beach (in San Pedro). Parking can be difficult, and sometimes expensive, but it's better to pony up for a legit space than have your vehicle towed while you're off having fun.

For more information on the beach of your choice, call the **Department of Beaches & Harbors** on 1-310 305 9503. For the best places to surf, *see page 229* **Sport & Fitness**. For gay-friendly beaches, *see page 189* **Gay & Lesbian**. The following are the pick of LA's beaches, from north to south:

El Matador State Beach

Small, beautiful and dominated by rocky outcrops, El Matador looks more like a European beach. It's six miles (9.5km) north of Malibu and just past Zuma Beach, then a walk down a steep gravelly path. Wear shoes and don't bring too much heavy gear or picnic paraphernalia. There are no lifeguards or other facilities, so you should be able to

Frolic on **Santa Monica beach**...

find some privacy here; spread your towel in the cupped hands of the rocks. Arriving early or staying late should reward you with a memorable dawn or sunset. Nearby **El Pescador** and **La Peidra** beaches are also worth visiting.

Zuma

Quintessentially Southern California, Zuma Beach is about as good as it gets. Four miles (6.5km) north of Malibu, enduring the sometimes long and traffic-clogged drive on the Pacific Coast Highway (PCH), you come upon a long sprawl of sand and surf. The water is clean and the waves strong enough to endanger your bikini top. Zuma can get crowded, but dish out the $5 to park (a must, because the parking enforcers here are ruthless) and you're set for the day. Lifeguards patrol the beach and there are toilets, showers and a few hot dog and soda carts; it's wise to bring your own food and drink. Although there are often volleyball games and surfing, Zuma is best for long beach walks, swimming, sunbathing and beach fun with friends and family.

Malibu

Unfortunately, the nicest beaches in Malibu are the private property of the rich and famous (most, by law, must have public access, but finding the routes down to them can be very difficult). The public beaches, spotted with commercial restaurants, are nothing out of the ordinary, making tourists wonder where the real Malibu could be. Nonetheless, swimming, sunning and playing here is popular, especially among those who enjoy watching the do-or-die surfers riding the waves at **Surfrider Beach**, between Malibu Pier and the lagoon. There are also tidepools, a marine preserve and volleyball and picnic areas. Drive out towards **Point Dume** to see the opulent houses of the rich and famous – some built precariously on the edge of rocky bluffs – with lush gardens and ocean views.

Santa Monica

Accessible and near LA proper, this big beach is usually crowded and has a fun, festive, summer-holiday feel to it. **Santa Monica Pier** is one of the highlights. Recently renovated, it is about three city blocks in length and offers typical and endearingly low-tech distractions: pier fishing, video arcades, free twilight dance concerts in summer, fortune tellers, shops, fairground games, snack foods, rides and an 11-storey Ferris wheel – from the top of which, on a clear day or night, you can see forever. The carousel is a national historic monument. It's touristy, but fun.

...or have your photo snapped with a celeb on **Santa Monica Pier**.

Venice

Venice Beach is a country all of its own, with the least homogeneous set of residents and visitors you could imagine. People-watching is the *raison d'être* here, and you'll soon tick off every last category in your *I Spy* book, California wackos included. Pedestrian-only **Ocean Front Walk** offers shops, restaurants, food stands and one of the most varied selection of cheap sunglasses on earth. Seawards from the Walk, jump into the flow of the winding **Venice Boardwalk**, where you can rollerblade or cycle, watch or play volleyball or basketball, check out the Incredible Hulk-sized men and women who work out endlessly at **Muscle Beach**, the almost legendary (but now rather outmoded) outdoor gym, or just enjoy the sun-warmed sand. **Venice Pier**, to the south, is amusing, but second fiddle to Ocean Front Walk. There are several beachside parking lots – try the end of Rose Avenue or Windward Avenue, off Pacific Avenue, where you'll pay $5-$7. Street parking is usually jammed solid, and in any case can be dodgy.

The South Bay

Manhattan, **Huntington** and **Hermosa Beaches** are the best of the South Bay beaches (though less cosmopolitan in their mix of people). Right out of a postcard of Southern California, they offer clean water, sand that stretches out of sight, small piers and all the accoutrements: volleyball, sailing and beachfront paths for walking, running, cycling and rollerblading. The charm of these beaches is the local flavour; visitors can swim, picnic and bask in the sun alongside residents and local fishermen as well as other tourists. The surf's not bad either: Huntington Beach picks up swells from a variety of directions, which makes for good waves, and the waters are often less crowded than at Surfrider Beach in Malibu. For those who prefer dry land, Manhattan Beach hosts an annual Volleyball Open, which is televised and attended by throngs of enthusiasts.

BEST BEACHES FOR...

...surfing

Surfrider Beach in Malibu, where the ocean teems with surfers hanging ten on the curvy surf, and the varying breaks and multi-directional swells of **Huntington Beach**.

...clean water

Zuma Beach, which is far enough north to escape the pollution of Santa Monica Bay – though the water there has improved under the auspices of Heal the Bay (1-310 581 4188), an outfit devoted to monitoring pollution levels and keeping local waters clean.

...catching a game of volleyball

Manhattan Beach, where the young and the beautiful play as if they were born with a volleyball in their hands.

...rollerblading

The stretch of **boardwalk** (paved beach path) between Will Rogers State Beach, just north of Santa Monica, and Venice Beach is marked for two-way traffic, which is essential due to the sharp twists and turns and the sheer number of joggers, cyclists and skaters. Group lessons are available at the rollerblade rental booths.

...people-watching

Venice Beach, where freaks are the norm and no one minds if you stare.

...people who don't like the water

Santa Monica Beach, with its busy, bright pier complete with food stalls and game arcades, as well as a camera obscura and Santa Monica Place shopping mall and Third Street Promenade all within walking distance.

Street and Rose Avenue. For a tour of the public artworks, many of which are near Ocean Front Walk (aka Venice Boardwalk), contact the Social and Public Art Resource (SPARC) on 1-310 822 9560. For more information on Frank Gehry's work, *see page 32* **Architecture**.

Many renowned Southern Californian artists have maintained studios in Venice for years, among them Laddie John Dill, Guy Dill, Billy Al Bengston, Ed Moses and Chuck Arnoldi. If you are here in May you might catch the yearly Venice Artwalk, a charitable event in aid of the Venice Family Free Clinic, in which you can tour more than 60 artists' studios.

Venice is also a mecca for kooky California culture – the **Psychic Eye** bookstore, incorporating the New Age Center (218 Main Street; 1-310 396 0110) is a must – and fitness fanaticism. Three of LA's most famous gyms are here, **Gold's** (*see page 227* **Sport & Fitness**), the Schwarzenegger-owned **World Gym** (812 Main Street; 1-310 399

9888) and **Powerhouse Gym** (245 Main Street; 1-310 314 8888). Their buff clientele can be seen strutting their stuff in many Venice locales; you can't miss them chowing down on protein-packed brunches at the **Firehouse Restaurant** (1-310 396 6810), a vivid, red-painted, former fire station on the corner of Rose Avenue and Main Street.

Other notable Venice spots include **St Marks** restaurant/club at the beach end of Windward Avenue – go there for salsa lessons on Sundays. This is one block south of Market Street, where you can take in the prominent **LA Louver** art gallery and trendy restaurant **72 Market Street** (*see page 119* **Restaurants**). The other key strip is **Rose Avenue**, an east-west commercial street at the north end of Venice. There are a few interesting second-hand shops, but the main attraction is the **Rose Café** (No.220; 1-310 399 0711), adorned with large painted roses; it's a self-serve and sit-down restaurant with an attractive garden and crafts store.

Readymade tours

If you want someone else to do the hard work and take you round LA's sights, try one of the following. For celeb-related tours, *see page 24* **Celebrity LA**.

Helinet Tours
Van Nuys Airport, Van Nuys (1-818 902 0229).
Bus 164, 236/I-405, exit Victory Boulevard west.
Cost *1-hour tour, 1-4 passengers* $575; *Dinner Tour* $279 per person (4 passengers minimum). **Credit** AmEx, MC, V.
From Van Nuys Airport, the one-hour tour spins you over Universal Studios, the Hollywood sign, Griffith Park, Dodger Stadium, Downtown and Beverly Hills, before a westward jaunt over Santa Monica, up the Malibu Coast and over, around and through some breathtaking canyons. The Dinner Tour is often organised for weddings and other special events: the helicopter takes you over the sparkling city as per the daytime tour, then drops you at the four-star Tower Restaurant on top of the TransAmerica Building. After dinner, a limo returns you to the airport or any other destination of your choice. The price includes everything except dinner drinks.

Los Angeles Conservancy Walking Tours
1-213 623 2489. **Tours** usually 10am, 11am Sat.
Cost $5.
Yes, it can be done on foot, especially Downtown. Try the Marble Masterpieces Tour, which explores the use of marble in historic and new buildings, from the 1931 One Bunker Hill Building to the postmodern Coast Savings Building. A shorter tour concentrates on the Biltmore, one of LA's most venerable and glamorous hotels. Other Conservancy walking tours, all one to two hours long, include Union Station, Pershing Square, and Little Tokyo and the Higashi Hongwanji Buddhist Temple. These tours are aimed at those interested in the preservation and

revitalisation of urban architectural heritage. They're popular and booking is required.

Nature Adventures for Kids
Information 1-310 998 1151/reservations 1-310 364 3591. **Cost** free; $5 donation per family requested.
These are nature walks in the Santa Monica Mountains and other wild areas of Los Angeles and Ventura Counties. They aim to introduce families to the outdoors while instilling respect for wilderness areas. Most are pushchair-accessible. They're run by the Children's Nature Institute, a non-profit organisation, which also offers various nature and animal-related festivals and events – phone for details.

Next Stage Tours
1-626 577 7880. **Cost** $30-$60. **No credit cards**.
If you're fed up of seeing the official sights, Next Stage will show you the LA that other tours ignore. Try the Insomniacs Tour: starting at 3am, it visits early-morning flower and produce markets, tai chi exercises and the 7am racehorse workout at Santa Anita, and promises a prime vantage point for sunrise as well as a generous breakfast. The Scentimental Journey introduces you to sundry odoriferous LA spots including a bakery/chocolatier, a rose garden, a coffee roaster's, a pine wood in the Santa Monica Mountains, an oceanfront pier, Armenian and Indian markets (for spices) and an aromatherapist's. Metatourists should try the LA Has Its Ups and Downs Tour, which takes you to numerous escalators and elevators from Downtown to the sea.

Oskar J's Sightseeing Tours
1-818 501 2217/1-800 458 2388. **Cost** $30-$60.
Credit AmEx, DC, MC, V.
Minibuses pick up from big hotels for tours of Sunset Strip, movie studios, the Farmers Market, Hollywood and celebrity homes, as well as shopping tours. Tours last from two to five hours.

For tourist information, check the Chamber of Commerce's website: www.venice.net.

Marina del Rey

An unsung aspect of Los Angeles life is its sailing. Many Angelenos keep boats, others live in them, at the **Marina del Rey Harbor**, a resort and residential complex just south of Venice in an area bounded by Washington Boulevard, Admiralty Way, Fiji Way and Via Marina. Conceived a century ago and finally completed in 1965, the Marina consists of a picturesque artificial harbour with eight basins named to evoke the South Seas (Tahiti Way, Bora Bora Way, Mindinao Way and so on). They are filled with 6,000 bobbing yachts, motor boats and flashy cruisers. This is surrounded by low- and high-rise apartment buildings and generic hotels, as well as many touristy restaurants.

Perceived as a haven for swinging singles, the Marina is actually home to many retirees and young families for whom the complex is a reasonably priced and charming – if somewhat sterile – place to live. It is livened up, however, by a motley crew of impecunious boat-dwellers. Simply to experience a pure 1970s period piece, the Marina is definitely worth seeing.

It's no place for culture vultures, however; except for a small public library, all the Marina's attractions are recreational. You can picnic, jog and cycle (the Marina is a link in the 21-mile coastal bike path) in the **Burton W Chace Park** and **Admiralty Park** at the northern end; fish from a dock at the west end of the Burton W Chace or rent a boat to go ocean-fishing at Fisherman's Village, 13755 Fiji Way, at Lincoln Boulevard (Green Boathouse). You can also rent boats or join excursions at a number of charter companies located in the Marina: there's whale-watching in winter. If you want to park your own boat, contact the visitors' information centre (*see below*).

There are plenty of touristy shops, most of them concentrated in **Fisherman's Wharf**, a cheesy replica of a New England fishing town. The many eateries are to be recommended for their waterside charm rather than for their food, which does not rank among Los Angeles's best. The **Cheesecake Factory** and the ultimate beach supershack, the **Warehouse Restaurant** (go on a full stomach), all on Admiralty Way, are among the better ones.

At the south end of Marina del Rey (just north of LAX) is **Playa del Rey**, a predominantly residential beach neighbourhood and an artificial lagoon. **Tanner's Coffee Company** (200 Culver Boulevard; 1-310 574 2739) is one of the more lively local cafés in an area whose attractions are mainly beach-oriented. Playa del Rey is also a magnet for nature lovers and birdwatchers, who come to observe the great grey herons, white egrets and other creatures that converge on the Ballona Wetlands, a natural sanctuary just east of Playa del Rey, in Playa Vista.

Marina del Rey Chamber of Commerce, Visitor & Convention Bureau

Oakwood Corporate Center, 4111 Via Marina, Marina del Rey, CA 90292 (1-310 821 0555).
Website: itlnet.com/marina

Pacific Palisades

Between Santa Monica and Malibu lies Pacific Palisades, a small, wealthy, residential community that has managed to keep a lower profile than its neighbours. The perfect, clipped, shiny green lawns and large bungalows of Pacific Palisades are straight out of *Leave It to Beaver* – but contained within its Santa Monica Mountains location are some wonderful places to visit.

The original Getty Museum, J Paul Getty's Roman fantasy, is just visible from Pacific Coast Highway but is closed to the public until it reopens as a museum for antiquities in 2001. For rugged nature, there's **Rustic Canyon Park** (1-310 454 5734), **Temescal Canyon Park** (1-310 459 5931) and **Will Rogers Historic State Park** (*see below*). The latter is the former home of famous American 'Cowboy Philosopher', trick roper, journalist and media personality Will Rogers. For a more manicured, but unbelievably lovely retreat, try the **Self-Realization Lake Shrine**.

Will Rogers State Beach has been used as a location for *Baywatch*. If you want to be part of the action, and have the requisite Barbie/Ken body, you could try asking Central Casting (1-818 562 2700) for work as an extra. By the way, the real male lifeguards are a lot hunkier than David Hasselhof, whose famously spindly legs are carefully kept out of the television frame.

Will Rogers Historic State Park

1501 Will Rogers State Park Road, at Sunset Boulevard, Pacific Palisades (1-310 454 8212). Bus 434/I-405, exit Sunset Boulevard west. **Open** 8am-sunset daily.
Will Rogers was a busy man. Humorist, writer, performer, cowboy and rope-trickster, he was also the first honorary mayor of Beverly Hills. Since Rogers was the only man in Hollywood who 'never met a man he didn't like', it seems fitting that upon his death, his ranch house and land became a national park welcoming one and all. The 31-room house is maintained as it was when the 1930s box-office star lived there, the living room full of Western-style furniture, Indian rugs and lariats. The grounds give access to some good hikes and also host polo matches on Saturdays and Sundays.
Parking $6.

Self-Realization Lake Shrine

17190 Sunset Boulevard, off PCH, Pacific Palisades (1-310 454 4114). Bus 2, 434/ I-10, exit PCH north. **Open** 9am-4.30pm Tue-Sat; 12.30-4.30pm Sun. **Admission** free.
Opened in 1950, this Buddhist retreat is an oasis of peace and beauty, run by the Self-Realization Fellowship Church. Surrounded by a spring-fed lake, trees, flowers, paths, birds

and turtles, you can stroll the grounds, ponder in private garden nooks or meditate in the Windmill Chapel. *Parking free.*

Pacific Palisades Chamber of Commerce
15330 Antioch Street, Pacific Palisades, CA 90272 (1-310 459 7963). **Open** 9.30am-5pm Mon-Fri.

Malibu

Malibu is not a place so much as a long stretch of the Pacific Coast Highway – 27 miles (43 kilometres) of it – which winds through some of Southern California's most magnificent coastal terrain. Parts of it are lined, on the ocean side, by beach houses of varying sizes and styles, with largely mediocre commercial buildings on the inland side, nestling against the Santa Monica Mountains.

The location is so desirable that residents are willing to live with the threat of seasonal – often destructive – fires and floods, and they form a cohesive community dedicated to preventing new development from marring their bucolic lifestyle. Finally incorporated as a city in 1990, Malibu is extremely wealthy (average income $150,000), due to its numerous entertainment industry residents, many of whom inhabit a private beachside street known as the Malibu Colony. But it also contains several trailer parks whose spectacular hillside locations make them the most enviable low-rent accommodation in the country.

Malibu has neither major industry nor major culture. Its treats lie mainly in the beaches, restaurants, cafés and canyons: within yards of the entrance to one of the many canyon trails you can be completely out of view of the city.

Malibu eating experiences include top-notch California cuisine at Wolfgang Puck's **Granita** (*see page 120* **Restaurants**), coffee and ornamental cakes at **Xanadu French Bakery** (3900 Cross Creek Road; 1-310 317 4818) or, if you prefer a grittier atmosphere, you can join bikers and surfers for burgers and all-day breakfast at the notorious **Malibu Inn & Restaurant** (22969 Pacific Coast Highway; 1-310 456 6106).

Malibu has one significant landmark, the **Adamson House** (23200 Pacific Coast Highway; 1-310 456 8432): a stunning 1929 Spanish-style building that sits, together with the **Malibu Lagoon Museum**, in Malibu Lagoon State Park. The house (open for guided tours 11am-3pm Wed-Sat) is adorned with decorative tiles manufactured at the once celebrated, now closed Malibu Tile Works. Visit the museum for more information about that and other Malibu historical artefacts.

Students study business and other subjects at the conservative **Pepperdine University** (24255 PCH, at Malibu Canyon Road). If you want to learn about conservation techniques for trees and flowers, take one of the Wednesday garden tours at La Diva Barbra's **Streisand Center for Conservancy Studies** (5750 Ramirez Canyon Road); tours costs $30 per person and you should book in advance on 1-310 589 2850).

Malibu Chamber of Commerce
23805 Stuart Ranch Road, suite 100, Malibu, CA 90265 (1-310 456 9025). **Open** 10am-4pm Mon-Fri. *Website: www.malibu.org*

Westside: inland

See Maps 3 & 4

West Hollywood

West Hollywood, which became an independent city in 1984, is actually three bustling communities in one. Most famously, perhaps, the tiny city (1.9 square miles/4.9 square kilometres) is the epicentre of gay and lesbian life in Los Angeles, with **Santa Monica Boulevard** as its main strip. But it is also home to the (straight scene) nightclubs of the fabled Sunset Strip. Both these communities are thriving impressively, thanks to the active nightlife that draws fun-seekers of every persuasion to Santa Monica and Sunset Boulevards, where a string of restaurants, coffee bars and nightclubs are hopping nearly every night of the week. The third community comprises immigrant Russians who live and run businesses in the east end of the city, around Fairfax: relations with their Western-hedonist neighbours are not especially harmonious.

Sunset Strip, the stretch of Sunset Boulevard (one of the longest streets in LA) that runs approximately from Doheny Drive to Laurel Canyon, was originally developed in 1924. By the 1930s it was Hollywood's playground, home to clubs like the Trocadero, Mocambo, the Players and Ciro's, where performers such as Lena Horne and Edith Piaf belted out their sets. In the 1940s and 1950s, mobsters Mickey Cohen and Bugsy Siegel called it home and in 1963 the **Whisky A Go-Go** (still breaking new acts; *see page 211* **Music**) became the first discotheque on the West Coast.

With Whisky's success, clubs such as Gazzarri's, the Zodiac, the Galaxy, Filthy McNasty's (named after a WC Fields movie) and the Trip opened. The Byrds, Love, the Doors and countless others played on the Strip, starting a musical revolution, which ended in a riot in 1966, when young club-goers protested in the streets against the proposed redevelopment of such key venues as Pandora's Box.

In the 1970s the moguls moved in: David Geffen, Phil Spector and disco giant Casablanca Records. The Strip is still home to Geffen Records, Island

Sunset Plaza, *in the heart of West Hollywood's fabled Sunset Strip.*

Records and other major record companies. Today, its glitzy, Las Vegas quality is kept alive by huge billboards: notably the Marlboro man and Absolut Vodka, plus murals of Elizabeth Taylor and James Dean painted on the sides of buildings.

The **Comedy Store** (*see page 218* **Nightlife**) helped break stars like Robin Williams, David Letterman and Whoopi Goldberg, and still hosts comedic legends, while music clubs, such as the **House of Blues**, the **Roxy**, and Johnny Depp's **Viper Room**, continue to present the latest sounds (for all, *see chapter* **Music**).

Restaurants such as **Le Dôme** (*see page 123* **Restaurants**), and hotels such as **Chateau Marmont** (where Greta Garbo lived and John Belushi died) and the **Mondrian**, still brim-full with celebs, also help to keep the legend of the Strip alive (for both, *see chapter* **Accommodation**). Bookshop **Book Soup** (*see page 154* **Shops & Services**) is well loved for its huge selection of literature and mags, and late opening. (For more Strip lore, *see page 210* **Music**.)

West Hollywood is one of the few districts that is easily walkable. Head a few blocks south of Sunset Boulevard to find exclusive restaurants such as **Morton's** on Melrose Avenue, the **Ivy** on North Robertson Boulevard (famed for its celebrity clientele and Hollywood deals), **Chaya Brasserie** on Alden Drive (more celebs and a good bar scene), **Le Colonial** on Beverly Boulevard, a string of excellent French restaurants along La Cienega Boulevard, and **Tail-o'-the-Pup** on North San Vicente Boulevard, a landmark 1946 hot dog stand built in the shape of a huge hot dog (for all, *see chapter* **Restaurants**).

Urth Caffè on Melrose Avenue is a popular spot (*see page 143* **Coffeehouses**), while next door the **Bodhi Tree** (*see page 154* **Shops & Services**) is a well-known Buddhist bookstore and lecture room. The **Sunset Marquis Hotel & Villas** (on Alta Loma Road, just south of Sunset Boulevard; *see page 103* **Accommodation**) is a music celeb hangout, while over on Robertson Boulevard, **LunaPark** is a popular restaurant and eclectic nightclub (*see page 219* **Nightlife**). Tucked away at the northern end of Kings Road, the **Schindler House** and its garden is an oasis of minimalist architecture (it's also known as the MAK Center; *see page 31* **Architecture**), and over on Doheny Drive the **Lloyd Wright Home and Studio**, designed by Frank Lloyd Wright's eldest son, is a masterpiece of quirky architecture.

The West Hollywood skyline is dominated by the **Pacific Design Center** (8687 Melrose Avenue, at San Vicente Boulevard). A gigantic blue and green glass building, it was designed by Cesar Pelli in 1975 to house outlets for the interior design trade. Fondly known as the 'Blue Whale', it is somewhat underused for its size except when it hosts the bustling West Week design convention each March. South of the PDC on Beverly Boulevard and La Cienega Boulevard is the monstrous **Beverly Center** mall, a huge 'grey whale' much bigger than the PDC, which houses the usual chainstore outlets and is where the Paul Mazursky film *Scenes from a Mall* was shot. Complete your consumer tour at **Koontz** (8914 Santa Monica Boulevard, at San Vicente Boulevard; 1-310 652 0123), which has the best selection of fixtures and fittings in LA and very helpful staff.

Beverly Hills

Swimming pools, movie stars, Rolls-Royces: when it comes to Beverly Hills, all the clichés are true. Expensively manicured and policed to the point of sterility, it comes on as a theme park for the rich, where shopping, eating and looking good in your car are the major activities. It's brimming with lavish mansions and celebrities – Douglas Fairbanks and Mary Pickford were the first to move here, to their mansion Pickfair, in 1920 – and is now populated by rich immigrants from Iran and Israel, with the second most-spoken language being Farsi. The area is replete with lushly planted streets, lilac-flowering jacaranda trees that bloom in April and May and every architectural style imaginable.

Beverly Hills extends either side of Santa Monica and Sunset Boulevards, south-west of West Hollywood. The best way to experience its opulent living is to drive around the residential streets that run north-south from Sunset to Santa Monica Boulevards, between Linden and Doheny Drives. Or check out the hillside houses in and around Benedict and Coldwater Canyons, north of Sunset. Just don't drive too slowly or the vigilant BH cops will be on your tail. Celeb-watchers should note that the public toilets in **Will Rogers Memorial Park**, at the intersection of Beverly Drive and Sunset Boulevard, is where singer George Michael was arrested in the spring of 1998. For locations of other celebrity landmarks, *see chapter* **Celebrity LA**.

The Spanish baroque-style **Civic Center**, which straddles Santa Monica Boulevard and Rexford Drive, is a unique reflection of the city's wealth, so carefully coiffed it looks like a movie set. In direct contrast is the **Union 76** gas station (on the corner of Little Santa Monica Boulevard and Rexford Drive), with its magnificent 1950s cantilevered concrete canopy.

The real reason most people visit Beverly Hills is the 'Golden Triangle' – the shopping area bounded by Wilshire Boulevard, Canon Drive and Little Santa Monica Boulevard that includes Rodeo Drive, Dayton Way and Brighton Way. It contains some of the most expensive shopping outlets in the world, among them Gucci, Armani, Ralph Lauren, Prada, Chanel, Cartier, Van Cleef & Arpels (for all, *see chapter* **Shops & Services**). **Two Rodeo Drive**, a $200 million ersatz European cobbled walkway that boasts an even greater selection of exclusive stores, is always busy with both window-shopping tourists and serious spenders.

If you're in the area, also take a look at the fairy-tale folly of **Spadena House**, also known as the Witch's House (at Carmelita Avenue and Walden Drive). Built in 1921, with peaked, shingled roofs, tilted windows and a fabulous witch-and-broomstick spirit, it was originally a film company's administration building and was often used as a movie set. It is now a private residence, so be careful not to incite the wrath of the resident witch, warlock or other homeowner.

The recently refurbished **Beverly Hills Hotel** on Sunset Boulevard, aka 'the Pink Palace', was one of the first buildings to be built in the city and remains a popular celebrity hangout (*see page 98* **Accommodation**). Its bar, the **Polo Lounge**, is still the place for power lunching and movie dealing (*see page 126* **Restaurants**). The **Peninsula Beverly Hills** on Little Santa Monica Boulevard is also a good place for celebrity-spotting (*see page 103* **Accommodation**), while next door stands the IM Pei-designed **CAA** (Creative Artists Agency) building, all minimalist white marble and cantilevered glass. The stretch of Beverly Drive south of Wilshire Boulevard to Pico Boulevard is a wonderful example of the kind of 1950s architecture that LA is renowned for.

Nate & Al on Beverly Drive is one of the best New York-style delis in the city, while upmarket diner **Kate Mantilini** on Wilshire Boulevard, named after a 1940s boxing promoter, is a feast of high-art architecture by noted firm Morphosis (for both, *see chapter* **Restaurants**).

Away from the shopping frenzy, **Greystone Mansion** (905 Loma Vista Drive; 1-310 550 4796), set in 18 landscaped acres (7.3 hectares), is an oasis of peace and quiet. Built in 1927 by oil millionaire Edward L Doheny, the 55-room Tudor-style home has been used in such films as *The Witches of Eastwick*, *The Bodyguard* and *Indecent Proposal*. The gardens are open 10am-6pm daily.

UCLA & Westwood Village

The University of California at Los Angeles (UCLA) is a sprawling 400-acre (162-hectare) campus, originally built on a bean field in the city of Westwood in 1929. Diverse architectural styles blend in beautifully landscaped grounds, highlighting the enormous wealth and influence of the school. The university is noted for its library holdings (among the largest in the world), school of business administration, centre for health sciences and sports facilities. **Schoenberg Hall** – named after the composer, who taught here in the 1940s – and **Royce Hall** are popular concert and performance venues (for both, *see* **UCLA Center** *page 234* **Theatre & Dance**).

Due to the sheer size of the campus, students are always buzzing around the area. Nearby Westwood Village – just south of UCLA and one of the few walkable neighbourhoods in Los Angeles – is a good place for inexpensive food and, south of Wilshire Boulevard, for bookshops and Italian and Persian restaurants.

Westwood Memorial Cemetery (1218 Glendon Avenue; 1-310 474 1579), on the edge of

Will Rogers Memorial Park, *Beverly Hills.*

the Village, is famous for its celebrity graves, including those of Marilyn Monroe and Natalie Wood, but the **Mormon Temple** (best seen from Santa Monica Boulevard) is by far the most powerful presence in the area. The 257-foot (84-metre) tower, crowned with a 15-foot (4.6-metre) gold-leaf statue of the angel Moroni, is the largest temple of the Church of Jesus Christ of Latter-day Saints outside Salt Lake City, Utah. The temple itself is only open to church members (there is a visitor centre for infidels; 1-310 474 1549), but the beautifully green, manicured lawn and clean, white stone building, which is lit up at night, always provide an awe-inspiring sight.

Rhino Records and **Border's Books & Music** are both fine and famed outlets for music on Westwood Boulevard, south of Wilshire Boulevard: the former for its knowledgeable, friendly staff and more eclectic selection of CDs and vinyl; the latter for the sheer volume of merchandise (for both, see *chapter* **Shops & Services**).

Westside Pavilion on Pico Boulevard is the epitome of the many 1980s shopping malls in Los Angeles: pastel colours juxtaposed with a glass-vaulted atrium and the obligatory selection of high-fashion stores that are in every other mall. However, it also houses the excellent **Samuel Goldwyn** four-screen cinema, which often has exclusive runs of independent films. Also notable

for its adventurous, independent movie screenings is the **Nuart**, one of LA's last surviving movie repertory houses, on Santa Monica Boulevard in West LA, south of Westwood (*see page 181* **Film**).

Across the road from Westside Pavilion is the **Apple Pan** (*see page 128* **Restaurants**), home of the homely hamburger and waiters who have worked there 40 years or more. **John O'Groats** (10516 W Pico Boulevard, at Beverly Glen Boulevard; 1-310 204 0692) is a Scottish-style eaterie with great fish and chips, and porridge (honest).

Bel Air

Bel Air is a posh, sleepy, hillside community between Brentwood and Beverly Hills: developed by Alphonzo E Bell in the early 1920s, it rapidly became a preferred location for celebrities who valued privacy and a good view. There's not much for the outsider to see along the winding roads, as the best houses are hidden from the street behind huge, imposing walls. Celebs who still inhabit the area include Joni Mitchell, Tom Jones, Barry Manilow, Elizabeth Taylor and Lionel Ritchie.

There's not much to do in Bel Air either, except take a jaunt to the **Hotel Bel-Air** on Stone Canyon Road (*see page 101* **Accommodation**). This ultra-expensive inn reflects the tranquil, dripping-with-money neighbourhood with beautifully manicured gardens, a lake full of swans, fireplaces in the rooms and a cosy bar. It has an expensive but delicious Sunday brunch and is also rumoured to entertain Prince Charles for a drink or two when he's in town. Grace Kelly lived here during her Hollywood years.

Century City

This tiny city, between Beverly Hills and West LA, was once a movie backlot and the site of Tom Mix Westerns. It was bought by Alcoa from 20th Century Fox in 1961 and today is still dominated by Fox studios and an over-abundance of high-rise office buildings: 8.6 million square feet (800,000 square metres) of office space on only 176 acres (71.3 hectares). Amid these nondescript buildings, however, are two buildings designed by Minoru Yamasaki (who also designed New York's World Trade Center towers): the triangular **Century Plaza towers** and the **Century Plaza Hotel** (*see page 98* **Accommodation**), a huge, high-rise ellipse enlivened at night by orange lighting and a blue-lit fountain that sits in front of the hotel.

Century City Shopping Center is a vast upmarket mall with a bustling foodcourt and Steven Spielberg's submarine-themed restaurant **Dive!** (*see page 177* **Children**). It is also home to the **AMC Century 14** (1-310 553 8900), claimed to be the second-largest cinema in the States. **Houston's** (*see page 129* **Restaurants**) is a good place to grab a Martini and a pizza after a film.

Brentwood

Novelist Raymond Chandler wrote *High Window* and *Lady in the Lake* while living at 12216 Shetland Place, and Marilyn Monroe died a lonely death just down the road at 12305 Fifth Helena Drive. This exclusive residential neighbourhood west of Beverly Hills was farms and fields until 1915, when a real estate agent named Bundy developed them into streets. Landscape architects and engineers were commissioned to create 'flora, arbor and artistic park attractions'. Everything that suggested a formal city street was avoided, which means Brentwood is like a small town and the main street, San Vicente Boulevard, has a line of coral trees (the official tree of Los Angeles) running down its centre.

The hills north of San Vicente are very rustic, very expensive and, needless to say, home to yet more celebrities. One in particular, OJ Simpson, has done much to put the neighbourhood on the map. The condo of murdered Nicole Brown Simpson on Bundy Drive became a regular tourist attraction, but has now been re-landscaped to deter ghoulish sightseers; OJ's own house, on Rockingham Avenue, was bulldozed in the summer of 1998.

The **Cheesecake Factory** (11647 San Vicente Boulevard, at Barrington Avenue; 1-310 826 7111) has a busy bar scene, while the **New York Bagel Company** (11640 San Vicente Boulevard, at Barrington Avenue; 1-310 820 1050), designed by Frank Gehry, is the place to have breakfast. **Dutton's** (11975 San Vicente Boulevard, between Bundy Drive and Montana Avenue; 1-310 476 6263) is one of the best bookstores in LA, sprawling its collection of books both new and used over four requisitioned condo units.

Nowadays, most people visit Brentwood to see the hugely popular, gleaming, brand new **Getty Center** (*see page 198* **Museums & Galleries**), an extension of the original J Paul Getty Museum in Malibu. Set in the Santa Monica Mountains, this complex houses everything but the Greek and Roman collections, which remain in Malibu.

Culver City

An incorporated city with its own police force, Culver City, at the south-eastern crux of the I-10/I-405 intersection, is renowned for being safe, if boring. At one time it was the home of three major motion picture studios – Metro Goldwyn Mayer, Hal Roach Studios and Selznick International Studios – and produced half the films made in the US. MGM, which claimed to have 'more stars than there are in heaven', gave up its last piece of turf to the producers of *Dallas* and *Falcon Crest*. Sony Film Studios dominates the area and a host of art and photography warehouse conversions by some of LA's most progressive architects, such as the late Frank Israel

and Eric Owen Moss, fill in the rest. The old Helms Bakery building now houses a collection of furniture stores, both contemporary and antique, as well as jazz venue the **Jazz Bakery** (3233 Helms Avenue, at Venice Boulevard; *see page 213* **Music**). Further west is **Versailles** (10319 Venice Boulevard), a cheap and cheerful Cuban restaurant worth visiting; there's another branch nearby on La Cienega Boulevard (*see page 129* **Restaurants**).

Hollywood & Midtown

See Maps 4 & 5

Hollywood

Hollywood does not exist. Actually, it's debatable whether or not it ever did: the floodlit paradise of filmic immortality that the name conjures up was mostly the creation of over-imaginative press officers. There was genuine glamour, too – but much of it has gone today. In any case, you are about as likely to spot a bona-fide movie star strolling along Hollywood Boulevard as you are to see Zeus cavorting on Mount Olympus. The area has no official status, either: it's merely part of the City of Los Angeles, while, confusingly, West Hollywood is an independent city.

You can see glimpses of what **Hollywood Boulevard** used to be in the wonderfully opulent façades of **Mann's Chinese Theater** (*see below*) and **El Capitan Theater** (*see page 181* **Film**), but these days the famous street is just a dirty and depressing stretch of boarded-up storefronts, tacky souvenir shops and teenage runaways with mohican haircuts.

The **Walk of Fame** (on Hollywood Boulevard between La Brea and Argyle Avenues), with its 2,000-plus star-shaped pavement plaques bearing the names of entertainment greats, still exists, but the bloom is well off the rose there, too: these days, it seems as if anyone with $7,500 and a decent publicity agent can score a star of their own.

Still, it's worth making a brief pilgrimage to the area's remaining landmarks. A first glimpse of the huge **Hollywood sign** (*see below*) is always a thrill. The **Hollywood Bowl** (*see page 207* **Music**) won't disappoint either, especially if you take a picnic to a summer evening concert. Further bucolic pleasures can be had at the **Hollywood Reservoir & Dog Park**, while **Sunset Ranch** and **Yamashiro** restaurant offer, respectively, horse riding and Japanese cuisine in an ancient pagoda with phenomenal views (for all, *see below*).

Any worth-their-salt music fan will experience a sense of wonder on seeing the **Capitol Records**

*The iconic **Capitol Records** building.*

building (on Vine Street, just north of the intersection with Hollywood Boulevard) – it's shaped like a stack of records and topped with a stylus, allegedly the idea of songwriter Johnny Mercer and singer Nat 'King' Cole – while the art deco interior of the **Pantages Theater** (6233 Hollywood Boulevard; *see page 209* **Music**) is so beautiful and disorienting that it verges on the psychedelic.

Anyone with a fetish for underwear or a taste for the camp should pay a visit to the **Celebrity Lingerie Hall of Fame** – an exhibition of underwear worn by stars both living and dead – at Frederick's of Hollywood (6608 Hollywood Boulevard; *see page 200* **Museums & Galleries**). Underwear shop **Playmates of Hollywood** (No. 6438) occasionally holds transvestite lingerie shows that are not to be believed.

Unleash the tourist within and pay a visit to the **Hollywood Wax Museum** (No.6767) or the **Guinness World of Records Museum** (No.6764), but make sure you leave off psychedelic drugs beforehand – both contain exhibits that, if viewed in a fragile state of mind, could warp you for life. More intentional oddness can be found at **Ripley's Believe it or Not!** (No.6780; 1-213 466 6335), a tourist trap of bizarre 'facts' that stretches the definition of the term museum.

Those looking for a more reverent view of Hollywood history should check out the mini-museum of cinematic memorabilia on the second-floor mezzanine of the **Clarion Hollywood Roosevelt Hotel** (No.7000; *see page 107* **Accommodation**), while memorabilia collectors and film fans should plan to drop some cash at **Hollywood Book & Poster** (No.6349), a shop jammed to the rafters with obscure videos, rare lobby cards (promotional signs that used to be displayed in cinema lobbies) and stills from just about every movie ever made.

Sunset Boulevard east of Fairfax Avenue is pretty sleazy as well (Hugh Grant was nicked in this part of town), but it somehow seems a lot more vital than its counterpart to the north. Maybe it's the constant, furtive comings and goings from the hourly rate motels or the equally busy string of guitar stores. Anyone interested in the latter should pay a visit to the **Guitar Center** (No.7425; *see page 160* **Shops & Services**): the selection of axes is dizzying in the extreme, and it's entertainment enough just to listen to the 'Hey, dude!' patois of the long-haired, beflannelled shop assistants and customers.

Crossroads of the World (No.6671), a charming little outdoor shopping plaza built in 1936, predates Los Angeles's strip mall explosion by 50 years: too bad its successors couldn't follow the example of its eye-catching English, French, Moorish and Spanish architecture.

After Mann's Chinese Theater, the 1960s **Cinerama Dome** (No.6360; *see page 181* **Film**), the only geodesic dome in the world made entirely of concrete, is the best place in town to see a movie, even if the wide-screen Cinerama process has long since thrown in the towel (the El Capitan is also splendid, but screens only new Disney releases). Once you've experienced the gigantic screen and plush seats, you'll never want to go to your local multiplex again. Unfortunately, plans are presently afoot to build a mall and parking structure around the dome, which will leave the cinema intact but hide the eye-popping exterior from view. See it now, while you still can.

The buildings that comprise **A&M Records** (1416 N La Brea Avenue) have resonated not only to the sounds of the Rolling Stones and the Carpenters (among the thousands of other acts that have recorded here over the past few decades), but with cinematic history as well: the core of the complex was built in 1918 by Charlie Chaplin, who used it as his movie studio. Jazz musician Herb Alpert purchased the place for A&M in 1966, but concrete prints of Chaplin's feet are allegedly still visible outside studio three.

In the end (no pun intended), the best place to look for the Ghost of Hollywood Past is at **Hollywood Memorial Cemetery** (6000 Santa Monica Boulevard; 1-323 469 1181). Located just north of **Paramount Studios** (*see page 182* **Film**), it is the final resting place of such luminaries as

Tyrone Power, Cecil B DeMille, Douglas Fairbanks Snr, Adolph Menjou, Nelson Eddy, studio mogul Harry Cohn (who wanted to be buried facing his beloved Columbia Studios), Peter Lorre, Peter Finch and Rudolph Valentino; legend has it that a mysterious 'Woman in Black' still stalks the place, mourning for the latter. The grounds are incredibly peaceful, the decades-old monuments unique in design and, overall, it's much less of a downer than a stroll along Hollywood Boulevard. As the headstone of Mel Blanc – the voice of Porky Pig, Elmer Fudd et al – reads: 'That's all, folks!'

Hollywood Reservoir & Dog Park
Lake Hollywood Drive, Hollywood Hills. Bus 420/US 101, exit Barham Boulevard north.
Set in the Hollywood Hills, above the Hollywood Bowl and below the Hollywood sign and Madonna's enormous estate, Hollywood Reservoir attracts runners, walkers and the occasional cyclist. It's at its best when the gates open at 6.30am: the aroma of dew-moist pines envelops you as you run or walk on the three-mile (5km) pebbly dirt road around the reservoir. From one side of the reservoir, you get a fantastic view of the Hollywood sign. Tucked behind the reservoir up Beachwood Canyon is the Hollywood Dog Park. It's not uncommon to catch a glimpse of a jogging celeb who thinks they're incognito under their baseball cap.

Hollywood sign
See also p80 **Take a hike**.
This perennially fascinating sign, symbol, logo, sculpture and icon in one stands north of Hollywood on Mount Lee. A good place from which to see it is the corner of Sunset Boulevard and Bronson Avenue; another is Paramount Studios, at Melrose Avenue and Gower Street. Built in 1923, the gargantuan sign was originally an advert for a real-estate development called 'Hollywoodland'. In 1949, the city tore down the last four of the 50ft (15m) letters and kept the rest as a landmark. It has now become such a potent symbol of stardom that it's a surprise to hear that it's been the jumping-off point for only one suicide – a young starlet, Lillian Millicent Entwistle, known as Peg, who threw herself off the 'H' one breezy September night in 1932 after RKO studios declined to pick up her option when they saw her first film.

Today, the sign is repainted five times a year and defended by a million-dollar security system. But even this cannot keep out the trespassers who want to get their messages out to the world. For brief moments, the sign and its 5,000 lights have become 'Ollywood' (after Iran-Contra messenger Colonel Oliver North), 'Holly-weed' (in appreciation of the powers of marijuana) and a support message to the US troops fighting in the Gulf War, when a massive yellow ribbon was tied around the letters.

Hollywood Wax Museum
6767 Hollywood Boulevard, at Highland Avenue, Hollywood (1-323 462 5991/recorded information 1-323 462 8860). Bus 1, 163, 180, 181, 210/I-10, exit La Brea Avenue north. **Open** 10am-midnight Mon-Thur, Sun; 10am-2am Fri, Sat. **Admission** $9.95; $8.50 seniors; $6.95 6-12s. **Credit** AmEx, MC, V. **Map 5 A1**
Rather ragged around the edges, the Wax Museum is still amusing, even if the sets do seem to have been locked in a time capsule for a decade. Many of the celebrities, presidents, athletes and historical figures immortalised here look more like relatives of the people they're supposed to portray: some close, others long-lost and some only by marriage. Its redeeming feature is the Chamber of Horrors, which despite its campness can be a bit spooky. Combo discount admission is available for the Hollywood Wax Museum and the Guinness World of Records Museum across the street.

Mann's Chinese Theater
6925 Hollywood Boulevard, between Highland & La Brea Avenues, Hollywood (1-323 461 3331/recorded information 1-323 464 8111). Bus 1, 26, 213/I-10, exit Highland Avenue. **Admission** $8; $5.50 students; $5 under-12s, seniors. **Credit** MC, V. **Map 5 A1**
Mann's is where you'll find the famous courtyard where movie greats have made imprints of their hands and feet. Master showman Sid Grauman, in true Hollywood style, commissioned architects Meyer and Holler to create a Chinese temple as a new stage on which to perform his prologues. Legend insists that Norma Talmadge accidentally stepped into the wet cement outside the new building and, in spirited response, Sid fetched Mary Pickford and Douglas Fairbanks to repeat the 'mistake' with their feet and hands. And so it began. Mann's was the spot where the first gala premières took place – limousines, fur-wrapped starlets, the works. The courtyard is sometimes choked with camera-snapping tourists measuring their own hands and feet against the likes of John Wayne, Jimmy Stewart and Judy Garland, but the cinema itself is well preserved, clean and still a great place to catch a movie.

Sunset Ranch
3400 N Beachwood Drive, at Franklin Avenue, Hollywood (1-323 469 5450). US 101, exit Beachwood Drive north. **Open** 9am-5pm daily. **Horses** $15 per hour.
Sunset Ranch offers riding lessons, moonlight rides and hourly rentals in the Hollywood Hills. Don't miss the evening Margarita ride, up and over the hills and into the Valley, where you stop at a Mexican restaurant – at least one person always falls off on the way home.

Yamashiro
For listings, see p131 **Restaurants**.
Now one of Hollywood's best-known Japanese restaurants, this imported oriental pagoda in the Hollywood Hills (originally a brothel, according to legend) is more than 600 years old, making it the oldest building in LA. You can have a drink in the bar or a full meal, but it's the view that matters. Book a window seat.

Fairfax District

Although LA's first major Jewish community settled in the East LA neighbourhood of Boyle Heights, the stretch of Fairfax Avenue between Beverly Boulevard and Melrose Avenue has been Los Angeles's main Jewish drag since the 1940s. If you're shopping for a new menorah or the latest in Israeli pop music, this is the place to go: and the neighbourhood's heavy Hasidic population makes it the safest place in LA to jog on a Friday evening.

Kosher grocers, butcher's shops, restaurants and bakeries line the street; all are excellent, and almost all are closed on Saturdays. Open 24 hours a day, however, is the legendary **Canter's** (419 N Fairfax Avenue; *see page 132* **Restaurants**), a World War II-era kosher restaurant, deli and bakery. The food is delicious and authentic (homesick New Yorkers eat here regularly), and portions are generous. Another good lunch spot is **Eat-a-Pita** (No.465), a pleasant outdoor stand that serves some of the best Middle Eastern fast food (falafel and so on) in town.

Just south of the Beverly-Fairfax intersection lies **CBS Television City**, home to many a game

For an authentic Jewish deli, visit **Canter's** on Fairfax Avenue (page 63).

show and sitcom. Next door is the retail experience of the **Farmers Market**.

Farmers Market

6333 W Third Street, at Fairfax Avenue, Fairfax District (1-213 549 2140). Bus 16, 217/I-10, exit Fairfax Avenue north. **Open** 9am-7pm Mon-Sat; 10am-6pm Sun. **Admission** free. **Map 4 B2**
Originally a co-op where people could buy produce from local farmers, today the Farmers Market has more than 165 stalls selling foods both homely and exotic, as well as shops offering knick-knacks, clothes and tourist tat. It's best on Thursday and Saturday evenings (7-9pm), when bands play; Friday-night karaoke is also popular. Plans to turn the neighbouring car park into a mall bode ill for the low-key atmosphere. For the more authentic farmers markets that are held all over LA, *see p51*.

Miracle Mile & Midtown

So named because of its tremendous commercial growth during the 1920s, Miracle Mile's appellation now seems somewhat ironic, given the rate at which businesses on the strip – which stretches along Wilshire Boulevard from Fairfax to La Brea Avenues – have been shutting their doors.

The saga of the **May Co** department store (6067 Wilshire Boulevard) pretty much sums up the situation. Opened in 1940, the store was one of the commercial mainstays of the district, but the recent shift in consumer habits (huge malls such as the Beverly Center now reign supreme) and the psychological residue of the 1992 riots (as far as most suburbanites were concerned, anywhere south of Ventura Boulevard was South Central)

forced it to close in 1993. The impressive façade, once slated for demolition, still stands, and the LA County Museum of Art supposedly has plans to renovate it, but it seems that it will be a while before the doors open again.

The neighbouring diner, **Johnie's** (No.6101), is a rare and rather run-down example of 1950s 'Googie' architecture. It looks gorgeous when lit up at night – but is best viewed from the outside at any time, as the food is, frankly, lousy.

This stretch of Wilshire is also known as Museum Row, and for good reason. The **Los Angeles County Museum of Art**, the **Petersen Automotive Museum**, the **Carole & Barry Kaye Museum of Miniatures** and the **George C Page Museum of Tar Pit Discoveries** are all within easy walking distance of each other. The latter features the added attraction of the **La Brea Tar Pits**: a huge, bubbling swamp of primordial ooze, it remains, after millions of years, a great place to ruminate on the brevity of your existence. Most of the park is currently closed for construction, but the large Lake Pit is still accessible. For all, *see chapter* **Museums & Galleries**.

The renovated **El Rey Theatre** (No.5519), built in 1936 in the Streamline Moderne style, was a popular rock concert venue for several years, although conflicts with the neighbours have temporarily put the kibosh on live music bookings. It is still an active nightclub, though; see *page 209* **Music** and **Coven 13** *page 215* **Nightlife**.

The area just south of the Miracle Mile is primarily residential, inhabited by an integrated, middle- and lower-middle-class community. Some of the finest soul food north of South Central can be found here, at **Maurice's Snack 'n' Chat** (5549 W Pico Boulevard) and **Roscoe's House of Chicken 'n' Waffles** (No.5006; for both, *see chapter* **Restaurants**), while **Uncle Darrow's** (5301 Venice Boulevard) dishes up the best no-frills Cajun cooking in town.

A few miles and many generic strip malls to the east, the **Wiltern Center** (at Wilshire Boulevard and Western Avenue) is thriving nicely. A breathtaking, green, art deco pile built in 1931, it lingered in a state of advanced decrepitude during much of the 1970s and 1980s before being rescued from the wrecking ball and turned into a performing arts and commercial centre. Pop acts regularly strut their stuff inside the stunning **Wiltern Theater** (*see page 209* **Music**) on the corner of the Center, which also regularly hosts such popular black theatrical productions as *Beauty Shop* and *Mama I'm Sorry*. The neighbouring **Atlas Bar & Grill** (*see page 133* **Restaurants**) is a must for Californian cuisine and cabaret in a deliciously camp interior.

The **Ambassador Hotel** (No.3400) – known to most as the site of Robert F Kennedy's assassination on the eve of the 1968 California primary elections – is certainly due for a revival, but plans to reopen the building have recently been delayed; there is talk, in fact, that it might be razed to make way for a school. But new life has come to the glorious **Bullocks Wilshire** (No.3050); one of the first department stores to open (in 1929) outside Downtown, it closed its doors in the wake of sagging revenues and the 1992 riots. Now, however, it has been reopened as a law school.

Revitalisation is still light years away, however, for **Lafayette Park** and its larger neighbour, **MacArthur Park** (Wilshire Boulevard, between Alvarado and Park View Streets). The latter, with its recently restored lake and 500-foot (150 metre) high water spout, is an especially grand example of urban landscaping – that is, if you can ignore the crackheads, the drug dealers and the Central American gang members who populate it. It's a shame; even in its present state, it's still not difficult to see how the park could have inspired Jimmy Webb's epic ballad. But this time, the only thing left out in the rain is the park's resident encampment of homeless individuals.

Two notable remnants of the neighbourhood's better days are the imposing **Park Plaza Hotel** (607 S Park View Street) and **Langer's Delicatessen** (704 S Alvarado Street). The latter, considered by many to have the best pastrami sandwich in town, has a kerbside takeaway service for customers too scared to park their cars on the surrounding mean streets. Hamburger fans should

also seek out nearby **Cassell's** (3266 W Sixth Street; *see page 133* **Restaurants**), where the home-made patties may well be the best you've ever tasted.

Hancock Park

A gorgeous residential neighbourhood dating back to 1910, Hancock Park is home to some of the most jaw-droppingly opulent mansions found outside Beverly Hills and Bel Air. Bounded by Wilshire Boulevard and Van Ness, Highland and Melrose Avenues, Hancock Park is best toured by car – the local security services are apt to be suspicious of anyone on foot. Historically an Anglo enclave, it excluded blacks and Jews (who moved west) until 1948, when Nat 'King' Cole was the first African-American to live there. (Don't confuse the area with Hancock Park, an actual park further west on Wilshire Boulevard.)

Stop for refreshment on the nearby stretch of Larchmont Boulevard (between Beverly Boulevard and First Street) known as **Larchmont Village**. This charming couple of blocks has a variety of restaurants, antique shops and other small businesses, many of them housed in buildings built in the 1920s. The residents of Larchmont Village take great pride in the area's period feel, and protested vociferously when a Blockbuster Video franchise moved in a few years back.

Koreatown

Torched during the 1992 riots, Koreatown – the Midtown neighbourhood roughly comprising the area south of Wilshire Boulevard and along Pico Boulevard between Western and Vermont Avenues – has made a remarkable comeback. Tensions between the Korean and African-American communities (and the area's Central American population) haven't exactly abated, but, for the shopowners, at least, things seem to be back to business as usual. Korean banks, men's clubs, shopfront grocers and golf driving ranges abound, especially along Pico and Olympic Boulevards, and several Korean car dealerships are currently thriving.

There are also plenty of Korean eateries, of course. Although Korean cooking, with its heavier, meat-based dishes, hasn't quite caught on with non-Koreans, adventurous eaters should take the opportunity to have a spot of lunch in the area. The pricey **Woo Lae Oak** (623 S Western Avenue; *see page 134* **Restaurants**) gets regular raves, while holes-in-the-wall such as **Ham Hung** (809 S Ardmore Avenue; 1-213 381 1520) offer delicious but cheaper regional cooking. For a carnivorous – and non-Korean – experience, try **Taylor's Steakhouse** (3361 W Eighth Street; 1-213 382 8449), a chop house with enormous buttoned-and-tufted booths and almost equally enormous steaks.

Downtown

See Map 7

It's hard to imagine now, but Downtown LA was once quite literally the heart of the city: a place where lavish film premières were held, where movie stars socialised in swanky restaurants and where a large portion of Angelenos actually went to work on a daily basis. These days, there are plenty of LA residents who have never been to Downtown at all, except perhaps to board a train at Union Station or catch the latest hot musical at the Mark Taper Forum. It's a pity, really; though its best days may well be behind it, Downtown still offers plenty of enjoyment.

After years of post-war decline, the area attracted a lot of investment in the 1980s, much of it from the Far East. Now it's packed during the week with commuting office workers, while the main drag, Broadway, is a buzzing Latino shopping zone, particularly at weekends.

Downtown is one of the few areas of LA where it's better to walk than drive. Everything can be seen in a day and DASH buses (*see page 254* **Directory**) serve the area at frequent intervals. Although it's not the best place in Los Angeles for star-spotting, you may well see film crews at work: it's a popular location for movies and TV shows. Most notably, perhaps, Ridley Scott immortalised Downtown's skyline and its landmark Bradbury Building in *Blade Runner*, a seminal LA movie.

No one really knows how many people live in Downtown and it's certainly not a conventional residential area. It also attracts a considerable number of homeless people. Avoid walking round the area at night and, if you're arriving or departing from the Greyhound terminal on Seventh Street, be careful in its immediate vicinity.

Chinatown

Located at the northern end of Downtown and starting where Broadway meets Sunset Boulevard, Chinatown has suffered in recent years from an exodus of residents to the San Gabriel Valley, now *the* place for Chinese food. Nevertheless, this small but busy neighbourhood is home to an estimated 30,000 people and remains the spiritual centre of LA's Chinese community. **North Broadway** and **North Spring Street** are the main thoroughfares – the site of banks, businesses and traditional markets – while the streets running off them are also worth a look: the small row of shops between **Bamboo Lane** and **Bernard Street** is an especially good place for souvenir shopping. Every February, giant dragons snake down Broadway during celebrations for Chinese New Year (*see page 90* **Los Angeles by Season**).

There are plenty of restaurants in the area. **Ocean Seafood** (Chunsan Plaza, 747 N Broadway, between Ord and Alpine Streets) and **Yang Chow** (819 N Broadway, between Alpine and College Streets) are both good bets, though the former can get very busy at weekends. Apart from eating, there's little to do here at night.

Olvera Street

Just across Sunset Boulevard from Chinatown is **El Pueblo de Los Angeles Historical Monument** (1-323 628 1274), a 44-acre (18-hectare) historic park and outdoor museum on the site of the original settlement of Los Angeles. In fact, the very first settlement was about half a mile (800 metres) from here, but no trace of it remains: LA's official birthday is 4 September 1781, the day that the first Spanish settlers began farming and building ranches. The museum courtyard is occupied by taco stands and a gift shop. Next door is the oldest Catholic church in LA: Our Lady, Queen of the Angels, known as **La Placita**. Established in 1784, it's still in use and has some impressive ceiling murals.

Cross Main Street and you reach the **Plaza**. With a bandstand in the middle, it's a popular place for performances by dancers and musicians and the trees offer some shade from the sun. In one corner is the Mexican Cultural Institute. The Plaza is the site of two annual festivals, the **Blessing of the Animals** at Easter and **Las Posadas** just before Christmas. The annual **Cinco de Mayo** celebrations include a parade down Olvera Street and then a fiesta commemorating the Mexican victory at the battle of Puebla (for all, *see chapter* **Los Angeles by Season**).

Running off the eastern side of the Plaza is **Olvera Street**, a narrow thoroughfare full of stalls selling postcards and Mexican handicrafts. Renovated in 1930 as a Mexican marketplace, it's now just a tourist trap – albeit a vibrant and generally enjoyable one. The **El Pueblo Gallery**, which shows local art, is worth checking out.

Olvera Street also contains **Avila Adobe**, the oldest house in Los Angeles. Built in 1818, this small ranch-style house has been restored, furnished with period pieces and now operates as a museum. There are also numerous Mexican restaurants along Olvera, all pretty average. If you're not in the mood for Mexican or Chinese, try **Phillipe Original** (1001 N Alameda Street; *see page 134* **Restaurants**), an ancient eaterie two blocks north of Olvera Street, which has been serving up delicious 'French Dip' sandwiches and 10¢ coffee for the best part of the past century. It's open 24 hours a day, and always crowded.

Visible from the Plaza is **Union Station** (800 N Alameda Street), one of the most accomplished structures in the city. Opened in 1939 on the site of the original Chinatown, which was later moved to its present location, it was the last of the great American train stations to be built and unified the three railroads that then served LA. With its distinctive, Spanish mission-style exterior, marble floors, high ceilings and gorgeous decorative tiles, it's an evocative place at which to arrive or depart from LA (but don't confuse Union Station with the imposing piece of Spanish colonial architecture that stands next to it: that's just the post office).

Union Station is also home to the easternmost stop on the **Red Line**, LA's new subway. The shortness of the line (currently it takes you along Wilshire Boulevard only as far as Western Avenue, a 15-minute ride) makes it pretty useless to most Angelenos, but it does offer visitors a convenient means (especially on rainy days) by which to buzz around the Downtown area. Unlike the subway systems in New York or Chicago, the Red Line is spotlessly clean and almost entirely free of grafitti. We'll see how long that lasts.

Little Tokyo

Head south down Alameda Street for a few blocks, past Temple Street, and you reach the **Geffen Contemporary** wing of MOCA (152 N Central Avenue). It is housed in an old warehouse converted by Frank Gehry. It's a more flexible space than MOCA's other site (at California Plaza, 250 S Grand Avenue) and concentrates mainly on post-World War II art. The always-provocative exhibitions change frequently (for both, *see chapter* **Museums & Galleries**).

Just down Central Avenue from MOCA, on the corner of First Street, is the **Japanese American National Museum** (369 E First Street). It's an appropriate place to start a tour of Little Tokyo, which begins at First Street and spreads west and north. The museum is dedicated to recording and relating the extensive history of the Japanese-American community – Little Tokyo has been in existence for over a century – and mixes exhibits with films and, occasionally, performance art.

Cross First Street from the museum and you enter the **Japanese Village Plaza** (335 E Second Street), a two-storey mini-mall with restaurants, shops and karaoke bars. Pop into **Rascal's** or **Frying Fish** for good ramen or sushi, respectively. Restaurants here generally stay open later than most of LA's eating places: you can turn up after midnight and still get served.

At the end of the plaza is the **Fire Tower** with its distinctive tiled roof. Nearby is the **Japanese American Cultural and Community Center** (244 S San Pedro Street), which has an art gallery and Japanese garden. Kabuki, dance and music performances are held in the **Japan America Theater** on the same site (*see page 206* **Music**). Also in the area is the **Higashi Honganji**

Welcome to **Chinatown**.

Buddhist Temple (505 E Third Street, at Central Avenue). With its subtle roof, it blends neatly into its very Western surroundings.

St Vibiana's Cathedral (114 E Second Street) is also nearby. Built in 1876 and now in very poor condition, it was recently the subject of a battle between the diocese, which wants to tear it down and build a new one, and conservationists, who want to preserve it. The diocese appears to have won, but the structure may still be standing when you get here. If so, it's definitely worth a look.

If you continue west past the Higashi Temple, you'll enter the **Artists'/Loft District**. The name is something of a misnomer: there are more homeless people here than artists. During the 1980s, when both Downtown and the LA art scene were booming, artists began converting the derelict warehouses that are scattered throughout this area into studios and apartments. Developers quickly started doing the same thing in the hope of reproducing New York's SoHo on the West Coast, but the expected rush of tenants never materialised.

Civic Center

A few blocks north of Little Tokyo along First Street is the area where many of LA's administrative and political institutions are based. The first you'll encounter is the **Times-Mirror Building**, home to the *Los Angeles Times* (202 W First Street, at Spring Street). The building is a slightly tatty example of 1930s architecture and the newspaper is the subject of derision for East Coasters (with good reason), but it's an important LA institution, founded by the Chandler family, one of the élite WASP families that ran Los Angeles in the late 1800s and played a major part in the development of Downtown.

Conveniently for *Times* reporters, **City Hall** (200 N Spring Street) is just across the road. Surrounded by uninspired modern office blocks, its graceful art deco lines have appeared in many movies (it was destroyed most memorably in *War of the Worlds*) and television shows. Until 1957 it was the tallest building in LA.

Nearby, in the Los Angeles Mall, an utterly soulless shopping area, is the **Los Angeles Children's Museum** (*see page 178* **Children**). Partly designed by the ubiquitous Frank Gehry, it's an ambitious and fun museum with plenty of interactive exhibits and installations. Around the corner, on Aliso and Los Angeles Streets, is the **Metropolitan Detention Center**, LA's newest hi-tech prison. Designed to blend in with the office blocks around it, the building looks nothing like a conventional jail; local legend has it that a group of Japanese tourists once tried to check into it, thinking it was a hotel. Also of note is the **Los Angeles County Courthouse**: located on Temple Street between Spring Street and Broadway, this imposing structure was the scene of the OJ Simpson trial.

Shopping on **Olvera Street** *(p66).*

Broadway

If you want a taste of what a real Mexican shopping street looks like, as opposed to the tourist tack of Olvera Street, then **Broadway** is the place to explore. Running the whole length of Downtown, it's one of the most fascinating streets in the area: a place where old Los Angeles, in the shape of the once grandiose and now mostly decrepit buildings that line it, meets the new, increasingly Hispanic city.

Back in the 1920s and 1930s it was the most fashionable shopping and entertainment zone in the city. But the post-war decline of Downtown hit Broadway hard and many of the buildings are boarded up or in a state of disrepair. Despite this, there's a vitality to the street, particularly at the weekends, that you don't find anywhere else in LA. The stores sell mainly electronic goods, cut-price clothes (this is a good place to buy jeans) and jewellery (LA's jewellery district starts below Fifth Street and Broadway) – but you don't come here for the shopping so much as the atmosphere.

Start at Second Street and Broadway and wander south. At the corner of Third Street and Broadway, you'll find the **Bradbury Building**, one of the

unquestionable highlights of the city's architecture (*see page 29* **Architecture**). Across the street, there's the **Million Dollar Theater**, first opened by Sid Grauman in 1918 and now an evangelical church. Next door is **Grand Central Market** (315 S Broadway), an enclosed market in the Mexican tradition. It's one of the busiest places in Downtown, with a host of fresh fruit stalls, butchers and fishmongers. If you want lunch and a beer, there are also plenty of taco stands, Chinese fast-food counters and pizza joints.

Alternatively, further down Broadway, just past Sixth Street, you can eat at **Clifton's Brookdale Cafeteria** (648 S Broadway). Built in the 1930s, the restaurant boasts a sumptuous array of inexpensive food items, but is also notable for its bizarre interior, which is half hunting lodge, half redwood forest. Just across the street is the **Los Angeles Theater**, which was built in 90 days for the première of Charlie Chaplin's *City Lights* in 1930. It's now boarded up, but the extravagant façade is still visible.

The only one of the old Broadway movie palaces that's still a working cinema is the huge **Orpheum** (842 S Broadway, at Eighth Street): built in 1926, it's a wacky blend of colonial Spanish and French Gothic styles. Across the street from the Orpheum is the old **Eastern Columbia Building**, a gorgeous, 13-storey, turquoise art deco pile built in 1929 by Claude Beelman. For a break from the hustle of Broadway, turn west at Fifth Street and head for **Pershing Square**. Named after the commander of the US Army in World War I, the square hosts free jazz, blues and salsa concerts during the summer and is a good place to catch your breath. Dominating the western corner of the square is the **Regal Biltmore** hotel, built in 1923 and one of the grandest hotels in Los Angeles (*see page 110* **Accommodation**). Winston Churchill used to stay there when he was in town.

Financial District

A block west of Pershing Square and you enter the land of the skyscraper. The major banks have their huge, gleaming offices here, dwarfing everything around them. This neighbourhood used to be known as Bunker Hill: a century or so ago it was where LA's rich built their houses, but most of those mansions are now long gone. The only remnant of that era is **Angels Flight**, the world's shortest railway (Hill Street, between Third and Fourth Streets). Opened in 1901, this funicular track was designed to connect Bunker Hill with the business district that was then located around Hill and Spring Streets; it saved the residents from having to walk the steep slope back to their houses. The railway reopened in 1996; a ride costs 25¢ and takes a mere two minutes (up and down).

A minute west of Bunker Hill and you reach the **Central Library** (630 W Fifth Street). Completed in 1926 and recently refurbished after a fire, it's an excellent library and has a dramatic, tiled pyramid tower (*see page 260* **Directory**). Virtually opposite is the **Westin Bonaventure Hotel** (*see page 111* **Accommodation**), the most distinctive skyscraper in Downtown. With its interior pools and bubble-shaped elevators, it offers a refreshing change from the uniformity of most of the district's tall buildings.

If you feel the need to watch a movie while in the area, head for **Laemmle's Grande** (349 S Figueroa Street), a modern four-screen cinema that's rarely crowded. Also near here is the **Los Angeles Convention & Visitors Bureau**, the main information centre for the city (685 S Figueroa Street; *see page 265* **Directory**).

Backtrack from the library down Fifth Street to Grand Avenue and then head north up the sharp little hill: the Wells Fargo Center is on your left. Apart from being the headquarters of the Wells Fargo bank, it also houses the **Wells Fargo History Museum**, which tells the story of the bank founded in the heyday of the California Gold Rush. There's a 100-year-old stagecoach and gold nuggets on display.

Just up from the Wells Fargo Center on the other side of the road is the other **MOCA** site (*see page 196* **Museums & Galleries**). Part of the billion-dollar **California Plaza** development, the muse-

Civic grandeur: **LA Central Library**.

um is unmissable: there's a huge Swiss Army knife, designed by Claes Oldenburg, in front of it.

Carry on walking up Grand Avenue and on the left you'll come to the vast Music Center (at First Street). Gathered together in one complex are the **Dorothy Chandler Pavilion** (*see page 205* **Music**), where the Oscars take place and the LA Philharmonic lives, the **Mark Taper Forum** and the **Ahmanson Theater**, regarded as two of LA's better theatres (*see chapter* **Theatre & Dance**). Guided tours are available.

East of Hollywood

See Map 6

The area was home to a number of film studios during the silent era: DW Griffith built his gigantic set for *Intolerance* at the north-east corner of Sunset Boulevard and Hillhurst Avenue, now the site of the Vista (*see page 181* **Film**), a fine single-screen cinema offering the most leg room of any in Los Angeles. On the culinary side, two good bets in this part of town are **Jitlada** (5233 W Sunset Boulevard, at Harvard Boulevard; 1-323 667 9809) and **Zankou Chicken** (5065 W Sunset Boulevard, at Normandie Avenue; 1-323 665 7845). The former offers excellent Thai cuisine at extremely reasonable prices, while the latter serves up cheap and simple but very tasty Middle Eastern food, the potent garlic balanced by munching pickled beets.

Griffith Park

Mining tycoon Griffith J Griffith donated 4,000 acres (1,600 hectares) to the city in 1896. Today, this land is the largest city-run park in the US (five times the size of New York's Central Park) and, despite recent fires and the flooding from El Niño that followed, is a paradise for hikers, picnickers, cyclists, families and tennis, golf, soccer and horse-riding enthusiasts.

The park's myriad attractions include the spectacular view from **Griffith Park Observatory** (*see* photo), **Los Angeles Zoo**, Western memorabilia at the **Autry Museum** (*see page 200* **Museums & Galleries**), open-air concerts at the 1930 **Greek Theater**, Andy Gibb's burial slot at **Forest Lawn Memorial Park** and a 1926 merry-go-round (as seen in the film *Face/Off*). There are 53 miles (85 kilometres) of hiking trails – the 1,625-foot (495-metre) peak of Mount Hollywood is only a half-hour hike from the Observatory – and the **Sierra Club** (1-213 387 4287) organises regular guided hikes and moonlight rambles. The park is open 10am-5pm daily; for more information, call 1-213 665 5188. For details of the four golf courses, 24 tennis courts and Los Angeles Equestrian Center, *see chapter* **Sport & Fitness**.

a gander at the Foucault pendulum, the cosmic ray cloud chamber and the giant Tesla coil.
Parking free.
Website: www.griffithobs.org

Griffith Park Observatory

2800 E Observatory Road (1-323 664 1181/recorded information 1-213 664 1191/Laserium 1-818 901 9405). Bus 96/I-5, exit Los Feliz Boulevard west. **Open** *summer* 12.30-10pm daily; *winter* 2-10pm Tue-Fri; 12.30-10pm Sat, Sun. **Admission** *telescope* free (cloudless nights only); *Planetarium shows* $4; $3 seniors; $2 5-12s; *Laserium shows* $7; $6 seniors, 5-12s; under-5s not admitted. **Credit** MC, V (Laserium only).

The outside deck at the Observatory, at the southern edge of the park, provides the best overview of the sprawl of LA, and even when the curdled haze of smog inhibits visibility, the view stretches over Chavez Ravine into East LA, down Western Avenue towards Inglewood and across Sunset Boulevard towards Santa Monica. On the odd clear night when the city sparkles below, the beauty of LA's psychogeography is mind-blowing.

The bronze domes of the Observatory have been part of the Hollywood Hills landscape since 1934 ('If every person could look through that telescope,' declared Griffith J Griffith, 'it would revolutionise the world.'). The formidable deco-modern building has been featured in many films, from the acclaimed (*Rebel Without a Cause, Terminator 2* and Wim Wenders's *The End of Violence*) to the disdained (*Flesh Gordon*). It houses a triple-beam solar telescope and a 12in Zeiss refracting telescope, permitting viewing of the next Leonid meteor shower, a thrice-a-century event expected around 18 November 1999. When there are eclipses or comets to be seen, local astronomy clubs set up 'scopes on the lawn and talk shop to anyone who will listen.

The Planetarium is traditional, while the laser shows include rock music. Leave time for the Hall of Science and

Los Angeles Zoo

5333 Zoo Drive (1-323 666 4650). Bus 96/I-5, exit Zoo Drive west. **Open** 10am-5pm daily. **Admission** $8.25; $5.25 seniors; $3.25 2-12s. **Credit** AmEx, Disc, MC, V.

One of the park's biggest draws for families, the LA Zoo continues to make improvements, such as the recent addition of a blind cavefish cave and the impending completion of the Great Ape Forest, a grass-and-wood world for the chimps. And when your visit to the more than 1,200 reptiles, birds, mammals and amphibians threatens to become too much, cool down in the eucalyptus forest environment inside the Ahmanson Koala House. If you've got kids in tow, take them to Adventure Island, specially designed for small children; phone in advance to see what special children's programmes are being offered, such as the summertime Wild Weekends series with food, music and puppetry.
Parking free.
Website: www.lazoo.org

Travel Town Museum

5200 Zoo Drive (1-323 662 5874). Bus 96/Hwy 134, exit Zoo Drive south. **Open** 10am-5pm Mon-Fri; 10am-6pm Sat, Sun. **Admission** free.

A fine outdoor museum featuring restored railroad cars from the Union Pacific, Atchison and Santa Fe lines, an early twentieth-century milk delivery truck, over a dozen steam and diesel locomotives and a nifty miniature train that gives visitors a ride around the museum grounds.
Website: www.scsra.org/~scrsa/ttown/ttown.html
Parking free.

Visitors with a taste for the seedier side of life can pay a visit to the **Sunset Theater** at the corner of Sunset Boulevard and Western Avenue, one of the town's few remaining triple-X grind houses ('Free admission for ladies'), or grab a seat at **Jumbo's Clown Room** (5153 Hollywood Boulevard, between Normandie Avenue and Winona Boulevard; 1-323 666 1187), a popular strip club with the vibe of a neighbourhood bar, whose patrons include David Lynch.

At the opposite end of the cultural spectrum is the lush oasis known as **Barnsdall Art Park**. Set on a hill high above a subway station slated to open in 2000, this peaceful, verdant park is home to the lovely **Hollyhock House** (built between 1917 and 1920, it was Frank Lloyd Wright's first Los Angeles commission), an art gallery and a number of arts and crafts centres, all of which are overseen by the City of Los Angeles Department of Cultural Affairs. Though the once delightful view of the city is now largely blocked by a nearby hospital complex, Barnsdall Art Park remains an enjoyable escape from the madness of LA (*see page 195* **Museums & Galleries**).

Los Feliz

Los Feliz is a truly cohesive neighbourhood, a casual coffee-klatch community whose largely on-the-go youth mixes with a significant Armenian population and elderly pensioners. In the Los Feliz Hills (where Madonna has chosen to bring up baby), above Los Feliz Boulevard and just below Griffith Park, there are posh, secluded homes, including the famous **Lovell House**, designed by Richard Neutra in 1929 and recently featured in *LA Confidential*. The spine of Los Feliz, **Vermont Avenue**, is further south – and very much alive and kicking.

Vermont Avenue's multicultural cocktail of clothing shops, bookshops and bars has a lot to offer. Its resurgent hipness has resulted in a number of fly-by-night outfits, but certain mainstays are worth visiting. A good recent addition is the free art at **George's Gallery** (1756 N Vermont Avenue), which takes its name from an old-time greasy spoon up the street that was ousted to make way for a garish and overpriced fake diner. Bookworms can stop at **Amok Books** (No.1764) for its eclectic offerings, **Skylight Books** (No.1818) for its wide selection and frequent literary readings, and **Aldine Books** (4663 Hollywood Boulevard) for its mounds of cheap, used paperbacks. **Onyx Sequel** is a popular, late-night coffeeshop (*see page 144* **Coffeehouses**). For vinyl record hounds, **Fat Beats** (No.1722) has a comprehensive selection of hip-hop and rare groove, while the **Record Recycler** (4659 Hollywood Boulevard) offers a staggering selection of all types of affordably priced second-hand

vinyl and some used CDs; for both, *see page 160* **Shops & Services**.

When in need of a quick bite, get a delicious $2.70 Yucatan pork burrito at the tiny stand **Yuca's** (2056 Hillhurst Avenue). At cocktail hour, the fabulously upholstered, white leather **Dresden Room** is a classy joint, featuring the lounge musical stylings of Marty and Elayne in the evening, while another swinging watering hole is the **Good Luck Bar** with its Chinese opium den-style interior. The true swingers, however, are shoehorned into the **Tiki-Ti**, a tiny, rarely open bar with fruity potent drinks such as Ray's Mistake and the Head Hunter Cooler (for details of all three, *see chapter* **Bars**). A young swing-dancing crowd is centred around the **Derby** (*see page 215* **Nightlife**) with its large parquet dancefloor and circular bar.

Silver Lake

Heading eastward – and a little further down the economic totem pole – Los Feliz gives way to Silver Lake, populated by an equally vital mix of artists and labourers (and home to folk rapper Beck), with a small pocket of wealthier individuals ensconced in homes overlooking the Silver Lake Reservoir, many of whom hobnob while their trophy pooches trot at the dog park adjacent to the reservoir. Some of LA's finest architects, including RM Schindler, Richard Neutra and John Lautner, built houses in this area in the 1920s and 1930s.

This bohemian segment of LA continues to experience an upswing in popularity. Although an article in *Vanity Fair* dubbing Silver Lake 'the coolest neighbourhood in Los Angeles' is indicative of its recent gentrification, cheesy chainstores have yet to truly invade and independently owned shops and restaurants give it an undeniable flair.

Casual eating out includes **Netty's** (1700 Silver Lake Boulevard), famed for its cornbread and blackened snapper, and the superb Mexican fare at **Alegria** (3510 Sunset Boulevard), as well as classic breakfasts at **Millie's** (3524 Sunset Boulevard). **Tang's Donuts** (4341 Sunset Boulevard, at Fountain Avenue) is hot and stinky, but the cappuccinos are cheap and the tables always crammed with chess enthusiasts hunkered over their boards. **Café Tropical** (2900 Sunset Boulevard, corner of Parkman Avenue; 1-323 661 8391) is a more upmarket coffeehouse serving potent café con leche and guava empanadas.

Most of the shops are found along the sun-baked stretch of Sunset Boulevard between Sanborn Avenue and Silver Lake Boulevard. At **You've Got Bad Taste** (3816 Sunset Boulevard), a novelty boutique co-owned by Exene Cervenka, former vocalist of LA punk band X, you can browse through stacks of obscure albums, mass-murderer paperbacks and other punk junk before heading

Driving lessons

Yes, you can get around Los Angeles by bus, but everyone should see the city through a windscreen at least once – it's what the place was designed for.

Wilshire Boulevard

Running 16 miles (25km) from the eastern edge of Downtown to the Pacific Ocean, Wilshire Boulevard is essentially the spinal cord of Los Angeles. Taking a trip west along Wilshire from Grand Avenue to Ocean Avenue is one of the few ways left to commune with the various phases of the city's history, and also a chance to observe the staggering cultural diversity of the City of Angels first-hand. It can take a good 90 minutes to drive the whole length, but there are exit points on to the I-10 if it all gets too much.

Heading from Downtown, you'll pass MacArthur and Lafayette Parks, once a genteel residential neighbourhood, now steeped in Central American culture, followed by the art deco gem of the former Bullocks Wilshire department store and, a mile or so on, Koreatown. Note the jade-green art deco Wiltern Center on your left at the intersection with Western Avenue.

A couple of miles later, you reach Miracle Mile, where some of LA's best museums are clustered, along with Hancock Park, home of the La Brea Tar Pits. From here, Wilshire Boulevard progresses through upmarket Beverly Hills, crossing Rodeo Drive; traffic is usually jammed in Beverly Hills so you'll get plenty of cruising time to check out the posh shops. Wilshire then continues through Westwood into Santa Monica, where it passes Third Street Promenade on its way to join Ocean Avenue at the seafront.

Mulholland Drive

Winding and precariously narrow, the ridge that Mulholland Drive follows boasts some alarming hairpin turns and a view that would make anyone fall in love with the city below. It's at its most glorious at night, when the City of Angels is alive with winking lights.

One of the best stretches is the three or so miles between Laurel Canyon Boulevard and Coldwater Canyon Drive, where there are places to pull over, get out of the car, stand on the edge of the city and look down. Mulholland Drive has inspired many celluloid tributes, notably Roman Polanski's *Chinatown*.

Pacific Coast Highway

The Pacific Coast Highway (Highway 1), more commonly known as PCH, hugs the LA coastline for most of its length, north to Malibu and beyond and south to the end of Orange County. We don't suggest that you drive the whole thing, but the northern section from Venice to Malibu and above is particularly scenic. This stretch is incredibly prone to mudslides, however, and may well be blocked during the winter months.

Griffith Park

Less hair-raising than the ride along Mulholland Drive, a looping spin through Griffith Park offers a refreshing respite from the more oppressive urban aspects of Los Angeles, as well as great views of the city and a chance to see such landmarks as the Griffith Park Observatory, LA Zoo and Forest Lawn Memorial Park. The 20-mile (32km) drive will take at least one hour, depending on how long you stop en route.

From Franklin Avenue, head north on Cahuenga Boulevard and then take a right on to Barham Boulevard. Continue for about two miles (3km), then take a right on to Forest Lawn Drive, which will take you past the entrance to the cemetery of the same name. Go right on to Zoo Drive, which runs along the northern perimeter of Griffith Park and through the LA Zoo (the Autry Museum of Western Heritage is also located nearby), whereupon it turns into Crystal Springs Drive. After passing through the Wilson and Harding public golf courses, Crystal Springs becomes Griffith Park Drive; continue south to Los Feliz Boulevard, and take Los Feliz west to Hillhurst Avenue. Head back up into the hills on Hillhurst, which becomes Vermont Canyon Road, and follow the signs to the Griffith Park Observatory.

From there, Western Canyon Road snakes lazily back down to Los Feliz Boulevard, the posher end of the Los Feliz area. A right turn there will lead you back to Franklin Avenue; head west, past the avenue's trendy neighbourhood bars and restaurants, and you're back at Cahuenga Boulevard where you started.

---

next door to the **Darby Crash Memorial Punk Rock Museum**. Hot tip: when you're in the neighbourhood, tune in to local radio station **KBLT** (104.7 FM).

At the annual **Sunset Junction street fair** in late August, a mile of Sunset Boulevard is blocked off to traffic for three days, allowing celebrants to stroll the bazaar of craft stalls, ethnic food stands, live entertainment stages and beer trucks without incident (for more details, *see page 90* **Los Angeles by Season**).

Echo Park

Echo Park is the final funky link between Hollywood and the predominantly Latino East LA, although most LA residents only venture into

the area to visit **Dodger Stadium** (1000 Elysian Park Avenue), home of the Los Angeles Dodgers baseball team. Defined as the area to the north of the Hollywood Freeway (US 101) and east of Alvarado Street, Echo Park was a nineteenth-century farming area that used Echo Park Lake for irrigation, and the area's winding hills retain a rustic feel. **El Carmelo Bakery** (1800 W Sunset Boulevard, between N Alvarado Street and Glendale Boulevard; 1-213 484 9255) is a gem, an obscure Cuban restaurant with delicious soups, sandwiches and coffee.

Although surrounded by some particularly dicey blocks, the 1300 block of **Carroll Avenue** is worth visiting for its painstakingly restored Victorian mansions, colourful remnants of the area's brief 1880s incarnation as a popular suburb for the

*Streetlife in **East LA**, the heart of LA's Latino community.*

monied classes. **Echo Park** itself (just below the junction of Sunset and Glendale Boulevards), laid out in the 1890s by architect Joseph Henry Taylor to resemble an English garden, serves during the summer as a focal point for various festivals presented by the neighbourhood's Cuban, Filipino, Vietnamese and Samoan communities. At the lake you can take an intimate paddle-boat ride through the blossoming lotuses.

East LA

East LA is not rich: its average annual income per capita is $5,000, 30 per cent of its households live below the poverty line, it is the site of some of the most noxious industries in LA and it suffers from virulent gang problems. And in the past its political clout was so negligible (these days Latinos have much more power) that it was torn asunder in the late 1960s by freeway construction: the intersection of the I-5, the I-10 and Highway 60 is a feat of engineering remarkable to behold, but it destroyed a neighbourhood and severed East LA from Downtown and the western part of the city.

Despite these negatives, East LA is a lively and characterful area. One thing that's distinctive about it, for starters, is the number of people hanging out on the streets, which makes it feel more alive than the typically more private residential areas in LA. It's also very colourful, with bright colours and murals decorating many of the buildings. Some of the best LA murals can be seen in East LA – and on Broadway in Downtown, which many consider East LA's Main Street.

El Este extends, unofficially, east from the Los Angeles River to just beyond Atlantic Boulevard, and from Olympic Boulevard north to the I-10. Officially, it starts even further east, at Indiana Avenue, but the true spiritual starting point is **Olvera Street**, at the corner of Cesar E Chavez Avenue and Alameda Street in Downtown: pretty much all that remains from the days of Spanish, then Mexican rule, and now a touristy street of mariachi singers and stalls selling Mexican trinkets.

Much of the action in East LA takes place on **First Street**, **Whittier Boulevard** and **Cesar E Chavez Avenue**. The latter (renamed a few years ago after the United Farm Workers Union president) is actually a continuation of Sunset Boulevard and runs from north of Downtown through Boyle Heights into East LA. At the intersection of Cesar E Chavez and Soto Street, in Boyle Heights, you can see several **murals** by local artists on such subjects as the social, economic and political life of the Mexican people and East LA neighbourhood scenes. For tours of these and other East Side murals, contact **SPARC** (Social and Public Art Resource) on 1-310 822 9560 or Robin Dunnitz on 1-310 470 8864. At the same intersection is the **Paseo of Peace**, a landscaped memorial walkway honouring local veterans of the Vietnam war.

Chavez Avenue is home to immigrant Latino street vendors, selling bargain silver, bootleg

Tiled sculpture of the Virgin Mary at Latino arts gallery **Self-Help Graphics**.

tapes, fresh mangoes and papayas, and strolling musicians who will play a romantic bolero or two on their well-worn guitars for a reasonable fee as you dine at **La Parilla** (2126 Cesar E Chavez Avenue; *see page 127* **Restaurants**). You can get fresh Mexican pastries at **La Mascota Bakery** (2715 Whittier Boulevard; 1-323 263 5513).

Just east of Downtown, at First Street and Boyle Avenue, is the famous **Mariachi Plaza**, one of the largest congregations of freelance mariachi musicians outside Mexico City's Garibaldi Square. Sporting traditional black ranchero outfits, they assemble at **Olympic Donut Shop** (1803 E First Street) and wait for passing drivers to hire them to play at social and family events. Also on First Street is the relatively expensive **La Serenata di Garibaldi** (*see page 127* **Restaurants**), which specialises in Mexican haute cuisine, and, further east, **El Mercado** (No.3425), a multi-level marketplace reminiscent of those found in Mexican cities. Upstairs are restaurants with duelling mariachi bands, each seeking to lure clientele from the others, while downstairs teems with stalls selling all manner of goods and produce.

On Chavez Avenue you'll also find one of East LA's best-known arts institutions, **Self-Help Graphics** (3802 Cesar E Chavez Avenue; 1-213 264 1259), with its distinctive façade of multicoloured pottery encased in plaster walls. The gallery shows work by established and up-and-coming Latino artists and also runs community art workshops: it has launched the careers of several successful Latino artists. The annual **Dia de Los Muertos** (Day of the Dead) celebration at the gallery in autumn has become an East LA tradition, presenting the cream of the Latino counter-culture crowd of poets, performance artists and agit-prop theatre groups; it's a 'must be seen at' event for Latino and other local hipsters (*see page 90* **Los Angeles by Season**).

For breakfast or lunch, head west on Chavez Avenue to Evergreen Avenue and hang a right to the always crowded **El Tepeyac Café** (812 N Evergreen Avenue; 1-323 268 1960) to try a 'Hollenbeck Special', an oversized burrito that could choke a horse. Or amble south to **Ciro's** (705 N Evergreen Avenue; 1-323 267 8637) for more traditional Mexican food.

East LA also boasts a very pleasant park, **Lincoln Park**, at 3540 N Mission Road, north of the I-10. It contains statues of Mexican revolutionary heroes and the **Plaza de la Raza**, a popular arts centre in a converted boathouse by the lake, which offers arts classes to children after school and hosts evenings of music, dance and theatre. There's more culture on display at the **Bilingual Foundation of the Arts** (421 N Avenue 19; 1-323 225 4044), a theatre group that presents modern and classical productions, in both Spanish and English.

South of Highway 60, in the southern end of East LA, is **Whittier Boulevard**, known as 'the Boulevard', the street some consider the unofficial 'capital' of East LA. This stretch of Whittier Boulevard, heading east towards Atlantic Boulevard, offers a wealth of clothes shops, restaurants, department stores, botanicas selling healing herbs and incense, bakeries, nightclubs, bars and other commercial establishments. On 29 August 1970, the Boulevard was the scene of a 'police riot' when a Chicano anti-war demonstration in a nearby park was attacked by police. Noted Chicano journalist Ruben Salazar was killed in the Silver Dollar Café on Whittier Boulevard by a police tear-gas pellet to the head. Salazar's death was thought by many to be retribution for his criticism of the sheriff's department's abusive behaviour towards people of colour. The park was renamed **Salazar Park** in his honour and is a symbol of the 1970s Chicano Movement.

Whittier Boulevard also used to be the main drag for fabulous displays of lowrider hot rod cars – until police shut them down. But East LA continues to be the LA capital of hot rod design, and if you're lucky, you'll see a spectacular example cruising the street. Look out for customised lowrider motorbikes, too: turning bikes into bejewelled fantasies fit only for display, not functional use, is as much a craze in Latino culture as customising cars. (If you want to find out more about goings-on in the hot rod world, pick up a copy of *Hot Rod Magazine* from newsstands.)

East LA life also spills over into its north-eastern neighbour, the city of **Monterey Park**. Try **Luminarias** (3500 Ramona Boulevard; 1-323 268 4363) or **Baby Doe's** (1-323 264 8426) next door, for dinner and a night of salsa, merengue and more contemporary music. From their hilltop perch,

both offer a splendid view of the San Gabriel Mountains to the north.

For other typically Mexican entertainments in East LA, the banda or norteño aficionado could try **La Zona Rosa** (1010 E Cesar E Chavez Avenue; 1-323 223 5683).

And for a feast of burritos and tacos, do as the Romans do and head east to **King Taco** (4504 E Third Street; 1-323 264 4067). Open 24 hours, it began as a solitary taco truck and is now a chain of restaurants (there's another branch on Cesar E Chavez Avenue and Soto Street) and a cultural icon – as well as an early-morning stop for many an Eastsider on their way home after a hectic night of partying.

South Central

South Central owes its black identity to the era of restrictive covenants – legal restrictions on who could reside in a property or neighbourhood – that were instituted in the early part of this century and finally repealed in 1948. These heinous laws, which also put restrictions on Jews, Chinese and Mexicans and helped shape Los Angeles into the relatively segregated place it still is, confined African-Americans to a tight area around Central Avenue. Though congested, Central Avenue enjoyed a cultural boom in the jazz age. Following the lifting of restrictive covenants, blacks gradually moved west, making the Crenshaw District its

Get a cut and a shave in **Crenshaw** *(see page 76).*

cultural and commercial centre, and, in the past two decades, they have vacated South Central in growing numbers to head to the suburbs.

Their homes have been taken over by Latino families, who've made their mark in the form of brightly painted mercatos, cheap Mexican restaurants and the numerous hole-in-the-wall evangelical churches that are wooing Latinos away from the Catholic Church. While South Central is not necessarily dangerous – it's highly unlikely you'll get caught in the crossfire between the rival gangs that riddle the area – it is bleak. Many of the homes and gardens in South Central are as pretty and sizeable as the single-family bungalows throughout the LA region, but missing are shops, restaurants, public landscaping and parks. Unrelieved by hills or sea, South Central seems to consist of relentless flatlands of concrete and asphalt. But it has a rich history and some neighbourhoods are worth checking out.

Central Avenue

At the turn of the century, the black community lived in what is now Little Tokyo in Downtown. Following World War I, Los Angeles's black population increased sharply as stories of the successes of local blacks circulated around the country. Thus began the steady migration of blacks west and south along the Central Avenue corridor, to which they were then restricted.

Central Avenue's significance in the history of black Los Angeles cannot be underestimated. It was the West Coast equivalent of Ellis Island to migrating blacks between the 1920s and the 1950s and home to some of the first financial enterprises, theatres, churches and social institutions established exclusively to serve blacks.

Built in 1928 by a wealthy professional couple, the **Dunbar Hotel** (4231 S Central Avenue) was the first hotel built by and for blacks. Along with several nightclubs in the area, including the now extinct Club Alabam, it brought to Central Avenue a worldwide reputation for its jazz scene, recreated every August with the free **Central Avenue Jazz Festival** (see page 90 **Los Angeles by Season**). To get a vivid picture of pre- and post-war Central Avenue, read Walter Mosley's Easy Rawlins detective mysteries.

Modern-day Central Avenue is far less alluring – many of its buildings are vacant and in disrepair – but the Dunbar, now operated by the Dunbar Economic Development Corporation as low-income residential units, continues to be a centre of jazz culture.

Watts

After the jazz era, blacks continued their migration south along Central Avenue towards Watts, known primarily for the **Watts Towers** (see below) – designed, in fact, by an Italian but adopted as a symbol of black pride – and the rioting in 1965 and 1992. Though many areas are in neglect, Watts is cautiously re-emerging as a centre for black community pride, embodied by the **Watts Labor Community Action Center** (10950 S Central Avenue; 1-323 563 5600), about a mile (1½ kilometres) from the towers, a one-stop social and cultural centre. A victim of both the 1965 and 1992 riots, it has now been completely rebuilt. The WLCAC's public art piece, *The Mother of Humanity*, is the largest bronze sculpture of a black woman in the world, and the building's main façade is the setting for *Mudtown Flats*, a mural depicting historic sites on Central Avenue.

The centre showcases work by local inner-city artists, hosts live performances and houses Countdown to Eternity, an exhibit on the 1960s Civil Rights movement and the final days of Martin Luther King, plus interactive installations on the history of the movement.

Watts Towers & Arts Center

1727 & 1765 E 107th Street, between Alameda Street & Central Avenue, Watts (1-213 847 4646). Metro 103rd Street/bus 56, 251/I-10, exit Century Boulevard north. **Open** *arts centre* 10am-4pm Tue-Sat; noon-4pm Sun. **Admission** free.

Working in construction by day, Italian Simon Rodia kept his sleeves rolled up into the night and spent 33 years (1921-54) building his Eiffel Tower in Watts. A plasterer, Rodia created the 92ft (28m) high towers with only his artistic vision to keep him company. Structuring his towers from salvaged steel rods and cast-off pipe structures, bed frames and cement, Rodia incorporated pieces of broken bottles, ceramic tiles, organic materials and china cups and plates into his folk-art masterpieces. He scaled the towers on a window-washer's belt and bucket and decorated them with over 25,000 seashells; so encrusted became the surface that the towers look as if they were made of nothing more than calcified coral and shell. Rodia deeded Watts Towers to the neighbourhood, and they have since become a source of black civic pride. Unfortunately, the towers are currently under restoration and hidden by scaffolding; they should reopen in 2000.

The adjacent community art centre hosts exhibitions of Third World and African-American art, workshops and a couple of festivals a year, including the **Day of the Drum/Simon Rodia Watts Towers Jazz Festival** in September (see page 90 **Los Angeles by Season**).

The Crenshaw District

The Crenshaw District is the area surrounding Crenshaw Boulevard south of the I-10 as far as Florence Avenue. It was the site of the 1932 Olympic Village (now Village Green Apartments on Rodeo Road, near La Brea Avenue) and of the first airport in Los Angeles. Though it's now one of the few predominantly black communities in LA County, the influence of earlier Japanese residents who moved there and established themselves as landscape gardeners after returning from World War II internment camps is still visible, notably in residential landscaping.

*Murals abound in thriving neighbourhood **Leimert Park** (see page 78).*

The Hills – Baldwin, Windsor and View Park, west of Crenshaw Boulevard around Slauson Avenue – are home to some of LA's most prominent upper middle-class and professional blacks. At the base of these well-manicured hills is an area known as the **Jungle**. The name originally derived from its lush tropical plantings, but the Jungle is better known these days as a haven for drug dealing and other illicit activities, so exercise caution.

In the 1940s, the first shopping plaza in the USA was built at the intersection of 'King' and Crenshaw Boulevards (the former is properly called **Martin Luther King Jr Boulevard**, formerly Santa Barbara Boulevard). Now transformed into the **Baldwin Hills Crenshaw Plaza**, it is the perfect place to park and see most of what's going on in this community. While there, visit the **Magic Johnson Theaters** (*see page 182* **Film**). Owned by basketball great Irvin 'Magic' Johnson, these cinemas have the friendliest staff in Los Angeles and show first-run films. And going to movies there is an experience: the audience doesn't simply watch the picture, it joins in with the action, loudly rooting for, shouting advice to and yelling at the actors.

For memorable soul food, leave your car in the plaza parking lot and walk half a block east on King to **M&M's Soul Food** (1-323 299 1302; *see page 139* **Restaurants**), required eating for locals, and get in line. Or walk half a block west to **Boulevard Café** (no.3710; 1-323 292 7900) on the outside edge of the floundering Santa Barbara Plaza, a dilapidated mall that is about to be turned into a large CityWalk-style entertainment retail centre by Magic Johnson's company, Magic Johnson Enterprises. One good eaterie in the plaza

itself is **Golden Bird Fried Chicken** (1-323 735 5686). Don't, incidentally, expect the same stellar service as at the Magic Theaters: some of these restaurants are well known for their rude, temperamental staff and less-than-attractive décor. And leave your diet behind: the food is salty and loaded with fat and calories, but it's worth every artery-clogging bite.

Also worth visiting is the **Museum of African American Art** (on the third floor of the Robinsons-May store in Baldwin Hill Crenshaw Plaza; 1-323 294 7071).

For a rousing black religious experience, visit the **West Angeles Church of God** on Crenshaw Boulevard at Exposition Boulevard (*see page 14* **Let's get spiritual**). Presided over by preacher Charles Blake, it is one of the most popular black Pentecostal churches, with 16,000 members – including celebrities such as Denzel Washington and Magic Johnson. With the help of fat donations from these two ($5 million from Johnson, $2.5 million from Washington), Blake is now building a new cathedral. The West Angeles Church of God is more than just a church, it is a major economic generator in the area. Not only does it have a school, an arts centre and a bookstore, but it also invests in housing and economic development. Together, the church and Magic Johnson's company are kick-starting the revitalisation of the Crenshaw District.

On the far west side of Crenshaw, sprawling between La Cienega Boulevard and La Brea Avenues north of Stocker Street, is an unsung public amenity, the **Kenneth Hahn State Recreation Area**. Named after a former and much-beloved councillor, this park is a delight. It's huge, with a pond that you can fish in, ducks, swans, a Japanese bridge over a gurgling waterfall, undulating hills, volleyball and basketball courts and fab views (from an unusual vantage point) of Los Angeles.

Once a year for the last three weekends in August, the Crenshaw District lights up with the **African Marketplace**, a celebration of diverse African cultures with a feast of foods, crafts and non-stop entertainment (for details, *see page 90* **Los Angeles by Season**).

Leimert Park

Leimert Park (pronounced 'Luh-murt'), anchored by the park itself and 43rd Street, is LA's most talked-about black neighbourhood. In recent years it has experienced the stirrings of a cultural revolution, with art galleries, shops and restaurants replacing the pawn shops and beauty salons that once lined the streets. On most weekends you will find street fairs in the Leimert Park village, be they large, organised events or a band of self-proclaimed prophets talking to whoever will listen. Don't miss the annual **Leimert Park Jazz Festival** (*see page 90* **Los Angeles by Season**) if you're visiting at the end of the summer.

For terrific live entertainment, **Fifth Street Dick's Coffee Company** (*see page 212* **Music**) is famous for its jazz and the chess games that take place on tables outside; **Babe's & Ricky's** (4339 Leimert Park; *see page 212* **Music**), relocated from Central Avenue, for the blues; and **World Stage** (4344 Degnan Boulevard (1-323 293 2451) for a mix of live music and poetry. Along Degnan Boulevard, there are also several Afrocentric art galleries and shops.

Off Degnan Boulevard at 4307 Leimert Boulevard, you'll find the famous **Phillip's Barbecue** (1-323 292 7613): prepare to wait in line for a take-out order of some of the best ribs in town. **Earle's Wieners** (4326 Crenshaw Boulevard; 1-323 299 2867) has an assortment of hot dogs, links (sausages) and vegetarian finger foods, or try **Coley's Kitchen** (No.4335; 1-323 290 4010) for Caribbean fare.

Inglewood

Although outside the Los Angeles city limits, Inglewood is often considered part of South Central. It is best known for being the home of the **Great Western Forum**, where the Los Angeles Lakers basketball and Los Angeles Kings hockey teams currently play (in 2000, they will switch locations to the Staples Center, a sports stadium and retail complex now under construction in Downtown). Just south of the Forum is the **Hollywood Park Race Track**. For details of both, *see chapter* **Sport & Fitness**.

The Valleys

San Fernando Valley

The history of the San Fernando Valley, presented in fictional form in the movie *Chinatown*, is one of the most colourful stories in US history. Early this century, LA's land barons hoodwinked voters into approving bonds for a water aqueduct and then diverted the water away from the city to the San Fernando Valley so they could cash in on the increased land values. Once an agricultural Eden, the Valley has become known as the archetypal suburb, immortalised in the 1980s by the movie and Frank and Moon Unit Zappa's song *Valley Girl*. Most recently, it has been the target of hilarious barbs from Sandra Tsing Loh, author of *Depth Takes a Holiday*, who at once celebrates its increasingly multi-ethnic culture and trashes it for suburban monotony.

The Valley is still part of the City of Los Angeles, but recently separatists have been working hard to secede and create a separate city. A vote appears likely within the next few years. If the Valley does become independent, it would be the sixth largest city in America, with a population of 1.3 million. The contracted Los Angeles, with a population of about two million, would be only the third largest, behind Chicago, and very different demographically: fewer whites, more Latinos and Asians.

The massive 1994 Northridge earthquake had its epicentre here; most damage has since been repaired. The Valley is also home to California State University, Northridge, and is a business centre, linked to Los Angeles by three freeways – US 101 (Hollywood Freeway), the I-405 (San Diego Freeway) and I-5 (Golden State Freeway) – and numerous winding canyon roads.

Like much of LA, some parts of the Valley are developing pleasant walking districts, especially along Ventura Boulevard near Van Nuys Boulevard in Sherman Oaks and further east on Ventura in Studio City. **Glendale** and **Burbank**, which are separate cities, also feature small-town-like, walkable downtowns that have been revived in recent years. Glendale is also home to the **Forest Lawn Memorial Park** (1712 S Glendale Avenue), the final resting place of a stack of celebrities including Walt Disney, Errol Flynn, Spencer Tracy, Humphrey Bogart, Nat 'King' Cole, Clark Gable and Carole Lombard. Unfortunately, the place is so huge and the staff so unhelpful that you'll have trouble finding famous graves.

The Valley has some 1950s and 1960s gems, including the Googie-style diner **Bob's Big Boy** in Burbank (4211 Riverside Drive, at Alameda Avenue; 1-818 843 9334), where muscle-car aficionados gather on Friday nights to show off their El Camino motors in true LA fashion.

The Valley is also the gateway to the **Santa Monica Mountains**, one of the country's most beautiful and environmentally fragile urban mountain ranges. Separating the Valley from the city basin and the ocean, the Santa Monicas are covered with hiking and biking trails, and the site of many ranches that once belonged to movie stars and studios. One highlight is **Paramount Ranch** (2813 Cornell Road, off Kanan Road, Agoura), where Paramount Studios' Western town set is still used today for the TV series *Dr Quinn, Medicine Woman*. The ranch is run by the National Park Service: for more information on the area, contact the Santa Monica Mountains National Recreation Area, 30401 Agoura Road, suite 100, Agoura Hills, CA 90265 (1-805 370 2300).

Six Flags California theme park (*see below*) is in Santa Clarita at the north end of the Valley. For a glimpse of history along the way, make the easy detour to one of the earliest Californian missions, **Mission San Fernando Rey de España** in Mission Hills, founded in 1797 and rebuilt after the 1971 Sylmar earthquake (*see* **On a mission** *page 246* **Trips Out of Town**).

Though Hollywood is 'over the hill', a good deal of glitz (not to mention a thriving porn film industry) can be found in the Valley – especially in **Burbank** and at **Universal City**, both located off US 101 at the Valley's east end. Warner Brothers, NBC and Walt Disney Studios are all located in Burbank's 'Media District', along Riverside Drive. The Disney complex is hard to miss: the animation building, designed by Robert Stern, has a two-storey wizard's hat like the one worn by Mickey in *The Sorcerer's Apprentice* and the word 'animation' spelt out in 14-foot (4.3-metre) high capital letters. Studio tours aren't usually available (except at Warner Brothers), but free tickets to TV show tapings often are (for both, *see* chapter **Film**).

From Burbank, it's just a short drive on Barham Boulevard into Cahuenga Pass, home of the **MCA-Universal Studios** complex. The Universal Studios tour (*see below*), formerly a jolly tram trip across the back lot, has evolved into a theme park to rival Disneyland. Burbank and Universal are close to the northern edge of **Griffith Park**, home to Los Angeles Zoo, the Griffith Park Observatory and sundry other attractions (*see page 70*).

Six Flags California

Magic Mountain Parkway, off the I-5, Valencia (1-805 255 4100/recorded information 1-805 255 4111). I-5, exit Magic Mountain Parkway. **Open** *from 10am daily; call for closing hours; Hurricane Harbor closed in winter.* **Admission** *Magic Mountain $36; $20 over-55s; $18 children under 48in; Hurricane Harbor $19; $12 over-55s, children under 48in; both parks free for children 2 years and under.* **Credit** *AmEx, MC, V.*

Six Flags California comprises **Six Flags Magic Mountain** and its new watery cousin, **Six Flags Hurricane Harbor**. They have rollercoasters and water rides for every level of screamer, the most famous being the Colossus, the largest wooden-framed rollercoaster ever built. Those whose idea of fun is to feel their kidneys and liver shifting around inside should not miss the Viper, a loop-the-loop rollercoaster. The upside-down, track-above-your-head Backlot is also out there. Raging Waters, undeniably wet, is a ball, as is the new Superman, the Escape: technological wizardry catapults you straight up a 41-storey tower at 100mph – in seven seconds – then you freefall down at the same speed. Set scenically on the hip of the San Fernando Mountains, this is fun with a screamingly huge capital 'F'. *Parking $7.*

The famous **Rose Bowl** *in Pasadena (see page 82).*

Take a hike

Nobody walks in Los Angeles, they say – but, believe it or not, it's an excellent place to hike. Blessed with an amazing variety of wilderness, the metropolis offers mountain, ocean and desert landscapes – often minutes away from bustling city streets.

None of the hikes described below requires specialised gear – a decent pair of sneakers and a large bottle of water will do – but you will need a car to reach them. Remember that most trails are hot in the summer, so it's best to hike in the early morning or late afternoon. Watch out for snakes and avoid shiny, tri-leafed foliage; it may be poison oak.

Sierra Club

Los Angeles chapter: 3435 Wilshire Boulevard, suite 320, Los Angeles, CA 90010-1904 (1-213 387 4287/fax 1-213 387 5383).
If hiking's your thing, you might want to contact the Sierra Club: founded in 1892, it a non-profit organisation devoted to lobbying for the preservation of wild environments and promoting public enjoyment and experience of same. The website has details of organised hikes and outings. *Website: www.sierraclub.org*

Hollywood Hills

This portion of the Santa Monica Mountains extends from Griffith Park to Beverly Hills and includes notable city views.

Griffith Park Observatory to Mount Hollywood

3½ miles (5½km); easy.
From Vermont Avenue, north of Los Feliz Boulevard, follow signs to the Observatory. From the north end of the parking lot, follow a wide sandy track across a bridge and continue for 1 mile (1½km) around curves that offer a good view of the Hollywood sign. At the fork, bear medium left (not hard, uphill left) and continue on the main road for ½ mile (800m) to Dante's View, a beautiful garden oasis that offers magical views of Downtown. A few feet beyond,

enjoy views of Burbank, Glendale and the San Gabriel Mountains. Continue bearing left ¼ mile (400m) to Mount Hollywood for a 360° view of the Los Angeles basin. Reverse to return, or try other paths, always keeping the Observatory in sight.

For a great two-hour bright-lights-big-city experience, try the Griffith Park/Sierra Club Guided Night Hikes (1-213 387 4287), with levels from beginner to strenuous. The hikes meet at 7pm on Tuesdays, Wednesdays and Thursdays, all year round, at the upper merry-go-round parking lot; enter from Los Feliz Boulevard.

Bronson Canyon & Batcaves

3-4 miles (5-6½km); initially steep.
Park at the end of Bronson Avenue (north of Franklin Avenue). Ascend the fire road for about 1 mile (1½km). At the top, find a beautiful 'road to nowhere' with Hollywood and city views. Head left towards the Hollywood sign or right towards the Griffith Park Observatory. Return the same way. Just below the parking lot, 4 miles (6½km) along a dirt road, you will find a group of freestanding caves probably familiar from the *Batman* TV series. This eerie, magical setting recalls cowboy shoot-'em-ups and affords an excellent view of the Hollywood sign for non-hikers.

Hollywood sign

3½ miles (5½km); steep.
Park at the northern end of Beachwood Drive (north of Franklin Avenue). Walk right on Hollyridge Drive 30 yards (25m) to the dirt track on the left. Ascend (ignoring the downhill trail to the stables) for ½ mile (800m) to a fork. Turn left uphill and continue to an asphalt road. Turn right and continue all the way up to the radio towers. This hike offers canyon, city and San Fernando Valley views, including the Burbank film studios and Forest Lawn cemetery. At the top, you'll find yourself behind and above the famous sign, observing that the letters have corrugated backs, with Madonna's former house (notable for its red and yellow stripes) and Lake Hollywood in the near distance. Don't attempt to climb down; it's dangerous and illegal.

Fryman Canyon

3 miles (5km); moderate.
Start at Fryman Road, off Laurel Canyon Boulevard, just to the south of Studio City. Begin this pretty walk at the

Universal Studios & CityWalk

100 Universal City Plaza, Universal City (1-818 508 9600). Bus 420/US 101, exit Universal Center Drive. **Open** *winter* 10am-6pm daily; *summer* 10am-6pm Mon-Fri; 10am-9pm Sat, Sun; last tram tour 4.15pm. **Admission** $38; $33 over-60s; $28 3-11s. **Credit** AmEx, DC, Disc, MC, V.

Unless you like pre-packaged cheese, doing Universal can seem like a rite of passage: you're glad you did it, but only when it's over. You can watch animal acts, stroll round the Lucille Ball museum, experience the Back to the Future flight simulator, go on rides such as Waterworld and Jurassic Park or see shows inspired by recent TV programmes and movies – but the best thing is the tram. The ride takes you through the back lot of the working studio, where you will see the likes of King Kong (all 13,000lb/6,000kg of him), moving rather arthritically, the shark from *Jaws* leaping out of the water and snapping its mechanical mouth at you, the part-

ing of the Red Sea, the 'Big One' earthquake simulation (nothing like the real thing), the *Psycho* house and the flames of *Backdraft*. The best part of the ride is that you glimpse slices of studio life: casts and crews rushing about, dilapidated old props stashed here and there.

It all lasts five to seven hours: allow a full day and start early to make the most of the complex, which also houses one of LA's big concert venues, Universal Amphitheater, the 18-screen Universal City Cinemas and Universal CityWalk, an LA-themed shopping (and eating) 'street'. CityWalk has been ridiculed for its fake, collaged architecture – but what could be more appropriate for Tinseltown?

San Gabriel Valley

Even more than the San Fernando Valley, the San Gabriel Valley – located east and north-east of

Wilacre Park sign. The fire-road trail is among the greenest in springtime, offering San Fernando Valley views and a chance to visit the TreePeople Nature Preserve at the top (*see p178* **Children**). This is very popular with dog-walkers as an 'off-lead' spot. Alternatively, start from above, at the intersection of Coldwater Canyon Boulevard and Mulholland Drive.

Santa Monica Mountains

While the Hollywood Hills are technically part of this range, these hikes represent the West LA section, from Brentwood to Malibu.

Sullivan Canyon

2-4 miles (3-6½km); easy.

Follow Sunset Boulevard 2½ miles (4km) west from the I-405 and turn right on to Mandeville Canyon Road. Turn left on to Westridge Road, then left on to Bayliss Road, then left on to Queensferry Road and go on ¼ mile (400m) to the end. (Take careful note of the street signs as to where you can park in this area.) The asphalt road at the left leads to a cement flood-control apron. Turn right to enter this lovely, quiet canyon and amble through shady oak and sycamore groves with frequent creek crossings. Retrace your steps to return.

Malibu Creek State Park

3½-4½ miles (5½-7km); easy.

From the Pacific Coast Highway, head 6½ miles (10½km) inland on Malibu Canyon Road, or, from US 101, take Las Virgenes Road 4 miles (6½km) south, to the park entrance. From the parking lot, follow the fire road to a fork. Take the high road right over a bridge and follow the Gorge Trail upstream to a spectacular volcanic gorge recognisable from Tarzan movies. When you're done frolicking in the water, ascend on the high road, bearing left towards Century Lake, taking in valley views and weird rock outcrops. End here, or continue on the fire road to the former site of the *M*A*S*H* set.

Sycamore Canyon

1½ miles (2½km); easy.

From Santa Monica, drive about 32 miles (51km) north on Pacific Coast Highway and turn right at the well-marked Sycamore Canyon ($6 to park). From the parking

lot, proceed past the campground and through the gate to the marked Scenic Overlook Trail on your immediate left. The trail crosses a seasonal stream and continues uphill through dense chaparral for about ¾ mile (1¼km). At a trail intersection, turn left toward the bluffs where you'll find spectacular views of the Pacific Ocean and, on a clear day, Anacapa and Santa Cruz islands.

Angeles National Forest

This portion of the Angeles National Forest includes hikes in the San Gabriel Mountains. You'll need to purchase a $5 day-use permit in advance at ranger stations or nearby stores for all hikes in the forest.

Sturtevant Falls

3½ miles (5½km); easy.

From the I-210 in Arcadia, exit on Santa Anita Avenue and drive 6 miles (9½km) north to Chantry Flat, where the road dead-ends into a parking lot. Descend a winding paved road on the Gabrielino Trail to a bridge that leads to a trail junction. Follow the well-marked path that veers right, follows Big Santa Anita Creek through canopies of sycamores and alders and passes several woodland cabins en route to the impressive 50ft (15m) waterfall. More adventurous hikers can continue on to Spruce Grove Camp, an 8-mile (13km) round trip, or Mount Wilson, a punishingly steep 16-mile (25½km) round trip that climbs 4,000ft (1,220m).

Switzer Falls

4 miles (6½km); easy.

From the Angeles Crest Highway (Highway 2), drive 10½ miles (17km) from La Cañada north to the Switzer Picnic Area and park. Descend on a paved road from the parking area to the river, cross the bridge and head down the canyon. A mile (1½km) takes you to Commodore Switzer Trail Camp, where film stars such as Clark Gable and Mary Pickford stayed at this one-time riparian resort in the 1930s. Cross the stream and follow the trail as it climbs above the falls. At a trail junction about ¼ mile (400m) hence, go left, dropping into the gorge below the falls. When you reach the creek, go upstream a short way to Switzer Falls. Retrace your steps to return.

---

downtown Los Angeles – hides a collection of charming small towns. Though crowded with suburban development and often choking with traffic and smog, the Valley is set picturesquely against the striking San Gabriel Mountains to the north. You can reach it from Los Angeles via a series of east-west freeways, including the I-210 (Foothill Freeway), I-10 (San Bernardino Freeway) and US 60 (Pomona Freeway), as well as the north-south I-110 (Pasadena Freeway).

Modern settlement of the Valley originated with **Mission San Gabriel Archangel**. It's now perhaps LA's most diverse area, with Asian and Latino communities scattered throughout. Unlike the San Fernando Valley, the San Gabriel Valley

is not part of the City of LA but is divided into many small suburban communities.

If the Valley has an image in America's popular imagination, it's the 'white trash heaven' of the 1950s and 1960s described vividly by crime writer James Ellroy in his book *My Dark Places* – a search for the killer of his mother, who was murdered in the San Gabriel Valley community of El Monte. This town still has its dark side: a few years ago, it hit the headlines after Thai sweatshop workers were discovered living in virtual slavery. But the San Gabriel Valley towns that pre-date this era are charming and pleasant: **Pasadena**, San Marino and La Verne contain some of LA's most beautiful neighbourhoods. Pasadena, the jewel of the

Valley, was first settled by wealthy retired farmers from the Midwest and remains one of the most attractive towns in the area.

Old Town Pasadena (centred on Colorado Boulevard and bounded by Arroyo Parkway, De Lacey Avenue and Holly and Green Streets) is a 1920s retail district turned shopping and entertainment centre. Its revival has been astonishing: as late as the mid-1980s, it was a run-down collection of boarded-up commercial buildings. Today it is so popular that it is often impossible to move along the sidewalk as late as midnight. Demand for retail space has become so great that even alleys have been opened up, redesigned and decorated with public art. A few vestiges of the past remain: musty used bookstores and the odd porno shop. But even the latter have gone upmarket. With their neon signs and tasteful décor they don't look out of place along Colorado Boulevard next to popular restaurants.

Pasadena has a clutch of museums, including the **Norton Simon Museum**, the **Pacific Asia Museum** (for both, *see page 197* **Museums & Galleries**) and **Kidspace** for children (*see page 178* **Children**). It is also home to the **California Institute of Technology** (CalTech) and the **Jet Propulsion Laboratory**, one of the nerve centres of the US space programme: tours can be arranged at both, but you can't just drop in. The **Rose Bowl** is in Brookside Park, and each New Year the **Rose Parade** is held (*see page 91* **Los Angeles by Season**).

The **Gamble House** (*see page 29* **Architecture**), designed by Charles and Henry Greene in 1908, is the leading example of Southern California's indigenous 'Craftsman' bungalow, influenced – in typical Californian fashion – by both Japanese and Swiss architecture. The Greenes also built many other houses in adjacent streets, notably Aroyo Terrace and Grand Avenue.

North-west of Pasadena is the picturesque hillside community of La Cañada Flintridge, home of the beautiful and peaceful **Descanso Gardens** (*see below*). And just south of the town is the expensive suburb of **San Marino**, developed by land and railroad baron Henry Huntington. His former estate (*see below*) now houses a world-class collection of books and manuscripts and includes some of the most beautiful gardens in Southern California. Pasadena's Lake Street district and the Fair Oaks area of South Pasadena, both near San Marino, are pleasant walking and shopping areas.

To the east of Pasadena is the lovely town of **Arcadia**, home of **Santa Anita Park**, one of LA's best-known race tracks (*see page 230* **Sport & Fitness**). Though dwarfed by a surrounding sea of suburbia, many older foothill communities along the Foothill Freeway, including **Sierra Madre** and **Monrovia**, have charming early twentieth-century downtowns. Both are north of

the I-210; Sierra Madre is reached by the Santa Anita exit, Monrovia by the Mountain exit. They lie in the shadow of the **San Gabriel Mountains**, one of the most geologically unstable mountain ranges in the world.

Further south in the Valley, modern suburbs tend to blend in an undifferentiated mass, but some of them have a distinctive identity. **Monterey Park** (take the Garfield Avenue or Atlantic Boulevard exits off the I-10) is the leading Chinese suburb in the US. Most of the population is Chinese or Chinese-American – many of them immigrants from Taiwan and Hong Kong – but a significant minority is Latino. The commercial strips of Atlantic Boulevard and Garfield Avenue may seem nondescript, but they contain some of the best Chinese restaurants in the US; local Chinese flock to them on Sunday mornings.

The San Gabriel Valley is also home to several universities, including **California State University** (off the I-10 in East LA) **California State Polytechnic University** in Pomona – a beautifully landscaped campus off the Kellogg Drive exit of the I-10 – and the **Claremont Colleges**, a collection of six distinguished colleges near East Foothill Boulevard in **Claremont**. The town of Claremont and the campus offer shady streets and an academic vibe reminiscent of East Coast Ivy League schools. Claremont's 'Village' (east of Indian Hill Boulevard, between First and Fourth Streets) is another delightful small downtown, featuring buildings from the 1920s, many restaurants and a train station (you can get there from Downtown LA via Metrolink).

The eastern San Gabriel Valley is the site of the **Los Angeles County Fair**, held at the Fairplex in Pomona each year from mid-September to mid-October. LA County remains an important agricultural centre, and this fair is one of the largest in the nation.

Descanso Gardens

1418 Descanso Drive, La Cañada (1-818 952 4400). Hwy 2, exit Verdugo Boulevard. **Open** 9am-4.30pm daily. **Admission** $5; $3 seniors, students; $1 5-12s. **Tram tour** daily; $1.50.
Descanso Gardens is another delightful tribute to the horticultural magic of Southern California. It includes more than 600 varieties of camelias (best between mid-February and early May) and five acres of roses in the International Rosarium. There are also lilac, orchid, fern and California native plant areas, as well as an Oriental Tea House donated by the Japanese-American community.

The Huntington Library, Art Collections, & Botanical Gardens

1151 Oxford Road, second entrance at corner of Orlando Road & Allen Avenue, San Marino (recorded information 1-626 405 2141). Bus 79/I-110, exit Arroyo Parkway north. **Open** noon-4.30pm Tue-Fri; 10.30am-4.30pm Sat, Sun. **Admission** $8.50; $7 seniors; $5 students; free under-12s; free first Thur of month. **Credit** MC, V.
Founded in 1919 by Henry E Huntington, his institution reflects the passions of this savvy businessman (besides business): books, art and gardens. The library holds six million

Mingle with the young and beautiful in surfing mecca **Manhattan Beach**.

items: the star attractions are a Gutenberg *Bible*, the earliest known edition of Chaucer's *Canterbury Tales* and several early Shakespeares, with an impressive supporting cast of rare books and manuscripts on British and American history and literature. The museum contains one of the most comprehensive assemblies of British and French art from the eighteenth and nineteenth centuries. The vast (130-acre/53-hectare) gardens, meanwhile, grow over 14,000 different plant varieties, including fantastic cacti in the 12-acre (5-hectare) Desert Garden. An enchanting place to spend an afternoon, topped off with high tea in the Rose Garden Tea Rooms. *Website: www.huntington.org*

The South Bay & Long Beach

The South Bay

El Segundo, Manhattan Beach, Hermosa Beach & Redondo Beach

Getting to the South Bay is half the fun. The road Vista del Mar, which runs right along the beach, starts about a mile (1½ kilometres) south of Marina del Rey, off Culver Avenue at Dockweiler State Beach, and it's the most picturesque gateway to the area. Zip past LAX and you're in the district of **El Segundo**. The best non-aquatic attraction here, and true to its Mayberry-on-Mar sensibility, is an old-fashioned cinema: the **Old Town Music Hall** (140 Richmond Street), open weekends only, features pre-1960s classics, a pipe organ and singalongs.

But for a true flavour of the South Bay, continue south on Vista del Mar (which becomes Highland Avenue) until you reach Manhattan Beach Boulevard and then make a right towards the ocean. On sunny weekends, the **Manhattan Beach** strand and pier are mobbed with skaters, cyclists and sun-worshippers. Cleaner than Venice, the strands in Manhattan and neighbouring Hermosa Beach offer some of the same people-watching pleasures (though with a less ethnically diverse crowd). Good casual dining is available nearby at the **Kettle** (at the corner of Highland Avenue and Manhattan Beach Boulevard), easily one of the best 24-hour restaurants in the LA area, and a French/Italian/Japanese mix at the recently opened **Michi** (*see page 140* **Restaurants**).

The surfside flavour continues southward into **Hermosa** and **Redondo Beaches**. Visitors might even catch a pro beach volleyball championship, surf festival or rollerblading exhibition. Those who prefer shade to sun can check out the **Lighthouse Café** (30 Pier Avenue, off the coastal Hermosa Avenue), a watering hole since the 1950s where volleyball players and scenesters hang and listen to live music; the **Comedy & Magic Club** (1018 Hermosa Avenue; 1-310 372 1193) where the likes of Jay Leno are said to try out new material; **Either/Or** (124 Pier Avenue), a bookstore that Thomas Pynchon supposedly patronised when he lived nearby; **Java Man Coffee** (157 Pier Avenue), a trendy place to sip a latte; **Spot** (110 Second Street; 1-310 376 2355), a legendary vegetarian restaurant that, rumour has it, is a favourite with Paul McCartney; **Ragin' Cajun**, an authentic Louisiana-style café (422 Pier Avenue; 1-310 376

7878); and **Coffee Cartel** (1916 Manhattan Avenue – the coast road; 1-310 316 8623), a cool place for live music and poetry.

Continuing south, Redondo Beach's **King Harbor** (at the end of Portofino Way) – with shops, restaurants, fish markets and marina – is one of the most developed local piers. Purists might find it a bit naff, but Redondo is the most family-oriented of these beaches. In the nearby inland city of **Torrance**, there's a phenomenal neighbourhood restaurant, **Gina Lee's Bistro** (211 Palos Verdes Boulevard; 1-310 375 4462).

Palos Verdes & San Pedro

One of the best ocean drives in SoCal is the loop around scenic Palos Verdes Peninsula. Take the Pacific Coast Highway (Highway 1, aka PCH) south to Palos Verdes Boulevard (at Redondo State Beach, a mile or so south of the eponymous city), go south again to Palos Verdes Drive West and then Palos Verdes Drive South. On the way, stop at the lovely glass and stone **Wayfarer's Chapel** (5755 Palos Verdes Drive S), the most visited building by architect Lloyd Wright (Frank's son), and the **South Coast Botanic Gardens** (26300 Crenshaw Boulevard; 1-310 544 6815), 87 acres (35 hectares) of botanical beauty.

Ironically, ritzy **Palos Verdes** shares the peninsula with one of LA's most colourful working-class communities, **San Pedro**. The traditional home of fishermen, dockworkers, Navy staff and Mediterranean immigrants, San Pedro – home of the massive Port of Los Angeles – often used to seem more Boston than Burbank. Gentrification and cuts in defence spending have changed much of that, but a walk along quaint Sixth Street and a Greek meal at **Papadakis Taverna** (301 W Sixth Street; 1-310 548 1186), a Yugoslavian one at **Ante's** (729 S Palos Verdes Street; 1-310 832 5375) or a classic film at the **Warner Grand Theatre** (478 W Sixth Street), a restored 1931 movie palace, can make the years vanish.

A spectacular view of the Pacific can be seen from nearby **Angels Gate Park** (3601 S Gaffey Street), home to the giant Korean Friendship Bell, a Bicentennial gift to the US from South Korea. Below this bluff, **Point Fermin Park**, with its 1874 wooden lighthouse, is a great picnic spot.

For families, the **Cabrillo Marine Aquarium**, housed in a Frank Gehry-designed building (*see page 178* **Children**), and the **Los Angeles Maritime Museum** (Berth 84, at the end of Sixth Street) are fun to explore.

Long Beach

Long Beach is easy to reach by public transport: it takes about an hour from Downtown LA on the Metro Blue Line. The city has always been given

short shrift by its more well-heeled neighbours to the north and south: the Long Beach of popular imagination is one of dockworkers, swing shifts and drunken sailors on leave. But since the factories closed and Navy work dwindled in the 1980s, it has changed almost out of recognition.

The city's latest attempt to shake off its gritty past is the **Long Beach Aquarium of the Pacific** (*see below*), opened to fanfare in the summer of 1998: with 10,000 creatures representing 550 Pacific Ocean species, it ranks as one of the US's largest and most spectacular aquariums. The aquarium is the first fruit of redevelopment for the area known as Queensway Bay: shortly after the turn of the century, there should be a public park with a lighthouse, shops, cinemas and restaurants. (Note: the circular building with fish painted on its exterior is not the aquarium but the **Long Beach Arena** where the local ice hockey team, the feisty **Ice Dogs**, play – the building was given its oceanic theme in 1992 by famed Southern California muralist Wyland.)

But there's more to the LBC – as local rappers called Long Beach – than a fishtank. An anchor's toss from the aquarium is the **Queen Mary** (*see below*), one of the largest passenger ships ever built, now a hotel and restaurants. It's not the *Titanic* but it's the next best thing.

Downtown Long Beach has sprouted some cool restaurants in recent years, such as the beautifully designed **La Traviata** (301 Cedar Avenue; 1-562 432 8022), the nouveau-Brazilian **Cha Cha Cha** (762 Pacific Avenue; 1-562 436 3900) and a string of hip haunts along or near once-blighted Pine Avenue. Try café/art gallery **M**, formerly System M (No.213A), pool hall/dance club/rock club **Jillian's** (No.110; 1-562 628 8866), dance club **Cohiba** (110 Broadway, entrance through Mum's restaurant at 144 Pine Avenue; 1-562 491 5220) and rock club **Blue Café** (210 The Promenade N; 1-562 983 7111).

Every April, the streets of downtown come alive with the sound of revving engines, when the **Long Beach Grand Prix** takes over for three days (*see page 91* **Los Angeles by Season**). Lesser-known things to do: catch a performance by the extremely avant-garde **Long Beach Opera** (Carpenter Performing Arts Center, 6200 Atherton Street; 1-562 439 2580), arguably the most eccentric opera company in the US; visit the small but ambitious **Long Beach Museum of Art** (2300 E Ocean Boulevard; 1-562 439 2119), which shows mainly contemporary Californian artists and is located in a seaside house built in 1912; or try the **Museum of Latin American Art** (628 Alamitos Avenue; 1-562 437 1689).

Also worth exploring are eclectic **Broadway** (between Alamitos and Ximeno Avenues) with such remarkable restaurants as the 1920s bordello-themed **House of Madam Jo Jo's** (2941 E

The new **Long Beach Aquarium**.

Broadway); **Fourth Street** (near Cherry Avenue), a funky strip of thrift stores; **Belmont Shore** (Second Street, from Park to Bayshore Avenues), where Cal State students shop and bar-hop; and what is unofficially called **Little Phnom Penh** – Anaheim Street, between Atlantic and Cherry Avenues – a struggling area and home to many Cambodian shops and eateries.

Naples (off Second Street, between Bay Shore and Marina Avenues) is an expensive neighbourhood laid out around picturesque canals like Venice up the coast, but with none of the latter's decay. Gondola rides are offered by **Gondola Getaway** (reservations required; 5437 E Ocean Boulevard; 1-562 433 9595).

In recent years, Long Beach has earned a rep for its rap scene. Snoop Doggy Dogg, Warren G and Dove Shack are some of the local hitmakers. Unfortunately, many of these performers have left the city and there is no hip-hop club as such. However, **VIP Records** (1012 E Pacific Coast Highway), an R&B/rap record store/studio where many of these acts got their start, is a good place to soak up the atmosphere.

Avoid the beaches here: pollution is a problem in this industrial town, especially since break-waters were built years ago to hold back the (cleansing) waves. Long Beach and San Pedro are both jumping-off points for nearby **Catalina Island** (*see page 237* **Trips Out of Town**).

Long Beach Aquarium of the Pacific
100 Aquarium Way, at Shoreline Drive (1-562 590 3100). Metro First Street or Transit Mall/Long Beach Transit bus C/I-710, exit Shoreline Drive east.
Open 10am-6pm daily. **Admission** $13.95; $11.95 over-60s; $6.95 3-11s. **Credit** MC, V.

The $117 million, 156,735sq ft (14,561sq m) aquarium with its wave-shaped profile has been turning 'em away since opening in June 1998 – and it's easy to see why. A three-storey high predator tank, coral reef and kelp forest are among the simulated underwater environments; a life-size replica of a blue whale with calf hangs from the ceiling of the Great Hall of the Pacific.
Parking $6.
Website: www.aquariumofpacific.org

Queen Mary
1126 Queens Highway (1-562 435 3511/hotel booking 1-800 437 2934). Metro Transit Mall/I-405, exit I-710 south. **Open** *winter* 10am-6pm daily; *summer* 9am-9pm daily. **Admission** $13; $11 over-55s; $8 4-11s.
Credit AmEx, DC, MC, V.
Having retired from active duty in 1967, the *Queen Mary* is now a popular tourist target. Though only mildly diverting unless you have a thing for cruise ships, the majestic liner offers fun like the Ghost Tour and the Engine Room Tour. The ship was used for interiors for the film *The Poseidon Adventure* and guides are happy to share shooting anecdotes. There are shops and restaurants aboard and in the adjacent shopping 'village'. Attendance has jumped recently thanks to the popularity of the movie *Titanic* and the addition of the *Scorpion*, a decommissioned Russian submarine, which gives those bored with the ship something else to do.
Parking $6-$8.

Long Beach Chamber of Commerce
1 World Trade Center, Long Beach, CA 90831 (1-562 436 1251). **Open** 8.30am-4.30pm Mon-Fri.
Visitor information and literature.

Orange County

The South Coast

Seal Beach and Sunset Beach, near the LA County border, begin the 50-mile (80-kilometre) expanse of beach bliss that is coastal Orange County. The Pacific Coast Highway (Highway 1, or 'PCH') runs the length of it. While **Seal Beach** and **Sunset Beach** give unpretentious fun, the real action starts just to the south in **Huntington Beach**, aka 'Surf City'. Hang out at the pier (Main Street, off PCH) or on the sand and you'll see how the city got its nickname. From dawn until dark, surfers are out searching for the perfect wave; the best appear in the many pro championships held every summer.

Unfortunately, bland, modern Main Street has a reputation for attracting misfits and malcontents. Skinheads have roughed up 'undesirables' and Independence Day celebrations have sometimes veered out of control. However, in recent years, police crackdowns have quashed many of the more obvious confrontations.

Newport Beach, further south, is something else altogether. From the multi-million-dollar homes overlooking Newport Harbor to the outdoor **Fashion Island** mall and the **Newport Harbor Art Museum** (850 San Clemente Drive, at Santa Barbara Drive; 1-949 759 1122), which specialises in California art, Newport Beach is where the American leisure class can live out its life in sun-soaked splendour.

Balboa Island (Jamboree Road Bridge and PCH) and **Balboa Peninsula** (Balboa Boulevard and PCH) are both prime walking areas and a ferry ushers visitors between the two. The island is full of small shops, restaurants and homes; perhaps the best activity is walking and browsing. On the peninsula, everyone seems to be rollerblading or cycling, and things are more downmarket. The **Balboa Pavilion** (at the end of Main Street), once a Victorian bathhouse, is the jumping-off point for harbour tours and winter whale-watching outings as well as trips to **Catalina Island**. The bars and restaurants along Balboa Boulevard are prime hangouts.

Laguna Beach began as an artists' colony and is the home of the admired **Laguna Beach Museum of Art** (307 Cliff Drive, at the PCH; 1-949 494 6531), which also collects California art. It's the artistic lineage that partly explains why this area is the most liberal in notoriously conservative OC. **Main Beach**, with its pick-up basketball and volleyball games, is a must for people-watching. Scuba diving is also good here.

Further down the coast, **San Juan Capistrano** is famous for the swallows that return to **Mission San Juan Capistrano** (Camino Capistrano and Ortega Highway) each year. But the 1776-built mission is worth visiting on its own account (*see* **On a mission** *page 246* **Trips Out of Town**). And one of the area's best rock clubs, the **Coach House** (33157 Camino Capistrano; 1-949 496 8930), is nearby.

At the county's end, **San Clemente** has all the sun and waves but few of the crowds of its neigh-bours. Richard Nixon's western White House, a Spanish-inspired mansion called Casa Pacifica, can be seen from San Clemente State Beach.

Central Orange County

Costa Mesa (which isn't on the coast) likes to bill itself as another city of the arts. It's the home of the **Orange County Performing Arts Center** (*see page 234* **Theatre & Dance**) and the much-admired **South Coast Repertory Theatre Company** (655 Town Center Drive; 1-714 708 5500). But it's really a city of commerce, thanks to an array of malls including **South Coast Plaza**, one of the largest in the world; the über-expensive **Crystal Court**; the **Lab**, 'the anti-mall' for the young and the pierced, which houses two of OC's best eateries, the **Gypsy Den** café (home to a Sunday-night ambient/techno space; 1-714 549 7012) and **Habana**, a post-modern Cuban restaurant (1-714 556 0176); and **Triangle Square**, a massive altar to consumerism that includes Nike Town and Virgin Megastore.

Antiseptic **Irvine**, an early masterplanned 'new town', is home to the University of California, Irvine (so futuristic when built in the 1960s that *Planet of the Apes* was filmed here), and the large **Irvine Spectrum** outdoor mall with its 3-D IMAX cinema. The city also has an 'alternative' scene at **Metropolis** (4255 Campus Drive; 1-949 856 9800), one of the county's most progressive dance clubs.

Santa Ana to the north gets a bad rap as Orange County's gang territory. True, the heavily Latino city contains some of the county's toughest areas – but it also has one of its most distinctive. Strolling along busy **Fourth Street**, between French and Ross Streets, with its colourful store-fronts and hum of Spanish, is like strolling through a small city in Mexico. Santa Ana is also home to the **Bowers Museum** (2002 N Main Street, at 20th Street; 1-714 893 6066), which has a strong collection of Latin and African arts and crafts, and a budding artists' district between Broadway and Bush, First and Third Streets. Near the Costa Mesa border is the **Galaxy** (3503 S Harbor Boulevard; 1-714 957 0600), a dinner theatre turned music venue with great sightlines.

Another lively neighbourhood is **Little Saigon** in Westminster, the largest Vietnamese community outside Vietnam. It's too big to walk, but well worth a visit for the Vietnamese and Chinese food served at places such as **Seafood Paradise** (8602 Westminster Boulevard; 1-714 893 6066).

Anaheim & inland

This area of Orange County is filled with some of the best-known icons of middle Americana, of which **Disneyland** (*see below*) is king. The area around Disneyland, for years known for cheap

*The **Lab**: Costa Mesa's hip shopping mall.*

*Discover Latino life on **Fourth Street** in Orange County's Santa Ana.*

motels and strip mall seediness, is being revitalised. Anaheim Stadium, where baseball team the California Angels play, has been redesigned, given a bit of personality and rechristened **Edison International Field**. The glitzy, new **Arrowhead Pond** of Anaheim is a huge arena showing everything from the Mighty Ducks hockey team to Barbra Streisand concerts. Just down the road, in the city of **Orange**, **Hop City** (1939 S State College Drive, at Katella Avenue; 1-714 978 3700) is *the* place to hear blues, and long-running **Linda's Doll's Hut** (107 S Adams Street, at Manchester Boulevard; 1-714 533 1286) is the cramped rock club where such OC bands as the Offspring got started.

For a more traditional slice of American pie, hop over to Beach Boulevard near La Palma Avenue in **Buena Park**. Here are **Knott's Berry Farm** (*see below*) – a smaller, more homely Disneyland – **Movieland Wax Museum**, and **Medieval Times**, the knights-and-knaves eatery where food is beside the point.

Two other shrines to the American way of life deserve a visit. The **Crystal Cathedral**, an all-glass house of worship (*see page 32* **Architecture**), is a marvel of sheer excess, while the **Nixon Library and Birthplace** in Yorba Linda (*see page 204* **Museums & Galleries**) is, as these places generally are, a combination of library and propaganda machine.

At the other end of the scale, some alternative, college-style life can be found around the Cal State campus in **Fullerton**, including **Club 369** (1641 N Placentia Avenue, at Yorba Linda Boulevard; 1-714 572 1816), where thrash, roots and pop bands play loud and fast.

Disneyland

1313 Harbor Boulevard, Anaheim, Orange County (1-714 999 4000). Bus 460/I-5, exit Harbor Boulevard. Open winter 10am-6pm Mon-Fri; 9am-10pm Sat, Sun;
summer 8am-midnight Mon-Thur, Sun; 8am-1am Fri, Sat; hours can vary, so call in advance. Admission $34; $30 seniors; $26 3-11s. Credit AmEx, MC, V.

Called 'the Happiest Place on Earth', Disneyland is all it's cracked up to be, if you like that kind of thing. If you don't, you may need sectioning after your visit. In this immaculate world (deliveries and rubbish removal are all done underground), new rides come on line with movie-studio productivity. But some of the old favourites still draw enormous crowds: Space Mountain, which takes you, in utter darkness, on a fast, scream-inducing ride through time, space and black holes; the Matterhorn, where you take a bobsled rollercoaster ride around a Swiss Alp; the Haunted Mansion, where Disney ghosts trill and smile; and Pirates of the Caribbean, where pirates sing during a drunken spree. A word of advice: if you hate having a song stick in your head, skip It's a Small World, which is outdated and no more than an incitement to strangle the composer of the inane tune. Disneyland is fun, but get there early to beat the crowds, be prepared to queue and pace yourself – it's big.
Parking $6.

Knott's Berry Farm

8039 Beach Boulevard, at La Palma Avenue, Buena Park, Orange County (1-714 220 5200/5220). Bus 420/I-5, exit Beach Boulevard south. Open winter hours vary, so call ahead; summer 9am-midnight daily. Admission $29.95; $19.95 seniors, 3-11s; after 4pm $14.95 adults, seniors. Credit AmEx, DC, Disc, MC, V.

Knott's Berry Farm started as a farm stand selling the homemade preserves of one Mrs Cordelia Knott. Although Ma Knott and family are long gone, her jams are still for sale, as are tasty fried chicken dinners at the restaurant outside the gates. Inside the park, which portrays an idealised, kinder America, there are water rides, the 20-storey Sky Jump parachute ride, and Montezooma's Revenge, a seemingly tame rollercoaster that still gives you a stomach-flying-out-of-your-mouth sensation. Many of the buildings in the park have been transplanted from old mining towns, which heightens the feeling of nostalgia that hovers in the air. Children will like Ghost Town, featuring smiling can-can girls and gun-slinging cowboys.
Parking $5.

Anaheim/Orange County Visitor & Convention Bureau

800 W Katella Avenue, Anaheim, CA 92802 (1-714 999 8999/recorded information 1-714 635 8900). Open 8am-5.30pm Mon-Fri.

Los Angeles by Season

From Chinese New Year to Cinco de Mayo, jazz festivals to surfing competitions, there are celebrations galore in multicultural LA.

Los Angeles, somewhat tiresomely known as a 'place with no seasons', managed to slip that moniker in 1998, when its seasons came in unpredictable and paradoxical packages: by the time this guide went to press, the lingering effects of El Niño – two to three times the normal annual rainfall and the worst beach and ground water conditions in eight summers – were wearing off, only to be replaced by sisterly La Niña: cold, dry winds that by early 1999 may create drought (not to mention fire) conditions across the Southland.

Not that its natives necessarily take much notice; most Angelenos clock the seasons by celebrating traditions imported from their place of origin, which results in the diverse displays of cultural pride that the city is celebrated for. Here are some of the more notable attempts in and around Los Angeles to keep a seasonal timetable by throwing a damn fine party.

The *Los Angeles Festival Guide*, a free booklet available at the LA Convention & Visitors Bureau (*see page 265* **Directory**), lists over 150 different festivals by the, er, 'season' they take place in. For details of LA's numerous film festivals, *see page 182* **Film**, and for more on local weather patterns, *see chapter* **Geography & Climate**.

National holidays

New Year's Day (1 Jan); Martin Luther King Jr Day (third Mon in Jan); President's Day (third Mon in Feb); Memorial Day (last Mon in May); Independence Day (4 July); Labor Day (first Mon in Sept); Columbus Day (second Mon in Oct); Election Day (first Tue in Nov); Veteran's Day (11 Nov); Thanksgiving Day (fourth Thur in Nov); Christmas Day (25 Dec).

Spring

The Academy Awards

Usually at Dorothy Chandler Pavilion, Music Center, 135 N Grand Avenue, at First Street, Downtown. **Date** mid/late Mar.

You'll have to camp out all night and hang out all day for even the vaguest chance of spotting any celebs – best to watch the whole shebang on TV, like the rest of the world. Work usually stops mid-afternoon to give everyone time to get in front of the telly for the late-afternoon start. Alternatively, since the stars are otherwise engaged, this is a choice night to get a good table at any posh restaurant that's not holding its own Oscars party. If you have friends in town, you're certain to be invited

to join an unofficial Oscars bash – everybody has them. The ceremony is meant to be moving to a new home on Hollywood Boulevard in 2001. *See also p24* **Celebrity LA.**

Santa Clarita Cowboy Poetry & Music Festival

Information 1-805 255 4910. Melody Ranch, Santa Clarita. **Date** late Mar/early Apr.

Relive the old West with a weekend of trail rides, poetry, storytelling, Western swing dance, chuck wagon food and music by top cowboy artists, held at Gene Autry's former ranch, as seen in the movies *High Noon* and *Gunsmoke.*

City of Los Angeles Marathon

Information 1-310 444 5544. Citywide; check newspapers for route. **Date** first Sun in Mar.

With 20,000 runners taking part, it's an all-city traffic-clogging festival, so if you're located within the course, join in the fun. Eleven 'entertainment centres' and more than 100 live bands and performers line the route.

Blessing of the Animals

Information 1-213 628 7164. Pueblo de Los Angeles Historical Monument, Olvera Street, Downtown LA. **Date** Easter Sat.

A bedecked cow leads a procession of farm animals and local pets to be sprinkled with holy water by the Cardinal of Los Angeles in a tradition dating from the fourth century.

Thai New Year (Songkran Festival)

Information 1-818 785 9552. Wat Thai of Los Angeles, 8225 Coldwater Canyon Avenue, at Roscoe Boulevard, North Hollywood. **Date** mid-Apr.

Visit this Buddhist temple to pay homage to the orange-robed monks, watch Thai boxing, classical dance and the Miss Songkran beauty contest and eat authentic delicacies.

Spring Festival of Books

Information 1-800 528 4637. Dickinson Plaza, UCLA campus, Westwood. **Date** Apr.

A weekend-long grey-matter gathering with more than 200 writers, poets, readings, storytellers and children's activities. Call ahead for tickets to the popular talks that feature many big names in the creative and business ends of publishing.

Fiesta Broadway/Cinco de Mayo

Information 1-310 914 0015. Broadway, Hill & Spring Streets, Downtown LA. **Date** last Sun in Apr.

Billed as 'the nation's largest Cinco de Mayo celebration', but actually a bit commercial. Ignore the corporate sponsors and zero in on a feast of Latino music.

Los Angeles Cuban Cultural Festival

Information 1-213 485 0709. Plaza Jose Marti, 1020 Glendale Boulevard, Echo Park. **Date** May.

The rich traditions of pre- and post-Castro Cuba can be

experienced in this one-day festival's mix of dance, theatre, readings, food, visual arts and, yes, cigar-rolling contests.

Topanga Banjo Fiddle Contest, Dance & Folk Arts Festival

Information 1-818 382 4819. Paramount Ranch, entrance on Cornell Road, Agoura. **Date** mid-May.
A bluegrass blowout, with old-time, railroad and hobo music, cowboy poetry and traditional dance demonstrations. Bring your instrument and a blanket.

Summer

Summer is the season for outdoor concerts. The most famous are at the **Hollywood Bowl**, the summer home of the LA Philharmonic (for details, *see page 207* **Music**).

Los Feliz Village Street Fair

Information 1-323 662 7747. Hillhurst Avenue, between Franklin & Finley Avenues, Los Feliz. **Date** June.
A low-key opportunity to experience the quaint, scruffy quality of one of LA's more interesting neighbourhoods. The one-day event includes free music and entertainment, food from the area's best restaurants, carnival games and raffles for hundreds of prizes.

Playboy Jazz Festival

Information 1-310 449 4070. Hollywood Bowl, 2301 N Highland Avenue, Hollywood. **Date** June.
The place to be if you love jazz. All strains of this singular art form – Latin, fusion, bebop, avant-garde, big band, blues and Dixieland – are represented in two days (over 17 hours) of continuous entertainment. The event is sponsored by *Playboy* magazine.

Woodland Hills Concerts in the Park

Information 1-818 704 1587. Warner Park, 5800 Topanga Canyon Boulevard, Woodland Hills. **Date** Sun, June-Aug.
Warner Park is the setting for this viable alternative to the crowded Hollywood Bowl. The 13-week programme (Sundays only) features big bands, classical recitals, Latin combos, reggae bands and much more – all on the grass, under the moon and next to a picnic basket.

The Will Geer Theatricum Botanicum

Information 1-310 455 3723. 1419 N Topanga Canyon Boulevard, at Cheney Drive, Topanga. **Tickets** $15.
Date mid-June to mid-Sept.
Shakespeare and other theatrical classics are presented on a wooded hillside in LA's last remaining hippy stronghold.

Gay & Lesbian Pride Celebration

Information 1-323 860 0701. Festival in West Hollywood Park, 647 N San Vicente Boulevard, at Robertson Boulevard, West Hollywood. Parade goes along Santa Monica Boulevard, from Crescent Heights Boulevard to the park. **Tickets** festival $10. **Date** late June.
A weekend of free concerts, two-day festival and Sunday parade. Politics and pride, flamboyance and freedom. Fun. *See also chapter* **Gay & Lesbian**.

Independence Day

Date 4 July.
Americana, LA-style. Picnic, barbecue, go to the beach, take in a parade and watch some fireworks. Check the papers for details of the 50 or so fireworks displays, from the Rose Bowl to Dodger Stadium, Marina del Rey to Magic Mountain, as well as oddities such as the Mr & Ms Muscle Beach Venice Physique Contest.

Lotus Festival

Information 1-213 485 1310. Echo Park Lake, Glendale Boulevard, at Bellevue Avenue, Echo Park. **Date** second weekend in July.
With the largest lotus bed in the States, this festival celebrates Asia and the Pacific Islands with dance, music, martial arts, exotic plants and, best of all, dragon boat races.

Santa Monica Pier Twilight Dance Series

Information 1-310 458 8900. Santa Monica Pier, at Colorado & Ocean Avenues, Santa Monica. **Date** 7.30-9.30pm Thur; July-Labor Day.
Santa Monica Pier rocks with stellar performers, from blues to regional, world beat to straight-out rock 'n' roll.

Brazilian Summer Festival

Information 1-818 566 1111. John Anson Ford Theater, 2580 Cahuenga Boulevard, at Vine Street, Hollywood. **Tickets** $15. **Date** July.
LA's vibrant Brazilian community makes this a happening like no other, with music, arts, food and capoeira.

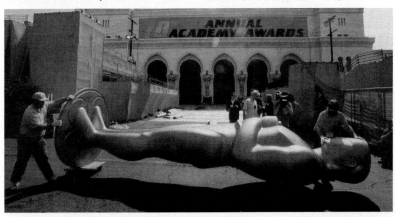

The Academy Awards: *some people will go to any lengths to take home an Oscar.*

Best of LA
Information 1-888 237 8635. Santa Monica Civic Auditorium, 1855 Main Street, Santa Monica. **Tickets** $10. **Date** July.
After the lamented demise of LA à la Carte a few years ago, *Los Angeles* magazine has sponsored this outdoor mass taste-test of over 100 LA eateries, as well as fashion shows, live music, kids' activities and (of course) a cigar lounge.

Festival of the Chariots
Information 1-310 836 2676. Venice Beach Pavilion, Venice. **Date** first Sun in Aug.
The best thing this side of Benares. See Krishna transported from Santa Monica Pier to Venice on three ornate 60ft (18m) chariots. Booths promote Indian culture and there's also dancing, rock 'n' roll and food.

Nisei Week Japanese Festival
Information 1-213 687 7193. Little Tokyo, Downtown. **Date** Aug.
This eight-day event includes martial arts, the tea ceremony, Taiko drumming, Japanese arts, a parade and lots more.

Sunset Junction Street Festival
Information 1-323 661 7771. Sunset Boulevard, between Edgecliff & Fountain Avenues, Silver Lake. **Tickets** $2. **Date** Aug.
One of the few legitimate street fairs in a city where pedestrians are generally regarded with suspicion, Sunset Junction's popular weekend event offers a great opportunity for everyone from Latino gang members to outrageously camp transvestites to strut their stuff in a festive and friendly environment. There are also carnival rides, three stages and a disco and more than 100 food and craft vendors. Don't forget to bring your camera.

Central Avenue Jazz Festival
Information 1-213 485 2437. Around the Dunbar Hotel, Central Avenue, between 42nd & 43rd Streets, LA. **Date** Aug.
The ghosts of Dizzy Gillespie, Charlie Parker, Miles Davis et al still haunt this West Coast jazz mecca. Extending from Downtown to Watts, Central Avenue was the gold vein of black LA from the 1920s to the 1950s, and this two-day festival recaptures the excitement of those times with jam sessions by local musicians.

LA African Marketplace & Cultural Faire
Information 1-323 734 1164. Rancho Cienega Park, 5001 Rodeo Road, at Martin Luther King Jr Boulevard, Baldwin Hills. **Date** last three weekends in Aug.
A dusty African village environment where over 350 merchants show their wares and six stages provide non-stop entertainment. African, Afro-Caribbean, roots and contemporary African-American music, dance and food.

Autumn

Leimert Park Jazz Festival
Information 1-323 960 1625. Leimert Park Village, 43rd Place & Crenshaw Boulevard, Crenshaw. **Date** late Aug-early Sept.
Top jazz artists converge on a neighbourhood that is the creative centre of LA's African-American community.

Garlic Festival
Information 1-888 222 2917. Federal Building, Wilshire & Veteran Boulevards, Westwood. **Tickets** $2-$10. **Date** late Sept.
Los Angeles's most odiferous festival celebrates the 'sinful apple' that is *allium sativum*. Two days of music, food, raffles, Margaritas – and, of course, no vampires anywhere in the vicinity.

Day of the Drum/Simon Rodia Watts Towers Jazz Festival
Information 1-213 485 1795. 1727 E 107th Street, between Willowbrook Avenue & 103rd Street, Watts. **Date** late Sept.
These back-to-back events feature international drumming, jazz, gospel and R&B bands. A great excuse to visit one of Los Angeles's quirkiest and most beautiful landmarks.

Hallowe'en in West Hollywood
Information 1-323 848 6547. Santa Monica Boulevard, between La Cienega & Robertson Boulevards, West Hollywood. **Date** 31 Oct.
In a city full of parties, this one is probably LA's most popular spot for costume viewing. Expect food, music and entertainment – the lip-sync competition is a must. Dress up, but be prepared to make live in; parking is a nightmare.

Day of the Dead (Dia de Los Muertos)
Information 1-323 881 6444. Self-Help Graphics, 3802 César E Chavez Avenue, at Gage Avenue, East LA. **Date** 2 Nov; art exhibition until end of month.
This hip organisation of Latino artists brings together art, altars and musical and theatrical groups to celebrate the Mexican tradition of honouring the dead. Skeletons galore.

Hollywood Christmas Parade
Information 1-323 469 2337. Hollywood: parade travels west on Sunset Boulevard, from Van Ness to Highland Avenues, north to Hollywood Boulevard, and east to Bronson Avenue. **Date** Sun after Thanksgiving.
If Hollywood is a state of mind, its namesake boulevard is a tacky embarrassment. Join one million fans for an evening of over 100 B-list celebrities, bands and equestrian units.

Winter

Mariachi Festival
Information 1-213 485 2437. Intersection of First, Boyle & Pleasant Streets, Boyle Heights. **Date** mid-Nov.
A fun and funky opportunity to experience a range of mariachi styles – right beside the doughnut shop that serves these musicians as an employment agency. Great Mexican food.

Downtown Tree Lighting Ceremony
Information 1-213 236 3900. Citicorp Plaza, 777 S Figueroa Street, Downtown. **Date** first week of Dec.
LA's answer to New York's Rockefeller Plaza Christmas tree is the lighting of Citicorp's 70ft (21m) white fir, the focus of a host of free events such as carol singing, orchestral concerts, refreshments and photos with Santa and his elves.

Las Posadas
Information 1-213 485 9777. Olvera Street, Downtown LA. **Date** 7pm, 16-24 Dec.
A candlelit procession re-enacts Joseph and Mary's search for shelter, finishing with traditional Mexican Christmas music and a piñata party for children.

Parades of Lights & Marina del Rey Christmas Boat Parade
Information 1-310 821 7614. Marina del Rey. **Date** second Sat in Dec.
Southern California's temperate weather lets locals take the tradition of Christmas decorations afloat. Check the press for details of ceremonies at marinas from Santa Barbara to San Diego. The best in-town offering is at Marina del Rey.

Chinese New Year
Information 1-213 617 0396). Chinatown; parade along N Broadway, between Cesar E Chavez Avenue & Bernard Street. **Date** Sat before President's Day.
A street fair, races and, best of all, the Golden Dragon parade.

Events outside Los Angeles

Tournament of Roses Rose Parade

Information 1-626 795 4171. Pasadena; route begins at S Orange Grove Boulevard & Ellis Street, turns east on Colorado Boulevard, turns north on Sierra Madre Boulevard, ends at Paloma Street. **Date** 8.05am, 1 Jan.
What is supposedly the world's largest parade started as a marketing ploy to show off California's great climate. And it still works.

Riverside County Fair & National Date Festival

Information 1-800 811 3247. Riverside County Fairgrounds, at US 111, Indio, Riverside County. **Date** Feb.
This ten-day event presents a uniquely Middle Eastern take on the traditional American county fair. In addition to agricultural exhibits, expect to find daily camel and ostrich races, date milkshakes and weirdly costumed desert denizens.

Ragga Muffins/Bob Marley Day

Information 1-562 436 3661. Long Beach Convention Center, E Shoreline Drive, Long Beach. **Date** mid-Feb.
Jamaica exports its top acts – from Burning Spear and Judy Mowatt to Sugar Minott – for this three-day festival, and LA's rastas and reggae enthusiasts show up in force.

California Poppy Festival

Information 1-805 723 6077. Lancaster City Park, 43011 Tenth Street W, between Avenues L & K-8, Lancaster. **Date** second weekend in Apr.
Yes, it's just like the *Wizard of Oz*, especially after a rainy winter. Take advantage of helicopter rides and free shuttles from the park to the California Poppy Reserve. Call the Wildflower Hotline (1-818 768 3533) for details of what's blooming where.

Long Beach Grand Prix

Information 1-562 436 9953. Downtown Long Beach. **Date** mid-Apr.
Thousands come to watch this annual motor race – a 1.85-mile (3-km) loop around downtown Long Beach – which celebrates its 25th anniversary in 1999 (16-18 April). It's a serious affair, with world-class racing drivers taking part as well as Hollywood stars in a separate celebrity challenge (Paul Newman is a regular). Tickets usually go on sale in January.
Website: www.longbeachgp.com

Temecula Balloon & Wine Festival

Information 1-909 676 6713. Lake Skinner, 37701 Warren Road, Temecula, Riverside County. **Tickets** $12 Sat; $10 Sun. **Date** last weekend in Apr.
There are antique cars, wine-tasting and live jazz and rock – but the real reason to visit the rolling hills of this wine district is to witness the mass ascension of more than 60 hot-air balloons. Get up early to catch this breath-taking 7am sight.

Ramona Pageant

Information 1-800 645 4465/1-909 658 3111. Ramona Bowl, 27400 Ramona Bowl Road, Hemet, Riverside County. **Date** late Apr-early May.
With a cast of 350, this hokey/wonderful spectacular is based on an early California interracial love story. Set in a stunning mountain amphitheatre, the show features mariachis, dancing, Native American rituals and hordes of charging horsemen. A then-unknown Raquel Welch once took part.

Annual Cajun & Zydeco Festival

Information 1-310 427 3713. Rainbow Lagoon Park, behind Long Beach Convention Center, E Shoreline Drive, Long Beach. **Tickets** $20 on gate; $15 in advance. **Date** first weekend in June.
Louisiana exports its best for a weekend of music, food, dancing and more. Work off the calories at this taste of LA in LA.

Pageant of the Masters & Sawdust Festival

Information Pageant of the Masters 1-714 494 1145; Sawdust Festival 1-714 494 3030. Irvine Bowl, 650 Laguna Canyon Road, Laguna Beach, Orange County. **Tickets** $15-$40. **Date** July-Aug.
Famous works of art are recreated with astonishing accuracy with Laguna locals posing in 'tableaux vivant', presented nightly in the beautiful Irvine Bowl. Spend the day enjoying yourself at the Sawdust Festival's arts and crafts displays.

US Open of Surfing & 'Surf City' Beach Exposition

Information 1-888 672 6737. Huntington Beach Pier, Main Street, at PCH, Huntington Beach, Orange County. **Date** first week in Aug.
Part of the ASP World Championships tour, this six-day event draws many internationally top-rated surfers, as well as 400 other competitors. Enthusiasts cheer them on at summer's biggest beach party.

Southern California Indian Center Pow Wow

Information 1-714 663 1102. Orange County Fairgrounds, 88 Fair Drive, between Fairview & Arlington Roads, Costa Mesa, Orange County. **Date** early Aug.
The biggest Native American event of the year features a weekend of drumming and dancing, food and exhibits from American Indians across the United States.

Doodah Parade

Information 1-626 449 3649. Old Town Pasadena; parade starts at Raymond Avenue & Holly Street, travels west on Colorado Boulevard, ends at Union Street.
Date 2pm, Sun before Thanksgiving.
A spoof version of the Rose Parade with just-plain-folks goofing on whatever is topical. Perennial favourites include the Precision Marching Briefcase Drill Team and the Lounge Lizards, a group of Sinatra-crooning reptiles.

The Glory of Christmas

Information 1-714 971 4000/reservations 1-714 544 5679. Crystal Cathedral, 12141 Lewis Street, at Chapman Avenue, Garden Grove, Orange County. **Date** late Nov-Dec.
Hollywood values make this spectacular 'living nativity' a must. Set in the famous glass-and-steel church with a cast of hundreds, a breathtaking starlit sky and live camels. At the ministry known for originating drive-in churches (*see also p32* **Architecture**).

Welcome to New York.

Now get out.

The obsessive guide to impulsive entertainment

On sale at newsstands in New York
Pick up a copy!

To get a copy of the current issue or to subscribe, call *Time Out New York* at 212-539-4444.

Consumer LA

Accommodation

Los Angeles is home to some of the world's most luxurious – and expensive – hotels, where you'll be treated like a movie star. But if budgets are tight, go for an authentic motel experience or a homely travellers' hangout.

Like most things in Los Angeles, its hotels are all about image. Many have been around since Hollywood's golden years, and whatever identity each chooses, most take it over the top in an only-in-California way. This means that the price of the room buys you not only a place to crash but also a scene and an attitude.

LA is so huge that where you choose to stay will dictate what kind of holiday you have. A room in Santa Monica guarantees quick shoreline access, a cooler climate and a beachy California vibe; Beverly Hills has the most expensive hotels and plenty of star-sightings, with exclusive shopping and dining; anything on the Sunset Strip puts you in the centre of Hollywood glamour and action-packed nightlife; West Hollywood celebrates gay culture and is easily navigable on foot; most Hollywood pads are gritty, cheap motels surrounded by star-paved streets, cheesy tourists, souvenir shops and shady characters; and Downtown digs generally cater to conventioneers.

PRICES & SERVICES

Expect to pay $60-$110 in a budget hotel (for a double room, per night); $90-$200 in a mid-range hotel; and from about $200 to any sum you like in a first-class hotel. The cheapest form of accommodation (bar camping) is to get a shared room in a hostel; these start from around $17 per person per night. Budget chain motels can be quite cheap, too (*see p110* **Hotel chains**), especially if there are four of you: double rooms usually have two large double beds, so you can end up paying as little as $25 per person for four for a room across the road from the beach. The rates will be lower the further out you go, but it can be worth the commute, especially since motels are never far from the freeway.

Remember that the quoted rates are 'rack rates' ('official', published rates): the actual cost can be half as much. Ask

about corporate, AAA, weekend, promotional and any other kind of discount you can think of. However, rates do not include hotel taxes, which range from 12-15 per cent (depending on which city the hotel is in).

Except in hostels, you will almost always get cable TV, a radio and a telephone (expect to pay a service charge, from 25¢ for a local call, for using it) in your room – they're as much part of the furniture as a bed – and most places can accommodate disabled guests. You can also expect parking facilities: it's usually free at budget and mid-range hotels, but be warned that the hefty rates at the larger and more costly places can increase your bill substantially (charges quoted in the listings below are per night). No-smoking rooms are now more common than smoking ones, so if you want the latter, ask. For hotels catering specifically for a gay clientele, *see chapter* Gay & Lesbian.

BOOKING & RENTAL SERVICES

If you want someone else to search for the options in your price range, contact any of the following services. They'll not only give you a list of hotels, B&Bs and motels, but also make your reservation for you. The exception is the Los Angeles Convention & Visitors Bureau, which will not book your room for you, but will forward an extensive list of accommodation throughout the area.

Bed & Breakfast International *PO Box 282910, San Francisco, CA 94128 (1-800 872 4500/1-650 696 1690/ fax 1-650 696 1699); website: www.bbintl.com*
Hotel Reservations Network *8140 Walnut Hill Lane, suite 203, Dallas, TX 75231 (1-800 964 6835/1-214 361 7311/fax 1-214 361 7299); website: www.180096 hotel.com*
Los Angeles Convention & Visitors Bureau *685 S Figueroa Street, LA, CA 90017 (1-213 689 8822/ fax 1-213 236 2395).* **Open** *8am-5pm Mon-Fri; 8.30am-3pm Sat.*
Preferred Hotels & Resorts Worldwide *10877 Wilshire Boulevard, suite 403, LA, CA 90024 (1-800 323 7500/1-888 755 9876/fax 1-310 374 7025); website: www.preferredhotels.com*

HOTELS ONLINE

There are hundreds of websites featuring accommodation in LA. At most sites, you can also make a reservation online.

The best resource is *www.gola.miningco.com/travel/.* Once at the site, click on 'Los Angeles for Visitors', then click on 'Hotels & More'.
Digital City *http://losangeles.digitalcity.com/travel/*
Discount Los Angeles Hotels
www.vacationweb.com/hotels/la/index.html
Hostels in Los Angeles *www.hostels.com/us.ca.la.html*
Snap! *www.snap.com/*
Yahoo! Travel *www.allhotels.com/usa/california/la.html*

Westside: beach towns

First-class

Hotel Oceana

849 Ocean Avenue, between Montana & Idaho Avenues, Santa Monica, CA 90403 (reservations 1-800 777 0758/ front desk 1-310 393 0486/fax 1-310 458 1182/ beachsuite@aol.com). Bus 22, 322/I-10, exit Fourth-Fifth Street north. **Rates** *executive suite $250; one-bedroom suite $265-$295; two-bedroom suite $425-$495.* **Credit** *AmEx, DC, Disc, JCB, MC, V.* **Map 2 A1/2**

Enjoy the private beach and tropical garden at the mid-priced **Casa Malibu.**

The quaint Oceana has unobstructed views to Santa Monica beach and is two blocks away from Third Street Promenade. Each of the 63 suites aims to recall the art deco era of the Côte d'Azur, with vibrant patterns, vibrant patterns, wrought iron and wicker. Bonuses include granite and marble bathrooms, free daily newspapers and, in the larger suites, fully equipped kitchens. Many rooms have large balconies facing on to Ocean Avenue, while others overlook the swimming pool in the courtyard. There is no on-site restaurant, but in-suite gourmet dining is provided by Wolfgang Puck's Café.
Website: www.smweb.com/oceana
Hotel services *Air-conditioning (limited). Babysitting. Bar. Continental breakfast. Fax. Laundry. Parking (self-park $10; valet $17.50). Room service (11.30am-9.30pm). Rooms for disabled. Spa.* **Room services** *Fax/modem line. Hairdryer. Minibar. Refrigerator. Stereo with CD player. VCR (on request).*

Loews Santa Monica Beach Hotel

1700 Ocean Avenue, between Colorado Avenue & Pico Boulevard, Santa Monica, CA 90401 (reservations 1-800 235 6397/front desk 1-310 458 6700/fax 1-310 458 6761). Bus 20, 22, 33, 320, 322, 333, 434, Santa Monica 1, 7, 8, 10/I-10, exit Fourth-Fifth Street north. **Rates** *single/double $290-$465; suite $600-$2,750.* **Credit** *AmEx, DC, Disc, JCB, MC, V.* **Map 2 A3**
The Loews is just what you'd expect from Southern California: light and airy, warm and beachy, casual but elegant. The four-storey atrium lobby takes full advantage of its scenic surroundings, offering views of the beach and beyond. The beach is just across the street and the oceanfront park, pier, restaurants and Third Street Promenade a painless stroll away. Food highlights include a good Sunday brunch and the revered French restaurant Lavande.
Website: www.loewshotels.com
Hotel services *Air-conditioning. Babysitting. Bar. Beauty salon. Conference facilities. Fax. Gym. Jacuzzi. Laundry. Parking (self-park $15.40; valet $18). Pool. Restaurants (2). Room service (24-hour). Rooms for disabled. Sauna. Steam room.* **Room services** *Fax. Hairdryer. Minibar. Refrigerator. VCR.*

Shutters on the Beach

1 Pico Boulevard, at Ocean Avenue, Santa Monica, CA 90405 (reservations 1-800 334 9000/hotel operator 1-310 458 0030/fax 1-310 458 4589). Bus 20, 33, 320, 434, Santa Monica 1, 7, 10/I-10, exit Fourth Street south. **Rates** *single/double $280-$450; suite $600-$2,450.* **Credit** *AmEx, DC, Disc, MC, V.* **Map 2 A3**
Shutters opened in 1993 and is the only hotel in Santa Monica that's actually on the beach. Its location, along with its New England beach-home styling and luxury amenities, make it one of the most popular destinations in the area. Beyond the lobby – with its two fireplaces and original artworks by David Hockney and Roy Lichtenstein – are 198 rooms and 12 suites, custom-furnished in luxury beach décor.
Website: www.shuttersonthebeach.com
Hotel services *Air-conditioning. Babysitting. Bar. Bike hire. Conference facilities. Currency exchange. Fax. Gym. Laundry. Parking (self-park $17; valet $17; daytime $3 first 3 hours, $2 each additional hour). Pool. Restaurants (2). Room service (24-hour). Rooms for disabled. Spa.* **Room services** *Hairdryer. Minibar. Safe. VCR.*

Mid-range

Casa Malibu

22752 Pacific Coast Highway, between Malibu Pier & Los Flores Canyon, Malibu, CA 90265 (reservations 1-800 831 0858/front desk 1-310 456 2219/fax 1-310 456 5418/casamalibu@earthlink.net). Bus 434/I-10, exit PCH north. **Rates** *single/double $99-$199; suite $189-$299.* **Credit** *AmEx, MC, V.*

Hollywood's very own French castle: **Chateau Marmont** *(p98).*

Owners Joan and Richard Page are slowly renovating this small (21 rooms and two suites), two-storey motel – and what they've done so far makes it the best choice in its price range along the northern shore. Each room has classy furnishings and a coffeemaker; some have fireplaces, kitchens and/or private decks. Upgraded rooms include Italian tiling and the kind of seriously stunning bathrooms you'd expect from a luxury hotel. The buildings are covered with flowing vines and surround a garden courtyard and a brick patio that looks directly on to the hotel's private beach.
Hotel services. *Air-conditioning (limited). Fax. Laundry. Parking (free). Private beach.* **Room services** *Fax/modem line. Hairdryer. Refrigerator. VCR.*

Shangri-La

1301 Ocean Avenue, at Arizona Avenue, Santa Monica, CA 90401 (reservations 1-800 345 7829/front desk 1-310 394 2791/fax 1-310 451 3351/nanniluigi@ aol.com). Bus 4, 20, 22, 33, Santa Monica 1, 7, 8, 10/ I-10, exit Fourth-Fifth Street north. **Rates** single/double $115; one-bedroom suite $155-$235; two-bedroom suite $265-$450; penthouse £375-$455. **Credit** AmEx, DC, Disc, JCB, MC, V. **Map 2 A2**

Across from oceanfront Palisades Park, the 1939 art deco Shangri-La prides itself on its spacious rooms and great ocean views. The 55 rooms and suites are nothing fancy, but they are large, and adorned with deco furniture that is mostly beautiful though sometimes scuffed and occasionally tacky. There are full kitchens in almost every room and the bathrooms are clean and roomy. Downsides? There's no pool, room service, restaurant or bar.
Website: www.shangrila-hotel.com
Hotel services *Air-conditioning. Continental breakfast. Fax. Gym. Laundry. Parking (free).* **Room services** *Hairdryer. Refrigerator.*

Budget

Bayside Hotel

2001 Ocean Avenue, at Bay Street, Santa Monica, CA 90405 (front desk 1-310 396 6000/fax 1-310 451 1111). Bus 20, 22, 320, 322, Santa Monica 1, 7, 10/I-10, exit Fourth Street south. **Rates** single/double $104-$119. **Credit** AmEx, Disc, MC, V. **Map 2 A3**

A few blocks south of Santa Monica's shopping and dining action and across from the beach, the Bayside is casual but surprisingly well appointed, considering it's an elderly motel. The 44 rooms range from box to suite, decorated in beiges and pastels with huge windows, somewhat spongy mattresses and ancient coffeemakers; note that none has a phone. Tables and chairs along the balcony walkway are a perfect perch for afternoon sun-catching. A few extra bucks will get you a kitchen or an unobstructed ocean view. Weekly rates.
Hotel services *Air-conditioning. Fax. Parking (free). Phones.* **Room services** *Refrigerator.*

Belle Blue Inn by the Sea

1670 Ocean Avenue, between Pico Boulevard & Colorado Avenue, Santa Monica, CA 90401 (front desk 1-310 393 2363/fax 1-310 393 1063). Bus 20, 22, 320, 322, 434, Santa Monica 1, 7, 10/I-10, exit Fourth Street south. **Rates** single $60-$90; double $65-$110; two-bedroom suites $225. **Credit** AmEx, MC, V. **Map 2 A3**

Sandwiched between the **Loews** hotel (*see p95*) and a string of commercial properties, the two-storey Belle Blue is a half-block stroll from the beach and has 25 cosy rooms and suites entered from a gated cul-de-sac lined with private houses and greenery. The newly renovated rooms are on the small side, with bland, minimalist décor and tiny basic bathrooms. However, many have leather sofas and hardwood floors. The courtyard terrace is the only place you can smoke.
Hotel services *Fax. Parking (free).* **Room services** *Refrigerator.*

The Cadillac

8 Dudley Avenue, at Speedway, Venice, CA 90291 (front desk 1-310 399 8876/fax 1-310 399 4536). Bus 33, 436, Santa Monica 1, 2/I-10, exit Lincoln Boulevard south. **Rates** hostel bed $20; single/double $79-$90; suite $110-$125. **Credit** AmEx, JCB, MC, V. **Map 2 A4**

This four-storey hotel's front yard is the heart of Venice Beach, complete with restaurants, rollerbladers, bikers and sunbathers, and is as vibrant as its beachfront surroundings. It's a hangout for young world travellers, who like the location, amenities and revamped deco interior – a mixture of artistic and vibrant, tasteful and cheesy. The hotel has private rooms (on the tackier side of deco, with black lacquer furnishings and industrial carpeting) and hostel rooms, each with two bunk beds and a shared bath. Common areas include a sun deck and a lounge with pool table. Built in 1905, the hotel was once the summer residence of Charlie Chaplin.
Website: www.leconcierge.com/cadillachotel
Hotel services *Babysitting. Fax. Gym. Laundry. Parking (free). Rooms for disabled. Sauna.*
Room services *Safe.*

Cal Mar Hotel Suites

220 California Avenue, between Second & Third Streets, Santa Monica, CA 90403 (reservations 1-800 776 6007/ front desk 1-310 395 5555/fax 1-310 451 1111). Bus 20, 22, 320, 322, Santa Monica 2, 3, 8, 9/I-10, exit Fourth-Fifth Street north. **Rates** single/double suite $109-$159. **Credit** AmEx, Disc, MC, V. **Map 2 A2**

Visitors from around the world choose the Cal Mar because of its location 2½ blocks from the beach and its enormous apartment-style suites, which are one of the best deals in town. The 36 suites surround a courtyard pool and each can host as many as four people. Almost all the rooms were recently renovated: the décor is mix-matched and homely and each unit has a full kitchen, living room (with a sofa bed) and bedroom (with either one king-size or two twin beds). The Third Street Promenade and oceanfront restaurants are a brief stroll away.
Hotel services *Fax. Parking (free). Pool.*

Hotel Carmel by the Sea

201 Broadway, at Second Street, Santa Monica, CA 90401 (reservations 1-800 445 8695/front desk 1-310 451 2469/fax 1-310 393 4180). Bus 4, 33, 434, Santa Monica 7, 8, 10/I-10, exit Fourth-Fifth street north. **Rates** shared bath $60; single $90; double $129; suite $169. **Credit** AmEx, DC, Disc, JCB, MC, V. **Map 2 A2**

Shutters on the Beach: *see p95.*

Hotel Carmel's 74-year-old walls show their age, but that doesn't stop young tourists from packing the place: its location one block from the beach and around the corner from Third Street Promenade plus its cheap rates make one of the best combos in the area. The 102 rooms (including 13 with shared bathrooms) have wooden furnishings and colourful bedspreads; bathrooms are basic. Suites have refrigerators. **Hotel services** Currency exchange. Fax. Hairdryer. Laundry. Parking ($7.70).

Ocean Lodge Santa Monica Beach Traveler's Hotel

1667 Ocean Avenue, between Colorado Avenue & Pico Boulevard, Santa Monica, CA 90401 (1-310 451 4146/ fax 1-310 393 9621). Bus 20, 22, 320, 322, 434, Santa Monica 1, 7, 10/I-10, exit Fourth Street north. **Rates** $125-$225. **Credit** AmEx, MC, V. **Map 2 A3**
Opposite the **Belle Blue** (see p97) and Santa Monica beach, and near Third Street Promenade, this motel is perfect if you simply want a roof over your head. The 15 rooms are clean and basic and, aside from free parking, there are no ancillary amenities to speak of. If you pack four people in a room with two beds, it'll cost you around $25 per night.
Website: twinnet.com/olhotel
Hotel services Parking (free). **Room services** Hairdryer. Fax. Modem line. Refrigerator.

Venice Beach House Historic Inn

15 30th Avenue, at Washington Boulevard & Pacific Avenue, Venice, CA 90291 (1-310 823 1966/fax 1-310 823 1842). Bus 108, Culver City 1, Commuter Express 437/I-10, exit Fourth-Fifth Street south. **Rates** single/ double $85-$165. **Credit** AmEx, MC, V. **Map 2 A5**
Unlike the larger, less personal hostels, the nine-room Venice Beach House provides luxurious yet informal B&B accommodation on a quaint and quiet Venice street. Built in 1911, it's impeccably furnished with dark wood, rich fabrics and antique everything – right down to the beautiful and well-appointed shared bathrooms. You get a full breakfast, coffee and tea and a peaceful, romantic environment, just 80 steps from the beach. The garden adds to the serene atmosphere. For a jolt back to reality, step outside and walk along the beachfront, where freaks, tourists and bikini-clad California girls are in full force. No smoking inside the hostel.
Hotel services Fax. Parking (free).

Westside: inland
First-class

The Argyle

8358 Sunset Boulevard, betweeen Sweetzer Avenue & La Cienega Boulevard, West Hollywood, CA 90069 (reservations 1-800 225 2637/ front desk 1-323 654 7100/fax 1-323 654 9287). Bus 2, 3, 429, West Hollywood A, B/I-10, exit La Cienega Boulevard north. **Rates** single/double $190-$325; suite $350-$1,500. **Credit** AmEx, DC, MC, V. **Map 4 A/B1**
This is a magnificent 1931 art deco building (previously the Saint James Club) in the heart of the wild side of Sunset Boulevard. The rooms capture the essence of deco luxury with custom-made Italian furniture, including an oval scalloped bed, a postcard desk and even a cute-enough-to-steal deco ice-bucket. Add a stereo system, VCR and a TV that electronically sinks into its own custom-made deco credenza, plus the wild bar scene downstairs, and you've got one of the prime spots in town. The bathrooms are equally stylish, and some have steam showers with Jacuzzi tubs. Rent one of the spacious penthouses (where John Wayne once lived) with rooftop balcony and you're living large. In mid-1998, restaurant **Fenix** started doubling as a 'young Hollywood' nightclub, accessible only if you're a guest of the hotel or on the coveted 'list' (see p121 **Restaurants** and p147 **Bars**).

Hotel services Air-conditioning. Babysitting. Bar. Concierge (24-hour). Conference facilities. Currency exchange. Fax. Gym. Laundry. Parking ($17). Pool. Restaurant. Room service (24-hour). Rooms for disabled. **Room services** Fax. Hairdryer. Minibar. Safe.

Beverly Hills Hotel & Bungalows

9641 Sunset Boulevard, at Rodeo Drive, Beverly Hills, CA 90210 (reservations 1-800 283 8885/front desk 1-310 276 2251/fax 1-310 887 2887). Bus 2, 429/I-405, exit Sunset Boulevard east. **Rates** single/double $300-$400; suite $600-$3,000; bungalow $300-$3,000. **Credit** AmEx, DC, MC, V. **Map 3 B1/2**
A celebrity favourite since its 1912 opening, it has hosted such regulars as Elizabeth Taylor (who bungalowed here with six of her seven husbands) and, after its $100 million renovation (by new owner the Sultan of Brunei), has become a parading ground for the nouveaux riches. The hotel's biggest draw is its true Hollywood feel – grandiose, glamorous and expensive. The décor is pink 'n' palatial, with banana-leaf wallpapered hallways. Each room is giddy with trinkets, gilded mirrors, a great stereo system, two phones with voicemail and a fax. Bathrooms are extravagantly oversized. Lounge in the lobby at teatime, walk in the 12-acre grounds, sunbathe at the fabulous pool (with cabanas for $100 per day) or hang out at the happening **Polo Lounge** (see p126 **Restaurants**) – you can't help but feel that Beverly Hills vibe.
Website: www.thebeverlyhillshotel.com
Hotel services Air-conditioning. Babysitting. Bar. Beauty salon. Conference facilities. Currency exchange. Gym. Jogging trails. Laundry. Parking ($15). Pool. Restaurants (4). Room service (24-hour). Rooms for disabled. **Room services** Hairdryer. Minibar. Modem line. Stereo. Telephones (3). VCR.

Century Plaza Hotel & Tower

2025 Avenue of the Stars, at Constellation Boulevard, Century City, CA 90067 (reservations 1-800 228 3000/ front desk 1-310 277 2000/fax 1-310 551 3355). Bus 22, 27, 28, 316, 328, Santa Monica 5, Antelope Valley 786/ I-405, exit Santa Monica Boulevard east. **Rates** single/ double $245-$270; suite $750-$950; tower single/double $295-$370; tower suite $900-£3,000. **Credit** AmEx, DC, MC, V. **Map 3 B3**
The Century Plaza's 20-storey, high, block-long main building is so enormous that it screams 'convention hotel'. However, the business pill is sweetened by good service, class and respectable style. The rooms (over 1,000 of them) have just undergone a $25 million renovation, but are still stately and come with a desk, coffeemaker, a small balcony with table and chairs plus views (partly obstructed by surrounding high-rises). Bathrooms can be small. The best common areas are by the pool, where swimming is accompanied by fitness facilities and patio lunches. Its location, near the ABC Entertainment Center, Schubert Theater, Century City Shopping Center and Beverly Hills, makes entertainment and retail cravings easy to satisfy.
Website: www.centuryplaza.com
Hotel services Air-conditioning. Babysitting. Bars (2). Beauty salon. Conference facilities. Currency exchange. Fax. Gym. Laundry. Parking (self-park $10; valet $19.50). Pool. Restaurants (2). Room service (24-hour). Rooms for disabled. **Room services** Hairdryer. Minibar. Safe.

Chateau Marmont

8221 Sunset Boulevard, between Sweetzer Avenue & Havenhurst Drive, Hollywood, CA 90046 (reservations 1-800 242 8328/front desk 1-323 656 1010/fax 1-310 655 5311). Bus 2, 3, 429/I-10, exit La Cienega Boulevard east. **Rates** single/double $195-$240; suite $700-$1,400; bungalow $700-$800. **Credit** AmEx, DC, MC, V. **Map 4 B1**

Since 1933, stars like Greta Garbo, Clark Gable, Roman Polanski, Jim Morrison and the unfortunate John Belushi (who overdosed in a bungalow here) have called the Marmont home. Standing just above Sunset Strip, it's a seven-storey structure modelled after the Loire Valley's Château Amboise. A steady stream of partying rock stars took its toll on the place until 1990, when the new owners returned it to its original funky-but-chic aesthetic. Rooms are large and unpretentious (ask for a bungalow for the ultimate home-from-home feel), furnishings are straight out of a Barbara Stanwyck movie and the service is casual and discreet. Add the too-cool and famous clientele, the hotel's lounge and outdoor dining patio, the popular next-door **Bar Marmont** (*see p148* **Bars**) and immediate access to Sunset Boulevard, and you've got one of the hippest hotels in Los Angeles.

Hotel services *Air-conditioning. Babysitting. Bar. Fax. Gym. Laundry. Parking ($12.50). Pool. Restaurant. Room service (24-hour).* **Room services** *CD player & CD library. Hairdryer. Minibar. Refrigerator. Safe. Telephones with voicemail (2). VCR.*

Four Seasons Beverly Hills

300 S Doheny Drive, at Burton Way, Beverly Hills, CA 90048 (reservations 1-800 332 3442/front desk 1-310 273 2222/fax 1-310 859 9048). Bus 27, 316, 576/I-10, exit Robertson Boulevard north. **Rates** *single $295-$365; double $325-$415; suite $475-$4,500.* **Credit** *AmEx, DC, JCB, MC, V.* **Map 3 C2**

Look through any doorway in the first-floor common areas, filled with original art and bountiful flower arrangements, and you'll see beautifully landscaped gardens. At weekends, when press junkets are in full force, you'll probably sight a famous face, too. The rooms have been renovated in soothing colours, but the walkout balcony, three phones, armoire and impeccable bathrooms remain. The clinchers, however, are the chi-chi, fourth-floor pool, with cabanas, an awning-covered outdoor gym, a luncheon patio, restaurants renowned for power breakfasts and formal dinners and the schmoozy cocktail lounge – all sprinkled with the beautiful people. Utterly refined.

Website: www.fourseasons.com

Hotel services *Air-conditioning. Babysitting. Bar.*

The hippest hotel in town: the Philippe Starck-designed **Mondrian**. *See page 101.*

Continental breakfast. Conference facilities. Currency exchange. Fax. Gym. Laundry. Parking (self-park free; valet $18). Pool. Restaurants. Room service (24-hour). **Rooms for disabled. Room services** Hairdryer. Minibar. Refrigerator.

Hotel Bel-Air

701 Stone Canyon Road, at Bellagio Road, Bel Air, CA 90077 (reservations 1-800 648 4097/front desk 1-310 472 1211/fax 1-310 476 5890). Bus 2, 302, 429, 576/ I-405, exit Sunset Boulevard east. **Rates** single/double $325-$435; suite $525-$2,500. **Credit** AmEx, Disc, JCB, MC, V.

The 12-acre, 92-room Bel-Air is sophisticated, luxurious, romantic and surprisingly pastoral – and stars and bigwigs have been retreating here since long before Marilyn booked her room by the pool. Heaven begins at the bridged entryway surrounded by Swan Lake (yes, real swans) and continues with the lavish sculpted-wilderness gardens, cocktails in the wood-panelled bar and the pool surrounded by palms and bougainvillea. The rooms, in two-storey, pink stucco, 1920s mission-style buildings, are impeccably stylish: each has a private entrance from the gardens. The dining room is a local favourite, so it's not unusual to see celebs (Nancy Reagan still lunches and Jack Nicholson's daughter was wed here), but don't attempt commemorative pics – exclusivity means no cameras are allowed.

Hotel services Air-conditioning. Babysitting. Bar. Beauty salon. Conference facilities. Currency exchange. Fax. Gym. Laundry. Parking (free). Restaurant. Room service (24-hour). Rooms for disabled. **Room services** Hairdryer. Minibar. VCR.

L'Ermitage Beverly Hills

9291 Burton Way, at Elm Drive, Beverly Hills, CA 90210 (reservations 1-800 800 2113/front desk 1-310 278 3344/fax 1-310 278 8247). Bus 27, 576/I-405, exit Wilshire Boulevard east. **Rates** rooms $385-$448; suites $700-$3,800. **Credit** AmEx, Disc, JCB, MC, V.
Map 3 C2

When it comes to amenities, the new L'Ermitage beats any luxury hotel in the state. After a $65 million renovation, this 124-room, fibre-optic-wired retreat caters to its wealthy visitors with an extensive and comfortable lobby lounge, formal dining room, rooftop restaurant with panoramic view, VIP cigar lounge, rooftop swimming pool and cabanas, spa, top-notch gym, steam room and sauna, and a staff that never says 'No'. But that's just for starters. The standard rates may be the highest in town, but the price tag includes huge, minimalist-modern rooms, massive bathrooms with whirlpool baths, a mobile phone, 40in TVs, DVD players and discs (including Pamela & Tommy Lee's renowned home movie), and a slew of freebies such as Aveda bathroom unguents, free local calls and gourmet chocolates upon check-in. Phew. And there's no charge for room service.

Website: www.lermitagehotel.com
Hotel services Air-conditioning. Bar. Beauty salon. Concierge. Currency exchange. Fax. Garden. Gym. Laundry. Limo service. Massage. Parking ($21). Pool. Restaurants (2). Room service (24-hour). Rooms for disabled. Smoking floors (2). **Room services** Business facilities. CD/DVD player. Dataports (4). Fax/printer/copier. Minibar. Safe. Telephones (5, plus cellphone on room's direct line). TVs (living room & bathroom; Web TV on request).

Hotel Nikko at Beverly Hills

465 S La Cienega Boulevard, at Clifton Way, LA, CA 90048 (reservations 1-800 645 5624/hotel operator 1-310 247 0400/fax 1-310 247 0315). Bus 27, 105, 576/ I-10, exit La Cienega Boulevard north.
Rates single $270-$345; double $295-$370; suite $600-$1,800. **Credit** AmEx, DC, DC, Disc, JCB, MC, V.
Map 4 B3

Worldly business travellers know the Nikko is one of the finest contemporary hotels in LA. The marble lobby is dominated by a Japanese-style rock garden with fountains and a towering atrium; behind the Hana Lounge is the pool area (as seen in the film *Indecent Proposal*); and upstairs, the 302 rooms range from 'deluxe' to the $1,800-per night Presidential Suite. Each has contemporary Japanese-style furnishings, subdued lighting and luxuriously soft, canopied beds. Bathrooms are huge; some have sunken Japanese tubs. Most impressive are the suites, combining full-blown luxury with New York apartment appeal, and offer all the facilities a businessperson could want.

Hotel services Air-conditioning. Babysitting. Bar. Conference facilities. Currency exchange. Fax. Gym. Laundry. Parking (self-park free; $16.50 valet). Pool. Restaurant. Room service (24-hour). Rooms for disabled. Sauna. **Room services** CD player. Hairdryer. Minibar. Refrigerator. Safe. VCR.

Mondrian Hotel

8440 Sunset Boulevard, at La Cienega Boulevard, West Hollywood, CA 90069 (reservations 1-800 525 8029/ front desk 1-323 650 8999/fax 1-323 650 5215). Bus 2, 3, 429/I-10, exit La Cienega Boulevard north. **Rates** single/double $240-$310; suite $300-$900; penthouse $2,100-$2,600. **Credit** AmEx, DC, Disc, JCB, MC, V. **Map 4 A/B1**

Ian Schrager Hotels, renowned for its Paramount and Royalton hotels in New York and the Delano in Miami, acquired this giant, 12-storey property and transformed it into the hottest hotel in town (read: snobby and swarming with celebrities). The environment plays on scale and illusion, with huge terracotta pots cradling short trees around the panoramic pool area, indoor furniture outside and vice versa, freeform light sculptures in the lobby and excessive Hollywood attitude. The chic, minimalist monotone rooms

Regent Beverly Wilshire: *see p103.*

usually come with kitchens, large windows and wannabe-Zen messages on the walls. One of the biggest draws of being a guest here is access to the super-fashionable **SkyBar** (*see p148* **Bars**).

Hotel services *Air-conditioning. Babysitting. Bar. Beauty salon. Children's play area. Conference facilities. Currency exchange. Fax. Gym (24-hour). Jacuzzi. Laundry. Parking ($17.50). Pool. Restaurant. Room service (24-hour). Rooms for disabled. Sauna. Steam room.* **Room services** *Hairdryer. Minibar. Safe.*

The Peninsula Beverly Hills

9882 Little Santa Monica Boulevard, at Wilshire Boulevard, Beverly Hills, CA 90212 (reservations 1-800 462 7899/front desk 1-310 551 2888/fax 1-310 788 2319). Bus 4, 304/I-405, exit Wilshire Boulevard east. **Rates** *single/double $325-$500; suite $650-$3,000.* **Credit** AmEx, DC, Disc, JCB, MC, V.
Map 3 B2/3

Bellhops in snappy white uniforms and gold-crested caps greet the famous, the wealthy and the corporate élite at the Peninsula's discreet location, eight blocks off Rodeo Drive. The mahogany lobby bar packs in the cigar-smokers, gold-diggers and men on the prowl. The enormous **Living Room** (*see p143* **Coffeehouses**) is an out-and-out luxury lounge, where guests sip tea or champagne and look out on to the sculpted garden. There are just under 200 rooms and suites: conservative and refined, they are fitted out with Tiffany amenities and Rodeo's finest linens. The pool is a fabulous spot, with patio dining and a Jacuzzi overlooking the city and the hills. Dining is five-star, of course.

Hotel services *Air-conditioning. Babysitting. Bar. Concierge. Conference facilities. Fax. Laundry. Limo service. Gym. Parking ($17). Pool. Restaurants (3). Room service (24-hour). Rooms for disabled. Spa.* **Room services** *Fax/modem line. Hairdryer. Minibar. Refrigerator. Safe. VCR.*

The Regent Beverly Wilshire

9500 Wilshire Boulevard, between Rodeo & El Camino Drives, Beverly Hills, CA 90212 (reservations 1-800 421 4354/front desk 1-310 275 5200/fax 1-310 274 2851). Bus 20, 21, 22, 320, 322/I-10, exit Wilshire Boulevard east. **Rates** *single/double $270-$500; suite $495-$7,500.* **Credit** AmEx, Disc, MC, V. **Map 3 C2**

This 275-room, Italian Renaissance-style hotel (as featured in *Pretty Woman*) is one of LA's favourite luxury hotels. Built in 1928, it is renowned for its old-world opulence and high-brow and famous clientele. Rooms are in two wings: the original Wilshire wing and the more recently constructed Beverly. The latter is currently being renovated, but the cognoscenti prefer the Wilshire wing anyway (Warren Beatty, at the height of his playboy career, shacked up here for 12 years). There's a cosy bar frequented by cigar-smoking businessmen, tourists and expensively dressed women. Visiting heads of state go for the $7,500- or $5,000-a-night Presidential Suites.
Website: www.rih.com
Hotel services *Air-conditioning. Babysitting. Ballroom. Bar. Beauty salon. Conference facilities. Currency exchange. Fax. Gym. Health spa. Hot tubs. Laundry. Parking ($18). Pool. Restaurants (3). Room service (24-hour). Rooms for disabled.* **Room services** *Hairdryer. Minibar. Refrigerator. Safe. VCR.*

Renaissance Beverly Hills

1224 S Beverwil Drive, at Pico Boulevard, LA, CA 90035 (reservations 1-800 228 9290/front desk 1-310 277 2800/fax 1-310 203 9537). Bus 3, Santa Monica 7, 13/I-10, exit National Boulevard/Overland Avenue north. **Rates** *single/double $160-$225; suite $325-$850.* **Credit** AmEx, DC, Disc, MC, V.
Map 3 C3

This whimsical, colourful and artistic hotel is masked by

*The tropical **Hotel Del Capri**: see p104.*

its bland 1970s-style, high-rise exterior. The lounge is pure creative fantasy and the rooms boldly follow suit in a whirlwind of colour and design detail. All rooms have a balcony, some looking on to the nearby hills to the north (sadly, across the parking lot), others to the flatlands to the south. Bathrooms have plenty of elbow room and granite detail. The three 'Club Level' floors cost around $45 extra, for which you get a special lobby serving light meals and a limited bar. It's not a walkable part of Beverly Hills, but then again, it's peaceful because of it.
Website: www.renaissancehotels.com or www.marriott.com
Hotel services *Air-conditioning. Babysitting. Bar. Conference facilities. Currency exchange. Fax. Gym. Laundry. Parking ($15.40). Restaurant. Room service (24-hour). Rooms for disabled.* **Room services** *Fax. Hairdryer. Minibar.*

Sunset Marquis Hotel & Villas

1200 N Alta Loma Road, at Sunset Boulevard, West Hollywood, CA 90069 (reservations 1-800 858 9758/front desk 1-310 657 1333/fax 1-310 652 5300). Bus 2, 3, 20, 27, 429/I-10, exit La Cienega Boulevard north. **Rates** *suite $255-$5,000; villa $350-$1,330.* **Credit** AmEx, DC, MC, V.

Bang in the middle of West Hollywood, this 114-room, three-storey building was once part of Lionel Barrymore's estate. Now it's divided into one- and two-bedroom suites with private patios and balconies, many overlooking the pool. The 12 private villas clustered around a smaller, more exclusive pool have boarded stars such as Julio Iglesias and Aerosmith's Steven Tyler and come with their own private butler. The hotel's Whiskey Bar is a popular watering hole.

Hotel services *Air-conditioning. Babysitting. Bar. Conference facilities. Fax. Laundry. Gym. Parking ($15). Pool. Restaurant. Room service (24-hour). Rooms for disabled.* **Room services** *CD player. Hairdryer. Safe. VCR.*
Branch: Westwood Marquis, 930 Hilgard Avenue, Westwood, CA 90024 (reservations US 1-800 421 2317/UK 0800 897529/front desk 1-310 208 8765/fax 1-310 824 0355).

Wyndham Bel Age Hotel
1020 N San Vicente Boulevard, at Sunset Boulevard, West Hollywood, CA 90069 (reservations 1-800 996 3426/front desk 1-310 854 1111/fax 1-310 854 0926). Bus 2, 3, 105, 302, 429/I-10, exit La Cienega Boulevard north. **Rates** *corporate $169-$199; one-bedroom suite $235-$325; two-bedroom suite $275-$475; Grand Class suite $400-$700.* **Credit** AmEx, DC, Disc, JCB, MC, V.
Map 4 A1
Located just below Sunset Strip and around the corner from the infamous **Viper Room** nightclub (*see p217* **Nightlife**), this nine-storey, brown stucco structure contains 200 one- and two-bedroom suites. Other attractions include the top-class Diaghilev Restaurant and the La Brasserie nightclub. A kitschy collection of sculptures and artworks in the common areas add a dash of flavour to the décor, and the rooftop pool allows for fun in the sun. The suites are large and comfortable and should be completely renovated by early 1999.
Hotel services *Air-conditioning. Babysitting. Bars (2). Beauty salon. Conference facilities. Fax. Gym. Jacuzzi. Laundry. Parking ($16; daytime $6 2 hours, $2 each additional hour). Pool. Restaurants (2). Room service (24-hour). Rooms for disabled.* **Room services** *Hairdryer. Minibar. Refrigerator.*

Mid-range

Beverly Plaza
8384 W Third Street, at Orlando Avenue, LA, CA 90048 (reservations 1-800 624 6835/front desk 1-323 658 6600/fax 1-323 653 3464). Bus 16/I-10, exit La Cienega Boulevard north. **Rates** *single/double $169-$218.* **Credit** AmEx, DC, JCB, MC, V. **Map 4 B3**
The trendy Beverly Plaza is an arty 98-room hotel with fanciful décor and a popular restaurant. Nearby are Miracle Mile's shopping and La Cienega Boulevard's 'restaurant row'. The oversized rooms were renovated in 1996 with custom furnishings, hand-painted headboards and plenty of taupe. Bathrooms are on the small side, but the perks – including dressing gowns, 'natural' shampoos and soaps, chocolates, free newspapers and $10 taxi coupons per day – plus eager-to-please staff make up for such shortcomings.
Website: wwwcalendarlive.com/beverlyplazaht1
Hotel services *Air-conditioning. Babysitting. Bar. Beauty services. Conference facilities. Laundry. Parking ($13). Pool. Room service (24-hour). Rooms for disabled. Sauna. Spa.* **Room services** *Hairdryer. Minibar.*

Hilgard House Westwood Village
927 Hilgard Avenue, at Le Conte Avenue, Westwood, CA 90024 (reservations 1-800 826 3934/front desk 1-310 208 3945/fax 1-310 208 1972). Bus 2, 21, 429, 576, Santa Monica 1, 2, Culver City 6/I-405, exit Wilshire Boulevard north. **Rates** *single/double $109-$139.* **Credit** AmEx, DC, Disc, MC, V.
Across from the Westwood Marquis is the understated but elegant 47-room Hilgard House. The lobby looks like an English library while the rooms are cosy European in style. It lacks extras – there's no pool, gym, bar or restaurant – but with the free continental breakfast, free parking and good

location (surrounded by UCLA and Westwood shopping) you've got yourself a darn good deal.
Hotel services *Air-conditioning. Babysitting. Continental breakfast. Fax. Laundry. Parking (free).* **Room services** *Hairdryer. Refrigerator.*

Hotel Del Capri
10587 Wilshire Boulevard, at Westholme Avenue, West LA, CA 90024 (reservations 1-800 444 6835/front desk 1-310 474 3511/fax 1-310 470 9999). Bus 20, 21, 22/I-405, exit Wilshire Boulevard east. **Rates** *single $85-$140; double $95-$140; suite $120-$140.* **Credit** AmEx, Disc, MC, V.* **Map 3 A3**
This hotel is a floral oasis offering splendid respite from the surrounding Westwood high-rises and Wilshire Boulevard traffic. It's a favourite with touring dance companies and Europeans, who enjoy the community atmosphere, and is adorned with tropical fish tanks, fountains and other decorative touches rarely found in such affordable lodgings. Service is superlative. The 80 rooms and suites are divided between a hotel block and a motel-style building around a lovely courtyard pool, ensconced among lush flowers and trumpet vines. Perks include continental breakfast delivered at any time of day, meeting rooms, a coin-operated laundry, and close proximity to Westwood Village and UCLA, which are both six blocks away. The pool is open 24 hours and VCRs are available for $8 per day.
Hotel services *Air-conditioning. Conference facilities. Continental breakfast. Fax. Laundry. Parking (free). Pool. Safe. Whirlpool.* **Room services** *Fax/modem line. Hairdryer. Refrigerator. Safe.*

Le Montrose Suite Hotel

900 Hammond Street, at San Vicente Boulevard & Doheny Drive, West Hollywood, CA 90069 (reservations 1-800 776 0666/front desk 1-310 855 1115/fax 1-310 657 9192). Bus 2, 3, 105, 429/I-405, exit Santa Monica Boulevard east. **Rates** *junior suite $270; executive suite $360; one-bedroom suite $440.* **Credit** *AmEx, DC, JCB, MC, V.* **Map 4 A2**

What Le Montrose lacks in service and amenities, it makes up for with affordable, comfortable rooms and its central location (just two blocks south of Sunset Boulevard). Each of the 125 suites is spotless, tastefully furnished in contemporary style and wired for modem hook-up, and the beds are wonderfully large. The rooftop pool has a commanding view of LA, looking out over the nearby Beverly Center, and is the only one in town with free cabanas. Ideal for families and couples wanting a comfortable weekend hideaway.
Website: www.travelweb12000.com/
Hotel services *Air-conditioning. Babysitting. Bicycles. Conference facilities. Currency exchange. Fax. Gym. Laundry. Parking ($14). Pool. Restaurant. Room service (24-hour). Rooms for disabled.* **Room services** *Hairdryer. Minibar. Refrigerator. Safe.*

Ramada West Hollywood

8585 Santa Monica Boulevard, between La Cienega Boulevard & Rugby Drive, West Hollywood, CA 90069 (reservations 1-800 228 2828/front desk 1-310 652 6400/fax 1-310 652 2135). Bus 4, 105, 304/I-10, exit La Cienega Boulevard. **Rates** *single/double $95-$149;*

suites $169-$275. **Credit** AmEx, DC, Disc, JCB, MC, V.
Map 4 A2
Slap-bang in the middle of gay West Hollywood, within walking distance of Sunset Strip and the Beverly Center and next door to a very popular Starbucks and a fabulous health food supermarket, the Ramada is a plain but friendly chain hotel. Although it's a bit motel-like in atmosphere and look, it has some nice neo-art deco touches and was completely redecorated in mid-1998. The 175 rooms include 45 suites (each with a refrigerator, minibar, microwave, coffeemaker and hairdryer), of which 20 are double-storey, with the sleeping area above the living space and bathroom. Best of all are the two, humungous corner suites with spiral staircases and giant beds. The entrance is easy to miss: look for the wiggly coloured metal sculptures.
Website: www.ramada-wh.com
Hotel services *Air-conditioning. Bar. Business centre. Parking ($12). Car rental. Concierge. Fax. Fitness centre (off-site, 24-hour, $15). Laundromat. Pool. Restaurant. Safe. Shuttle service.* **Room services** *Fax/modem line. Telephones with voicemail (2).*

Summit Hotel Rodeo Drive

360 N Rodeo Drive, at Brighton Way, Beverly Hills, CA 90210 (reservations 1-800 468 3541/front desk 1-310 273 0300/fax 1-310 859 8730). Bus 20, 21, 22/I-405, exit Wilshire Boulevard east. **Rates** *single/double $130-$239; suite $375-$440.* **Credit** *AmEx, DC, Disc, JCB, MC, V.* **Map 3 C2**
The 88-room Summit is squeezed into the middle of Rodeo's exorbitant shopping action – the optimum spot for folks in

Best for...

...pooling it

Four Seasons' rooftop pool offers panoramic views, but you're more likely to focus on the Bronzed and the Beautiful who lounge cabana-side or work out in the adjoining open-air gym. Runners-up are the **Beverly Hills Hotel**, where handsome young poolhands cater to your every whim, and the **Peninsula Beverly Hills**, whose Jacuzzi is surrounded by a rooftop lawn and is perhaps the perfect place in the metropolis to catch a romantic sunset. Hard-bodied extroverts prefer the **Mondrian**, where poolside performance is viewed by visitors to the SkyBar.

...partying on the patio with celebs

The SkyBar, the bar LA loves to hate at the **Mondrian**, maintains its celebrity clientele by enforcing a red-rope policy, which means if you're not a guest of the hotel, a famous face or on 'the list', you're not through the door. While the ratio of celebs to normal Joes is lower than it was in its prime, the spectacular views and parade of prowling singles keep everyone from Leonardo DiCaprio and Jerry Seinfeld to Denzel Washington and Puff Daddy stopping by for a drink.
Ditto for the nearby **Argyle**, where on weekend nights you might have a brush with Hugh Hefner, members of the Counting Crows or a slew of upcoming actors and models.

...escaping LA chaos

Spend even an afternoon at the pastoral **Hotel Bel-Air** and you'll feel pampered and rejuvenated. The **Ritz-Carlton** hotels **Huntington** and **Laguna Niegel** also do the trick, combining grand surroundings with impeccable service and an air of exclusivity.

...fine dining

Even locals venture to **Loews Santa Monica** to dine at its French Lavande restaurant. **Hotel Bel-Air**'s stellar menu, whether served in the formal dining room or on the bougainvillea-draped terrace, makes it one of the town's top dining spots, while in West Hollywood the **Wyndham Bel Age**'s Diaghilev restaurant provides excellent cuisine and an impressive selection of top vodkas, served by the shot.

...making new friends

Stay at the funky **Cadillac** on Venice Beach and you can't help but meet up with adventurous young Europeans on holiday. The ultra-budget **Banana Bungalow**'s resort-like atmosphere also allows for plenty of mingling.

...ghost-spotting

The **Clarion Hollywood Roosevelt** has housed some of Hollywood's greatest bygone entertainers. Apparently, some still haven't checked out.

...breaking the bank

L'Ermitage comes with all the bells and whistles – and then some – but you'll have to pay the big bucks to take advantage of the plethora of little touches.

...budget bargains

Beverly Laurel Motor Hotel's strategic location, hip décor and adjoining restaurant, combined with its rock-bottom prices, make it a best bet (*see* **photo**). The **Best Western Hollywood Hotel**'s cheery disposition and Hollywood access provide another top choice. In Downtown, even the luxury hotels don't have the atmosphere that comes free at the **Hotel Figueroa**.

Budget Inn

In the heart of Hollywood
Located on the World Famous Sunset Strip

Within walking distance to:
- Hollywood Walk of Fame
- Mann's Chinese Theater
- Hollywood Bowl

Easy access to:
- Universal Studios
- Planet Hollywood
- Hard Rock Café
- World Famous Night Clubs
- Venice Beach
- Santa Monica
- Beverly Hills

Room Rates: $45 – $80 + tax, based on availability.
- Free Continental Breakfast
- Free Parking
- New Rooms
- Refrigerators
- Door-to-Door Airport Shuttle
- All Major Sight Seeing Tours Available

Budget Inn

682 Sunset Boulevard, Hollywood, CA 90028
Phone: (213) 465 7186 Fax: (213) 962 7663
Toll Free: 1-800-405-MOTEL
All Major Credit Cards Accepted

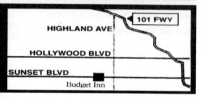

★★

Hollywood Best Inn

Daily Rate: $32.95 and up
excluding weekends/holidays
Weekly Rates Available

WALKING DISTANCE TO: Hollywood
Walk of Fame, Mann's Chinese
Theatre • Universal Studio's Package
available, Hollywood Bowl & clubs
(everything 2 miles)

**Newly renovated
Remote color TV • HBO
A/C • Refrigerator &
Microwave in select rooms
Continental Breakfast
Free parking**

TOUR FOR MAJOR ATTRACTIONS
DIRECTIONS: EXIT 101 (CAHUENGA BOULEVARD)
AIRPORT SHUTTLE AVAILABLE

Hollywood Best Inn

1822 North Cahuenga Boulevard
Hollywood, California 90028

TEL 213/467.2252
FAX 213/465.8316

★★

need of a little retail therapy. Built in 1962, the hotel is undergoing renovation and may close for a while. There's not much public space: only a second-floor sun deck and an adjoining restaurant – the kitchen is currently closed (it should be back in action in January 1999), but a limited menu is still available. There is, however, a free shuttle to Summit's Bel Air property, which has a pool and sports facilities. Once the renovation is complete, expect to find contemporary-chic décor and small but well-appointed bathrooms.
Website: www.summithotel.com
Hotel services *Air-conditioning. Babysitting. Bar. Fax. Laundry. Parking (valet $16). Pool & sports facilities (off-site). Restaurant. Room service (6.30-10.30am, noon-10pm).* **Room services** *Hairdryer. Minibar.*

Budget

Beverly House Hotel

140 S Lasky Drive, at Little Santa Monica Boulevard, Beverly Hills, CA 90212 (reservations 1-310 271 8141/ front desk 1-310 271 2145/fax 1-310 276 8431). Bus 4, 20, 21, 22, 27/I-405, exit Santa Monica Boulevard east. **Rates** *single $99; double $109.* **Credit** *AmEx, DC, JCB, MC, V.* **Map 3 B3**
This quiet, quaint European-style hotel, located behind the Peninsula Hotel and close to Rodeo Drive, is far less glitzy than its surroundings, but remarkably affordable, clean and accommodating. A cornucopia of antiques grace the front lounge and extend into the three levels of 50 simple guest rooms. The adjoining first-floor 'suite' is ideal for families. Perks include a free continental breakfast, parking and homely touches missing in most LA hotels. Some rooms have fridges and VCRs.
Hotel services *Air-conditioning. Continental breakfast. Fax. Laundry. Parking (free).*

The Secret Garden

PO Box 46164, Los Angeles, CA 90046 (1-323 656 8111/fax 1-323 656 9992). **Rates** *single/double without en suite shower $65; with shower $85.* **No credit cards.**
LA's best B&B is so secluded that the management asked us not to print the address. But we can reveal that it's tucked away at the bottom of Laurel Canyon, within walking distance of the most buzzing shopping/eating complex in the area, and is an oasis of tranquillity. Run by the ex-maître d' of the famous industry restaurant Chasen's, the Secret Garden boasts five beautiful rooms, some with en suite showers and, as its name suggests, a gorgeous fairy-tale garden complete with Jacuzzi. While serving his home-cooked breakfasts, your host Raymond is also happy to regale his guests with delicious tales of celeb goings-on at Chasen's.
Hotel services *Breakfast. Jacuzzi. Laundry. Parking (free). Piano.*

The Standard

8300 Sunset Boulevard, at Sweetzer Avenue, West Hollywood, CA 90069 (1-323 650 9090/fax 1-323 650 2820). Bus 2, 3, 429/I-10, exit La Cienega Boulevard north. **Rates** *double from $145.* **Credit** *AmEx, DC, MC, V.* **Map 4 B1**
Chateau Marmont's owner recently purchased this three-storey Sunset Strip retirement home, and as we go to press is converting it into what will undoubtedly be the hippest budget hotel in town. The 143 rooms are being transformed into retro 1960s digs. The outdoor pool has the same coveted views as the nearby Mondrian, but for a whole lot fewer bucks. A similarly styled diner, which faces the boulevard, promises to attract Hollywood hipsters as well as fashionable young travellers.
Hotel services *Air-conditioning. Bar. Fax. Gym. Laundry. Parking. Pool. Restaurant. Room service (24-hour). Rooms for disabled.* **Room services** *CD player. Fax/modem line. Minibar. Refrigerator. VCR.*

Hollywood & Midtown

First-class

Hotel Sofitel Los Angeles

8555 Beverly Boulevard, at La Cienega Boulevard, West Hollywood, CA 90048 (reservations 1-800 521 7772/ front desk 1-310 278 5444/fax 1-310 657 2816). Bus 14, 16, 105, DASH Fairfax, Hollywood/I-10, exit La Cienega Boulevard north. **Rates** *single/double $230-$250; suite $265-$500.* **Credit** *AmEx, DC, MC, V.* **Map 4 A/B 2/3**
The mature and tasteful, French-owned, 311-room Sofitel attracts guests with its calming and well-appointed lobby, its location – directly across the street from the Beverly Center and near 'restaurant row' – and rooms decorated with flowery wallpaper, adobe-coloured paint and above-par fabrics. There's no wacky Hollywood vibe here, just peaceful surroundings and fashionably classic décor, which attract plenty of foreigners and an older business clientele. Guests get a freshly baked baguette upon check-out.
Website: www.hotelsofitel.com
Hotel services *Air-conditioning. Babysitting. Bar. Conference room. Currency exchange. Fax. Gym (24-hour). Laundry. Parking ($16.50). Pool. Restaurants. Room service (24-hour). Rooms for disabled. Safe. Sauna.* **Room services** *Fax/modem line. Hairdryer. Minibar. Telephones with voicemail (2).*

Mid-range

Clarion Hollywood Roosevelt Hotel

7000 Hollywood Boulevard, between N Highland & N La Brea Avenues, Hollywood, CA 90028 (reservations 1-800 252 7466/front desk 1-323 466 7000/fax 1-323 466 9376). Bus 1, 180, 181, 212/US 101, exit Highland Avenue south. **Rates** *single $109-$119; double $129-$139.* **Credit** *AmEx, DC, Disc, JCB, MC, V.* **Map 5 A1**
In the middle of gritty Hollywood Boulevard stands the surprisingly pleasant 320-room Hollywood Roosevelt, a 1927 landmark building that was once the hub of Hollywood hullabaloo. The first Academy Awards were held here, Marilyn Monroe lived here for eight years and legend has it that Bill 'Bojangles' Robinson taught Shirley Temple how to tap dance up the lobby staircase. The staff say the place is haunted by Montgomery Clift and Marilyn (her room is still intact, her wardrobe mirror hangs in the lower lobby and some claim they've seen her face in it), and you can't help but feel the old Hollywood magic in the air. The two-storey Spanish Colonial lobby, with hand-stencilled ceilings and arched doorways, is impressive and well kept. The rooms are less glamorous, but are individually decorated. There's a David Hockney painting on the bottom of the pool.
Website: www.hotelchoice.com
Hotel services *Air-conditioning. Babysitting. Bars (2). Conference facilities. Currency exchange. Fax. Gym. Laundry (valet). Parking ($9.50). Pool. Restaurant. Room service (6am-11pm). Rooms for disabled.* **Room services** *Minibar. Safe.*

Budget

Best Western Hollywood Hills Hotel

6141 Franklin Avenue, between N Gower Street & Vista del Mar, Hollywood, CA 90028 (reservations 1-800 287 1700/front desk 1-323 464 5181/fax 1-323 962 0536). Bus 26, Community Connection 208/US 101, exit Gower Street north. **Rates** *single/double $50-$85.* **Credit** *AmEx, DC, Disc, MC, V.* **Map 5 B1**
No cheap hotel celebrates Hollywood and festivity like this one. Located near the 101 freeway, the family-run hotel's exterior looks grim; but inside, the lobby is swank and

MODERN PAINTERS

Major British and American writers contribute to the U.K.'s most controversial art magazine:

- JULIAN BARNES

- WILLIAM BOYD

- A.S.BYATT

- PATRICK HERON

- HILTON KRAMER

- JED PEARL

- CHARLIE FINCH

- MATTHEW COLLINGS

- DAVID SYLVESTER

Britain's best-selling quarterly journal to the fine arts.

moody, walls throughout are adorned with murals and posters of movie stars and cartoon characters, and every guest room has a glittery star on the door. There are two buildings: the 'new' one, renovated in 1998, is motel-like, with outdoor entrances looking down on the courtyard pool and dapper, modern décor in the rooms; the older building has larger, less formal rooms. All rooms have coffeemakers, refrigerators, kitchenettes and access to the pool and laundry. The **Hollywood Hills Coffee Shop**, the old-fashioned coffeeshop/liquor store off the lobby (open for breakfast, lunch and dinner) is a favourite stopover for hip celebrities such as Quentin Tarantino and various grunge bands, along with guests ranging from young Europeans to families (*see p131* **Restaurants**).
Hotel services *Air-conditioning. Fax. Laundry. Parking (free). Pool. Restaurants.* **Room services** *Hairdryer. Kitchenette. Refrigerator.*

Beverly Laurel Motor Hotel

8018 Beverly Boulevard, at Laurel Avenue, LA, CA 90048 (1-213 651 2441/fax 1-213 651 5225). Bus 14, 217, DASH Fairfax/I-10, exit La Cienega Boulevard north. **Rates** *single $55-$65; double $60-$70.*
Credit AmEx, DC, MC, V. **Map 4 B2**
Its exterior looks like a dive and it's priced like a dive, but the owners' artistic flare has turned the Beverly Laurel into one of the most tasteful and stylish motels around, with gold-and-black checkered bedspreads, wooden headboards inlaid with black-and-white photos, black vinyl chairs and groovy deco tables. In most rooms, one wall is painted brilliant blue. This is one of the best deals in town – especially for larger parties. Some rooms have kitchens. The adjoining restaurant, Swingers (1-323 653 5858), is a popular breakfast and late-night spot for West LA hipsters.
Hotel services *Air-conditioning. Continental breakfast. Fax. Parking (free). Pool. Restaurant.* **Room services** *Microwave oven. Refrigerator.*

Bevonshire Lodge Motel

7575 Beverly Boulevard, at Curson Avenue, LA, CA 90036 (1-323 936 6154/fax 1-323 936 6640). Bus 14, DASH Fairfax/I-10, exit La Brea Avenue north. **Rates** *single $43.89; double $48.45.* **Credit** AmEx, MC, V. **Map 4 C2**
The enormous rubber tree growing from a hole in the Bevonshire's lobby carpet and extending along the two-storey windows is an indication of how long this motel has been around. Though a splash of paint is needed in some areas, every bathroom has just been remodelled and new carpeting has been laid. Rooms are sizeable and many come with complete kitchens ($6 extra); all circle the courtyard pool. There's no restaurant, but the popular Authentic Café is across the street and many of Beverly's trendy boutiques and eateries are nearby.
Hotel services *Air-conditioning. Fax. Parking (free). Safe.* **Room services** *Refrigerator.*

Dunes Sunset Motel

5625 Sunset Boulevard, between N Wilton & Saint Andrews Places, Hollywood, CA 90028 (reservations 1-800 452 3863/front desk 1-323 467-5171/fax 1-323 469 1962). Bus 2, 3, 207, 357/US 101, exit Sunset Boulevard east. **Rates** *single/double $49-$58.*
Credit AmEx, Disc, MC, V. **Map 5 C1/2**
If your idea of a Hollywood vacation has a *Leaving Las Vegas* scenario, check into the gritty and cheap Dunes. It ain't pretty – just basic motel rooms that are in serious need of TLC – but the parking's free, there's an adjoining diner, and you'll feel at home nursing a hangover behind closed curtains. This section of Sunset, which is closer to Los Feliz, is anything but glamorous (don't stroll at night), but you won't find rates cheaper than these.
Hotel services *Air-conditioning. Bar. Parking (free). Restaurant.* **Room services** *Refrigerator.*

The great-value **Best Western**. See p108.

Highland Gardens Hotel

7047 Franklin Avenue, at La Brea Avenue, Hollywood Hills, CA 90028 (reservations 1-800 404 5472/ front desk 1-323 850 0536/fax 1-323 850 1712). Bus 1, 2, 3, 4, 212, 420/US 101, exit Highland Avenue south. **Rates** *single $60-$80; double $60-$80; suite $80-$110.* **Credit** AmEx, MC, V.
Map 5 A1
Rooms at the Highland Gardens may be reminiscent of a *Brady Bunch* set, but they're huge, dirt cheap and only a few blocks from star-paved Hollywood Boulevard. Common areas consist of a breakfast room (with free coffee and pastries), a simple lobby and a heated courtyard pool. The rooms surround the pool and offer the basics in 1970s colours and décor, with enormous bedrooms, kitchens and/or living rooms. Per square foot, no hotel in town can touch this for value. A ghoulish fame claim is that Janis Joplin overdosed here – room 105 – on 4 October 1970, when the hotel was called the Landmark.
Hotel services *Air-conditioning. Continental breakfast. Fax. Laundry. Parking (free). Pool.* **Room services** *Hairdryer. Refrigerator. Safe.*

Magic Hotel

7025 Franklin Avenue, between La Brea & Orange Avenues, Hollywood, CA 90028 (reservations 1-800 741 4915/front desk 1-323 851 0800/fax 1-323 851 4926/ info@magichotel.com or reservations@magichotel.com). Bus 1, 180, 181, 212, 217, 429/US 101, exit Highland Avenue north. **Rates** *single $55-$69; executive suite $69-$85; deluxe suite $79-$109; two-bedroom suite $105-$139.* **Credit** AmEx, DC, JCB, MC, V.
Across the street from the Highland Gardens is the motel-like Magic Hotel. Here, too, rooms are large and tidy, with newer furnishings and carpeting and stiff mattresses. Old magic show posters adorn the walls, in reference to the neighbouring Magic Castle, a private magicians' club. All rooms surround the courtyard, which has a pool and lounge furniture, and all (bar the singles) have a kitchen. The deluxe rooms have safes.
Website: www.magichotel.com
Hotel services *Air-conditioning. Fax. Laundry. Parking (free). Pool.* **Room services** *Refrigerator.*

Hotel chains

There are hundreds of chain hotels, ranging from budget to luxury, throughout Los Angeles. Contact any of the following and they're likely to have a property in the area of your choice.

First-class

These hotels often have swimming pools, a concierge, restaurants, transportation to and from the airport and other services usually associated with very large luxury hotels. Rates change constantly, but you may be able to secure a reservation for around $100 a night (excluding the Ritz, which won't start much under $200); rack rates go up to $350.

● **Ritz Carlton** *1-800 241 3333*
The three properties in the area all come with expected Ritz panache, excellent service and lovely grounds.
● **Hilton Hotels** *1-800 445 8667*
Hilton's enormous Beverly Hills location is the most highly regarded. More mid-range options include its convention hotel-like Burbank, LAX airport and Universal City locations.
● **Hyatt** *1-800 233 1234*
Locations include Downtown, Century City and the more moderately priced West Hollywood hotel.
● **Sheraton Hotels & Inns** *1-800 325 3535*
The most popular outpost is the Santa Monica location. There are also hotels in Downtown and near LAX.

Mid-range

These tend to have full-service facilities, including pools, restaurants and standard large hotel amenities. They're less luxurious than first-class and, in most cases, less expensive. Rates vary, but you can generally count on securing a reservation for under $150 a night, with $70-$80 the rock bottom.

● **Holiday Inn** *1-800 465 4329*
Its 42 locations in Los Angeles County cover everywhere from Hollywood to Downtown, LAX and Anaheim. Prices begin at under $100 for the 'Express' (budget) properties. For 'Luxury' (full-service), expect to pay about $150.
● **Howard Johnson** *1-800 654 2000*
Inns in Hollywood, Anaheim and throughout LA County.
● **Marriott** *1-800 228 9290*
Its full-service hotels/resorts are more expensive and include 42 locations throughout the area; there are also five motels, including one in Anaheim.
● **Radisson** *1-800 333 3333*
Its 11 LA County properties include Midtown, Beverly Hills Santa Monica, the Valleys, Culver City and Anaheim.

Budget

The cheapest accommodation is usually a motel, which may or may not have a pool, restaurant or other amenities. There are literally hundreds in Southern California, with rates varying dramatically. You can count on well-kept rooms, and often some of the best prices around, starting at under $40 a night.

Best Western *1-800 528 1234*
Comfort Inns *1-800 228 5150*
Days Inn *1-800 325 2525*
Motel 6 *1-800 446 8356*
Super 8 *1-800 800 8000*
Travelodge *1-800 578 7878*

Downtown

First-class

Hotel Inter-Continental

California Plaza, 251 S Olive Street, at Second Street, LA, CA 90012 (reservations 1-800 442 5251/front desk 1-213 617 3300/fax 1-213 617 3399/ losangeles@ interconti.com). Metro Civic Center/Tom Bradley/bus 14, 24, 420, Commuter Express 418, 425/ I-110, exit Fourth Street east. **Rates** *single $150-$240; double $210-$250; suite $375-$1,300.* **Credit** *AmEx, Disc, MC, V.*
Map 7 B2
A welcome departure from generic business hotels, the new high-rise Inter-Continental, located next door to the Museum of Contemporary Art, blends the traditional with the boldly creative – and the result is impressive. An enormous, light lobby, with grand floral arrangements, a huge, bright yellow sculpture and calming orchestral music give way to soothing taupe-and-olive rooms. Each has an en suite bath and shower, a chaise longue, a comfy love seat and an oversized desk: all a step above corporate. 'Club level' guests are housed on floors 16 or 17, with access to the hotel's business centre. This is the hotel where OJ Simpson's jury stayed.
Website: www.interconti.com
Hotel services *Air-conditioning. Babysitting. Bar. Conference facilities. Currency exchange. Fax. Laundry (valet). Parking (self-park $18; valet $20; daytime $2.20 per 20 mins). Pool. Restaurants (2). Room service (24-hour). Rooms for disabled. Sauna. Steam room.*

Room services *Hairdryer. Minibar. Modem line. Refrigerator. Telephone with voicemail.*

Regal Biltmore

506 S Grand Avenue, at Fifth Street, LA, CA 90071 (reservations 1-800 245 8673/front desk 1-213 624 1011/fax 1-213 612 1545). Metro Seventh Street/Metro Center/bus 16, 18, 78, 96, Foothill Transit 492/I-110, exit Sixth Street east. **Rates** *single/double $145-$235; suite $290-$2,000.* **Credit** *AmEx, Disc, JCB, MC, V.*
Map 7 B3
Built in 1923, the 11-storey Biltmore is the oldest hotel in Downtown LA, and still maintains the Italian-Spanish Renaissance elegance that enticed such VIPs as Winston Churchill, Princess Margaret and Presidents Truman, Kennedy, Ford, Carter and Reagan to pay a visit. The cathedral-like lobby and common areas are masterpieces, with hand-painted frescos (by Italian artist Giovanni Smeraldi, who also contributed to the White House and the Vatican), bas-relief décor, a fountain, wooden floors, beautifully ornate ceilings with glass inlay and hand-painted detail, and stupendous floral arrangements. Some rooms look a little worn. Best is the executive floor, which has newly decorated rooms with twice-daily maid service. The health club has a Roman-style steam room, pool, Jacuzzi and sauna.
Website: www.thebiltmore.com
Hotel services *Air-conditioning. Babysitting. Bars (3). Beauty salon. Conference facilities. Currency exchange. Fax. Gym. Jacuzzi. Laundry. Parking ($17.50). Pool. Restaurants (3). Room service (24-hour). Rooms for disabled. Sauna. Steam room.*

Room services *Minibar (most rooms). Refrigerator (most rooms). Telephone with voicemail.*

Wyndham Checkers Hotel

535 S Grand Avenue, between Fifth & Sixth Streets, LA, CA 90071 (reservations 1-800 996 3426/front desk 1-213 624 0000/fax 1-213 626 9906). Metro Seventh Street/Metro Center/bus 37, 78, 79/I-110, exit Sixth Street east. Rates single $159-$259; double $179-$279. Credit AmEx, DC, Disc, JCB, MC, V.
Map 7 B3
Combine first-class service and a boutique environment and you've got Checkers, a Downtown favourite. The recently renovated, Asian-influenced lobby is full of worldly visitors chatting over cappuccino, while the award-winning Checkers restaurant serves lofty fare to a wealthy clientele. Light and airy rooms are individually decorated in understated luxury, with original art and marble side tables and bathrooms.
Website: www.wyndham.com
Hotel services *Air-conditioning. Babysitting. Bar. Conference facilities. Fax. Laundry. Parking ($18). Pool. Restaurant. Room service (24-hour). Rooms for disabled. Sauna. Whirlpool.* Room services *Fax/modem line. Hairdryer. Minibar. Telephones with voicemail (3).*

Mid-range

Hotel Figueroa

939 S Figueroa Street, at Olympic Boulevard, LA, CA 90015 (reservations 1-800 421 9092/front desk 1-213 627 8971/fax 1-213 689 0305). Metro Seventh Street/ Metro Center or Westlake/Macarthur Park/bus 27, 28, 81, 328, 427, Commuter Express 419/I-110, exit Ninth Street east. Rates single/double $78-$150. Credit DC, JCB, MC, V. Map 7 A4
An exotic oasis near the Convention Center, the 285-room Figueroa is Southwestern funky-chic. It's a whirlwind of hand-painted everything, including elevators, doors and ceilings, with Mexican tables and chairs and huge pots filled with exotic plants. Some rooms are large, some small and each is uniquely decorated; the older TVs and furnishings could be ugly on their own, but in combination they create a style. Especially cool are the Clay Pit Indian restaurant and the crowded Verandah Bar, which overlooks the pool and garden. Most rooms have refrigerators.
Hotel services *Air-conditioning. Bar. Fax. Laundry. Parking (free). Restaurants (2).*

Westin Bonaventure Hotel & Suites

404 S Figueroa Street, at Fourth Street, LA, CA 90071 (reservations 1-800 228 3000/front desk 1-213 624 1000/fax 1-213 612 4800/labon@westin.com). Metro Seventh Street/Metro Center/bus 53, 60, 471, Montebello 40/I-110 north, exit Third Street east. Rates single $139-$177; double $139-$195; suite $219-$239. Credit AmEx, DC, Disc, JCB, MC, V.
Map 7 A/B2
Five gargantuan, cylindrical, mirrored towers fused together, the Bonaventure is a major contributor to Downtown LA's skyline. From the outside, it's a visual wonder; from the inside, a mini-city. Occupying an entire city block, the hotel has 12 glass elevators that shoot you to your (rather small) room (one of 1,368). Each room has floor-to-ceiling windows, wall safes, voicemail and a modem port. Tower suites are twice the size. There's an 85,000sq ft (7, 900sq m) health, tennis and fitness centre, a revolving rooftop lounge, Top of Five (*see p150* Bars) and a shopping gallery with over 40 shops and restaurants. There's also one all-suite tower with a Japanese guest floor (24-hour translation, Japanese newspapers, TV and breakfast), and sky bridges to the World Trade Center.
Website: www.westin. com
Hotel services *Air-conditioning. Bars (3). Beauty salon.*

Conference facilities. Currency exchange. Fax. Gym. Laundry. Parking ($18.15). Pool. Restaurants (2). Room service (24-hour). Rooms for disabled. Spa.
Room services *Fax/modem line. Hairdryer. Safe. Telephone with voicemail.*

Budget

Kawada Hotel

200 S Hill Street, at Second Street, LA, CA 90012 (reservations 1-800 752 9232/front desk 1-213 621 4455/fax 1-213 687 4455). Metro Civic Center/Tom Bradley/bus 420, 425/I-110, exit Ninth Street east. Rates single $79-$109; double $89-$119; corporate single/ double $75. Credit AmEx, MC, V. Map 7 B2
What the four-storey Kawada lacks in décor, it more than makes up for with cleanliness and value. Take the slow lift to spotless rooms, complete with kitchenette, coffeemaker and desk. Though watercolour paintings, pot-pourri, pretty soaps and a bathroom phone attempt to make the place feel upmarket, rooms here are hardly luxurious. Some can be small (request a larger one), there's no closet (just a clothing nook) and most offer a view that will inspire you only to keep the blinds drawn. However, the only real bummer is that parking is uncovered and half a block away.
Website: www.hotelbook.com
Hotel services *Air-conditioning. Bar. Conference facilities. Fax. Laundry. Parking ($6.60). Restaurant. Room service (7am-2pm, 5-11pm). Rooms for disabled. Shuttle to Downtown (free).* Room services *Kitchenette. Refrigerator. VCR.*

Stillwell Hotel

840 S Grand Avenue, between Eighth & Ninth Streets, LA, CA 90017 (front desk 1-800 553 4774/1-213 627 1151/fax 1-213 622 8940). Metro Seventh Street/Metro Center or Pershing Square/bus 40, 78, 79, 96, DASH C, E/I-110, exit Ninth Street east. Rates single $39-$49; double $49-$59. Credit AmEx, DC, MC, V. Map 7 B3
Aged and ultra-budget, the 232-room Stillwell ain't much to look at, but it's certainly cheap and located only a few blocks from the LA Convention Center and the California Mart, which makes it perfect for convention-goers. The staff can be unfriendly, but they offer an all-you-can-eat Indian buffet lunch for $7.95, as well as authentic barflies in Hank's Bar (*see p150* Bars), and a budget restaurant.
Hotel services *Air-conditioning. Bar. Conference facilities. Fax. Laundry. Parking ($3). Restaurants (3). Rooms for disabled.* Room services *Refrigerator.*

The Valleys

First-class

Ritz-Carlton Huntington

1401 S Oak Knoll Avenue, at Wentworth Avenue, Pasadena, CA 91106 (reservations 1-800 241 3333/front desk 1-626 568 3900/fax 1-626 568 3700). Bus 485/ I-110, exit Glenarm Street east. Rates single $185-$295; double $200-$1,310; suite $400-$2,000. Credit AmEx, DC, Disc, JCB, MC, V.
On 23 pristine acres in Pasadena, the Ritz's 1907 palace stands amid Japanese gardens and vast grassy expanses. It's a perfect escape from the traffic and crowds of LA; Jim Carrey rents the Presidential Suite when he's in the neighbourhood. Rooms and cottages are elegant and the service divine. Splash in the pool, stroll through the gardens, snack on sushi, swing dance on Friday night or indulge in Sunday's champagne brunch: whatever you do, you'll be hard-pressed to find a reason to leave this peaceful (albeit pricey) retreat.
Hotel services *Air-conditioning. Babysitting. Bar. Beauty salon. Bicycles. Conference facilities. Currency*

exchange. Fax. Gym. Laundry. Parking ($15). Pool & swimming lessons. Restaurants (2). Room service (24-hour). Rooms for disabled. Sports facilities. **Room services** *Hairdryer. Minibar. Refrigerator. Safe. Telephones (3). VCR.*

Mid-range

Sheraton Universal

333 Universal Terrace Parkway, at Lankershim Boulevard, Universal City, CA 91608 (reservations 1-800 325 3535/front desk 1-818 980 1212/fax 1-818 985 4980). Bus 420, 425, 522/US 101, exit Lankershim Boulevard north. **Rates** *single/double $225-$275; suite $325-$1,500.* **Credit** *AmEx, DC, Disc, MC, V.*

Renovated in 1994, the 444-room Sheraton Universal is an attractive corporate-style hotel near burgeoning Universal CityWalk, Universal Studios and all the major freeways. There's a respectable gym, complimentary shuttle to Universal Studios and special holiday packages that include admission to the Universal Studios Tour. Club-level rooms offer plenty of perks.

Website: www.sheraton.com

Hotel services *Air-conditioning. Babysitting. Bar. Conference facilities. Fax. Games room. Gym. Laundry. Parking ($14). Pool. Restaurant. Room service (6am-midnight). Rooms for disabled. Whirlpool.* **Room services** *Fax/modem line. Hairdryer. Minibar. Safe. Telephone with voicemail.*

First-class

The Disneyland Hotel

1150 W Cerritos Avenue, between West & Walnut Streets, Anaheim, CA 92802 (reservations 1-714 956 6400/front desk 1-714 778 6600/fax 1-714 956 6597). Bus 460/I-5, exit Ball Avenue west. **Rates** *single/double $180-$275; suites $350-$2,000.* **Credit** *AmEx, DC, MC, V.* **Hotel services** *Air-conditioning. Babysitting. Bar. Concierge. Conference facilities. Currency exchange. Fax. Gym. Laundry. Parking ($10). Pools (3). Restaurants (11). Room service (5am-1am). Rooms for disabled. Shops.* **Room services** *Hairdryer. Minibar.*

The Disneyland Pacific Hotel

1717 S West Street, at Katella Avenue, Anaheim, CA 92802 (1-714 999 0990/fax 1-714 776 5763). Bus 460/I-5, exit Ball Road west. **Rates** *tower $180-$215; concierge level $240-$270; suite $350-$450.* **Credit** *AmEx, DC, MC, V.* **Hotel services** *Air-conditioning. Babysitting. Bars (2). Business centre (concierge level only). Conference facilities. Currency exchange. Fax. Gym. Laundry. Parking ($10). Restaurants (2). Room service (5.30am-1am). Rooms for disabled.* **Room services** *Hairdryer. VCR (concierge level only).*

Both of Disney's properties are adjacent to the theme park and surrounded by restaurants, a pond (used as an ice rink in winter), paddle boats, an outdoor pool with a sandy shore and volleyball court, shops and the monorail that picks passengers up and shuttles them to Disneyland. The rooms themselves are rather disappointing: not in quality, but because they're not fantastical enough. The Disneyland Hotel (1,000-plus rooms) features traditional Disney (Mickey, Donald et al) while the Pacific (500 rooms) honours modern Disney (such as *The Lion King*). Kids are especially fond of the Disneyland's Goofy's Kitchen, where they can breakfast with their favourite Disney characters. The Pacific, the fancier of the two, is currently less central, but when Disney's enormous new extension is completed (in 2001), the hotel will look directly on to the new park. Big bonus: with the purchase of a basic Disney passport guests can enter the park 1½ hours before the general public.

Website: www.disney.com/Disneyland/plan/resort_hotels/

Ritz-Carlton Laguna Niegel

33533 Ritz-Carlton Drive, at Pacific Coast Highway, Dana Point, CA 92629 (reservations 1-800 241 3333/front desk 1-714 240 2000/fax 1-714 240 0829). Bus Orange County Transit 1/I-5, exit Crown Valley Parkway west. **Rates** *single/double $215-$415; club floor $275-$475; suite $500-$2,750.* **Credit** *AmEx, DC, Disc, MC, V.*

California's only five-star and five-diamond resort perches on a 150ft (46m) bluff in Dana Point, overlooking the adjoining golf course and the shimmering Pacific Ocean. The four-storey Mediterranean-style hotel is about as good as it gets, with an art gallery, three renowned restaurants and every type of resort recreation you could wish for (including two miles of hotel-front beach). The kids' programme will keep young folk busy all day while parents relax, and you can always blast over to Disneyland, 35 miles (56km) away. The rooms have private balconies, many overlooking the ocean.

Hotel services *Air-conditioning. Babysitting. Bars (2). Beauty salon. Business centre. Car & limo hire. Conference facilities. Currency exchange. Room service (24-hour). Rooms for disabled. Fax. Golf. Gym. Laundry. Parking ($17). Pools (2). Restaurants (3). Sauna. Sports facilities. Whirlpool.* **Room services** *Hairdryer. Minibar. Refrigerator. Safe. Telephones (3).*

Mid-range

Candy Cane Inn

1747 S Harbor Boulevard, at Katella Avenue, Anaheim, CA 92802 (1-800 345 7057/front desk 1-714 774 5284/fax 1-714 772 5462). Bus 460/I-5, exit Harbor Boulevard south. **Rates** *single/double $69-$119.* **Credit** *AmEx, DC, Disc, MC, V.*

Ask locals where to stay and they're likely to direct you to the Candy Cane Inn. No, it's not pink and stripy: the name dates back to the Inn's beginnings in the early days of Disneyland, but it's come a long way since then. Today, it is one of the best mid-range options in the area. The 192 rooms have recently been renovated (work on other areas continues as we go to press) and there's plenty of greenery plus a pool with a children's wading area. And the management really cares about its guests.

Hotel services *Air-conditioning. Continental breakfast. Fax. Laundry. Parking (free). Rooms for disabled. Shuttle to Disneyland (free).*

Budget

Penny Sleeper Inn

1441 S Manchester Avenue, at Harbor Boulevard, Anaheim, CA 92802 (reservations 1-800 854 6118/front desk 1-714 991 8100/fax 1-714 533 6430). Bus 460, Orange County Transit 43, 46/I-5, exit Harbor Boulevard south. **Rates** *single/double $36-$46.* **Credit** *AmEx, Disc, MC, V.*

You're likely to hear cars passing on the neighbouring freeway, and the beds and furniture look like they haven't been updated since the 1970s (think bright orange), but if you're looking for a clean crash pad with a pool for next to nothing, this 192-room hotel is the spot.

Website: www.pennysleeper.com

Hotel services *Air-conditioning. Babysitting. Continental breakfast. Fax. Laundry. Parking (free). Pool. Rooms for disabled. Shuttle to Disneyland (free).* **Room services** *Hairdryer. Safe.*

Relax poolside at the **Banana Bungalow.**

Hostels

Banana Bungalow Hollywood

2775 W Cahuenga Boulevard, between Mulholland Drive & Franklin Avenue, Hollywood, CA 90068 (reservations 1-800 446 7835/front desk 1-323 851 1129/fax 1-213 883 1960). Bus 163, 420/US 101, exit Hollywood Bowl/Highland Avenue north. **Rates** *shared room $18-$20; single/double $55.* **Credit** *MC, V.*

This small international village just above the Bowl is the perfect place from which to explore Hollywood. Forty-five well-kept bungalows (sleeping four to six, each with its own bathroom) make up the dormitory accommodation and there are ten private rooms, each with a TV, lockers and bathroom. Guests have access to a pool, kitchen, pool table, video games, a simple restaurant serving sandwiches and burgers for under five bucks, and three dance parties a week. Its location is a bit removed from the action, but the hostel provides daily shuttles to attractions and nightlife.

Website: www.bananabungalow.com
Hotel services *Airport, bus & train pick-up (free). Fax. Gym. Internet access. Kitchen. Laundry. Market. Parking (free). Pool. Restaurant. Theatre. Vending machines.*
Room services *Lockers.*

Hostelling International Los Angeles

1436 Second Street, at Santa Monica Boulevard, Santa Monica, CA 90401 (reservations 1-800 909 4776/front desk 1-310 393 9913/fax 1-310 393 1769). Bus 4, 20, 33, 434, Santa Monica 1, 2, 3, 10/I-10, exit Fourth-Fifth Street south. **Rates** *members bed in dorm with 8-10 beds $20.16; in 6-bed dorm $21.28; in 4-bed-dorm $22.40;*

single/double $56; *non-members* $3 extra per night.
Credit MC, V. **Map 2 A2**
If a beach vacation is your thing, book in advance at this enormous Santa Monica hostel located two blocks from the shore and a few strides from Third Street Promenade. Rooms are either dorm-style (sleeping four, six, eight or ten) or private. The latter are small and basic – just a bed, side table, lamp, mirror and dresser (no wardrobe) – but spotless. Bring flip-flops to wear in the shower. No en suite baths.
Website: www.hostelweb.com
Hotel services *Bike storage. Conference facilities. Fax. Games room. Kitchen. Laundry. Library. Lockers. Pool table. Restaurant.*

YMCA of Glendale

140 N Louise Street, at Wilson Avenue, Glendale, CA 91206 (1-818 240 4130/fax 1-818 500 1737). Bus 177, 180, 181, 201, Glendale B Line 4/US 134, exit Central Avenue south. **Registration** 7am-10pm. **Rates** bed in dorm $19.80; $99 per week; key deposit $3.
No credit cards.
The maximum stay in this 75-room hostel is 'as long as we're happy with you', and there's no restriction on coming back any time of day or night. Note that the Hollywood Wilshire YMCA no longer has rooms.
Website: www.ymca.net
Hotel services *Gym/sports centre. Lounge. Microwave. Parking (free). Payphone. Storage facilities. Vending machine.*

Camping

It's worth considering camping in LA: obviously it's cheap, but it's also pleasant – state campgrounds tend to be located in beautiful surroundings and each site has a picnic table and fire ring. Yes, it involves a drive – but what doesn't in LA?

Leo Carrillo State Beach

35000 Pacific Coast Highway, just north of Mulholland Highway, Malibu, CA 90265 (reservations 1-800 444 7275/1-818 880 0350). Bus 434/I-10, exit PCH north. **Rates** $17-$18 per site. **Credit** AmEx, MC, V.
Tent camping is allowed in the park, except on the north side of the beach, which is tarmac and so open only to camper vans. There are 127 sites, bathrooms, pay showers, a small shop and access to the beach and hiking/biking trails.
Website: www.cal-parks.ca.gov

Malibu Beach RV Park

25801 Pacific Coast Highway, at Corral Canyon & Puerco Canyon Road, Malibu, CA 90265 (reservations 1-800 622 6052/1-310 456 6052). Bus 434/I-10, exit PCH north. **Rates** tents from $20.16; RVs $30-$42.
Credit AmEx, Disc, MC, V.
A commercial (and so less lovely) site largely aimed at recreational vehicle (RV) campers, but with 50 tent sites and plenty of facilities, including a Jacuzzi.
Website: www.malibubeachrv.com

Rented accommodation

Rent is relatively cheap in Los Angeles, but most rental agreements are for a minimum of one year. If you're staying for at least two weeks, you could try **Oakwood Corporate Housing**, a nationwide organisation specialising in short-term lets in purpose-built apartment complexes. Most rents are for a minimum of one month, though its Marina del Rey location will rent apartments for two weeks. Call 1-800 888 0808 for its central office and price details (website: www.oakwood.com).

Restaurants

If LA is a melting-pot of the world's cultures, just imagine what the restaurants are like. Here's the menu.

More than ever, Los Angeles is in the fast track when it comes to modish restaurants. The city's sprawling geography means that dining out is often not just the main event of an evening out, but its only attraction. So restaurateurs try to outdo one another in impressing, indulging and satiating all their clients' senses.

This has given rise to the renaissance of the supper club – such as **Lucky Seven**, **Atlas Bar & Grill**, the **Conga Room**, **Dominick's**, **North**, **360** and the soon-to-open **Supperclub 180** – where entertainment is laid on. Then there are restaurants where the design is paramount – **Tahiti**, **Vida** and **Jones** – and others where the vibe is such that regulars spend hours there: some such as **Lola's**, the **Los Angeles Palm**, **Voda**, **Indochine**, **Coco Pazzo**, **Drai's** and **Morton's**. And there are restaurants so pretty and chic – **Les Deux Café** and the **Little Door** – that it hardly seems to matter whether you even eat.

One person who understands more than most the importance of restaurants – whether you're there to make deals, conduct a romance or simply break bread – is Barbara Lazaroff, wife of chef **Wolfgang Puck** and partner and designer of **Spago of Beverly Hills**, absolutely the city's restaurant of the moment. Puck, the ultimate celebrity chef, rules over a culinary empire: he's the official chef for the Academy Awards banquet and owns three restaurants – **Chinois on Main**, **Granita** and **Spago of Beverly Hills**, as well as myriad Wolfgang Puck cafés around the country and his own frozen-food company.

Following him, other top-ranking restaurant owners have expanded from their flagships. **Patina**'s Joachim Splichal has launched the more affordable chain of **Pinot** bistros. **La Cachette**'s Jean-François Meteigner has opened **829 Bistro**. Pierro Selvaggio, who owns the sublime **Valentino**, also has Primi and **Posto**.

While Pacific New Wave – also known as 'fusion' or 'global' cooking – is still very much a fundamental part of California cuisine – and ever evolving, with inventive chefs at **Splash!**, **Michi**, **Xiomara** and **Jozu** – there is also a growing contingent of diners returning to more purist roots. Indeed, even Puck, one of the early practitioners of eclectic cuisine, is putting some rather sturdy Austrian dishes on his menu, while **L'Orangerie** – which some say is the only true classical French

restaurant in town – and **Valentino** – Italian food only, however inventive – are still two of the town's most respected and popular eating spots.

Los Angeles's multi-ethnic community also offers myriad (and cheaper) dining experiences, from Korean barbecue through superb Oaxacan specialities and Thai treasures. All in all, it's a city where those with a sense of culinary adventure, regardless of budget, are well indulged.

INSIDE INFORMATION

Although this used to be a city with a reputation for closing early, Angelenos are rediscovering their sense of joie de vivre and restaurants are staying open later and later. It's always best to book, to valet park and show your appreciation with a minimum 15% tip; 20% is not considered exorbitant. Average prices given are for a typical meal for that restaurant: thus, for three courses at a more formal restaurant, two at a more casual one. Drinks are not included.

Also, check out the bold letter on the front of the establishment you're intending to dine at. The LA County Health Services Department now grades restaurants on their health-code compliance. A 'C' rating or lower is questionable. And you can now enjoy smoke-free eating, thanks to the city's new anti-smoking law.

LA International Airport

Encounter

For listings, see p147 **Bars**. **Lunch** 11am-4pm, **dinner** 5-10pm, daily. **Average** $30. **Credit** AmEx, DC, Disc, MC, V.

The food and service at the space-age Encounter, inside the fabulous 1960s Theme Building, are reminiscent of one too many other airport eateries. But it's a fun place to have a drink and enjoy the entertaining retro-futuristic décor if you have time to kill before a flight.

Valet parking $5.

Landrey's

Sheraton Gateway Hotel, 6101 W Century Boulevard, between Airport & Sepulveda Boulevards, Westchester (1-310 642 4820). Bus 40, 117/I-405, exit La Tijera Boulevard west. **Dinner** 6-10pm Mon-Sat. **Average** $28. **Credit** AmEx, DC, Disc, MC, V.

Landrey's is the answer to fine dining at LAX. Indonesian-style lobster cakes, smoked salmon rolled in a grain pancake, and rabbit stuffed with sun-dried tomatoes and herbs are a few of the daring creations in chef Dana Taus's repertoire. There's also a sushi and cigar bar.

Parking free up to 2 hours with validation.

*Enjoy country cooking, in Santa Monica, at **Blueberry**.*

Westside: beach towns

Santa Monica

Blueberry
510 Santa Monica Boulevard, between Fifth & Sixth Streets, Santa Monica (1-310 394 7766). Bus 4, 304, Santa Monica 1, 7, 10/I-10, exit Fourth-Fifth Street north. **Open** 8am-3pm daily. **Average** $12.
Credit MC, V. **Map 2 A2**
Cutting-edge breakfast and lunch place where a white picket fence surrounds the tiny upstairs mezzanine and waitresses dressed in denim overalls, white T-shirts and bright blue scarves serve country food: blueberry pancakes with blueberry compôte and blueberry ice-cream, some mighty fine Southern fried chicken and big, two-hand sandwiches.

The Broadway Deli
1457 Third Street Promenade, at Broadway, Santa Monica (1-310 451 0616). Bus 33, 304, 434, Santa Monica 2, 4/I-10, exit Fourth-Fifth Street north. **Breakfast** 7am-3pm Mon-Fri; 8am-3pm Sat, Sun. **Lunch** 11am-5pm daily. **Dinner** 5pm-midnight Mon-Thur, Sun; 5pm-1am Fri, Sat. **Average** $18. **Credit** AmEx, MC, V. **Map 2 A2**
A vast, airy deli with a long counter and many booths, which is conveniently close to several cinemas and treats its New York Jewish fare with the same respect one would haute cuisine. You'll like the gravadlax and smoked salmon served with chewy country breads – but it's all good.
Valet parking $3.50.

Chez Jay
1657 Ocean Avenue, between Pico Boulevard & Colorado Avenue, Santa Monica (1-310 395 1741). Bus 20, 33, 333, 320, 434, Santa Monica 1, 7, 10/I-10, exit Fourth-Fifth Street north. **Breakfast** 9am-2pm Sat, Sun. **Lunch** noon-2pm Mon-Fri. **Dinner** 6-10.30pm Mon-Sat; 5.30-11pm Sun. **Average** $17. **Credit** AmEx, MC, V. **Map 2 A3**

Ten tables (some in booths), a dozen barstools, a massive schooner wheel, real portholes and sawdust on the floor: this is the beachfront roadhouse that owner Jay Fiondella opened in 1959. It's low-key and funky, and the clientele includes a few celebrities in search of anonymity (Sean Penn, Warren Beatty and Henry Kissinger). The simple fare (steak or fish in old-fashioned, heavy sauces) isn't bad, either.
Valet parking $2.

Chinois on Main
2709 Main Street, at Hill Street, Santa Monica (1-310 392 9025). Bus 33, 333, Santa Monica 1, 2, 10/I-10, exit Fourth Street south. **Lunch** 11.30am-2pm Wed-Fri. **Dinner** 6.30-10.30pm Mon-Sat; 6.30-10pm Sun. **Average** $45. **Credit** AmEx, DC, Disc, MC, V. **Map 2 A4**
Some people believe this Wolfgang Puck eaterie is his finest. The cuisine goes by the name of Pacific New Wave, which means a mélange of different ethnicities (Asian, French, Californian) rolled into one, sometimes creating confusion, sometimes delighting, all topped off with wife Barbara Lazaroff's kitsch design and a slew of deliriously friendly waiting staff. We suggest barbecued baby pork ribs in a honey-chilli sauce and Shanghai lobster in spicy curry.
Valet parking $3.25.

The Jamaican Café
424 Wilshire Boulevard, between Fourth & Fifth Streets, Santa Monica (1-310 587 2626). Bus 20, 21, 22/I-10, exit Fourth-Fifth Street north. **Lunch** noon-3pm Tue-Thur; noon-6pm Fri. **Dinner** 6-10pm Tue-Thur; 6-11pm Fri; 3-11pm Sat; 3-9pm Sun. **Average** $18. **Credit** AmEx, Disc, MC, V. **Map 2 A2**
No longer Jamaican-owned but an authentic Jamaican restaurant nevertheless, where the jerked meats are the signature dishes, along with the curried goat and wonderful fruit punch.

JiRaffe
502 Santa Monica Boulevard, at Fifth Street, Santa Monica (1-310 917 6671). Bus 434, Santa Monica 2, 3, 9/I-10, exit Fourth-Fifth Street north. **Lunch** noon-2pm

THE ACTIVE ISSUE NO.172 · photographed by elfie semotan january/february 98

£2.50 US$6

i-D

i-Deas,fashion,clubs,music,people

steady...

Subscribe now to i-D to receive 12 issues
full of the latest i-Deas, fashion, clubs, music and people.

- -

SUBSCRIPTIONS

annual subscription rates
(please choose)

uk
a (£30.00)

europe
a (£40.00)

world[airmail]
a (£60.00)

Mastercard/Visa/Amex number:

☐ ☐ ☐ ☐ ☐ ☐ ☐ ☐ ☐ ☐ ☐ ☐ ☐ ☐ ☐ ☐

Signature:_____

Expiry date:_____

Name:_____

Address:_____
_____
_____

Tel:_____

Date:_____

If you do not have a credit card send a cheque/ postal otder in pounds sterlingmade payable to
Levelprint Ltd. Do not forget to fill in your name and address. Return the above form to i-D, Universal
House, 251-255, Tottenham Court Road, London, W1P OAE. For enquiries please call 0171 813 6170

Tue-Fri. **Dinner** 6-10pm Tue-Fri; 5.30-11pm Sat; 5.30-9pm Sun. **Average** $16-$32. **Credit** AmEx, DC, MC, V. **Map 2 A3**

Young, goatee-ed chefs Josiah Citrin and Raphael Lunetta have been buddies since they were 12, and have been cooking together for the past six years. Breathtaking dishes include rock shrimp ravioli with tomatoes and green onions, and scallops with braised endive in a rich, dark gravy. The décor is white and unpretentious. This is one of Santa Monica's best restaurants.
Parking $3.50.

Michael's

1147 Third Street, between California Avenue & Wilshire Boulevard, Santa Monica (1-310 451 0843). Bus 20, 22, Santa Monica 2, 3/I-10, exit Fourth-Fifth Street north. **Lunch** 11.30am-2.30pm Tue-Fri. **Dinner** 6-10.30pm Tue-Sat. **Average** $45. **Credit** AmEx, JCB, MC, V. **Map 2 A2**

One of LA's oldest and most celebrated restaurants – and also one of the prettiest. Sit in the garden beside trickling fountains and consume some of the best nouvelle food where it was first conceived. It's pretty expensive, though.
Valet parking $3.50.

1 Pico

For listings, see **Shutters on the Beach** *p95*
Accommodation *(1-310 587 1717).* **Lunch** 11.30am-2.30pm Mon-Sat. **Dinner** 6-10.30pm daily. **Brunch** 11am-2.30pm Sun. **Average** $35. **Credit** AmEx, DC, Disc, MC, V.

Think ocean, sunsets and Ralph Lauren and you've got 1 Pico. Dip your toes in the sand before settling into a well-prepared meal, served with grace. We recommend brunch.
Parking $3.

Patrick's Roadhouse

106 Entrada Drive, at Pacific Coast Highway, Santa Monica (1-310 459 4544). Bus Santa Monica 9/I-10, exit PCH north. **Open** 8am-3pm Mon-Fri; 9am-3pm Sat, Sun. **Average** $15. **No credit cards. Map 2 A1**

Funky beachside diner. Hot for breakfast (Billy Crystal likes his eggs 'Jewish-style' with salami) and burger-type lunches (Bill Clinton thinks they're among the best). Large on cholesterol and portions, long on queues, star-spotting and attitude. Short on sophistication.
Parking free-$3.

Rae's

2901 Pico Boulevard, at 29th Street, Santa Monica (1-310 828 7937). Bus Santa Monica 7/I-10, exit Bundy Drive north. **Open** 5.30am-10pm daily. **Average** $8. **No credit cards. Map 2 C3**

Slick, turquoise, classic 1950s diner, so popular there are often lines around the block. Breakfast is recommended. Try the '2 plus 2': two eggs, two strips of bacon or sausages and two pancakes.

Rix

1413 Fifth Street, between Broadway & Santa Monica Boulevard, Santa Monica (1-310 656 9688). Bus 33, 304, 434, Santa Monica 2, 4/I-10, exit Fourth-Fifth Street north. **Dinner** 6-10pm Mon-Tue; 6-10.30pm Wed; 6-11pm Thur-Sat. **Average** $25. **Credit** AmEx, MC, V. **Map 2 A2**

Another trendy, happening spot. It has a restaurant serving California-eclectic food downstairs, a tiki room, Martini bar and cigar lounge upstairs, and a patio jazz stage outside.
Parking $4.

Röckenwagner

2435 Main Street, at Ocean Park Boulevard, Santa Monica (1-310 399 6504). Bus 33, 333, Santa Monica 1, 8, 10/I-10, exit Fourth Street south. **Lunch** 11.30am-

2.30pm Tue-Fri; 9am-2pm Sat, Sun. **Dinner** 6-10pm Tue-Fri; 5.30-10pm Sat, Sun. **Brunch** 9am-2pm Sat, Sun. **Average** $23. **Credit** AmEx, DC, MC, V. **Map 2 A3**

Located in architect Frank Gehry's sculptural Edgemar Complex, this is the high-end restaurant that put German chef Hans Röckenwagner on the map. It epitomises California cuisine in its marriage of eclectic and artistic food and décor. The most popular item is the crab soufflé with sliced mango and lobster-butter sauce.
Valet parking $2.75.

Rosalynn Thai Restaurant

2308 Lincoln Boulevard, at Pearl Street, Santa Monica (1-310 397 2647). Bus Culver City 1, 7, Santa Monica 3, 7, 8/I-10, exit Lincoln Boulevard south. **Open** 11am-10pm daily. **Average** $12. **Credit** MC, V. **Map 2 B3**

Thai restaurants are two-a-penny in the Southland, but it's hard to find an exceptional one. This place is distinctive, with its 76-item menu, some unusual dishes and attentive service. Recommendations: krathongtong, spicy scallops, duck salad, pad see yew, shrimp curry, and ginger ice-cream.

Critic's choice

Class acts

Campanile (Miracle Mile)
Citrus (Melrose)
Hotel Bel-Air (Bel Air)
L'Orangerie (West Hollywood)
Patina (Hollywood)
Valentino (Santa Monica)

Best for brunch

Café del Rey (Marina Del Rey)
Campanile (Miracle Mile)
Geoffrey's (Malibu)
Hotel Bel-Air (Bel Air)
Joe Joe's (Sherman Oaks)
Off Vine (Hollywood)

LA landmarks

Apple Pan (West LA)
Chez Jay (Santa Monica)
Dan Tana's (West Hollwood)
The Los Angeles Palm (West Hollywood)
Musso & Frank Grill (Hollywood)
The Pacific Dining Car (Downtown)
The Polo Lounge (Beverly Hills)

Hip & happening

Coco Pazzo (West Hollywood)
Indochine (West Hollywood)
Les Deux Café (Hollywood)
The Little Door (West Hollywood)
Nic's (Beverly Hills)
Tahiti (Fairfax)
Vida (Los Feliz)

Best ethnic

Brazilian **Itana Bahia** (West Hollywood)
Chinese **Harbor Village** (Monterey Park)
Ethiopian **Nyala Ethiopian Restaurant** (Midtown)
Indian **India Café** (Culver City)
Jamaican **Coley's Place** (South Central)
Korean **Woo Lae Oak** (Koreatown)
Thai **Talesai** (West Hollywood)

Old-fashioned fun at the legendary **Fountain Coffee Shop** *(p126).*

Royal Star Seafood Restaurant

3001 Wilshire Boulevard, at Stanford Avenue, Santa Monica (1-310 828 8812). Bus 20, 21, 22/I-10, exit Bundy Drive north. **Lunch** 11am-3pm, **dinner** 5.30-10pm, daily. **Average** $25. **Credit** MC, V. **Map 2 C2**

Outstanding Hong Kong-style Chinese food in opulent surroundings. Try the giant shrimp and the duck served with dumpling-like pancakes.
Parking free.

Typhoon

Santa Monica Airport, 3221 Donald Douglas Loop S, at 28th Street, Santa Monica (1-310 390 6565). Bus Santa Monica 14/I-10, exit Bundy Drive south. **Lunch** noon-3pm Mon-Fri. **Dinner** 5.30-10.30pm daily. **Brunch** 11.30am-3pm Sun. **Average** $28. **Credit** AmEx, DC, Disc, MC, V. **Map 2 C4**

This Pan-Asian restaurant sits right on the runway of Santa Monica Airport, providing a fabulous view of planes taking off and landing, as well as the mountains and the city. You can also sample excellent food from more than seven countries and scan for celebrities: Robert De Niro, Goldie Hawn and Val Kilmer love this place.
Parking free.

Valentino

3115 Pico Boulevard, at Centinela Avenue, Santa Monica (1-310 829 4313). Bus Santa Monica 7/I-10, exit Centinela Avenue south. **Lunch** 11.30am-2.30pm Fri. **Dinner** 5-11pm daily. **Average** $55. **Credit** AmEx, DC, Disc, MC, V.

Piero Selvaggio has awards coming out of his ears for this, his flagship restaurant; according to *Wine Spectator* magazine, it is one of the top Italian restaurants in the country. He also garners endless praise for his wine collection; some say it is the finest restaurant cellar in the United States. Ask Piero to put together a 'tasting plate' for you, and if you've got the money, splurge.
Parking $3.

Voda

1449 Second Street, between Broadway & Santa Monica Boulevard, Santa Monica (1-310 394 9774). Bus 33, 304, 434, Santa Monica 2, 4/I-10, exit Fourth-Fifth Street north. **Dinner** 6pm-midnight Tue-Sat. **Average** $28. **Credit** AmEx, DC, Disc, MC, V. **Map 2 A2**

An integral part of the city's new lounge scene, doubling as a caviar-and-Martini bar, Voda (the name supposedly means 'water' in 22 languages) is designed as a modern speakeasy. The menu focuses on appetisers such as pizza, Asian lettuce cups, steamed clams and, of course, caviar served over a flowered ice block with condiments. Leave your car at home. *Valet parking at 217 Broadway $3.*

Also recommended

Fritto Misto (Italian) *601 Colorado Avenue, Santa Monica (1-310 458 2829);* **Remi** (Italian) *1451 Third Street Promenade, Santa Monica (1-310 393 6545);* **Ristorante di Giorgio Baldi** (Italian) *114 W Channel Road, Santa Monica (1-310 573 1660).*

Venice

A Votre Santé

1025 Abbot Kinney Boulevard, between Westminster Avenue & Main Street, Venice (1-310 314 1187). Bus 33, 36, 333, Santa Monica 1, 2/I-10, exit Fourth Street south. **Open** 11am-10pm Mon-Fri; 9am-10pm Sat; 9am-9pm Sun. **Average** $15. **Credit** AmEx, DC, Disc, MC, V. **Map 2 A4/5**

Some people swear by this health-conscious, low-fat, vegetarian chain. The wraps – sandwiches using chapati bread – are worth a try, as are the veggie burgers.

The Fig Tree

429 Ocean Front Walk, at Rose Avenue, Venice (1-310 392 4937). Bus Santa Monica 2/I-10, exit Fourth Street south. **Open** 9am-9pm daily. **Average** $15. **Credit** AmEx, DC, MC, V. **Map 2 A4**

Get front seats for the spectacle that is Venice Boardwalk

and eat healthily and heartily at the locals' fave oceanside brunch hangout. All the vegetables are organic; cakes and desserts are sweetened only with honey or fruit juice. Highly recommended, if you go on an empty stomach, are the oat or cornmeal pancakes stuffed with blueberries or banana and served with apple butter and pure maple syrup.

Hal's Bar & Grill

1349 Abbot Kinney Boulevard, at California Avenue, Venice (1-310 396 3105). Bus Santa Monica 2/I-10, exit Lincoln Boulevard north. **Lunch** 11.30am-3pm Mon-Fri. **Dinner** 6-10.30pm, **late dinner** 10.30pm-midnight, daily. **Brunch** 10am-3pm Sat, Sun. **Average** $22. **Credit** AmEx, DC, Disc, JCB, MC, V.
Map 2 A5
A mainstay for the local Venetian bourgeoisie, real and wannabe artists and artistes. The place is a bit like an aircraft hangar, with the same horrible acoustics, but the bar is long, the booths enticing and the American food upmarket (though overpriced). Supposedly an excellent pick-up spot.

Joe's

1023 Abbot Kinney Boulevard, between Broadway & Westminster Avenue, Venice (1-310 399 5811). Bus 33, 333, 436, Santa Monica 1, 2/I-10, exit Lincoln Boulevard south. **Lunch** 11.30am-2.30pm Tue-Fri. **Dinner** 6-11pm Tue-Sun. **Brunch** 11am-3pm Sat, Sun. **Average** $28. **Credit** AmEx, MC, V. **Map 2 A4/5**
Joe's unassuming shopfront stands out wildly in this restaurant-heavy, artsy section of town. The place has a low-key feel, but the Californian-French food will bring tears to your eyes. Try warm onion tart with gravadlax and crème fraîche, followed by roast pork tenderloin, potatoes, wild mushrooms and roasted garlic juice. There's a small bar, a small patio and a fixed-price menu, too.
Parking $2.50.

Rebecca's

2025 Pacific Avenue, at N Venice Boulevard, Venice (1-310 306 6266). Bus Culver City 1/I-10, exit Fourth Street south. **Dinner** 6-10pm Mon-Thur, Sun; 6-11pm Fri, Sat. **Average** $38. **Credit** AmEx, DC, MC, V.
Map 2 A5
This evening-only joint, designed by Frank Gehry, teems with hip, loud, young things who like to party. The food is nouvelle Mexican. There is also a raw bar (oysters, clams and shrimp) and they serve great tropical drinks.
Valet parking $2.75.

72 Market Street

72 Market Street, between Pacific Avenue & Speedway, Venice (1-310 392 8720). Bus 33, Culver City 1, Santa Monica 2/I-10, exit Lincoln Boulevard south. **Lunch** 11.30am-2.30pm Mon-Sat. **Dinner** 6-10pm Mon-Thur; 6-11pm Fri, Sat; 5.30-10.30pm Sun. **Average** $35. **Credit** AmEx, MC, V. **Map 2 A5**
The local artist community make up the backbone of this upmarket restaurant housed in a minimalist space. Chef Roland Gibert – who took over when Leonard Schwartz went off to open **Maple Drive** (*see p126*) – gives a French, Asian and even Latin twist to the fare. But the staple American comfort foods instituted by Schwartz – such as the kick-ass chilli, the meatloaf and the best mashed potatoes west of Ireland – linger proudly on the menu. The oyster bar and grand piano remain, and you may catch sight of the founding owners – actor Dudley Moore and film-maker Tony Bill.
Valet parking $2.50.

Venus of Venice

1202 Abbot Kinney Boulevard, between Westminster & California Avenues, Venice (1-310 392 1987). Bus Santa Monica 2/I-10, Lincoln Boulevard south. **Open** 11.30am-8.30pm Mon-Fri; 9.30am-8.30pm Sat, Sun. **Average** $12. **No credit cards. Map 2 A5**

This is one of a kind, reminiscent of a Southern truckstop wherein eccentric owner Venus is a law unto herself. She whispers like Blanche Dubois, usually dresses in long pink numbers and serves up an array of home-made, vegetarian health food at a leisurely pace.

Also recommended

Abbot's Pizza (pizza) *1407 Abbot Kinney Boulevard, at California Avenue, Venice (1-310 396 7334).*

Marina del Rey

Alejo's Trattoria

4002 Lincoln Boulevard, at Washington Boulevard, Marina del Rey (1-310 822 0095). Bus Culver City 1, 2, Santa Monica 3, 7, 8/Hwy 90, exit Lincoln Boulevard north. **Open** 11am-10pm Mon-Fri; 4-10.30pm Sat, Sun. **Average** $15. **Credit** AmEx, Disc, MC, V.
This Italian-Argentinian-owned joint is a fabulous, cheap and fun place to eat spaghetti with clams or any other authentic Italian trattoria-style food you care to name. They have no licence, so pop to the shop next door and buy some wine to accompany your meal.

Aunt Kizzy's Back Porch

Villa Marina Marketplace, 4325 Glencoe Avenue, between Mindanao Way & Maxella Avenue, Marina del Rey (1-310 578 1005). Bus 108, 220/Hwy 90, exit Mindanao Way north. **Lunch** 11am-4pm Mon-Sat. **Dinner** 4-10pm Mon-Thur, Sun; 4-11pm Fri, Sat. **Average** $12. **Credit** AmEx.
Signed photos of black celebs line the walls of this cheerful, popular soul-food haunt tucked away in a mini-mall. If you're not cholesterol-conscious, it's a great place to sample comfort food, Southern style.

Benny's BBQ

4077 Lincoln Boulevard, between Maxella Avenue & Washington Boulevard, Marina del Rey (1-310 821 6939). Bus Culver City 1, 2, Santa Monica 3, 7/Hwy 90, exit Lincoln Boulevard north. **Open** 11am-10pm Mon-Fri; noon-10pm Sat; 3-10pm Sun. **Average** $11. **Credit** AmEx, MC, V.
This is a Marina del Rey institution, providing the neighbourhood with smoky ribs and fab hot links (sausages) from an oakwood barbecue.
Free parking at Brennan's next door.

Café del Rey

4451 Admiralty Way, between Bali & Palawan Ways, Marina del Rey (1-310 823 6395). Bus 108, Santa Monica 3/Hwy 90, exit Mindanao Way west. **Lunch** 11.30am-2.30pm Mon-Sat. **Dinner** 5.30-10pm Mon-Thur; 5.30-10.30pm Fri, Sat; 5-10pm Sun. **Brunch** 10.30am-2.30pm Sun. **Average** $25. **Credit** AmEx, DC, Disc, MC, V.
A beautiful setting overlooking the marina coupled with an excellent fusion of French and Pacific Rim cuisine by executive chef Katsuo Nagasawa. Excellent choice for Sunday brunch, a watery dinner or simply when you're peckish after dropping off someone at LAX. Prices are reasonable.
Parking $3.

Killer Shrimp

523 Washington Street, at Ocean Avenue, Marina del Rey (1-310 578 2293). Bus 108, Culver City 1/Hwy 90, exit Lincoln Boulevard north. **Open** 11.30am-10pm Mon-Thur, Sun; 11.30am-11pm Fri, Sat. **Average** $16. **Credit** MC, V. **Map 2 A5**
For some of the best shrimp west of the Bayou, head for this chow house, part of a chain. Eat shrimps, peeled or unpeeled, with Bayou butter or pepper sauce, served with bread, rice or spaghetti and on paper plates.

Malibu

Geoffrey's

27400 Pacific Coast Highway, at Latigo Canyon Road, Malibu (1-310 457 1519). Bus 434/I-10, exit PCH north.
Open noon-10pm Mon-Thur; noon-11pm Fri; 11am-11pm Sat; 10.30am-10pm Sun. **Brunch** noon-4pm Sat, Sun. **Average** $32. **Credit** AmEx, MC, V.
Dining on Geoffrey's cliffside deck, you could swear you're on the French Riviera. But the hearty, eclectic Californian menu, the California-heavy wine list and the Ray-Ban-clad waiters soon set you straight. During the 1940s it was a motel as well, called the Holiday House – it's rumoured Marilyn Monroe and JFK spent a weekend or two here. The good food, exceptional view (featured in movies *The Player* and *Guilty by Suspicion*) and the harmonious service make the drive worthwhile. A good choice for brunch.
Valet parking $3.

Gladstone's 4 Fish – Malibu

17300 Pacific Coast Highway, at Sunset Boulevard, Malibu (1-310 454 3474). Bus 2, 434/I-10, exit PCH north. **Open** 7am-11pm Mon-Thur, Sun; 7am-midnight Fri, Sat. **Average** $20. **Credit** AmEx, DC, Disc, MC, V.
The busiest Greyhound refuelling stop on the PCH: seagulls and tourists alike flock here for fresh seafood right on the beach. If you don't like having your name called over a megaphone and being treated like one of the hungry 3,000 (which is the average number of customers served per day), this isn't the place for you.
Parking $2.75.

Granita

23725 W Malibu Road, at Webb Way, Malibu (1-310 456 0488). Bus 434/I-10, exit PCH north. **Lunch** 11.30am-2pm Wed-Fri; 11am-2pm Sat, Sun. **Dinner** 6-10pm Mon-Fri; 5.30-11pm Sat, Sun. **Brunch** 11am-2pm Sat, Sun. **Average** $32-$45. **Credit** MC, V.
Wolfgang Puck's restaurant in Malibu Colony Plaza. The food is California-Provençal with Asian influences; the interior is beach chic, styled, as always, by Puck's wife and partner Barbara Lazaroff. The open kitchen allows you to see new chef Jennifer Naylor prepare such dishes as crispy tempura soft-shell crab with radicchio-kaiware salad, pickled ginger and black bean vinaigrette. The bar has become beach-hip central and a place to spy celebs from the Colony.

Neptune's Net

42505 Pacific Coast Highway, just north of Leo S Carrillo State Beach, Malibu (1-310 457 3095). Bus 434/ I-10, exit PCH north. **Open** 10.30am-8pm daily. **Average** $14. **Credit** AmEx, MC, V.
An affable seafood joint that's been around for 30 or so years, where you'll find plenty of locals diving into steamed, grilled or fried plates of shellfish. Eat inside or outside.

Taverna Tony

23410 Civic Center Way, at Cross Creek Road, Malibu (1-310 317 9667). Bus 434/I-10, exit PCH north. **Open** 11.30am-11.30pm daily. **Average** $27. **Credit** AmEx, Disc, MC, V.
A Greek taverna loved by locals for its good food, hospitable service, the general party atmosphere and the breathtaking views of the Santa Monica Mountains from the outside patio. It's also the only Greek restaurant in Malibu.
Valet parking $2.

Tra di Noi

3835 Cross Creek Road, at Pacific Coast Highway, Malibu (1-310 4456 0169). Bus 4324/I-10, exit PCH north. **Lunch** 11.30am-3pm, **dinner** 5.30-10.30pm, daily. **Average** $25. **Credit** AmEx, MC, V.
Popular if a little pricey local haunt with a delightful patio, serving some solid, upscale Italian favourites.

West Hollywood & Melrose

Barney's Beanery

8447 Santa Monica Boulevard, at La Cienega Boulevard, West Hollywood (1-323 654 2287). Bus 4, DASH West Hollywood/I-10, exit La Cienega Boulevard north. **Open** 10am-2am daily. **Average** $10. **Credit** AmEx, Disc, MC, V. **Map 4 A2/B1**
Popular and noisy West Hollywood haunt, now in its 78th year, where they serve a mean bowl of chilli and the biggest selection of beer in the city, maybe even the state – 37 on tap, 250 bottled brands. You can also practise your pool in this fun late-nighter, where people have been known to disobey LA's recent smoking ban.

Book Soup Bistro

8800 Sunset Boulevard, at Holloway Drive, West Hollywood (1-310 657 1072). Bus 2, 3, 105, 302, 429, DASH West Hollywood/I-10, exit La Cienega Boulevard north. **Lunch** noon-4pm Tue-Fri. **Dinner** 4-10pm Tue-Sun. **Brunch** 11am-4pm Sat, Sun. **Average** $25. **Credit** AmEx, DC, Disc, MC, V. **Map 4 A1**
Owner Glen Goldman opened this Californian-French bistro as a natural extension of Book Soup, his hip independent bookstore and newsstand (*see p154* **Shops & Services**). Wolf down a delicious plate of paglia e fieno with New Zealand mussels or prop up the long, wooden bar and pick on a crispy duck confit salad while shooting the breeze with the cocktail-shaking Harry.
Parking $1.25 per hour; free after 6pm & on weekends.

Boxer

7615 Beverly Boulevard, between Curson & Stanley Avenues, West Hollywood (1-323 932 6178). Bus 14/ I-10, exit La Cienega Boulevard north. **Lunch** 11.30am-2.30pm Tue-Sat. **Dinner** 6.30-11.30pm Tue-Sun. **Brunch** 10am-2pm Sat, Sun. **Average** $32. **Credit** AmEx, DC, Disc, MC, V. **Map 4 C2**
Owner Steven Arroyo wanted to give a certain 'punchiness' to his one-room, storefront restaurant – hence the name. It attracts a stylish but unpretentious crowd who are serious about their food. The inventive Cal-eclectic menu makes decision-making difficult, but we recommend the Israeli couscous and shrimp with saffron.

Cadillac Café

359 N La Cienega Boulevard, between Beverly Boulevard & Oakwood Avenue, West Hollywood (1-310 657 6591). Bus 14, 104/I-10, exit La Cienega Boulevard north. **Open** 11am-11pm Mon-Thur; 11am-midnight Fri; 10am-midnight Sat, Sun. **Average** $14. **Credit** AmEx, MC, V. **Map 4 A/B2**
Funky, friendly café serving up some very competent American comfort food with an ironic twist in a kitschy Jetson-style setting. We cannot recommend the French toast enough. Try the amaretto biscuits with orange maple syrup for brunch and the blackened meatloaf with a side order of 'curly Q' fries – cooked to look like onion rings – for lunch or dinner. They are planning to open a bar next door.

Café Med

8615 Sunset Boulevard, at Sunset Plaza, West Hollywood (1-310 652 0445). Bus 2, 3, 302, 429/I-10, exit La Cienega Boulevard north. **Open** 11am-11.30pm Mon-Thur; 11.30am-midnight Fri-Sun. **Average** $22. **Credit** AmEx, Disc, MC, V. **Map 4 A1**
This could be the least pretentious and most fun of the Sunset Plaza sidewalk restaurant/cafés – if it weren't for the Eurotrash clientele. Try piadina bread with stracchino cheese and arrugala nope (herb seasoning), then the pasta al mare with a beautifully dressed tricolore salad.
Parking free.

Coco Pazzo

For listings, see **Mondrian Hotel** *p101* **Accommodation**
(1-323 848 6000). **Lunch** 11.30am-3.30pm, **dinner**
6-11pm, **late dinner** 11.30pm-2am, daily. **Average** $45.
Credit AmEx, DC, JCB, MC, V.

Enter Ian Schrager's ultimately hip creation through *Alice
in Wonderland*-like giant doors. Before your eyes blink in
astonishment, the white-attired valets will have whisked
your car away and you will be in the oh-so-Philippe Starck
interior. Coco Pazzo beckons. Sit inside the minimalist, all-
white interior (where the table legs have painted socks) or
outside between gargantuan flower pots, overlooking the
pool or the city, or gaze longingly at the **SkyBar** (*see p148*
Bars) - it may be the closest you'll get to it. Try the calf's
liver sautéed with onion and dried figs, served with polenta,
and the garganelli pasta with pumpkin and wild mushrooms.
The prices are sky-high. But oh, what a setting!
Valet parking $10.

Chaya Brasserie

*8741 Alden Drive, at Robertson Boulevard, West
Hollywood (1-310 859 8833). Bus 14, 16, 105, DASH
Fairfax/I-10, exit La Cienega Boulevard north.* **Lunch**
11.30am-2.30pm Mon-Fri. **Dinner** 6-10.30pm Mon-Thur;
6-11pm Fri, Sat; 6-10pm Sun. **Late dinner** 10.30pm-
midnight Mon-Sat. **Average** $40. **Credit** AmEx, DC,
MC, V. **Map 4 A3**

This posh but friendly restaurant serves excellent
Mediterranean-French dishes with some Pacific Rim influences, in a pretty colonial-style setting, with large trees
stretching to the high ceiling. It's been a mainstay of the
neighbourhood for some time, attracting surgeons from
nearby Cedars Sinai hospital, film executives from New Line
Cinema, and art and antique dealers from Robertson
Boulevard and Beverly Hills.
Valet parking $3.50.

Chianti Cucina

*7383 Melrose Avenue, at Martel Avenue, Melrose
District (1-323 653 8333). Bus 10, 11/I-10, exit Fairfax
Avenue north.* **Open** *Chianti* 5.30-10.30pm Mon-Thur;
5.30-11pm Fri, Sat; 5.30-10pm Sun. *Cucina* 11.30am-
11.30pm Mon-Thur; 11.30am-midnight Fri, Sat; 4-11pm
Sun. **Average** $32. **Credit** AmEx, DC, MC, V.
Map 4 C2

Two restaurants that share the same kitchen. On the left is
Chianti: opened in 1938, it's dark, formal, expensive and
romantic, with a bar. On the right is Cucina, contemporary
and airy. The food in both places is outstanding modern
northern Italian.
Parking $3.

Citrus

*6703 Melrose Avenue, at Citrus Avenue, Melrose District
(1-323 857 0034). Bus 10, 11/I-10, exit La Brea Avenue
north.* **Lunch** noon-2.30pm Mon-Fri. **Dinner** 6.30-
10.30pm Mon-Fri; 6-11pm Sat. **Average** $40. **Credit**
AmEx, DC, MC, V. **Map 5 A3**

One of LA's most imaginative menus (Californian-French)
in a carelessly classy 'outside inside' setting. Sit under white
umbrellas and watch masterful chefs create in their glass
kitchen. Try the smoked salmon terrine, the snails in white
wine and mushroom sauce, the sea bass dipped in a sauce of
black chanterelles, the wafer-thin onion rings, and the chocolate hazelnut bars. Out of this world.
Valet parking $3.50.

Dan Tana's

*9071 Santa Monica Boulevard, at Doheny Drive, West
Hollywood (1-310 275 9444). Bus 4, DASH West
Hollywood/I-405, exit Santa Monica Boulevard east.*
Dinner 5pm-1am daily. **Average** $32. **Credit** AmEx,
DC, Disc, MC, V. **Map 4 A2**

This friendly, vivacious late-night restaurant and bar has

been hanging in there since 1964 and is still bursting at the
seams with film and TV stars, sports personalities and the
rank and file of the movie industry. It offers consistently
good, if simple, old-fashioned Italian food served with
panache and humour by a loyal staff.
Parking $3.50.

Dominick's

*8715 Beverly Boulevard, between Robertson & San
Vicente Boulevards, West Hollywood (1-310 652 7272).
Bus 14, 220, DASH West Hollywood/I-10, exit La
Cienega Boulevard north.* **Dinner** 7pm-12.30am
Mon-Thur, Sun; 7pm-2am Fri, Sat. **Average** $29.
Credit AmEx, MC, V. **Map 4 A2**

This old Hollywood hangout (Warren and Jack were regulars) has reopened one door down with different owners. It's
certain to become one of the city's coolest old/new places.
The décor is by Fred Southerland, designer of *Vida* (*see
p135*), and Sandy Gendel, formerly of Table 29 in Napa and
classy **Campanile** (*see p133*), cooks up the coastal Italian
menu with a rare and ironic continental twist.
Parking $3.50.

Drai's

*730 N La Cienega Boulevard, at Sherwood Drive, West
Hollywood (1-310 358 8585). Bus 4, 10, 11, 305/I-10,
exit La Cienega Boulevard.* **Dinner** 6pm-1am Mon;
6.30-10.30pm Tue-Sat. **Average** $45. **Credit** AmEx, DC,
MC, V. **Map 4 A/B2**

Hollywood restaurateurs are often celebrities in their own
right: Victor Drai is a former film producer and well known
around town. On any given night of the week the valet
parking here is usually packing half a dozen Rolls-Royces,
any number of Mercedes and a handful of Jags. Inside, the
maître d' is usually packing his share of celebs, seated on
the leopard skin banquettes in the fussy, European-inspired
main dining room or in the cutesy garden room, complete
with astroturf. It's defiantly a place to be seen - though the
French-Californian food isn't bad, either. There's a strong
bar scene, especially when they have live music on Monday
and Friday nights.
Parking $3.50.

829 Bistro

*829 N La Cienega Boulevard, between Waring &
Willoughby Avenues, West Hollywood (1-310 360 9064).
Bus 4, 10, 105, 304/I-10, exit La Cienega Boulevard
north.* **Dinner** 6pm-2am Tue-Sun; 6pm-4am Thur-Sat.
Average $28. **Credit** AmEx, DC, MC, V. **Map 4 A/B2**

One of LA's new wave of French bistros, an offshoot of Jean-
François Meteigner's **La Cachette** (*see p129*). It offers pretty Provençal interior details and dishes. Too bad the patio
is on busy La Cienega.
Valet parking $3.50.

El Coyote

*7312 Beverly Boulevard, between Poinsettia Place &
Fuller Avenue, Melrose District (1-323 939 2255). Bus
14/I-10, exit La Brea Avenue north.* **Open** 11am-10pm
Mon-Thur, Sun; 11am-11pm Fri, Sat. **Average** $10.
Credit MC, V. **Map 4 C2**

People generally don't come here for the food but to soak up
the carefree atmosphere and the Margaritas. After 65 years
in business, it's an institution, maybe because of its anti-snob
vibe. It has a newly added patio.
Parking $1.50.

Fenix at the Argyle

For listings, see **Argyle Hotel** *p98* **Accommodation.**
Breakfast 7-11am Mon-Sat. **Lunch** 11.30am-2.30pm
Mon-Fri. **Dinner** 6-10pm Mon-Thur; 6-11pm Fri, Sat.
Brunch 10am-3pm Sat, Sun. **Average** $45.
Credit AmEx, DC, MC, V.

A delightful, upmarket spot for brunch, lunch or dinner in

Enjoy brunch in style at **Campanile**. *See page 133.*

this authentic art deco hotel serving Californian food. We recommend Sunday brunch or Tuesday dinner, when they host an evening of live jazz. Request the patio overlooking the pool for an extraordinary view of the city.
Parking $6.50.

Gaucho Grill

7980 Sunset Boulevard, at Crescent Heights Boulevard, West Hollywood (1-323 656 4152). Bus 2, 3, 105, 302, DASH West Hollywood/I-10, exit Fairfax Avenue north. **Lunch** 11am-5pm Mon-Sat; noon-5pm Sun. **Dinner** 5-11pm Mon-Thur, Sun; 5pm-midnight Sat. **Average** $8. **Credit** AmEx, DC, MC, V. **Map 4 B1**
Fun, economically priced Argentinian restaurant chain. This one is perfectly located for a bite before or after a movie or a browse around the Virgin Megastore at the adjacent Sunset 5 complex. Excellent beef ribs and boneless, skinless, spicy chicken dishes served with rice and 'curly Q' fries.
Parking free.
Branch: 1251 Third Street Promenade, between Arizona Avenue & Wilshire Boulevard, Santa Monica (1-310 394 4966).

Georgia

7250 Melrose Avenue, at Alta Vista Boulevard, Melrose District (1-323 933 8420). Bus 10, 11/I-10, exit La Brea Avenue north. **Dinner** 6.30-11pm Mon-Sat; 5.30-10.30pm Sun. **Average** $26. **Credit** AmEx, MC, V. **Map 4 C2**
Former Laker player Norman Nixon and Brad Johnson, owners of the legendary (now closed) Roxbury Club on Sunset Boulevard, created Georgia with backing from celebrities such as Denzel Washington and Eddie Murphy, so, inevitably, this pretty restaurant with a huge patio attracts a large movie star following. The Georgia peach Daquiri is required drinking and the Southern food is downhome *and* health-oriented.
Parking $3.

The House of Blues

For listings, see p211 Music. **Lunch** 11.30am-4pm daily. **Dinner** 4-11pm Mon-Thur, Sun; 4pm-midnight Fri, Sat. **Brunch** sittings at 9.30am, noon, 2.30pm Sun. **Average** $15; *brunch* $24; $12 4-12s. **Credit** AmEx, DC, Disc, MC, V.
This bizarre upstairs restaurant inside the well-styled music venue serves hearty but refined Southern tucker and a wild 'Gospel Brunch' on Sundays.
Valet parking $8.

Indochine

8225 Beverly Boulevard, between Harper & La Jolla Avenues, West Hollywood (1-323 655 4777). Bus 14/I-10, exit Fairfax Avenue north. **Dinner** 6-11pm daily. **Average** $27. **Credit** AmEx, DC, Disc, JCB, MC, V. **Map 4 B2**
This Vietnamese restaurant housed in the old Monkey Bar quarters has become as much an institution in LA as has its cousin in Manhattan, attracting a bustling crowd of luminaries, artistes, beautiful people and lookey-loo star-gazers who enjoy the sultry tropical décor and the naturally light fare. Try the oxtail broth with sliced fillet of beef, rice noodles and bean sprouts or the spicy sliced chicken breast with lemongrass, Asian basil and sweet-potato crisps.
Valet parking $3.50.

Itana Bahia

8711 Santa Monica Boulevard, between Hancock Avenue & Huntley Drive, West Hollywood (1-310 657 6306). Bus 2, 3, 302, 429/I-10, exit La Cienega Boulevard north. **Open** noon-11pm Tue-Fri; noon-10pm Sat, Sun. **Average** $14. **Credit** AmEx, MC, V. **Map 4 A2**
A tiny and increasingly popular Brazilian restaurant decorated with indigenous musical instruments, serving some of the more exotic and challenging foods of the Bahia region.
Parking free.

The Ivy

113 N Robertson Boulevard, between Third Street & Beverly Boulevard, West Hollywood (1-310 274 8303). Bus 20, 21, 22, 220, 320/I-10, exit Robertson Boulevard north. **Lunch** 11.30am-4.30pm, **dinner** 5-11pm, daily. **Average** $50. **Credit** AmEx, MC, V. **Map 4 A3**
The service sometimes borders on rude or inattentive, but that doesn't seem to affect the status of this landmark California restaurant in a converted house with an adorably pretty patio. It's a great star-spotting place, especially at lunchtime, and they serve some excellent salads, crab cakes and fresh fish dishes. The white-chocolate lemon and walnut cake covered in flowers and fruit is other-worldly.
Valet parking $3.50.

Jozu

8360 Melrose Avenue, between Flores Street & Kings Road, West Hollywood (1-323 655 5600). Bus 10, 11/I-10, exit La Cienega Boulevard north. **Dinner** 6-10pm Mon-Thur, Sun; 5.30-10.30pm Fri, Sat. **Average** $32. **Credit** AmEx, DC, Disc, MC, V. **Map 4 B2**
One of LA's newer A-list restaurants, offering tranquillity, exquisite Pacific New Wave dishes and a very long sake list.
Parking $3.50.

Jones

7205 Santa Monica Boulevard, between Poinsettia Place & Formosa Avenue, West Hollywood (1-323 850 1726/7). Bus 4, 212/I-10, exit La Brea Avenue north. **Lunch** noon-4.30pm Mon-Fri. **Dinner** 7.30pm-1.30am daily. **Average** $24. **Credit** AmEx, Disc, MC, V. **Map 4 C1**
Will Karges and Sean MacPhearson have the trend thing down. Their 1930s-retro restaurant/bar has a nightclub atmosphere and attracts the hippest younger set plus a spattering of celebs. Try the Caesar salad with a pizza and ignore the sometimes supercilious attitude of the other diners.
Valet parking $3.50.

Joss

9255 Sunset Boulevard, at Doheny Drive, West Hollywood (1-310 276 1886). Bus 2, 3, 429/I-10, exit La Cienega Boulevard north. **Lunch** noon-3pm Mon-Fri. **Dinner** 6-10.30pm Mon-Thur, Sun; 6-11pm Fri, Sat. **Average** $25. **Credit** AmEx, DC, MC, V. **Map 4 A1**
At last, a restaurant where you can eat dim sum for both lunch and dinner. An upmarket, minimalist-design, celeb hangout where the food is innovative and the atmosphere cool. If you're very lucky, you'll be served by the tall maître d', Martin Buckler, who will bend down to table level and help you order from an eclectic mix of Cantonese, Mandarin and Szechuan dishes. Lobster is a speciality.
Parking $2.50.

Le Colonial

8783 Beverly Boulevard, at Robertson Boulevard, West Hollywood (1-310 289 0660). Bus 14, 16, 220, DASH Fairfax/I-10, exit La Cienega Boulevard north. **Lunch** 11.30am-2pm daily. **Dinner** 5.30-11pm Mon-Wed, Sun; 5.30pm-midnight Thur-Sat. **Average** $40. **Credit** AmEx, DC, MC, V. **Map 4 A2**
Athough the designers have outdone themselves evoking a French-Vietnamese colonial joint, with a hip and inviting lounge bar, some say it's quicker to order a pizza on a mobile phone; it will arrive long before the waitress does. However, if you can get a table outside, it's really very romantic and the banh cuon (Vietnamese ravioli stuffed with shrimp, chicken and mushroom) will take a long time to forget.
Valet parking $3.50.

Le Dôme

8720 Sunset Boulevard, between Horn Avenue & Sunset Plaza Drive, West Hollywood (1-310 659 6919). Bus 2, 3, 105, DASH West Hollywood/I-10, exit La Cienega

Boulevard north. **Open** noon-11.30pm Mon-Fri;
6pm-midnight Sat. **Average** $45. **Credit** AmEx, DC,
Disc, MC, V. **Map 4 A1**
An LA institution where all the major players of the film
industry chow down for lunch and sometimes dinner: where
they seat you, dahling, is everything. Personally, we prefer
the new front patio. There are some creative and hedonistic
dishes on the New French menu, with quite a few options for
those ever-shrinking 'salad girls'.
Parking $2.50.

The Little Door

*8164 W Third Street, at La Jolla Avenue, West
Hollywood (1-323 951 1210). Bus 16, DASH Fairfax/
I-10, exit Fairfax Avenue north.* **Dinner** 6.30pm-
midnight daily. **Average** $29. **Credit** AmEx, MC, V.
Map 4 B3
One of the prettiest restaurants in West Hollywood and so
hip, in fact, that it doesn't even need a sign out front. Alas,
the place is so overrun with Eurotrash clad in attitude,
leather pants and rakish hairstyles, smoking madly, it's hard
to get a table inside or outside on the idyllic patio. Avoid
such frustrations: go for a drink and a gander at the scene.

Lola's

*945 N Fairfax Avenue, at Romaine Street, West
Hollywood (1-213 736 5652). Bus 4, 217/I-10, exit
Fairfax Avenue north.* **Dinner** 5.30pm-2am daily.
Average $26. **Credit** AmEx, MC, V. **Map 4 B2**
As much a place to hang out as a restaurant, Lola's has an
exceptional Martini list (we recommend the dark-and-white-
chocolate variety) and an international menu that allows you
to snack (crispy calamari, crab cakes and chicken satay) at
the bar, in the living room or while playing a game of pool.
Or dine more sedately (on mesquite grilled steak or rack of
lamb) in the dining room or on the patio.
Valet parking $3.50.

L'Orangerie

*903 N La Cienega Boulevard, between Melrose Avenue &
Santa Monica Boulevard, West Hollywood (1-310 652
9770). Bus 4, 10, 11, 105, 304/I-10, exit La Cienega
Boulevard north.* **Dinner** 6-11pm Tue-Sun. **Average**
$50. **Credit** AmEx, DC, Disc, JCB, MC, V. **Map 4 A/B2**
Classic French cuisine in an aristocratic setting, now celebrating its 20th year. Owners Gérard Ferry and his wife
Virgine have imported 26-year-old Ludovic Lefèbvre, who
worked at two three-star restaurants in Paris, and the food
is as inspired as ever. The restaurant is dripping with towering flower arrangements and the more private garden
room has a ceiling that pulls back to reveal the stars. Plenty
of stars seated at the tables, too.
Parking $3.50.

Lumpy Gravy

*7311 Beverly Boulevard, between Fuller Avenue &
Poinsettia Place, Melrose District (1-323 934 9400). Bus
14/I-10, exit La Brea Avenue north.* **Lunch** noon-3pm
Mon-Fri. **Dinner** 6-11pm Mon-Thur; 6pm-midnight Fri,
Sat. **Average** $25. **Credit** MC, V. **Map 4 C2**
At last, a restaurant dedicated to and inspired by the genius
of Frank Zappa – a place where art, food and music collide.
Whatever you think of the wacky design, the internation-
al menu is fun and the entertainment often notable. Try the
vegetarian filo spring roll, smoked duck mushu and Fire
Walker prawns.
Parking $3.40 Tue-Sat (evenings only).

The Mandarette

*8386 Beverly Boulevard, at Orlando Avenue, West
Hollywood (1-323 655 6115). Bus 14, 105/I-10, exit La
Cienega Boulevard north.* **Open** 11am-10.30pm Mon-Fri;
2-11.30pm Sat, Sun. **Average** $22. **Credit** AmEx, DC,
Disc, MC, V. **Map 4 B2**

We love the Mandarette. It's a high-ceilinged, reasonably
priced neighbourhood Chinese, popular with a well-heeled
young crowd looking for inspired food. The sort of joint
where you can nibble appetisers such as onion pancakes or
dumplings or satisfy a yen for something heartier – maybe
the colourful orange peel chicken or crispy sesame beef.
Parking $2.50.
Branch: 9513 Santa Monica Boulevard, Beverly Hills
(1-310 385 1188).

Manhattan Wonton Company

*8475 Melrose Place, at La Cienega Boulevard, West
Hollywood (1-323 655 6030). Bus 10, 11, 105, DASH
Fairfax/I-10, exit La Cienega Boulevard north.* **Lunch**
noon-2.30pm Mon-Fri. **Dinner** 6-10pm, **dim sum**
10-11pm, daily. **Average** $30. **Credit** AmEx, MC, V.
Map 4 A/B2
Traditional Chinese food in a non-traditional setting. Owner
Paul Heller (nephew of scribe Joseph) is a former agent/
producer who now puts on a show of a different kind at his
beautiful Brooklyn-Cantonese-style restaurant. Be sure to
sample the Company Shrimp, the minced chicken with pine
nuts in lettuce cups and the Peking duck. One of Leonardo
DiCaprio's favourite dinner spots.
Parking $3.

Morton's

*8764 Melrose Avenue, at Robertson Boulevard, West
Hollywood (1-310 276 5205). Bus 10, 11, 105, 220,
DASH West Hollywood/I-10, exit Robertson Boulevard
north.* **Lunch** noon-3pm Mon-Fri. **Dinner** 6-11.30pm
Mon-Sat. **Average** $40. **Credit** AmEx, DC, MC, V.
Map 4 A2
Hard Rock Café founder Peter Morton owns this upmarket
restaurant – a bastion of the power-luncheon crowd and
always popular on Monday nights. Reminiscent of a cosy aircraft hangar, if you can imagine such a thing, it offers a tranquil setting whether at tables masked by tall palms or at the
bar presided over by Jack Martin (voted LA's best bartender
by *Los Angeles* magazine). The American menu with a
Californian twist isn't overly ambitious, but very serviceable.
Parking $3.50.

Orso

*8706 W Third Street, at Hamel Road, West Hollywood
(1-310 274 7144). Bus 16, 27, 220, 316, 576, DASH
West Hollywood/I-10, exit La Cienega Boulevard north.*
Open 11.45am-11pm daily. **Average** $28. **Credit** MC, V.
Map 4 A3
Sitting on the back patio, you feel like you're taking a vacation from LA – if it weren't for all those celebrities. Regular
Faye Dunaway is known to the waiting staff as Fadin' Away.
Julia 'You'll never eat lunch in this town' Phillips likes this
place because they *do* serve her. Timid Jennifer Jason Leigh
chooses a corner table, close to the foliage. The house wine
is excellent, the pizzas are thinner than the girls that dine on
them and the liver and onions is tremendous. The décor is a
replica of the related London and New York restaurants, but
with less of a theatrical bent.
Parking $3.

The Los Angeles Palm

*9001 Santa Monica Boulevard, at Robertson Boulevard,
West Hollywood (1-310 550 8811). Bus 4, 220/I-10, exit
La Cienega Boulevard north.* **Open** noon-10.30pm
Mon-Fri; 5-10.30pm Sat; 5-9.30pm Sun. **Average** $45.
Credit AmEx, MC, V. **Map 4 A2**
A spin-off of the Palm in NYC, which opened in the 1920s,
the LA version has survived intact for 21 years and is still
doing a rip-roaring trade. Expect to wait for your table. The
chop house fare – steaks and lobsters – are all man-sized
portions, only fitting for the predominantly macho crowd
who come to celebrate their freshly inked deals.
Parking $3.75.

Classic diner **Apple Pan**, *in business for over 50 years (see page 128).*

Pink's Hot Dogs

709 N La Brea Avenue, at Melrose Avenue, Melrose District (1-323 931 4223). Bus 10, 11, 212/I-10, exit La Brea Avenue north. **Open** *9.30am-2am Mon-Thur, Sun; 9.30am-3am Fri, Sat.* **Average** *$7.* **No credit cards.** **Map 4 C2**

This little hot dog stand has been pulling in the punters since Paul Pink started his business with a pushcart in 1939. His chilli dogs went on to become the most popular in Los Angeles, drawing celebrities along with a citywide clientele. It's one of LA's few late-night eateries – and the burgers and dogs are OK, too.

The Shark Bar

826 N La Cienega Boulevard, between Willoughby & Waring Avenues, West Hollywood (1-310 652 1520). Bus 104, DASH West Hollywood/I-10, exit La Cienega Boulevard north. **Open** *6-11pm Mon-Wed, Sun; 6pm-midnight Thur; 6pm-12.30am Fri, Sat.* **Average** *$32.* **Credit** *AmEx, DC, Disc, MC, V.* **Map 4 A/B2**

Braised shrimp, chicken and sausage-laden Big Easy Gumbo – you might think you're in heaven, or at least been transported down South. But no, it's just Keith Clinkscale and Chris Hale's latest restaurant and bar – they have others in Manhattan, Chicago and Atlanta. The food is best described as 'modern soul', with a strong Southern influence rooted in Cajun, Creole, African, Caribbean and Native American food. Hugely popular with the sports and entertainment worlds. *Valet parking $3.50.*

Tail-o'-the-Pup

329 N San Vicente Boulevard, at Beverly Boulevard, West Hollywood (1-310 652 4517). Bus 14, 16, DASH West Hollywood/I-10, exit La Cienega Boulevard north. **Open** *6am-5pm Mon-Sat.* **Average** *$7.* **No credit cards.** **Map 4 A2**

You don't visit Tail-o'-the-Pup for a gourmet experience. You visit it for a taste of the carefree, pre-cholesterol-conscious LA of the 1950s. It's a classic: a hot dog stand shaped like a giant hot dog, one of the few remaining examples of the buildings-as-signs that used to proliferate here. The Mexican Olé chilli dog and the Baseball Special are recommended.

Talesai

9043 Sunset Boulevard, at Doheny Drive, West Hollywood (1-310 275 9724). Bus 2, 3, 429/I-10, exit La Cienega Boulevard north. **Lunch** *11.30am-2.30pm Mon-Fri.* **Dinner** *6-10.30pm Mon-Sat.* **Average** *$27.* **Credit** *AmEx, MC, V.* **Map 4 A1**

The city is jammed with bargain Thai restaurants, but this is the upgraded gourmet version and it's well worth the trip to its cool and dark interiors. Order the Hidden Treasures (Thai versions of dim sum served in little clay covered pots), the pineapple fried rice and Phuket chicken. *Parking $3.*

Yujean Kang's

8826 Melrose Avenue, at Robertson Boulevard, West Hollywood (1-310 288 0806). Bus 4, 220, DASH West Hollywood/I-10, exit Robertson Boulevard north. **Lunch** *noon-2.30pm,* **dinner** *6-10.30pm, daily.* **Average** *$30.* **Credit** *AmEx, DC, Disc, MC, V.* **Map 4 A2**

The second startlingly good gourmet Chinese restaurant with a modern California twist from chef Yujean Kang, making Melrose and Robertson one of the hottest restaurant corners in West Hollywood. It's a cavernous contemporary space, offset with antiques, that is, sadly, never full. *Parking $3.50.*

Also recommended

Authentic Café (Southwestern) *7605 Beverly Boulevard, West Hollywood (1-323 939 4626);* **Caffè Luna** (Italian) *7463 Melrose Avenue, Melrose District (1-323 655 8647);* **Chin Chin** (Californian-Chinese) *8618 Sunset Boulevard, West Hollywood (1-310 652 1818);* **Duke's** (diner) *8909 Sunset Boulevard, West Hollywood (1-310 652 3100);* **Hugo's** (American-Italian) *8401 Santa Monica Boulevard, West Hollywood (1-323 654 3993);* **Marix Tex Mex Café** (Mexican) *1108 N Flores Street, West Hollywood (1-323 656 8800);*

Mishima (Japanese) *8474 W Third Street, West Hollywood (1-323 782 0181);* **The Newsroom Café** (healthy) *120 N Robertson Boulevard, West Hollywood (1-310 652 4444);* **North** (American) *8029 Sunset Boulevard, West Hollywood (1-323 654 1313);* **Pane e Vino** (Italian) *8265 Beverly Boulevard, West Hollywood (1-323 651 4600).*

Beverly Hills

Barney Greengrass, the rooftop restaurant atop exclusive department store Barneys of New York (*see p152* **Shops & Services**), offers indoor and patio dining and one of the best views into Beverly Hills and the Hollywood Hills. The menu's big feature is smoked fish.

Ed Debevic's

134 N La Cienega Boulevard, at Wilshire Boulevard, Beverly Hills (1-310 659 1952). Bus 20, 105, 320, 322/ I-10, exit La Cienega Boulevard north. **Open** 11.30am-3pm Mon-Thur; 11.30am-midnight Fri, Sat; 11.30am-10pm Sun. **Average** $10. **Credit** AmEx, DC, Disc, MC, V. **Map 4 B3**

Extremely loud 1950s diner-cum-tourist-trap, plastered with fun memorabilia. Worth visiting just for the ridiculous waiting staff and their entertaining schtick (not for the faint of heart) or if you have kids in tow. But it's probably best to eat first, unless you *like* burgers and fries served in a plastic basket, accompanied by a malt or a shake. *Parking $2.50.*

The Fountain Coffee Shop

For listings, see **Beverly Hills Hotel** *p98* **Accommodation** *(1-310 276 2251).* **Open** 7am-7pm daily. **Average** $13. **Credit** AmEx, MC, V.

This cute pink-and-pistachio soda bar is just as much the stuff of legend as the hotel's **Polo Lounge** (*see below*). Sit on one of the 20 barstools at the counter (built in 1949) and order omelettes, pancakes, waffles or French toast for breakfast or salads, sandwiches or burgers for lunch or dinner. Wash it all down with a soda, float or a homemade ice-cream. *Parking $6.*

Kate Mantilini

9101 Wilshire Boulevard, at Doheny Drive, Beverly Hills (1-310 278 3699). Bus 20, 21, 22/I-10, exit Robertson Boulevard north. **Breakfast** 7.30-11.30am, **lunch** 11am-5pm, Mon-Fri. **Dinner** 5pm-1am Mon-Thur; 5pm-2am Fri; 4pm-midnight Sat, Sun. **Brunch** noon-4pm Sat; 10am-4pm Sun. **Average** $30. **Credit** AmEx, MC, V. **Map 4 A3**

This is a cavernous restaurant with some rather strange 1980s artworks suspended from the high ceiling. The large American menu is nothing to write home about, but it's open late (by LA standards), there are some inviting wooden booths and, if you're careful what you order, you can have an enjoyable if overpriced meal, served by white-aproned, friendly staff. *Valet parking $2.50.*

L'Ermitage Beverly Hills

For listings, see p101 **Accommodation** *(1-310 385 5307).* **Breakfast** 6.30-11am, **lunch** 11.30am-2.30pm, **dinner** 6-11pm, daily. **Average** $37. **Credit** AmEx, Disc, JCB, MC, V.

Beverly Hills' newest hotel houses this elegant and intimate restaurant, with a domed ceiling and huge glass windows. Chef Serge Falesitch offers the sublime and inspired dishes that he calls Cuisine du Soleil (Mediterranean with an Asian influence), complemented by Angela Hunter's desserts. *Free valet parking.*

Maple Drive

345 N Maple Drive, at Burton Way, Beverly Hills (1-310 274 9800). Bus 27, Commuter Express 576/I-10, exit Robertson Boulevard north. **Lunch** 11.30am-2.30pm Mon-Sat. **Dinner** 6-10pm Mon-Thur, Sun; 6-11pm Fri, Sat. **Average** $50-$65. **Credit** AmEx, DC, Disc, MC, V. **Map 3 C2**

Maple Drive has been a lunchtime fave for years with the entertainment crowd and a dinnertime choice for Beverly Hills residents. Sit in an intimate booth, listening to the jazz combo, chill out on the patio or loll at the long maple-wood bar, where cigars can be puffed and, at happy hour, hors d'oeuvres are free. Wherever you sit, you cannot fail to be impressed by Leonard Schwartz's fine New American food. *Valet parking $3.*

Mr Chow's

344 N Camden Drive, between Wilshire Boulevard & Brighton Way, Beverly Hills (1-310 278 9911). Bus 20, 21, 22, Beverly Hills BT/I-405, exit Wilshire Boulevard east. **Lunch** noon-2.30pm Mon-Fri. **Dinner** 6-11.30pm daily. **Average** $40. **Credit** AmEx, DC, MC, V. **Map 3 C2**

Breathe a sigh of relief as you enter the comforting cocoon that is Mr Chow's. Started in London, opened in Manhattan, now the old favourite, celebrity-popular Chinese dining spot is in posh Beverly Hills. The night we were there, Steven Seagal and producer Joel Silver were chewing on some tender duck. Be prepared to pay top dollar. *Valet parking $3.50.*

Mulberry Street Pizzeria

347 N Canon Drive, between Brighton & Dayton Ways, Beverly Hills (1-310 247 8100). Bus 3, Beverly Hills BT, BD, RP/I-405, exit Santa Monica Boulevard east. **Open** 11am-midnight Mon-Sat; 11am-11pm Sun. **Average** $16. **Credit** MC, V. **Map 3 C2**

A no-frills pizza joint that looks like it might have been lifted from a Scorsese movie. The idea is not so far-fetched: the owner is *Raging Bull* co-star Cathy Moriarty. The walls are covered in autographed photos of her celebrity friends and clientele and you may even find Ms Moriarty herself, with sleeves rolled high, serving you some fine pizza or old-fashioned Sicilian favourites like spaghetti and meatballs.

Nate & Al

414 N Beverly Drive, between Brighton Way & Little Santa Monica Boulevard, Beverly Hills (1-310 274 0101). Bus 4, 20, 27, Beverly Hills BT, RP/I-405, exit Santa Monica Boulevard east. **Open** 7.30am-8.45pm daily. **Average** $13. **Credit** AmEx, MC, V. **Map 3 C2**

Despite its tawdry exterior, this 50-year-old establishment is a big industry hangout, serving excellent, traditional Jewish deli fare. The blintzes are recommended.

Nic's

453 N Canon Drive, between Brighton Way & Santa Monica Boulevard, Beverly Hills (1-310 550 5707). Bus 3, Beverly Hills BT, BD, RP/I-10, exit Robertson Boulevard north. **Lunch** 11.30am-2.30pm Tue-Fri. **Dinner** 6-9pm Mon-Thur; 9-11pm Fri, Sat. **Average** $42. **Credit** MC, V. **Map 3 C2**

A smooth new restaurant and Martini lounge where the muted décor, fine art and smart waiting staff set a comfortable and sophisticated tone that is a perfect accompaniment to owner/chef Larry Nicola's fabulous Californian-eclectic food. Recommended: everything on the menu. *Valet parking $3.50 (evenings only).*

The Polo Lounge

For listings, see **Beverly Hills Hotel** *p98* **Accommodation** *(1-310 276 2251).* **Breakfast** 7-11am, **lunch** 11am-4pm, **appetisers** 4-5.30pm, **dinner** 5.30-11pm, **late night dinner** 11pm-1.30am, daily.

Best Mexican

Los Angeles is supposed to have great Mexican food – but, for the most part, it doesn't. Here are the exceptions:

Border Grill

1445 Fourth Street, between Broadway & Santa Monica Boulevard, Santa Monica (1-310 451 1655). Bus 4, 304, Santa Monica 1, 2, 3, 7, 8/I-10, exit Fourth Street north. **Dinner** 5-10pm Mon-Thur; 5-11pm Fri; 4.30-11pm Sat; 4.30-10pm Sun. **Average** $30. **Credit** AmEx, DC, Disc, MC, V. **Map 2 A2**
With its orange walls, vivid paintings, sharp Margaritas, pulsating music, crowded bar and dining area and spicy New Mexican cuisine, this place is hot. Celebrity chefs/owners Mary Sue Milliken and Susan Fenniger (who host a television food show called *Too Hot Tamales*) have been instrumental in putting healthy, gourmet cuisine on the map. Recommended: green corn tamales with salsa fresca, and Pescado Veracruzano – Chilean sea bass, pan-seared in a white wine broth with olives, tomatoes, onions and jalapeños. For dessert, try the key lime pie or Oaxacan mocha cake.

Guelaguetza

3337½ W Eighth Street, at Irolo Street, Koreatown (1-213 427 0601). Bus 66/I-10, exit Vermont Street north. **Open** 8am-11pm daily. **Average** $11. **No credit cards. Map 5 C4**
A spotless and informal restaurant painted in happy colours and dedicated to the food of Oaxaca – the region famed for its seven moles (sauces). Here you can try at least four: mole negro, made with four types of chilli, sesame seeds, tomatoes, garlic, onions, bananas, raisins and secret spices, usually served over chicken; red mole coloradito, made with chillis, spices, chocolate, sugar and peanuts, eaten with chicken or pork backbone; or the green and yellow moles.

La Parilla

2126 Caesar E Chavez Avenue, between Cummings & St Louis Streets, East LA (1-323 262 3434). Bus 68/

Hwy 60, exit Whittier Boulevard east. **Open** 8am-11pm daily. **Average** $15. **Credit** AmEx, MC, V.
Slap-bang in the middle of Boyle Heights, this hospitable Mexican restaurant is the real thing. Its speciality is grilled meats, especially the sweet and spicy spare ribs, as well as seafood, mole sauce, cactus and sangria. Beware of the parillada for two: it's way too large.

La Serenata di Garibaldi

1842 E First Street, between State Street & Boyle Avenue, Boyle Heights (1-323 265 2887). Bus 30, 31/ I-10, exit Boyle Avenue north. **Open** 11am-10.30pm daily. **Average** $18.
Credit AmEx, DC, MC, V.
In run-down Boyle Heights, this small, simple place serves fresh fish in exquisite sauces. Call ahead, get directions, park in the back and you'll dine at red-and-white checkered tables with Mexican families, mariachis and Downtown artists. **La Serenata Gourmet** is the less formal and less expensive Westside version – try the fish tacos and empanadas stuffed with pink shrimp, and be prepared to wait for your table – while the newest branch is in Santa Monica.
Branch: 1416 Fourth Street, between Broadway & Santa Monica Boulevard, Santa Monica (1-310 656 7017); **La Serenata Gourmet** 10924 W Pico Boulevard, at Westwood Boulevard, West LA (1-310 441 9667).

Sonora Café

180 S La Brea Avenue, between First & Second Streets, Mid Wilshire (1-213 857 1800). Bus 16, 212, 316, DASH Fairfax/I-10, exit La Brea Avenue north. **Lunch** 11.30am-5pm Mon-Fri. **Dinner** 5.30-10pm Mon-Thur; 5.30-11pm Fri; 5-11pm Sat; 5-9pm Sun. **Average** $21. **Credit** AmEx, DC, Disc, MC, V. **Map 4 C3**
A huge and hugely successful Southwestern restaurant, immaculately done up in an elegant style, with lush carpets, roaring fireplaces, heavy wooden furniture – and some great grub.
Valet parking $3.50.

Brunch 11am-4pm Sun. **Average** $40. **Credit** AmEx, DC, MC, V.
A-not-to-be-missed piece of Old Hollywood where the power breakfast was invented and having a telephone brought to your table was made a famous Hollywood tactic. The lounge was renamed after Darryl F Zanuck and his polo-playing buddies, such as Will Rogers, Tommy Hitchcock and Spencer Tracy. The hotel was recently overhauled, but the lounge has been left intact and million-dollar deals are still sealed over eggs Benedict, while romantic interludes are shared on the charming patio over a plate of pasta adorned with the house-smoked chicken. It also offers the best hamburger in town.
Parking $3.

Spago of Beverly Hills

176 N Canon Drive, between Clifton Way & Wilshire Boulevard, Beverly Hills (1-310 385 0880). Bus 20, 21, 22/I-405, exit Wilshire Boulevard east. **Lunch** 11.30am-2pm, **dinner** 5.30-10pm, daily. **Average** $45.
Credit AmEx, DC, Disc, JCB, MC, V. **Map 3 C2**
Wolfgang Puck started the original Spago off Sunset Boulevard umpteen years ago. Hew was one of the first celebrity American chefs: perfecting talk-show banter, endorsing

credit cards and franchising cafés. In 1998 he and his partner/designer/wife Barbara Lazaroff opened Spago of Beverly Hills. It's his first and much-anticipated try at a classic restaurant: it's a stunning 11,500sq ft (1,070 sq m) extravaganza with Italian glass chandeliers, a romantic garden, an impressive art collection including a Hockney and a Picasso, a 22ft (6.7m) long bar and a huge expanse of glass that exposes the chefs at work. They create most of Puck's original classic dishes, such as the designer pizzas and the light California cuisine with Far Eastern influences, but with the addition of Puck's spin on sturdier Austrian dishes. It's a must-visit for the Beverly Hills vibe (classy without being stuffy), some rather good food and some even finer celebrity spotting.
Valet parking $4.50.

Supperclub 180

180 N Robertson Boulevard, between Clifton Way & Wilshire Boulevard, Beverly Hills. Bus 20, 21, 22, 220/ I-10, exit La Cienega Boulevard north. **Map 3 A3**
At press time, Stephen Noriega and chef Ken Barnoski's proposed fabulously fine supper club – at present housed in a beautiful, two-tiered deco building – had not opened. Watch out: this might become LA's hottest ticket for dining and dancing in old-world style.

X'ian

*362 N Canon Drive, between Brighton & Dayton Ways,
Beverly Hills (1-310 275 3345). Bus 3, Beverly Hills BT,
BD, RP/I-405, exit Wilshire Boulevard east.* **Open** 11am-
9.30pm Mon-Thur; 11am-10pm Fri, Sat; 5-10pm Sun.
Average $27. **Credit** DC, Disc, MC, V. **Map 3 C2**
In downtown Beverly Hills, X'ian is the new upmarket
Chinese health spot on the block. In a contemporary mini-
malist setting, or at the few pavement tables, enjoy your
favourite Chinese dishes. Hearts dot the extensive menu,
signifying healthy, low-fat, low-sodium ingredients.

Also recommended

Bombay Palace (Indian) *8690 Wilshire Boulevard,
Beverly Hills (1-310 659 9944);* **Café Caretta**
(Californian-eclectic) *456 N Bedford Drive, Beverly Hills
(1-310 858 7000);* **Il Buco** (pizza) *107 N Robertson
Boulevard, Beverly Hills (1-310 657 1345);* **McCormick
& Schmick's** (seafood) *Two Rodeo, 206 N Rodeo Drive,
Beverly Hills (1-310 859 0434);* **Porta Via** (Italian) *424
N Canon Drive, Beverly Hills (1-310 274 6534).*

Westwood & UCLA

Maui Beach Café

*1019 Westwood Boulevard, between Kinross & Weyburn
Avenues, Westwood (1-310 209 0494). Bus 21, 429,
Culver City 6, Commuter Express 431, Santa Monica 1,
2, 3/I-405, exit Wilshire Boulevard east.* **Lunch** 11.30am-
10.30pm Mon-Thur, Sun; 11.30am-11.30pm Fri, Sat.
Average $16. **Credit** AmEx, DC, MC, V.
The all-day menu is as much fun as the décor, and both are
designed to put you in mind of the best from Hawaii and
Maui. Try tea-smoked pot-stickers with a lilikoi sweet and
sour sauce for an appetiser, followed by macadamia nut-
dusted swordfish with fresh banana salsa and mashed potatoes, polished off with jasmine rice pudding with fresh
papaya – paradise on a plate.
Parking $2.

Shaharazad

*1442 Westwood Boulevard, at Ohio Avenue, Westwood
(1-310 470 3242). Bus Santa Monica 1, 8, 12/I-405, exit
Wilshire Boulevard east.* **Open** 11.30am-midnight
Mon-Thur; 11.30am-4am Fri, Sat. **Average** $11.
Credit AmEx, DC, Disc, MC, V.
Good Persian food at great prices – and it's open late.
Branch: 138 Beverly Drive, Beverly Hills (1-310 859
8585).

Also recommended

Asuka (Japanese) *1266 Westwood Boulevard, Westwood
(1-310 474 7412);* **The Gardens on Glendon**
(Californian) *1139 Glendon Avenue, Westwood (1-310
824 1818);* **Thai House** (Thai) *1049 Gayley Avenue,
Westwood (1-310 208 2676).*

Bel Air, Brentwood & West LA

Apple Pan

*10801 W Pico Boulevard, at Glendon Avenue, West LA
(1-310 475 3585). Bus Culver City 3, Santa Monica 7, 8,
12, 13/I-10, exit Overland Avenue north.* **Open** 11am-
midnight Tue-Thur; 11am-2am Fri, Sat. **Average** $10.
No credit cards. **Map 3 A4**
The Baker family bought a vacant lot in 1947 and literally
built the Apple Pan from the ground up. It was an instant
hit, and at lunchtime people still line up three deep for one
of the 26 coveted stools at the 1950s horseshoe counter, to
eat from the simple menu of seven sandwiches. They're all
served on paper plates and washed down with Coke, Dr
Pepper or root beer served in paper cups. For dessert, pick
from one of their myriad home-baked cream pies.

Bali Place

*2530 Overland Avenue, between Cushdon & Esther
Avenues, West LA (1-310 204 4341). Bus Culver City 3,
Santa Monica 7, 13/I-10, exit Overland Avenue north.*
Open 11.30am-10pm Mon-Tue, Thur, Fri; noon-10pm
Sat, Sun. **Average** $16. **Credit** AmEx, DC, MC, V.
Map 3 A5
A simple Balinese restaurant, offering a menu as extensive
as it is enticing, good for vegetarians and carnivores alike.

Hotel Bel-Air

For listings, see p101 **Accommodation**. **Breakfast**
7-10.30am Mon-Sat; 7-9.30am Sun. **Lunch** 10am-2pm
Mon-Sat. **Dinner** 6.30-10pm daily. **Brunch** 11am-2pm
Sun. **Average** $45. **Credit** AmEx, DC, Disc, MC, V.
Driving up Stone Canyon Road to the mission-style Hotel
Bel-Air, originally a series of stables and the planning office
for the development of Bel Air in the 1920s, is a romantic
experience in itself. Crossing the wooden bridge by the swan
garden is an added bonus; but taking a leisurely brunch,
lunch or dinner on the bougainvillea-draped terrace with
inventive British chef Gary Clauson in the kitchen makes for
the earthbound version of heaven, where all your senses are
toyed with and always satisfied.
Valet parking (tip only).

Bombay Café

*12113 Santa Monica Boulevard, at Bundy Drive, West
LA (1-310 820 2070). Bus 4, 304, Santa Monica 1, 10,
14/I-405, exit Santa Monica Boulevard east.* **Lunch**
11.30am-3pm Tue-Sun. **Dinner** 3-10pm Tue-Thur;
3-11pm Fri; 4-11pm Sat; 4-10pm Sun. **Average** $4-$15.
Credit MC, V.
Expect queues at this highly popular Californian-Indian
restaurant housed on the second floor of an unprepossess-
ing mini-mall. Try the masala dosas or the Frankies (egg-
dipped tortillas, filled burrito-style with chicken, lamb or
cauliflower), accompanied by Indian beer or chai (tea). Top
it off with rice pudding or home-made mango or ginger kulfi.

Chan Dara

*11940 W Pico Boulevard, at Bundy Drive, West LA
(1-310 479 4461). Bus Santa Monica 7, 10, 14/I-10, exit
Bundy Drive north.* **Lunch** noon-3.30pm Mon-Thur, Sun.
Dinner 5-10.30pm Mon-Thur, Sun; 5-11.30pm Fri, Sat.
Average $20. **Credit** AmEx, DC, Disc, MC, V.
The best of this very popular chain of rock 'n' roll Thai
restaurants. The food is reliably good: try the spicy garlic
chicken and the Thai bouillabaisse with brown rice. Some
joke that people come less for the good food and more for the
pretty, provocatively dressed waitresses.
Valet parking $3.35.

The Chez

For listings, see **Renaissance Beverly Hills** *p103*
Accommodation *(1-310 772 2999).* **Breakfast**
7-11am, **lunch** 11.30am-2.30pm, Mon-Fri. **Dinner**
5.30-10pm Mon-Thur; 5.30-11pm Fri, Sat; 5.30-9pm Sun.
Brunch 8am-2.30pm Sat, Sun. **Average** $22.
Credit AmEx, DC, MC, V.
The first Westside venture for South Bay restaurateurs
Michael Franks and Robert Bell, offering an eclectic menu.
At lunchtimes, it's packed with execs from the nearby 20th
Century Fox lot, while evenings are popular with locals from
Cheviot Hills and leftovers from the studio. Eat inside or out-
side on the pretty patio.
Parking $2.50.

Delmonico's Seafood Grille

*9320 W Pico Boulevard, between Beverly & Doheny
Drives, West LA (1-310 550 7737). Bus Santa Monica 3,
5, 7, 13/I-10, exit Robertson Boulevard north.*
Open 11.30am-10pm Mon-Sat; 5-10pm Sun. **Average**
$25. **Credit** AmEx, MC, V. **Map 3 C3**

While its sign 'If it swims we've got it' may not be entirely true, Delmonico's is dependable for a few fishy things. The Maine lobster is reliable and there are some good variations on grilled and sautéed fish, but too often the dishes are drowning in old-fashioned, rich sauces.
Parking $2.50.
Branch: 16358 Ventura Boulevard, Encino (1-818 986 0777).

Four Oaks Restaurant

2181 N Beverly Glen Boulevard, at Scenario Lane, Bel Air (1-310 470 2265). Bus 429, 578, 302/I-405, exit Sunset Boulevard east. **Dinner** 6-9.30pm daily. **Brunch** 10.30am-2pm Sun. **Average** $18-$28. **Credit** AmEx, MC, V.
Once a speakeasy, now a romantic hideaway cottage in rustic Beverly Glen Canyon, with chef Peter Roelant – formerly of **L'Orangerie** (*see p124*) – at the helm. The complex menu offers starters such as lavender-wood smoked salmon cake with crisp potato and horseradish, while main courses include white-feather quails with pecan, apricot and mushroom stuffing and port and shallot sauce. Sit indoors by the fire or outside near the fountain.
Valet parking $3.

Hymie's Fish Market

9228 W Pico Boulevard, between Oakhurst & Palm Drives, West LA (1-310 550 0377). Bus Santa Monica 3, 5, 7, 13/I-10, exit Robertson Boulevard north. **Lunch** 11.30am-2pm Mon-Sat. **Dinner** 4.30-9.30pm Mon-Sat; 5-9pm Sun. **Average** $23. **Credit** AmEx, DC, Disc, MC, V. **Map 3 C3**
Fish market by day, pricey fish restaurant at night. The fish is very fresh, the preparation simple and the service painstaking. All in all, a bare-bones sort of place.
Valet parking $2.50.

Milky Way

9108 W Pico Boulevard, at Doheny Drive, West LA (1-310 859 0004). Bus Santa Monica 3, 5, 7, 13/I-10, exit Robertson Boulevard north. **Lunch** 11.30am-2.30pm daily. **Dinner** 4.30-9.30pm Mon-Thur, Sun. **Average** $21. **Credit** AmEx, Disc, MC, V. **Map 3 C3**
A strictly kosher restaurant owned by Steven Spielberg's mother, offering some rare dishes. Recommended are the cheese blintzes, pistachio nut pasta, Cajun blackened snapper and warm atmosphere. 'Reservations are sometimes a good idea here,' says a modest Mrs Spielberg Sr.

Versailles

1415 S La Cienega Boulevard, at Pico Boulevard, West LA (1-310 289 0392). Bus Santa Monica 5, 7, 12, 105/ I-10, exit La Cienega Boulevard south. **Open** 11am-10pm daily. **Average** $12. **Credit** AmEx, MC, V.
Map 4 B4
Well-known, funky, no-frills Cuban joint where the food is good, the prices great (even the LAPD can afford it) and the service to the point. Try the garlic chicken served with sweet raw onion and fried plantains on white rice and black beans.
Parking $2.50.
Branch: 10319 Venice Boulevard, Culver City (1-310 558 3168).

Vincenti

11930 San Vicente Boulevard, between Bundy Drive & Montana Avenue, Brentwood (1-310 207 0127). Bus 22, 322, Santa Monica 3, 14/I-10, exit Sunset Boulevard west. **Dinner** 6-10pm Tue-Sun. **Average** $40.
Credit AmEx, DC, MC, V.
New on the scene, Vincenti offers flawless and exciting contemporary Italian cuisine in a sleek but warm setting – wood floors accompany the teal-and-aubergine walls. Specialities are the meat and whole fish dishes from the wood-burning rotisserie. Frequented by the local haute bourgeoisie.
Parking $3.50.

VIP Harbor Seafood Restaurant

11701 Wilshire Boulevard, at Barrington Avenue, West LA (1-310 979 3377). Bus 20, 329, Santa Monica 2/ I-405, exit Wilshire Boulevard west. **Lunch** 11am-3pm Mon-Fri; 10am-3pm Sat, Sun. **Dinner** 5-10pm Mon-Fri; 3-10pm Sat, Sun. **Average** $40. **Credit** AmEx, MC, V.
Popular Cantonese-style seafood restaurant with live tanks of lobster, crab, abalone and shrimp. Excellent dim sum is served every day until 3pm.
Valet parking free.

Also recommended

Asahi Ramen (Japanese) *2027 Sawtelle Boulevard, West LA (1-310 479 2231);* **Delphi** (Greek) *1383 Westwood Boulevard, Westwood (1-310 478 2900);* **Koutoubia** (Moroccan) *2116 Westwood Boulevard, West LA (1-310 475 0729);* **Pizzicotto** (Italian) *11758 San Vicente Boulevard, Brentwood (1-310 442 7188);* **Sushi Sasabune** (Japanese) *11300 Nebraska Avenue, West LA (1-310 268 8380);* **U-Zen** (Japanese) *11951 Santa Monica Boulevard, West LA (1-310 477 1390).*

Century City

Partly owned by Steven Spielberg, submarine-styled, fast-food restaurant **Dive!** (*see page 177* **Children**) is worth checking out.

Houstons

Century City Shopping Mall, 10250 Santa Monica Boulevard, between Century Park W & Avenue of the Stars, Century City (1-310 557 1285). Bus 22, 27, 28, 316, Santa Monica 5, Commuter Express 534, 573/ I-405, exit Santa Monica Boulevard east. **Open** 11.30am-11pm Mon-Thur, Sun; 11.30am-midnight Fri, Sat. **Average** $25. **Credit** AmEx, MC, V.
Map 3 B3
It's a frenetic place, so relax, if you can, at the bar and wait for your pager to go off, signalling that your table is ready. The food is consistently good, fast-food-type fare; try the very thin pizzas, hickory burgers or the barbecue ribs. The décor is upmarket and womb-like: plenty of dark wooden panels and booths.
Parking 2 hours free with validation.

La Cachette

10506 Little Santa Monica Boulevard, at Fairburn Avenue, Century City (1-310 470 4992). Bus 4, 304/ I-405, exit Santa Monica Boulevard east. **Lunch** noon-3pm Mon-Fri. **Dinner** 6-9.30pm daily. **Average** $36.
Credit AmEx, DC, Disc, MC, V. **Map 3 A3**
This is the flagship restaurant of Jean-François Meteigner, arguably the top French chef in town. He apprenticed in Paris at the three-star L'Archestrade and the two-star Chiberta. In LA he worked as the executive chef at **L'Orangerie** (*see p124*) before opening Cicada, then this award-winning place and, more recently **829 Bistro** (*see p121*). He prepares original French cuisine, though with a restrained use of butter and cream. His signature dishes include Muscovy duck with sherried brandy sauce, rock-shrimp ravioli with lobster sauce, and tarte tartin.
Valet parking $2.75.

Yin Yang

Century City Shopping Mall, 10250 Santa Monica Boulevard, between Century Park W & Avenue of the Stars, Century City (1-310 556 3333). Bus 22, 27, 28, 316, Santa Monica 5, Commuter Express 534, 573/ I-405, exit Santa Monica Boulevard east. **Open** 11.30am-9pm Mon-Thur, Sun; 11.30am-11pm Fri, Sat. **Average** $15. **Credit** AmEx, MC, V.
Map 3 B3
A high-energy restaurant with a good and interesting mix

of different regional Chinese dishes. The Hong Kong-style dim sum is excellent. Try the new wok specials – dishes cooked in individual baby woks brought to the table. *Parking 2 hours free with validation.*

Culver City

Café Brasil
10831 Venice Boulevard, at Westwood Boulevard, Culver City (1-310 837 8957). Bus 33, Commuter Express 431/I-10, exit Overland Avenue south. **Open** 11am-10pm daily. **Average** $14. **Credit** MC, V.
A funky shack that prides itself on its low-priced authentic Brazilian food – fish and meat marinated and grilled and served with rice and beans and Brazilian salsa. *Free parking.*

India Café
10855½ Venice Boulevard, between Midvale Avenue & Westwood Boulevard, Culver City (1-310 836 9696). Bus 33, Commuter Express 431/I-10, exit Overland Avenue south. **Lunch** 11am-2.30pm, **dinner** 5-9pm, daily. **Average** $15. **Credit** AmEx, DC, Disc, MC, V.
This unique Indian restaurant serves hard-to-find, rather

spicy dishes from Kerala: avial (green bananas and mixed vegetables cooked with coconut milk), fish curries that will light up more than your tongue and many other delights.

Also recommended
Tito's Tacos (Mexican) *11222 Washington Place, at Sepulveda Boulevard, Culver City (1-310 391 5780).*

Hollywood & Midtown

Hollywood

Csardas
5820 Melrose Avenue, at Vine Street, Hollywood (1-323 962 6434). Bus 10, 11, 163/US 101, exit Melrose Avenue west. **Open** noon-10pm daily. **Average** $17. **Credit** AmEx, MC, V. **Map 5 B3**
Old-fashioned Hungarian eaterie serving up the good ol' hearty staples of dumplings and Weiner Schnitzel. Try the set dinner or their champagne brunch on Sundays ($12.95).

Hollywood Canteen
1006 Seward Street, at Santa Monica Boulevard, Hollywood (1-323 465 0961). Bus 4, 420/I-10, exit

Best Japanese

There are hundreds of Japanese restaurants in Los Angeles; these are the outstanding ones:

Hirozen Gourmet
8385 Beverly Boulevard, at Orlando Avenue, West Hollywood (1-323 653 0470). Bus 14/I-10, exit La Cienega Boulevard north. **Lunch** 11.30am-2.30pm Mon-Fri. **Dinner** 6-10pm Mon-Sat; closed last Sat of the month. **Average** $15. **Credit** AmEx, DC, Disc, MC, V. **Map 4 B2**
Tucked inside a nondescript strip mall in West Hollywood, known only to locals and clever people, sits Hirozen, a sublime gourmet Japanese restaurant and sushi bar. Owner/chef Hiro prepares delicate and unusual cooked dishes, good-looking salads and vegetable plates, while his co-workers attend to some pretty smashing sushi. Be warned: it's small and it fills up fast. *Parking free.*

Ita Cho
6775 Santa Monica Boulevard, between Highland & Las Palmas Avenues, Hollywood (1-323 871 0236). Bus 4, 304, 420, 426/I-10, exit La Brea Avenue north. **Dinner** 6.30-11pm daily. **Average** $35. **Credit** AmEx, DC, Disc, MC, V. **Map 5 A2**
Small and unusual Japanese restaurant with some out-of-the-ordinary cooked dishes and good sashimi, but absolutely no sushi. It's located in a mini-mall with some unsavoury characters in the vicinity, but worth the trip. Check out the spicy lotus root, Japanese jalepeño peppers, the aubergine with sweet miso paste and the dozen or so different sakes.

Matsuhisa
129 N La Cienega Boulevard, between Wilshire Boulevard & Clifton Way, Beverly Hills (1-310 659 9639). Bus 20, 21, 22, 105, 320/I-10, exit La Cienega Boulevard north. **Lunch** 11.45am-2.15pm Mon-Fri. **Dinner** 5.45-10.15pm daily. **Average** $60. **Credit** AmEx, DC, MC, V. **Map 4 B3**

Chef Nobuyuki Matsuhisa's fusion of Japanese and Peruvian cuisines attracts celebrities and expense-account eaters. Although traditional sushi is available, his additions of garlic, fresh chilli and special sauces are a shrewd delight. Try the squid 'pasta' with garlic sauce, or sea scallops filled with black truffles and topped with caviar. *Parking $2.50.*

Myagi's
8225 Sunset Boulevard, between Havenhurst Drive & Sweetzer Avenue, West Hollywood (1-323 650 3524). Bus 2, 3, 429/I-10, exit La Cienega Boulevard north. **Open** 5pm-2am daily. **Average** $17. **Credit** AmEx, MC, V. **Map 4 B1**
On the site of the infamous, defunct West Hollywood nightclub the Roxbury, Myagi's is a huge, three-floor Japanese restaurant unlike any other in LA. The pale wood top floor comprises one main bar, several mini sushi bars, a stream running through the floor, a waterfall and wall-mounted TVs. One floor down, there's a dark cosy bar that also serves food and, on the entry level, another bar, a pool table and an outside dining area. The sushi and assorted entrées are fresh, delicious and very reasonably priced. *Parking $1.50.*

Noshi Sushi
4430 Beverly Boulevard, at N Hobart Place, Koreatown (1-213 469 3458). Bus 14, 207, 357/I-10, exit

La Brea Avenue north. **Lunch** 11.30am-5.30pm Mon-Fri, Sun. **Dinner** 6-10pm daily. **Average** $20. **Credit** AmEx, MC, V. **Map 5 A2**
Bang in the middle of Nowheresville, surrounded by film post-production houses, is this cool, retro grill. A simple sushi bar greets you in the front, while a more sophisticated collection of booths furnishes the centre room, and there's also a small garden, with a silver Airstream trailer for decoration. The menu offers good Caesar salads, pastas, chowders, steaks and fish.

Hollywood Hills Coffee Shop

6145 Franklin Avenue, between Gower & Vine Streets, Hollywood (1-323 467 7678). Bus 26, Community Connection 208/US 101, exit Gower Street north. **Open** 7am-4pm Mon, Sun; 7am-10pm Tue-Sat. **Average** $10. **Credit** AmEx, Disc, MC, V. **Map 5 B1**
A banner outside alerts motorists to the 'Last cappuccino before the 101 freeway'. This non-greasy spoon diner is favoured by celebs like Sandra Bullock, Quentin Tarantino and Tim Roth as a great place to meet or simply to read the morning paper with a terrific breakfast of blueberry pancakes or huevos rancheros.

Les Deux Café

1638 Las Palmas Avenue, between Hollywood Boulevard & Selma Avenue, Hollywood (1-323 465 0509). Bus 26, 163, 181, 217/US 101, exit Highland Avenue south. **Breakfast** 8.30-11.30am, **dinner** 6-11pm, Mon-Sat. **Lunch** 11.30am-3.30pm Mon-Fri. **Average** $35. **Credit** AmEx, MC, V. **Map 5 A1**
Michele Lamy, former manageress of the nearby Café des Artistes has got her work cut out now she's opened her own place. Despite its almost secret location (through the back of Grant's Parking), she has attracted a madly fashionable crowd. Admittedly, it's pricey, reservations are often not honoured and when they are the service can be erratic. But the French food can be good and the ambience is a sort of Euro-chic only found in Los Angeles.
Parking $2.

Lucky Seven

1610 N Vine Street, between Hollywood Boulevard & Selma Avenue, Hollywood (1-323 463 7777/reservations after 1pm 1-323 463 7957). Bus 163, 180, 212, 217/US 101, exit Vine Street south. **Dinner** 7pm-1am Mon-Sat. **Average** $30. **Credit** AmEx, DC, MC, V. **Map 5 B1**
Lucky Seven is a new supper club refurbished out of the

Western Avenue north. **Open** 11.30am-9pm Tue-Sun. **Average** $12. **No credit cards. Map 5 C3**
This is the perfect complement to an expensive day at the Beverly Hot Springs Spa (*see p170* **Shops & Services**), across the street. It's almost a fast-food sushi bar: basic, cheap and popular with the masses. Try the halibut sushi in special sauce or spicy tuna handrolls.

Sushi Nozawa

11288 Ventura Boulevard, between Tujunga & Vineland Avenues, Studio City (1-818 508 7017). Bus 420, 424, 522/US 101, exit Vineland Avenue south. **Lunch** noon-2pm Mon-Fri. **Dinner** 6-10pm Mon-Sat. **Average** $30. **Credit** MC, V.
The Valley's best-kept secret, hidden in a ordinary-looking strip mall. Queue with others in the know who adore this no-frills café-style restaurant where they serve just one thing: sushi. Above the somewhat taciturn chef's head is a large sign that brusquely announces 'No California Roll' and 'Tonight's Special: Trust Me'. Trust us: you will become a devotee.

Sushi Roku

8445 W Third Street, between La Cienega Boulevard & Orlando Avenue, West Hollywood (1-323 655 6767). Bus 14, 16, 105, 316, DASH Fairfax, West Hollywood/I-10, exit La Cienega Boulevard north. **Lunch** 11.30am-2.30pm Mon-Fri. **Dinner** 5.30pm-midnight daily. **Average** $30. **Credit** AmEx, DC, MC, V. **Map 4 B3**
An elegant sushi bar and restaurant (*see* **photo**) with a very contemporary design and a divine patio. The food is for the most part inventive, though the sushi is sometimes anaemic-looking and slight in size, particularly when you consider the high prices. And the crowd, too, is anything but modest.
Parking $3.

Yabu

521 N La Cienega Boulevard, between Melrose & Rosewood Avenues, West Hollywood (1-310 854 0400). Bus 10, 11, 104, DASH West Hollywood/I-10, exit La Cienega Boulevard north. **Lunch** 11.30am-2.30pm daily. **Dinner** 6-10.30pm Mon-Thur; 6-11pm Fri-Sun. **Average** $18. **Credit** AmEx, DC, Disc, MC, V. **Map 4 A/B2**

Adorable, upmarket version of the original noodle shop in West LA. The small shopfront has been redesigned with a vaulted wooden ceiling and small Japanese-style patio. Noodles are the mainstay, but a sushi bar offers some unusual cooked and raw fish dishes and feather-light tempura.
Branch: 11820 W Pico Boulevard, at Granville Avenue, West LA (1-310 473 9757).
Parking $3.

Yamashiro

1999 N Sycamore Avenue, at Franklin Avenue, Hollywood (1-213 466 5125). Bus 1/US 101, exit Highland Avenue. **Dinner** 5.30-10pm Mon-Thur, Sun; 5.30-11pm Fri, Sat. **Average** $27. **Credit** AmEx, MC, V. **Map 5 A1**
You don't visit Yamashiro for the so-so Japanese food. You visit it for the chance to consume cocktails and so-so Japanese food in a truly magnificent setting: a hilltop palace (imported from Kyoto, complete with ornamental gardens) with a spectacular, panoramic view of LA. No shorts allowed. *See also p63* **Sightseeing**.

Yuu

11043 Santa Monica Boulevard, at Sepulveda Boulevard, West LA (1-310 478 7450). Bus 4, 304, Culver City 6/ I-405, exit Santa Monica Boulevard east. **Open** 6pm-2am Tue-Sun. **Average** $20. **Credit** MC, V.
If you're a tad tired of all the Californianised Japanese restaurants, pay Yuu a visit to try more authentic dishes from its expansive and exotic menu.

Zipangu

802 Broadway, at Lincoln Boulevard, Santa Monica (1-310 395 3082). Bus 4, 304, Santa Monica 1, 7, 9, 10/ I-10, exit Lincoln Boulevard north. **Lunch** noon-2.30pm Mon-Fri. **Dinner** 6-10.30pm Mon-Thur, Sun; 6-11pm Fri, Sat. **Average** $22. **Credit** AmEx, MC, V. **Map 2 A/B2**
Informal yet elegant and slightly off the beaten track, Zipangu offers a Californian combination of Italian and Japanese cooking at tables or a long sushi bar. The rare tuna steak, served as a starter or main course, is a gem. Service can be inconsistent, so allow plenty of time.
Parking $3.50.

ashes of the legendary Vine Street Bar & Grill where the Ink Spots and Shirley Horn once performed. On Monday nights the house musician, Jeff Goldblum (yes, that one), can be found tinkling the ivories. Relax at the bar or in the comfortable booths and choose from the comfort food menu. Cool, cool, cool. But book, book, book.

Musso & Frank Grill

For listings, see p149 Bars.
In 1919, Musso & Frank's opened its double doors on what was just a muddy strip of Hollywood Boulevard. Everything about the neighbourhood has changed, but this old-style grill lives on, with its original, high-backed, red leatherette booths, dark stained wood and faded hunting-scene wallpaper. If you're not deterred by the undertaker demeanour of the waiting staff nor by a menu that hasn't changed in 70 years (lamb kidneys, short ribs and sauerbraten) and you don't mind ruining your palate with a Sidecar or a Highball, this is a landmark must. Hollywood dining at its most vintage.
Parking 2 hours free with validation.

Off Vine

6263 Leland Way, at Seward Street, Hollywood (1-323 962 1900). Bus 2, 3, 210, 310, Commuter Connection 208/US 101, exit Sunset Boulevard west. **Lunch** 11.30am-2.30pm Mon-Fri. **Dinner** 5.30-10pm Mon-Thur; 5.30-11.30pm Fri; 5-11.30pm Sat; 5-10pm Sun. **Brunch** 11am-2.30pm Sun. **Average** $25. **Credit** AmEx, MC, V. **Map 5 A2**
California-chic casual restaurant where the food is a mite ambitious, but the Arts and Crafts cottage hideaway setting (with a marlin through its roof) is just too cute to pass up. The dessert soufflés alone are worth coming for.
Parking $2.75.

Patina

5955 Melrose Avenue, at Cahuenga Boulevard, Hollywood (1-213 467 1108). Bus 10, 11/US 101, exit Melrose Avenue west. **Dinner** 6-9.30pm Mon-Thur, Sun; 6-10.30pm Fri, Sat. **Average** $40. **Credit** AmEx, DC, Disc, MC, V. **Map 5 B3**
Chef/owner Joachim Splichal cooks some of the best food in town. But a glance at his menu tells you not to take his offerings too seriously: tomatoes are not sun-dried but 'Hollywood roof-dried' and rabbit kidneys, liver and heart served with polenta gnocchi are termed 'everything from the rabbit'. Creative potato dishes are his signature. The setting is classy, if a little austere and noisy. Splichal's wife/partner Christine takes care of business at the front of house.
Parking $3.50.

Pinot Hollywood

1448 N Gower Street, at Sunset Boulevard, Hollywood (1-213 461 8800). Bus 10, 11/US 101, exit Gower Street south. **Open** 11.30am-1am Mon-Fri; 5.30pm-1am Sat. **Average** $24. **Credit** AmEx, DC, Disc, MC, V. **Map 5 B2**
Also owned by Joachim Splichal, this is a sparky, upmarket French bistro, with a great bar and patio dining. It's the only posh restaurant in the heart of Hollywood, and worth a visit even if you're not already on this side of town.
Valet parking $3.50.

Roscoe's House of Chicken 'n' Waffles

1514 N Gower Street, between Selma Avenue & Sunset Boulevard, Hollywood (1-213 466 7453). Bus 2, 3, DASH Hollywood/US 101, exit Gower Street south. **Open** 9am-midnight Mon-Thur; 9am-3am Fri; 8.30am-3am Sat; 8.30am-midnight Sun. **Average** $9. **Credit** AmEx, MC, V. **Map 5 B1/2**
One of a chain of funky Southern joints that are beloved for their late opening, low prices and tasty down-home dishes.

Also recommended

Lucy's Café El Adobe (Mexican) *5536 Melrose Avenue, Hollywood (1-323 462 9421);* **Prizzi's Piazza** (pizza) *5923 Franklin Avenue, Hollywood (1-323 467 0168);* **360** (supper club) *6290 Sunset Boulevard, Hollywood (1-323 461 8600).*

Fairfax & Midtown

Canter's

419 N Fairfax Avenue, at Oakwood Avenue, Fairfax (1-323 651 2030). Bus 14, 217, DASH Fairfax/I-10, exit Fairfax Avenue north. **Open** 24 hours daily. **Average** $12. **Credit** MC, V. **Map 4 B2**
Visiting 50-year-old Jewish deli Canter's is a unique experience. The service can be charmless and the food tasteless, but, hell, it's open 24 hours. They make their own pickles and sell some excellent chocolate-chip rugala and bagels covered with melted cheddar and poppy seeds. After midnight, the restaurant develops quite a scene of young folk in search of sustenance after a night of clubbing. There's also the Kibbutz Room, a bar with live entertainment nightly.

Mimosa

8009 Beverly Boulevard, at Edinburgh Avenue, Fairfax (1-323 655 8895). Bus 14/I-10, exit Fairfax Avenue. **Lunch** 11.30am-3pm Mon-Fri. **Dinner** 5.30-10.30pm Mon-Thur; 5.30-11pm Fri, Sat. **Average** $30. **Credit** AmEx, MC, V. **Map 4 B2**
Beautifully decked out in bewitching Mediterranean hues, Mimosa offers excellent French bistro fare – mussels marinière, fried steak and andouillette sausages in French bread – for your enjoyment inside or on the pavement patio.

Nyala Ethiopian Restaurant

1076 S Fairfax Avenue, between Olympic Boulevard & Whitworth Drive, Midtown (1-323 936 5918). Bus 27, 28, 217, 328/I-10, exit Fairfax Avenue north. **Open** 11.30am-11pm Mon-Thur; 11.30am-midnight Fri-Sun. **Average** $16. **Credit** AmEx, DC, Disc, MC, V. **Map 4 B4**
Spicy food scooped up with bread, eaten with your mitts only, served by Ethiopian waitresses, often to the accompaniment of live music. An unusual and fun experience.

Tahiti

7910 W Third Street, at Fairfax Avenue, Fairfax (1-323 651 1213). Bus 16, DASH Fairfax/I-10, exit Fairfax Avenue north. **Lunch** 11.30am-2.30pm Mon-Fri. **Dinner** 6-10pm Mon-Thur, Sun; 6-11pm Fri, Sat. **Average** $20. **Credit** AmEx, MC, V. **Map 4 B3**
Leopard- and alligator-print booths, peacock-feather lamps, giant turtles climbing up the walls, thatched umbrellas, oversized Ali Baba urns and a small lava rock and bamboo garden exemplify the theatricality of this restaurant, designed by film designer Damon Medlen. The food is just as striking and whimsical, inspired by the islands, cooked up by Tony Di Lembo, formerly a personal chef to Barbra Streisand: Yucatan-style Chilean sea bass, baked in banana leaves, with achote spices, orange sticks and chillis; chicken in red curry coconut sauce; plus pizzas and an unbeatable beer menu.
Valet parking $3.50.

Also recommended

Du-Par's (diner) *Farmers Market, 6333 W Third Street, Fairfax (1-323 933 8446);* **Vim** (Thai) *831 S Vermont Avenue, Midtown (1-213 386 2338).*

Miracle Mile & Mid Wilshire

Al Amir

5750 Wilshire Boulevard, at Courtyard Place, Mid Wilshire (1-323 931 8740). Bus 20, 21, 22, 320/I-10, exit La Brea Avenue north. **Open** 11.30am-9.30pm

Mon-Thur; 11.30am-1am Fri; 5.30pm-1am Sat. **Average** $23. **Credit** AmEx, DC, Disc, MC, V. **Map 4 C3**
Upmarket Lebanese restaurant, housed in the courtyard of the contemporary Museum Square office complex. Perfect for supper after a browse around the LA County Museum opposite (*see p196* **Museums & Galleries**).
Parking $3.

Atlas Bar & Grill
3760 Wilshire Boulevard, at Western Avenue, Mid Wilshire (1-213 380 8400). Metro Wilshire/Western/bus 20, 21, 22, 207, 357/I-10, exit Crenshaw Boulevard north. **Lunch** 11.30am-3pm daily. **Dinner** 6-10pm Mon-Thur; 6-11pm Fri, Sat. **Average** $30. **Credit** AmEx, DC, MC, V. **Map 5 C4**
Atlas is the legacy of flamboyant restaurateur Mario Tomayo, who died of AIDS in his early 30s after establishing three highly successful restaurants in run-down neighbourhoods. Atlas followed the smaller **Cha Cha Cha** (still going; *see p135*) and Café Mambo (now closed) and instantly attracted a mixed Midtown business and gay crowd with its golden painted room the size of a tennis court, super-camp décor (by Conga Room designer Ron Meyers) and charming waiters. Its eclectic menu is fine if not exceptional, but, with live blues, jazz and Latin music most nights, dining here is more than just eating out.
Valet parking $3.50.

Campanile
624 S La Brea Avenue, between Sixth Street & Wilshire Boulevard, Miracle Mile (1-323 938 1447). Bus 20, 21, 22, 212, 316/I-10, exit La Brea Avenue north. **Lunch** 11.30am-2.30pm Mon-Fri. **Dinner** 6-10pm Mon-Thur; 5.30-11pm Fri, Sat. **Brunch** 8am-1.30pm Sat, Sun. **Average** $36. **Credit** AmEx, DC, Disc, MC, V. **Map 5 A4**
One of the city's prettiest restaurants, housed in what were intended as offices for Charlie Chaplin. Chef/owner Mark Peele has worked with Wolfgang Puck and at Michael's in Santa Monica, where he met his wife-to-be Nancy Silverton. She provides the now-famous breads and pastries that are sold all over town and complement Mark's original spin on Mediterranean fare – risotto and barley cake with roasted autumn vegetables, or duck breasts stuffed with Swiss chard and dried cherries, in a port sauce. We recommend Sunday brunch and Monday for the well-priced set meals.
Parking: brunch $2.50; dinner $3.50.

Cassell's
3266 W Sixth Street, at Berendo Street, Mid Wilshire (1-213 480 8668). Bus 18, 204, 354/I-10, exit Vermont Avenue north. **Open** 10.30am-4pm Mon-Sat. **Average** $9. **No credit cards. Map 6 A5**
Perhaps hamburgers are to Americans what pizzas are to Italians: the discourse can be endless as to where to commandeer the best in town. Many are faithful to this storefront, lunch-only joint, which serves up a mean and greasy burger with home-made mayonnaise and great potato salad.

The Conga Room
For listings, see p213 **Music. Dinner** 7-11pm Thur-Sat. **Credit** AmEx, MC, V.
The Latino-American-owned club is decked out in 1950s tropical style with some unusual Latin artwork and hosts some of the best Latin dance music in the world: José Feliciano, Tito Nieves and Celia Cruz have all played here. And the restaurant serves up some very palatable nuevo Latino food, care of Alfonso Ramirez. It's a sizzlin' groove!
Parking $4-$6.

El Cholo
1121 S Western Avenue, between Pico & Olympic Boulevards, Mid Wilshire (1-323 734 2773). Bus 27, 28, 30, 207, 328, 357, Commuter Express 534/I-10, exit

Western Avenue north. **Open** 11am-10pm daily. **Average** $12. **Credit** AmEx, DC, MC, V. **Map 5 C5**
This LA landmark opened in 1927. The service is old-style ceremonious by ladies in flowing floral dresses and the Mexican food is traditional CalMex – basically Mexican but favouring dishes that have done well in California. What to order: tortilla soup and blue corn enchilada.
Valet parking $2.50.
Branch: 1025 Wilshire Boulevard, between Tenth & 11th Streets, Santa Monica (1-310 899 1106).

Farfalla
143 N La Brea Avenue, between First Street & Beverly Boulevard, Mid Wilshire (1-323 938 2504). Bus 14, 212/I-10, exit La Brea Avenue north. **Lunch** noon-3pm daily. **Dinner** 5.30-10.30pm Mon-Thur, Sun; 5.30-11.30pm Fri, Sat. **Average** $25. **Credit** AmEx, MC, V. **Map 4 C2/3**
A very popular Italian restaurant that attracts a hip thirty-something crowd. Sample the pizzas and the pastas, many of which are home-made: especially good is the fusilli dell' aristocratico – truffle oil, roasted artichokes, shiitake mushrooms and crumbled ricotta. There is live music upstairs some nights.
Parking $3.

Gadsby's
672 S La Brea Avenue, at Wilshire Boulevard, Miracle Mile (1-323 936 8471). Bus 20, 21, 22, 212/I-10, exit La Brea Avenue north. **Lunch** noon-3pm Mon-Fri. **Dinner** 6-10pm Mon-Sat. **Average** $32. **Credit** AmEx, MC, V. **Map 5 A4**
Etched glass panels, 20ft (6m) high ceilings and grey stone floors are the visual keynotes of Englishman Robert Gadsby's chic, minimalist joint. Each dish is diminutive, enticing patrons to mix and match many times over. We smiled when we sampled a slither of granita perfumed by rose petals followed by a dainty mimosa salad. We laughed when the crispy oysters beignet touched with pineapple arrived and nearly sobbed at the sight of Eccles cakes laden with crimini and Portabella mushrooms. The 'chef's tasting' dinner (seven courses) costs just $45 and the 'beggars' bar' (three-course) lunch $25.
Free parking.

La Fonda
2501 Wilshire Boulevard, at Coronado Street, Westlake (1-213 380 5055). Bus 21, 22, 29, 320/I-10, exit S Vermont Avenue north. **Lunch** 11am-2pm Mon-Fri. **Dinner** 5pm-1am Mon-Thur; 5pm-2am Fri, Sat. **Average** $17. **Credit** AmEx, DC, MC, V. **Map 6 B5**
People have come to La Fonda for 30 years, principally to hear the famous mariachi musicians, Los Camperos, but also to eat Mexican food. A fun place for a party.
Parking $5.

Maurice's Snack 'n' Chat
5549 W Pico Boulevard, at Sierra Bonita Avenue, Mid Wilshire (1-213 931 3877). Bus Santa Monica 5, 7, 12, 13/I-10, exit Fairfax Avenue north. **Open** 9am-10pm daily. **Average** $12. **Credit** DC, Disc, MC, V. **Map 4 C4**
Visit Maurice at her funky soul-food restaurant. She makes the best home-fried chicken in town, as well as great liver and onions, and smothered pork chops with brown sauce, cooked with a low-fat content – that's what she says, anyway!

Hancock Park

Girasole
2252 N Larchmont Boulevard, between Beverly Boulevard & W First Street, Hancock Park (1-323 464 6978). Bus 14/US 101, exit Melrose Avenue west. **Lunch** 11.30am-3pm Tue-Fri; 12.30-3pm Sat. **Dinner** 6.30-10pm Wed-Sat. **Average** $23. **Credit** AmEx, MC, V. **Map 5 B3**

Authentic Italian trattoria run by a northern Italian couple. Ermanno takes care of things out front, while Sonia cooks up a storm in the back. The rigatoni with sausage, olives and a slightly spicy tomato sauce is notably excellent.

Prado

244 N Larchmont Boulevard, at Beverly Boulevard, Hancock Park (1-323 467 3871). Bus 14, 16/US 101, exit Melrose Avenue west. **Lunch** 11.30am-3pm Mon-Sat. **Dinner** 5-10pm daily. **Average** $23. **Credit** AmEx, DC, Disc, MC, V. **Map 5 B3**

Prado is split into two, with the themes of night and day depicted on the walls and ceilings. Try the Prado Sampler: moist corn tamales served with sour cream, caviar and tomatillo sauce, shrimp in black pepper sauce, crab cake with tartare sauce and a portion of Pacifico-style chilli relleno. The tarte tatin – a brief European excursion – is sublime.

Koreatown

Dong Il Jang

3455 W Eighth Street, at Hobart Boulevard, Koreatown (1-213 383 5757). Metro Wilshire/Western/bus 66, 67, 207, 357/I-10, exit Western Avenue north. **Open** 11am-10pm daily. **Average** $20. **Credit** AmEx, MC, V. **Map 5 C4**

An upmarket affair in the heart of Koreatown. Dine at the sushi bar, in a booth, or more privately, sitting on cushions on the floor. For traditional Korean barbecue, we recommend the galbi-marinated beef short ribs, which you cook at your table yourself. These will arrive with myriad side dishes, pickled vegetables, sweet potatoes, glass noodles and rice. Shika, made from rice and sugar, is a good way to wash your palate at the end of the meal.

Soot Bull Jeep

3136 W Eighth Street, between Berendo & Catalina Streets, Koreatown (1-213 387 3865). Bus 66/I-10, exit Vermont Avenue north. **Open** 11am-11pm daily. **Average** $12. **Credit** AmEx, MC, V. **Map 6 A5**

One of the best Korean barbecue joints in town. Even before you're seated, a waitress scatters a trowel full of glowing coals into a pit set in the middle of your table.

Woo Lae Oak

623 S Western Avenue, between Wilshire Boulevard & Sixth Street, Koreatown (1-213 384 2244). Metro Wilshire/Western/bus 18, 20, 21, 22, 207, 320, 327/I-10, exit Western Avenue north. **Open** 11.30am-10.30pm daily. **Average** $23. **Credit** AmEx, Disc, MC, V. **Map 5 C4**

A traditional Korean barbecue restaurant: you can cook a custom-made meal on your own hwaro (table-top grill). The sister restaurant in Beverly Hills serves near-psychedelic dishes culled from a mixture of French and Korean cuisines. We suggest the ke sal mari (crab and spinach crêpes), chap chae (fried glass noodles and assorted vegetables) and pajun (seafood and spring onion pancakes). **Branch:** 170 N La Cienega Boulevard, at Wilshire Boulevard, Beverly Hills (1-310 452 4187).

Downtown LA

Café Pinot

700 W Fifth Street, between Flower Street & Grand Avenue, Downtown (1-213 239 6500). Bus 16, 78, 96, Foothill 92, DASH E/I-110, exit Sixth Street east. **Lunch** 11.30am-2.30pm Mon-Sat. **Dinner** 5.30-9pm Mon-Wed, Sun; 5.30-10pm Thur-Sat. **Average** $30. **Credit** AmEx, DC, Disc, MC, V. **Map 7 B3**

Surreally located in the shadow of the newly renovated and splendidly deco Central Library, this restaurant is almost

entirely made of glass: even if you're not seated on the pretty patio outside, you feel just as liberated. It's part of the Pinot family, so expectation is high, but it is more than fulfilled by chef Bernhard Renk's Californian-French menu. *Valet parking $5.50.*

Empress Pavillion

Bamboo Plaza, suite 201, 988 N Hill Street, at Bernard Street, Downtown (1-213 617 9898). Bus 45, 46, 83, 84, 85, 345/I-110, exit Hill Street east. **Open** 9am-3pm, 3.30-9.45pm, daily. **Average** $20. **Credit** DC, MC, V.

Come with a crowd to this vast, outstanding Cantonese-style restaurant so you can flag down more of the dim sum waitresses. The rest of the menu is good, too.

Mon Kee's

679 N Spring Street, at Ord Street, Downtown (1-213 628 6717). Metro Union Station/bus 68, 76, 83, 84, 85, DASH B/I-110, exit Hill Street east. **Lunch** 11.30am-3pm daily. **Dinner** 3-9.45pm Mon-Thur, Sun; 3-10.15pm Fri, Sat. **Average** $25. **Credit** AmEx, DC, MC, V. **Map 7 C1**

Arguably the best Chinese seafood in the area. Pick out your own live Maine lobster or crab and have it cooked in garlic sauce, or get down and dirty with crispy whole shrimp served with a secret-recipe sauce. *Parking $2.50.*

The Pacific Dining Car

1310 W Sixth Street, at Witmer Street, Downtown (1-213 483 6000). Bus 18/I-110, exit Third Street west. **Open** 24 hours daily. **Average** $40. **Credit** AmEx, MC, V. **Map 7 A3**

Imagine the **Los Angeles Palm** (*see p124*) with a little more class and a lot less attitude. When this 24-hour, all-American steak house opened in 1921, LA barely extended west of Downtown and it was immediately adopted as a hangout by local politicians, businessmen, lawyers and sportsmen (from nearby Dodgers Stadium). The front room resembles a Pacific Rail dining car, service is attentive, the wine list has been voted seventh-best in the city and the menu is fastidiously realised: corn-fed beef from the Midwest, which the chefs age themselves and cook over mesquite charcoal, a good selection of fish and shellfish and inventive breakfast dishes such as eggs Sardu (with spinach) and roast beef hash.

Phillipe Original Sandwich Shop

1001 N Alameda Street, at Ord Street, Downtown (1-213 628 3781). Bus 71, 78, 79/US 101, exit Alameda Street north. **Open** 6am-10pm daily. **Average** $8. **No credit cards. Map 7 C1**

Philippe Mathieu invented the French Dip Sandwich in 1908: freshly carved roast beef, lamb, pork or turkey served on a soft bun dipped in the meat's juices. Choose from a fine selection of wines by the glass to accompany said creation.

Trax

Union Station, 800 N Alameda Street, between Cesar E Chavez Avenue & US 101, Downtown (1-213 625 1999). Metro Union Station/bus DASH B/US 101, exit Alameda Street north. **Lunch** 11am-5pm Mon-Fri. **Dinner** 5-10pm Mon-Sat. **Average** $23. **Credit** AmEx, MC, V. **Map 7 C1**

Newly opened restaurant on the concourse of Union Station, wittily incorporating some of the station's deco architectural details. The Cal-French food is excellent, with such creations as endive with gorgonzola and walnuts, lamb sandwiches and pumpkin risotto with shrimp. *Free parking with validation.*

Also recommended

Yagura Ichiban (Japanese) *Japanese Village Plaza Mall, 335 E Second Street, Downtown (1-213 623 4141);* **R-23** (Japanese) *923 E Third Street, Downtown (1-213 687 7178).*

Wolfgang Puck's latest venture, the very classy **Spago of Beverly Hills** *(p127).*

East of Hollywood

Cha Cha Cha

656 N Virgil Avenue, at Melrose Avenue, Silver Lake (1-323 664 7723). Bus 10, 26/I-10, exit Vermont Avenue north. **Open** 8am-10pm Mon-Thur, Sun; 8am-11pm Fri, Sat. **Average** $20. **Credit** AmEx, DC, Disc, MC, V. **Map 6 A3/4**

One of Mario Tomayo's restaurants: a festive, funky place whose Latin American menu draws all the best people to the worst neighbourhood. *See also p133* **Atlas Bar & Grill**. *Parking $2.50.*

Electronic Lotus

4656 Franklin Avenue, at Vermont Avenue, Los Feliz (1-323 953 0040). Bus 1, 180, 181, 204, 217, 354/ US 101, exit Vermont Avenue north. **Open** noon-midnight daily. **Average** $10. **Credit** AmEx, MC, V. **Map 6 A1**

Just opened at press time, an Indian restaurant with a chic, contemporary interior – brightly coloured plastic chairs – and traditional live entertainment every night. A must-see.

Chef Larry Nicola (left) of **Nic's** *(p126).*

Fred 62

1850 N Vermont Avenue, at Russell Avenue, Los Feliz (1-213 667 0062). Bus 1, 180, 204, 217, Community Connection 203/US 101, exit Vermont Avenue north. **Open** 24 hours daily. **Average** $8. **Credit** AmEx, DC, Disc, MC, V. **Map 6 A2**

At the latest whimsical venture of Fred Eric (of *Vida* fame; *see p135*) on the increasingly hipper-than-thou Vermont Avenue, you can satisfy your hunger pangs at any time of day or night. The menu is stylised fast food, with a vegetarian and health-conscious edge: there's 62 Chopper Salad and a fine array of 'Noo*Del' soups. It's a 1950s diner with some 1960s style overlap, and a jukebox stacked with 1970s funk to add into the mix.

Millie's

3524 W Sunset Boulevard, between Maltman Avenue & Griffith Park Boulevard, Silver Lake (1-323 664 0404). Bus 1, 2, 3, 4/US 101, exit Silver Lake Boulevard north. **Open** 8am-10pm Mon-Thur, Sun; 8am-midnight Fri, Sat. **Average** $7. **No credit cards. Map 6 B3**

This quaint little all-American diner – complete with a counter-top jukebox that plays everything from Tony Bennett to Nick Cave – has gone through a lot of owners since it opened in 1926. Local eccentrics swarm here for home-made food at economical prices. Or is it because you can bring your own booze? Try the Eleanor R (for Roosevelt): two eggs over easy, cheddar, salsa and sour cream on rosemary potatoes.

Vida

1930 Hillhurst Avenue, between Franklin & Clarissa Avenues, Los Feliz (1-323 660 4446). Bus 26, 180, 181/ US 101, exit Vermont Avenue north. **Dinner** 6-11.30pm daily. **Average** $29. **Credit** AmEx, DC, MC, V. **Map 6 A2**

One of the new wave of Californian restaurants that serve inventive, off-beat, usually vertically constructed and whimsically named food. There is an array of different corners at which you can dine, and a busy bar. The crowd is chic. *Parking $3.*

THE STINKING ROSE

A GARLIC RESTAURANT

Full Bar

Open Every Day
Untill 2:00 am

Four Dining Rooms

Great for Large Parties

11:00 am - 2:00 am
Seven Days A Week

Located on
Restaurant Row
in Beverly Hills

Outside Dining

Cigar Patio

55 N. La Cienega Blvd. (at Wilshire)
Beverly Hills

1(310)N-LA-ROSE   1(310) 652-7673

www.thestinkingrose.com

Loud, colourful and funky: **Cadillac Café** in West Hollywood (see page 120).

Also recommended

El **Chavo** (Mexican) *4441 W Sunset Boulevard, Los Feliz (1-213 664 0871)*; **Jay's Jay Burger** (hamburgers) *4481 Santa Monica Boulevard, Silver Lake (1-323 666 5204)*; **Katsu** (Japanese) *1972 Hillhurst Avenue, Los Feliz (1-323 665 1891)*.

East LA

Boca del Rio

3706 E Whittier Boulevard, at Indiana Street, East LA (1-323 268 9339). Bus 18, 65, 318/Hwy 60, exit Whittier Boulevard east. **Open** 9am-9pm daily. **Average** $12. **Credit** AmEx, Disc, MC, V.
This family place specialising in food from Veracruz (in the southern part of Mexico) provides simple and complex tastes alike: grilled lobster; steamed and stuffed crab served with rice, flavoured with enough garlic to ward off the most persistent vampires; or red snapper marinated with garlic and dried chillis. A convivial atmosphere, excellent food: what more could one ask for at the end of another sunny day in Los Angeles?

Semitas Poblanas

3010 E First Street, at Evergreen Avenue, East LA (1-323 881 0428). Bus 30, 31, 253/I-10, exit Cesar E Chavez Avenue east. **Open** 10am-10pm daily. **Average** $8. **No credit cards.**
Need a fast snack in East LA? Then head here for the puebla-style beef sandwiches.

South Central

Coley's Place

5035 W Slauson Avenue, between S La Cienega & La Tijera Boulevards, South Central (1-310 672 7474). Bus 108/Hwy 90, exit Slauson Avenue east. **Open** 7am-10pm

Mon-Thur, Sun; 7am-11pm Fri, Sat. **Average** $16. **Credit** AmEx, MC, V.
A very hospitable Jamaican restaurant where you will be greeted by an-out-of-this-world shrimp St James: tender shrimp surrounded by okra nestling in a coconut cream sauce and airy conch fritters. Or there's chicken Lockerton, a breast of chicken stuffed with bananas before being deeply fried. Don't even think about asking for the bill before you've indulged in an order of peach cobbler.

Harold & Belle's

2920 W Jefferson Boulevard, between Arlington Avenue & Crenshaw Boulevard, South Central (1-323 735 9023). Bus 38/I-10, exit Crenshaw Boulevard south. **Open** noon-10pm Mon-Thur; 1-11pm Fri, Sat; 1-10pm Sun. **Average** $18. **Credit** AmEx, Disc, MC, V.
If you have a hankering for upmarket Southern food, you're in luck (though the area is not the safest for visitors – be careful). Once inside, you're cosseted in elegance and, of course, good ol' Southern hospitality. Try breaded fish with crayfish sauce, soft-shell crabs or Louisiana oysters. *Valet parking $2.*

Try **Tahiti** for a taste of the islands (p132).

http://www.timeout.com

AMSTERDAM BARCELONA **BERLIN**
BOSTON **BRUSSELS** BUDAPEST
CHICAGO DUBLIN **EDINBURGH**
FLORENCE **GLASGOW** LAS VEGAS
LISBON LONDON **LOS ANGELES**
MADRID **MIAMI** MOSCOW
NEW ORLEANS NEW YORK **PARIS**
PHILADELPHIA **PRAGUE** ROME
SAN FRANCISCO SYDNEY **TOKYO**
VENICE **WASHINGTON DC**

Jacob's Café

4705 S Broadway, at 47th Street, South Central (1-323 233 3803). Bus 45, 46/I-110, exit Vernon Avenue east. **Open** 10am-4pm daily. **Average** $12. **Credit** MC, V.
Sit at tables, booths or a small counter in this peach and green joint, a traditional Southern eatery that's been open since 1947. Fried chicken, catfish, baked turkey wings, oxtail and pig feet, and they bake their own cornbread all day.

M&M Soul Food Café

9506 S Avalon Boulevard, at 95th Street, South Central (1-323 777 9250). Bus 51/I-110, exit Century Boulevard east. **Open** 7.30am-8pm Tue-Sat; 8am-6pm Sun. **Average** $13.
Although all the branches of this soul-food chain claim to be the original, this one has been around for 30 years. With only five burgundy leatherette booths, seven stools at the counter and four tables in the middle, it's a small, basic place. People who try the newer, more user-friendly branches generally end up back here; because, quite simply, its short ribs (served barbecued or smothered), oxtails, pork chops and chitlins – 'chitterlings' to carnivore Brits – are the best.

The Valleys
San Fernando Valley

Art's Deli

12224 Ventura Boulevard, at Laurel Grove Avenue, Studio City (1-818 762 1221). Bus 424, 425, 522, DASH Van Nuys/US 101, exit Laurel Canyon Boulevard south. **Open** 6.30am-10.30pm Mon-Thur; 6.30am-11.30pm Fri, Sat; 6.30am-10pm Sun. **Average** $10. **Credit** AmEx, DC, Disc, MC, V.
Many people think this is one of LA's best delis. Seating is mainly in booths, with large photos of their famous sandwiches on the walls: try the corned beef and pastrami.
Valet parking $2.

Café N'Awlins

122 San Fernando Boulevard, between Angeleno & Olive Avenues, Burbank (1-818 563 3569). Bus 92, 93, 94, 152, 183/Hwy 134, exit Buena Vista Street north. **Lunch** 11.30am-3pm, **dinner** 6-9pm, Tue-Fri. **Open** 1-10pm Sat, Sun. **Average** $16. **No credit cards.**
Mark Foster, who worked with world-famous chef Paul Prudhomme in New Orleans, is cooking up a storm of traditional Cajun-Creole fare – seafood gumbo, braised shrimp, po'boys (sandwiches) and fried seafood.

Joe Joe's

13355 Ventura Boulevard, between Fulton Avenue & Valley Vista Boulevard, Sherman Oaks (1-818 990 8280). Bus 424, 522/US 101, exit Coldwater Canyon Boulevard south. **Lunch** 11.30am-2.30pm Mon-Fri. **Dinner** 5.30-10pm daily. **Brunch** 11am-2pm Sat, Sun. **Average** $25. **Credit** AmEx, MC, V.
This casual, one-room place is adorned with illustrations from children's books, and although chef Thomas Munoz's food is frequently presented in the hip, vertical pile-up style, it is also grounded in earthiness. Appetisers include grilled scallops with caramelised figs and warm onion tart with smoked salmon and crème fraîche. Favourite entrées include lamb sirloin crusted with porcini mushrooms, tarragon lamb au jus and a plate of shrimp towering over saffron risotto, crowned with shredded and sautéed carrots and green beans. A heart-warming bet for brunch, lunch or dinner. The four-course set menu is tough to beat at $28.
Valet parking $2.50.

Pinot Bistro

12969 Ventura Boulevard, between Coldwater Canyon Avenue & Valley Vista Boulevard, Studio City (1-818 990

0500). Bus 424, 522/US 101, exit Coldwater Canyon Boulevard south. **Lunch** 11.30am-2.30pm Mon-Fri. **Dinner** 6-10pm Mon-Thur; 5.30-10.30pm Fri, Sat; 5.30-9.30pm Sun. **Average** $35. **Credit** AmEx, DC, Disc, MC, V.
Joachim Splichal (of **Patina**; *see p132*) and executive chef and partner Luciano Beccerra created this French bistro-style eatery almost five years ago. The smart (if a mite staid and masculine) décor of wood panelling, ochre walls and chequered floor, the attentive service and the eclectic menu make it one of the most prized spots in the neighbourhood. Beccerra excels at new- wave 'compressed' dishes, such as a salad of radiccio, vertically constructed with dates, figs and manchego cheese, drizzled with pistachio oil.
Valet parking $3.50.

Poquito Mas

3701 Cahuenga Boulevard W, between Lankershim Boulevard & Universal Center Drive, Studio City (1-818 760 8226). Bus 96, 152, 420, 424, 425/US 101, exit Lankershim Boulevard south. **Open** 10am-midnight Mon-Thur, Sun; 10am-1am Fri, Sat. **Average** $8. **Credit** AmEx, MC, V.
The strongest link in this chain of fast-food Mexican joints, serving some of the freshest fish this side of Baja. You can eat on the small patio or take out. Try the shrimp tacos San Felipe or the ahi tuna tacos – and the beans, of course.

Posto

14928 Ventura Boulevard, at Kester Avenue, Sherman Oaks (1-818 784 4400). Bus 96, 236, 522, 561; DASH Van Nuys/US 101, exit Sepulveda Boulevard south. **Lunch** 11.30am-2.30pm Mon-Fri. **Dinner** 5-10.30pm Mon-Sat. **Average** $34. **Credit** AmEx, DC, MC, V.
The chief of Piero Selvaggio's **Valentino** restaurant on the Westside (*see p118*), Posto achieves the impossible: serious class without pretension. Luciano Pelligrini's elegant dishes are understated in their daring. Try the arrugala salad of watercress, mushrooms, Parmesan and raspberry vinaigrette, or venison dressed with cabbage and diminutive artichokes. Finish with chocolate ravioli with saffron ice-cream and pistachio sauce. Posto also boasts one of the finest wine collections in California. Go on, spoil yourself.
Valet parking $2.50.

Saddle Peak Lodge

419 Cold Canyon Road, off Piuma Road, Calabasas (1-818 222 3888). Bus 434/PCH, exit S Malibu Canyon Road north. **Dinner** 6-10pm Wed-Fri; 5.30-10pm Sat; 5-10pm Sun. **Brunch** 11am-2pm Sun. **Average** $42. **Credit** AmEx, MC, V.
This is a fabulous escape from the city: it's only a 30-minute drive from Santa Monica to a rustic hunting lodge country setting, complete with fireplaces, waterfalls and Malibu views. Game is the speciality: antelope, kangaroo, buffalo, venison, pheasant and even ostrich are usually on the menu. It's an impossibly romantic hideout, if you don't mind being stared at by stuffed deer heads at almost every turn.
Parking $2.50.

Wat Thai

8225 Coldwater Canyon Drive, between Roscoe Boulevard & Strathern Street, North Hollywood (1-818 780 4200). Bus 152, 167, 418/Hwy 170, exit Roscoe Boulevard west. **Open** 8am-3pm daily. **Average** $15. **No credit cards.**
This is an ornate Thai Buddhist temple, where they serve lunch at weekends. Join the saffron-robed monks, worshippers and small children who throng throughout the massive grounds and line up for chicken satay, wheat pancakes, crabs in papaya salad or noodle soups with Thai iced tea.

Also recommended

The California Canteen (Mediterranean) *3311 Cahuenga Boulevard W, Universal City (1-213 876 1702).*

San Gabriel Valley & Pasadena

All India Café
*39 S Fair Oaks Avenue, between Green Street &
Colorado Boulevard, Pasadena (1-626 440 0309). Bus
180, 181, 256, 483/I-110, exit Colorado Boulevard west.*
Open 11.30am-10pm Mon-Thur; 11am-11pm Fri, Sat.
Average $16. **Credit** AmEx, MC, V.
An excellent eclectic Indian restaurant with distinguished
curries and innumerable vegetable dishes.

Harbor Village
*111 N Atlantic Boulevard, at Garvey Avenue, Monterey
Park (1-626 300 8833). Bus 70, 260, Monterey Park 1, 2/
I-10, exit N Atlantic Boulevard south.* **Lunch** 11am-
2.30pm Mon-Fri; 10am-2.30pm Sat, Sun. **Dinner** 5.30-
10pm daily. **Average** $14. **Credit** AmEx, DC, Disc, MC, V.
Possibly the best dim sum you'll eat outside of Hong Kong.
Also good are the shark's fin soup, Peking duck and lobster.

Lake Spring Cuisine
*219 E Garvey Avenue, at Russell Avenue, Monterey Park
(1-626 280 3571). Bus 70, 262/I-10, exit Garfield
Avenue south.* **Open** 11.30am-3pm, 5-9.30pm, daily.
Average $15. **Credit** MC, V.
This is an awe-inspiring Shanghainese café, a place to
experiment with hairy crabs, pork pump (pork encased in
fat) and jade shrimp.

Xiomara
*69 N Raymond Avenue, at Walnut Drive, Pasadena
(1-626 796 2520). Bus 188, 264, 267, 483, Foothill
Transit 187, 690, Commuter Express 549/Hwy 110, exit
Colorado Boulevard west.* **Lunch** 11.30am-2.30pm
Mon-Fri. **Dinner** 5.30-10.30pm daily. **Average** $32.
Credit AmEx, MC, V.
Nuevo Latino restaurant. A mystical, one-of-a-kind experi-
ence, owned by Cuban-born Xiomara Ardolina, with fellow
Cuban Roberto Ferrer masterminding in the kitchen.
Valet parking $3.50.

Also recommended
Arirang (Korean) *114 W Union Street, Pasadena (1-626
577 8885);* **Damon's Steakhouse** (diners & grills) *317
N Brand Boulevard, Glendale (1-818 507 1510);*
Market City Caffè (Italian) *33 S Fair Oaks Avenue,
Pasadena (1-626 568 0203);* **The Raymond**
(Californian) *1250 S Fair Oaks Avenue, Pasadena (1-626
441 3136);* **Sushi Polo** (Japanese) *927 E Colorado
Boulevard, Pasadena (1-626 356 0099).*

The South Bay

Chez Melange
*Palos Verdes Inn, 1716 Pacific Coast Highway, between
Prospect & Palos Verdes Avenues, Redondo Beach
(1-310 540 1222). Bus 225, 232/I-405, exit Artesia
Boulevard west.* **Breakfast** 7-11.15am Mon-Fri.
Brunch 7.30am-2.30pm Sat; 8am-2.30pm Sun.
Lunch 11.30am-2.30pm Mon-Fri. **Dinner** 5-10pm
Mon-Thur, Sun; 5-11pm Fri, Sat. **Average** $25.
Credit AmEx, DC, Disc, MC, V.
In 1982, in the middle of the recession, Englishman Michael
Franks and New Yorker Robert Bell walked into a bank with
no collateral and came out with a $200,000 loan to build Chez
Melange. They've beat that into five hugely successful
restaurants in the South Bay. The food at their flagship
operation is nouvelle eclectic, but doesn't take itself too seri-
ously – how could it, when it's housed in a late-1950s diner?
There are also vodka, champagne and caviar bars. Also
Frank & Bell establishment in the area is **Depot** (1250
Cabrillo Avenue, Torrance; 1-310 787 7501), an old train
depot serving great Californian cuisine.

French 75
*1464 S Pacific Coast Highway, between Calliope &
Mountain Streets, Laguna Beach (1-949 494 8444).
Bus OCT 1/Hwy 133, exit PCH south.* **Open** 5.30-10pm
Mon-Thur, Sun; 5.30-11pm Fri, Sat. **Average** $35.
Credit AmEx, MC, V.
This is the hottest thing to hit Laguna Beach in years: a little Parisian bistro and champagne bar, with oversized tables,
overstuffed chairs, a surfeit of velvet and a patio from which,
if you crank your head enough, you can see the ocean. Dishes
run the gamut from heavenly to earthbound: langoustine and
crayfish cappuccino and 'rustic French soul food' dishes.

Michi
*903 Manhattan Avenue, at Ninth Street, Manhattan
Beach (1-310 376 0613). Bus 126, 439, Commuter
Express 438/I-405, exit Hawthorne Boulevard north.*
Lunch 11.30am-2.40pm Tue-Fri. **Dinner** 6-10pm
Mon, Tue; 6-10.30pm Wed, Thur; 6-11pm Fri, Sat.
Average $27. **Credit** AmEx, DC, MC, V.
Michi Takahashi is becoming one of the Southland's hippest
chefs thanks to the cross-cultural culinary experience –
inspired by French, Italian and Japanese cuisines – he serves
at his newly opened restaurant. We recommend the oysters
on roast potatoes as an appetiser, the seafood paella for two
as an entrée and absolutely anything for dessert.

Splash!
*350 N Harbor Drive, at Beryl Street, Redondo Beach
(1-310 798 5348). Bus 130, 439/Hwy 134, exit Colorado
Boulevard east.* **Breakfast served** 6.30-10.30am
Mon-Fri; 7-11am Sat; 7-11.30am Sun. **Lunch** 11.30am-
2pm Mon-Fri; noon-2pm Sat, Sun. **Dinner** 6-9.30pm
Mon-Thur, Sun; 6-10.30pm Fri, Sat. **Average** $40.
Credit AmEx, DC, Disc, MC, V.
Ever sampled fruit sushi? Come to Splash!, where Serge
Burckel never tires of reinventing fusion cuisine. Well, he
worked in Hong Kong and Paris for years. The fantastical,
eclectic menu is hard to choose from here, so are some ideas:
lobster in cinnamon tea, with mangoes and Thai parsley;
crab in a cucumber seafood broth flavoured with dill; and
fried stuffed aubergine on an apple saffron, vinegar sauce,
raspberry coulis. His barman creates his own fun, concoct-
ing way-out cocktails. If you come in a group, request the
Chef's Table, where Serge will personally delight you.
Parking $2 (self-parking); $2.50 (valet).

Also recommended
The Crab Pot (seafood) *215 Marina Drive, Long Beach
(1-562 430 0272);* **Café Zoolu** (Californian) *860
Glenneyre Street, Laguna Beach (1-714 494 6825);*
Five Feet (Californian) *328 Glenneyre Street, Laguna
Beach (1-714 497 4955);* **L'Opéra** (Italian) *101 Pine
Avenue, Long Beach (1-562 491 0066);* **Reed's** (New
American-French) *2640 N Sepulveda Boulevard,
Manhattan Beach (1-310 546 3299).*

Orange County & Anaheim

JW's
*Anaheim Marriott, 700 W Convention Way, at Harbor
Boulevard, Anaheim (1-714 750 8000). Bus 43/I-5, exit
Harbor Boulevard south.* **Dinner** 5-11pm daily.
Average $35. **Credit** AmEx, DC, MC, V.
You have to see it to believe it. A French château, or at least
a good facsimile thereof, slap-bang in the middle of the
Marriott hotel. Seafood and game prepared in the French
manner, with typically fussy hotel service. At least it's a safe
haven from Disneyland.

Also recommended
The White House (Italian) *887 S Anaheim Boulevard,
at Vermont Street, Anaheim (1-714 772 1381).*

Coffeehouses

The cult of the coffee bean has Angelenos in its grip. Power breakfasters and sleep-spurning clubbers alike can be sure of finding their dream coffeehouse vibe, with a brew to match.

If you go out for a drink in Los Angeles, it's most likely to be caffeinated. Coffee is chic and, unlike alcohol, doesn't get in the way of driving or early starts at the office – two landmarks of the LA lifestyle. LA's coffeehouses probably outnumber bars by about five to one. Also, many coffeehouses have outdoor areas where smoking is permitted, whereas most bars are now scarily smoke-free.

Coffee is also big business, as the Seattle-based chain **Starbucks** realised some years ago. Four chains are now fighting to snap up prime locations: besides Starbucks, there's **Buzz**, **Coffee Bean & Tea Leaf** and **Peet's Coffee & Tea**. Starbucks has even been eclipsed for trendiness by Coffee Bean & Tea Leaf, perhaps because it has a few too many branches – and perhaps also thanks to the famed ice-cold 'frappuccino' that Coffee Bean & Tea Leaf claims to have invented. The advantage of the chains is simple: you know what you'll get and that it will be good. The same can't be said for every streetcorner coffeeshop; but, for the most part, the horrible coffee of old-fashioned diners is a thing of the past.

More of a problem than bad coffee is the sheer variety of the stuff available: asking for a plain old cup of joe is a bit like asking for 'a beer'. Regular coffee is still the cheapest option, but you can also get anything from a non-fat vanilla latte to a power frappuccino to an extra-hot triple espresso with bells on top. There is a bewildering variety of whiteners on offer, from 'half and half' (half whole milk, half cream; any coffee called 'breve' is made with this) to '1 per cent' (milk with 1 per cent fat) to soy milk. Sizes can also be confusing. Most coffeehouses have followed the Starbucks trend of 'small' meaning small, 'tall' meaning 'large' and 'grande' meaning 'biggest'.

A growing LA trend is the coffeeshop-within-a-shop, usually a bookshop. Chains such as Barnes & Noble are constantly adding coffeeshops to their larger stores, so one can pleasantly idle away an afternoon test-driving books over a long cool iced coffee; call 1-888 257 6397 to check the location of the nearest such luxury. For your closest reliable chain establishment, try any of the following: **Buzz** (1-213 938 9964); **Coffee Bean & Tea Leaf** (1-800 832 5323); **Peet's Coffee & Tea** (1-800 999 2132); or **Starbucks** (1-800 235 2883).

For coffeehouses serving a specifically gay or lesbian clientele, *see chapter* **Gay & Lesbian**.

Westside: beach towns

Santa Monica

Borders Books & Music
1415 Third Street Promenade, between Broadway & Santa Monica Boulevard, Santa Monica (1-310 393 9290). Bus 4, 304, Santa Monica 1, 2, 3, 7/I-10, exit Fourth Street north. **Open** 9am-11pm Mon-Thur, Sun; 9am-midnight Fri, Sat. **Credit** AmEx, MC, V. **Map 2 A2**
People-watch in Santa Monica's best shopping location from the outdoor tables, or publication-watch inside while sipping excellent coffee and nibbling equally delightful snacks.

Interactive Café
215 Broadway, at Second Street, Santa Monica (1-310 395 5009/intrcafe@cafe.net). Bus 4, 33, 434, Santa Monica 7, 8, 10/I-10, exit Fourth Street north. **Open** 6.30am-1am Mon-Thur, Sun; 6.30am-2am Fri, Sat. **Credit** MC, V. **Map 2 A2**
Around the corner from Third Street Promenade, this spacious and airy café is furnished with cushy velvet sofas, Henry VIII-style chairs and flower arrangements that dwarf anyone under 5ft. Popular for its top-notch coffee, incredible fruit shakes, smoothies, home-made sandwiches and desserts, Interactive also sells cards, newspapers and mags.

Legal Grind
2640 Lincoln Boulevard, at Ocean Park Boulevard, Santa Monica (1-310 452 8160/legalgrind@msn.com). Bus Santa Monica 3, 7/I-10, exit Lincoln Boulevard. **Open** 6.30am-6.30pm Mon-Thur; 6.30am-2pm Fri-Sun. **No credit cards**. **Map 2 B3/4**
No, not a hangout for Ally McBeal wannabes: it's a law centre/café combo, providing not only a small legal library but also nine flesh-and-blood lawyers who will dispense free advice – over great pastries and creamy mochas – on everything from car trouble to divorce. Call ahead to find out which attorney will be there when and don't forget to leave a small donation to keep the resource centre running. California State Bar-certified.
Website: www.legalgrind.com

Novel Café
212 Pier Avenue, at Main Street, Santa Monica (1-310 396 8566). Bus 33, 436, Santa Monica 1, 2, 10/I-10, exit Lincoln Boulevard south. **Open** 7am-1am Mon-Fri; 7.30am-1am Sat, Sun. **Credit** AmEx, MC, V. **Map 2 A4**
'This bookstore is dedicated with respect and humility to the Chinese god, Wei D'to, protector of books against fire, pillaging, decay and dishonest borrowers…' So reads the sign in the library room at this café/second-hand bookshop. The coffee and treats are nothing special, but the books, the boho atmosphere and the location – just off Main Street and a hop, skip and a jump from the beach – make up for such shortcomings in spades.

Starbucks

*334 Third Street Promenade, at Wilshire Boulevard,
Santa Monica (1-310 260 9947). Bus 4, 304, Santa
Monica 1, 2, 3, 7/I-10, exit Fourth Street north.* **Open**
7am-11pm Mon-Thur; 7am-1am Fri, Sat; 8am-11pm Sun.
Credit AmEx, MC, V. **Map 2 A2**
Located slap-bang in the middle of Santa Monica's dream
street for shoppers, this branch of Starbucks provides a
welcome respite from shopping and is a wonderful spot
from which to examine an excellently eclectic group of
passers-by. Annoyingly, though, it does not have a toilet
for customers.

Venice

Abbot's Habit

*1401 Abbot Kinney Boulevard, at California Avenue,
Venice (1-310 399 1171). Bus Santa Monica 2, Venice
33/I-10, exit Lincoln Boulevard south.* **Open** 6am-11pm
daily. **No credit cards. Map 2 A5**
Abbot's Habit attracts a strange yet fascinating crowd of
Venice locals, from yuppies who live on the canals to artists
surviving on a shoestring. Local art is displayed on the walls;
depending on the week and the artist, your morning coffee
could be a soothing experience amid pastel abstracts or a
rude awakening with huge, Munch-like faces. The muffins
and other baked goods are delicious, even the fat-frees.

Van Go's Ear

*796 Main Street, between Rose Avenue & Abbot Kinney
Boulevard, Venice (1-310 396 1987). Bus 33, 436, Santa
Monica 1, 2/I-10, exit Fourth Street south.* **Open** 24
hours daily. **No credit cards. Map 2 A4**
This colourful, slightly seedy, 24-hour coffeehouse – with a
patio and upstairs porch – attracts Venice hippies as well as
the buff and beautiful beach gang. Dishes with names like
the John Belushi (an overstuffed omelette), the Pee-Wee
Herman (a Cajun blackened-chicken 'samwitch', according
to the menu), and the Karen Carpenter (an almost calorie-free
bowl of oatmeal and fruit) are creatively prepared and
downright tasty. Don't miss the Fruit Fuck.

Marina del Rey

Cow's End

*34 Washington Boulevard, at Pacific Avenue, Marina del
Rey (1-310 574 1080). Bus 108, Culver City 1,
Commuter Express 437/I-10, exit Lincoln Boulevard
south.* **Open** 6am-midnight daily. **No credit cards.**
Map 2 A5

The best...

strong coffee Kings Road Café, West Hollywood
high-calorie snack German chocolate cake at
Onyx Sequel, Los Feliz
**cardboard contraption to stop your fingers
getting burnt** Buzz coffeeshops everywhere
coffeehouse to ogle beautiful people Kings
Road Café, West Hollywood
mall coffee Starbucks in the Beverly Center,
West Hollywood
coffeeshop in a bookshop Barnes & Noble on
Third Street Promenade, Santa Monica
coffeehouse to spot celebs Buzz at 8000 Sunset
Boulevard, West Hollywood
sofas Insomnia, Fairfax District

With two floors and outdoor seating, the kitsch Cow's End
is a prime spot, whether for playing backgammon on the
house boards or reading in an oversized, over-upholstered
chair. Most of the cakes and sweet breads are home-made
and worth the calories – especially the banana bread. Take
advantage of the small newsstand on the first floor and enjoy
the cow paraphernalia.

Also recommended

Anastasia's Asylum *1028 Wilshire Boulevard,
between Tenth & 11th Streets, Santa Monica (1-310 394
7113);* **The Bean Queen** *1513 Park Row, at Windward
Avenue, Venice (1-310 450 4945);* **Mani's Bakery**
*2507 Main Street, at Ocean Park Boulevard, Santa
Monica (1-310 396 7700);* **Prebica** *4325 Glencoe
Avenue, at Mindanao Way, Maxella & Lincoln
Boulevard, Marina del Rey (1-310 823 4446);*
Wednesday's House *2409 Main Street, between
Hollister Avenue & Ocean Park Boulevard, Santa Monica
(1-310 452 4486).*

Westside: inland

West Hollywood

Basix

*8333 Santa Monica Boulevard, at Flores Street, West
Hollywood (1-323 848 2460). Bus 4, 304/I-10, exit
La Cienega Boulevard north.* **Open** 7am-11pm daily.
Credit AmEx, MC, V. **Map 4 B1**
For connoisseurs of moist, home-made muffins, Basix is
undoubtedly the place: try the pear nutmeg, banana bran
or zucchini cinnamon flavours. Then move on to the pastas
and mouthwatering salads, sandwiches and thin-crust pizzas.
Although a little too popular for its own good, Basix has
plenty of outdoor and indoor seating where you can enjoy
the bustle of this pedestrianised area. Like anywhere on LA's
premier gay strip, Basix is fairly mixed during the day and
very gay in the evenings.

Buzz Coffee

*8000 Sunset Boulevard, at Crescent Heights Boulevard,
West Hollywood (1-323 656 7460). Bus 26, 163, 212,
217/I-10, exit Fairfax Avenue north.* **Open** 7am-12.30am
Mon-Thur, Sun; 7am-1.30am Fri, Sat. **Credit** AmEx, MC,
V. **Map 4 B1**
The most accurately titled of all the branches of Buzz, being
in Los Angeles's buzziest location. The 8000 Sunset location
also houses Crunch, the gym *du jour* and Sunset 5, the indie
cinema *du jour* – plus the Virgin Megastore, Wolfgang Puck
Café, Burke-Williams Day Spa and Sam Ash music store.

Coffee Bean & Tea Leaf

*8591 Sunset Boulevard, at Sunset Plaza Drive, West
Hollywood (1-310 659 1890). Bus 2, 3, 105, DASH West
Hollywood/I-10, exit La Cienega Boulevard north.* **Open**
6.30am-midnight Mon-Fri; 7am-midnight Sat, Sun.
Credit MC, V. **Map 4 A1**
A good place for people-watching, this branch is almost
directly opposite the shopping/eating/posing paradise that
is Sunset Plaza. Jennifer Aniston is just one of countless
celebs who can't do without their blended mochas here.

Kings Road Café

*8361 Beverly Boulevard, at Kings Road, West Hollywood
(1-323 655 9044). Bus 14/I-10, exit La Cienega
Boulevard north.* **Open** 7.30am-11pm daily. **Credit** MC,
V. **Map 4 B2**
Kings Road Café is one of those rare LA breeds – a trendy
coffeeshop that is as trendy now as when it opened in 1990.
If you want to glimpse LA's young beautiful things during
the day, there's no better place. It's also a prime hot actor-
spotting location: everyone from Brad Pitt to Alec Baldwin

Feel like royalty at **Kings Road Café**.

and shady refuge from heat and relentless shoppers. Though somewhat overpriced, it serves delicious salads and other creative dishes along with baked fare and sandwiches made with breads baked on the premises. We recommend olive or walnut yam. A fine site for people-watching.

Beverly Hills

Caffe Latte
6254 Wilshire Boulevard, at Crescent Heights Boulevard, Beverly Hills (1-323 936 5213). Bus 20, 21, 22/I-10, exit La Cienega Boulevard north. **Open** 7am-9pm Mon-Fri; 8am-3.30pm Sat, Sun. **Credit** AmEx, MC, V. **Map 4 B3**
In one of LA's off-street mini-malls, within spitting distance of Miracle Mile, Caffe Latte is a favourite spot for locals. It offers some boast-worthy snacks such as cinnamon swirl French toast and the Jody Maroni sausage sandwich, plus coffees from beans roasted on the premises and spirit-rejuvenating yogi teas (plain or with a halo of steamed milk). Breakfast is popular, especially on the weekends.

The Living Room
Peninsula Hotel, 9882 Little Santa Monica Boulevard, at Wilshire Boulevard, Beverly Hills (1-310 551 2888). Bus 4, 304/I-405, exit Wilshire Boulevard east. **Open** 8am-midnight Mon-Thur, Sun; 8am-1am Fri, Sat; reservations required. **Credit** AmEx, DC, Disc, JCB, MC, V. **Map 3 B2/3**
If you can get in (on weekends it's usually booked three weeks in advance) you will be pampered by the Beverly Hills version of English High Tea. Each day at 3pm you can choose from a dizzying array of leaves – from Earl Grey and Justin Lloyd to Temple of Heaven and Russian Caravan – and sample the mouthwatering salmon-on-pumpernickel sandwiches and the luscious tea cakes. It ain't cheap, though: $24 for the lot will transport you back to reality.

Michel Richard
310 N Robertson Boulevard, between Third Street & Burton Way, Beverly Hills (1-310 275 5707). Bus 27, 220, 316, 576/I-10, exit Robertson Boulevard north. **Open** 8am-10pm Mon-Sat; 9am-4pm Sun. **Credit** AmEx, DC, MC, V. **Map 4 A3**
Started by popular chef Michel Richard (though he has long since moved on), this fancy pastry shop – on fashionable Robertson Boulevard, with a hedged-in patio and spacious interior – brings in local regulars as well as film and music industry bigwigs. It's no secret that someone was shot at a patio table years back, but this doesn't deter the customers.

West LA

Lulu's Alibi
1640 Sawtelle Boulevard, at Santa Monica Boulevard, West LA (1-310 479 6007). Bus 4, 304, Santa Monica 1, 5/I-405, exit Santa Monica Boulevard west. **Open** 8.30am-1am Mon-Thur, Sun; 8.30am-2am Fri, Sat. **Credit** AmEx, MC, V.
If there is a story about Lulu's Alibi, no one's telling, beyond the fact that the original owner's name was Luanna. Choose from a wide variety of coffee drinks as well as sandwiches, salads, sweet breads, cookies and desserts – the most popular being tiramisu – and many Brazilian dishes, including the hearty national dish, feijoada. With cosy indoor and outdoor seating, Lulu's Alibi attracts a vibrant crowd of all ages and is a favourite with playgoers at the nearby Odyssey Theatre. It also holds poetry nights: phone for details.

Also recommended
The Abbey *692 N Robertson Boulevard, at Santa Monica Boulevard, West Hollywood (1-310 289 8410);* **The Conservatory** *10117 Washington Boulevard, at Motor Avenue, Culver City (1-310 558 0436);*

has taken meetings here. Handily placed for caffeine-hungry shoppers – it's just a few blocks from the Beverly Center shopping mall – Kings Road offers large cups of frighteningly strong coffee, delicious muffins and cakes and popular breakfasts. Coffee is reasonably priced (refills are cheaper) while food and cakes are a tad pricey and the service often leaves much to be desired. It has its own store next door, which sells café blend, decaf and regular coffee for $10/lb, and there's also a good international newsstand outside.

Urth Caffè
8565 Melrose Avenue, at Westmount Drive, West Hollywood (1-310 659 0628). Bus 10, 11, 105/I-10 east, exit La Cienega Boulevard north. **Open** 6.30am-11pm Mon-Thur, Sun; 6.30am-midnight Fri, Sat. **Credit** AmEx, MC, V. **Map 4 A2**
Urth was the first certified organic coffee and tea store in the US. It opened only after the owners had devoted two years to visiting coffee roasters, companies, plantations and tea importers throughout America and Europe. The delicious food includes wholehearted savouries and lo-cal desserts that will forever change your tune about dieting; don't even think of leaving without trying the famous three-layer cheesecake. Complete with sprawling outdoor porch and relaxing music, Urth offers coffeehouse life at its percolating best. It rivals Kings Road Café as the trendiest spot in the area and is also well situated on a newly hip strip of Melrose Avenue west of La Cienega.

Vienna Café/Melrose Baking Company
7356 Melrose Avenue, at Fuller Avenue, West Hollywood (bakery 1-323 851 8808/café 1-323 651 3822). Bus 10, 11/I-10, exit Fairfax Avenue north. **Open** 7.30am-9pm Mon-Thur, Sun; 7.30am-midnight Fri, Sat. **Credit** MC, V. **Map 4 C2**
Set on fashionable Melrose Avenue, Vienna Café is a quiet

You don't have to be a **Bourgeois Pig** *to enjoy this Hollywood hotspot.*

Il **Fornaio** *301 N Beverly Drive, at Dayton Way, Beverly Hills (1-310 550 8330);* **Petterson's Frisch Röst Coffees** *10019 Venice Boulevard, at Overland Avenue, Culver City (1-310 839 3359);* **Revival Café** *7149 Beverly Boulevard, at Detroit Street, West Hollywood (1-323 930 1210);* **Sweet Lady Jane** *8360 Melrose Avenue, at Kings Road, West Hollywood (1-213 653 7145).*

Hollywood & Midtown

Bourgeois Pig
5931 Franklin Avenue, at Beachwood Drive, Hollywood (1-323 962 6366). Bus 26, Community Connection 208/ US 101, exit Gower Street north. **Open** *9am-1.30am daily.* **No credit cards.** **Map 5 B1**
Set in a seriously funky row of shops and restaurants at the bottom of the Hollywood Hills in Beachwood Canyon, this dark and smoky café, furnished with elderly couches and chairs, has a pool table in the back room and perennially interesting company. Next door there's an excellent gift shop and newsstand.

Highland Grounds
742 N Highland Avenue, between Melrose & Waring Avenues, Hollywood (1-323 466 1507). Bus 10, 11/I-10 east, exit La Brea Avenue north. **Open** *9am-6pm Mon; 9am-12.30am Tue-Thur; 9am-1am Fri, Sat; 10am-9pm Sun.* **Credit** *MC, V.* **Map 5 A3**
Moments after stepping inside this airy two-floor café or the adjacent patio, you forget you are in the middle of LA. Started by some of the founders of **Caffe Latte** (*see p143*), this family establishment serves exceptional food, ranging from hamburgers on grainy brown bread with thin French fries to guacamole and tortilla chips. The coffee and teas are almost unbeatable (the yogi tea is the best in town), and the café's liquor licence draws big crowds to the nightly music and entertainment scene.

Insomnia
7286 Beverly Boulevard, at N Poinsettia Place, Fairfax District (1-323 931 4943). Bus 14/I-10, exit Fairfax Avenue north. **Open** *9am-4am daily.* **No credit cards.* **Map 4 C2**

As you might expect from its name, Insomnia stays open very late, serving clubbers wanting to party till dawn as well as those who simply can't sleep. It has stuck to the tried-and-tested formula of long hours, comfy seats and living-room-style surroundings, one of the few such places still open. Though Eric Stoltz is no longer a partner, Insomnia attracts actors and screenwriters by the car-load, so much so that one can feel out of place without a laptop or script to tote on your way in.

Also recommended
Hollywood Hills Coffee Shop & Café *Best Western Hollywood Hills Hotel, 6145 Franklin Avenue, between Gower & Vine, Hollywood (1-323 467 7678).*

East of Hollywood

Onyx Sequel
1804 N Vermont Avenue, between Melbourne & Russell Avenues, Los Feliz (no phone). Bus 1, 26, 180, 181/ US 101, exit Sunset Boulevard east. **Open** *8am-4am daily.* **No credit cards.** **Map 6 A2**
Slap-bang in the middle of hyper-trendy Vermont Avenue in Los Feliz, the Onyx, as it's known locally, is much less fancy than **Fred 62**, the hip restaurant up the street (*see p135* **Restaurants**). Its shabby chic feel attracts most of the area's hipsters and especially the party crowd since it's open until 4am (so long as there are java-seeking night owls in attendance). The Onyx serves tea, coffee and local delicacies, including the 'hippie roll', fancy bread stuffed with all manner of healthy vegetables, and assorted, unusually flavoured and thoroughly delicious muffins. There have been sightings of Leonardo DiCaprio here.

Say Cheese
2800 Hyperion Avenue, between Rowena Avenue & Griffith Park Boulevard, Silver Lake (1-323 665 0545). Bus 175/I-5, exit Los Feliz Boulevard west. **Open** *8am-6.30pm daily.* **Credit** *AmEx, MC, V.* **Map 6 B1/2**
Ignore the cutesy name: this is a peaceful coffeehouse and deli serving invariably fresh coffee in large café-au-lait cups. Fabulous deli sandwiches are made to order, hot or cold: a favourite is the California Melt, made with cheese, turkey,

onions, tomatoes and home-made dressing. One of the few coffeehouses – and a good one at that – in the area.

The Valleys

Boom Boom Room

11651 Riverside Drive, at Colfax Avenue, North Hollywood (1-818 753 9966). Bus 96/US 101, exit Laurel Canyon Boulevard north. **Open** 8am-1am Mon-Thur; 8am-3am Fri; 9am-3am Sat; 9am-1am Sun. **No credit cards.**

The perfect pitstop to recover from the oppressive heat of the San Fernando Valley with the help of an iced coffee. Decorated with old furniture and lamps with tasselled shades, it has the charm of a beloved and eccentric aunt's parlour. A great find in an area with limited coffee choices.

Hot House Café

12123 Riverside Drive, at Laurel Canyon Boulevard, North Hollywood (1-818 506 7058). Bus 96, 230/US 101, exit Laurel Canyon Boulevard north. **Open** 7am-midnight daily. **No credit cards.**

Actually a coffeehouse/performance space/used paperback bookstore, specialising in lurid detective and pulp fiction, and bizarre furniture. It adds a bit of life to the dreary North Hollywood neighbourhood, especially when George Thorogood, a pal of owner Karl Dovaston, drops by for an impromptu solo show.

Lulu's Beehive

13203 Ventura Boulevard, between Coldwater Canyon & Fulton Avenue, Studio City (1-818 986 2233). Bus 424, 522/US 101, exit Coldwater Canyon south. **Open** 8am-1am Mon-Fri; 8am-2am Sat; 11am-2am Sun. **No credit cards.**

Old Los Angeles hands may know this as Emerson's, its pre-Lulu identity. It's owned by the same person who started **Lulu's Alibi** in West LA (*see p143*); here she's jollying up an unthrilling neighbourhood by introducing art, comedy and poetry nights.

Horseshoe Coffeehouse

14568 Ventura Boulevard, at Cedros Avenue, Sherman Oaks (1-818 986 4262). Bus 424, 522/US 101, exit Van Nuys Boulevard south. **Open** 8am-2am daily. **Credit** MC, V.

Usually crowded indoors and out with the twentysomething crowd, what sets this café apart is its nightly music scene: soft love songs on Mondays, Hebrew/Mediterranean music on Tuesdays, big band on Wednesdays, jazz on Thursdays, world beat and reggae on Fridays, 1950s-1970s music on Saturdays and Euro hits and oldies on Sundays. It offers great food, plus board games, decks of cards and two pinball machines. Highly recommended.

Peet's Coffee & Tea

605 S Lake Avenue, at California Boulevard, Pasadena (1-626 795 7413). Bus 177, 485/I-210, exit Lake Avenue south. **Open** 6.30am-10pm Mon-Fri; 7am-10pm Sat; 7am-8pm Sun. **Credit** DC, Disc, MC, V.

After 30 years, San Francisco's Peet's Coffee & Tea brings its enterprise – intense, motor-oil-strength coffee – to Pasadena. It also brings the kind of dusky ambience that makes you wonder whether the owners have paid their electricity bill. The French Roast or any of the darker blends are Peet's specialities.

Also recommended

Seattle's Best Coffee *12265 Ventura Boulevard, at Laurel Canyon Boulevard, Studio City (1-818 761 8085).*

Cybercafés

There's no need to go electronically incommunicado while in LA. Head for a cybercafé, whether you want to send a digital postcard or peruse airline schedules online. While 24-hour computer/photocopying shops such as **Kinko's** (Hollywood branch: 7630 Sunset Boulevard, at Stanley Avenue; 1-323 845 4501) have machines for hire, the environment is often pressured and sterile: cybercafés are much more fun. There aren't as many fully fledged outfits in LA as one might expect; but there are a handful of pleasant spots to check your e-mail while downing a latte. Expect to pay $5-$9 an hour, though some places give time free if you buy a coffee.

Cyber Java

1029 Abbot Kinney Boulevard, at Broadway, Venice (1-310 581 1300/info@cyberjava.com). Bus 33, 436, Santa Monica 1, 2/I-10, exit Lincoln Boulevard south. **Open** 7am-2am daily. **Credit** DC, Disc, MC, V. **Map 2 A4**

Equipped with nine computers – both Macintosh and PC – as well as fax, laser printing, photocopying and colour scanning services, Cyber Java is usually packed, especially in the evenings. Terminals can be hired for $9 per

hour or $2.25 per 15 minutes; workshops and Internet classes are also available. The coffee and food – such as salads, sandwiches, myriad desserts and baked goods – are delicious and good value. The new Hollywood branch has 12 PCs and is open 24 hours.
Branch: 7080 Hollywood Boulevard, at La Brea Avenue, Hollywood (1-323 466 5600).
Website: www.cyberjava.com

Also recommended

Dolphin Café
1732 Abbot Kinney Boulevard, at Venice Boulevard, Venice (1-310 822 1415/dreamadolphin@earthlink.net/website: www.dreamadolphin.org).
Two Macintoshes, black-and-white printer. Children can use the equipment for free.
iBrowse Coffee & Internet
11 W Main Street, at Garfield Avenue, Alhambra (1-626 588 2233/website & e-mail: www.ibrowsecoffee.com).
Four PCs, three Macs, no printer; ½ hour free with a drink.
Megabyte Coffeehouse
4135 E Anaheim Street, at Ximeno Avenue, Long Beach (1-562 986 6892/Mark@megabytecoffee.com/website: www.megabytecoffee.com).
Nine PCs, scanner, colour printer.
World Café *2820 Main Street, at Ashland Avenue, Santa Monica (1-310 392 1661/teck@interworld.net).*
Two PCs, printer; restricted hours.

Bars

In clean-living, car-driving, hard-working LA, bars recall a more dissolute age. From faded splendour to seedy dives, here's where to start.

For all the pleasures that Los Angeles has to offer, the sad fact remains that there are precious few places in town where you can get a decent mixed drink. As most LA bartenders are actors marking time until their next job, bruised Martinis and warmed-over Cosmopolitans often seem the rule rather than the exception.

Then again, LA residents are hardly discerning drinkers. Bars are a much less important part of social life here than elsewhere; the city's poor public transport does not encourage drunken binges (keep in mind that the local police are extremely unsympathetic towards intoxicated motorists), and most of the hip and happening places are too far apart to make walking from one to another at all convenient.

Besides, the early-to-bed, early-to-rise ethos of the entertainment industry clears out many bars well before closing time, and '12-step' meetings (Alcoholics Anonymous and so on) have notoriously supplanted bars as popular pick-up spots. Still, LA's bar scene is more vibrant than it has been in years, thanks to the recent 'Lounge Revival' (which, unfortunately, came a few years too late to save some classic Polynesian-themed 'tiki' bars) and the appearance of several local watering holes in films such as *LA Confidential* and *Swingers*.

To be on the safe side, you can always order a beer; but don't expect an inspiring variety of brews. Compared to drinkers in New York, San Francisco, Chicago, Portland or Seattle, Angelenos tend to be rather undiscerning about their beer preferences. With the microbrew boom of the early 1990s replaced by today's Martini revivalism, most LA bars tend to stick to such insipid American standbys as Budweiser and Rolling Rock; Newcastle Brown, Bass, Harp and Guinness are the most commonly found foreign beers.

Note that smoking is now banned in bars. The government enforces the law erratically at best, and many bar owners would prefer to pay the $500 fine (smokers themselves are not fined), rather than suffer the greater financial hit that would go with losing their smoking customers. Smart, high-profile bars tend to enforce the ban more stringently than dark and dingy dives, but asking your bartender for an ashtray is the simplest way to ascertain whether or not you can light up.

Helpful hint: it's proper etiquette to tip the bartender. The simple act of tipping one or two dollars per round will win you a friend for life – or, at least, good service throughout the evening. In return, you can expect that most bartenders will be happy to call a cab for you.

For bars serving a specifically gay or lesbian clientele, *see chapter* **Gay & Lesbian**. Some bars have live music: if so, you may have to pay a cover charge of up to $5.

BOOZE & THE LAW

All bars are subject to California's strict alcohol laws: you have to be over 21 to buy and consume the stuff (take photo ID even if you look older), and alcohol can be sold only between the hours of 6am and 2am. Virtually every bar calls last orders at around 1.45am – technically, staff are obliged to confiscate unconsumed alcohol after 2am. Also, the Hollywood police department has, for several years, been making a concerted effort to bust bartenders for 'overserving', even taking allegedly inebriated customers into custody as 'evidence'. Therefore, unless you feel like cooling your heels down at the local precinct station, it would be wise not to make a show of your intoxication.

Westside: beach towns

The Arsenal
12012 W Pico Boulevard, at Bundy Drive, West LA (1-310 479 9782). Bus 30, 31, 209/I-10, exit Bundy Drive north. **Open** 10am-2am daily. **Credit** AmEx, DC, Disc, JCB, MC, V.
Boasting an alarming array of decorative weapons on its walls, this tiny restaurant/bar more than lives up to its name. The service is friendly, however, and in the unfearsome Happy Hour (4-6pm) – you'll pay only $1.50 for 'well' drinks (cheap, standard spirits).

Bob Burns
202 Wilshire Boulevard, at Second Street, Santa Monica (1-310 393 6777). Bus 4, 304, Santa Monica 1, 2, 3, 7/I-10, exit Fourth-Fifth Street north. **Open** 11.30am-midnight daily. **Credit** AmEx, DC, Disc, MC, V. **Map 2 A2**
Step out of consumer din into a quieter, bygone Los Angeles. Wood panelling, black leatherette booths, tartan carpets and older hipsters in pillbox hats and demi-furs make this place seem like an eerie holdover from the 1940s (it actually dates from the 1960s). An excellent cocktail bar, a menu that includes prime rib, oysters and pizza, and the guy at the grand piano who's been playing here since the place opened, combine to give Burns its unique character.

'Star Trek' meets Austin Powers at **Encounter** – *for that stiff drink before take-off.*

Circle Bar

*2926 Main Street, at Pier Avenue, Santa Monica
(1-310 392 4898). Bus 33, 333, Santa Monica 1, 2,
10/I-10, exit Lincoln Boulevard south.*
Open noon-2am daily. **No credit cards.**
Map 2 A4
If you like your bars dark, poky and steeped in cigarette
smoke, then this one's a must. The Circle Bar – an oval bar
in a shoebox-sized room opening off Main Street – remains
one of the last bastions of seediness in Santa Monica and,
boy, are the locals proud of it.

Encounter

*209 World Way, between Terminals 2 & 6, LAX
(1-310 215 5151). Bus 11, 42, 120, 225, 232, Culver
City 6, 11/I-405, exit La Tijera Boulevard west.*
Open 11am-midnight Mon-Thur, Sun; 11am-2am Fri, Sat.
Credit AmEx, DC, JCB, MC, V.
The service is terrible, the drinks are expensive and
ineptly mixed and the food is mediocre at best, but the Star
Trek-meets-Austin Powers vibe of this nostalgically futur-
istic restaurant/bar (hanging aloft in LAX's fabulous 1960s
Theme Building) makes it more than worth the trip. Lava
lamps adorn the kidney-shaped bar, Esquivel's *Harlem
Nocturne* plays endlessly in the elevators and you can
watch the endless parade of flight departures and arrivals
while sipping your beverage. Altogether an essential Los
Angeles experience.
Valet parking $5.

Liquid Kitty

*11780 W Pico Boulevard, between Barrington Avenue &
Bundy Drive, West LA (1-310 473-3707). Bus 30, 31,
209/I-10, exit Bundy Drive north.* **Open** 6pm-2am.
No credit cards.
This small, dimly lit establishment brings a touch of lounge-
revival elegance to an otherwise drab stretch of Pico
Boulevard. Obscure drink requests are handled with aplomb,
and live bands and DJs often stoke the atmosphere with
appropriately retro sounds.

Red Carpet Lounge

*Bay Shore Bowl, 234 Pico Boulevard, between Main &
Third Streets, Santa Monica (1-310 399 7731). Bus 20,
33, 434, Santa Monica 1, 7, 8/I-10, exit Lincoln
Boulevard south.* **Open** 9am-midnight Mon-Thur, Sun;
9am-1am Fri, Sat. **Credit** AmEx, MC, V. **Map 2 A3**
Identical twins Jean and Pat preside over this Googie-style
bowling alley's bar, mixing incredible $2.75 Martinis. The
lure of this place – where the Coen brothers threw *The Big
Lebowski*'s wrap party – is its seedy, supine, unintentional
re-creation of a Southern brothel. *See also* **Bay Shore Bowl**
p224 **Sport & Fitness**.

Ye Olde King's Head

*116 Santa Monica Boulevard, between Ocean Avenue
& Second Street, Santa Monica (1-310 451 1402).
Bus 4, 20, 22, 33, Santa Monica 1, 7, 8, 10/I-10,
exit Fourth-Fifth Street north.* **Open** 11am-1.30am Mon-
Thur; 10am-1.30am Fri, Sun. **Credit** AmEx, DC, MC, V.
Map 2 A2
Santa Monica's populous British contingent pretty much
keeps this pub in business. Darts, fish and chips, and stout
in abundance make a suitable home away from home; it's
also the best place in the area to watch televised European
soccer matches, which is why you'll usually find the members of Oasis hanging out here when they're in town.

Also recommended

My Father's Office *1018 Montana Avenue, between
Tenth & 11th Streets, Santa Monica (1-310 451 9330).*

Westside: inland

Argyle Hotel Bar

*8358 Sunset Boulevard, between Sweetzer Avenue &
La Cienega Boulevard, West Hollywood (1-213 654
7100). Bus 2, 3, 429, West Hollywood A, B/I-10, exit La
Cienega Boulevard north.* **Open** 11am-1.30am daily.
Credit AmEx, DC, Disc, MC, V. **Map 4 B1**

Located in the breathtaking art deco structure that is the Argyle Hotel, this bar – which made a brief appearance in Robert Altman's *The Player* – has one of the finest selections of whisky in town. Dress to impress.
Valet parking usually $3.50.

Bar Marmont

8171 Sunset Boulevard, between Sweetzer Avenue & Crescent Heights Boulevard, West Hollywood (1-213 650 0575). Bus 2, 3, 429/US 101, exit Highland Avenue south. **Open** 6pm-1.30am daily. **Credit** AmEx, MC, V. **Map 4 B1**
This bar's luxurious interior hides within a deceptively ugly, shanty-like structure down the street from the Chateau Marmont hotel on Sunset Boulevard. Bar Marmont has become *the* place for Hollywood's élite to lap up prohibitively priced but nicely confected libations. Sunday nights often feature poetry readings by famous actors and actresses who should know better, which can be a highly entertaining experience.
Parking $3.50 Mon-Wed, Sun; $5.50 Thur-Sat.

C

8442 Wilshire Boulevard, at Hamilton Drive, Beverly Hills (1-213 782 8157). Bus 20, 21, 22, 320/I-10, exit La Cienega Boulevard north. **Open** 5.30pm-2am Mon-Fri; 6.30pm-2am Sat, Sun. **Credit** AmEx, DC, Disc, JCB, MC, V. **Map 4 B3**
Prepare to dress well and pay through the nose for a classy, deco-era LA experience. This is a small bar and restaurant whose architecture dates back to 1929 and looks it: sumptuous, red-stained African wood panelling, real leather booths, bronze-toned drapes, plus smoked windows to keep the real world at bay. The globe-trotting assortment of vodkas, vintage champagnes, malt Scotches, ports, cognacs and tequilas sure helps, too.
Free validated parking at the Flynt Building or the Great Western Bank.

SkyBar

Mondrian Hotel, 8440 Sunset Boulevard, at La Cienega Boulevard, West Hollywood (1-213 848 6025). Bus 2, 3, 429/I-10, exit La Cienega Boulevard north. **Open** 11am-2am daily. **Credit** AmEx, DC, JCB, MC, V. **Map 4 A/B1**
This grotesquely trendy watering hole in the Mondrian Hotel is a great place for spotting celebs, provided you actually get in – to gain entry, you must first make reservations by phone (and even if you're staying at the hotel, you're allowed only two guests). The unceasing parade of beautiful Hollywood types (including the servers) is the main visual interest: the fixed décor is rather plain, and the view from the windows is far from impressive – don't be fooled by the high-flying name, as the bar is actually situated on one of the Mondrian's lower floors.
Valet parking $10.

Trader Vic's

Beverly Hilton Hotel, 9876 Wilshire Boulevard, at Santa Monica Boulevard, Beverly Hills (1-310 274 7777). Bus 4, 20, 21, 22, 27/I-405, exit Wilshire Boulevard east. **Open** 5pm-1am daily. **Credit** AmEx, DC, Disc, MC, V. **Map 3 B2**
Renowned for its absurdly overpriced Polynesian menu and its expensive-but-worth-it tropical drinks, Trader Vic's is an old-school 'tiki' bar. Wizened old bartenders of South Sea descent create alchemical wonders with various liquors and fruit juices – ordering the ridiculously potent Tiki Puka-Puka will earn you their undying respect and admiration – while Hawaiian entertainer Don Ho's 1960s classic *Tiny Bubbles* seems to play at five-minute intervals. Extremely crowded with the young and beautiful of Beverly Hills at weekends, the place usually has a barstool or two free most nights of the week.

Also recommended

Barney's Beanery *8447 Santa Monica Boulevard, at La Cienega Boulevard, West Hollywood (1-213 654 2287);* **bo kaos** *8689 Wilshire Boulevard, at S Hamel Drive, Beverly Hills (1-310 659 1200);* **Cava** *8384 W Third Street, at Orlando Avenue, West Hollywood (1-213 658 8898);* **Coronet Pub** *370 N La Cienega Boulevard, between Melrose Avenue & Beverly Boulevard, West Hollywood (1-310 659 4583).*

Hollywood & Midtown

Boardner's

1652 N Cherokee Avenue, at Hollywood Boulevard, Hollywood (1-323 462 9621). Bus 1, 180, 181, 210, 212/ US 101, exit Highland Avenue south. **Open** 11am-2am daily. **No credit cards. Map 5 A1**
Cheap beer and even cheaper entertainment – that is, if you find drunken former members of popular 1980s heavy metal acts entertaining – make a trip to this Hollywood mainstay worthwhile. Multiple bars and an airy back patio add to the frayed-at-the-edges appeal. Smoking is definitely not discouraged here.

Burgundy Room

16212 N Cahuenga Boulevard, at Hollywood Boulevard, Hollywood (1-323 465 7530). Bus 1, 180, 210, 212/ US 101, exit Cahuenga Boulevard south. **Open** 8.30pm-2am daily. **No credit cards.** **Map 5 B1**
Once your eyes adjust to the darkness, you'll notice that this ragged-but-right Hollywood dive has an amazing jukebox – full of obscure punk and soul singles – and that it's in dire need of a good dusting. Motorcycle jackets are pretty much the required uniform.

Cat & Fiddle Pub

6530 Sunset Boulevard, between Highland Avenue & N Cahuenga Boulevard, Hollywood (1-323 468 3800). Bus 2, 3, DASH Hollywood/US 101, exit Sunset Boulevard west. **Open** 11.30am-2am daily. **Credit** AmEx, MC, V. **Map 5 A2**
This popular spot for expatriate Brits and visiting rock musicians, run by former Creation/Ashton Gardner & Dyke bassist Kim Gardner, offers good fish and chips as well as several English brews on tap. The front patio is an exceedingly pleasant place to enjoy a pint.
Valet parking $2.75.

Coach & Horses

7617 Sunset Boulevard, at Stanley & Curson Avenues, Hollywood (1-323 876 6900). Bus 2, 3, 429/US 101, exit Highland Avenue south. **Open** 11.30am-2am Mon-Thur; noon-2am Sat; 5pm-2am Sun. **No credit cards. Map 4 C1**
A dartboard, a variety of lagers and a crew of unbelievably ill-tempered barmaids attract many of Los Angeles's British subjects to this tiny pub on Sunset Boulevard's 'Guitar Row'. Billy Idol is often seen here, which may be a reason for avoiding/visiting the place, depending on your point of view.

El Carmen

8138 W Third Street, between Kilkea Drive & La Jolla Avenue, Fairfax District (1-213 852 1556). Bus 16, DASH Fairfax/I-10, exit Fairfax Avenue north. **Open** 5pm-2am Mon-Fri; 7pm-2am Sat, Sun. **Credit** AmEx, MC, V. **Map 4 B3**
Arguably the best tequila bar in Los Angeles, this haven for Mexican kitsch is always packed for good reason: it stocks over 60 brands of mescal and tequila, from Patrón to Chicicapa. Bring a designated driver.
Valet parking $3.

Ye Olde King's Head *(page 147): home away from home for Santa Monica's Britpack.*

Formosa Café

7156 Santa Monica Boulevard, at Formosa Avenue,
Hollywood (1-323 850 9050). Bus 4, 212, West
Hollywood A, B/I-10, exit La Brea Avenue north. **Open**
11.30am-2am daily. **Credit** AmEx, MC, V. **Map 4 C1**
One of the few real remnants of Old Hollywood. The dark-
ened interior of this charming Chinese box – which boasts
the world's largest collection of Elvis decanters – is covered
with autographed photos of movie stars who have imbibed
here during the past six decades. The place has experienced
a surge in popularity, thanks to its memorable appearance in
LA Confidential, but the recent addition of an outdoor bar
area (sidestepping the smoking ban) helps to keep it from getting unbearably crowded. Take a seat at the bar or in an overstuffed leather booth, order a drink and pretend you're a
private detective or a matinée idol. But steer clear of the food.
Valet parking free with validation.

Frolic Room

6245 Hollywood Boulevard, at Vine Street, Hollywood
(1-323 462 5890). Bus 1, 180, 181, 217, 429/US 101,
exit Hollywood Boulevard west. **Open** 10am-2am daily.
No credit cards. Map 5 B1
Stepping over the squatter overflow from the lobby of the
neighbouring Pantages Theater will work up a thirst in even
the hardiest of individuals, so refresh yourself with a visit
to this hard-boiled relic from the 1940s, which was featured
in several scenes of *LA Confidential*.

Lava Lounge

1533 N La Brea Avenue, at Sunset Boulevard, Hollywood
(1-323 876 6612). Bus 2, 3, 212, 302, 429/I-10, exit La
Brea Avenue north. **Open** 9pm-2am daily. **Credit** Disc,
MC, V. **Map 4 C1**
Located in a fairly grim strip mall, Lava Lounge updates the
Polynesian pleasure palaces of the Eisenhower era with an
attractive mirrors-and-bamboo look, while the triangle-
backed leather barstools are the last word in bachelor-pad

luxury. Along with the usual beers and hard liquor, the bartenders mix a mean selection of tropical drinks.

Lola

945 N Fairfax Avenue, at Romaine Street, West
Hollywood (1-323 736 5652). Bus 14, 217/I-10, exit
Fairfax Avenue north. **Open** 5.30pm-2am daily. **Credit**
AmEx, DC, MC, V. **Map 4 B2**
This trendy nightspot is one of the few new establishments
in town to specialise in excellent Martinis – although, at $8
a pop, they'd better be excellent. The faux Tuscan décor and
trendy clientele are attractive, though the slow service and
oppressive noise levels can make the experience unbearable.

Molly Malone's Irish Pub

575 S Fairfax Avenue, at Sixth Street, Miracle Mile
(1-323 935 1577/music hotline 1-323 935 2707). Bus
20, 21, 22, 217/I-10, exit Fairfax Avenue north. **Open**
10.30am-2am daily. **Credit** AmEx, MC, V. **Map 4 B3**
Irish to the *n*th degree, Molly's stout-brown walls are
adorned with paintings of Brendan Behan, James Joyce and
Ms Malone herself. A friendly and comfortable place to enjoy
a pint of Guinness – though it can become uncomfortably
crowded on weekend nights – the pub attracts an odd mix
of musicians, twentysomething actors and actresses and
incredibly aged Irishmen. It also books a rootsy combination
of country, folk and Irish-influenced musical talent.

Musso & Frank Grill

6667 Hollywood Boulevard, at Cherokee Avenue,
Hollywood (1-323 467 7788). Bus 163, 180, 181, 212,
DASH Hollywood/US 101, exit Highland Avenue south.
Open 11am-11pm Tue-Sat. **Credit** AmEx, DC, MC, V.
Map 5 A1
Dinner at this remnant of Hollywood's golden age (it opened
in 1919) can cost you an arm and a leg, but plenty of
Angelenos come just to sit at the bar, sip Martinis (possibly
the best in town) and soak up the wood-panelled atmosphere.

Author and poet Charles Bukowski, in his relatively flush later years, ate and drank here regularly. *Parking 2 hours free with validation.*

The Room

1626 N Cahuenga Boulevard, between Selma Avenue & Hollywood Boulevard, Hollywood (1-323 462 7196). Bus 1, 180, 210, 212/US 101, exit Sunset Boulevard west. **Open** 8pm-2am daily. **Credit** MC, V. **Map 5 B1**

This dark dive's hard-to-find location (the entrance is down an alley at the back of the building) makes it the ultimate in 'if you don't know, don't go' hipness, though the atmosphere inside is friendly and very laid-back. The extremely spacious booths and seemingly endless bar ensure there's almost always a place to sit and sip, even at weekends.

Three Clubs

1123 Vine Street, at Santa Monica Boulevard, Hollywood (1-323 462 6441). Bus 4, 210, 420, 426/US 101, exit Vine Street south. **Open** 8.30pm-2am daily. **Credit** AmEx, MC, V. **Map 5 B2**

Cloaked in anonymity on the edge of one of Hollywood's more dilapidated strip malls – look for the 'Bargain Clown Mart' sign overhead, or you'll miss it completely – the Three Clubs is a cavernous wonder, complete with flocked velvet wallpaper and a ceiling decorated to look like a sparkling night sky. Although it looks (on the inside, at least) like the sort of place that Don Vito Corleone would hold court in, you're more likely to find beautiful twenty-somethings packed into the dark booths, exchanging phone numbers to the music of yesterday's easy-listening icons. Be warned: the bouncers can become surly at the slightest provocation.

Windows on Hollywood

Holiday Inn, 1755 N Highland Avenue, at Hollywood Boulevard, Hollywood (1-323 462 7181). Bus 1, 210, 212/US 101, exit Highland Avenue south. **Open** 6pm-1am Tue-Sat. **Credit** MC, V. **Map 5 A1**

Looking like the UFO from the *X-Files* movie crashed into the 23rd floor of the Hollywood Holiday Inn, this pleasingly morbid cocktail lounge boasts a stunning panoramic view of Hollywood Boulevard and vicinity. The atmosphere can't help but be casual in a place where many come alone to contemplate the smog sunset. Even the menu evokes broken dreams, with 'Tinseltown Prime Rib' and 'Universal Studios Salmon'. The entire lounge rotates from south to north and back again, which sort of drives the knife in and twists it a little. *Valet parking $8.*

Also recommended

HMS Bounty *3357 Wilshire Boulevard, at S Catalina Street, Mid Wilshire (1-213 385 7275).*

Downtown

Hank's Bar

Stillwell Hotel, 840 S Grand Avenue, between Eighth & Ninth Streets, Downtown (1-213 623 7718). Metro Seventh Street/Metro Center or Pershing Square/bus 40, 78, 79, 96, DASH C, E/I-110, exit Ninth Street east. **Open** 10am-2am daily. **Credit** AmEx, MC, V. **Map 7 B3/4**

If you're strolling around Downtown, be sure to stop in at this piece of Los Angeles history, a popular meeting place for policemen, reporters and politicians since before World War II. Just about the only thing that's changed since then is the price of the drinks.

Top of Five

Westin Bonaventure Hotel, 404 S Figueroa Street, at Fourth Street, Downtown (1-213 624 1000). Metro Seventh Street/Metro Center/bus 53, 60, 471, Montebello

---

40/US 101 north, exit Third Street south. **Open** 5.30-10pm daily. **Credit** MC, V. **Map 7 A/B2**

If the idea of watching the sunset from a slowly revolving bar at the top of a Downtown hotel appeals to you, give this place a visit. The drinks are nothing special, but the view is – on a clear day, you get a panoramic eyeful of the city – and the ride in the glass elevator isn't bad, either.

Also recommended

Otani Hotel *120 S Los Angeles Street, at E First Street, Downtown (front desk 1-213 629 1200).*

East of Hollywood

The Dresden Room

1760 N Vermont Avenue, between Franklin Avenue & Hollywood Boulevard, Los Feliz (1-213 665 4294). Bus 26, 180, 181, Community Connection 203/US 101, exit Vermont Avenue north. **Open** 11am-2am Mon-Sat; 3-10pm Sun. **Credit** AmEx, MC, V. **Map 6 A2**

This Los Feliz landmark has experienced something of a renaissance in the past few years, thanks to its appearance in *Swingers*. An eye-popping white leather and corkboard interior – and regular appearances by lounge duo Marty & Elayne – are the main attractions, but experienced bartenders also make it a real pleasure for discerning drinkers. *Valet parking $1.50.*

Good Luck Bar

1514 N Hillhurst Avenue, at Hollywood & Sunset Boulevards, Los Feliz (1-323 666 3524). Bus 1, 2, 3, 26, 302/US 101, exit Hollywood Boulevard east. **Open** 7pm-2am Mon-Fri; 8pm-2am Sat, Sun. **Credit** MC, V. **Map 6 A2**

This popular spot is packed to the rafters most nights of the week, which can make it hard to appreciate (or even see) its gloriously gaudy oriental décor. Many intriguing Chinese liqueurs and brandies are listed on the drinks menu, although the predominantly college-age crowd seems to prefer shots and beers (Tsingtao, of course). *Valet parking $3-$4.*

Smog Cutter

864 N Virgil Avenue, between Normal & Burns Avenues, Silver Lake (1-323 667 9832). Bus 26/US 101, exit Melrose Avenue east. **Open** noon-2am daily. **No credit cards. Map 6 A3**

If karaoke's your passion, make sure to include the Smog Cutter on your itinerary. Tough-talking Asian barmaids encourage you to have another, while folks from all walks of life get up to take their turn at the microphone – kd lang occasionally stops by to sing Patsy Cline numbers.

Tiki-Ti

4427 W Sunset Boulevard, between Hillhurst & Fountain Avenues, Silver Lake (1-213 669 9381). Bus 1, 2, 3, 26, 175/US 101, exit Vermont Avenue north. **Open** 6pm-2am Wed-Sat. **No credit cards. Map 6 A/B2**

A tiny Polynesian gem in the shadow of Silver Lake's KCET television studios, the Tiki-Ti dares ask the inebriated question: how much Pacific Ocean-related junk can you pack into an outhouse-sized shack while still leaving room for a few customers? Despite the cramped conditions, dedicated sybarites come from near and far to sample such potent tropical concoctions as Ray's Mistake, Blood and Sand and The Stealth – although it's virtually impossible to drink more than two without throwing up, passing out or going into severe insulin shock.

Also recommended

Red Lion Tavern *2366 Glendale Boulevard, at Silver Lake Boulevard, Silver Lake (1-213 662 5337).*

Shops & Services

Whatever your yen you can find it in Los Angeles, the city that made acquisitiveness and pampering less a leisurely pastime and more a 24/7 job.

The City of Angels, which blossomed largely as a result of the movie industry, with its emphasis on vanity and superficiality, loves to shop till it drops and simply adores to be spoiled. Whether or not you want to partake personally, it's a great place just to marvel at others' frivolity, made more pleasant by the clement weather and well-planned shopping areas – designed, of course, around use of the car.

Shop opening hours are usually 10am-7pm or 8pm, depending upon the area, or 11am-9pm in some shopping malls. Return policies in the chain-stores are nearly always in the buyer's favour; but watch out for smaller boutiques, which will go to the other end of the world to avoid giving you your money back. Parking is usually not too difficult, but if you're visiting the more expensive shops, use their valet parking: it's a small indulgence (compared to what you'll be laying out for the merchandise) and far better than a traffic ticket.

Los Angeles County adds an 8.25% sales tax to the marked price of all merchandise and services; Orange County taxes at 7.75%.

The shopping districts

Beverly Hills, particularly the Rodeo Collection and Two Rodeo on **Rodeo Drive**, is for those with money to burn and less-than-radical taste. Hidden among the Chanels and Pradas, however, are the odd, one-off boutique and hip California designer. It's also home to some of the best department stores, such as Neiman Marcus and Barneys New York. **Brentwood** has a range of upmarket restaurants, bookshops, clothing boutiques and the petite Brentwood Gardens mall. **Sunset Plaza** on Sunset Strip is another posh neighbourhood, scattered with high-end shops and sidewalk cafés, and great for a spot of people-watching.

North La Brea Avenue is Rodeo Drive's younger, hipper, cheaper sibling, the place for retro fashion and clubwear. **Robertson Boulevard** between Alden Drive and Third Street in West Hollywood is teeming with antique and design shops and is getting more fashionable by the nano-second, with a flurry of hip, upmarket boutiques and shoe shops moving in. **Hollywood Boulevard**, not unlike the **Venice Boardwalk**, is fun and seedy, packed with one-off vendors selling T-shirts, trashy lingerie, cloned designer goods, sunglasses, bargain leather and naff gifts.

Melrose Avenue is akin to the King's Road in London, once hip and avant-garde and now a somewhat tired-looking row of shops, cafés and restaurants that change hands quicker than a dealer at a poker table. It also suffers from a

Third Street Promenade, *Santa Monica.*

lack of decent parking. However, it's still popular with the young and a great place to spot young girls baring their pierced belly buttons. **Larchmont Village** is an oddity in Los Angeles – a four-block stretch of boutiques, shops and restaurants plonked slap-bang in the middle of expensive, residential Hancock Park – and not to be missed.

Westwood offers the kind of shopping you would find in a mall, but without the structure. It also has a very limited choice of shops. Its popularity has been usurped by **Third Street Promenade** in Santa Monica, which, rather like **Old Town Pasadena**, is a retro-fitted downtown area that emulates the mall experience.

Main Street in the Ocean Park area of Santa Monica is a revamped turn-of-the-century seaside resort, made into a delightful shopping experience with antique shops, fashion outlets, art galleries and speciality shops. On **Montana Avenue** (in the northern part of Santa Monica) you are spoilt for choice with furniture shops, antique and gift shops, restaurants, cafés, galleries, clothing shops and gourmet food shops. It combines high quality with eclectic range and has a pleasant, albeit affluent, neighbourhood vibe.

Downtown is home to the garment district, jewellery trade centres, flower and furniture markets and the California Mart, the country's largest wholesale apparel centre. **Seventh Street** has the city's largest collection of shoe shops and its original department stores. **Little Tokyo**, **Chinatown**, bustling **Broadway** and Mexican **Olvera Street** offer a good few hours of fun. Broadway is one of LA's main Latino streets and is full of discount clothing and knick-knack shops, bodegas (which sell religious kitsch and folkloric remedies for everything from indigestion to unrequited love), jewellers' shops and also features the vibrant Grand Central Market, which is a must.

Universal CityWalk in Universal City has the feel of a futuristic shopping centre with a mélange of shops and cafés. The sheer magnitude of the place and the wacky designs of the buildings make it well worth a visit.

Department stores

Barneys New York

9570 Wilshire Boulevard, at Camden Drive, Beverly Hills (1-310 276 4400). Bus 20, 21, 22/I-10, exit Robertson Boulevard north. **Open** 10am-7pm Mon-Wed; 10am-8pm Thur-Sat; noon-6pm Sun. **Credit** AmEx, JCB, MC, V. **Map 3 C2**

A good facsimile of the now legendary New York store, with four floors of cosmetics, jewellery, shoes, the best in designer clothes for both sexes, lingerie and home accessories. Above sits more elegance: Barney Greengrass, a bar and first-rate rooftop restaurant with one of the best views into Beverly Hills. It also sells gourmet foods.

Bloomingdales

Century City Shopping Center, 10250 Santa Monica Boulevard, between Century Park W & Avenue of the Stars (1-310 772 2100). Bus 22, 27, 28, 316, Santa Monica 5, Commuter Express 534/I-405, exit Santa Monica Boulevard east. **Open** 10am-9pm Mon-Fri; 10am-8pm Sat; 11am-6pm Sun. **Credit** AmEx, Disc, JCB, MC, V. **Map 3 B3**

Upmarket clothing, shoes, jewellery and accessories.

Branches: Beverly Center, 8500 Beverly Boulevard, at La Cienega Boulevard, West Hollywood (1-310 360 2700); Fashion Square, 14060 Riverside Drive, at Woodman Avenue, Sherman Oaks (1-818 325 2200).

Macy's

Beverly Center, 8500 Beverly Boulevard, at La Cienega Boulevard, West Hollywood (1-310 854 6655). Bus 14, 104/I-10, exit La Cienega Boulevard north. **Open** 10am-9.30pm Mon-Sat; 11am-7pm Sun. **Credit** AmEx, MC, V. **Map 4 A/B2**

Having bought out all its competitors, Macy's is the 800lb gorilla of US retail. Sensible, standard products.

Branches: check the phone directory for your nearest.

Neiman Marcus

9700 Wilshire Boulevard, at Roxbury Drive, Beverly Hills (1-310 550 5900). Bus 4, 20, 21, 22/I-10, exit Wilshire Boulevard north. **Open** 10am-6pm Mon-Fri; 10am-7pm Sat; noon-6pm Sun. **Credit** AmEx. **Map 3 B2**

Although Neiman's is nicknamed 'Needless Markups', nothing is really overpriced here. It's simply a store selling top-of-the-line goods that, naturally, cost a lot of money. It has one of the best women's shoe departments in town, a fine confectionery counter and a good cosmetics department.

Saks Fifth Avenue Beverly Hills

9600 & 9634 Wilshire Boulevard, at Bedford Drive, Beverly Hills (1-310 275 4211). Bus 4, 20, 21, 22/I-405, exit Wilshire Boulevard east. **Open** 10am-6pm Mon-Wed,

Fri, Sat; 10am-8.30pm Thur; noon-5pm Sat. **Credit** AmEx, MC, V. **Map 3 B/C2**

Saks has been a part of Beverly Hills since 1938 and offers everything you could possibly want in expensive glamour. It now offers even more, thanks to its expansion into a prime deco building (formerly inhabited by I Magnin, now known as Saks West), which has made Saks the largest Beverly Hills store. The new men's department, the Fifth Avenue Club for Men, is claimed to offer the most comprehensive personal shopping service in the country.

Sears

5601 Santa Monica Boulevard, at Western Avenue, Hollywood (1-323 769 2600). Bus 4, 20, 175, 207, 357/ US 101, exit Santa Monica Boulevard west. **Open** 10am-9pm Mon-Fri; 10am-7pm Sat; 10am-6pm Sun. **Credit** AmEx, Disc, MC, V. **Map 5 C2**

Despite its ugly brown exterior, this is a useful department store for all domestic appliances and inexpensive utility items. A blue-collar kinda place.

Branch: check the phone directory for your nearest.

Shopping malls

Shopping malls sprang up in the 1950s and 1960s to service suburbanites newly lured away from downtown areas. In LA, the ultimate suburban sprawl, malls have all but taken over, and a visit to the mall often takes the place of other activities, since it combines dining, shopping, exercise, movie-going and driving in one experience.

The same shops and franchises appear again and again – Ann Taylor, Z Gallerie, the Gap, Banana Republic, the Limited, Express, Hold Everything, Crabtree & Evelyn, Victoria's Secret, Joan & David – usually anchored by a generic department store, adding to the general homogeneity. Malls also usually house fast-food venues, cafés, cinemas and often a large supermarket, as well as the occasional restaurant or individually owned shop.

Beverly Center

8500 Beverly Boulevard, at La Cienega Boulevard, West Hollywood (1-310 854 0070). Bus 14, 104/I-10, exit La Cienega Boulevard north. **Map 4 A/B 2/3**

All you could possibly want in a mall, including two department stores (Macy's and Bloomingdales), a good selection of shoe shops, a MAC Cosmetics, some high-end, one-off boutiques, a multi-screen cinema and the Hard Rock Café.

Beverly Connection

100 N La Cienega Boulevard, between Beverly & Third Streets, West Hollywood (1-323 651 3611). Bus 14, 104/ I-10, exit La Cienega Boulevard north. **Map 4 B2/3**

A small, slightly shabby mall, opposite the Beverly Center, with a Strouds, Bookstar, Starbucks and Sport Chalet.

Brentwood Gardens

11677 San Vicente Boulevard, at 26th Street, Brentwood (1-310 820 7646). Bus 22, 322, Santa Monica 4, 8/ I-405, exit Wilshire Boulevard west.

A mini-mall with some excellent designer-filled boutiques.

Century City Shopping Center

10250 Santa Monica Boulevard, between Century Park W & Avenue of the Stars (1-310 277 3898). Bus 22, 27, 28, 316, Santa Monica 5, Commuter Express 534/I-405, exit Santa Monica Boulevard east. **Map 3 B3**

An outdoor set-up, comprehensive for both shopping, eating and movie-watching.

*The **Beverly Center**: West Hollywood's favourite shopping mall.*

Glendale Galleria

At Central Avenue & Broadway, Glendale (1-818 240 9481). Metrolink Glendale/bus 92/I-5, exit Colorado Street east.
It has a Neiman Marcus, so we approve.

Sherman Oaks Galleria

15301 Ventura Boulevard, at Sepulveda Boulevard, Sherman Oaks (1-818 382 4100). Bus 183, 234, 424, 425, 522, DASH Sherman Oaks/I-405, exit Ventura Boulevard west.
One of LA's original malls. Only in the Valleys can they create tackiness this extreme.

Westside Pavilion

10800 W Pico Boulevard, at Westwood Boulevard, Century City (1-310 474 6255). Bus Culver City 3, Santa Monica 7, 8, 12, 13, Commuter Express 431/I-10, exit Overland Boulevard north. **Map 3 A4**
This Westside shopping complex has some good kids' toys and clothes shops, the only Nordstrom department store in the city (great for reasonably priced clothes), a fine art-house cinema – and difficult parking.

Factory outlets

If you're willing to drive further afield, factory outlet stores offer factory seconds and some very good deals on major brand names such as Sony, Nike and Guess.

However, some items are not returnable and may not be the most up-to-date models.

Citadel Factory Stores

5675 E Telegraph Road, at Citadel Drive, City of Commerce (1-323 888 1220). Bus 462/I-5, exit Washington Boulevard north. **Open** 10am-8pm Mon-Sat; 10am-6pm Sun.

The Cooper Building

860 S Los Angeles Street, at Ninth Street, Downtown (1-213 622 1139). Bus 27, 28, 40, 42, 83, 84, 85/I-110, exit Ninth Street east. **Open** 8.30am-5.30pm Mon-Sat; 11am-5pm Sun.

Antiques

Antique shops

Ludy Strauss/The Quilt Gallery

1025 Montana Avenue, at Tenth & 11th Streets, Santa Monica (1-310 393 1148). Bus 3, Santa Monica 3/I-10, exit Lincoln Boulevard north. **Open** 11am-5pm Mon-Sat. **Credit** MC, V. **Map 2 B1**
North American quilts and hooked rugs from 1800 to 1940 plus American folk art, furnishings and paintings.

Off the Wall

7325 Melrose Avenue, at Fuller Avenue, Melrose District (1-323 930 1185). Bus 10, 11/I-10, exit La Brea Avenue north. **Open** 11am-6pm Mon-Sat. **Credit** AmEx, MC, V. **Map 4 C2**
Antiques and weird stuff, from the turn of the century to art deco to twentieth-century Americana, such as (at press time) a sofa converted from a 1960 Cadillac and myriad Wurlitzer jukeboxes from the 1940s.

Thanks for the Memories

8319 Melrose Avenue, between Sweetzer Avenue & Kings Road, Melrose District (1-323 852 9407). Bus 10, 11/I-10, exit La Cienega Boulevard north. **Open** noon-6pm Mon-Sat. **Credit** AmEx, Disc, MC, V. **Map 4 B2**
This Melrose store has probably one of the most comprehensive collections of art deco and Streamline Moderne in the city. It's populr with the stars: Johnny Depp purchased an oversized, burled walnut, 1930s Austrian cabinet here; Patricia Arquette bought some Murano glass for husband Nic Cage to add to his collection; and Diane Keaton bought some Mexican silver jewellery as gifts for friends.

Best bookshops

Angelenos are not the illiterates that the rest of the world thinks. They haven't the same opportunities to read on trains and buses that other urbanites do, but nevertheless publishers do a very brisk trade in Southern California. And bookshops have remade themselves into coffeehouses, entertainment centres with author readings and book groups, and meeting places – safe places to encounter interesting people, the 1990s version of the aerobics class.

There are three main bookshop chains, with branches all over town, many with in-shop cafés. Phone one branch to find the nearest to you: **Barnes & Noble** (Westwood branch: 1-310 475 4144); **Border's Books & Music** (Santa Monica branch: 1-310 393 9290); and **Bookstar** (Beverly Connection branch: 1-310 289 1734). Below are the best of the independent, specialist and second-hand bookshops.

Bodhi Tree

8585 Melrose Avenue, at Westbourne Drive, West Hollywood (1-310 659 1733). Bus 10, 11, 105, DASH Fairfax, West Hollywood/I-10, exit La Cienega Boulevard north. **Open** 10am-11pm daily.
Credit MC, V. **Map 4 A2**
Once a place frequented only by underground mystics, hippies and some pretty odd people (it was mentioned in Shirley Maclaine's first book, *Out on a Limb*), the Bodhi Tree is now recognised as the best metaphysical bookshop in Los Angeles and attracts many international questers. It also hosts 'alternative' workshops, poetry readings and seminars. The annexe at 606 Westbourne Drive sells second-hand books.

Book Soup

8818 Sunset Boulevard, at Horn Avenue & Holloway Drive, West Hollywood (1-310 659 3110). Bus 2, 3, 105, 302, 429, DASH West Hollywood/I-10, exit La Cienega Boulevard north. **Open** 9am-midnight daily. **Credit** AmEx, DC, Disc, MC, V.
Map 4 A1
If you only have time to visit one bookshop in LA, Book Soup is definitely the most pleasurable place to dip your nose into the delicious smell of fresh print, whether your penchant is for Raymond Chandler in paperback or the photos of Bruce Weber in hardback, or if you just want to lose track of time at its extensive domestic and international newsstand. Readings and signings are held, and **Book Soup Bistro** (*see p120* **Restaurants**) is a handy place for a quick cappuccino or a full meal.

Children's Book World

1058034 W Pico Boulevard, between Prosser & Manning Avenues, Rancho Park (1-310 559 2665). Bus Culver City 3, Santa Monica 7, 13, Commuter Express 431/I-10, exit Overland Avenue north. **Open** 10am-5.30pm Mon-Fri; 10am-5pm Sat. **Credit** MC, V.
Map 3 A/B4
A huge children's bookstore near Westside Pavilion shopping mall, with devoted and knowledgeable staff. There are storytelling sessions three Saturdays a month.

Cook's Library

8373 W Third Street, between Kings Road & Orlando Avenue, West Hollywood (1-323 655 3141). Bus 16, DASH Fairfax/I-10, exit La Cienega Boulevard north. **Open** 1-5pm Mon; 11am-6pm Tue-Sat. **Credit** MC, V.
Map 4 B3
Salivate over 4,000-plus books on food and wine from around the world, the collection of owner Ellen Rose.

Elliot M Katt

8568 Melrose Avenue, at Westmount Drive, West Hollywood (1-310 652 5178). Bus 10, 11, DASH Fairfax, West Hollywood/I-10, exit La Cienega Boulevard north. **Open** 11am-5.45pm Mon-Sat.
Credit AmEx, MC, V. **Map 4 A2**
An extensive array of books on any and every aspect of the performing arts in the United States. Prices range from $20 to $20,000.

Hollywood Book City

6627 Hollywood Boulevard, between Cherokee & Whitely Avenues, Hollywood (1-323 466 2525). Bus 1, 163, 180, 181, DASH Hollywood/US 101, exit Cahuenga Boulevard south. **Open** 10am-10pm Mon-Fri; 9am-9pm Sat; 10am-8pm Sun. **Credit** AmEx, DC, Disc, MC, V. **Map 5 A1**
A gargantuan, well-organised space filled with used books on myriad subjects.

Larry Edmunds Cinema & Theater Bookshop

6644 Hollywood Boulevard, between Cherokee & Whitely Avenues, Hollywood (1-323 463 3273). Bus 1, 163, 180, 181, DASH Hollywood/US 101, exit Cahuenga Boulevard south. **Open** 10am-6pm Mon-Sat.
Credit MC, V. **Map 4 A1**
Cinema and theatre books, movie magazines, scripts, posters and memorabilia.

Midnight Special

1318 Third Street Promenade, between Arizona Avenue & Santa Monica Boulevard (1-310 393 2923). Bus 4, Santa Monica 1, 7, 8/I-10, exit Fourth/Fifth Street north. **Open** 10.30am-11pm Mon-Thur; 10.30am-11.30pm Fri, Sat; 11am-11pm Sun. **Credit** AmEx, MC, V. **Map 2 A2**
This shop specialises in politics and culture, although it also has a good selection of general literature as well as a phenomenal range of magazines – and it's open late. Cultural events include open poetry evenings, book readings by authors and documentary film screenings.

Mysterious Bookshop

8763 Beverly Boulevard, between Robertson & San Vicente Boulevards, West Hollywood (1-310 659 2959). Bus 14, 16, 220/I-10, exit La Cienega Boulevard north. **Open** 10am-6pm Mon-Sat; noon-5pm Sun. **Credit** AmEx, Disc, MC, V. **Map 4 A2**
LA's oldest and largest mystery bookshop, selling new, second-hand and rare mystery, spy, detective and crime books and thrillers. Come here for a dose of LA noir.

Samuel French Theater & Film Bookshop

7623 Sunset Boulevard, at Stanley Avenue, West Hollywood (1-323 876 0570). Bus 2, 3, 429/I-10, exit

*Read all about it at **Book Soup** in West Hollywood.*

Fairfax Avenue north. **Open** 10am-6pm Mon-Fri; 10am-5pm Sat. **Credit** AmEx, Disc, MC, V. **Map 4 C1**
Stocks just about every film script in print, myriad theatre scripts and many books about drama and film.
Branch: 11963 Ventura Boulevard, at Laurel Canyon Boulevard, Studio City (1-818 762 0535).

Thomas Brothers Maps & Travel Bookstore

521 W Sixth Street, between Grand Avenue & Olive Street, Downtown (1-213 627 4018). Metro Pershing Square or Seventh Street/Metro Center/bus 442, 444, 446, 447, Foothill 488, Montebello 40, Santa Monica 10/I-110, exit Sixth Street east. **Open** 9.30am-5.30pm Mon-Fri. **Credit** AmEx, Disc, MC, V. **Map 7 B3**
The place to pick up your Thomas street guide to LA, and plenty of other maps. A browsing favourite for Downtown workers on their lunch break.

Vroman's

695 E Colorado Boulevard, between El Molino & Oak Knoll, Pasadena (1-626 449 5320). Bus 180, 181, 188, 256, 401/I-110, exit Colorado Boulevard east. **Open** 9am-9pm Mon-Thur, Sat; 9am-10pm Fri; 10am-7pm Sun. **Credit** AmEx, Disc, MC, V.
Vroman's is the largest independent bookshop in Southern California, with a 32,000sq ft (3,000sq m) shopfloor. It's 102 years old and still going strong. You'll find books, magazines, stationery, audio books, rentals and, soon, a coffee bar.

W&V Dailey Rare Books

8216 Melrose Avenue, between Harper & La Jolla Avenues, Melrose District (1-323 658 8515). Bus 10, 11/I-10, exit Fairfax Avenue north. **Open** 11am-5pm Tue-Sat. **Credit** AmEx, MC, V. **Map 4 B2**
Rare and wonderful books and first editions. William Dailey also does book appraisals and completed the late Timothy Leary's archive.

Wells

2209 Sunset Boulevard, at Mohawk Street, Silver Lake
(1-213 413 0558). Bus 1, 2, 3, 4, 200, 304/US 101, exit
N Alvarado Boulevard north. **Open** 11am-6pm Mon-Sat.
Credit AmEx, MC, V. **Map 6 C4**
Probably the largest collection of Southern Californian
antique tiles and pottery, from 1900 to the 1940s.

Antique malls

Pasadena Antique Center (1-626 449 7706),
open 10am-6pm daily, is also worth a visit.

Cranberry House

12318 Ventura Boulevard, between Whitsett & Laurel
Grove Avenues, Studio City (1-818 506 8945). Bus
424, 522/US 101, exit Laurel Canyon south.
Open 11am-6pm daily.
Some 15,000sq ft (1,395sq m) of antique clothing, furniture
and accessories on two floors of a 1930s building. The ambience and service are markedly welcoming.

Santa Monica Antique Market

1607 Lincoln Boulevard, between Colorado Avenue &
Olympic Boulevard, Santa Monica (1-310 314 4899).
Bus Santa Monica 9/I-10, exit Lincoln Boulevard north.
Open 10am-6pm Mon-Sat; noon-5pm Sun.
Map 2 A/B3
This 20,000sq ft (1,860sq m) mall has 200 different dealers.

Flea markets

The best flea market in town is held at the **Rose
Bowl** in Pasadena on the second Sunday of the
month; details on 1-213 588 2727.

Pasadena City College

1570 E Colorado Boulevard, between S Hill & Bonnie
Avenues, Pasadena (1-626 585 7123). Bus 181, 188,
401, Foothill Transit 187/I-110, exit Colorado Boulevard
east. **Open** 8am-4pm first Sun of month.
Admission free.
A manageable-sized market selling furniture, clothing,
jewellery and nostalgia items.

Long Beach Outdoor Antique &
Collectible Market

5000 Lew Davis Street, at Conant Street, Long Beach
(1-562 655 5703). Bus Long Beach Transit 112/I-405,
exit Lakewood Boulevard north. **Open** 5.30am-3pm third
Sun of the month. **Admission** $4.50; early $10.
The largest antiques and collectibles market in the West.

Art supplies

Aaron Brothers Art Mart

1645 Lincoln Boulevard, between Colorado Avenue &
Olympic Boulevard, Santa Monica (1-310 450 6333).
Bus Santa Monica 9/I-10, exit Lincoln Boulevard north.
Open 9am-9pm Mon-Sat; 10am-6pm Sun. **Credit** AmEx,
Disc, MC, V. **Map 2 A/B3**
The Westside's biggest art supply shop. Discount prices.

The Art Store

7301 W Beverly Boulevard, at Poinsettia Place, West
Hollywood (1-323 933 9284). Bus 14/I-10, exit La Brea
Avenue north. **Open** 9am-8pm Mon-Fri; 9am-6pm Sat;
11am-6pm Sun. **Credit** AmEx, MC, V.
Map 4 C2
Everything from frames, portfolios, oils, pastels, clay, faux
finishes and easels to greeting cards and art books.

Pearl Art & Craft Supplies

1250 La Cienega Boulevard, at Pico Boulevard, Midtown.
Bus 105, Santa Monica 5, 7, 12/I-10 exit La Cienega
Boulevard north. **Open** 10am-8.30pm Mon-Sat;
11am-6pm Sun. **Credit** AmEx, MC, V. **Map 4 B4**
Humungous warehouse seething with paints, portfolios and
fine art books. You name it, they got it!

Dry cleaners

Effrey's

8917 Melrose Avenue, between Robertson Boulevard &
Doheny Drive, West Hollywood (1-310 858 7400).
Bus 4, 220/I-10, exit Robertson Boulevard north.
Open 8am-5.30pm Mon-Fri; 8am-1pm Sat. **Credit**
AmEx, MC, V. **Map 4 A2**
For the ultimate in dry cleaning. They won't hurry it and it
will cost the earth, but take your treasured items elsewhere
at your peril. Pick-up and delivery is, of course, available.

Michael Faeth Studio Cleaners

10800 Washington Boulevard, between Midway &
Overland Avenues, Culver City (1-310 838 1801).
Bus Culver City 1, 3/I-10, exit Overland Avenue south.
Open 24 hours Mon-Fri; 9am-3pm Sat.
No credit cards.
This outfit services many of the film studios' costume depart-
ments; they cleaned up on *Batman and Robin* and *Waterworld*.

Electronics & computers

The large electronic chainstores can be rather
intimidating places to shop, but offer the best bargains. One shop will often make a promise to
match another's lower price, so check the Sunday
papers to see who's offering the top deal in town.
Chainstore the **Good Guys** has a handy branch
at the Beverly Connection mall in West
Hollywood (1-310 659 6500). Beware of buying
costly items with a warranty that won't be valid
outside the US.

Circuit City

1839 La Cienega Boulevard, between 18th & Sawyer
Streets, Midtown (1-310 280 0700). Bus 105/I-10, exit
La Cienega Boulevard north. **Open** 10am-9pm Mon-Sat;
11am-6pm Sun. **Credit** AmEx, Disc, MC, V. **Map 4 B5**
A vast shop that stocks everything from personal elec-
tronics and stereo systems to washers and dryers.
Branches: check the phone directory for your nearest.

CompUSA

11441 Jefferson Boulevard, between Slauson Boulevard
& the I-405, Culver City (1-310 390 9993). Bus 108,
110, 561, Culver City 2, 4, 6/I-405, exit Jefferson
Boulevard east. **Open** 9am-9pm Mon-Fri; 10am-7pm Sat;
11am-7pm Sun. **Credit** AmEx, MC, V.
Computer supplies and systems. At last, a shop that celebrates Macintosh (whaddya think this book was built on?).
Branch: 761 N San Fernando Road, at Burbank
Boulevard, Burbank (1-818 848 8588).

Fry's

3600 Sepulveda Boulevard, at Rosecrans Avenue,
Manhattan Beach (1-310 364 3797). Bus 125, 232/I-
405, exit Rosecrans Avenue west. **Open** 8am-9pm Mon-
Fri; 9am-8pm Sat; 9am-7pm Sun. **Credit** Disc, MC, V.
A dizzying array of computers, software and gadgetry, plus
an excellent choice of games.

Flower power

Head for the **The Woods** *in Brentwood for floral finery.*

To order flower deliveries in the US and internationally, call **Florist Transworld Delivery** (1-800 736 3383; it's based in Illinois).

Campo dei Fiori
648 Martel Avenue, between Clinton Street & Melrose Avenue, West Hollywood (1-323 655 9966). Bus 10, 11/ I-10, exit Fairfax Avenue north. **Open** 9am-6pm Mon-Fri. **Credit** AmEx, MC, V. **Map 4 C2**
Fashion-conscious florist selling everything from country-cottage garden arrangements with hydrangeas and wild roses to exotic tropicals. Closed at the weekend.

LA Flower Market
754 Wall Street, between Seventh & Eighth Streets, Downtown (1-213 622 1966). Bus 10, 11, 20, 21, 22, 48, 51, DASH D/I-110, exit Ninth Street east. **Open** 8am-noon Wed, Fri; 6am-11am Tue, Thur, Sat. **Admission** $2. **Map 7 C3**

The smell is intoxicating and the bustle of the city's retailers buying their blooms at wholesale prices is worth the trip. You don't have to be trade to buy here, though.

The Woods
11711 Gorham Avenue, between San Vicente Boulevard & Barrington Avenue, Brentwood (1-310 826 0711). Bus 22, 322, Santa Monica 3, 14/ I-405, exit Wilshire Boulevard west. **Open** 8am-8pm Mon-Thur; 8am-9pm Fri, Sat; 9am-7pm Sun. **Credit** AmEx, MC, V.
A spectacular contemporary florist in Brentwood. The arrangements are an expression of the beauty of all things growing – not just flowers, but fruit, vegetables and herbs, too. Meg Ryan favours the luscious garden roses, grown especially for the store; John Travolta likes to buy arrangements flowing from customised silver treasure chests; and Jim Belushi is always using the Woods to express his thanks to various women in his world.

Fashion

If you think fashion begins and ends with Paris, London and New York, think again, cookies. LA has its own distinctive style. Anything goes. The climate often dictates. So do the stars. Status labels have always carried their weight here, but you should check out LA's rising young designers, such as John Eshaya, Monah Li and Anna Hueling for women and the Fever label for men. Sportswear is also crucial, and, in fact, probably LA's biggest contribution to the fashion scene.

Reliable chainstores the **Gap** (Santa Monica branch: 1-310 453 4551; website: www.gap.com) and **Banana Republic** (Beverly Hills branch: 1-310 858 7900) are plentiful; call any branch to find the nearest to you.

Atlantis Clothing Café

3900 Cross Creek Road, suite 2, between Cross Creek & Palm Canyon Lanes, Malibu (1-310 456 5773). Bus 434/I-10, exit PCH north. **Open** 10am-6pm daily.
Credit MC, V.
Love-inspired 1960s fashions endure at this hip clothing shop for yuppie mums and girls way too young to know what happened at Woodstock. It also has sensual oils for healing, elixirs, crystals, jewellery, mystical things, poetry readings and channelling sessions. 'We're a total goddess, boheme, movie star funky shop,' says manager Susan Dupre.

Booth 7

7576 Melrose Avenue, between Curson & Sierra Bonita Avenues, Melrose District (1-323 651 1373). Bus 10, 11/ I-10, exit Fairfax Avenue north. **Open** 11am-8pm Mon-Sat; noon-8pm Sun. **Credit** AmEx, MC, V. **Map 4 C2**
Places open and close so fast on Melrose Avenue, but at press time this was an excellent bet for trendy clubwear for boys and girls.

Brooks Brothers

601 S Figueroa Street, at Sixth Street, Downtown (1-213 629 4200). Metro Seventh Street/Metro Center/bus 20, 21, 22, 26, 51, 60, DASH C, E/I-110, exit Sixth Street east. **Open** 9.30am-6pm Mon-Fri; 9am-6pm Sat; noon-5pm Sun. **Credit** AmEx, Disc, JCB, MC, V.
Map 7 A3
Now you don't have to fly to New York for your button-down, preppie men's shirts.
Branches: check the phone directory for your nearest.

CP Shades

2937 Main Street, at Marine & Pier Avenues, Santa Monica (1-310 392 0949). Bus 33, 333, Santa Monica 1, 2/I-10, exit Lincoln Boulevard south. **Open** 11am-7pm Mon-Fri; 11am-6pm Sat; noon-5pm Sun. **Credit** AmEx, MC, V. **Map 2 A4**
Comfortable sportswear for men and women, all in muted and solid colours.
Branches: check the phone directory for your nearest.

Curve

154 N Robertson Boulevard, between Clifton Way & Wilshire Boulevard, Beverly Hills (1-310 360 8008). Bus 20, 21, 22, 220/I-405, exit Wilshire Boulevard east. **Open** 11am-7pm daily. **Credit** AmEx, MC, V.
Map 4 A3
Thirty-year-old Delia Seaman and 22-year-old Nevena Borissova have combined their fashion styles – Delia's is classic and conservative and Nevena's street-funky – and opened Curve, a women's clothing and accessory shop.

Fred Segal/Ron Herman Melrose

8100 Melrose Avenue, at Crescent Heights Boulevard, Melrose District (1-323 651 4129). Bus 10, 11/I-10, exit La Cienega Boulevard north. **Open** 10am-7pm Mon-Sat; noon-6pm Sun. **Credit** AmEx, MC, V. **Map 4 B2**
Fred Segal is the answer to one-stop fashion shopping for those with style, taste and money. A cornucopia of shops under one roof, with everything from hip casual wear to expensive designer gear for men, women and small children, plus gifts, furniture and beauty goods.
Branch: 500 Broadway, at Fifth Street, Santa Monica (1-310 393 4477).

Gisele Tune

12660 Ventura Boulevard, at Whitsett Avenue, Studio City (1-818 980 1196). Bus 422, 424, 522, DASH Van Nuys/US 101, exit Laurel Canyon Boulevard south. **Open** 11am-7pm Mon-Sat; 11am-6.30pm Sun.
Credit AmEx, MC, V.
Upmarket boutique with all the latest funky, contemporary togs, from Aviatic jeans to Espace 'pedicure' sandals.

Golf Punk/Golf Punk Girl

7550 Melrose Avenue, at Sierra Bonita Avenue, Melrose District (1-323 653 5386). Bus 10, 11/I-10, exit Fairfax Avenue north. **Open** noon-7pm Mon, Sun; 11am-7.30pm Thur-Sat. **Credit** MC, V. **Map 4 C2**
You'll find crazy, fun and very *aujourd'hui* clothing for young men and women in this tiny shop. Mainly T-shirts.

Iceberg

280 N Rodeo Drive, between Dayton Way & Wilshire Boulevard, Beverly Hills (1-310 777 0067). Bus 4, 20, 21, 320, DASH Beverly Hills/I-405, exit Wilshire Boulevard. **Open** 10am-7pm Mon-Sat; noon-6pm Sun.
Credit AmEx, MC, V. **Map 3 C2**
Fabulous, upmarket but daring clothing is made for Iceberg by different designers each season, for men and women.

Jay Wolf

517 N Robertson Boulevard, at Melrose Avenue, West Hollywood (1-310 273 9893). Bus 10, 11, 220/I-10, exit Robertson Boulevard north. **Open** 11am-7pm Mon-Fri; 10.30am-6pm Sat. **Credit** AmEx, MC, V.
Map 4 A2
Expect a very personal service in this boutique, which carries Hugo Boss and Paul Smith labels for men and Paul Smith and Margaret Howell for women.

J Crew

3 Colorado Boulevard, at Fair Oaks Avenue, Pasadena (1-626 568 2739). Bus 180, 181, 188, 256, 402, 483, Foothill Transit 187/I-110, exit Fair Oaks Avenue north. **Open** 10am-9pm Mon-Sat; 10am-7pm Sun.
Credit AmEx, MC, V.
One of the few shops for this high-quality catalogue designer: the ultimate in preppie-style casual togs for both sexes.
Branches: check the phone directory for your nearest.

Jonathan A Logan

8336 Melrose Avenue, between Sweetzer Avenue & Kings Road, West Hollywood (1-323 653 9155). Bus 10, 11/ I-10, exit La Cienega Boulevard north. **Open** 8am-7pm Mon-Fri; 10am-5pm Sat; by appointment Sun.
Credit AmEx, MC, V. **Map 4 B2**
Custom-designed leather made from over 3,000 types of skins, in myriad colours. Film credits include *City of Angels* and *US Marshall*.

Kate Spade

105 N Robertson Boulevard, at Alden Drive, Beverly Hills (1-310 271 9778). Bus 20, 21, 22, 420/I-405, exit Wilshire Boulevard east. **Open** 11am-7pm Mon-Sat; noon-5pm Sun. **Credit** AmEx, Disc, MC, V. **Map 4 A3**

CDs, tapes & records

Los Angeles has the overwhelming selection of recorded music that you'd expect to find in a big city and, as a music industry hub, is also fantastic for used vinyl. A whole 'beat junkie' culture has grown around finding rare records for next to nothing, but even the casual buyer can make great finds.

And if you want to make music rather than just listen to it, visit the **Guitar Center** in Hollywood (7425 Sunset Boulevard, at N Martel Avenue; 1-323 874 1060). It stocks most kinds of musical instruments as well as vintage guitars.

A-1 Record Finders

5639 Melrose Avenue, at Larchmont Boulevard, Hollywood (1-323 732 6737). Bus 10, 11, 210, 310, 426/ US 101, exit Melrose Avenue west. **Open** noon-6pm Mon-Sat. **Credit** AmEx, MC, V.
Map 5 B3
A-1 will scour the earth for your hard-to-find penchant, if it doesn't already have it in stock – and it probably will – but only if it's on vinyl. Insanely pricey, though.

Aron's Record Shop

1150 N Highland Avenue, between Lexington Avenue & Santa Monica Boulevard, Hollywood (1-323 469 4700). Bus 4, 304, 420, 426/US 101, exit Highland Avenue south. **Open** 10am-10pm Mon-Thur, Sun; 10am-midnight Fri, Sat. **Credit** AmEx, MC, V.
Map 5 A2
New and used, every genre, every format. Plus videos (used movies and new music videos) and magazines.

Fat Beats

1722 N Vermont Avenue, between Hollywood Boulevard & Franklin Avenue, Silver Lake (1-323 663 3717). Bus 1, 180, 181, 204, 206, 354/US 101, exit Vermont Avenue north. **Open** noon-9pm Mon-Thur; noon-10pm Fri, Sat; noon-6pm Sun; closed last Sun of the month. **Credit** MC, V. **Map 6 A2**
A comprehensive hip-hop shop with over 200 wall-mounted racks selling the newest of the new, complemented nicely by a rare groove wall.

The Record Recycler

4659 Hollywood Boulevard, at Vermont Avenue, Los Feliz (1-323 666 7361). Bus 1, 180, 206, 354/US 101, exit Vermont Avenue north. **Open** 11am-8pm Mon-Sat; noon-6pm Sun. **Credit** AmEx, Disc, MC, V. **Map 6 A2**
A place for vinyl buffs, with a huge selection of clean, well-filed, used vinyl, with decks to listen before you buy.

Rhino Records

1720 Westwood Boulevard, between Massachusetts Avenue & Santa Monica Boulevard, Westwood (1-310 474 8685). Bus 4, 304, Santa Monica 1, 8, 12/I-

The famous New York handbag/purse designer lands in LA with her wacky bags and small line of classic clothes.

Madison

106 N Robertson Boulevard, between W Third Street & Alden Drive, Beverly Hills (1-310 275 1930). Bus 20, 21, 22, 220, 320/I-10, exit Robertson Boulevard north. **Open** 11am-7pm Mon-Sat; noon-5pm Sun. **Credit** AmEx, MC, V. **Map 4 A3**
A good mix of hiply classic clothes for sophisticated women. As well as Madison's own label, you'll find clothing by Alberto Biani, Blumarine, Tocca and Ann Demeulemeester and shoes and handbags by Miu Miu and Dolce & Gabbana.

Marshalls

11239 Ventura Boulevard, between Tujunga & Vineland Avenues, Studio City (1-818 753 1301). Bus 96, 166, 424, 522/US 101, exit Vineland Avenue south. **Open** 9.30am-9.30pm Mon-Sat; 11am-7pm Sun. **Credit** AmEx, Disc, MC, V.
This discount shop sells clothes, gifts and household stuff. The best place to buy Calvin Klein underwear at low prices.

Maxfields

8825 Melrose Avenue, at Robertson Boulevard, West Hollywood (1-310 274 8800). Bus 10, 11, 220/I-10, exit Robertson Boulevard north. **Open** 11am-7pm Mon-Sat. **Credit** AmEx, DC, Disc, MC, V. **Map 4 A2**
This the Sistine Chapel of designer gear and accessories for cutting-edge men and women: Gigli, Gucci, Prada, Comme des Garçons, Yohji Yamamoto, Jil Sander, Gaultier, Galliano, Dries Van Nouten. Enjoy the personal service and drink the shop's own-label designer water while you mix and match.

Scott Hill

100 N Robertson Boulevard, at Alden Drive, Beverly Hills (1-310 777 1190). Bus 20, 21, 22, 220, 322/I-10, exit Robertson Boulevard north. **Open** 11am-6pm Mon-Sat; noon-5pm Sun. **Credit** AmEx, MC, V. **Map 4 A3**
Scott Hill will put together a whole wardrobe for you – or catalogue and co-ordinate your existing one. Business and casual menswear, with designs by Donna Karan, Calvin Klein, Giorgio Armani, Kiton, Luciano Barbera and Isaia.

The Swell Store

126 N La Brea Avenue, between First Street & Beverly Boulevard, West Hollywood (1-213 937 2096). Bus 14, 212/I-10, exit La Brea Avenue north. **Open** 11am-8pm Mon-Sat; noon-7pm Sun. **Credit** AmEx, MC, V. **Map 4 C2/3**
Check out the huge Hush Puppy sitting on top of the shop, then venture inside to find clothes and shoes for the young, hip, club crowd.

Sunny's

1007 Fair Oaks Avenue, at El Centro Street, South Pasadena (1-626 799 8764). Bus 176, 483/Hwy 110, exit Fair Oaks Avenue south. **Open** 11am-7pm Mon-Sat; noon-5pm Sun. **Credit** AmEx, MC, V.
Clothes, jewellery, knick-knacks, home furnishings and gifts from India to Japan. A fun experience.

Syren

7225 Beverly Boulevard, between Alta Vista Boulevard & Formosa Avenue, West Hollywood (1-323 936 6693). Bus 14, 212/I-10, exit La Brea Avenue north. **Open** 11am-6pm Tue-Sat. **Credit** AmEx, MC, V. **Map 4 C2**
Syren designed the suit for Michelle Pfeiffer's Catwoman, a dress for a Cindy Crawford *Vogue* shoot and outfits for Madonna and Appolonia. Although this is couture latex, don't be intimidated: you can pick up a basic strap dress in rubber for $160.

405, exit Santa Monica Boulevard east. **Open** 10am-11pm Mon-Thur, Sun; 10am-midnight Fri, Sat. **Credit** AmEx, Disc, MC, V. **Map 3 A4**
For serious collectors and ol' fashioned lovers of fine rock, jazz, blues, folk and reggae. New and second-hand records and all other formats, indie and imports, plus regular live performances in the shop.

Tower Records

8801 Sunset Boulevard, at Horn Avenue, West Hollywood (1-310 657 7300). Bus 2, 3, 429/I-10, exit La Cienega Boulevard north. **Open** 9am-midnight daily. **Credit** AmEx, MC, V. **Map 4 A1**
You can't ignore Tower (*see* **photo**), but it doesn't always carry the range you would expect, forcing customers to flee to the nearby Virgin Megastore.

Virgin Megastore

8000 Sunset Boulevard, at Crescent Heights Boulevard, West Hollywood (1-213 650 8666). Bus 2, 3, 217, 302, 429/I-10, exit La Cienega Boulevard north. **Open** 9am-midnight Mon-Thur, Sun; 9am-1pm Fri, Sat. **Credit** AmEx, Disc, MC, V. **Map 4 B1**
Hurray for Richard Branson. Not only are there well-stocked sections of everything from soul to classical, an in-house DJ, easy access and free parking, but you get a whole floor dedicated to movies, videos, laserdiscs and computer games.

*Delve for designer labels at ultra-fashionable **Maxfields**. See page 161.*

Tag Rag

363 N Beverly Drive, between Brighton & Dayton Ways, Beverly Hills (1-310 275 2131). Bus 3, 4, 14, 20, DASH Beverly Hills/I-405, exit Wilshire Boulevard. **Open** 10am-6.30pm Mon-Sat; noon-5pm Sun. **Credit** AmEx, MC, V. **Map 3 C2**

LA designer of casual, club and sports clothing for hip boys and girls who like to shop with the grown-ups in Bev Hills.

2000BC Stoned Age Hemp Shop

8260 Melrose Avenue, between Harper & La Jolla Avenues, Melrose District (1-323 782 0760). Bus 10, 11/ I-10, exit Fairfax Avenue south. **Open** 11am-7pm Mon-Sat; noon-6pm Sun. **Credit** Disc, MC, V. **Map 4 B2**

'Everything to do with the whole hemp lifestyle': bongs, pipes and lots of hemp clothing.

Theodore Beach

23733 W Malibu Road,at Webb Way, Malibu (1-310 456 7719). Bus 434/I-10, exit PCH north. **Open** 10am-6pm Mon-Sat; noon-5pm Sun. **Credit** AmEx, DC, MC, V.

Everything for the rich hippy chick, from footwear to a tremendous selection of T-shirts.

Tracy Ross

8595 Sunset Boulevard, between Alta Loma Road & La Cienega Boulevard, West Hollywood (1-310 854 1996). Bus 4, West Hollywood A, B/I-10, exit La Cienega Boulevard north. **Open** 10am-7pm Mon-Sat; noon-5pm Sun. **Credit** AmEx, MC, V. **Map 4 A1**

T-shirts, mini-dresses, pyjamas and perfumes for the cool girl-woman about town.

Union

110 N La Brea Avenue, between First & Second Streets, Fairfax District (1-323 549 6950). Bus 212/I-10, exit La Brea Avenue north. **Open** 11am-7pm Mon-Sat; noon-6pm Sun. **Credit** AmEx, MC, V. **Map 5 A3/4**

Casual clothes and activewear by hot young designers.

Worn Out West

645 N Martel Avenue, at Melrose Avenue, Melrose District (1-323 653 5645). Bus 10, 11/I-10, exit La Brea Avenue north. **Open** 11.30am-7pm Mon-Sat; noon-7pm Sun. **Credit** AmEx, Disc, MC, V. **Map 4 C2**

Renowned for its large selection of used Levi's, cowboy boots, workshirts and military outfits.

X-Large & X-Girl

1756 N Vermont Avenue, between Hollywood Boulevard & Franklin Avenue, Los Feliz (1-323 666 3483). Bus 1, 180, 181, 204, 217, 354/ US 101, exit Vermont Avenue north. **Open** noon-7pm Mon-Sat; noon-6pm Sun. **Credit** AmEx, MC, V. **Map 6 A2**

Three lines of actionwear clothes for grown-up boys and girls – Grand Royal, X Large and Mini – plus work by other hip designers, including Sophia Coppola's Milk Fed line.

Designer

The area in Beverly Hills bounded by Crescent Drive, Wilshire Boulevard and Little Santa Monica Boulevard is known as the 'Golden Triangle'; it contains the swanky shopping meccas of **Rodeo Drive** and **Brighton Way**, where you'll find outlets for most of fashion's top names. In **Two Rodeo**, a European-style outdoor shopping complex at the corner of Rodeo Drive and Wilshire Boulevard, you'll find **Christian Dior** (1-310 859 4700). On Rodeo Drive itself top designers include **Hermès** (No.343; 1-310 278 6440), **Chanel** (No.400; 1-310 278 5500), **Giorgio Armani** (No.436; 1-213 271 5555) and **Gucci** (No.443; 1-310 278 3451), while Brighton Way is home to **Emporio Armani** (No.9533; 1-310 271 7790) and **Prada** (No.9521; 1-310 276 8889).

Agnès B

100 N Robertson Boulevard, at Alden Drive, Beverly Hills (1-310 271 9643). Bus 20, 21, 22, 220, 320, 322/I-10, exit Robertson Boulevard north. **Open** 11am-7pm Mon-Sat; noon-6pm Sun. **Credit** AmEx, MC, V.
Map 4 A3
Modern-day classics for men and women and a new line for teenagers, entitled Lolita.

Ann Taylor

357 N Camden Drive, between Wilshire Boulevard & Brighton Way, Beverly Hills (1-310 858 7840). Bus 20, 21, 22/I-405, exit Wilshire Boulevard east.
Open 10am-7pm Mon-Fri; 10am-6pm Sat; noon-5pm Sun.
Credit AmEx, MC, V. **Map 3 C2**
Well-priced, sensible day and evening wear for women.

Betsey Johnson

7311 Melrose Avenue, between Poinsettia Place & Fuller Avenue, Melrose District (1-323 931 4490). Bus 10, 11/ I-10, exit La Brea Avenue north. **Open** 11am-7pm Mon-Sat; noon-6pm Sun. **Credit** AmEx, MC, V.
Map 4 C2
Hip, sexy, affordable fashion for women with little girls' hearts. Everything from polyester minis to Lurex trousers.
Branches: check the phone directory for your nearest.

DNA Clothing Company

411 Rose Avenue, between Fourth & Fifth Streets, Venice (1-310 399 0341). Bus 33, Santa Monica 1, 2, 10/I-10, exit Lincoln Boulevard south. **Open** 11am-8pm Mon-Sat; 11am-7pm Sun. **Credit** AmEx, Disc, MC, V. **Map 2 A4**
Famous contemporary clothing for men and women and jeans, always at wholesale prices or less.

Ghost

125 N Robertson Boulevard, at Wilshire Boulevard, Beverly Hills (1-310 246 0567). Bus 20, 21, 22, 220/ I-10, exit Robertson Boulevard north. **Open** 11am-7pm Mon-Sat. **Credit** AmEx, MC, V. **Map 4 A3**
Tania Sarne's British label opened here in 1998. Its traditional romantic image, reinforced by embroidery and flowing shapes, has recently been augmented by sharper pieces in silk jersey and lightweight wool.

Laura Urbinati

8667 Sunset Boulevard, at Sunset Plaza Drive, West Hollywood (1-310 652 3183). Bus 2, 3, 429/I-10, exit La Cienega Boulevard north. **Open** 10am-7pm Mon-Fri; 10am-6pm Sat; noon-5pm Sun. **Credit** AmEx, MC, V.
Map 4 A1
Two floors of Urbinati wear, including her famous bathing suits in earth-toned cottons and knitwear, along with a few other classy, wearable designers-with-edge such as Helmut Lang, Costume National and Martin Margiela.

Todd Oldham

7386 Beverly Boulevard, at Martel Avenue, Melrose District (1-323 936 6045). Bus 14, DASH Fairfax/I-10, exit La Brea Avenue north. **Open** 11am-7pm Mon-Sat; noon-6pm Sun. **Credit** AmEx, MC, V. **Map 4 C2**
This fantasy shop designed by Texan design king Oldham is a mosaic of coloured glass chandeliers, real shells embossed on surfaces and innumerable pages from a thousand books pasted on the floor. It's worth a visit to scope out the décor even if you don't have a yen (or a pound, or a dollar) for his hip, brightly coloured clothes.

Richard Tyler

7290 Beverly Boulevard, between Poinsettia Place & Alta Vista Boulevard, Melrose District (1-323 931 6769). Bus 14, DASH Fairfax/I-10, exit La Brea Avenue north.
Open 10am-6pm Mon-Fri; 11am-6pm Sat. **Credit** AmEx, MC, V. **Map 4 C2**

Although Tyler doesn't actively discourage off-the-street business (if you ring the bell they should let you in), staff here do spend most of their time with by-appointment clients known to include Julia Roberts, Brad Pitt and Seal, who come for ballgowns and fine tailored suits. It's all very Melrose.

Discount

Loehmans

333 La Cienega Boulevard, between Third & Wilshire Boulevards, Mid Wilshire (1-310 659 0674). Bus 28, 105, 328/I-10, exit La Cienega Boulevard north.
Open 10am-9pm Mon-Sat; 11am-7pm Sun. **Credit** Disc, MC, V. **Map 4 B3**
Discount women's and men's clothes and shoes. Be sure to check out the Back Room, devoted to more upmarket designer names, including Perry Ellis and Bill Blass.

Ross Dress for Less

1751 Westwood Boulevard, at Santa Monica Boulevard, Westwood (1-310 477 1707). Bus 4, 304, Santa Monica 1, 8, 12/I-405, exit Wilshire Boulevard east. **Open** 9.30am-9pm Mon-Sat; 9.30am-7pm Sun. **Credit** AmEx, MC, V. **Map 3 A4**
Men's and women's clothing and accessories.

Saks SFO

652 N La Brea Avenue, between Clinton Street & Melrose Avenue, Melrose District (1-323 939 3993). Bus 10, 11, 212/I-10, exit La Brea Avenue north.
Open 11am-8pm Mon-Fri; 11am-7pm Sat, Sun.
Credit MC, V. **Map 4 C2**
Many a bargain for men, women and children.
Branch: 9608 Venice Boulevard, at Robertson Boulevard, Culver City (1-310 559 5448).

Children

Gap Kids is everywhere (general information 1-800 427 7895; Beverly Hills branch: 1-310 273 1685). Many of the shops listed elsewhere also sell children's clothes; see individual entries.

98% Angel

Malibu Country Mart, unit 5A, 3835 Cross Creek Road, off Pacific Coast Highway, Malibu (1-310 456 0069). Bus 434/I-10, exit PCH north. **Open** 10am-6pm Mon-Sat; 11am-5pm Sun. **Credit** AmEx, MC, V.
A hip shop for all your little darlings' wardrobe needs, overlooking a sandbox in a cute shopping plaza in the heart of Malibu. Brands carried include Mini Man, Metropolitan Prairie and Cacharel.

Lee & Life Size at Fred Segal

For listings, see p159 **Fred Segal/Ron Herman Melrose**.
Adorable clothes for ages four to 14, and even more adorable stuff for trend-setting babies with dosh-laden parents.

Pixie Town

400 N Beverly Drive, at Brighton Way, Beverly Hills (1-323 272 6415). Bus 3, 4, 14, 20, 21, 22, DASH Beverly Hills/I-10, exit Robertson Boulevard north. **Open** 10am-6pm Mon-Sat. **Credit** AmEx, MC, V. **Map 3 C2**
Pricey designer clothing and shoes for upwardly mobile newborns and kids up to age 15.

Pom D'Api

9411 Brighton Way, between Beverly & Canon Drives, Beverly Hills (1-310 278 7663). Bus DASH Beverly Hills/ I-10, exit Robertson Boulevard north. **Open** 10am-6pm Mon-Sat; noon-5pm Sun. **Credit** AmEx, MC, V.
Map 3 C2

Tony Brand opened this cool kids' shoe shop, the only one of its kind in the US (the chain started in France), where he stocks a smorgasbord of chic French footwear, from 'Smellies' (scented plastic beach sandals) to clogs in crazy colours. For kids and teens.

Flap Happy

2330 Michigan Avenue, at Cloverfield Avenue, Santa Monica (1-310 453 3527). Bus Santa Monica 9/I-10, exit Cloverfield Avenue north. **Open** 10am-5pm Mon-Sat. **Credit** Disc, MC, V. **Map 2 C3**
Colourful, patterned cotton clothes (up to age five) from this Venice-based clothing manufacturer.

FlapJack's

2462 Overland Avenue, at Pico Boulevard, West LA (1-310 204 1896). Bus Santa Monica 7, Culver City 3, Commuter Express 13, 431/I-10, exit Overland Avenue north. **Open** 10am-6pm Mon-Sat. **Credit** AmEx, MC, V. **Map 3 A4**
Visit this West LA shop for a huge selection of second-hand clothes (up to age ten).

Vintage & second-hand

Aardvark's

7579 Melrose Avenue, between Curson & Sierra Bonita Avenues, Melrose District (1-323 655 6769). Bus 10, 11/I-10, exit Fairfax Avenue north. **Open** 11am-9pm Mon-Sat; 11am-7pm Sun. **Credit** AmEx, Disc, MC, V. **Map 4 C2**
An old favourite, offering funky 1950s to 1970s clothing.
Branch: Aardvark's Odd Ark, 85 Market Street, at Pacific Avenue, Venice (1-310 392 2996).

American Rag

150 N La Brea Avenue, between First & Second Streets, Fairfax District (1-323 935 3154). Bus 212/I-10, exit La Brea Avenue north. **Open** 10am-9pm Mon-Sat; noon-7pm Sun. **Credit** AmEx, DC, MC, V. **Map 4 C3**
One of the largest collections of vintage clothing in Los Angeles, in a relaxed, warehouse-sized setting. The shop also has new clothes and housewares.

Decades

8214 Melrose Avenue, at Harper Avenue, Melrose District (1-323 655 0223). Bus 10, 11/I-10, exit Fairfax Avenue north. **Open** 11.30am-6pm Mon-Sat. **Credit** AmEx, MC, V. **Map 4 B2**
Specialising in vintage couture for men and women, Decades has a fascinating repository of rare designer fashions and accoutrements, primarily from the 1960s and 1970s, including Gucci, Hermès, Pucci and Courreges.

Deja Vu USA

7600 Melrose Avenue, at Curson Avenue, Melrose District (1-213 653 8252). Bus 10, 11/I-10, exit La Brea Avenue north. **Open** 11am-8pm daily. **Credit** AmEx, MC, V. **Map 4 C2**
For the perfect pair of used jeans, look no further.

Greenspan's

3422 Tweedy Boulevard, at Elizabeth Avenue, South Gate (1-213 566 6964). Bus 117/I-105, exit Long Beach Boulevard north. **Open** 10.30am-6pm Mon-Thur; 10.30am-7pm Fri, Sat. **Credit** AmEx, Disc, MC, V.
In 1928, Edward Greenspan started to buy up unfashionable men's and boys' clothes at bargain prices. People thought he was crazy. Now movie studios and rappers collide in their quest for authentic clothing from the 1930s to the present day – workwear, inner-city, dresswear and hats. Much of it is still in the original packaging.

It's a Wrap

3315 W Magnolia Boulevard, at California Street, Burbank (1-626 567 7366). Bus 183/Hwy 134, exit Pass Avenue north. **Open** 11am-8pm Mon-Fri; 11am-6pm Sat, Sun. **Credit** MC, V.
This place specialises in film wardrobe purchases and sales. You could find yourself (almost) wearing Bruce Willis's trousers from *Die Hard* or Elizabeth Berkley's get-up from *Showgirls*. Or maybe something from *Days of Our Lives*, *Seinfeld* or *Beverly Hills 90210*.

Lily

9044 Burton Way, between Doheny & Wetherly Drives, Beverly Hills (1-310 724 5757). Bus 316, 562/I-405, exit Wilshire Boulevard east. **Open** 10am-6pm Mon-Fri; 11am-4pm Sat. **Credit** AmEx, MC, V. **Map 3 C2**
Not a thrift shop, but a place to discover treasures from the past. An excellent range of clothes from the 1920s to the 1960s, in splendid condition.

The Paper Bag Princess

8700 Santa Monica Boulevard, at La Cienega Boulevard, West Hollywood (1-310 358 1985). Bus 4, West Hollywood A, B/I-10, exit La Cienega Boulevard north. **Open** noon-7pm Mon-Sat; noon-5pm Sun. **Credit** MC, V. **Map 4 A2**
For top-of-the-line, second-hand stuff, the Paper Bag Princess is it, ladies. You never know who you might run into here, but owner Elizabeth Mason is certain to fill you in as you're trying on an item no doubt formerly owned by a celebrity. It has everything from little black cocktail dresses to collector shoes.

Rebecca's Dream

16 S Fair Oaks Avenue, at Green Street, Old Town Pasadena (1-626 796 1200). Bus 180, 181, 188, 256, 402, 483/I-110, exit Arroyo Parkway north. **Open** 11am-9pm Mon-Thur; 11am-11pm Fri, Sat; 11am-8pm Sun. **Credit** AmEx, Disc, MC, V.
This Pasadena store calls itself the Nordstrom's of vintage. It stocks everything a man or woman could desire in the way of clothes and accessories from the 1930s to the 1960s, including vintage clothes patterns for keen dressmakers.

Re-Mix

7605½ Beverly Boulevard, between Curson & Stanley Avenues, Fairfax District (1-323 936 6210). Bus 14, DASH Fairfax/I-10, exit Fairfax Avenue north. **Open** noon-7pm Mon-Sat; noon-6pm Sun. **Credit** AmEx, MC, V. **Map 4 C2**.
Unworn shoes for both genders from the 1930s to the 1970s, plus some clothing, still in its original packaging.

Dress hire

One Night Affair

2370 Westwood Boulevard, between Tennessee Avenue & Pico Boulevard, West LA (1-310 652 4334/474 7808). Bus Culver City 3, Santa Monica 7, 8, 12, 13/I-10, exit Santa Monica Boulevard east. **Open** 11am-7pm Tue-Sat; by appointment only. **Credit** AmEx, Disc, MC, V. **Map 3 A4**
Women's wear, from cocktail dresses to wedding gowns, by designers from Gianni Versace to Bill Blass.

Tuxedo Center

7360 Sunset Boulevard, at N Martel Avenue, West Hollywood (1-323 874 4200). Bus 2, 3, 429/I-10, exit La Brea Avenue north. **Open** 9am-7pm Mon, Fri; 9am-6pm Tue-Thur; 9am-5pm Sat; 11am-3pm Sun. **Credit** AmEx, MC, V. **Map 4 C1**
Traditional formal wear for men.

Fashion accessories

Jewellery

Harry Winston

371 N Rodeo Drive, at Brighton Way, Beverly Hills (1-310 271 8554). Bus 4, 20, 21, 22, 320, DASH Beverly Hills/I-405, exit Wilshire Boulevard north. **Open** 10am-5.30pm Mon-Fri; 10am-5pm Sat. **Credit** AmEx, DC, JCB, MC, V. **Map 3 C2**

This is where Oscar nominees get their shinies for the big night. Winston's has been in business for more than 100 years, supplying the rarest and finest diamonds, rubies, sapphires and emeralds in traditional settings. Prices run from $800 to several million.

New Stone Age

8407 W Third Street, between Orlando Avenue & La Cienega Boulevard, West Hollywood (1-213 658 5969). Bus 16, DASH Fairfax/I-10, exit La Cienega Boulevard north. **Open** 11am-6pm Mon-Sat; noon-5pm Sun. **Credit** MC, V. **Map 4 B3**

This West Hollywood shop sells hip jewellery from over 20 different designers, costing from $20-$400, plus ceramics in a colourful, folky setting.

Tiffany & Co

210 N Rodeo Drive, between Dayton Way & Wilshire Boulevard, Beverly Hills (1-310 273 8880). Bus 20, 21, 22/I-405, exit La Cienega Boulevard north. **Open** 10am-6pm Mon-Fri; noon-6pm Sat, Sun. **Credit** AmEx, DC, JCB, MC, V. **Map 3 C2**

The West Coast branch of the Fifth Avenue breakfast joint, er, classic jeweller.

Lingerie

Lingerie chain store **Victoria's Secret** (Beverly Center shop: 1-310 657 2958) has branches everywhere; call one to find the nearest to you.

Frederick's of Hollywood

6608 Hollywood Boulevard, at Highland Avenue, Hollywood (1-800 323 9525/1-323 466 8506). Bus 1, 26, 310, DASH Hollywood/US 101, exit Hollywood Boulevard west. **Open** 10am-9pm Mon-Fri; 10am-7pm Sat; 11am-6pm Sun. **Credit** AmEx, Disc, MC, V. **Map 5 A1**

This legendary Hollywood shop has survived earthquakes, riots and even subsidence (caused recently by the building of the Metro subway). Don't forget to visit the **Celebrity Lingerie Hall of Fame** in the back (*see p200* **Museums & Galleries**).

Trashy Lingerie

402 La Cienega Boulevard, at Oakwood Avenue, West Hollywood (1-310 652 4543). Bus 14, 104/I-10, exit La Cienega Boulevard north. **Open** 10am-7pm Mon-Sat. **Credit** AmEx, Disc, MC, V. **Map 4 A/B2**

Drew Barrymore and Elizabeth Berkley are among the celebs who frequent this shop full of leather, lace, made-to-measure corsets and G-strings. You have to become a member to shop; it's only a formality, though.

Shoes, luggage & repairs

Shoe chainstore **Payless Shoes** (Hollywood branch: 1-323 469 5926) offers all the high street fashions at discount prices. For an outrageously large selection of Hush Puppies, try the **Swell Store** (*see page 161*).

Artistic Shoe Repair

9562 Dayton Way, at Rodeo Drive, Beverly Hills (1-310 271 1956). Bus 4, 20, 21, 22, 320/I-10, exit Robertson Boulevard north. **Open** 8.30am-5.30pm Mon-Fri; 8.30am-3pm Sat. **No credit cards. Map 3 C2**

John Yegeyan and Mike Shadoian have been mending shoes for the Beverly Hills set for more than 15 years.

Beverly Hills Luggage

404 N Beverly Drive, at Brighton Way, Beverly Hills (1-310 273 5885). Bus 4, 20, 27, DASH Beverly Hills/I-10, exit Robertson Boulevard north. **Open** 9.30am-6pm Mon-Fri; 9.30am-5.30pm Sat. **Credit** AmEx, MC, V. **Map 3 C2**

This shop is over 100 years old, sells all major brands of luggage and will repair anything you bring in.

Charles David

Beverly Center, 8500 Beverly Boulevard, at La Cienega Boulevard, West Hollywood (1-310 659 7110). Bus 14, 104/I-10, exit La Cienega Boulevard north. **Open** 10am-9pm Mon-Fri; 10am-8pm Sat; 10am-6pm Sun. **Credit** AmEx, MC. **Map 4 A/B 2/3**

An excellent selection of up-to-the-moment designs in a good array of colours and materials.

Cole Haan

Two Rodeo, 260 N Rodeo Drive, between Dayton Way & Wilshire Boulevard, Beverly Hills (1-310 859 7622). Bus 20, 21, 22/I-10, exit Wilshire Boulevard east. **Open** 10am-7pm Mon-Sat; noon-5pm Sun. **Credit** AmEx, DC, Disc, JCB, MC, V. **Map 3 C2**

Solidly traditional US designs to complete your uptown preppie look. Cole Haan's signature loafers and moccasins have become quite a status symbol and are particularly popular in Australia and Germany.

Delvaux

8647 Sunset Boulevard, at Sunset Plaza Drive, West Hollywood (1-310 289 8588). Bus 2, 3, 429/I-10, exit La Cienega Boulevard north. **Open** 10am-6pm Mon-Sat. **Credit** AmEx, DC, Disc, MC, V. **Map 4 A1**

Exclusive, exclusive, exclusive. Founded in 1829, Delvaux was once the licensed supplier of quality luggage to the Belgian Court. It now makes scarfs, handbags, briefcases and gloves; this is its only US shop and there is a feeding frenzy for its limited stock of haute-couture designs.

Freelance

113 N Robertson Boulevard, between Alden & Third Streets, Beverly Hills (1-310 247 8727). Bus 14, 16, 105, DASH Fairfax/I-10, exit Roberston Boulevard north. **Open** 11am-7pm Mon-Sat; noon-5pm Sun. **Credit** AmEx, DC, Disc, JCB, MC, V. **Map 4 A3**

Eclectically chic footwear with a grand sense of fun, care of French designing brothers Yvon and Guy Rautureau, lands with a resounding, happy thud in West Hollywood.

Kenneth Cole

8752 Sunset Boulevard, between San Vicente & La Cienega Boulevards, West Hollywood (1-310 289 5085). Bus 2, 3, 105, 429, West Hollywood A, B/I-10, exit La Cienega Boulevard north. **Open** 10am-7pm Mon-Thur, Sat; 10am-8pm Fri; noon-5pm Sun. **Credit** AmEx, MC, V. **Map 4 A1**

This New York-based shoe company offers designer shoes, briefcases and outerwear at affordable prices. Outside the shop are footprints in the concrete, including those of Richard Gere, Liz Taylor and Matthew Modine, and on their respective birthdays, 10% of the shop's proceeds that day go to the star's choice of AIDS charity.

Branches: Third Street Promenade, Santa Monica (1-310 458 6633); Century City Shopping Center, 10250 Santa Monica Boulevard, Century City (1-310 282 8535).

Maraolo

*9546 Brighton Way, between Rodeo & Camden Drives,
Beverly Hills (1-310 274 8181). Bus DASH Beverly Hills/
I-10 exit Robertson Boulevard north.* **Open** 10am-6pm
Mon-Sat; noon-5pm Sun. **Credit** AmEx, MC, V.
Map 3 C2

This Neopolitan company has its own line of shoes and
handbags and also manufactures for Armani, Donna Karan
and Polo Ralph Lauren.

The Nike Store

*9560 Wilshire Boulevard, at Rodeo Drive, Beverly Hills
(1-310 275 9998). Bus 3, 20, 21, 22, 320, DASH
Beverly Hills/I-10, exit Robertson Boulevard north.*
Open 10am-7pm Mon-Wed; 10am-8pm Thur; 10am-7pm
Fri, Sat; noon-6pm Sun. **Credit** AmEx, DC, Disc, JCB,
MC, V. **Map 3 C2**

A vast array of Nike shoes and clothing.

Peter Fox Shoes

*712 Montana Avenue, between Lincoln Boulevard &
Seventh Street, Santa Monica (1-310 393 9669). Bus 3,
Santa Monica 3/I-10, exit Lincoln Boulevard north.*
Open 10am-6pm Mon-Sat; noon-5pm Sun. **Credit** AmEx,
MC, V. **Map 2 A/B1**

Handmade shoes inspired by ladies' footwear from the
Victorian era to the 1940s, with a 1970s edge. Not unlike
Patrick Cox shoes. Too cute for words.

Vans

*400 Broadway, at Fourth Street, Santa Monica (1-310
394 1413). Bus 4, 20, 21, 22, 320, 561, Santa Monica
2, 3, 7, 9/I-10, exit Fourth Street north.* **Open** 10am-8pm
daily. **Credit** AmEx, Disc, MC, V. **Map 2 A2**

Visit this Santa Monica store for a multitude of designs from
the leading trainer/casual shoe brand.
Branches: check the phone directory for your nearest.

Ethnic food shops

Aloha Grocery

*4515 Centinela Boulevard, between Washington and
Culver Boulevards, Culver City (1-310 822 2288). Bus
108, Santa Monica 14/I-405, exit Culver Boulevard
west.* **Open** 9am-7pm Mon-Sat; 9am-5pm Sun.
Credit AmEx, Disc, MC, V.

The one-stop shopping mecca for Hawaiian foods. Poi
(vegetable root), ti leaves, Hawaiian crackers, taro chips
and lomi lomi (salmon).

Bangkok Supermarket

*4757 Melrose Avenue, between Normandie & Western
Avenues, Hollywood (1-323 662 9705). Bus 10, 11,
207/ US 101, exit Melrose Avenue west.* **Open** 9am-
9pm daily. **Credit** AmEx, MC, V. **Map 5 C3**

One of LA's landmark Thai markets and an excellent
source of all ingredients for your Thai meal. Be prepared
– not all products are labelled in English.

Bharat Bazaar

*11510 W Washington Boulevard, at Sepulveda
Boulevard, Culver City (1-310 398 6563). Bus 68,
Culver City 1/I-405, exit Washington Boulevard
west.* **Open** 11am-7pm Mon, Wed-Sun. **Credit** AmEx,
MC, V.

Breathe in the aromas at this well-stocked Indian market
in Culver City, a good place to hunt for spices, chutneys
and baked delicacies.

El Camaguey Market

*10925 W Venice Boulevard, at Veteran Avenue,
Culver City (1-310 839 4037). Bus 33/I-405, exit
Venice Boulevard east.* **Open** 8am-8pm Mon-Sat;
8am-6pm Sun. **Credit** AmEx, Disc, MC, V.

Although this market originated as a Cuban haunt – as
still evidenced by the hand-rolled cigars perched by the
cash register – it also purveys foodstuffs from the rest of
South and Central America.

Grand Central Market

*317 S Broadway, between Third & Fourth Streets,
Downtown (1-213 624 2378). Metro Pershing Square/
bus 1, 2, 4, 45, 92, 93, 345, 410, 418, Commuter
Express 413, 423/I-110, exit Third Street east.*
Open 9am-6pm Mon-Sat; 10am-6pm Sun.
No credit cards. Map 7 B2

It's worth a visit just for the overwhelming fun of it all.

With Korean vendors who speak fluent Spanish, Latin-
style seafood cocktails at Maria's Fresh Seafood and
forditas at Ana-Maria's, you can't go wrong.

India Sweets & Spices

*9409 Venice Boulevard, at Bagley Avenue, Culver City
(1-310 837 5286). Bus 33, 220, 333, 436, Culver City
1, 4, 5, Santa Monica 12/I-10, exit Robertson
Boulevard south.* **Open** 9.30am-9.30pm daily.
Credit AmEx, Disc, MC, V.

One of a chain of shops, which are all individually owned
and vary drastically. This Culver City branch is friendly
and sells a good array of Indian spices and some excellent takeaway food.

Juanito's Tamales

*4214 E Floral Drive, at Eastern Avenue, East LA
(1-323 268 2365). Bus 30/I-710, exit Floral Drive
west.* **Open** 9am-6pm Mon-Fri; 7am-6pm Sat; 7am-3pm
Sun. **Credit** AmEx, Disc, MC, V.

Some claim this is the best tamale shop in town. Watch
the ladies make them and pick up either sweet or savoury
versions to take away.

Koreatown Plaza Market

*928 S Western Avenue, at Ninth Street, Koreatown
(1-213 385 1100). Bus Wilshire/Western/bus 27,
28, 207/I-10, exit Western Avenue north.*
Open 10am-9pm daily. **Credit** MC, V. **Map 5 C5**

The Harrods of Korean supermarkets, displaying a spectacular selection of fresh produce and prepared foods.

LA Man Wah

*758 New High Street, between Alpine & Ord Streets,
Chinatown (1-213 613 1942). Metro Union
Station/bus 68, 76, 83, 84, 85, Santa Monica 10/
I-110, exit Hill Street south.* **Open** 8.30am-7pm daily.
No credit cards. Map 7 C1

A good, all-round, old-fashioned Chinese supermarket.

Safe & Save

*2030 Sawtelle Boulevard, at Olympic Boulevard, West
LA (1-310 479 3810). Bus Santa Monica 5, 9, 10/
I-405, exit Santa Monica Boulevard west.* **Open** 10am-
7pm Mon-Sat; 10am-6pm Sun. **Credit** MC, V.

Though small, this market has all the fixings for sushi
and sukiyaki, with good advice from the friendly staff.

Film memorabilia

Chick a Boom

6817 Melrose Avenue, between Orange Drive & Mansfield Avenue, Melrose District (1-323 931 7441). Bus 10, 11/I-10, exit La Brea Avenue north. **Open** 11am-6pm Mon-Sat. **Credit** AmEx, Disc, MC, V. **Map 5 A3**
Toys, magazines, ads, movie posters and bumper stickers from the 1930s to the 1970s.

Cinema Collectors

1507 Wilcox Avenue, at Sunset Boulevard, Hollywood (1-323 461 6516). Bus 1, 163, 180, 181, 212, 217/ US 101, exit Cahuenga Boulevard south. **Open** 10am-6pm Mon-Sat; noon-5pm Sun. **Credit** AmEx, MC, V. **Map 5 A2**
Posters and photographs.

Food & drink

For details of LA's popular farmers markets, *see page 51* **Sightseeing**.

Bakeries

Beverlywood Bakery

9128 Pico Boulevard, at Oakhurst Drive, Beverly Hills (1-310 550 9842). Bus 3, Santa Monica 5, 7/I-10, exit Robertson Boulevard north. **Open** 6am-6.30pm Mon-Fri; 6am-6pm Sat; 6am-5pm Sun. **No credit cards.** **Map 3 C3**
Old-fashioned Jewish bakery, an institution in the neighbourhood: it still gives free biscuits to children and sells some of the best challah, rye bread and rugelach to their parents.

Mani's Bakery

519 S Fairfax Avenue, between Fifth & Sixth Streets, Miracle Mile (1-323 938 8800). Bus 217/I-10, exit Fairfax Avenue north. **Open** 6.30am-11pm Mon-Thur; 6.30am-midnight Fri; 7.30am-midnight Sat; 7.30am-11pm Sun. **Credit** AmEx, Disc, MC, V. **Map 4 B3**
Hip, back-to-basics bakery. Mani's uses only fruit juice to sweeten, and the flour is organic. You can sup coffee and cake (fat-free, of course) on the premises. Eat in or take out.
Branches: check the phone directory for your nearest.

La Brea Bakery

624 S La Brea Avenue, between Wilshire Boulevard & Sixth Street, Mid Wilshire (1-323 939 6813). Bus 20, 21, 22, 217/I-10, exit La Brea Avenue north. **Open** 7.30am-6pm Mon-Fri; 8am-6pm Sat; 8am-4pm Sun. **No credit cards.** **Map 4 C3**
LA's most high-profile bakery, supplying many of the better markets and restaurants with owner Nancy Silverton's outstanding sour-dough baguettes and some more arcane bready delights – chocolate cherry, rye currant and focaccia. Go early in the morning before supplies run out.

Noah's New York Bagels

200 S Beverly Drive, at Charleville Boulevard, Beverly Hills (1-310 550 7392). Bus 3/I-10, exit Robertson Boulevard north. **Open** 6.30am-6pm Mon-Fri; 7am-6pm Sat; 7am-5pm Sun. **Credit** MC, V. **Map 3 C3**
Set to become the McDonald's of bagels, there's a Noah's in almost every shopping area, selling a wild variety of bagels and some inventive smears. Eat in or take out.
Branches: check the phone directory for your nearest.

Sweet Lady Jane

8360 Melrose Avenue, at Kings Road, West Hollywood (1-323 653 7145). Bus 10, 11/I-10, exit La Cienega Boulevard north. **Open** 8.30am-11.30pm Mon-Sat.

Credit AmEx, DC, Disc, JCB, MC, V.
Map 4 B2
A West Hollywood institution, loved for its cheesecake, lemon meringue tarts and signature three-berry cake.

Beer & wine

Du Vin

540 N San Vicente Boulevard, at Melrose Avenue, West Hollywood (1-310 855 1161). Bus 10, 11, 105, 220, West Hollywood A, B/I-405, exit Santa Monica Boulevard east. **Open** 10am-7pm Mon-Sat. **Credit** AmEx, MC, V. **Map 4 A2**
If the cardboard champagne sign is out on the street, Du Vin is open. Enter via a cobblestoned courtyard that seems more European than West Hollywood – it looks like someone's personal, albeit large, wine cellar, full of sophisticated Italian, French and Californian wines. There's also a good selection of grappas, eaux de vie and caviars.

Wally's

2107 Westwood Boulevard, between Mississippi Avenue & Olympic Boulevard, West LA (1-310 475 0606). Bus Santa Monica 5, 8, 12/I-405, exit Santa Monica Boulevard east. **Open** 9am-8pm Mon-Sat; 10am-6pm Sun. **Credit** AmEx, MC, V. **Map 3 A4**
One of the best wine and beer shops in town, with a great selection of grappas, cognacs and single malts, and a full-service gourmet deli. It also offers gift baskets and delivery.

Gourmet

Chalet Gourmet

7880 Sunset Boulevard, at Fairfax Avenue, West Hollywood (1-323 874 6301). Bus 2, 3, 429/US 101, exit Highland Avenue south. **Open** 9am-10pm daily.
Credit AmEx, DC, MC, V. **Map 4 B1**
This rather pricey place has excellent meat, fish and fresh produce departments, an interesting deli and bakery, a fine selection of wines and beers plus a thousand things you never thought you needed. It's also a source of hard-to-find British chocolate.

Gelsons Market

Century City Shopping Center, 10250 Santa Monica Boulevard, between Century Park W & Avenue of the Stars, Century City (1-310 277 4288). Bus 22, 27, 28, 316, Santa Monica 5, Commuter Express 534/I-405, exit Santa Monica Boulevard east. **Open** 8am-10pm daily.
Credit AmEx, Disc, MC, V. **Map 3 B3**
First-rate gourmet market. You dream it up, they deliver it.
Branches: check the phone directory for your nearest.

Trader Joe's

7304 Santa Monica Boulevard, at Poinsettia Place, West Hollywood (1-323 851 9772). Bus 4, DASH Hollywood/ I-10, exit La Brea Avenue north. **Open** 9am-9pm daily.
Credit Disc, MC, V. **Map 4 C1**
Angelenos swear by this store, which sells dry goods, organic produce and fantastic pre-packed meals with a health bent at bargain prices.
Branches: phone 1-800 746 7857 and punch in your zip code to find your nearest branch.

Organic & wholefood shops

Beverly Hills Juice

8382 Beverly Boulevard, at Orlando Avenue, Beverly Hills (1-323 655 8300). Bus 14/I-10, exit Robertson Boulevard north. **Open** 8am-6.30pm Mon-Fri; 10am-6pm Sat. **No credit cards.** **Map 4 B2**
Wonderful fruits and veggies are squeezed daily into

Old-fashioned service and cheeses galore at the **Cheese Store of Beverly Hills**.

delightful drinks to go. There are also smoothies and a dairy-free ice-cream called Banana Manna.

Co-Opportunity

1525 Broadway, at 16th Street, Santa Monica (1-310 451 8902). Bus 4, 304, Santa Monica 1, 10/I-10, exit Cloverfield Avenue/26th Street north. **Open** 8am-10pm daily. **Credit** AmEx, Disc, MC, V. **Map 2 B2**
A wide range of macrobiotic and organic foods and complementary/alternative medicines. The shop is a collective, owned and run by subscribing members, who get a 5% discount. You don't have to join to shop here, though.

Erewhon Natural Foods

7660 Beverly Boulevard, at Stanley Avenue, Fairfax District (1-323 937 0777). Bus 14, 220/I-10, exit Fairfax Avenue north. **Open** 8am-10pm Mon-Sat; 9am-9pm Sun. **Credit** AmEx, Disc, MC, V. **Map 4 C2**
Organic produce, food supplements, cosmetics and a deli.

Wholefoods

239 N Crescent Drive, between Clifton & Dayton Ways, Beverly Hills (1-310 274 3360). Bus 20, 21, 22, 320, 322, DASH Beverly Hills/I-10, exit Wilshire Boulevard east. **Open** 8am-9pm daily. **Credit** AmEx, Disc, MC, V. **Map 3 C2**
Arguably the best in natural gourmet food shopping. Great fish, meat, cheese and deli counters. Excellent fresh pastas.

Speciality foods

Also try **Barney Greengrass** at department store Barneys New York (*see page 152*).

Al Gelato

806 S Robertson Boulevard, between Olympic & Wilshire Boulevards, Beverly Hills (1-310 659 8069). Bus 28, 220, 328/I-10, exit Robertson Boulevard north. **Open** 10am-midnight daily. **No credit cards. Map 4 A3**

Forget Häagen-Dazs, this is ice-cream heaven: a wicked selection of intense and exotic flavours.

Aristoff Caviar & Fine Foods

321 N Robertson Boulevard, at Rosewood Avenue, West Hollywood (1-310 271 0576). Bus 14, 220/I-10, exit Robertson Boulevard north. **Open** 9.30am-6pm Mon-Fri; 10.30am-4pm Sat. **Credit** AmEx, DC, Disc, MC, V. **Map 4 A2**
Purveyors of fine caviar: beluga, sevruga and American paddle fish. Savvy Jack Nicholson plumps for the latter – it's half the price of the famous sturgeon varieties.

Cheese Store of Beverly Hills

419 N Beverly Drive, at Santa Monica Boulevard, Beverly Hills (1-310 278 2855). Bus 4, 20, 21, 22, 320, DASH Beverly Hills/I-10, exit Santa Monica Boulevard east. **Open** 10am-6pm Mon-Sat. **Credit** AmEx, MC, V. **Map 3 C2**
A fabulous store. You'll find every cheese known to science, fresh cornichons (little French gherkins), olives, baguettes, foie gras, pâté, sausages, wines, balsamic vinegars and olive oils, housed in an old-world setting and served by men in long denim pinnies.

Delmarus Lox

9340 W Pico Boulevard, at Rexford Drive, Beverly Hills (1-310 273 3004). Bus Santa Monica 7, 13/I-10, exit Robertson Boulevard north. **Open** noon-6pm Mon-Fri; 9am-6pm Sat; 8am-3pm Sun. **Credit** AmEx, Disc, MC, V. **Map 3 C3**
Lox (smoked salmon) in weird flavours – lemon-dill, rosemary-mint and jalapeño-cilantro.

Divine Pasta Company

615 N La Brea Avenue, between Clinton Street & Melrose Avenue, Melrose District (1-323 939 1148). Bus 10, 11, 212/I-10, exit La Brea Avenue north. **Open** 11am-8pm Mon-Sat. **Credit** AmEx, MC, V. **Map 4 C2**
An extraordinary array of fresh pasta, home-made sauces,

and all the things that go with them. There are branches in Santa Monica, Beverly Hills and Studio City.
Branches: check the phone directory for your nearest.

Godiva Chocolatier

Beverly Center, 8500 Beverly Boulevard, at La Cienega Boulevard, West Hollywood (1-323 651 0697). Bus 14, 104/I-10, exit La Cienega Boulevard north. **Open** 10am-9pm Mon-Fri; 10am-8.30pm Sat; 11am-6.30pm Sun.
Credit AmEx, MC, V. **Map 4 A/B 2/3**
The place for excellent chocolates, beautifully presented in ritzy gold packaging, at high prices.

Los Angeles Fish

420 Stanford Avenue, at Central Avenue & E Fourth Street, Downtown (1-213 629 1213). Bus 14, 40, DASH A, D/US 101, exit Fourth Street west. **Open** 6am-noon, 1-3pm, Mon-Fri; 6-10.30am Sat. **No credit cards**.
Map 7 C3
A division of American Fish, suppliers to large supermarket chains and some of the best restaurants in town, this LA Downtown cash-and-carry outlet is one of the finest sources of fish imaginable. It's not in the most salubrious location, but there are security guards in the parking lot. It's also well refrigerated, so wear more than a T-shirt.

Noonan's Ribs

6601 S Western Avenue, between Florence & Gage Avenues, South Central (1-213 752 0032). Metro Florence/bus 40, 207/I-110, exit Gage Avenue west. **Open** 7am-3pm Tue-Fri. **Credit** AmEx, MC, V.
It's worth a trip to this none-too-charming neighbourhood for baby back ribs that have less fat and a terrific marinade.

Santa Monica Seafood

1205 Colorado Boulevard, at 12th Street, Santa Monica (1-310 393 5244). Bus 4, 304, Santa Monica 9, 11/I-10, exit Lincoln Boulevard north. **Open** 9am-7pm Mon-Fri; 9am-6pm Sat. **Credit** AmEx, MC, V. **Map 2 B3**
The Cigliano family – six brothers, a sister and a father – has run this wholesale and retail enterprise since 1969, supplying hotels and restaurants throughout Southern California. The shop is beautiful: aquamarine tiles, sunken ceiling lights and glistening silver fixtures set off a heavenly array of fish and shellfish. They also have a great selection of prepared foods, from smoked trout cakes to breaded frogs' legs for that sublime TV snack.

Say Cheese

2800 Hyperion Avenue, between Rowena Avenue & Griffith Park Boulevard, Silver Lake (1-323 665 0545). Bus 175/I-5, exit Los Feliz Boulevard west. **Open** 8am-6.30pm daily. **Credit** AmEx, DC, MC, V.
Map 6 C1/2
An excellent selection, from your regular Jack to more esoteric varieties, served to you with style and class. There's a small café if you're feeling peckish.

Gifts & stationery

Museum and art gallery shops are often a good source for gifts: think clocks, glassware, posters, games and pottery. Two worth visiting are the **Getty Center** and **MOCA** shops (*see chapter* **Museums & Galleries**).

Hammacher Schlemmer

309 N Rodeo Drive, between Brighton & Dayton Ways, Beverly Hills (1-310 859 7255). Bus 3, 20, 21, 22, 320, DASH Beverly Hills/I-10, exit Robertson Boulevard north. **Open** 10am-6pm Mon-Sat; noon-5pm Sun. **Credit** AmEx, DC, Disc, MC, V. **Map 3 C2**

Hi-tech gadgetry and non-essential gift items for people with an excess of greenbacks – for example, the world's smallest camera and a posture feeder for dogs with back conditions.

Necromance

7220 Melrose Avenue, between Alta Vista Boulevard & Formosa Avenue, Melrose District (1-323 934 8684). Bus 10, 11/I-10, exit La Brea Avenue north. **Open** noon-7pm Mon-Sat; 1-7pm Sun. **Credit** MC, V. **Map 4 C2**
Owner Nancy calls her gaff a natural history shop. She sells animal skulls, mounted insects, beetles and butterflies, jewellery made from teeth and bones, and antique medical and funerary tools and products.

Panpipes Magickal Marketplace

1641 Cahuenga Boulevard, between Selma Avenue & Hollywood Boulevard, Hollywood (1-323 462 7078). Bus 1, 163, 180, 181, 212/US 101, exit Cahuenga Boulevard south. **Open** 11am-7pm Mon-Sat. **Credit** AmEx, MC, V. **Map 5 B1**
LA's oldest full-service occult shop, selling everything from voodoo dolls and mojo bags (for casting spells) to crystal balls. The place to visit if you want to improve your love life or your bank account.

Planet Blue

Malibu Country Mart, 3835 Cross Creek Road, off Pacific Coast Highway, Malibu (1-310 317 9975). Bus 434/I-10, exit PCH north. **Open** 9.30am-6.30pm Mon-Fri; 9.30am-7pm Sat, Sun. **Credit** AmEx, MC, V.
A beautiful shop filled with things you may well not need, but will certainly want to buy: candles, beauty products, perfumes, bedding, towels, underwear and hip clothes.

The Pleasure Chest

7733 Santa Monica Boulevard, between Genesee & Stanley Avenues, West Hollywood (1-323 650 1022). Bus 4, West Hollywood A, B/I-10, exit Fairfax Avenue north. **Open** 10am-midnight Mon-Thur, Sun; 10am-12.45am Fri, Sat. **Credit** AmEx, DC, MC, V. **Map 4 C1**
The best in naughty, erotic and X-rated toys, and said to be Madonna's favourite shop. Worth a visit if only to view the limos parked in the lot and the oddly dressed folk inside.
Website: www.pleasurechest.com

Soolip Paperie & Press/
Soolip Bungalow

8646 Melrose Avenue, at Norwich Drive, West Hollywood (1-310 360 0545). Bus 10, 11/I-405, exit Santa Monica Boulevard east. **Open** 11am-7pm Mon-Sat; noon-5pm Sun. **Credit** AmEx, MC, V. **Map 4 A2**
The Paperie & Press sells scented ink, exotic ribbons, notepaper made of bamboo, a huge array of cards and exquisite wrapping paper and also offers a calligraphy service. The Bungalow is through the adjacent garden courtyard and has sleek pyjamas, ethereal bed linen, satin pillows, sensuous candles and beauteous bath products.

Yamagushi's

2057 Sawtelle Boulevard, at Olympic Boulevard, West LA (1-310 479 9531). Bus 4, 304, Santa Monica 9, 10/ I-405, exit Santa Monica Boulevard west. **Open** 9.30am-7pm Mon-Fri; 9.30am-6pm Sat. **Credit** MC, V.
A Japanese-style gift shop where colourful koi kites set off other Asian accessories, cookware and clothing.

Y-Que

1770 N Vermont Avenue, at Hollywood Boulevard, Los Feliz (1-323 664 0021). Bus 1/US 101, exit Vermont Avenue north. **Open** noon-7pm Mon-Sat; noon-6pm Sun. **Credit** AmEx, MC, V. **Map 6 A2**
A tiny space packed with funky, kitschy stuff, from a Virgin of Guadalupe holy water holder to 1970s lunch boxes.

Shops

Fred Segal The Apothia

For listings, see p159 **Fred Segal/Ron Herman Melrose**.
Part of the Fred Segal empire, this is a beauty paradise for spoilt princesses, carrying a rainbow of skin, body and hair-care products, including Kiehls, Jean Laporte, Comptoir Sud Pacifique, Thymes and Molton Brown.

Herb Products Company

11012 Magnolia Boulevard, between Vineland Avenue & Lankershim Boulevard, North Hollywood (1-818 761 0351). Bus 420/Hwy 170, exit Magnolia Boulevard east. **Open** 9am-5.30pm Mon-Fri; 9am-5pm Sat. **Credit** MC, V.
Medicinal herbs, myriad hard-to-find oils and pot-pourri served up by a knowledgeable staff.

Larchmont Beauty Centre

208 N Larchmont Boulevard, at Beverly Boulevard, Hancock Park (1-323 461 0162). Bus 14/I-10, exit La Brea Avenue north. **Open** 8.30am-7pm Mon-Sat (Nov, Dec 11am-5pm Mon-Sat). **Credit** AmEx, Disc, MC, V. **Map 5 B3**
This Larchmont Village shop has everything you could ever want to pretty yourself up: high-end hair and skincare products by Decleor, Thymes, JF Lazartigue and Neal's Yard as well as aromatherapy products by Aroma Vera, Tisserand and Essential Elements.

MAC Cosmetics

133 N Robertson Boulevard, at Beverly Boulevard, West Hollywood (1-310 854 0860). Bus 14, 16, 220, DASH Fairfax/I-10, exit Robertson Boulevard north. **Open** 10.30am-7pm Mon-Sat; noon-5pm Sun. **Credit** AmEx, Disc, MC, V. **Map 4 A2**
This is a Canadian-based outfit that sells politically sound cosmetics (they have not been tested on animals), in an enormous array of colours and formulas.

Complementary & alternative medicine

Sun Moon Acupuncture Health Clinic

300 S Beverly Drive, suite 105, at Dayton Way, Beverly Hills (1-310 286 1598). Bus 3, 328, DASH Beverly Hills/ I-10, exit Robertson Boulevard north. **Open** 10am-8pm Mon-Sat. **No credit cards**. **Map 3 C2**
If you want to lose a few pounds, give up smoking or drinking, quieten your mind, rid yourself of asthma, depression or any physical pain, Baljit Khalsa will acupuncture your troubles away. He does house calls, and also teaches yoga and meditation and creates his own herbal tinctures. His wife Martha has her own essential oil and offers otherworldly massage treatments.

Gurutei Jaur Khalsa

Information 1-323 930 2803.
When you're out of sync, Gurutei, who is Sikh and has been a Kundalini yoga teacher for almost 30 years, will heal you with Raj Yog, using external sound (gongs and bells), vibrations (colour and light), warm chakra pillows and essential oils to change energy flow and release old patterns that contribute to stress and disease.

Spas & masseurs

The **Regent Beverly Wilshire** hotel (*see page 103* **Accommodation**) has a delightful spa facility, which is open to non-residents as long as you have a treatment, while **Kenny Nakaji** (1-213 599 1935) offers shiatsu-anma massage and reflexology. For more on spas and retreats further out of Los Angeles, *see page 240* **Trips Out of Town**.

Aida Thibiant's European Day Spa

449 N Canon Drive, at Little Santa Monica Boulevard, Beverly Hills (1-310 278 7565). Bus 3, 4, 14, 27/ I-405, exit Santa Monica Boulevard east. **Open** 9am-6pm Mon-Wed, Fri, Sat; 9am-7pm Thur. **Credit** AmEx, Disc, MC, V. **Map 3 C2**
This is an upmarket, totally aesthetic experience. Purified air and an 18ft (5.5m) waterfall are some of the bonuses here, as well as the usual range of face and body treatments. You might even run into Michelle Pfeiffer, Ali MacGraw or Rachel Hunter.

Beverly Hot Springs

308 N Oxford Avenue, between Oakwood & Beverly Boulevards, Mid Wilshire (1-323 734 7000). Bus 14, 207, 357/I-10, exit Western Avenue north. **Open** 9am-9pm daily. **Admission** $40. **Credit** AmEx, Disc, MC, V. **Map 5 C3**
In the middle of the hurly-burly that is LA sits BHS, the city's only natural spring. Spend the day jumping from hot to cold baths, relaxing in a funky artificial grotto, steam rooms, massage rooms and facial rooms, or get the full body treatment: lie naked and be scrubbed, hosed down and anointed with milk, sesame oil and cucumber (for an extra $110).

Burke Williams

8000 Sunset Boulevard, at Crescent Heights Boulevard, West Hollywood (1-323 822 9007). Bus 2, 3, 429/US 101, exit Sunset Boulevard west. **Open** 9am-10pm daily. **Admission** $25. **Credit** AmEx, MC, V. **Map 4 B1**
Treatments to uplift your body and spirit, from a mundane manicure or prosaic scalp treatment to a more exotic herbal wrap. Create your own simple rejuvenation package: enjoy the Jacuzzi, heated at a balmy 105°F (41°C), cool down in the plunge pool iced at 60°F (16°C), then detoxify in the sauna and steam rooms.
Branch: 1460 Fourth Street, at Broadway, Santa Monica (1-310 587 3366).

Hahm's Rejuvenation Center

8474 W Third Street, suite 204, at La Cienega Boulevard, Beverly Hills (1-323 966 4141). Bus 16, DASH Fairfax/I-10, exit La Cienega Boulevard north. **Open** 9am-9pm daily. **Credit** AmEx, DC, Disc, MC, V. **Map A3**
Experience the most uplifting 55 minutes in Los Angeles with the blind Korean master of shiatsu massage, Suk Hahm. Follow your massage with a sizzling steam bath and bracing body scrub.

Healing Waters

*136 N Orlando Avenue, between First & Third Streets,
West Hollywood (1-323 651 4656). Bus 14, 16, DASH
Fairfax/I-10, exit La Brea Avenue north.* **Open** 1-5pm
Mon-Sat. **No credit cards. Map 4 B3**
At this cute West Hollywood shop, where terracotta angels
adorn the windows and glass wind chimes hang from the
door, you can get a Bach Flower or an Aura-Soma Color con-
sultation by appointment. Both are intended to rejuvenate
mind and spirit.

Ron Teagarden's Herbal Emporium

*9001 Beverly Boulevard, at Wetherly Drive, West
Hollywood (1-310 205 0104). Bus 14/I-10, exit La
Cienega Boulevard north.* **Open** 11am-7pm Mon-Sat;
noon-5pm Sun. **Credit** AmEx, MC, V.
Map 4 A2
When you're suffering from a nervous crisis, leave your
therapist and run to Ron Teagarden's for Shen Chinese
herbs. If your libido is lacking, forget Viagra, purchase
extract of deer antler.

24-hour drugstore

Rite-Aid Drugs

*300 N Canon Drive, at Brighton Way, Beverly Hills
(1-310 273 7293). Bus 3, 4, 14, 27, 304/I-405, exit
Wilshire Boulevard east.* **Open** 24 hours daily.
Credit AmEx, MC, V. **Map 3 C2**
Everything from pet food, beer and stationery to cosmetics
and first aid supplies.
Branches: check the phone directory for your nearest.

Hairdressers

Art Lunar Salon

*8930 Keith Avenue, at Robertson Boulevard, West
Hollywood (1-310 247 1383). Bus 4/I-10, exit Robertson
Boulevard north.* **Open** 9am-6pm Tue-Sat. **Credit** MC, V.
Map 4 A2
Enter a quaint garden, dripping with exotic blooms, and go
through a white wooden door to a 1940s cottage. This is Art
Lunar's workplace and, unlike most hair salons, is a tranquil
refuge. Angelica Huston, Michelle Pfeiffer and Winona Ryder
are among his clients. Expect to pay $100-$200 for a cut.

Clark Nova

*8118½ W Third Street, at Crescent Heights Boulevard,
Fairfax District (1-323 655 1100). Bus 16/I-10, exit La
Cienega Boulevard north.* **Open** 10am-6pm Tue, Wed;
10am-8pm Thur, Fri; 9am-6pm Sat. **Credit** MC, V.
Map 4 B3
For both men and women. Have Eusebio trim you up – since
he and Mick opened their doors, the wig-whacking hasn't
stopped. Cuts cost $50-$75; call for an appointment.

Doyle Wilson

*8006 Melrose Avenue, between Edinburgh & Laurel
Avenues, West Hollywood (1-323 658 6987). Bus 10, 11/
I-10, exit Fairfax Avenue north.* **Open** 9am-8pm Wed;
11am-8pm Thur, Fri; 9am-6pm Sun. **Credit** AmEx, MC,
V. **Map 4 B2**
The talk here is far cheaper than the haircut, but you may
end up getting a rinse next to Faye Dunaway or listening to
the horrible nightmare it was on the set of so-and-so's last
movie. And, male or female, you'll leave looking fabulous.
Expect to pay $70-$100 for a cut, up to $160 for colour.

Estilo

*7402 Beverly Boulevard, at Martel Avenue, Fairfax
District (1-323 936 6775). Bus 14, DASH Fairfax/I-10,
exit La Brea Avenue north.* **Open** 9am-5pm Tue-Sat.
No credit cards. Map 4 C2

One of Los Angeles's fashion-forming salons: Chris
McMillan invented the Jennifer Aniston cut and also prunes
Patricia Arquette's mop.

Juan Juan

*9667 Wilshire Boulevard, at Bedford Drive, Beverly Hills
(1-310 278 5826). Bus 3, 20, 21, 22, 320, DASH
Beverly Hills/I-10, exit Robertson Boulevard north.*
Open 9am-6pm Tue, Wed, Fri, Sat; 9am-8pm Thur.
Credit MC, V. **Map 3 B/C2**
This is one of Beverly Hills' élite beauty salons, with a surprisingly low-key and young vibe. Juan Juan, as you might
expect with a name like that, has a clientele that reads like
the Oscar nominations, including Uma Thurman, Diane
Keaton, Brad Pitt, Robert De Niro and Robin Williams. Enjoy
a royal pampering, relax at the cappuccino bar and then take
home some 'J' products.

Louis Licari Color Group

*450 N Canon Drive, between Santa Monica Boulevard &
Brighton Way, Beverly Hills (1-310 247 0855). Bus 3, 4,
14, 27, 304/I-10, exit Santa Monica Boulevard east.*
Open 8am-6pm Mon-Sat. **Credit** AmEx, MC, V.
Map 3 C2
Otherwise known as the King of Colour, this New Yorker
who trained as a painter is now using his palette of tints on
women's hair.

The Magnificent Brothers

*4267 Crenshaw Avenue, between Stocker & W 43rd
Street, Crenshaw (1-213 299 0223). Bus 42, 105, 210,
310, DASH Crenshaw, Leimert-Slauson/I-10, exit
Crenshaw Boulevard.* **Open** 9am-7pm Mon-Sat.
No credit cards.
Old-fashioned barber's, specialising in hair of African
descent. Come for the ambience and to catch up on the local
gossip as much as for a cut or shave.

Privé

*8458 Melrose Place, at La Cienega Boulevard, West
Hollywood (1-323 651 5045). Bus 10, 11, 105, DASH
Fairfax/I-10, exit La Cienega Boulevard north.*
Open 9am-7pm Mon-Sat. **Credit** AmEx, MC, V.
Map 4 B2
Everything here starts with an 'L' for Eduardo Laurent. The
Biarritz native is one of the best hairdressers in town. He
gave Melrose Place starlette Josie Bisset her gamine short
coiffe and tends the divine Sophia Loren's locks. Also request
Eduardo's customised organic scalp treatment, part science
and part his grandmother's secret recipe.

Make-up artists

The Cloutier Agency

*1026 Montana Avenue, between Tenth & 11th Streets,
Santa Monica (1-310 394 8813). Bus 3, Santa Monica 3/
I-10, Lincoln Boulevard north.* **Open** 9am-6pm
Mon-Thur; 9am-5.30pm Fri. **No credit cards.**
Map 2 B1
Some of Chantal Cloutier's top make-up artists, usually
booked out for several thousand dollars per day on com-
mercials and fashion shoots, are now available to paint your
face. They will come to your home or hotel. Go glamour, girl!

Valerie – Cosmetics Boutique & Studio

*460 N Canon Drive, at Little Santa Monica Boulevard,
Beverly Hills (1-310 274 7348). Bus 3, 20, 21, 22, 320,
DASH Beverly Hills/I-10, exit Robertson Boulevard north.*
Open 10am-6pm Tue-Sat. **Credit** AmEx, MC, V.
Map 3 C2
Ex-make-up artist extrordinaire Valerie launched her own
line of cosmetics and opened this shop. Don't leave without
the 'Secret Weapon' foundation or 'Fairy Dust', a face and
body powder with the airiest of finishes.

Manicure & pedicure

Kendall at Lather Hair Shop
727 N Fairfax Avenue, at Melrose Avenue, Melrose District (1-323 658 8585). Bus 10, 212, 217/I-10, exit Melrose Avenue north. **Open** 10am-7pm Mon-Sat. **Credit** AmEx, MC, V. **Map 4 B2**
One of the best manicurists in the city.

Kimberly's Nails
8046 W Third Street, at Crescent Heights Boulevard, West Hollywood (1-323 653 5342). Bus 16, DASH Fairfax/I-10, exit La Cienega Boulevard north. **Open** 9am-7pm Mon-Sat; 10am-5pm Sun. **No credit cards**. **Map 4 B3**
You can get a basic manicure and pedicure for $14, a full set of acrylics for $25, wraps for $30 and the ever-popular French manicure for $8. Ask for Christina.

Skin & body care

Esthetica
931½ La Cienega Boulevard, between Santa Monica Boulevard & Waring Avenue, West Hollywood (1-310 659 5152). Bus 105/I-10, exit La Cienega Boulevard north. **Open** by appointment only. **Credit** AmEx, MC, V. **Map 4 A/B2**
In a secluded, quaint cottage screened from the hustle and bustle of La Cienega Boulevard, ex-model Brandy provides a sanctuary where she pampers you with revolutionary facials, body treatments, waxing and tinting. For both men and women.

Georgette Klinger
131 S Rodeo Drive, at Wilshire Avenue, Beverly Hills (1-310 274 6347). Bus 3, 20, 21, 22/I-10, exit Robertson Boulevard north. **Open** 9am-6pm Mon, Tue, Thur-Sat; 9am-8.30pm Wed; 10am-6pm Sun. **Credit** AmEx, DC, Disc, MC, V. **Map 3 C2**
It's pristine and well designed, without too many frills, and professionally run, without the sycophantic pandering that one comes to expect with Beverly Hills beauty joints. Hell, Mrs Hillary Clinton likes it! There's a separate area for men.

Lisa Wilson Skin Care
Alex Roldan Hair Salon, Wyndham Bel Age Hotel, 1020 N San Vicente Boulevard, at Sunset Boulevard, West Hollywood (1-310 657 5791). Bus 2, 3, 105, 302, 429, DASH West Hollywood/I-10, exit La Cienega Boulevard north. **Open** 9am-5pm Mon; 9am-6pm Tue-Sat. **Credit** AmEx, MC, V. **Map 4 A1**
Expat Brit Lisa works solo and provides some of the best skincare and body therapies in town, using traditional treatment techniques with modern ingredients (including the Dermalogica line).

Sona Chaandi Beauty Center
18307 Pioneer Boulevard, at 183rd Street, Artesia (1-562 924 7274). Metro Artesia/bus 362/I-91, exit Pioneer Boulevard south. **Open** 11am-8pm Tue-Sun. **Credit** AmEx, MC, V.
If you happen to be shopping in Artesia for Indian saris, stop at this immaculate salon that offers great deals on mehndi (henna body painting), threading (a form of hair removal) and other Indian beauty and hair treatments.

Tattooing & body piercing

Body Electric
7274½ Melrose Avenue, at Poinsettia Place, Melrose District (1-323 954 0408). Bus 10, 11/I-10, exit La Brea Avenue north. **Open** noon-8pm Wed-Sun. **Rates** $45-$100. **Credit** AmEx, MC, V. **Map 4 C2**

Riley Baxter is one of four tattoo artists working out of this parlour above Angeli's Italian restaurant.

The Gauntlet
872 Huntley Drive, at Santa Monica Boulevard, West Hollywood (1-310 657 6677). Bus 4, 304/I-10, exit La Cienega Boulevard north. **Open** noon-7pm Mon-Sat; noon-5pm Sun. **Rates** from $10. **Credit** MC, V. **Map 4 A2**
One of the best places for body-piercing in the city.

Household & furniture

Crate & Barrel
Century City Shopping Center, 10250 Santa Monica Boulevard, between Century Park W & Avenue of the Stars, Century City (1-310 551 1100). Bus 22, 27, 28, 316, Santa Monica 5, Commuter Express 534/I-405, exit Santa Monica Boulevard east. **Open** 10am-9pm Mon-Fri; 10am-7pm Sat; 11am-6pm Sun. **Credit** AmEx, Disc, MC, V. **Map 3 B3**
Accessories so beautifully displayed you'll want 'em all.

Diva
8801 Beverly Boulevard, at Robertson Boulevard, West Hollywood (1-310 278 3191). Bus 14, 220/I-10, exit Robertson Boulevard north. **Open** 9.30am-6pm Mon-Fri; 11am-6pm Sat. **Credit** AmEx, MC, V. **Map 4 A2**
The place for high-style contemporary furnishings and accessories, especially light fixtures.

Plastica
4685 Hollywood Boulevard, at Vermont Avenue, Los Feliz (1-323 644 1212). Bus 26, 180, 181/US 101, exit Hollywood Boulevard east. **Open** noon-7pm Tue-Fri; noon-6pm Sat, Sun. **Credit** AmEx, MC, V. **Map 6 A2**
Everything's plastic, half of it's vintage, half new. From bags to chopsticks, plus stuff from Africa, all over the US, Japan and China.

Shabby Chic
1013 Montana Avenue, between Tenth & 11th Streets, Santa Monica (1-310 394 1975). Bus Santa Monica 3/ I-10, exit Lincoln Boulevard north. **Open** 10am-6pm Mon-Sat; noon-5pm Sun. **Credit** AmEx, Disc, MC, V. **Map 2 B1**
Furniture and accessories that are a hybrid of English rustic and California beach, with a client list that includes Bruce Springsteen and Tracey Ullman.

Williams Sonoma
339 N Beverly Drive, between Brighton & Dayton Ways, Beverly Hills (1-310 274 9127). Bus 4, 20, 27, DASH Beverly Hills/I-10, exit Robertson Boulevard north. **Open** 10am-6pm Mon-Fri; 10am-8pm Thur; 10am-6.30pm Sat; noon-5pm Sun. **Credit** AmEx, Disc, MC, V. **Map 3 C2**
Fabulous, expensive kitchen accessories almost – but not quite – too good-looking to use.

Opticians

Old Focals Retail in Old Town Pasadena (1-626 793 7073) supplies vintage specs for films (including 1950s cat-eye frames for Sally Field in *Forrest Gump* and metal-and-plastic frames as donned by Kevin Costner in *JFK*) and for regular folk.

Joe Roberts Optical
3507 W Magnolia Avenue, between Avon & Cordova Streets, Burbank (1-818 842 0666). Bus 163, 183/

Hwy 134, exit Pass Avenue north. **Open** 9am-5pm Tue-Fri; 9am-noon Sat. **No credit cards.**
Dispensing optician, custom gold soldering and difficult repairs. Often you can have your specs back the same day.

Oliver Peoples
8642 Sunset Boulevard, at Sunset Plaza, West Hollywood (1-310 657 2553). Bus 2, 3, 429/I-10, exit La Cienega Boulevard north. **Open** 10am-7pm Mon-Fri; 10am-6pm Sat. **Credit** AmEx, MC, V. **Map 4 A1**
A candy shop of machine-age-inspired frames as well as an optician. You'll find designs by Paul Smith, Eyevan and Ollie Peoples (for children), plus one-of-a-kind vintage frames.

Photography

For one-hour film processing, try **Fromex** (Santa Monica branch: 1-310 395 5177) or **One Hour Motophoto** (Midtown branch: 1-310 275 4685).

Frank's Camera
5715 N Figueroa Street, at Avenue 57, Highland Park (1-323 255 0123). Bus 81, 176, 256, DASH A/I-110, exit S Avenue 52 north. **Open** 10am-5.30pm Mon-Sat. **Credit** AmEx, MC, V.
In business for more than 30 years, Frank sells new and used cameras and will also process your film, send your camera out for repair and rent you a video camera.

Samy's Camera
200 S La Brea Avenue, between Second & Third Streets, Mid Wilshire (1-323 938 2420). Bus 16, 212, 316, DASH Fairfax/I-10, exit La Brea Avenue north. **Open** 8am-7pm Mon-Fri; 9.30am-6pm Sat. **Credit** AmEx, Disc, MC, V. **Map 5 A4**

For the outward-bound: **Adventure 16.**

Some 20,000sq ft (1,770sq m) of photographic heaven, including digital and video rentals and sales, for both amateurs and professionals. Also, film processing and repairs.

Sport & adventure

ZJ Boardinghouse (*see page 223* **Sport & Fitness**) is a great source of hard and soft goods for surfing, skating and snowboarding.

Adventure 16
11161 W Pico Boulevard, between Sepulveda Boulevard & the I-405, West LA (1-310 473 4574). Bus Santa Monica 7, Culver City 6/I-10, exit Overland Boulevard north. **Open** 10am-9pm Mon-Fri; 10am-6pm Sat; 11am-6pm Sun. **Credit** AmEx, MC, V. **Map 3 A5**
The best outward-bound shop in the city. Helpful staff cater for your every camping need, and there's a great selection of travel books.

Patagonia
2936 Main Street, at Marine Street, Santa Monica (1-310 314 1776). Bus Santa Monica 1/I-10, exit Fourth Street south. **Open** 10am-7pm Mon-Sat; 10am-5pm Sun. **Credit** AmEx, Disc, MC, V. **Map 2 A4**
This shop sells only, guess what? – Patagonia clothing.

PMB Golf
10581½ W Pico Boulevard, between Beverly Glen Boulevard & Overland Avenue, Century City (1-310 446 4555). Bus Santa Monica 7/I-10, exit Overland Avenue north. **Open** 10am-7pm Mon-Sat; 1-6pm Sun. **Credit** AmEx, Disc, MC, V. **Map 3 A/B4**
New and used clubs and all things to do with golf.

Sports Chalet
Beverly Connection, 100 N La Cienega Boulevard, at Beverly Boulevard, West Hollywood (1-310 657 3210). Bus 14, 104/I-10, exit La Cienega Boulevard north. **Open** 10am-9pm Mon-Fri; 9am-9pm Sat; 10am-7pm Sun. **Credit** AmEx, DC, Disc, MC, V. **Map 4 A/B 2/3**
This is the ultimate sports shop. Diving, mountaineering, boating – whatever your sport, Sports Chalet has the goods. **Branches:** check the phone directory for your nearest.

Val Surf & Sport
4810 Whitsett Avenue N, between Magnolia Boulevard & Riverside Drive, North Hollywood (1-818 769 6977). Bus 96/US 101, exit Laurel Canyon Boulevard north. **Open** 9am-8pm Mon-Fri; 9am-6pm Sat; 11am-5pm Sun. **Credit** AmEx, MC, V.
Snowboard rental is $27 a day; ski rental is $18. It also sells clothing and a full line of skateboards and related gear.

Wind n' Wave
11910 Pico Boulevard, at Bundy Drive, West LA (1-310 478 7537). Bus Santa Monica 7, 10, 14/I-10, exit Bundy Drive north. **Open** 10am-7pm Mon-Fri; 10am-6pm Sat, Sun. **Credit** AmEx, MC, V.
Purveyors of high-quality toys to perpetual adolescents, this is one of the largest windsurfing and snowboarding equipment and clothes shops in town.

Ticket agencies

For **Ticketmaster's** outlets, *see page 205* **Music**.

Absolut Tickets
144 N Larchmont Boulevard, between First Street & Beverly Boulevard, Hancock Park (1-323 957 6699). Bus 14/I-10, exit La Brea Avenue north. **Open** 9am-6.30pm

Mon-Fri; 10am-5pm Sat. **Credit** AmEx, Disc, MC, V.
Map 5 B3
These guys sell tickets for sporting events, concerts and
theatre shows. They usually have the first 15 rows in the
house along with preferential parking – and you will pay
top dollar for them.

Toys

The Glendale Galleria mall houses the famous New
York toyshop **FAO Schwarz** (1-818 547 5900)
while the Beverly Center has the educational but
fun store **Learningsmith** (1-310 854 7722).

Allied Model Trains
*4411 S Sepulveda Boulevard, at Braddock Drive, Culver
City (1-310 313 9353). Bus Culver City 5, 6/I-405, exit
Culver Boulevard east.* **Open** 10am-6pm Mon-Thur;
10am-7pm Fri; 10am-6pm Sat. **Credit** Disc, MC, V.
Housed in a replica of Union Station, this is the store where
you will find trains, trains, trains and any accessories to do
with trains. Makes include Thomas the Tank Engine, Brio
and Playmobile for small children, and Fleishmann, LGB,
Lionel and others for the serious enthusiast.

Lakeshore Learning Materials
*8888 Venice Boulevard, at National Boulevard, Culver City
(1-310 559 9630). Bus 33, 220, 333, 436, Santa Monica
12/I-10, exit National Avenue south.* **Open** 9am-6.30pm
Mon-Sat; 11am-5pm Sun. **Credit** AmEx, Disc, MC, V.
A warehouse full of stimulating, politically correct, educational toys. We recommend the Frog Hatchery Kit, the Giant
Ant Farm and the elephantine jigsaw puzzles.
Website: www.lakeshorelearning.com

Star Toys
*130 Barrington Place, at Sunset Boulevard, Brentwood
(1-310 472 2422). Bus Santa Monica 14/I-405, exit
Sunset Boulevard west.* **Open** 9.30am-6pm Mon-Sat;
10am-5pm Sun. **Credit** AmEx, MC, V.
This store has 2,200sq ft (205sq m) of toys, from boxed
games to collectable dolls. 'If Toys-R-Us carries it, I try not
to,' says the owner.

Toys-R-Us
*402 Santa Monica Boulevard, at Fourth Street, Santa
Monica (1-310 451 1205). Bus 4, Santa Monica 1, 2, 3,
7, 8/I-10, exit Fourth Street north.* **Open** 9.30am-9.30pm
Mon-Sat; 10am-7pm Sun. **Credit** AmEx, Disc, MC, V.
Map 2 A2
One of the largest branches of this toyshop chain.
Branches: check the phone directory for your nearest.

Wound & Wound Toy Company
*7374 Melrose Avenue, at N Martel Avenue, Melrose
District (1-323 653 6703). Bus 10, 212, 217/US 101,
exit Melrose Avenue west.* **Open** 11am-8pm Mon-Thur;
11am-11pm Fri, Sat; noon-7pm Sun. **Credit** MC, V.
Map 4 C2
Robots, hand puppets, model classic cars and trains.

Zany Brainy
*3842 Sepulveda Boulevard, at Hawthorne Boulevard,
Torrance (1-310 791 6200). Bus 444, Torrance Transit
8/I-405, exit Hawthorne Boulevard south.* **Open** 9am-
8pm Mon-Sat; 11am-6pm Sun. **Credit** AmEx, Disc, MC, V.
Part of a national chain of multimedia educational super-
stores, Zany Brainy proclaims it has 'a zillion neat things for
kids'. Indeed, there is a huge selection of toys, games, puzzles, audio tapes, video tapes, books, arts and crafts, software, dolls and electronic toys. Branches are due to open in
early 1999 in Santa Monica, Pasadena and Manhattan Beach.

Travel

For general travel services, try travel agency
Global Travel Management in Northridge
(1-818 701 7272); after 20 years in business, there's
not much they haven't done.

The Travel Medical Center
*131 N Robertson Boulevard, at Wilshire Boulevard,
Beverly Hills (1-310 360 1331). Bus 20, 21, 22, 320,
322/I-10, exit Robertson Boulevard north.* **Open** 9am-
5pm Mon-Fri; 11am-3pm Sat. **Credit** AmEx, DC, Disc,
MC, V. **Map 4 A3**
This is the place for one-stop shopping for all your medical
travel needs (vaccinations, customised first-aid kits for your
chosen destination), mosquito nets, travel-sized hairdryers
and much more.

Video rental

To find your nearest branch of the ubiquitous
Blockbuster chain, call 1-800 800 6767.

Eddie Brandt's Saturday Matinee
*5006 Vineland Avenue, between Magnolia Boulevard &
Camarillo Street, North Hollywood (1-818 506 4242).
Bus 420/US 101, exit Vineland Avenue north.*
Open 1-6pm Tue-Fri; 8.30am-5pm Sat. **Credit** AmEx,
Disc, MC, V.
This store has a highly eclectic selection of films, from
episodic TV to Japanese sex epics.

Rocket Video
*726 N La Brea Avenue, between Melrose & Waring
Avenues, Hollywood (1-323 965 1100). Bus 10, 11, 212/
I-10, exit La Brea Avenue north.* **Open** 11am-10pm Mon-
Thur, Sun; 11am-11pm Fri, Sat. **Credit** AmEx, MC, V.
Map 4 C2
The cinephile's video shop: Rocket is likely to have that
obscure masterpiece when no one else does.

Vidiots
*302 Pico Boulevard, at Third Street, Santa Monica
(1-310 392 8508). Bus Santa Monica 1, 2, 3, 7, 8/I-10,
exit Lincoln Boulevard north.* **Open** 10am-11pm Mon-
Thur, Sun; 10am-midnight Fri, Sat. **Credit** AmEx, MC,
V. **Map 2 A3**
Foreign and hard-to-find stuff plus regular commercial fare.

Rocket Video: *it's a blast.*

Arts & Entertainment

Children

In a city that trades in fantasy and is the home of Disney, blessed with endless beaches and a thousand varieties of fun, children are honoured guests.

Los Angeles is a great place for kids, from its sun-drenched beaches to its array of theme parks and children-centred museums. The region offers huge commercial attractions and a few large public green spaces rather than modest neighbourhood playgrounds, so you'll spend time getting about – but the effort will usually be worthwhile. Children are welcome at all but the most refined restaurants and shops, and LA's casual, fun-seeking atmosphere suits families perfectly.

For children's books, clothes and toys – and much else – *see chapter* **Shops & Services**.

Babysitters

Babysitters Agency of Santa Monica
1105 Garfield Avenue, Marina del Rey, CA 90291 (1-310 306 5437). **Open** 9am-5pm Mon-Sat. **No credit cards**.
Babysitters aged at least 21 will take the kids out for a bike ride, a swim or other activities. They need 24 hours' notice and charge $9 per hour ($10 per hour at hotels) plus transport costs, with a four-hour minimum.

Babysitters Guild
6399 Wilshire Boulevard, suite 812, Los Angeles, CA 90048 (1-323 658 8792/fax 1-323 852 1422). **Open** 8am-3pm Mon-Fri. **No credit cards**.
In business for 50 years, the Guild employs babysitters aged 21-70, who all speak English, have CPR (cardiopulmonary resuscitation) training and drive. They serve hotels all over the city at a cost of $8-$11 an hour plus $5 petrol fee and parking, with a four-hour minimum.

Mount St Mary's College – Student Placement Office
Chalon Campus, 12001 Chalon Road, Los Angeles, CA 90049 (1-310 954 4195/fax 1-310-954 4199). **Open** 8am-5pm Mon-Fri.
The Student Placement office will provide a list of college students who babysit, or you can put in a request by fax. You make the arrangements yourself; fees are $7-$10 an hour. *Website: www.msmc.la.edu*

Entertainment

For listings of theme parks, beaches and other family attractions, *see chapter* **Sightseeing**. For more entertainment suggestions, refer to the Calendar section of the Sunday *LA Times*, the *LA Weekly* and the monthly *LA Parent*, which can be found in any location that caters for kids. On weekdays during July and August, **Open House at**

Hollywood Bowl (*see page 207* **Music**) lays on performances and workshops of all varieties for children aged between three and 12.

Circuses & shows

Disney on Ice
LA Sports Arena, 3939 S Figueroa Street, at Martin Luther King Jr Boulevard, Exposition Park, Downtown (1-213 748 6131). Bus 81, 102, 200, 442, 444/I-110, exit Exposition Boulevard west. **Open** box office 10am-6pm Mon-Fri & days of games. **Tickets** $11.50-$32.50. **Credit** MC, V.
Part of the Disney marketing machine: stories from the animated features are skated out in costume on ice, for one week in winter, at the LA Sports Arena in Downtown. A big, good-natured spectacle that kids love.

LA Circus
Information 1-213 751 3486.
Sponsored by the Los Angeles Cultural Affairs Office, this delightful one-ring circus sets up in inner city parks for a one- or two-day show, and at other venues such as Universal Studios for longer stays. There are also children's circus workshops. Call for a performance schedule.

Ringling Brothers and Barnum & Bailey Circus
For listings, see above **Disney on Ice**.
The Ringling Brothers and Barnum & Bailey three-ring spectacle is the epitome of the US circus. This one's as big, loud and lavish as they come and plays at various area venues during the summer, such as the LA Sports Arena in Downtown, Great Western Forum in Inglewood and Arrowhead Pond in Anaheim.

Libraries

Most of the public libraries in and around LA have regular storytelling and workshops. To learn about other performances and events, ask for the *Children's Activities* pamphlet, available free at most branches.

Central Library
630 W Fifth Street, between Flower Street & Grand Avenue, Downtown (1-213 228 7000/children's tour reservation line 1-213 228 7055/children's library 1-213 228 7250). Metro Seventh Street/Metro Center/bus 16, 18, 78, 79, 96, DASH E, Foothill Transit 492/I-110 north, exit Sixth Street east. **Open** 10am-5.30pm Mon, Thur-Sat; noon-8pm Tue, Wed; 1-5pm Sun.
Map 7 B3
The children's library here is well equipped and very active. The Ronald McDonald multimedia centre features eight interactive workstations. To locate books, children can refer to Kid Cat, a computer catalogue system that uses icons – so there's no need to spell. The KLOS Story

Theater seats 60 people for music and dance, storytelling and puppet shows (2pm Sat). On any given day you will find storytelling, dancing, music, crafts and more throughout the library and its grounds.

Music

From October to May, **Open House at the Music Center** schedules a concert and workshop series for children aged from three upwards at the Dorothy Chandler Pavilion (*see page 205* **Music**).

Pasadena Symphony Musical Circus

Pasadena Civic Auditorium, 300 E Green Street, at Euclid Avenue, Pasadena (1-626 449 7360/Pasadena Symphony 1-626 793 7172). Bus 180, 181, 188, 256, Foothill Transit 187/I-110, exit Green Street east. **Credit** AmEx, MC, V.
Musicians and teachers help children aged 4-12 discover the joy of music-making through a hands-on session with a variety of orchestral instruments, an event that relates to the theme of that evening's concert.
Parking $5.

Will Geer Theatricum Botanicum

For listings, see p232 **Theatre & Dance**.
This rustically located open-air theatre welcomes children's performers on Sundays at 11am from July through to September.

Restaurants

With child-friendly fast-food joints and family dining chains, such as Denny's, endemic, the problem won't be where you can feed your kids, but how to get them out of there.

DC-3

2800 Donald Douglas Loop N, at 28th Street, Santa Monica (1-310 399 2323). Bus Santa Monica 8/I-10, exit Bundy Drive south. **Lunch served** 11.30am-2.30pm Mon-Fri. **Dinner served** 6-9.30pm Tue-Sat. **Credit** AmEx, MC, V. **Map 2 C4**
The city's most fashionable restaurant back in the late 1980s, DC-3 offers a service from Tuesday to Friday (6-9.30pm) whereby kids are entertained and fed by babysitters while their parents eat. Main courses cost $17-$26; kids' meals average $5.95. Children must be out of nappies and walking.

Dive!

Century City Shopping Mall, 10250 Santa Monica Boulevard, between Avenue of the Stars & Century Park W, Century City (1-310 788 3483). Bus 22, 27, 28, 316, 328, Santa Monica 5, Commuter Express 534, 573/ I-405, exit Santa Monica Boulevard east. **Open** 11.30am-10pm Mon-Thur, Sun; 11.30am-11.30pm Fri, Sat. **Credit** AmEx, DC, MC, V. **Map 3 B3**
Popular with kids of all ages. Partly owned by Steven Spielberg, this submarine-themed fast-food restaurant serves ribs, pasta, pizza, burgers and salads, but specialises, of course, in submarine sandwiches – a super-large hot dog-style roll with any number of absurd fillings.
Parking free first 2 hours.

Theatre/puppets

Bob Baker Marionette Theater

1345 W First Street, at Glendale Boulevard, Echo Park (1-213 250 9995). Bus 14/I-110, exit Third Street west. **Shows** 10.30am Tue-Fri; 2.30pm Sat, Sun. **Tickets** $10; $8 seniors. **Credit** AmEx, MC, V. **Map 6 C5**
Original marionette productions. Booking essential.
Free parking.

Santa Monica Playhouse

1211 Fourth Street, between Arizona Avenue & Wilshire Boulevard, Santa Monica (1-310 394 9779). Bus 20, 320, Santa Monica 2, 3, 8, 9/I-10, exit Fourth Street north. **Tickets** $8. **Credit** MC, V. **Map 2 A2**
Five or six original family musicals are staged each year by the Playhouse's Actors' Repertory Theatre Company.

Museums

In the new **California Science Center**, children can experience a simulated earthquake, watch chicks hatch, design a bicycle and see the body's inner workings in Tess, a recumbent 50-foot (15m) human model. The **Natural History Museum**, meanwhile, has an interactive gallery and a giant ant farm. At the Discovery Center at the **Skirball Cultural Center**, young archaeologists can play at being Indiana Jones, and woolly mammoths still roam the earth at the **George C Page Museum of La Brea Discoveries**. Also recommended is the **Petersen Automotive Museum**; for all, *see chapter* **Museums**. Below are museums aimed specially at kids.

Angels Attic Museum

516 Colorado Boulevard, between Fifth & Sixth Streets, Santa Monica (1-310 394 8331). Bus 434, Santa Monica 2, 3, 9/I-10, exit Fifth Street north. **Open** 12.30-4.30pm Thur-Sun. **Admission** $6.50; $4 seniors; $3 under-12s. **Credit** MC, V. **Map 2 A2/3**
Doll lovers can covet more than 60 antique dolls' houses and dolls from around the world at this museum, aimed at both adults and kids. Sit down to tea and cakes for $7.50 per person (book in advance).

*Take the plunge at **Dive!** restaurant.*

Los Angeles Children's Museum

310 N Main Street, at Temple Street, Downtown (1-213 687 8801/recorded information 1-213 687 8800). Metro Civic Center/Tom Bradley/bus 434, 436, 439, 442, DASH D/US 101, exit Los Angeles Street south. **Open** 11.30am-5pm Mon-Fri. **Admission** $5; free under-2s. **No credit cards.**
Map 7 C2

Children can record a song in a professional recording studio, make a TV show in the Videozone (US-format videos only), learn about recycling, make an animated cartoon and much more. The theatre hosts performances and related workshops by storytellers, musicians, dancers, actors, artists, animal handlers and writers.
Website: www.lacm.org

Kidspace Museum

390 S El Molino Avenue, between California & Del Mar Boulevards, Pasadena (1-626 449 9143). Bus 267/I-110 to Arroyo Parkway, exit California Boulevard east. **Open** Sept-May 1-5pm Mon, Wed-Fri, Sun; 1.30-5pm Tue; 10am-5pm Sat; June-Aug 1-5pm Mon-Thur, Sun; 10am-5pm Fri, Sat. **Admission** $5; $3.50 seniors; $2.50 1-2s. **Credit** MC, V.

At this children-oriented museum in Pasadena, curious kids can visit a simulated beach, shop in a mini-supermarket, make masks, observe animal and insect habitats and ecosystems, play with computers and a fire truck, be a TV news anchor and study California's night skies. There are also plenty of games and building blocks to play with and Toddler Territory, an area specially designed for wee ones, with padded walls and floors.
Free parking.

Museum of Flying

2772 Donald Douglas Loop N, at 28th Street, Santa Monica (1-310 392 8822). Bus Santa Monica 8/I-10, exit Bundy Drive south. **Open** 10am-5pm Wed-Sun. **Admission** $7; $5 seniors; $3 children. **Credit** AmEx, MC, V. **Map 2 C4**

There are more than 40 aircraft in and around this Santa Monica museum. Embryonic aviators can clamber into cockpits, attend workshops, watch videos and learn about designing and flying aircraft.
Website: http://pen.ci.santa-monica.ca.us/airport/

Outdoors

The rolling hills of **Griffith Park** (*see page 70* **Sightseeing**) make a great one-stop outdoor experience for children. There are picnic areas, miles of hiking and horse-riding trails, the Travel Town Museum, a merry-go-round – built in 1926 and operated daily during the summer and at weekends – Los Angeles Zoo and the famous Griffith Park Observatory.

In fact, all the parks are good for kids: also try **Will Rogers State Park** and **Kenny Hahn State Recreation Area**. For an in-depth look at LA's beaches, *see page 52* **Sightseeing**.

TreePeople Tours

12601 Mulholland Drive, at Coldwater Canyon Drive, Beverly Hills (1-818 753 4620/tour reservations 1-818 623 4859). US 101, exit Coldwater Canyon Boulevard south. **Open** 10am Wed, Thur, Fri. **Admission** $5 per child. **Credit** MC, V.

Spend a delightful, politically correct day with TreePeople. This non-profit group plants and cares for trees both native and exotic while enlightening the Los Angeles community

about protecting the environment. It's located in the 45-acre (18ha) Coldwater Canyon Park, where visitors can enjoy guided walks and educational displays at the centre. Children can garden, learn about conservation and explore the recycling area. Booking is essential for the tours.

Flora & fauna

The new **Long Beach Aquarium of the Pacific** is a must for children; for information *see page 85* **Sightseeing**.

Cabrillo Marine Aquarium

3720 Stephen White Drive, at Pacific Avenue, San Pedro (1-310 548 7562). Bus 446, MAX 3/I-110, exit Harbor Boulevard west. **Open** noon-5pm Tue-Fri, 10am-5pm Sat, Sun. **Admission** (suggested donation) $2; $1 children, seniors.

This 60-year-old aquarium is dedicated to California marine life. It's home to a jellyfish farm, a hands-on tidal pool exhibit and 30 ocean-life tanks. Special seasonal events include two-hour whale-watching trips, guided walks to the tidal pools at Point Fermin Marine Life Refuge and grunion runs (trips made during this small, pencil-sized fish's migrating season – an opportunity to catch and eat the grunion, but not recommended if you get seasick).
Website: www.cabrilloaq.org
Parking $6.50.

Hydrosphere

Information 1-310 230 3334/fax 1-310 230 3336/hydrosphere@juno.com. **Open** *office* 9am-5pm Mon-Fri. **Admission** $15-$399 and up. **Credit** MC, V.

Board the expedition vessel, the 64ft *Pacific Explorer,* in Long Beach and pick your destination, from the day-long Catalina Island Adventure or the Day Shark Expedition to a 2½-day expedition. An open-top snorkelling cage lets snorkelers and non-swimmers aged eight and over view sea life – sharks, sea lions, kelp forests and more – in a safe, protected setting. Experienced scuba divers are welcome. For a tamer but still fascinating experience, try an interactive exploration: from the *Pacific Explorer,* you can speak to the divers while they are underwater, and on-board naturalists give information and answer questions.
Website: www.hydrosphere-expedition.com

Los Angeles Zoo

For listings, see p70 **Sightseeing**.

Housing more than 1,600 animals in lushly landscaped settings, the zoo's highlights include a reptile house, a koala house, gorilla and tiger exhibits and animal shows. The Safari Shuttle, a tram that travels to many of the different environments, takes the pain out of the zoo's steep slopes. Phone for details of special workshops – where children can accompany zookeepers as they give the animals breakfast – and sleepovers, where children can have a night-time stroll with the keepers.
Website: www.lazoo.org
Free parking.

Sebastian Rainforest

6109 DeSoto Avenue, at Erwin Street, Woodland Hills (1-800 829 7322). Bus 243, Santa Clarita 796/US 101, exit DeSoto Avenue north. **Open** 9am-3pm Mon, Wed, Fri. **Admission** free.

Experience a miniature rainforest created inside the Sebastian haircare product corporation's building in the San Fernando Valley. The exhibit features artefacts made by rainforest inhabitants, a small aquarium and displays of rainforest animals and products. Guides give groups of ten to 25 people a 45-minute tour (booking required; children must be seven or older).
Free parking.

Film

You can't ignore film in LA – so why not wallow in its wealth of movie palaces, little-screened classics and eclectic festivals, catching the action at a location shoot on the way?

HOLLYWOOD: THE BEGINNINGS

The old film-makers liked to say that it was the perfect shooting weather that brought them to Hollywood as early as 1908, but the reality was more prosaic: Los Angeles was a long way from New York and the tough patent laws that controlled film-making there. The sunshine was an added advantage, though, and by the beginning of World War I, Hollywood was jammed with film companies operating out of old barns and warehouses.

Star actors soon became a big part of the fledgling movie business, notable among them Charlie Chaplin and Mary Pickford. As early as 1915, studio executives were complaining about the high price of stars' salaries. Carl Laemmle, who started Universal, even took out an advertisement to claim he was the first producer to 'buck the star system – the ruinous practice that has been responsible for high-priced but low-grade features'. Pickford, however, was a shrewd judge of her own worth and in 1919, along with Chaplin, Douglas Fairbanks and DW Griffith – America's first great movie director – she founded United Artists to distribute their own work, becoming, in the process, one of the richest women in America.

Hollywood's first golden age began in the 1920s. Legendary bosses such as Sam Goldwyn, Louis B Mayer and Carl Laemmle were running highly productive studios like MGM, RKO, Fox, Paramount, Universal and Columbia. Paramount alone was putting out four features a week. At the same time, Hollywood was rocked by a series of scandals, most notable the accusation that popular comedian Roscoe 'Fatty' Arbuckle was involved in the death of a starlet. Frightened of government censorship, the producers put in place a self-regulatory organisation, the Motion Picture Producers and Distributors of America, also known as the Hayes Office after its chief, Will Hayes.

The arrival of sound with *The Jazz Singer* in 1927 further consolidated the studios' power: the new technology meant immediate pay cuts for the silent stars, who had to prove they could make the transition to talkies. Not all of them did, but by now American talent was being bolstered increasingly by new arrivals from Europe. The Brits been here since the beginning, but the rise of Hitler prompted much of the German film industry, the artistic powerhouse of world cinema in the 1920s,

to up and move to Hollywood. LA was now the world capital of film-making, its lure so powerful that even Sergei Eisenstein, the great Soviet director, stopped by in 1932 for a brief visit.

THE PRODUCTION LINE

The Great Depression reached Hollywood four year after the stock market crash – but it hit hard. President Franklin Roosevelt came to the rescue with the National Industrial Recovery Act, which permitted certain monopolistic practices. It permitted the studios to control every aspect of movie-making, locking the talent into long-term contracts that granted them extravagant salaries while ensuring they had no control over what they did.

The studios were factories: actors and directors were assigned to projects whether they liked them or not, writers clocked in every day at the writers' building and an army of technicians kept the cameras rolling. This new corporate atmosphere displeased many actors and film-makers; but it meant there was no shortage of jobs, and some films were enormously accomplished.

The moguls also worked on Hollywood's somewhat dissolute public image. Nearly all were immigrants from Eastern Europe, but they were determined to make the film industry as American as baseball. Scandals were kept quiet, donations were made to political parties and the outbreak of World War II allowed Hollywood to show that it could wave the flag better than anyone.

After the war, the dark side of this studied patriotism emerged: studios hastily complied with a congressional inquiry into Communism in the motion picture industry. From 1947 into the early 1960s, hundreds of writers, actors and directors were blacklisted from working in Hollywood because of Senator Joe McCarthy's mission to root out Communist sympathisers in all walks of public life.

The 1940s also saw the first cracks in the studio system; by the end of the 1950s, competition from television and stars' desire to control their own destinies appeared to signal its demise. But after some lean times in the 1960s and 1970s, the studios have bounced back. They no longer have the stars on a string and are now owned by the Japanese, the banks and, in the case of Twentieth Century Fox, by Rupert Murdoch, but the studios

The ultimate movie palace: **Mann's Chinese Theater** *in Hollywood.*

are still here. In a town with a short history, they act as a reassuring constant. At present they're growing more powerful through their non-movie interests: merchandising, running theme parks and owning sports teams. And the flow of hopeful talent has never stopped. Tens of thousands of people pitch up in LA every year, lured by the same dreams that have been drawing the star-struck since 1912.

TINSELTOWN TODAY

It often seems as if every person you meet in Los Angeles either works in the film industry, knows someone who does, or wants to know someone who does. Much of the city closes down on the day of the **Academy Awards** (*see page 88* **Los Angeles by Season**).

In terms of actual cinema-going and film-related activities, this translates into a huge variety of choices. There are film courses aplenty at just about every college in and around Los Angeles, a couple of film festivals every month, workshops everywhere and, if you stay here for any length of time, you're almost certain to happen across a location shoot.

TICKETS & INFORMATION

The best sources are the *Los Angeles Times* Calendar section, the *LA Weekly* and *New Times*, which all list festivals and special screenings as well as standard movie reviews and info. There are thousands of cinema screens in Los Angeles; we have listed a selection of the most interesting below. For bog-standard local multi-screens, check the newspapers.

FILM RATINGS

Producers pay the Motion Picture Association of America to protect the innocent by rating their movies. 'NC-17' has replaced the 'X' rating, which embarrassed the MPAA because of its association with porn. The ratings are:

G unrestricted
PG parental guidance suggested
PG-13 under-13s must be accompanied by an adult
R under-17s must be accompanied by an adult
NC-17 no one under 17

The cinemas

Los Angeles isn't a good place to catch the latest European releases: only the big hits make it over. A lot of European cinema is shown in tributes, retrospectives and special seasons, however, and not just in art-house cinemas.

Classic, archive & experimental

American Cinematheque

Information 1-323 466 3456.
Specialising in tributes and retrospectives, the Cinematheque has a growing reputation for innovative programming. Screenings have been held at various locations, but in 1999 the group is getting a permanent home at the historic Egyptian Theater (6712 Hollywood Boulevard, near N Highland Avenue, Hollywood).

American Film Institute

Information 1-323 856 7600. **Open** 9am-5pm Mon-Fri.
Dedicated to preserving old films and advancing the cause of the moving image in general, the American Film Institute (AFI) also runs the LA International Film Festival and sometimes organises screenings for the general public at venues around the city.

IMAX

For listings, see **California Science Center** *p200*
Museums & Galleries.
The seven-storey-high and 70ft-wide screen at the IMAX cinema is perfectly suited to capturing vast landscapes and showing off the natural world – and documentaries on these subjects are what the theatre mostly screens. It's located at the California Science Center, which also has a 3-D theatre, where the prices are a dollar more.

LA County Museum of Art

For listings, see p196 **Museums & Galleries**. **Open** *box office* 10am-5pm Tue-Thur; 11am-9pm Fri; 11am-6pm Sat, Sun; *shows* 7.30pm Fri, Sat; 1pm Wed. **Tickets** $6; $4 seniors, students; $1 Tue. **No credit cards**.
The museum regularly runs film series seasons and tributes at the Leo S Bing Theater and on Tuesday afternoons screens classic movies for the bargain price of $1. One of Martin Scorsese's favourite rep venues.

Los Angeles Contemporary Exhibitions

6522 Hollywood Boulevard, at Wilcox Avenue, Hollywood (1-213 957 1777). Bus 180, 181, 217/I-101, exit N Cahuenga Boulevard south. **Open** *noon-6pm Wed, Fri; noon-8pm Thur; noon-5pm Sat, Sun.* **Map 5 A1**
LACE is famous for the unpredictable, but film and video are a staple part of its exhibitions. It provides a weekly venue for FilmForum (1-213 526 2911), a local underground institution, in addition to its own series. In 1997 it hosted the first Super 8 Film Festival. Most screenings are free.

Museum of Contemporary Art

For listings, see p196 **Museums & Galleries**. **Open** *box office* 11am-5pm Tue-Sun; call for show times. **Tickets** $6; $4 seniors, students. **No credit cards**.
Both MOCA sites in Downtown screen experimental and classic films and videos as part of exhibitions.

Tales Bookshop/Café

667 S La Brea Avenue, at Wilshire Boulevard, Miracle Mile (1-213 933 2640). Bus 20, 21, 22, 212, 320, 322/ I-10, exit La Brea Avenue north. **Open** *shows* 7.30pm Mon, Thur; 7.30pm, 9.30pm Fri; 3.30pm, 7.30pm, 9.30pm Sat, Sun.* **Tickets** $4. **Credit** MC, V. **Map 4 C3**
Half bookstore and half coffeehouse, Tales presents weekly screenings of classic 16mm prints. The screen is so large that you can sit in either the bookshop or the café – you can always see. Tales specialises in film noir.

UCLA Film & Television Archive

UCLA campus, 405 Hilgard Avenue, Westwood (admin 1-310 206 8013/box office 1-310 206 8365/recorded information 1-310 206 3456). Bus 2, 21, 429, 576, Culver City 6, Santa Monica 1, 2, 3/I-10, exit Sunset Boulevard east. **Open** *admin* 9am-6pm Mon-Fri; *box office* 1 hour before show. **Tickets** $6; $4 seniors, students. **No credit cards**.
UCLA's huge archives are a treasure trove of little-seen silents, classics from the 1930s heyday of Hollywood, newsreels and documentaries. But screenings aren't just limited to archive material: there's normally something for everyone in any week. The cinema operates year-round.

Repertory

Bear in mind that many of the cinemas listed above also act as rep venues.

Laemmle chain

The Laemmle chain of cinemas frequently has mini-seasons and tributes to individual directors. There are eight Laemmles scattered across Los Angeles and the Valleys, including the following:

Sunset 5 *8000 Sunset Boulevard, at Crescent Heights Boulevard, West Hollywood (1-213 848 3500).* **Map 4 B1**
Laemmle's Monica 4-Plex *1332 Second Street, between Santa Monica Boulevard & Arizona Avenue, Santa Monica (1-310 394 9741).* **Map 2 A2**
Laemmle's Royal *11523 Santa Monica Boulevard, between Butler & Colby Avenues, West LA (1-310 477 5581).*
Laemmle's Music Hall *9036 Wilshire Boulevard, at Doheny Drive, Beverly Hills (1-310 274 6869).* **Map 3 C2**

New Beverly Cinema

7165 Beverly Boulevard, at N Detroit Street, Fairfax District (1-213 938 4038). Bus 14, 212/I-10, exit La Brea Avenue north. **Open** *box office* 2 hours before show. **Tickets** $5; $4 students; $2.50 seniors. **No credit cards**. **Map 4 C2**
The New Beverly is nothing special in terms of comfort, but extraordinary in terms of programming. In addition to independent and foreign films, it also revives older films. The bill changes every couple of days.

Nuart

11272 Santa Monica Boulevard, at Sawtelle Boulevard, West LA (1-310 478 6379). Bus 4, 304, Santa Monica 1, 5/I-405, exit Santa Monica Boulevard west. **Open** *box office* from 5pm daily. **Tickets** $7.50; $4.50 seniors. **No credit cards**.
Owned by the Landmark chain, the Nuart is the best rep house on the Westside. It often gets exclusive engagements of independent and foreign movies. It also runs classics, including a Saturday-midnight screening of *The Rocky Horror Picture Show* as well as other midnight screenings.

Rialto

1023 Fair Oaks Avenue, at Oxly Avenue, South Pasadena (1-818 799 9567). Bus 176, 483/I-110, exit Fair Oaks Avenue south. **Open** *box office* from 4pm Mon-Fri; from noon Sat, Sun. **Tickets** $7; $4 seniors. **No credit cards**.
Another Landmark Theater where you can catch *The Rocky Horror Picture Show* (midnight Sat) as well as the latest art-house releases. Some people love the balcony, though the mediocre sound is worse up there. A useful standby if you're ever in Pasadena, and a charming looker to boot, this is where Tim Robbins's character in *The Player* comes to see *Bicycle Thieves*.

Movie palaces

There are some extravagant movie palaces in LA, dating from the early glamour days of the industry. The most famous of these is **Mann's Chinese Theater** in Hollywood (6925 Hollywood Boulevard; 1-323 464 8111), a bizarre re-creation of a Chinese temple, but also a good place to see a film (*see also p63* **Sightseeing**). Almost opposite it is the elegant Disney-owned **El Capitan Theater** (at Hollywood Boulevard and Highland Avenue; 1-323 467 7674). The El Capitan has been closed for earthquake renovations, but is known for fancy pre-film floor shows.

In Downtown, the 2,000-seat **Orpheum** (842 S Broadway, at Eighth Street; 1-213 239 0937) is the last of the great 1920s Broadway theatres still to operate as a cinema; the defunct **Los Angeles Theater** (615 S Broadway) is still worth a look, though.

Other notable cinemas include the **Cinerama Dome** (6360 Sunset Boulevard, at Ivar Avenue, Hollywood; 1-323 466 3401), with its giant screen and spectacular sound system; the very comfortable six-screen **GCC Hollywood Galaxy** (7021 Hollywood Boulevard, at Sycamore Avenue, Hollywood; 1-323 957 9246); the pleasant **Vista** (4473 Sunset Drive, at Sunset Boulevard, Los Feliz; 1-323 660 6639); the

AMC Century 14 (in Century City Shopping Mall, 10250 Little Santa Monica Boulevard, at the Avenue of the Stars, Century City; 1-310 553 8900); and the 18-screen Universal City 18 Cinemas (Universal CityWalk; 1-818 766 4317). The huge Mann Theaters, all in Westwood (general line 1-310 248 6266), are frequently used for big-name premières and are an ideal place to get the big-screen experience.

African-American cinema

Magic Johnson Theaters

4020 Marlton Avenue, near Crenshaw Plaza, Baldwin Hills (1-323 290 5900). Bus 105, DASH Crenshaw/ Midtown/I-10, exit Crenshaw Boulevard south. **Open** 10.30am-11.30pm daily. **Tickets** $7.50 after 6pm; $4.75 adults before 6pm, seniors, under-12s. **Credit** AmEx, MC, V.

Owned by the now-retired star of the Los Angeles Lakers, this is the one venue in the city that shows African-American films after they've left most mall multiplexes, as well as those that don't make it to general release. It also hosts the annual Pan-African Film Festival.

Drive-ins

Only a couple of drive-ins remain in LA County: they all show current releases and, for obvious reasons, screenings start at dusk. Tickets cost $5 and credit cards are not accepted.

Azusa Drive-In *675 E Foothill Boulevard, west of Citrus Boulevard, Azusa (1-626 334 0263).*
Vermont Drive-In *17737 S Vermont Avenue, at Artesia Boulevard, Gardena (1-310 323 4055).*

Preview screenings

As you'd expect, there are endless industry and press screenings in LA, but getting in isn't easy unless you have industry connections. However, on most weekends there are people outside the big multiplexes offering free tickets to previews and test screenings of soon-to-be-released movies. Try the **Laemmle's Monica 4-Plex** in Santa Monica and the **AMC Century 14** in Century City. Old Town Pasadena and Westwood are also swarming with movie recruiters. If you're aged under 30, you might just get asked inside. The **Bruin** (948 Broxton Avenue, near UCLA campus; 1-310 208 8998) is often used for previews of upcoming movies; they're advertised in advance in the *Los Angeles Times* and *LA Weekly*.

Film festivals

Festival seems the wrong word to use in Los Angeles, where such special programmes go on non-stop. Here are some highlights.

Cinecon Annual Film Festival

Information 1-760 770 9533.
Cinecon found the perfect home at the Alex Theatre (216 N Brand Boulevard, Glendale; 1-818 243 2539), a restored 1920s silent movie palace. The one-weekend show, usually in August, screens almost-never-seen early films.

The Last Remaining Seats

Information 1-213 623 2489.
On four Wednesdays in June you can see old films – both silents and talkies – with live musical accompaniment in the grand old movie palaces on Broadway reopened especially for the event.

Los Angeles Asian Pacific Film & Video Festival

Information 1-213 680 3004/1-310 206 3456.
Takes a look at what's coming out of the other side of the Pacific Rim each May.

Los Angeles Independent Film Festival

Information 1-323 937 9155.
Started in 1994, this has become a four-day marathon each April to show the work of young American film-makers.

Los Angeles International Film Festival

Information 1-323 856 7707.
This is the American Film Institute's festival (hence its 'AFI Fest' nickname). Held for two weeks in October, it always attracts big crowds for both American and foreign films.

Los Angeles International Latino Film Festival

Information 1-213 896 2419.
First held in 1997 and now planned as an annual October event, the festival focuses on movies from Mexico, Central and South America.

Outfest: The Los Angeles Gay & Lesbian Film Festival

Information 1-323 951 1247.
One of the most comprehensive festivals of its kind in the world, Outfest runs for ten days every July. Events tend to sell out quickly with advance bookings.

Pan-African Film Festival

Information 1-213 896 8221.
In addition to African-American films, this festival spotlights movies from Africa and from African communities on other continents. It has a permanent home at the Magic Johnson Theaters and runs in January or February.

Studio tours

The Universal Studios tour (*see page 80* **Sightseeing**) is justly famous for its spectacular rides, but if you want a tour that shows how a studio actually operates then you have to go to **Paramount** or **Warner Brothers**. Both promise to try to get you on to any sound stages they can, so you can actually see a film shooting. Don't expect to shake hands with the stars, though: at best, you'll see a few vaguely familiar faces being whisked around on the golf carts that serve as transport on the lots. Numbers are limited on both tours, so book a few days ahead. No children under ten are allowed.

Paramount Studios

5555 Melrose Avenue, at Gower Street, Hollywood (1-323 956 1777). Bus 10, 11/US 101, exit Gower Street south. **Open** 9am-2pm Mon-Fri; tours every hour. **Tickets** $15. **No credit cards. Map 5 B2/3**
The two-hour walking tour of Paramount is good value, spinning you round the oldest and most attractive studio in LA, and also the only one still in Hollywood: it has been in the same place, give or take a few hundred metres, since 1915.

Warner Brothers Studios

4000 Warner Boulevard, at Hollywood Way & Olive Avenue, Burbank (1-818 954 1744). Bus 96, 152, 163/ Hwy 134, exit Pass Avenue south. **Open** 10am-3pm Mon-Fri (later in summer); tours on the hour. **Tickets** $30. **Credit** AmEx, MC, V.

*Previews of new films are often shown at the **Bruin** cinema in Westwood.*

The Warner's tour is double the price of Paramount's for the same amount of time, and its lot doesn't have as much historical resonance. It is, however, the shooting location of most prime-time US television shows, including *Friends* and *ER*.

TV tapings

TV sitcoms often come with the pronouncement 'Filmed live before a studio audience', and if you want to see it happen, LA is the place. Tickets are free – but be warned, tapings can take over three hours. Unfortunately, drama programmes are made on closed sets, so there's no chance of watching a *Star Trek* or *ER* studio shoot.

Audiences Unlimited
100 Universal Plaza, Building 153, Universal City, CA 91608 (1-818 753 3470, ext 810).
This agency provides studio audiences for about 40 sitcoms, including *Third Rock from the Sun* and *Friends* (as well as *Donny & Marie*, an Osmond-fronted talk show). The easiest way to get a ticket is via its website, any time from 60 to two days before a show date. Or write (preferably at least a month in advance), saying which days you'll be in LA and which shows you'd like to see. Show schedules for the next seven to ten days are also available by phone.
Website: www.tvtickets.com

The Tonight Show with Jay Leno
Tickets, NBC Television Studios, 3000 W Alameda Avenue, Burbank, CA 91523 (1-818 840 3537).
The Tonight Show is recorded each afternoon at NBC's studios. Send an SAE along with a brief letter listing a preferred date of taping and three alternative dates.

How to be an extra

Back in the 1930s it was easy to get yourself into a feature film as an extra. You simply rolled up to the Central Casting building at Hollywood Boulevard and Western Avenue. David Niven got his start this way. Nowadays, however, things are different. Central Casting is no more and extras are usually recruited from agencies that charge a fee before they send you out on a job. Check the *LA Weekly*'s classified section for their ads and look in the actors' trade papers, *Drama-Logue* and *Back Stage West*, available at most newsstands.

Location shoots

About 150 crews take to the streets of Los Angeles each day for everything from TV to fashion to film shoots, providing your best chance of watching a movie being made. The disadvantage is that filmmaking makes a poor spectator sport.

EIDC Shoot Sheet
The website (www.eidc.com) of the Entertainment Industry Development Corporation (EIDC) provides a list of production companies and production titles shooting on location in LA over the next two weeks, with dates, times and location addresses. But note: this Shoot Sheet doesn't list directors and actors, and working titles may be uninformative. If you go to pick up a hard copy of the Shoot Sheet from the EIDC office, you'll pay $10 for the privilege.

That's entertainment!

The entertainment industry encompasses everything from Hollywood blockbusters to local TV 'infomercials', and ever since aerospace took a nosedive in the early 1990s, it has become Southern California's steadiest economic pillar.

Popular perception of the industry is riddled with myth, however. The actual neighbourhood of Hollywood, for instance, is now home to only one major studio, Paramount. Universal Studios is in Universal City, while Warner Brothers and Disney have set up headquarters in Burbank. To the west, Twentieth Century Fox is in Century City; Sony is in Culver City.

Also, most of the industry's product is for TV, not cinema. While the major networks – NBC, CBS, ABC – keep their news operations based in New York, the vast majority of fictional TV programmes are produced in the LA area. Warner Brothers Television produces more prime-time programmes than any other company on its lot in Burbank. Nearby is NBC's homestead. In Studio City, the CBS Studio Center was home to the supposed New Yorkers of *Seinfeld* for years; shows like *Third Rock from the Sun* still shoot on its sound stages.

A study by the Motion Picture Association of America (MPAA) revealed that the film and TV industry pumped $27.5 billion into the California economy in 1996, most of that in LA County. Here are some other indicators of how important the business of entertainment is in LA:

● American movie-goers spent $6.2 billion on tickets in 1997 – then an all-time record.
● About 400 movies got a theatrical release in 1996. On average, each cost $40 million to produce and $20 million to market. 'Low-budget' films cost anything from $100,000 to $15 million.
● Around 130 prime-time TV programmes film at least 20 episodes each season.
● Nearly 250,000 people worked in film or TV production or services in 1997. Another 16,000 jobs were expected to be added in 1998. Hundreds of thousands more work in distribution, exhibition and video.
● Most entertainment industry jobs are with small companies that provide services to the big studios.

More than 90% of the 7,000 motion picture or video production firms have ten or fewer employees.
● Film production workers earn, on average, more than $1,300 a week, enabling many to take long breaks between jobs.
● About 130,000 people belong to the Screen Actors Guild or the American Federation of Television and Radio Artists, the actors' unions. Only 30% of them earned more than $7,500 at their craft in 1997.
● The Writers Guild West, the union for screenwriters, has only 8,000 members. One must not only have written a script, but also sold it, to become a member.
● The Directors Guild of America has 11,200 members nationally, about 55% of whom are actually directors. The others are members of the directorial team – people with jobs ranging from assistant directors to unit production managers.

The black sheep of the entertainment industry lives in the San Fernando Valley, the undisputed pornography capital of the United States – and therefore the world. This suburban tract of post-war homes may seem an unlikely place for it, but, as chronicled in the 1997 film *Boogie Nights* (*see* **photo**), 'adult' movie producers gravitated here in the 1960s and 1970s, drawn by its proximity to Hollywood, the cheap rents, the comfortable weather (allowing outdoor filming) and the morally tolerant climate of Los Angeles. But the real reason to stick around was the huge pool of potential talent: countless actors and actresses looking for work – any kind of work.

Women who make it big in the porn business can earn as much as $200,000 a year. But there are also lots of downsides. Most careers last only two years. Few, if any, adult video actors have successfully crossed over to mainstream films. And a recent HIV scare has actors and actresses demanding that condoms be used while, um… shooting.

Still, the porn industry is booming, to the tune of $4.2 billion a year in sales and rentals. A few large Valley firms – like the suggestively named Vivid Video, Anabolic Video and Wicked Pictures – and other smaller shops turned out 70 per cent of the estimated 7,000 'X-rated' film and videos released in the US in 1997.

Gay & Lesbian

Welcome to gay Los Angeles. It's friendlier than New York, warmer than San Francisco, hipper than Miami and ready for fun.

Take a walk on the wild side at **Gay & Lesbian Pride***, held every June.*

The Los Angeles region holds every imaginable configuration of gay and lesbian life: tall, tan, tattooed beach bunnies and low-riding cholos; two-stepping cowgirls and dykes on bikes; homebound couples in Gap clothes with dogs, gardens and kids; muscle queens; and ultra-smooth, all-night dancers with pierced nipples, charged up with 'tina' (crystal meth, the current drug vogue/scourge, depending on your point of view). Gay Los Angeles is concentrated in West Hollywood, Hollywood and Silver Lake, with a few interesting places in the Valleys, at the beaches and in the central city area. It's truly a delight for gay and lesbian residents, and for visitors it's a garden of Eden where every Adam and Steve and Ada and Eve are welcome.

Resources

The **Community Yellow Pages** is LA's lesbian/gay telephone book, listing anything from plumbers to pet care to nightlife. Get a copy in the bookshops listed below.

LA Gay & Lesbian Center
1625 N Schrader Boulevard, at Hollywood Boulevard, West Hollywood (1-323 993 7400). Bus 1, 26, 163, 180,
213/US 101, exit Highland Avenue south. **Open** 9.30am-8pm Mon-Fri; 9.30am-1.30pm Sat. **Map 5 A1**
When in trouble or doubt, this is the place to go: it's the largest gay and lesbian community centre in the world, offering legal, medical, outreach and education services, among many others. The June Mazer Lesbian Collection, showcasing the history of lesbian women, is on the second floor. The centre also organises moonlight horse riding.
Website: www.gay-lesbian-center.org

The Village at Ed Gould Plaza
1125 McCadden Place, between Lexington Avenue & Santa Monica Boulevard, Hollywood (1-323 461 2633). Bus 4, 304/US 101, exit Santa Monica Boulevard west. **Open** 10am-10pm Mon-Sat; 9am-9pm Sun. **Map 5 A2**
The Gay & Lesbian Center's newest complex, which opened in June 1998, the Village offers workshops, galleries, performance space, meeting rooms, a cybercentre, a coffeeshop and many helpful organisations.

West Hollywood Convention & Visitors Bureau
Pacific Design Center, 8687 Melrose Avenue, suite M25, at San Vicente Boulevard, West Hollywood (1-800 368 6020/1-310 289 2525/WHCVB@aol.com). Bus 4, 10, 11, DASH West Hollywood/I-10, exit Robertson Boulevard north. **Open** 8.30am-5.30pm Mon-Fri. **Map 4 A2**
Free booklets on hotels, cafés, restaurants, art galleries and nightlife options in West Hollywood.

Gay

With a little digging you can find whatever your heart and hard-on might desire, with enough gyms, clubs, restaurants and bars to satisfy the most choosy or ardent pleasure-seeker. But stay safe: in the past couple of years, drug abuse and HIV have found a new foothold, thanks to steroids and crystal meth mixed with unsafe sex and all-night partying. Many thousands become infected each year with HIV in LA. Take care. Don't put yourself or your partner at risk. Otherwise, though, you can abandon your vacationer's anxiety: there isn't a lot of (reported) gay bashing (though it does go on, so keep your wits about you).

The biggest concentrations of gay good times are during **Mardi Gras** in spring (details from the West Hollywood visitors bureau), **Gay Pride** weekend in June and **Hallowe'en** in October (for both, *see chapter* **Los Angeles by Season**). Meanwhile, buckle up, tune in to 103.1 FM Groove Radio and enjoy Gay LA.

Information & shops

First, pick up a copy of **Circuit Noise** (1-818 769 9390; website: www.circuitnoise.com), **Odyssey** (1-323 874 8788), **Frontiers** (1-323 848 2222; website: www.frontiersweb.com), **qvmagazine** (1-818 766 0023) or **Edge** (1-323 962 6994): they're free and have all the latest what's what. You'll find them in bars, cafés, bookshops and other shops throughout West Hollywood. Website **www.west hollywood.com** is a useful gay guide.

A Different Light Bookstore
8853 Santa Monica Boulevard, at San Vicente Boulevard, West Hollywood (1-310 854 6601). Bus 2, 3, 105, 302, DASH West Hollywood/I-10, exit Santa Monica Boulevard north. **Open** 10am-midnight daily. **Credit** AmEx, MC, V. **Map 4 A2**
Largest selection of lesbian and gay books, magazines, cards and videos, with super-friendly service and special activities almost nightly. Check out the bulletin board in the back for events, rooms to rent, massages and whatnots.
Website: www.adlbooks.com/whe.html

Circus of Books
8230 Santa Monica Boulevard, between Harper & La Jolla Avenues, West Hollywood (1-323 656 6533). Bus 4, 304/I-10, exit Fairfax Avenue north. **Open** 6am-2am daily. **Credit** Disc, MC, V. **Map 4 B1**
There are two of them. They're sleazy and can be a lot of fun. Get a porn mag, some lube and maybe a date. **Branch:** 4001 Sunset Boulevard, at Sanborn Avenue, Silver Lake (1-323 666 1304).

Accommodation

Le Montrose is plush and in a residential neighbourhood of West Hollywood, while the **Ramada Inn** is a local institution right at the happening centre (for both, *see page 105* **Accommodation**).

The San Vicente Inn
387 N San Vicente Boulevard, between Beverly Boulevard & Rosewood Avenue, West Hollywood (1-310 854 6915/ fax 1-310 289 5929/info@gayresort.com). Bus 14, 550, DASH West Hollywood/I-10, exit La Cienega Boulevard north. **Rates** $59-$179. **Credit** AmEx, DC, Disc, MC, V. **Map 4 A2**
The Westside's only gay guesthouse, the San Vicente Inn features a fabulous pool, a tropical garden, nude sunbathing, proximity to local attractions and a high sexual temperature. *Website: www.gaywired.com/sanvicente/index.html* **Hotel services** *Complimentary breakfast. Parking (free). Pool. Spa. Sun deck.* **Room services** *Answering machine.*

Coffeehouses & restaurants

Gay dining in Los Angeles has finally crossed into the realm of the swallowable. The following establishments are all in West Hollywood. The most venerable institution is **French Quarter** (at French Market, 7995 Santa Monica Boulevard, at Laurel Street; 1-323 654 0898), while Margarita maniacs should head for **Cobalt Cantina** (616 N Robertson Boulevard, between Melrose Avenue & Santa Monica Boulevard; 1-310 659 8691). Eye-feasts can be had at **Koo Koo Roo** (8520 Santa Monica Boulevard, between La Cienega Boulevard & W Knoll Drive; 1-310 473 5858), where the boys come straight from the gym (we call it Mr Muscle's Disco Chicken), and **Tango Grill** (8807 Santa Monica Boulevard, at Hancock Avenue; 1-310 659 3663), which serves up Argentinian cuisine and grilled chicken. And if you're on Santa Monica Boulevard, but not really hungry, the **Buzz** and **Starbucks** coffeehouses are always hopping with homos.

The **Tsunami Coffee House** in Silver Lake (4019 Sunset Boulevard, at Sanborn Avenue; 1-323 661 7771) is also worth a visit.

The Abbey
692 N Robertson Boulevard, at Santa Monica Boulevard, West Hollywood (1-310 289 8410). Bus 4, 10, 220, DASH West Hollywood/I-10, exit Robertson Boulevard north. **Open** 8am-2am Mon-Thur, Sun; 7am-3am Fri; 8am-3am Sat. **No credit cards. Map 4 A2**
This largely outdoor coffeehouse in the heart of West Hollywood attracts a pretty mixed crowd during the day, thanks to its wonderfully scenic setting and smoker-friendly patio. By evening, the clientele is almost exclusively gay.

California Chicken Café
6805 Melrose Avenue, at Mansfield Avenue, Hollywood (1-323 935 5877). Bus 10, 11/I-10, exit La Brea Avenue north. **Open** 11am-10pm Mon-Sat. **Credit** AmEx, MC, V. **Map 5 A3**
This is a cheap, no frills place, serving roast chicken and salads. But the queues go out the door and all the boys from the gym are here, protein 'n' carbo-loading.

Cha Cha Cha
For listings, see p135 **Restaurants**.
The legacy of restaurateur Mario Tamayo lives. The Caribbean jerk chicken is excellent, as is the chicken sandwich. Tuesday night is Homo Happy Hour. Booking advised.

*Indulge your fantasies at **Circus of Books** in West Hollywood.*

Bars & clubs

The club scene in Los Angeles has never been hotter for gay men: every week there seems to be another reason to buy a tight shirt and do 1,000 sit-ups. Some of the old standbys are listed by area below; cover varies from $2-$10 and credit cards are not accepted.

Also try: the **House of Blues** on Sunset Strip (*see page 211* **Music**), which sometimes has a Sunday tea dance; **Cosmo** in Hollywood (at Selma Avenue and Cosmo Street; and check for gay nights at the El Rey Theatre (*see* **Coven 13** *page 215* **Nightlife**), including **Man-o-Rama** (1-323 769 6292), **Hooker** (1-323 360 7179; website: www.hookerla.com) and **Boy Trade** (1-323 350 3600).

West Hollywood

The West Hollywood strip tends to attract a cleaner, younger, fresh-from-the-gym crowd more interested in vertical communication than horizontal boot-banging.

Motherlode

8944 Santa Monica Boulevard, at San Vicente Boulevard (1-310 659 9700). Bus 2, 4, 10, 105, 304, DASH West Hollywood/I-10, exit La Cienega Boulevard north. **Open** noon-2am daily. **Map 4 A2**
Everyone's favourite beer bust on Sunday afternoons, Motherlode offers friendly guys playing pool and making small talk.

Rage

8911 Santa Monica Boulevard, between Larrabee Street & San Vicente Boulevard (1-310 652 7055). Bus 2, 4, 10, 105, 304, DASH West Hollywood/I-10, exit La Cienega Boulevard north. **Open** 1.30pm-2am Mon-Fri; 2pm-2am Sat, Sun. **Map 4 A2**
Nightly dancing in the quintessential West Hollywood gay dance club.

Revolver

8851 Santa Monica Boulevard, at Larrabee Street (1-310 659 8851). Bus 2, 4, 105, 304, DASH West Hollywood/I-10, exit La Cienega Boulevard north. **Open** 4pm-2am daily. **Map 4 A2**
At this entertaining video bar, you'll find plenty of guys having a good time watching each other have a good time.

Hollywood

Hollywood bars and clubs attract an entirely different crowd from those in West Hollywood. The music is better, the haircuts shorter, the muscles look bigger in the bad lighting and the nights begin and end much later.

Arena

For listings, see p215 **Nightlife**.
Gay nights at this huge Hollywood club, a former ice factory, include **Circus** (*see p215* **Nightlife**) and **Club 6655** on Thursdays (9pm-2.30am; $6). Muy caliente. The security parking is a bonus.

Probe

836 N Highland Avenue, between Waring & Willoughby Avenues (1-323 461 8301). Bus 10, 11/US 101, exit Highland Avenue south. **Open** 9pm-3am Wed, Fri, Sat. **Map 5 A2**
Everyone has to visit Probe at least once. Take your disco nap because you're going to be up late; arrive after midnight to see turned-on muscle queens with their shirts off. Be warned that when the club gets packed, the queue outside gets long and the bouncers get choosy.
Website: www.mightymen.com

Spike

7746 Santa Monica Boulevard, at Genesee Avenue (1-323 656 9343). Bus 4, 304/I-10, exit Fairfax Avenue north. **Open** noon-2am Mon-Thur, Sun; noon-4am Fri, Sat. **Map 4 C1**
A Levi's/leather bar, with an always interesting crowd: cruising guys with sex on their minds. Officially, it's at the eastern end of West Hollywood, but in atmosphere it's more part of the Hollywood scene. Free admission on Sundays.

The Study

1723 Western Avenue, between Hollywood Boulevard & Russell Avenue (1-323 464 9551). Bus 180, 181, 217, 357/US 101, exit Hollywood Boulevard east. **Open** 11am-2am daily. **Map 5 C1**

A neighbourhood bar with a pool table and friendly customers. The famous Coral Sands Hotel (nowadays frequently raided for the sex-and-drugs orgies enacted by its guests) is across the street.

Silver Lake

Bars and clubs in bohemian Silver Lake come in as many shapes and sizes as their clientele. If you're into tattoos, piercings, facial hair and leather, you'll find them here.

Cuffs

1941 Hyperion Avenue, between Fountain & Lyric Avenues (1-323 660 2649). Bus 175/US 101, exit Sunset Boulevard east. **Open** 4pm-2am Mon-Thur, Sun; 4pm-4am Fri, Sat. **Map 6 B2**

Quintessential Silver Lake. Nobody leaves empty-handed.

Faultline

4216 Melrose Avenue, at N Vermont Avenue (1-323 660 0889). Bus 10, 204, 354, Community Connection 203 /US 101, exit Vermont Avenue north. **Open** 4pm-2am Tue-Fri; 2pm-2am Sat, Sun. **Map 6 A3**

The leather ethic is observed here; fortunately, there's a leather store on the premises. The Sunday beer bust is always a kick in the rubber parts and on Tuesday nights it's positively teeming.

Cruising

Cruising around the block for the 38th time and still wondering if the guy in the striped shirt noticed you in your rented convertible? The only rules are: don't hit anyone or anything, and remember public sex or 'lewdness' is still a crime in LA (think George Michael and avoid Beverly Hills).

Vaseline Alley and neighbourhood

The City of West Hollywood gave us this cruiser's wet dream by installing several one-way and no-left-turn signs to create a loop-of-love sure to keep you busy for hours. Vaseline Alley, as it's commonly known, is the alley behind the West Hollywood Circus of Books shop (at La Jolla Avenue and Santa Monica Boulevard). The cruisy neighbourhood is the logical extension of Vaseline Alley into the residential area below. Park your car and walk. Before you know it, you'll have many new friends.

Griffith Park

Enter Griffith Park off Vermont Avenue north of Los Feliz Boulevard and turn right to the tennis courts any day of the week. Or for a special treat on Sunday afternoons, head to the 'circle' north of Los Feliz Boulevard just east of Western Avenue on Fern Dell Drive. It'll be up on your right after the concession stand.

Health & fitness

Your questions about HIV or drug abuse will be answered by **STORE** (Satellite Testing Office for Research and Education, 745 San Vicente Boulevard, at Santa Monica Boulevard, West Hollywood; 1-310 854 1310; open 11am-7pm Tue-

Sat). Or call **Friends Health Center** on 1-888 822 6384. **LA Shanti** in Hollywood (1616 N La Brea Avenue, at Sunset Boulevard; 1-323 962 8197; open 10am-6pm Mon-Fri) offers various services for individuals affected by HIV and AIDS, as well as seminars, a lesbian support group and Women for Positive Living. For other helplines, *see page 259* **Directory**.

Gyms

LA is full of gyms: the following will pump you up and make you hard. Don't miss the famous **Gold's** gym (*see page 227* **Sport & Fitness**): the Cole Avenue branch promises a fantasy land of porn performers, prom queens and soap stars: Hollywood truly is magical.

The Athletic Club

8560 Santa Monica Boulevard, at La Cienega Boulevard, West Hollywood (1-310 659 6630). Bus 4, 304, DASH West Hollywood/I-10, exit La Cienega Boulevard north. **Open** 5.30am-11pm Mon-Sat; 5.30am-9pm Sun. **Rates** $15 per day; $50 per week. **Credit** AmEx, Disc, MC, V. **Map 4 A/B1**

A West Hollywood institution: forget your shirt, bring your muscles.

Bathhouses & sex clubs

Everyone loves a good bathhouse and Los Angeles has some of the better ones. Take your own condoms. The **Hollywood Spa** (1650 Ivar Street, between Hollywood Boulevard and Selma Avenue; 1-800 772 2582/ 1-323 464 0445; $16-$20) is an LA bathhouse institution, with a DJ every night. It's open 24 hours and they'll give you the towel. If you're in Silver Lake, pop into **Flex** (4424 Melrose Avenue, between Normandie and Vermont Avenues; 1-323 663 5858; $5-$25), also open 24 hours..

About a decade ago, the stand-up sex club came into its own. The following have been around for a while. **Basic Plumbing** (1924 Hyperion Avenue, between Fernwood and Lyric Avenues; 1-323 953 6731) and **EXxILE** (1800 Hyperion Avenue, at Fountain Avenue; 1-323 661 9417) are Silver Lake neighbours that tend to fill up after the bars close. **Prowl** (1064 Myra Avenue, at Santa Monica Boulevard; 1-323 662 4726), also in Silver Lake, is just the way it sounds. **Zone** in Hollywood (1037 N Sycamore Avenue, between Romaine Street and Santa Monica Boulevard; 1-323 464 8881) is for the glamour boy in you.

Crunch

*8000 Sunset Boulevard, at Laurel Avenue, West
Hollywood (1-323 654 4550). Bus 2, 3, 217, 302/I-10,
exit Fairfax Avenue north.* **Open** 5am-11pm Mon-Thur;
5am-9pm Fri; 8am-8pm Sat, Sun. **Rates** $20 per day; $150
per week. **Credit** AmEx, MC, V. **Map 4 B1**
The scenery from the hill-view windows competes with the
sexy guys working out inside. Crunch insists all are welcome.

Fitness classes

If you want to leave LA a thinner and fit as a fiddle, try these
classes ($10 each): spinning at **Todd Tramp's** (624 N La
Cienega Boulevard, at Melrose Avenue, West Hollywood;
1-310 657 4140), and High Impact at **Voight by the Sea**
(1919 Broadway, between 19th & 20th Streets, Santa Monica;
1-310 453 4536).

Beaches

California beaches are a joy year round; these are
particularly gay-friendly areas. For more on LA's
beaches, *see page 52* **Sightseeing**.

South Laguna Beach

It's a long drive down to Laguna from LA, but the water is
clean and this beach is hot. It's on Pacific Coast Highway, just
past the pier: look for the gay flag (easy to miss), park on the
side of the road and take the stairs down to the beach. It's especially nice on a weekday. After the beach, head for the **Coast
Inn** (1401 PCH, at Mountain Road; 1-949 494 7588), where you
can stay the night or just check out the **Boom Boom Room**,
which offers dancing, drink specials and plenty of tanned
guys with their shirts off. Or grab a snack at **Wahoo's Fish
Tacos** (1133 PCH, at Oak Street; 1-949 497 0033).

Venice Beach

Head for the stretch where Windward Avenue meets the
beach, next to the wall, just down from Muscle Beach and in
front of the heart of the famed Venice boardwalk. Check out
the **Roosterfish** (1302 Abbot Kinney Boulevard; 1-310 392
2123), a friendly neighbourhood bar and a Venice Beach institution: no one should leave LA without a trip to 'the Fish'.

Will Rogers Beach

On PCH, north of the Santa Monica Pier, in front of the
Beach Club. On sunny weekends the beach is packed: it's
fun, it's free, it's got tons of guys playing volleyball and it
all lasts till sunset. Parking can be a drag, so it's best to bring
your $7, park in the lot and save some aggro. **Patrick's
Roadhouse** across the street is always good for a laugh.

Lesbian

Lesbian Los Angeles plays host to clubbers, coffee-
talk ladies, career professionals, homebound
couples, the single, the obsessed, the beloved and
the heartbroken. From lipstick, chapstick and hair-
spray to the 'natural' look, you name it, LA will
own up to it. West Hollywood has the nickname
'Boys' Town', but is there such a place as 'Girls'
Town'? Well, yes, but it's in little pockets here and
there. The main areas for lesbians, as for gay men,
are West Hollywood, Hollywood and Silver Lake;
others, such as Venice, Long Beach and the Valleys,
pop up now and again. Santa Monica Boulevard
between Robertson Boulevard and Fairfax Avenue
hosts a wide variety of lesbian hotspots.

Information & shops

Monthly magazines include **LA Girl Guide** (website: www.girlguide.com), a must-have if you're out
and about in LA, and **Female FYI** (e-mail:
fyizine@aol.com), a lesbian entertainment magazine covering San Francisco, LA and New York.
Lesbian News (website: www.lesbiannews.com)
is a national magazine covering news, entertainment and events worldwide.

If you want to join a wide variety of women of
all ages for bike riding, hiking, volleyball, camping, theatre trips, dinner parties and other activities, contact **Women on a Roll** (PO Box 5112,
Santa Monica, CA 90409-5112; 1-310 578 8888),
ideally before you get to town. Note that August
is 'Lesbian Visibility Month' in West Hollywood,
giving dykes the spotlight with dances, comedy
nights, social and educational forums and a day in
the park; check local gal mags for details.

The Pleasure Chest

For listings, see p170 **Shops & Services**.
Shopping for that certain leather bra for that big date? Look
no further. Erotic toys, clothes, magazines and videos for
every occasion and pleasure.

Sisterhood Bookstore

*1351 Westwood Boulevard, at Rochester Avenue,
Westwood (1-310 477 7300). Bus Santa Monica 1, 8, 12/
I-405, exit Wilshire Boulevard east.* **Open** 10am-8pm
daily. **Credit** Disc, MC, V.
This shop has a large selection of books, magazines, 'zines,
jewellery and crafts made by and for women, as well as
author readings and weekly book groups.
Website: www.sisterhood.com

Accommodation

The **Ramada Inn** (*see page 105* **Accommodation**)
is as popular with dykes as it is with gays.

Grove Guest House

*1325 N Orange Grove Avenue, between Fountain Avenue
& Sunset Boulevard, Hollywood (1-323 876 7778/fax
1-323 876 3170). Bus 1, 2, 3, 217, 302, 429/I-10, exit
Fairfax Avenue north.* **Rates** $150. **No credit cards.**
Map 4 B1
Imagine renting your own one-bedroom house with a full
kitchen, cable TV, a VCR, barbecue, pool and spa, in a quiet,
historical district. You can – if you call well in advance.
Worth every dime.

Coffeehouses & restaurants

Two of the main lesbian hangouts are the **Abbey**
coffeehouse and **French Quarter** restaurant (for
both, *see page 186*). The ladies with the British
accents tend to frequent **Van Go's Ear** (*see page
142* **Coffeehouses**), which gets going after hours.
For good food in a quiet, cosy atmosphere, try the
Coffee Table (2930 Rowena Avenue, between
Armstrong Drive and Hyperion Avenue, Silver
Lake; 1-323 644 8111). The following are also
worth seeking out:

Find a friendly smile at **Little Frida's**.

Little Frida's

*8730 Santa Monica Boulevard, between La Cienega &
San Vicente Boulevards, West Hollywood (1-310 854
5421). Bus 2, 4, 10, 11, 105, DASH West Hollywood/
I-10, exit La Cienega Boulevard north.* **Open** 11am-11pm
Mon-Thur, Sun; 11am-midnight Fri, Sat. **No credit
cards. Map 4 A2**
By day, this café is a ghost town and a good place to catch
up on some reading, but at night expect standing room only.
Events are scheduled nightly: recommended is Thursday's
Women with Balls comedy night.

Skewers

*8939 Santa Monica Boulevard, between Robertson & San
Vicente Boulevard, West Hollywood (1-310 271 0555).
Bus 4, 105, 220, 304, DASH West Hollywood/I-10, exit
La Cienega Boulevard north.* **Open** 11am-11pm daily.
Credit AmEx, MC, V. **Map 4 A2**
Ignore the naked male photos on the wall – the food is worth
it. Over-indulge yourself on the humus and home-made
mashed potatoes. You get free refills of Coke, too.

Swing Cafe

*8545 Santa Monica Boulevard, at Croft Avenue, West
Hollywood (1-310 652 8838). Bus 4, 304/I-10, exit La
Cienega Boulevard north.* **Open** 8.30am-11pm daily.
Credit AmEx, MC, V. **Map 4 B1**
Sit indoors or outside on the patio and enjoy a wide variety
of coffee, desserts – and women. Treat yourself – and her –
to breakfast on Sunday.

Bars & clubs

No shortage of nightlife options for women on the
razzle, but if your jaded taste longs for something
different, try skating at the **Moonlight Rollerway**
(*see page 225* **Sport & Fitness**) or break out your
cha-cha shoes for Salsa Con Clase at **Rudolfo's**
(*see page 217* **Nightlife**). Admission to the clubs
below is $3-$8 and credit cards are not accepted.

Fuel

Information 1-310 394 6541.
One of the newest and hippest roving theme clubs to hit the
West Coast, and never disappointing: when Fuel is on, the
women turn out in large numbers.

Girl Bar

*Fri: Axis, 652 N La Peer Drive, at Santa Monica
Boulevard, West Hollywood.
Sat: Love Lounge, 657 N Robertson Boulevard, between
Melrose Avenue & Santa Monica Boulevard, West
Hollywood.*

*Both information 1-323 460 2531. Bus 4, 10, 11, 220,
DASH West Hollywood/I-10, exit Robertson Boulevard
north.* **Open** 9pm-2am. **Map 4 A2**
One of the hottest lesbian clubs in town, with masterful DJs
mixing some of today's best beats and grooves and lots of
lovely ladies to see and seek out. Friday nights at Axis are
especially recommended.
Website: www.girlbar.com

Jewel's Catch One

*4067 W Pico Boulevard, at 12th Avenue, Midtown
(1-323 734 8849). Bus 30, 31, 210, 310/I-10, exit
Crenshaw Boulevard north.* **Open** 10pm-2am Tue-Thur;
10pm-4am Fri, Sat; 10pm-3am Sun.
Jewel's has a huge dancefloor and a diverse group of women.
It fills up quickly, so get there early.

Oil Can Harry's

*11502 Ventura Boulevard, between Berry & Ridgemore
Drives, Studio City (1-818 760 9749). Bus 424, 522/
US 101, exit Tujunga Boulevard south.* **Open** 9.15pm-
midnight Tue-Thur; 9pm-2am Fri, Sat.
Two-step and line dance with your best gal on your arm to
country music legends (lessons available on Tuesdays and
Thursdays, 7.45-9.15pm). Whether you go with a group of
friends or solo, there's always somebody to dance with. It's
the nicest bar in town and staff are very friendly.

The Palms

*8572 Santa Monica Boulevard, at La Cienega Boulevard,
West Hollywood (1-310 652 6188). Bus 4, 105, DASH
West Hollywood/I-10, exit La Cienega Boulevard north.*
Open 1pm-2am daily. **Map 4 A/B 1/2**
The oldest lesbian bar in LA, offering live entertainment,
many drink specials and DJ dancing treats. Dress is casual
and women range across ethnic backgrounds and ages. Call
for special events.

Health & fitness

Audre Lorde Lesbian Health Clinic

Information 1-323 993 7570. For listings, see p185
LA Gay & Lesbian Center.

Lesbian Health Clinic

*8240 Santa Monica Boulevard, at Harper Avenue,
West Hollywood (1-323 650 1508). Bus 4, 304, DASH
West Hollywood/I-10, exit La Cienega Boulevard north.*
Open 11am-6pm Mon-Fri. **Map 4 B1**
Both these clinics offer a wide range of therapies. The latter
has more than 20 years' experience, offering complete ob/gyn,
donor insemination, 24-hour HIV results, holistic health care
and workshops. If you can, book well ahead, though both
places can usually squeeze in an appointment within a week.

24 Hour Fitness

*8612 Santa Monica Boulevard, at W Knoll Drive, West
Hollywood (1-310 652 7440). Bus 4, 105, 304, DASH
West Hollywood/I-10, at La Cienega Boulevard north.*
Open 24 hours daily. **Rates** $15 per day. **Credit** AmEx,
Disc, MC, V. **Map 4 A2**
This gym may be in the heart of Boys' Town, but you'll be
surprised by the number of women you'll find there.

Women's Clinic

*9911 W Pico Boulevard, suite 500, between Beverly
Green & Roxbury Drives, Beverly Hills (1-310 203 8899).
Bus Santa Monica 7, 13/I-10, exit Robertson Boulevard
north.* **Open** 11am-6pm Mon, Tue; 8am-3pm Wed, Thur,
alternate Fri. **Map 3 B/C 3/4**
Offers health care and counselling services; Saturday and
evening appointments are usually available. The phone is
always busy, but keep hitting redial: it's worth the wait.

Media

LA's media landscape, dominated by the vast movie industry, features both outcrops of sanity and trackless badlands of weirdness. You'll need a map: here it is.

Newspapers & magazines

San Franciscans and other Northern Californians tend to view their neighbours to the south as superficial and unsophisticated. And as far as the media is concerned, they're not entirely wrong. Los Angeles, for the most part, is a town where everyone writes (mainly scripts, treatments and reviews) but no one actually reads. Part of the reason is that, while citizens of San Francisco, Chicago and New York do much of their newspaper and magazine reading during their morning and evening commute, car-bound Angelenos tend to rely on radio and television.

Films, of course, are the pinnacle of LA-based media, and also the major obsession of all the lesser forms. Given the sheer number of actors, directors, producers and screenwriters running around this town, it makes a twisted sort of sense that whatever happens before and behind the camera is much more important than the news of the day – unless the news happens to be a local disaster.

For gay publications, *see chapter* **Gay & Lesbian**. For the best websites from and about LA, *see page 266* **Directory**).

Dailies

The **Los Angeles Times** (35¢) is the only major daily newspaper in town. While extensive in its coverage of worldwide and local events, this centrist publication's lack of estimable competition (and regular staff cuts) is evident in its unbelievably sloppy editing and fact-checking: you can amuse yourself for hours playing 'Spot the Typo'. The paper's Calendar section devotes a lot of space to the arts, with a predictable emphasis on Hollywood films, while its music coverage is strictly middle of the road.

The **Wall Street Journal** (75¢) and **New York Times** ($1) are both widely available, but the **Washington Post** ($1.85) can be harder to track down. For British newspapers, head for the newsstand on Santa Monica's Third Street Promenade. Myriad foreign-language dailies – including **La Opinion** (25¢), published in LA and the largest Spanish-language newspaper in the country – are also available at newsstands and drop-boxes throughout the city.

Free weeklies

To get a sense of what's actually going on in Los Angeles, the city's free weeklies are your best bet. You can pick them up at just about every magazine stand, bookshop or record store. The **LA Weekly**, which belongs to the same company that owns New York's *Village Voice*, offers a *Voice*-like combination of dreadfully PC features (read by few) and wonderfully detailed arts listings (read by everyone). The *Weekly* is the publication to pick up when planning an evening of club- (or theatre- or gallery-) hopping.

Newer on the scene is the **New Times Los Angeles**, one in a series of 'alternative' weeklies published by the Phoenix, Arizona-based corporation New Times. This company generated a lot of local bad will in 1996 when it gutted weeklies the *LA Reader* and Westwood's *Village View* to make way for its new recruit. Since then, the paper's hamfisted editorial policy – which seems to confuse negative broadsides with investigative journalism – and reliance on out-of-town writers has won the *New Times* few friends.

Entertainment Weekly, a sort of bargain-basement *People Magazine*, is also available on newsstands free of charge. Also worth mentioning is **BAM**, a free music mag published twice a month. Its listings are often outdated, but *BAM* is filled with profiles of up-and-coming local bands – worth a look if you want a whiff of LA rock 'n' roll.

Tabloid weeklies

If celebrity sightings are your thang, you would do well to pick up one of the many weekly gossip magazines that reside next to the cash registers at grocery stores. Although the focus isn't strictly local, and the stories can be somewhat dubious, they often reveal helpful clues as to the latest Tinseltown hotspots. For instance, even if George Clooney and Sandra Bullock weren't actually 'spotted on a date' at a certain Sunset Strip bistro, the mention of the eaterie means it is a good bet for watching famous folk. Of the many tabloids, the **Star** ($1.29) is definitely the most Hollywood-intensive, and usually the most accurate: during the OJ Simpson trial, it regularly broke related stories ahead of the *LA Times*.

Monthlies

Though the venerable **Los Angeles** ($2.95) has tried to fashion itself as the West Coast's answer to *Vanity Fair* and the *New Yorker* rolled into one, it falls well short of either. But the recent demise of the slightly hipper *Buzz* means that *Los Angeles* now has little in the way of competition. **Venice** ($1.50) is a lower-budget composite of *Buzz* and *Los Angeles*, but with better coverage of what's going on in its titular 'hood.

Pornography aficionados should note that Larry Flynt – recently immortalised in celluloid by director Milos Forman – publishes *Hustler*, *Chic* and other monthly magazines from his imposing, brown-glass Flynt Publications Building at the intersection of La Cienega and Wilshire Boulevards in Beverly Hills. Deliciously ironic is the fact that a large equestrian statue of that self-appointed defender of American morality, John Wayne, stands proudly on the building's plaza.

Business

The **Hollywood Reporter** and **Daily Variety** (both dailies, costing $1.50) are Hollywood's twin bibles, with the latest scoops on industry manoeuvrings and projects in production. **Billboard** (weekly, $5.50) is the music industry equivalent. The **Los Angeles Daily Journal** ($2) provides California's legal news, while **Investors Business Daily** ($1) and **Los Angeles Business Journal** ($2.50) are business-focused newspapers. Upmarket business magazines include **Barron's** ($3), **Business Week** ($3.50), **Forbes** ($5), **Fortune** ($4.50) and **Money** ($3.50).

Outlets

Considering that no one in Los Angeles actually seems to read, the city has a surprising number of newsstands. One of the best is the stand outside West Hollywood's **Book Soup** (*see page 154* **Shops & Services**), which carries an impressive array of American, British and French periodicals, and stays open till 11.30pm. **Circus of Books** (8230 Santa Monica Boulevard, between Harper and La Jolla Avenues, West Hollywood; 1-323 656 6533) also stocks just about whatever you require.

The mother of them all is **World Book & News** (1652 N Cahuenga Boulevard, at Hollywood Boulevard, Hollywood; 1-323 465 4352). Nearly a full city block in length, the stand matches its overwhelming selection of international periodicals with an equally overwhelming selection of paperback books, including the entire published oeuvre of ghetto novelist Iceberg Slim.

On the Westside, a plethora of publications can be found at the newsstand on Third Street Promenade, at Arizona Avenue, Santa Monica.

Magazines galore at **Circus of Books**.

You want to watch television? Are you kidding? Let's face it: if you've seen American television before, LA television isn't going to offer much in the way of anything new.

Certainly, the argument could be made that, if you can only truly understand Homer by reading him in Greece, then only in Los Angeles can you fully comprehend *Baywatch* or *CHiPS*, even though television here generally sticks to the same mind-rotting morning- news-into-game-show-into-soap-opera-into-chat-show-into-evening-news-into-evening-soap-opera routine as it does in the rest of the country. If, however, you can't get through the day without bathing in cathode rays, there are plenty of television channels to keep you off the streets.

One thing that really is only possible in LA is watching television without a television – in other words, watching a show being made, either as part of a live studio audience (*Friends* and *Third Rock from the Sun* are both shot in LA) or at a location shoot; for information on both, *see chapter* **Film**.

For comprehensive information about what's on the box, pick up the ever-popular **TV Guide** ($1.19), which has a handy table telling you which channel each cable station can be found on. The *LA Times* also prints daily TV listings.

The networks

Like most US cities, Los Angeles has affiliates of the three major networks: CBS (**KCBS**, channel 2), **NBC** (**KNBC**, channel 4) and **ABC** (**KABC**, channel 7). The big three are now being given a serious run for their ratings by **Fox TV** (**KTTV**, channel 11), and the fledgling **Warner Brothers** network (**KTLA**, channel 5) is also beginning to seduce Angelenos. **KWHY** (channel 22), **KMEX** (channel 34) and **KVEA** (channel 52) serve the city's Latino population, while **KSCI** (channel 18) and **KDOC** (channel 56) offer a mix of Japanese, Korean, Chinese and Armenian programming, interspersed with infomercials.

Some of the more popular programmes include news shows *60 Minutes* (CBS, 7pm Sun), *Today* (NBC, 7am Mon-Fri) and *Good Morning America* (ABC, 7am Mon-Fri); comedies *Mad About You* (NBC, 8pm Tue), *Friends* (NBC, 8pm Thur) and *The Drew Carey Show* (ABC, 9pm Wed); and the late-night chat shows of David Letterman (CBS, 11.30pm Mon-Fri) and Jay Leno (NBC, 11.30pm Mon-Fri). The ever-popular *X-Files* appears on Fox (9pm Sun). The notorious *Jerry Springer Show* (KCAL, channel 9, 11pm Mon-Fri) is the place to turn for confessions like 'I Slept With My Sister's Dog' and 'My Father Stole My Boyfriend', while the completely over-the-top Sabado Gigante (KMEX, 8pm Sat) remains the best introduction to the freewheeling joys of Mexican variety shows. (Times, of course, may change.)

Cable TV

Although watching cable TV requires a monthly fee, many Angelenos subscribe in order to improve both reception and choice of programmes. At present, there are 38 cable channels (with more planned), including: **ESPN** (sports); **CNN** (24-hour international news); the **Discovery Channel** (anthropological and nature documentaries); **CRT** (Court TV, showing live trial footage); and the **Home Shopping Network**, which enables you to order ugly jewellery and useless appliances from the privacy of your own home. Public access cable features anything from religious puppet shows to experimental films.

The problem is that, due to a lack of regulation, different cable companies provide different services to different neighbourhoods: channel 96 may be MTV in your neighbourhood, but it could be the Disney Channel on the other side of town. Some cable networks, such as **E! Entertainment Television** (a pop-culture mix of celebrities and movie news), **Comedy Central** (24-hour comedy) or the **Sci-Fi Channel**, are limited to half-day programming (or aren't available at all) in various parts of the city, and each cable company publishes a different monthly schedule.

Most hotels worth their nightly rates offer cable as a standard feature, but if your room doesn't have a copy of your neighbourhood's cable guide, your best bet is to decode a copy of *TV Guide* or to channel-surf until you find what you're after.

Public TV

KCET (channel 28) is Los Angeles's local Public Broadcasting Service affiliate, providing all the ponderous, self-important programming we've come to expect from public television (as well as some of the BBC's finest). Now that the government has almost completely slashed PBS funding, the ungodly fundraisers seem to occur even more frequently than before.

Radio

Although the city has long been a major player in the history of American music, LA's present radio output is pretty dire. With the decline of heavy metal as LA's chief musical export, most of the city's rock stations have become clones of each other, rotating an ever-shrinking playlist of so-called alternative bands and puerile tag-team morning shows in an attempt to curry favour with the 18-25 demographic of MTV viewers. A great many Angelenos seem to listen to the radio solely for traffic reports, which you can hear at regular intervals on almost every station during the morning and evening rush hours.

Talk radio

Despite the post-Oklahoma City backlash against right-wing radio, Bill 'The Man' Handel (5-9am Mon-Fri) and Rush 'The Fat Idiot' Limbaugh (9am-noon Mon-Fri), both on KFI (640 AM), continue to deliver their dubious blend of fear-mongering and vaudeville – albeit with tamer tongues.

A more moderate sage is Larry Elder (3-7pm Mon-Fri, KABC, 709 AM), who is black, conservative and determined to return a bit of dignity and intelligence to drive-time 'politalk'. The more liberal, pipe-smoking contingent has the gracious Warren Olney, whose *Which Way LA?* (1-2pm Mon-Fri, rebroadcast 7-8pm, KCRW, 89.9 FM) is probably the best issues-forum radio programme in California and the biting commentary of Marc Cooper (4-5pm Mon-Fri, KPFK, 90.7 FM).

But if you are truly attracted to the perversity, cruelty and cynicism of American 'shock' radio, then Howard Stern (6-10am Mon-Fri, KSLX, 97.1 FM) won't disappoint : however crude he may be, Stern is at least consistently funny. You can also try *The Tilden and Minyard Show* (5am-9am Mon-Fri, KABC, 790 AM), which would sound like nothing more than a couple of white guys (they are) sittin' around reading the papers (they do) – except that Peter Tilden is downright hilarious.

If straight news is what you're after, **KNX** (1070 AM), **KFWB** (980 AM), **KNNS** (1260 AM) and **KNNZ** (540 AM) all offer 24-hour, up-to-the-minute coverage.

Classical

KUSC (91.5 FM), **KCSN** (88.5 FM) and **KKGO** (105.1 FM), while not round the clock, all offer classical music on a regular basis.

Jazz

On the off-chance that you're spending a Friday evening by the radio, *Jazz on the Latin Side*, hosted by Jose Rizo, on **KLON** (88.1 FM) will have you sambaing in your seat from 8pm to midnight. **KCLU** (88.3 FM), **KPCC** (89.3 FM) and **KCRW** (89.9 FM) also feature jazz at various times.

Dance & hip-hop

LA's two major dance and hip-hop stations are **KKBT** (92.3 FM) and **KPWR** (106.3 FM). The latter sticks to more of a hits-based playlist while the former gravitates towards harder and deeper grooves. Unlike most local stations, both insert a lot of local acts and artists into their daily rotation.

Rock & pop

KROQ (106.7 FM) is probably the most influential alternative rock station in America: when it adds a song to its playlist, similarly formatted stations across the country follow suit. **Y107** (107.1 FM) plays 'classic alternative' stuff from the 1980s and early 1990s, although the station's *Chris Carter Mess* (9pm-midnight Sun) presents a fairly adventurous mix of new pop from the US and UK. **KLOS** (95.5 FM) is the place to turn to for your daily dose of grunge, while **KIIS** (102.7 FM) is doubtless a godsend to the city's Mariah Carey fans. **KACE** (103.9 FM) rolls out soul and funk hits from the 1960s and 1970s; **KBIG** (104.3 FM) and **KRLA** (1110 AM) spin pop oldies from the 1950s and 1960s; and **KOST** (103.5 FM) serves up anthems of co-dependency, for all you lovers out there.

College & public radio

Loyola Marymount's **KXLU** (88.9 FM) provides noisy and nice indie sounds, although its weak signal can make it hard to find. Ditto for **KBLT**, an unlicensed pirate station broadcasting from somewhere around Downtown. USC's **KUSC** (91.5 FM) features heavy doses of classical and talk, while public stations **KCRW** (89.9 FM), **KPFK** (90.7 FM) and **KPCC** (89.3 FM) serve up the usual eclectic mix of talk shows, news, world music, alternative rock, jazz and classical.

Supported by a dedicated subscriber audience, **KCRW** is the standout public radio station, with

'Zine scene

Although fanzines have been around in one form or another since the 1920s, the current wave of independent 'zines grew out of the punk-era fanzines of the late 1970s and early 1980s. Local Los Angeles 'zines are as diverse, bizarre, silly and opinionated as the city they try to capture – as their titles often indicate (for example: *Blow My Colon, Hot Mexican Love Comics, Everything I Touch Turns to Shit and Garbage*).

By their nature, 'zines cover the extremes of viewpoint, taste and coherence, so be warned. Many are repetitive imitations of the punk-era music fanzines, but there are also a few worth picking up to take home as Los Angeles curios.

Adam Bregman's **Shithappy** ($2) contains the author's personal guide to LA as well as 'comics, rants, anarchy, sex, and some other junk'; **Ben Is Dead** ($5), a sort of anti-*Marie Claire*, was one of the pioneering publications of the radical feminist Riot Grrl movement; **Scram** ($4) is a pitch-potch-patch of, among other topics, Burt Reynolds movies, 'sinister' Disney land developments and 'the sexual subtext of bubblegum music'; Venice-based **Diabolical Clits** ($6) offers the 'best' in kitchen-sink erotica of all shapes and sizes; **Dragazine** ($6) covers Hollywood's transvestite scene; and **Giant Robot** ($4) caters to lovers of Pacific Rim culture (surreal cartoon shows, Sumo wrestling and Japanese rock music). Also look out for **Housewife Turned Assassin** and **Meat Hook**, two publications connected to Revolution Rising, a feminist social-change collective.

Good places to pick up 'zines include Destroy All Music (3818 Sunset Boulevard, Silver Lake; 1-323 663 9300); KOMA Books (1764 N Vermont Avenue, Los Feliz; 1-323 665 0956); Skylight Books (1818 N Vermont Avenue, Los Feliz; 1-323 660 1175); and the Velveteen Robot Bad Book Boutique (3932 Sunset Boulevard, Silver Lake; 1-323 660 1934). Happy reading.

excellent news programmes and original music shows. Unfortunately, recent staff shake-ups have left the station's schedule in a state of disarray, although the popular and influential *Morning Becomes Eclectic* (9am-noon Mon-Fri) continues to hang tough in its time slot: English host Nic Harcourt presents new music and insightful interviews with musicians from around the globe.

Museums & Galleries

There's more to LA culture than glitz and schmaltz. The city is home to several world-class museums and its independent art gallery scene has finally come of age.

Los Angeles's museums have a hard fight for attention in the world's entertainment capital. But they're in good health and taking their responsibilities more seriously than ever. The worst of the 1990s' budgetary crises seem to have passed, though individual museums may yet face constriction or even extinction (witness the late, lamented Craft & Folk Museum). Alongside sober, professionally curated institutions, LA also has a rich seam of lone devotees displaying eccentric amassments for the public's edification.

Meanwhile, the gallery scene continues to flourish. Having enjoyed spectacular growth in numbers and ambition in the later 1980s, LA's galleries weathered a downturn almost as profound in the recession of the early 1990s. Now they constitute a durable presence in the city's cultural life that was unthinkable a generation ago. Los Angeles has long attracted artists, but now it also has the critical mass of collectors (and curators and critics) that allows the artists to make a living.

Though galleries and museums tend to cluster in particular locations, these are beginning to overlap: you can find important galleries, for instance, in the museum-intensive Miracle Mile along Wilshire Boulevard, while there is now a museum at the heart of the region's premier gallery enclave, Bergamot Station in Santa Monica. Individual venues are scattered far and wide, so be prepared to venture out to Pasadena or Malibu, or to look for parking in Beverly Hills or Downtown. Your reward will be some of the best expressions of culture that Southern California – and the entire United States – has to offer.

Museums

Art & culture

Barnsdall Art Park

4800 Hollywood Boulevard, between Edgemont Street & Vermont Avenue, Los Feliz (1-323 660 4254/Hollyhock *House 1-213 913 4157/Junior Arts Center 1-213 485 4474/LA Municipal Art Gallery 1-213 485 4581). Metro Vermont Avenue/bus 1, 180, 181, 204, 217, Community Connection 203/US 101, exit Sunset Boulevard east.* **Open** *Junior Arts Center Gallery* 12.30-5pm Wed-Thur; Sat, Sun; 12.30-8.30pm Fri; *LA Municipal Art Gallery* noon-5pm Tue-Sun. **Admission** *LA Municipal Art Gallery* $1.50. **Map 6 A2**

The city's official 'art park', perched on a green hill where tawdry Hollywood meets bohemian Silver Lake, boasts a complex of small institutions, each housed in a structure designed by Frank Lloyd Wright and/or his son, the unjustly overshadowed Lloyd Wright. **Hollyhock House**, one of the senior Wright's signal middle-period residential structures, features architectural exhibits, while the **Municipal Art Gallery** and **Junior Arts Center** sponsor one-person and themed group shows of Southern Californian artists. The Center also runs a popular series of children's art programmes, and there are artists' talks, readings and concerts .

California African-American Museum

600 State Drive, at Figueroa Street, Exposition Park, Downtown (1-213 744 7432). Bus 81, 200, 442, 444, 445, DASH C/I-110, exit Exposition Boulevard west. **Open** 10am-5pm Tue-Sun. **Admission** free; donation requested.

A research library and museum focusing on the cultural and historical achievements of African-Americans, with permanent exhibits of sculpture, landscape painting and African tribal art. Past shows have included a survey of African puppetry, black art and black music in 1960s LA, the history of black children's book illustration and retrospectives of local African-American artists Betye Saar and John Outterbridge. Note that the CAAM should not be confused with the Museum of African American Art in Crenshaw (*see p77* **Sightseeing**).
Website: www.caam.ca.gov
Parking $5.

The Huntington Library, Art Collections & Botanical Gardens

For listings, see p82 **Sightseeing**.
Located in the Pasadena suburb of San Marino, the bequest of entrepreneur Henry E Huntington has some very, very rare old books and manuscripts, a large collection of eighteenth- and nineteenth-century British and French art and gorgeous gardens. And tea.

Japanese American National Museum

369 E First Street, at Central Avenue, Downtown (1-800 461 5266/1-213 625 0414). Bus 30, 31, 40, 42, 436, 445, 466, DASH A, D/I-110, exit Fourth Street east. **Open** 10am-5pm Tue, Wed, Fri-Sun; 10am-8pm Thur. **Admission** $4; $3 3-16s, students, seniors; free 5-8pm Thur and the third Thur of the month. **Map 7 C2**

The already capacious JANM, located in the heart of Little Tokyo, is expanding next door to new, much larger quarters (due to open in January 1999). The museum has an impressive record of documentary and art exhibitions, including a survey of Asian-influenced American art from the 1950s and 1960s, several collaborations with other ethnically based institutions, and wrenching yet nostalgia-laden displays of images and artefacts from the internment camps into which Japanese-Americans were herded during World War II. Its expansion makes the JANM (not to be confused with the nearby Japanese American Cultural Center) the largest of a growing number of museums devoted to the arts and culture of LA's polyglot population. Others include the Korean American Museum, the Korean Cultural Center, the newly established Latino Museum of History, Art and Culture and the Museum of Latin American Art in Long Beach.
Website: www.lausd.k12.ca.us/janm

Los Angeles County Museum of Art

5905 Wilshire Boulevard, between La Brea & Fairfax Avenues, Miracle Mile (1-323 857 6000). Bus 20, 21, 22, 320/I-10, exit Fairfax Avenue north. **Open** noon-8pm Mon, Tue, Thur; noon-9pm Fri; 11am-8pm Sat, Sun. **Admission** $7; $5 students, seniors; $1 6-17s; free second Tue of the month. **No credit cards.**
Map 4 C3
The multipurpose Getty Center may be vaster, but LACMA's five pavilions ringing a central courtyard constitute LA's largest purely museological complex. In some ways, it's more like the Getty than the Getty. It's got a bit of everything, but in certain areas stands with the world's greatest museums. Notable collections include: modern and contemporary masterpieces, including a small but impressive sculpture garden; textiles; photographs; and Indian, South-east Asian, pre-Columbian and Japanese art (a whole building is devoted to the latter). Recent temporary exhibitions have included surveys of Van Gogh, Soutine, Picasso, Yayoi Kusama, Arthur Dove, the Harlem Renaissance and a controversial show paying homage to William S Burroughs. There are also lectures, films and classical and jazz concerts.
Website: www.lacma.org
Parking $5 Wilshire Boulevard & Spaulding Avenue; free after 6pm.

Museum of Contemporary Art & Geffen Contemporary

MOCA: 250 S Grand Avenue, at Third Street, Downtown (1-213 621 2766/Patinette restaurant 1-213 625 1178). Metro Civic Center/Tom Bradley or Pershing Square/bus 30, 31, 40, 42, 436, 445, 466, DASH A, D/ I-110, exit Fourth Street east. **Map 7 B2**
Geffen: N Central Avenue, at First Street, Downtown (1-213 621 2766). Bus 30, 31, 40, 42, 436, 445, 466, DASH A, D/US 101, exit Alameda Avenue south.
Map 7 C2
Both **Open** 11am-5pm Tue, Wed, Fri-Sun; 11am-8pm Thur. **Admission** $6; $4 students, seniors; free under-12s; free 5-8pm Thur. **Credit** AmEx, MC, V.
The city's – and perhaps the American West's – premier showcase for art made after the middle of the twentieth century, MOCA started life in a vast bus barn on the edge of Little Tokyo, east of Downtown. Long known as the Temporary Contemporary, this building is now the Geffen Contemporary (with an interior designed by Frank Gehry). When MOCA's main building (the work of Japan's Arata Isozaki) was completed a block from the Civic Center, the museum was able both to mount ambitious survey exhibitions and to showcase items from an excellent and rapidly expanding permanent collection. Thus, upwards of half a dozen shows can be viewed at any time in the two MOCAs. Such recent displays as Out of Actions (an exhaustive history of post-war performance art), Hall of Mirrors (a similarly comprehensive look at the interaction of art and film since 1940), and retrospectives of artists such as Cindy Sherman,

Don't miss the **LA County Museum of Art**.

Ed Moses and Richard Serra have come from or travel to all corners of the world. The MOCA bookshop, including its offshoot at the Geffen, is one of the best places in LA to find publications about new art. Patinette, the gourmet café at the main building, serves light, sophisticated continental fare.
Website: www.moca-la.org
Parking at Grand Avenue & Second Street: $7 for 4 hours with validation from MOCA.

The Museum of Television & Radio

465 N Beverly Drive, at Little Santa Monica Boulevard, Beverly Hills (1-310 786 1000). Bus 14/I-10, exit Robertson Boulevard north. **Open** noon-5pm Wed-Sun; noon-9pm Thur. **Admission** $6; $4 students, seniors; $3 under-12s. **No credit cards.** **Map 3 C2**
The MT&R's permanent collection consists of nearly 100,000 TV and radio programmes, duplicating the holdings of the museum's New York counterpart and easily accessible via a computer catalogue. Does that make it a 'museum without walls', in André Malraux's phrase? (Perhaps it should be renamed 'Malraux's Place'.) Not entirely: the MT&R also has a lively, changing programme of artefacts, such as the wedding dresses from soap operas, costumes and make-up from *Star Trek*, and a history of *TV Guide* through its covers.
Website: www.mtr.org
Parking $1 per hour; free 2 hours with validation.

Museum of Tolerance at the Simon Wiesenthal Center for Holocaust Studies

9786 W Pico Boulevard, at Roxbury Drive, West LA (1-310 553 8403/Simon Weisenthal Center 1-310 553 9036). Bus 7/I-10, Robertson Boulevard exit south. **Open** 10am-5pm Mon-Thur; 10am-3pm (Nov-Mar 10am-1pm) Fri; 11am-5pm Sun. **Admission** $8; $6 seniors; $5 students; $3 3-12s. **Credit** AmEx, MC, V.
Map 3 C3

One section of the permanent exhibition area confronts contemporary racism in the US, with exhibits about the 1992 LA riots, the Civil Rights movement, hate groups and racial stereotypes; the other, more extensive area guides visitors through the Holocaust, with dioramas, photographs and stories. At the beginning of this section, you get a 'passport' with a child's photograph on it: their fate is revealed to you at the end of the tour. Upstairs, in the Multimedia Learning Center, you can explore the subject further by computer. Book in advance.
Website: www.wiesenthal.com
Free parking.

Norton Simon Museum of Art

411 W Colorado Boulevard, at Orange Grove Boulevard, Pasadena (1-626 449 6840). Bus 177, 180, 181/ I-110, exit Colorado Boulevard west. **Open** noon-6pm Tue-Sun. **Admission** $4; $2 students, seniors. **No credit cards**.
The Norton Simon features an impressive collection of Old Masters, notably superb examples of seventeenth-century Dutch and nineteenth-century French painting, as well as some excellent modern works. It is home to the Galka Scheyer collection of modern German painting, compiled by the woman who championed the work of Kandinsky, Klee, Feininger, Jawlensky and other Northern European abstractionists in Southern California. The museum is gradually learning to emphasise the different aspects of its collection more evenly, hanging choice items and programming special exhibitions with a wider perspective.
Free parking.

Pacific Asia Museum

46 N Los Robles Avenue, at Colorado Boulevard, Pasadena (1-818 449 2742). Bus 180, 181, 256, 267, 401, 402/I-110, exit Colorado Boulevard east. **Open** noon-5pm Wed-Sun. **Admission** $4; $2 students, seniors. **No credit cards**.
Art and artefacts from Asia and the Pacific Rim are displayed in the historic Grace Nicholson Building, a re-creation of a northern Chinese palace, with the charming Chinese Garden Court to match. Exhibitions include contemporary as well as traditional Asian arts. The museum's most popular events, however, are its family-oriented festival days, each featuring the culture and cuisine of a different Asian nation or people.
Free parking.

Santa Monica Museum of Art

Bergamot Station, 2525 Michigan Avenue, suite G1, at Cloverfield Boulevard, Santa Monica (1-310 586 6488). Bus Santa Monica 9/I-10, exit Cloverfield Boulevard south. **Open** 11am-6pm Wed-Sun; 11am-10pm Fri. **Admission** $3. **No credit cards. Map 2 C3**
After a two-year hiatus, Greater Los Angeles's best contemporary *kunsthalle* has reopened in a corner of Santa Monica (the area's most art-intensive neighbourhood) and resumed its lively programme of work by local and international artists, along with Friday Night Salon, a series of discussions and performances. Recent shows have included: collages and drawings by the late Fluxus-Happenings artist Al Hansen and his grandson, pop singer Beck; installations by Californian artists such as Liza Lou (who created a full-scale kitchen covered in coloured beads), Michael McMillen and Carl Cheng; and a survey of the elaborate auto-erotic photographs of French post-Surrealist Pierre Molinier.
Free parking.

Skirball Cultural Center & Museum

2701 N Sepulveda Boulevard, at the I-405, West LA (1-310 440 4500). Bus Culver City 6/I-405, exit Skirball Center/Mulholland Drive south. **Open** noon-5pm Tue-Sat; 11am-5pm Sun. **Admission** $8; $6 students, seniors. **Credit** MC, V.

Concerned mostly with American Judaism, this offshoot of Hebrew Union College houses a reconstruction of a Middle Eastern archeological dig, a room-sized exhibit devoted to religious decorative arts and a collection of art that chronicles Jewish migration to America. Its temporary exhibitions display both art and historical documentation, and often bridge over to cover LA's other ethnic groups. The Skirball also features lectures, readings and musical and theatrical performances. The University of Judaism, across the I-405, has a much smaller exhibition space, the Platt Gallery, which shows work by mainly Jewish local artists.
Free parking.

Southwest Museum

234 Museum Drive, at Avenue 43, Highland Park (1-213 221 2164). Bus 81, 83, DASH A/I-110, exit Avenue 43 north. **Open** 11am-5pm Tue-Sun. **Admission** $5; $3 students, seniors; $2 7-18s. **No credit cards**.
Located atop a hill in the Mount Washington area, in an impressive building that reconstructs the hacienda style of the area's Spanish settlers, the Southwest displays selections from its huge collection of Native American art and artefacts, as well as old-fashioned dioramas. The unusual entrance tunnel (originally installed in 1920 after the first director had a heart attack and died while climbing the hill) has recently been reopened and a new elevator installed.
Website: www.southwestmuseum.org
Free parking.

UCLA Armand Hammer Museum of Art & Cultural Center

10899 Wilshire Boulevard, at Westwood Boulevard, Westwood (1-310 443 7000). Bus 20, 21, 22, 320, 322, 429, Santa Monica 1, 2, 4, 8, 12/I-405, exit Wilshire Boulevard east. **Open** 11am-7pm Tue, Wed, Fri, Sat; 11am-9pm Thur; 11am-6pm Sun. **Admission** $4.50; $3 students, seniors; $1 UCLA students; free 6-9pm Thur. **Credit** AmEx, MC, V.
Industrialist Armand Hammer founded this museum in the plaza levels of his Occidental Petroleum building primarily to house his personal collection of art and then bequeathed it to nearby UCLA. After his death in 1990, the university moved its art collections and its substantial exhibition programme there. The latter favours modern and contemporary Western work, but pre-modern and non-Western art is also shown. There is a further bias towards Californian culture: recent shows have included a scholarly look at pre-war Californian modernist art; the controversial *Sunshine & Noir* exhibition that surveyed contemporary LA art from a European standpoint; and a huge show documenting the architecture and planning of Disney's amusement parks.
Website: www.arts.ucla.edu/hammer
Parking $2.75 first 3 hours with validation; $1.50 each additional 20 mins; $3 after 6pm Thur.

UCLA Fowler Museum of Cultural History

UCLA campus, between the Dance Building & Royce Hall, Westwood (1-310 825 4361). Bus 2, 21, 302, 561, Santa Monica 2, 8, 12/I-405, exit Sunset Boulevard east. **Open** noon-5pm Wed, Fri-Sun; noon-8pm Thur. **Admission** free.
Tucked away on the UCLA campus, the Fowler presents exhibitions on diverse ethnographic themes: shows have included Haitian voodoo flags, African headrests, Bornean war-ritual fabrics, photo-documentations of LA's Iranian communities and the Amish communities in middle America, and northern Mexican corrido ballads and their singers. The exhibitions are invariably well researched and handsomely installed.
Website: www.fmch.ucla.edu/
Parking $5.

The Getty Center

Los Angeles's very own acropolis opened at the end of 1997, after a gestation of 13 years. The Getty Center complex occupies the top of a hill in the Santa Monica Mountains, in the wealthy Westside neighbourhood of Brentwood, over-looking the 405 freeway, on land once destined to be the site of a co-operative housing development. The original Getty Villa, perched on another bluff directly over the ocean in Malibu, is closed until 2002 for extensive renovation. When it opens it will house the Getty's great collections of antiquities, which until then are being sampled in a cycle of exhibitions at the new museum.

The complex was conceived as a home for the hitherto disparate entities of the J Paul Getty Trust and was the brainchild of former CEO and president of the trust, Harold Williams. On taking over in 1981, he invested and substantially increased the late oil baron's $700 million bequest to the J Paul Getty Museum. He then expanded the trust's mission, created new institutes, announced a commitment to reaching out to the local community and hired a new museum director, John Walsh. Walsh has overseen the expansion of the museum's holdings from a laughable hodge-podge of gaudy rococco furniture and a few insignificant paintings to a competitive store of post-Renaissance European paintings, drawings and sculpture, decorative arts, antiquities and an outstanding photography collection.

The new campus was built partly to get rid of millions of spare dollars: to keep its tax-exempt status, the Getty has to spend 4.25 per cent of its endowment in three out of every four years (the endowment currently stands at $4.3 billion – work that out). In 1983, the trust bought the land and, the following year, hired East Coast-based Richard Meier, then America's most celebrated architect.

As the building slowly went up, stories about its excesses were legion – the escalation of cost from $733 million to $1 billion (due to an expanded programme and earthquake retro-fitting costs, explained the Getty); the 16,000 tons of split travertine blocks quarried in Italy; the first-of-its-kind, computer-operated tram installed to ferry people up the hill. Then there were the feuds between the architect and various antagonists: the locals, who objected to Meier's original plans for a white metal building; Walsh, who rejected Meier's minimalist interiors and instead hired interior designer Thierry Despont to create lavish backdrops; and artist Robert Irwin, selected over Meier's head to landscape the Central Garden.

When the Getty Center finally opened, it sur-prised many Doubting Thomases by turning out to be a stunner. Getting there to see it, however, is tiresome, to say the least. By car, it means a drive, invariably at a slow crawl, up the con-gested I-405, then a queue for the parking lot (you have to book a parking space in advance), then another queue for the tram, which, being state of the art, breaks down fairly regularly. But once you are on the little train, heading off into the clouds, leaving freeway and city behind, it becomes a truly marvellous – albeit slightly Disneyish – experience (some refer to the Getty as 'Gettyland').

On arrival at the top of the hill you find your-self in a large plaza with a stupendous panoramic view of Los Angeles, from the hills and ocean in the west right around to Downtown in the east. The complex is a little baffling because there are several buildings, some open to the public, others not, and signs are few and confusing.

To the west of the plaza is a self-service café (serving very decent, subsidised food), a restau-rant and the circular Research Institute, which houses a private scholarly centre and changing public exhibits. North are the other institutes (some off-limits to the public) and the Harold M Williams Auditorium, where you can catch a short film about the Getty, *Art Works: Behind the Scenes at the Getty*. To the south, up a grand Spanish Steps-style stairway, is the museum lobby, an airy, luminous rotunda that gives on to a fountain-filled open courtyard surrounded by the Getty Museum's six pavilions, housing the permanent collection and temporary exhibi-tions of paintings, decorative arts and photos. The courtyard follows the line of a promontory. – continue past the pavilions to cascading terraces and at the end you'll find a charmingly quirky garden of cacti and succulents, and an even more breathtaking view.

In its entirety, the collection of pristine build-ings, all clad in varying amounts of travertine and white metal panelling, does feel a little like a very expensive office park, and the Central Garden – an overly fussy pseudo-maze – is disappointing. But there is much to offset these shortcomings: the elegant modernism of some of the spaces; the glorious light (inside and out); the spaciousness; the fountains and pools; the pretty landscaping; the many outside terraces, balconies, nooks and crannies for panoramic viewing; and the Center's overall sense of civic grandeur, a quality that is almost anathema in Los Angeles.

The billion-dollar **Getty Center**, *LA's newest and extremely popular museum complex.*

Until its opening, and to some extent still now, the Center was criticised for keeping itself in monastic seclusion, in an affluent neighbourhood far removed from the polyglot city it claimed to serve. These charges increased as the opening approached, so, in a bid to prove how inclusive it was in multi-culti LA, the Center deluged the entire city with posters bearing the slogan 'Your Getty'. This pronouncement was taken quite literally by the public, which stormed the inaccessible mountain retreat. The result was outrage among the residents of Brentwood and Bel Air, in whose private streets visitors were parking, and chaos at the Getty Center itself, where people ran roughshod over the complex. A frazzled staff was reduced to hanging cardboard 'Keep Out' signs on Meier's pristine doorways.

The museum has proven so phenomenally successful – with almost double the expected attendance – that it has had to back-pedal from its initial statement that the Getty was open to all who could get there, whether by car, bus, bicycle, taxi, or on foot. It has now resorted to radio and print announcements beseeching the public to come back when they've booked a parking space. There is a similar shortage of toilets (a fact that the British press, of course, found fascinating) – so visitors should plan ahead.

Since the Getty Center was a Johnny-come-lately to collecting European art, its collection will never amount to that of the great old museums. Also, it does feel a little bizarre to be looking at Rubens paintings on a sunny mountain top in LA, albeit in a building designed to feel like a weighty European institution. Thus, the reason to go to the Getty is not primarily for its holdings. It is for the magical experience of this ravishing public space high above the city.

The Getty Center

1200 Getty Center Drive, at the I-405, Brentwood (information & reservations 1-310 440 7300/deaf or hearing-impaired 1-310 440 7305). Bus 561, Santa Monica 14/I-405, exit Getty Center Drive. **Open** 11am-7pm Tue, Wed; 11am-9pm Thur, Fri; 10am-6pm Sat, Sun. **Admission** free.
Parking reservations are required if coming by car.
Website: www.getty.edu
Parking $5.

Getting to the Getty

● Admittance to the Getty Center is assured only for those with parking reservations, but most parking spaces are, at the time of writing, booked months ahead. Probably the best times to try to book a space are the late afternoon or evening.
● To avoid a long wait when trying to book a parking space by phone, call the 24-hour information and reservations line on Mondays or any afternoon after 2pm.
● To avoid the parking problem altogether, catch a shuttle bus. Take a taxi or drive to the Veterans Administration Hospital parking lot on Constitution Avenue, at Sepulveda Boulevard near the I-405 ($5 parking), from where you can catch a bus ($5 round trip) to the tram stop at the Getty.

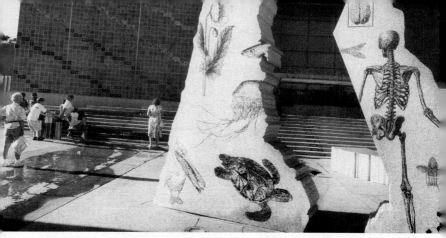

*Examine the building blocks of life at the **California Science Center**.*

Science

California Science Center

700 State Drive, between Figueroa & Menlo Streets, Exposition Park, Downtown (1-213 724 3626/IMAX 1-213 744 2014). Bus 81, 102, 200, 442, 444, 445, 446, 447/I-110, exit Exposition Boulevard west. **Open** 10am-5pm daily. **Admission** *museum* free; *IMAX* $4.75 18-21s; $4 children, seniors. **Credit** (IMAX) MC, V.
The recently opened Science Center, incorporating the California Museum of Science and Industry and the Aerospace Museum, consists of four themed wings: World of Life, Creative World, World of the Pacific and Worlds Beyond. World of Life unravels biological mysteries: its main feature is Gertie, a 50ft (15m) long transparent human female body. Creative World focuses on human adaptability and our relationship with technology. Not open at the time of writing, World of the Pacific will examine the varied forms nature and culture take on either side, and in the middle, of the ocean at LA's edge, while Worlds Beyond will head out past the earth's atmosphere and into deep space. The Center also houses the improved seven-storey 3-D IMAX cinema.
Website: www.casciencectr.org
Parking $5.

The George C Page Museum of La Brea Discoveries

5801 Wilshire Boulevard, between La Brea & Fairfax Avenues, Miracle Mile (1-323 934 7243/1-323 857 6311). Bus 20, 21, 22/I-10, exit La Brea Avenue north. **Open** 10am-5pm Tue-Sun. **Admission** $6; $3.50 students, seniors; $2 5-10s; free first Tue of month. **Credit** AmEx, Disc, V. **Map 4 C3**
Inside the half-underground Page museum, check out old bones found in the surrounding La Brea Tar Pits, along with reconstructed, life-size skeletons of mammoths, wolves, sloths and eagles and an animatronic sabre-toothed tiger. Walk around the park and look for stray puddles of oozing black tar, still seeping from the ground. In the summer, you can see paleontologists at work in the ongoing excavation of Pit 91 and smell the tang of tar in the air. A giant re-creation of a mastodon sinking into a pit as his 'wife' and 'child' look on is heart-rending.
Website: www.tarpits.org
Parking $7.50.

Los Angeles County Museum of Natural History

900 Exposition Boulevard, between Hoover & Menlo Streets, Exposition Park, Downtown (1-213 763 3466/ recorded information 1-213 744 3466). Bus 81, 102, 200, 442, 444, 445, 446, 447/I-110, exit Exposition Boulevard west. **Open** 10am-5pm Tue-Sun. **Admission** $8; $5.50 12-17s; $2 5-12s. **No credit cards**.
This is one of the few institutions in the area that actually feels like a 'proper' museum. The huge Spanish-Renaissance building opened in 1913 and is the third largest natural history museum in the US, its 35 halls and galleries packed with stuffed birds, mammals, gems, a Tyrannosaurus Rex skull and Native American pottery, textiles and baskets. Don't forget to visit the Insect Zoo, full of stick insects, Madagascan hissing cockroaches, scorpions, tarantulas and lots of ants.
Website: www.nhm.org
Parking $5.

Only in LA

Autry Museum of Western Heritage

4700 Western Heritage Way, opposite LA Zoo, Griffith Park (1-323 667 2000). Bus 96/I-5, exit Zoo Drive west. **Open** 10am-5pm Tue-Sun. **Admission** $7.50; $5 seniors, students; $3.50 2-12s. **Credit** AmEx, MC, V.
Angelenos are often accused of confusing the Hollywood version of the world with the real thing. Nowhere is this more evident than at the Autry Museum, where the real history of the West is presented side by side with images and props from its various silver-screen interpretations – such as a life-sized bronze sculpture of Gene Autry (aka 'The Singing Cowboy') and his horse, Champion. Kids will enjoy the re-creations of Wild West saloons and the 1873 fire engine. But, for all its confounding of art and artifice, the Autry Museum presents serious exhibitions that illustrate the history of the American West with critical depth. It has hosted, for example, an extensive survey of women artists in the pre-war West, revealing their significance in frontier regions. And to celebrate California's sesquicentennial, the museum displayed a sober, un-jingoistic documentary show about the Mexican-American War.
Website: www.autry-museum.org
Parking free.

Frederick's of Hollywood Celebrity Lingerie Hall of Fame

6608 Hollywood Boulevard, at Hudson Avenue, Hollywood (1-323 466 8506). Bus 1, 163, 180, 181, 210, 212, 217/US 101, exit Highland Avenue south. **Open** 10am-6.45pm Mon-Thur; 10am-9.45pm Fri; 10am-6pm Sat; noon-5pm Sun. **Admission** free. **Map 5 A1**

This museum is housed in a few rooms in the back of a well-known lingerie emporium. On display, next to an oil painting of founder Frederick Mellinger, are brassières with names like the 'peek-a-boo' and the 'depth charge'. Madonna's black-and-gold sequinned bustier can be found here, along with the bra Marilyn Monroe wore in *Let's Make Love*, and, inexplicably, a bra that was thrown on stage during a Kiss concert. Still as trashy as ever, the rest of the store is almost a museum itself. Amazing shoes, too.

Hollywood Entertainment Museum

7021 Hollywood Boulevard, at Sycamore Avenue, Hollywood (1-323 465 7900). Bus 1, 180, 181, 217/I-10, exit Highland Avenue south. **Open** 10am-6pm Tue-Sun.
Admission $7.50; $4.50 students, seniors; $4 children.
Credit AmEx, DC, MC, V. **Map 5 A1**
This huge (33,000sq ft/3,000sq m), state-of-the-museological-art facility is dedicated to the history of Hollywood, its people and its productions. It features original sets, Tinseltown memorabilia – including stars' wigs and cosmetics from the Max Factor Museum of Beauty, which the Entertainment Museum incorporates – an educational wing, a recording studio, a library and archives.
Website: www.hollywoodentertainment.com
Parking $2.

International Surfing Museum

411 Olive Avenue, between Main & Fifth Streets, Huntington Beach, Orange County (1-949 960 3483). Bus Orange County Transit 29/I-405, exit Beach Boulevard south. **Open** *summer* noon-5pm daily; *winter* noon-5pm Wed-Sun. **Admission** $2; $1 students.
Credit AmEx, MC, V.
Various exhibits honour Duke Kahanamoku, the father of surfing, celebrate surf music and showcase the women of surfing and the heroes of surf life-saving. This small museum is staffed with friendly volunteers full of stories – ask to hear about Dick 'King of the Surf Guitar' Dale's guitar, which was stolen from the museum's original building and now hangs in the rear gallery. Head for the beach if you want a taste of contemporary beach culture.
Website: www.surfingmuseum.org

Museum of Jurassic Technology

9341 Venice Boulevard, at Bagley Avenue, Culver City (1-310 836 6131). Bus 33, 220, 333, 436, Culver City 1, 4, 5/I-10, exit Robertson Boulevard south. **Open** 2-8pm Thur; noon-6pm Fri-Sun. **Admission** $4; $2.40 students, seniors. **No credit cards.**
From its name, you'd expect this museum to be included under the heading 'Science'. But this is science fiction, taken to an especially subtle and sublime level. The brainchild and handiwork of artist Richard Wilson, the MJT presents itself as a museum of curiosities, scientific wonders (such as a bat that can fly through walls without damaging either the walls or itself) and artistic miracles (the 'microminiature' painting of Hagop Sandaldjian, who painted on needles and sculpted human hair and specks of dust into the likenesses of famous people, including the Pope and several Disney characters). Fact (Hagop Sandaldjian did, indeed, craft such microscopic objects) is mixed with fiction through the elaborate museological treatment accorded each display, right down to extensive wall labels and dramatically lit vitrines. In the capital of spectacle, on the verge of the virtual century, the 'chamber of marvels' has itself become a marvel.

Carole & Barry Kaye Museum of Miniatures

5900 Wilshire Boulevard, between Ogden Drive & Spaulding Avenue, Miracle Mile (1-213 937 6464). Bus 20, 21, 22, 320/I-10, exit Fairfax Avenue north. **Open** 10am-5pm Tue-Sat; 11am-5pm Sun. **Admission** $7.50; $6.50 seniors; $5 students; $3 children. **Credit** MC, V. **Map 4 B/C3**

Beverly Hills entrepreneur Barry Kaye (author of *Die Rich and Tax Free*) and his wife Carole began collecting miniatures – miniature everything – a decade ago, acquiring items at such a rate that they had soon established their own museum. Classic and kitsch stand cheek by jowl in this aesthetic democracy: the museum features both a miniature 'Alexander's Siege Tent at Halicarnassus' and a Lilliputian version of the OJ Simpson trial. But the emphasis is on historic curios, such as those found in the Great Palaces of Europe permanent exhibit.
Website: www.museumofminiatures.com
Parking $3.60 ($1.80 with validation).

Museum of Neon Art

Grand Hope Park, 501 W Olympic Boulevard, between Hope Street & Grand Avenue, Downtown (1-213 489 9918). Metro Pico Street or Seventh Street/Metro Center/bus 27, 28, 38, 96, 327, 328/I-110, exit Ninth Street east. **Open** 11am-5pm Wed, Fri, Sat; 11am-8pm Thur; noon-5pm Sun. **Admission** $5; $3.50 students, seniors. **Credit** AmEx, MC, V. **Map 7 B4**
MONA is a celebration of the many uses of neon, including signage and fine art. Permanent exhibits include works by kinetic-art pioneers Lili Lakich and Candace Gawne and a rather fine neon interpretation of the *Mona Lisa*. You'll also find work by many other neon artists from around the country and the world.
Free parking.

Nethercutt Collection

15200 Bledsoe Street, at San Fernando Road, Sylmar (1-818 367 2251). Bus 94/I-5, exit Roxford Street east. **Tours** 10am, 1.30pm, Tue-Sat; duration 2 hours. **Admission** free; booking essential.
Within an innocuous building in an even more innocuous industrial suburb to the north of LA, Dorothy and JB Nethercutt, heirs to the fortune of a cosmetics company, have assembled a huge collection of functional objects, all of which somehow fit into their very personal concept of beauty. Their principles also dictate that everything on the premises must be in working order: the impressive Rolls-Royces are all driven to a picnic once a year and the gargantuan Mighty Wurlitzer Pipe Organ can be enjoyed during scheduled recitals. Visitors are also treated to a huge collection of Stueben Glass hood ornaments, nickeldoeons, French furniture, clocks and watches, and a painted ceiling depicting the members of the immediate family as cherubs. Shorts and jeans are prohibited out of respect for the stuff. It's about a 30-minute drive from West LA.
No under-12s and no jeans or shorts allowed.

Petersen Automotive Museum

6060 Wilshire Boulevard, at Fairfax Avenue, Miracle Mile (1-323 964 6315/recorded information 1-323 930 2277). Bus 20, 21, 22, 217, 320, 322/I-10, exit Fairfax Avenue north. **Open** 10am-6pm Tue-Sun. **Admission** $7; $5 students, seniors; $3 5-12s. **Credit** AmEx, MC, V. **Map 4 B3**
An oil-dribbled monster pick-up truck marks the entrance to LA's version of the car museum. Inside, life-sized dioramas of supermarkets, garages and restaurants recreate the early days of the drive-in lifestyle, complete with a full range of classic automobiles parked at the front. Upstairs, changing exhibitions showcase various aspects of car culture, from cars of the stars to fancy racing machines to motorcycles. In the lobby, there's an AM/PM mini-market to satisfy your craving for highway cuisine: have a beer and a spicy hot dog and ruminate about lacquer and chrome. Among the Petersen's recent shows was *It's a Duesy!*, with over 20 examples of the glamorous Duesenberg Model J (owned by, among others, Elvis Presley and Tyrone Power).
Website: www.nhm.org/petersen/index1.htm
Parking $5.

Art in the open

*The recently uncovered **America Tropical** mural in Downtown.*

The decentralised sprawl of Southern California is best seen, and understood, in motion, from behind car windows and windscreens. So you would expect the Los Angeles environment to be a prime locus for outdoor fine-artworks.

Murals are perhaps the most common artform: there are some 2,000 in the LA area, inside buildings and out, alongside freeways, everywhere – among them two particularly significant examples of Mexican mural-making. The better known is José Clemente Orozco's **Prometheus**, situated in Frary Hall's men's dining room on the Claremont Colleges campus in the eastern edge of the San Gabriel Valley (1-909 621 8000).

The other is less famed but was, in its day, more controversial. David Alfaro Siqueiros painted his bumptious anti-capitalist tract **America Tropical** in 1932 on Olvera Street in Downtown (at the corner of Main Street and Cesar E Chavez Boulevard). The mural – whitewashed almost as soon as it was finished – was only recently uncovered in a restoration project by the Getty Conservation Institute.

An African-American mural masterpiece,

The Negro in California History, resides in the lobby of the Golden State Mutual Life Insurance Company building on the edge of the Crenshaw district (1999 W Adams Boulevard, at Western Avenue). Painted in 1949 – and spared in the riots that rocked the neighbourhood 43 years later – the mural comprises two panels. Charles Alston painted *Exploration and Growth*, tracing black Californian history to 1850, while Hale Woodruff realised *Settlement and Development*, bringing the story up to date.

But most of Los Angeles's contemporary mural and public art is situated out of doors – often right beside the freeway. The bulk of such work has been created in the past 30 years, notably in the early 1970s and in the flurry of public art activity that accompanied the city's hosting of the 1984 Olympics. Kent Twitchell's photo-realist figures are the best known, best executed and most straightforward of these.

The most ambitious and exciting of the contemporary political murals is Judy Baca's **The Great Wall of Los Angeles**, a half-mile long historical frieze depicting LA's many cultural turning points, painted – and to a certain extent

Terry Allen's **Corporate Head**.

and Eighth Streets). Allen's life-sized, briefcase-bearing businessman would be just another trompe l'oeil bronze if he weren't sticking his head into the building's concrete skin. The sculpture was prescient: it was erected not long before heads rolled in Security Pacific's takeover.

The best non-objective public object, at least in Downtown, is at the corner of Ninth and Figueroa Streets. **Eugene Sturman**'s immense, elaborate concatenation of stems, springs and geometric solids effectively reinvents the optimism of the Soviet Constructivists.

Artists and architects can also work together very successfully, as demonstrated by Los Angeles's most ambitious art project to date: the new **Metro** train system. Artwork of some kind is integrated into almost every one of the stations; indeed, this is the prime motivation for most visitors to ride the predictably under-used system. The Blue and Red Lines tend to have the best art.

Except for one other reason: visible from one of the stops on the train down to Long Beach are the legendary, magical **Watts Towers** (*see page 76* **Sightseeing**). If the Hollywood sign is LA's Eiffel Tower, the Towers, blossoming in the middle of a once black, now Latino slum, is its Notre Dame, its Taj Mahal, its Guell Cathedral. Slowly emerging from an exoskeleton of scaffolding, the Towers (and the arts centre beneath them) can be visited easily and safely during the day. Anyone interested in art of any type must see the Towers, one of the world's great *art brut* monuments and certainly the most important, and most enchanting, public artwork in LA.

co-conceived – by her students on a wall of the Tujunga wash drainage canal on the Van Nuys/North Hollywood border (Coldwater Canyon Avenue, between Burbank Boulevard and Oxnard Street).

Compared to the murals, the rest of Los Angeles's public art is a disappointment. Principally, it's what might be called 'corporate plop art': more or less nondescript abstract sculpture deposited on the pavement in front of office buildings. The figurative outdoor sculpture is usually worse.

One notable exception is an equestrian statue of **John Wayne**, dramatically conceived and classically forged by Harry Jackson, America's premier Western sculptor. It stands before the erstwhile Great Western Bank building, now the home of porn magazine empire Larry Flynt Publications (at the corner of La Cienega and Wilshire Boulevards).

Terry Allen is responsible for LA's other outstanding piece of public figurative sculpture, **Corporate Head**, which is outside the former Security Pacific building in Downtown (now Citicorp 1, 725 S Figueroa Street, between Seventh

Mural Conservancy of Los Angeles

PO Box 86244, Los Angeles, CA 90086 (1-323 481 1186).
The Conservancy provides a map and brief history of *The Great Wall of Los Angeles* – and of nearly all other public wallworks in LA County. It also runs occasional mural tours ($25) conducted by the artists themselves – past tours by Kent Twitchell, Elliot Pinkey and Ernesto de la Loza have sold out months in advance (Twitchell had to split his into two, to accomodate the glut). Booking is essential; call 1-310 470 8664 and ask for Robin Dunnitz.

SPARC

685 Venice Boulevard, at Lincoln Boulevard, Venice (1-310 822 9560).
Since 1988, Judy Baca's Social and Public Art Resource Center has created more than 70 murals celebrating the ethnic heritage of various communities throughout Los Angeles. It also runs monthly thematic bus tours of mural art; call for details.
Website: www.sparcmurals.org

The LA area is home to two presidential libraries/museums. They are open for research, but the museums are also open to the general public. The tone of the two is very different: Reagan's banks on sentimentality, while Nixon's focuses more on the intellectual rigour required of a president. Both libraries are some way out of LA, in opposite directions.

Richard Nixon Library & Birthplace

18001 Yorba Linda Boulevard, at Rose Drive, Yorba Linda, Orange County (1-714 993 5075). Bus Orange County Transit 26/Hwy 90, exit Yorba Linda Boulevard west. **Open** 10am-5pm Mon-Sat; 11am-5pm Sun. **Admission** $5.95; $3.95 seniors; $2 8-11s. **Credit** AmEx, Disc, MC, V.

Located in the out-of-the-way suburb where Nixon was born, the library provides an overview of his presidency as well as a tour of the modest house, built from a kit by his father, in which Tricky Dicky was born. The gifts section includes a gun from Elvis Presley and a rock in the shape of Nixon's profile from Barry Goldwater, as well as the usual assortment of buckles and paintings. Richard and Pat Nixon are buried in the gardens.
Website: www.nixonfoundation.org
Free parking.

Ronald Reagan Library & Museum

40 Presidential Drive, at Madera Road, Simi Valley, Ventura (1-805 522 8444). Train Metrolink Simi Valley/US 101 to Hwy 23 north, exit Olsen Road north. **Open** 10am-5pm daily. **Admission** $4; $2 students, seniors. **No credit cards.**

Simi Valley has gained infamy in recent years as the site of the (first) LAPD trial that set off the 1992 riots. It's also home to this library; great for fans of the Gipper, but liberal types will probably see red. The museum has a CD-Rom display containing Reagan's most endearing quips, photos of him as a young lad with a football, a re-creation of the Oval Office plus awesome gifts received over the years, such as a beaded gown given to Nancy by Imelda Marcos and a White House-shaped Kleenex box made from white yarn.

Galleries

There were art dealerships in Los Angeles before World War II, and during the 1960s there was a lively gallery scene along La Cienega Boulevard. But LA came of cultural age only in the 1980s. The scene is still changing and expanding, as the hippest dealers and most advanced work in town move into neighbourhoods where galleries would have been unthinkable only a few months before. Those galleries sometimes have short lives, but at least the LA gallery scene can finally boast an overall stability.

WHERE TO GO

Most of the galleries are found in the oceanside enclave of Santa Monica, mainly in several 'art malls'. The most prominent of these by far is **Bergamot Station** (2525 Michigan Avenue, at Cloverfield Boulevard; 1-310 829 5854), a sprawling former tram terminal. Some 30 or so galleries, plus

several art-related outlets and the **Santa Monica Museum of Art** (*see page 197*), occupy a complex of large sheds ringing a capacious parking area. A few blocks away is the **Broadway Complex** (2042 Broadway, between 20th Street and Cloverfield Avenue) and, further west, a small 'business park' on **Colorado Avenue** (between Ninth and Tenth Streets) – but both are gradually losing their galleries to Bergamot.

In the meantime, the beyond-cool galleries that populated the so-called 'Baby Bergamot' complex down the street from the adult version have moved lock, stock and database to a similar warren of spaces around Miracle Mile, across Wilshire Boulevard from the Los Angeles County Museum of Art. Their number has doubled, and the City of LA finally has an art mall it can call its own.

La Brea Avenue, between Santa Monica Boulevard and Third Street, is dotted with galleries of all kinds, as is **Beverly Boulevard** to the west, albeit more sparsely. In artsy West Hollywood, a cluster of galleries has sprung up along **Melrose Avenue** and cross streets **Robertson Boulevard** and **Almont Street**. August outposts of New York blue-chip establishments and branches of Sotheby's and Christie's auction houses have gone where the money is, to glitzy **Beverly Hills**. Many artists still live in the SoHo-wannabe warehouse district east of Downtown and in Venice, but there are few galleries left in either area, though the ones that do exist are some of the city's best.

There was some hope that a gallery scene would coalesce around the relocation of two of the town's most important non-profit-making galleries, **Los Angeles Contemporary Exhibitions** (1-323 957 1777) and the **Los Angeles Center for Photographic Studies** (1-323 466 6232), on Hollywood Boulevard, between Schroeder and Wilcox Avenues (LACE is at No.6522 and LACPS is next door). No such luck. Instead, the second generation of LA's cutting-edge, fly-by-night galleries has emerged in Tinseltown's true bohemia, **Silver Lake**. These are shoestring operations, often just a gritty shopfront and sometimes literally nothing more than the gallerist's living room.

INFORMATION

Two monthly directories, *Art Scene* and *Art Now Gallery Guide* (available at all the galleries they list), provide a comprehensive briefing on LA's spaces. *Art Scene* is the more extensive and especially good for college and other non-commercial venues. The *LA Weekly* and the *LA Times*'s Sunday Calendar section also provide extensive listings. Bi-monthly art publications include the heady, flippant *Art Issues*, the even headier *Art & Text* and the yet more flippant *Coagula*, which covers New York as well as LA (all from bookshops and newsstands). Venues and phone numbers are constantly changing, so always ring first to save a wasted trip.

Music

Hardcore rock 'n' roll on Sunset Strip or hardcore minimalism from the LA Phil? Or you could practise 'ooh!'s and 'aah!'s at a Hollywood Bowl firework concert. It's all part of the LA sound.

Tickets & information

Big-name concerts – both classical and rock – often sell out, so buy tickets in advance if you can. It's always worth checking with the box office on the day of the show, as the promoters sometimes release excellent seats at that time. Whenever possible, try to get tickets directly from the venue in order to save on credit card booking charges. At smaller venues, you can usually pay on the door.

Alternatively, you can buy tickets through mega-service **Ticketmaster**, whose many (cash-only) outlets can be found in Blockbuster Music, Tower Records, Robinsons-May and Ritmo Latino stores. Tickets for selected shows are also available, without a service charge, at the Ticketmaster Box Office (6243 Hollywood Boulevard, between Vine and Gower Streets; 10am-6pm Mon-Sat). For credit card bookings (AmEx, Disc, MC, V), call 1-213 480 3232 or 1-714 740 2000; note that the 'convenience' charges are fairly high.

The most comprehensive music listings can be found in the *LA Weekly*, while the *LA Times* Sunday Calendar section is also a good source. For CD, record and tape shops, *see page 160* **Shops & Services**. For radio stations, *see page 193* **Media**.

Classical

Since the early 1970s, the Los Angeles Philharmonic has been belying its home city's reputation as a cultural wasteland. Under the baton of Zubin 'Macho Maestro' Mehta, it metamorphosed into a world-class orchestra and now has expanded into a multi-tiered organisation responsible for most classical performances in LA. Most of these are staged in the **Music Center** at the **Dorothy Chandler Pavilion** (October-May) and at the **Hollywood Bowl** (June-September; for both, *see below*).

Thanks to the interests of its present music director, the youthful Finnish heart-throb Esa-Pekka Salonen, the Philharmonic's programming consists of an unusually large contemporary repertoire, often side by side with the standard warhorses. Sir Simon Rattle, Pierre Boulez and former principal conductor Zubin Mehta have especially strong relationships with the orchestra and appear regularly. For more insight into its performances, the Philharmonic offers *Upbeat Live!*, a free pre-concert lecture in the Pavilion's Grand Hall starting half an hour before each performance.

LOS ANGELES OPERA

Having given its first performance in 1987, the LA Opera is one of the newest of the city's major arts companies. It specialises in high-concept stagings of familiar operas featuring international stars such as Maria Ewing, Placido Domingo and Galina Gortchakova, but has also been a welcoming home to famous productions such as the Peter Sellars/Salonen version of Debussy's *Pelléas et Mélisande* and Wagner's *Tristan und Isolde* designed by David Hockney.

OTHER ORCHESTRAS

Los Angeles Chamber Orchestra (1-213 622 7001; tickets $12-$48) is LA's foremost chamber ensemble, devoted to the entire repertoire from the seventeenth to the twentieth centuries. It performs at UCLA's Royce Hall (*see below*) and the Mark Taper Forum (*see* **Music Center** *page 231* **Theatre & Dance**). The **Da Camera Society's Chamber Music in Historic Sites** (1-310 440 1351; tickets $24-$68) presents concerts by first-rate chamber ensembles and soloists in some of the city's more interesting buildings, while the **Los Angeles Baroque Orchestra** (1-310 458 0425; tickets $25-$30) plays its authentic, period instruments in various churches and small halls around town. The presence of other good-to-excellent ensembles, such as the **Pasadena Symphony** (1-626 793 7172) and the **Long Beach Symphony** (1-562 436 3203; tickets $4-$60), testifies to LA's demand for high-quality classical programming.

Major venues

Dorothy Chandler Pavilion

Music Center of Los Angeles, 135 N Grand Avenue, at First Street, Downtown (1-213 972 7200/1-213 972 7211/LA Philharmonic 1-213 972 7300/LA Opera 1-213 972 7219/LA Master Chorale 1-213 972 7282). Metro Civic Center/Tom Bradley/bus 78, 79, 96, 379, 427, Commuter Express 423/I-110 north, exit Fourth Street east; I-110 south, exit Hill Street; I-101 north, exit Grand Avenue; I-101 south, exit Temple Street. **Open** box office 10am-6pm Mon-Sat. **Tickets** $6-$120. **Credit** AmEx, MC, V. **Map 7 B2**

The *grande dame* of the city's concert scene and the largest hall in town devoted (almost) entirely to classical music, the Pavilion is probably best known internationally for the one

*LA's premier classical music venue, the **Dorothy Chandler Pavilion**. See page 205.*

night each year that it hosts the Academy Awards. Movie stars in tuxes aside, the home of the LA Opera, the Los Angeles Philharmonic and the Los Angeles Master Chorale is the place to go for an evening of high culture.

Built in the early 1960s after a fund drive by Dorothy 'Buff' Chandler, wife of the *LA Times*'s publisher Norman, the Pavilion sits at the south end of the LA County-operated Music Center, a stone and marble edifice it shares with the Mark Taper Forum and the Ahmanson Theater. Sandwiched between the Criminal Courts Building and the Department of Water and Power, the Center is an oasis in what can be a fairly dodgy corner of Downtown. Further south from the Pavilion is the future site of the Disney Concert Hall, designed by Frank Gehry, a long-planned project whose construction should be under way shortly.

The Pavilion's comfortably plush house seats 3,200 amid dark wood panelling, muted colours and iridescent crystal chandeliers. Sound quality, acceptable everywhere in the building, is best on the upper floors, though the view from the top balcony can be vertigo-inducing.
Website: www.ioio.com/musiccenter
Parking evenings & weekends $7; weekdays $2.50 per 20 mins ($15 dollar maximum); valet parking $17.

Other venues

Leo S Bing Theater *Los Angeles County Museum of Art (see p196* **Museums & Galleries**). The Bing presents Sundays at Four (1-323 485 6873), a series of free concerts featuring chamber ensembles and soloists, as well as evening concerts (8pm, Mon, Wed; $7-$15).
Getty Courtyard *(1-213 365 3500).* **Tickets** $22. At 8pm on Saturday and Sunday evenings in summer, the Getty Center presents the music of ancient Greece.
Japan America Theater *(1-213 680 3700).* $25-$50. Modelled on a Japanese fan, this 840-seat venue hosts Japanese performing arts, from traditional Kabuki, Noh, Kageboschi (shadow-play) and Bunraku (puppet theatre) to contemporary music, comedy and dance.
Pasadena Civic Auditorium *(1-626 449 7360/ Pasadena Symphony 1-626 793 7172).* **Tickets** $18-$60. The Pasadena Symphony shares this facility with several musicals a year and the Emmy Awards.

College venues

Call the venues themselves for information on concerts and ticket prices.

Bovard Auditorium at USC *(1-213 740 7111).*
Gindi Auditorium at the University of Judaism *(1-310 476 9777).*
Harriet & Charles Luckman Fine Arts Complex at Cal State LA *(recorded information 1-323 343 6600/box office 1-323 343 6610).*
Schoenberg Hall & Royce Hall at UCLA *For listings, see* **UCLA Center** *p234* **Theatre & Dance**.

<h2 style="background:black;color:white">Rock, roots & jazz</h2>

Long an important player in American popular music, Los Angeles officially became the music industry capital of the United States – and, by inference, the world – in the early 1970s, when local record companies such as Elektra and A&M racked up hit after hit, and prominent labels like Motown and Atlantic moved their operations west. Although not a 'jazz town' like New York or a 'blues town' like Chicago, LA is still an important stop on any touring artist's itinerary and the city can hold its own when it comes to the quality and quantity of jazz and blues performances. The sheer size and diversity of the city's populace ensure that all the world's musics are represented, for better or worse; but it is the lasting rock 'n' roll mythology of the city that plays itself out every day in a very visible fashion, especially along the legendary **Sunset Strip**.

Ironically, while musicians from all over the country have relocated to LA in hope of attracting the attention of the music industry, relatively few local bands have been signed to major labels in

The Hollywood Bowl

A perennial favourite with both locals and tourists, this world-famous jewel of an outdoor amphitheatre has hosted concerts since its first LA Philharmonic performance on Easter morning 1921. Nestled in an aesthetically and acoustically blessed fold in the Hollywood Hills, the Bowl, it is said, was once a gathering spot for the area's Native American tribes. One of the theatre's first shells was designed by Lloyd Wright (son of Frank); much later it was given a going-over by Frank Gehry. It is a deceptively large venue, with a capacity of almost 18,000.

A balmy summer night at the Bowl is the quintessential LA experience and can bring out the romantic in even the terminally cynical. Closer to ritual than concert-going, the evening starts for most with an al fresco dinner eaten in the stands or one of the many picnic areas in the grounds. The Patio and Deck restaurants serve pre-concert meals and dinner picnic baskets can also be ordered.

EVENTS

The Bowl is the summer home of the LA Philharmonic and, since 1991, conductor John Mauceri's pops-oriented Hollywood Bowl Orchestra, which has taken over on most weekends, often joined by big-name talents such as Natalie Cole or Carol Burnett. Look out for the frequent performances that are capped off by a firework display. Jazz and rock concerts are also held frequently.

The Bowl is a country park and thus open to the general public during the day. During the summer, orchestra rehearsals (open to the public) are held several mornings a week.

TICKETS

The prized box seats at the front of the Bowl, sold by subscription for the classical and jazz series, are often handed down from generation to generation, making them virtually unobtainable. If budget isn't a limitation, check with the box office on the day of performance: these prime seats sometimes become available at short notice. But don't worry if you're a long way from the stage, as the sound system is updated virtually each year – though it's not so well suited to rock acts.

The $1 ($3 Fri, Sat) seats at the top, complete with enchanting vistas, are a great bargain.

2301 N Highland Avenue, at Odin Street, Hollywood (1-323 850 2000/restaurants 1-323 851 3588). Bus Hollywood Bowl/US 101, exit Highland Avenue/ Hollywood Bowl. **Open** *June-Sept* box office 10am-9pm Mon-Sat; noon-8pm Sun; rehearsals 9.30am-12.30pm day of performance. **Tickets** bench seats $1-$24 Tue, Thur; $3-$26 Fri, Sat; box seats $61-$75 Tue, Thur; $69-$90 Fri; $75-$95 Sat; other ticket prices vary; call to check. **Credit** AmEx, Disc, MC, V. **Map 5 A1** *Website: www.hollywoodbowl.org Parking Hollywood Bowl $10-$24.20; park & ride $5 round trip; shuttle $2.50 round trip.*

recent years. Industry types are still searching for the next Seattle, but LA is just too large and diverse to produce a unified sound. **Silver Lake**, the quasi-bohemian enclave east of Hollywood, experienced a recent flurry of record company interest when local boy Beck first hit the charts, but fellow Silver Lake acts such as the Geraldine Fibbers, Sissy Bar and the Negro Problem have (so far) proved too idiosyncratic for mass consump-tion. **Spaceland**, Silver Lake's only real music club, remains a great place to sample local sounds.

Although gangsta rap originated in neighbouring Compton and LA is home to such successful rap labels as Marion 'Suge' Knight's Death Row (somewhat quiet at present while it deals with a multitude of lawsuits) and Ruthless, don't count on seeing much of this urban African-American artform live in Los Angeles.

Based on past history and current stereotypes, promoters and their liability insurers are hesitant to get involved. Paradoxically, but in keeping with their commitment to black music, the corporate-run **House of Blues** has almost single-handedly kept rap and hip-hop in front of LA audiences.

One of the best ways to experience LA's diverse Latino culture is through its music. Well-known Latin pop stars appear frequently at mainstream venues such as the **Universal Amphitheater**, as well as more obscure locales such as the **Pico Rivera Sports Arena** (11003 Rooks Road, just off the I-605, Pico Rivera; 1-562 695 0509). Some weekends, merengue dances take place at the **Hollywood Palladium**. The salsa crowd does its thing weekly at the tiny **El Floridita** (1253 N Vine Street, at Lexington Avenue, Hollywood; 1-323 871 8612) and at other clubs such as the new **Conga Room**, which specialises in star line-ups.

The Rock en Español movement (passionate guitar-heavy rock 'n' roll, sung in Spanish) has experienced a huge burst of local popularity in recent years, and can be enjoyed at the **Palace** in Hollywood and various smaller clubs.

More assimilated, a talented contingent of East LA-based bands play multi-faceted music all over town, including world music hangout **LunaPark**. Up-and-coming acts include the ska-inflected Latin swingers Yeska and Ozomatli, whose nine-man line-up serves up a stimulating array of funky rhythms with jazzy flourishes.

Free shows of everything from roots to reggae to pop to world music take place during the summer at the **Santa Monica Pier** and at **California Plaza** in Downtown. For year-round festival information, contact the City's Department of Cultural Affairs (1-213 485 2433).

Take photo ID to every music venue. This will not only enable you to drink (if you are 21 or over), but in many cases allow you through the door. Some shows are open to 18s and over, depending on the venue's alcohol-licensing arrangement.

Major venues

Great Western Forum

3900 Manchester Boulevard, at Prairie Avenue, Inglewood (box office 1-310 673 1300). Bus 115, 211, 315, 442/ I-405, exit Manchester Boulevard east. **Open** box office 10am-6pm Mon-Fri; varies Sat, Sun. **Admission** varies. **Credit** AmEx, MC, V.
The Lakers play basketball and the Kings play hockey at this acoustically challenged classic in the concrete arena tradition. Superstar attractions such as Pearl Jam and the Spice Girls have played here recently. Although the venue has an undeniable energy when 18,000 souls are packing it, the flipside is that concert-goers shouldn't expect to be able to see the act's facial features or hear the musical subtleties of the performance (provided, of course, that there are any).
Parking $10.

Greek Theater

2700 N Vermont Avenue, at Los Feliz Boulevard, Griffith Park (1-323 665 1927/box office 1-323 665 5857). Bus Community Connection 203/US 101, exit Vermont Avenue north. **Open** June-Oct box office noon-6pm Mon-Fri; 10am-4pm Sat, Sun; until 9pm nights of shows. **Admission** varies. **Credit** MC, V. **Map 6 A1**
This bucolic, open-air, 6,000-seater in Griffith Park is a great place to catch pop and rock perennials such as John Fogerty, Santana or the Allman Brothers. One drawback: the intractable stack parking.
Parking $6-$25.

Henry Fonda Theater

6126 Hollywood Boulevard, at Gower Street, Hollywood (1-323 468 1700). Bus 1, 180, 181, 212, 217/US 101, exit Vine Street south. **Open** box office from 2pm day of show. **Admission** varies. **Credit** AmEx, MC, V. **Map 5 B1**
Occasional shows by adult-oriented acts such as the Charlie Watts Quintet or Ray Davies are a treat in this intimate Hollywood theatre (capacity 800). In 1994 it suffered earthquake damage and hasn't been very busy since.
Parking $6.

Hollywood Palladium

6215 Sunset Boulevard, between Argyle & El Centro Avenues, Hollywood (1-323 962 7600). Bus 2, 3, 210, 212/US 101, exit Vine Street south. **Open & admission** varies; call for schedule. **No credit cards. Map 5 B2**
Mosh pits are common at this venue, which has the tightest door policy in town; even pens and chewing gum are banned. Recently refurbished (not that you can tell), the faded ballroom, once ruled by the sounds of Glenn Miller and Tommy Dorsey, has now been claimed by successful alterna-bands like Rancid and alterna-swing acts like Cherry Poppin' Daddies. LA perennials X recently played a sold-out string of reunion dates here.
Parking $5-$7.

John Anson Ford Amphitheatre

2580 Cahuenga Boulevard E, at Vine Street, Hollywood (1-213 974 1396). Bus 163, 420/US 101, exit Cahuenga Boulevard north. **Open** 4 hours before show; call for

Multicultural LA band Ozomatli.

schedule. **Admission** varies. **Credit** (advance bookings only) Disc, MC, V.

The LA County-sponsored Summer Nights at the Ford series is the mainstay at this small (1,200 capacity) but enchanting outdoor amphitheatre, which presents everything from local choreographer and dance diva Naomi Goldberg's stunning Los Angeles Modern Dance & Ballet programmes to a samba-crazed Brazilian festival.
Parking $5.

The Palace

1735 N Vine Street, at Hollywood Boulevard, Hollywood (1-323 462 3000). Bus 163, 180, 181, 212, 217/US 101, exit Hollywood Boulevard west. **Open** 9pm-4am Thur-Sun; shows vary, so call for schedule. **Admission** varies. **Credit** AmEx, MC, V. **Map 5 B1**

In the heart of Hollywood, this small 1927 theatre holds 1,200 fans for shows mainly of the alternative rock variety. The upstairs balcony provides an escape from the downstairs crush, but don't expect the sound to be clear anywhere; you've probably been in bomb shelters with better acoustics. It turns into a disco at 10.30pm from Thursday to Saturday, so shows on those evenings start punctually.

Pantages Theater

6233 Hollywood Boulevard, between Vine Street & Argyle Avenue, Hollywood (1-323 468 1700). Bus 180, 181, 212, 217/US 101, exit Vine Street south. **Open &** **admission** varies; call for schedule. **Credit** AmEx, MC, V. **Map 5 B1**

Another smallish (2,200 capacity) theatre with an art deco design, the Pantages is a great place to see established acts. However, largely due to construction for the Metro subway, it isn't currently very active, apart from some musicals and a few award shows.
Parking $6.

Universal Amphitheater

100 Universal City Plaza, Universal City (1-818 777 3931/recorded information 1-818 622 4440). Bus 420/US 101, exit Universal Center Drive. **Open** box office 1-9pm Tue-Sun. **Admission** varies. **Credit** AmEx, MC, V.

This slick, semicircular room for major pop, rock, R&B and Latin acts is probably not what God had in mind when he invented rock 'n' roll. But clean sightlines and good acoustics (except below the balcony) make this a popular spot for under-age Valley girls and other music lovers.
Website: www.uniconcerts.com
Parking $6.

Veterans Wadsworth Theater

Veterans Administration Grounds, at Wilshire & San Vincente Boulevards, Westwood (1-310 825 2101/ Jazz at the Wadsworth 1-310 825 5706). Bus 20, 320, Santa Monica 2, 3/I-405, exit Wilshire Boulevard west. **Open & admission** varies; call for schedule.
Credit AmEx, MC, V.

Located on the Veteran Administration's Westwood grounds and run by UCLA, the 1,400-seater Wadsworth presents many of the university's performing arts series programmes, ranging from classical recitals to ethnic dance performances to world music shows as well as the occasional pop concert.
Parking $5.

Wiltern Theater

Wiltern Center, 3790 Wilshire Boulevard, at Western Avenue, Mid Wilshire (1-213 380 5005). Metro Wilshire/ Western/bus 20, 21, 22, 207, 357/I-10, exit Western Avenue north. **Open** box office noon-6pm Mon-Sat; venue 3 hours before show. **Admission** varies. **Credit** MC, V. **Map 5 C4**

An art deco gem renovated and energised ten years ago by the late rock impresario Bill Graham, the Wiltern draws a mostly older crowd for the likes of Cowboy Junkies, Neil Finn and the occasional dance troupe or musical. The venue's comfortable seating and human scale make up for the crummy surrounding neighbourhood.
Parking $5.

Rock

Al's Bar

305 S Hewitt Street, at Traction Avenue, Downtown (1-213 625 9703). Bus 16, DASH A, Montebello 40/I-10, exit Alameda Street east. **Open** 6pm-2am Mon-Thur, Sat, Sun; 3pm-2am Fri; shows 9pm daily. **Admission** $5; Tue, Wed free. **No credit cards.**

Al's has been a favourite of loft-living bohemians and low-living alcoholics for years. Some might find the deep Downtown location and heavy vibe a tad scary, but many of LA's more compelling bands have done time in its spartan digs. It's a place for those who take their beer drinking, pool playing and arty hard rocking seriously. First-time visitors should definitely go in the company of someone who's been there before; the haphazard street layout can make finding Al's almost impossible if you're unfamiliar with the area.

Bar Deluxe

1710 N Las Palmas Avenue, between Hollywood Boulevard & Yucca Street, Hollywood (1-323 469 1991). Bus 1, 26, 163, 181/US 101, exit Highland Avenue south. **Open** 9pm-2am nightly. **Admission** $5-$7. **No credit cards**.
Map 5 A1

Dark, dusty and always still dripping with sweat from the previous night's revels, this Hollywood joint regularly features some of the finest rockabilly, surf and trash-rock in Southern California. The sound often verges on the terrible, but with bands like Deadbolt and the Lazy Cowgirls, CD-quality sound is somewhat beside the point.

Chorus Club

237 N Vermont Avenue, between Beverly Boulevard & Council Street, Silver Lake (1-323 666-2407). Bus 14, 204, 354, Community Connection 203/US 101, exit Vermont Avenue south. **Open** 9pm-2am daily. **Admission** $3-$8. **No credit cards. Map 6 A4**

This tiny Koreatown bar, whose bizarre décor includes musical instruments suspended from the ceiling and walls hung with posters of 1980s metal bands, has recently become home to the Fold club, which features touring indie acts and obscure denizens of the nearby Silver Lake scene.

Dragonfly

6510 Santa Monica Boulevard, at Wilcox Avenue, Hollywood (1-323 466 6111). Bus 4, 420/I-10, exit La Brea Avenue north. **Open** 9pm-2am daily. **Admission** $5-$15. **Credit** AmEx, MC, V. **Map 5 A2**

A Hollywood rock emporium masquerading as a Middle Eastern harem, Dragonfly plays host to at least one band with a heavy music industry buzz pretty much every night, thus attracting record company talent scouts and scenesters alike. The sound is excellent, although the grab-bag booking policy – and the club's tendency to spin bad Eurodisco or New Age music between sets, whatever is on the bill – can make for a somewhat excruciating experience. The back patio offers a welcome respite from the music, as well as a good place to have a smoke.
Parking $3.50.

El Rey Theatre

For listings, see **Coven 13**, *p215* **Nightlife**.

Once a popular venue for touring acts like Stereolab and Spiritualized, the El Rey Theatre has been forced to cut its seating capacity in half due to conflicts with the fire marshal and uptight neighbours. As a result, larger acts are opting to play elsewhere, and the future of this gorgeous art deco relic looks troubled.

14 Below

*1348 14th Street, at Santa Monica Boulevard, Santa
Monica (1-310 451-5040). Bus 4/I-10, exit 26th Street
north.* **Open** *3pm-2am Mon-Fri; 4pm-2am Sat; 8pm-2am
Sun.* **Admission** *$8-$23.* **Credit** *MC, V.*
Map 2 B2

Grateful Dead tribute bands, washed-up 1980s acts like Dave
Wakeling and Gene Loves Jezebel and local pop groups like
Baby Lemonade and the Andersons are some of the acts to
appear regularly at this popular Westside nightspot (one of
the few decent ones left, thanks to the recent demise of the
Alligator Lounge). The long, narrow music room (and incom-
petent sound engineers) can occasionally render the stage
volume unbearable, but you can also watch the show on video
monitors in the adjacent billiard rooms.

The Garage

For listings, see p216 **Nightlife***.*

This funky Silver Lake hangout is best enjoyed on Sundays,
when Club Sucker presents a variety of cutting-edge local acts.
The sound system isn't great, but the crowd – a feisty mix of
straight and gay punks, musicians and artists – always makes
for an agreeably raucous time.

Genghis Cohen Cantina

*740 N Fairfax Avenue, between Melrose & Waring
Avenues, West Hollywood (1-213 653 0640). Bus 10, 11,
217, DASH Fairfax/I-10, exit Fairfax Avenue north.* **Open**
varies Mon; from 8.15pm Tue-Thur; from 9pm Fri, Sat;
from 8.30pm Sun. **Admission** *$4-$7.* **Credit** *AmEx, MC, V.*
Map 4 B2

Come for the tunes, not the food, at this small music room
and restaurant where singer-songwriters earnestly plug
away in an acoustic setting, hoping for that publishing deal.
Valet parking $2.50.

The Gig

*11637 W Pico Boulevard, between Barrington & Federal
Avenues, West LA (1-310 444 9870). Bus Santa Monica
7/I-10, exit Bundy Avenue north.* **Open** *8pm-2am daily.*
Admission *$5-$10.* **Credit** *AmEx, MC, V.*

Opened in 1997, this West LA joint still resembles its former
incarnation – a comedy club. Though the vibe is decidedly
un-rock 'n' roll (dig those cushy sofas and oversized pillows),
the sightlines are excellent and the sound system is loud without being overpowering. A wide variety of local reggae,
worldbeat, pop and avant-jazz acts perform nightly.

Goldfingers

For listings, see p216 **Nightlife***.*

Formerly the appropriately monikered Hell's Gate, this tiny
Hollywood club has been transformed into a swinging playpen
worthy of James Bond and Dean Martin. The miniscule stage
mostly accommodates hip cabaret acts and lounge combos.

Hollywood Athletic Club

*6525 Sunset Boulevard, at Schrader Boulevard, Hollywood
(1-323 962 6600). Bus 2, 3/US 101, exit Sunset Boulevard
west.* **Open** *11am-2am daily.* **Admission** *$8-$20.* **Credit**
AmEx, Disc, MC, V. **Map 5 A2**

Once a popular trysting place for gay stars of the silent
movie era, this has recently become a popular spot for local
promoters to stage rock shows. Most evenings are devoted
to dance DJs, but rumour has it that the venue – which
recently hosted sold-out shows by David Bowie and
Cornershop – will soon be adopting a bands-only policy.
Valet parking $4.

Largo

*432 N Fairfax Avenue, between Oakwood & Rosewood
Avenues, Fairfax District (1-213 852 1073). Bus 14, 217,
DASH Fairfax/I-10, exit Fairfax Avenue north.* **Open**
shows at 9pm daily. **Admission** *$2-$12.* **Credit** *AmEx,
MC, V.* **Map 4 B2**

Sunset Strip

In the 1960s, the stretch of Sunset Boulevard
bordered by Doheny Drive and Crescent
Heights Boulevard in West Hollywood became
known colloquially as the 'Sunset Strip'. A glit-
tering wonderland of nightclubs, restaurants
and pricey shops, the Strip became a magnet for
Southern California youth in the post-surf, pre-
hippy era. Acts ranging in hipness from the
Byrds and Buffalo Springfield to Johnny Rivers
and Trini Lopez performed at nightclubs such
as Ciro's and the Whisky A Go-Go; but mostly,
the kids came from the surrounding suburbs
less to see the bands than to hang out and meet
other kids. Their presence didn't sit too well
with the local shop owners, though, and soon
the local police were called in to clear the side-
walks of the youthful loiterers. The ensuing
confrontations passed into legend as 'the riot on
Sunset Strip', and put an end (at least for a
while) to the area's reputation as a teen mecca.

The Sunset Strip nickname still sticks today,
even though the past few decades have seen
the street undergo several transformations.
Briefly popular with the decadent glam-rock
crowd in the early 1970s, the Strip experienced
something of a renaissance in the mid-1980s,
when the local heavy metal scene began
churning out such nationally known acts as
Ratt, Quiet Riot and Guns N Roses. The metal
bands are mostly gone now, but the onerous
'pay-to-play' policies of Sunset Strip club
bookers have proved remarkably resilient.
Though it certainly exhibits far less character
than it once did, the Strip is still hopping; on a
good night, the following clubs still provide a
hint of that old Strip magic. One relatively new
kid on the Strip is Johnny Depp's **Viper Room**,
which doubles as a dance club and a music
venue (*see page 217* **Nightlife***).*

Coconut Teaszer

*8117 Sunset Boulevard, at Crescent Heights
Boulevard (1-323 654 4773). Bus 2, 3, 429/I-10,
exit La Cienega Boulevard north.* **Open** *6.30pm-2am
daily.* **Admission** *$10.* **Credit** *AmEx, MC, V.*
Map 4 B1

Located almost directly across from Canter's Delicatessen,
the Largo is an intimate pub specialising in fairly decent food
(call for reservations) and high-quality acoustic music. A
sizeable cult has developed around musical jack-of-all-trades
Jon Brion, so obtaining entry to his regular Friday-night
shows can be difficult – ditto for Andy Prieboy's monthly
performances of *White Trash Wins Lotto*, a musical version
of the Axl Rose story. The Divine Comedy has played here
several times, as has Robyn Hitchcock.

Many bands that play the Teaszer would probably kill their own grandmothers for a record deal, which gives the place an air of desperation to accompany its painful decibel levels. Downstairs, the Crooked Bar showcases mostly talented unknowns playing acoustic sets. *Parking $3-$5.*

House of Blues

8430 Sunset Boulevard, at Olive Drive (concert hotline 1-323 650 1451/box office 1-323 848 5100). Bus 2, 3, 429/I-10, exit La Cienega Boulevard north. **Open** box office 10.30am-midnight daily. **Admission** $10-$25. **Credit** AmEx, DC, Disc, MC, V. **Map 4 B1**
Brainchild of a Hard Rock Café founder, the flagship operation (*see* **photo**) of the wildly successful House of Blues string of club/music hall/restaurants is to the blues what fast-food chains are to the hamburger. While the bands (blues-related and otherwise) in this Disneyesque juke joint are extremely diverse and of top quality, the poor sightlines, cramped standing room, parking problems and surly staff may give you your own blues. But the food is excellent.
Website: www.hob.com
Valet parking $8.

Key Club

9039 Sunset Boulevard, at Doheny Drive (1-310 274 5800). Bus 2, 3, 429/I-10, exit La Cienega Boulevard north. **Open** 7pm-2am Wed-Sun; box office 10am-1am daily. **Admission** $10-$22.50. **Credit** AmEx, MC, V. **Map 4 A1**
Formerly known as Billboard Live, this high-tech, multilevel club (built on the foundations of legendary metal stronghold Gazzari's) has been only moderately successful in its attempts to compete with the House of Blues; if anything, this place is even less appealing.
Valet parking $7.

The Roxy

9009 Sunset Boulevard, between San Vincente Boulevard & Doheny Drive (1-310 276 2222). Bus 2, 3, 429 /I-10, exit La Cienega Boulevard north. **Open** from 8pm daily; call for show times. **Admission** $10-$15. **Credit** AmEx, DC, Disc, MC, V.
Map 4 A1
One of the Strip's few survivors from the 1970s, the Roxy has a history of career-making performances by top names such as Bob Marley, Neil Young and Bruce Springsteen. Nowadays, most shows of note are nouveau-punk and alternative bands booked by promoter Goldenvoice. Unless you're industry-connected, get there early to snag a table or it's more than likely that you'll be standing all night. Still, the sound system is excellent and the sightlines unencumbered.
Parking $5.

Whisky A Go-Go

8901 Sunset Boulevard, at Clark Street (recorded information 1-310 535 0579/office 1-310 652 4202). Bus 2, 3, 429/I-10, exit La Cienega Boulevard north. **Open** 8pm-2am daily; office 10am-7pm Mon-Fri. **Admission** $7-$15. **Credit** AmEx, DC, Disc, V. **Map 4 A1**
Perhaps LA's most famous music venue, the Whisky is still crazy after all these years. The Doors were at one time the house band and virtually all the significant pop acts of the past three decades have played this landmark club at one time or another. While nationally known talent appears regularly, the majority of the venue's fare is promising young bands, many of whom can be heard for free on Monday nights. Open to all ages.
Website: www.whiskyagogo.com
Parking $5.

LunaPark

For listings, see p219 **Nightlife.** **Open** shows usually 8pm daily. **Admission** $7-$12.
Impresario Jean-Pierre Bocarra has for the past several years presented an incredibly wide array of music – in addition to comedy and performance art – to a mixed crowd in this comfortable club. Enter through the restaurant and either go downstairs to the low-ceilinged cabaret or make your way to the main room in the back.

Martini Lounge

5657 Melrose Avenue, at El Centro Avenue, Hollywood (1-323 467 4068). Bus 10, 11/US 101, exit Hollywood Boulevard west. **Admission** free-$10. **No credit cards. Map 5 B3**
This poorly laid-out club (whoever thought it was a good idea to put a stage in the centre of a very narrow room should be bludgeoned repeatedly) plays host to local pop and rock bands, but is leaning more towards funk and acid-jazz.

Moguls

1650 N Schrader Boulevard, between Hollywood Boulevard & Selma Avenue, Hollywood (1-323 465 7449/ office 1-323 463 6451). Bus 1, 160, 180/US 101, exit Hollywood Boulevard west. **Open** call for schedule. **Admission** free-$10. **Credit** MC, V. **Map 5 A1**

Located in the very epicentre of Hollywood, Moguls has been through several incarnations in the past decade – coffeehouse, independent film screening room and now a comfortably spacious music venue. Tiger Mask, a club that usually takes place at weekends, is immensely popular with the pompadour-and-wallet-chain crowd thanks to its devotion to local and national surf, garage and rockabilly bands. Note that all shows have to end at midnight because of local zoning and curfew restrictions.

Spaceland

1717 Silver Lake Boulevard, at Effie Street, Silver Lake (1-213 833 2843/1-213 661 4380). Bus 201/US 101, exit Silver Lake Boulevard north. **Admission** $5-$8. **Credit** AmEx, MC, V. **Map 6 C3**

Still the most important (read: only) club of the much-hyped Silver Lake scene, Spaceland presents cutting-edge touring acts, as well as popular local acts such as the Negro Problem and WACO. Beck used to be a regular fixture, but the constant media and industry buzz surrounding the club has driven him (and many other Silver Lake scenesters) elsewhere. The sightlines and sound system are only so-so, but the mirror-and-neon interior (it was once a strip club) is amusing, the bartenders friendly and the mood convivial.

The Troubadour

9081 Santa Monica Boulevard, at Doheny Drive, West Hollywood (1-310 276 6168). Bus 4, DASH A, West Hollywood/I-405, exit Santa Monica Boulevard east. **Open** 1.30pm-2am Mon-Fri; 3pm-2am Sat, Sun. **Admission** $5-$12. **No credit cards. Map 4 A2**

Elton John made his US debut at the Troub in 1970 during the club's salad days, when it nurtured the careers of neofolkies Jackson Browne, Linda Ronstadt and David Crosby. Resurrected fairly recently from the depths of metaldom, the venue (which looks like an Alpine ski lodge) once again hosts acts of taste and substance. Along with the Whisky and the Roxy, it has one of the best sound systems in town. *Valet parking $3.50.*

Roots & blues

Country, folk and the music of Ireland can be heard at **Molly Malone's Irish Pub** (*see page 149* **Bars**). Swing mecca the **Derby** (*see page 215* **Nightlife**), which has become almost unbearably hip in the wake of its appearance in the movie *Swingers*, offers regular swing lessons for beginners.

Babe's & Ricky's Inn

4339 Leimert Boulevard, at 43rd Street, Leimert Park (1-323 295 9112). Bus 40, 105, 210, 310, DASH Crenshaw/I-10, exit Crenshaw Boulevard south. **Open** 10am-2am daily. **Admission** free-$5. **Credit** AmEx, MC, V.

One of LA's oldest blues joints, Babe's & Ricky's may be the only local blues club to actually reside in a predominantly black neighbourhood. The atmosphere is extremely friendly, the local blues acts more than respectable and Mama Laura's fried chicken alone is worth the trip. *Parking free.*

BB King's Blues Club

Universal CityWalk, 1000 Universal Center Drive, Universal City (1-818 622 5464). Bus 420/US 101, exit Universal Center Drive. **Open** 5pm-1am Mon-Thur, Sun; 5pm-2am Fri, Sat. **Admission** $10-$12. **Credit** AmEx, DC, Disc, MC, V.

Local guitar slingers and the odd national R&B name ply their trade at the LA branch of blues master King's Memphis supper club. This is the most down-to-earth joint on Universal City's hideously commercial and plastic CityWalk. *Parking $6.*

Club Fais Do-Do

5257 W Adams Boulevard, at Cloverdale Avenue, Culver City (1-213 954 8080). Bus 37/I-10, exit La Brea Avenue south. **Open** 7pm-midnight Tue, Wed, Sun; 7pm-2am Thur-Sat. **Admission** $5. **Credit** MC, V.

Specialising in the New Orleans sound, Fais Do-Do (Cajun dialect for 'dance party') can be counted on for a friendly, funky clientele grooving to the music and enjoying the good selection of tap beers. The opulent interior (the pre-World

The suits are sharp and swing is in at the **Derby** *in Los Feliz.*

War II building used to house a bank) only adds to the club's exotic, out-of-time vibe.
Valet parking $3 Fri, Sat.

The Conga Room

5364 Wilshire Boulevard, at Cloverdale Avenue, Miracle Mile (1-213 938 1696). Bus 20, 21, 22, 320/I-10, exit Fairfax Avenue north. **Open** 9pm-2am Thur-Sun. **Credit** AmEx, MC, V. **Map 5 A4**

Opened in 1998, this stylish, atmospheric club has been an extremely positive addition both to LA's music scene and an otherwise drab part of Miracle Mile. Consistently booking some of the hemisphere's top Latin and Afro-Cuban acts, the Conga Room also offers dance lessons and some very fine 'nuevo latino' cuisine. It ain't cheap (drinks run in the $8 range, and tickets cost three to four times as much), but if you've got a little salsa in your soul, make sure you put this place on your itinerary.
Valet parking $4.

Harvelle's

1432 Fourth Street, between Broadway & Santa Monica Boulevard, Santa Monica (1-310 395 1676). Bus 4, 304, Santa Monica 1, 2, 3, 7, 8/I-10, exit Fourth-Fifth Street north. **Open** 8pm-2am daily. **Admission** $3-$8. **No credit cards. Map 2 A2**

Santa Monica's self-styled 'home of the blues' is smokin' seven nights a week in a comfortable bar/lounge setting.

Jack's Sugar Shack

1707 Vine Street, at Hollywood Boulevard, Hollywood (1-323 466 7005). Bus 1, 163, 180, 181, 212/US 101, exit Gower Street south. **Open** 11.30am-2am, shows 9pm daily. **Admission** free-$15. **Credit** AmEx, Disc, MC, V. **Map 5 B2**

Retaining the Polynesian tiki-house look of its former location, Jack's serves up a healthy dose of blues, country and rockabilly as well as indie/alternative acts. Without a doubt, the friendliest, most attitude-free music club in town.
Valet parking $3.50.

McCabe's

3101 Pico Boulevard, at 31st Street, Santa Monica (1-310 828 4497/1-310 828 4403). Bus Santa Monica 7/I-10, exit Centinela Avenue south. **Open** 10am-10pm Mon-Thur; 10am-6pm Fri, Sat; 1-5pm Sun. **Admission** $10-$20. **Credit** AmEx, DC, Disc, MC, V. **Map 2 C3**

By day a guitar shop, by night (usually at the weekends) McCabe's intimate (and draughty) back room is renowned for acoustic pickin' and singin' by country-folk-rock types such as Rosanne Cash and Jorma Kaukonen. No alcohol is served, but coffee and cookies are available.

The Mint

6010 W Pico Boulevard, at Crescent Heights Boulevard, Midtown (1-323 954 9630). Bus Santa Monica 5, 7/I-10, exit La Cienega Boulevard north. **Open** 8pm-2am daily. **Admission** $5-$15. **Credit** AmEx, MC, V. **Map 4 B4**

Reopened a couple of years ago with an enlarged capacity, the Mint's line-up of blues, jazz and roots satisfies those looking for good, honest, downhome jams.
Valet parking $3.

Jazz

The Baked Potato

3787 N Cahuenga Boulevard, at Lankershim Boulevard, North Hollywood (1-818 980 1615). Bus 96, 152, 420, 424, 425/US 101 north, exit Lankershim Boulevard south. **Open** 7pm-2am, shows 9.30pm, 11.30pm, daily. **Admission** $10; two-drink minimum. **Credit** AmEx, Disc, MC, V.

Musician and owner Don Randi's pint-sized room spawned the LA jazz fusion sound in the 1970s and is still the site of

many a synth-driven romp, though local Latin jazz acts occasionally make an appearance. Don't miss the menu full of – guess what? – spuds.
Website: www.thebakedpotato.com

Catalina Bar & Grill

1640 N Cahuenga Boulevard, at Hollywood Boulevard, Hollywood (1-323 466 2210). Bus 1, 163, 180, 181, 212/ US 101, exit Cahuenga Boulevard south. **Open** 7pm-1am, shows 8.30pm, 10.30pm, daily. **Admission** $10-$20. **Credit** AmEx, Disc, MC, V. **Map 5 B2**

Catalina Popescu consistently pulls jazz's heaviest hitters into her highly civilised, peach-shaded establishment. With the venue's bent toward be-bop, a residence here is de rigueur for old-guard names such as McCoy Tyner and Pharoah Sanders as well as the new crop of jazz men typified by Branford Marsalis and Joshua Redman. Leave the cooking to the players, though: dining here isn't recommended.
Parking $3.

Fifth Street Dick's Coffee Company

3347 2½ W 43rd Place, at Degnan Boulevard, Leimert Park (1-323 296 3970). Bus 40, 105, 210, 310, DASH Crenshaw/I-10, exit Crenshaw Boulevard south. **Open** 4pm-2am Mon-Thur; 4pm-5am Fri; 1pm-5am Sat; 1pm-2am Sun; *shows* 9pm Mon-Thur; 9pm, 1am Fri, Sat; 5.30pm Sun. **Admission** free-$5. **No credit cards.**

Traditional jazz workouts last into the wee hours upstairs at Fifth Street Dick's as some of the city's most skilled practitioners (including Dale Fielder and Ron Muldrow) hone their chops, usually for free. Dick's Sock-It-To-Me cake alone is worth the trip. Note the late opening hours.

Jazz Bakery

3233 Helms Avenue, at Venice Boulevard, Culver City (1-310 271 9039). Bus 33, 436, Culver City 1, 4/I-10, exit La Cienega Boulevard south. **Open** shows 8.30pm Mon-Fri; 4pm, 8.30pm, Sat, Sun. **Admission** $12-$22. **No credit cards.**

Mostly jazz of the straight-ahead variety from members of the pantheon, such as Ahmad Jamal and Dave Grusin. The atmosphere is more than slightly stuffy – this place is for serious jazz aficionados only.
Parking free.

La Vee Lee

12514 Ventura Boulevard, at Whitsett Avenue, Studio City (1-818 980 8158). Bus 424, 522/US 101, exit Coldwater Canyon Boulevard. **Open** 8pm-2am daily. **Admission** $5-$10. **Credit** AmEx, V.

One of the Valley's more swingin' nightspots presents an enticing mixture of Brazilian beat, Latin jazz and fusion.
Valet parking $2.

Lunaria

10351 Santa Monica Boulevard, at Beverly Glen Boulevard, West LA (1-310 282 8870). Bus 4, 304/ I-405, exit Santa Monica Boulevard east. **Open** 10am-2am daily. **Admission** $6-$7. **Credit** AmEx, MC, V. **Map 3 A3**

Located in the shadow of the nearby Century City office towers, this elegant restaurant books a variety of high-quality Latin, swing and contemporary jazz bands in its lounge.
Valet parking $3.50.

St Mark's

23 Windward Avenue, at Pacific Avenue, Venice (1-310 452 2222). Bus Culver City 1, Santa Monica 2, DASH Venice/I-10, exit Lincoln Boulevard south. **Open** 7pm-2am, *shows* 9pm, Tue-Sun. **Admission** $5-$15. **Credit** AmEx, DC, MC, V. **Map 2 A5**

A relaxed beachside spot for contemporary jazz and R&B, with an active (straight) pick-up scene at the bar.
Parking $3.

Nightlife

Angelenos are more likely to start the evening early than stay out all night, but that doesn't mean there aren't plenty of clubs – dance, comedy and cabaret – to keep the good times rolling past the midnight hour.

Dance clubs

Clubbers will be happy to learn that Los Angeles has a vibrant dance music scene. Recent years have seen top DJs such as Carl Craig, Aphrodite, Louis Vega, Sasha, Fatboy Slim and Jon Carter become globe-trotting personalities with rock star reputations, and LA is definitely on such travelling DJs' itineraries, most notably at the **Viper Room** in West Hollywood.

The underground dance scene has become a more hit-and-run, one-off operation, often employing lauded local DJ talent such as Doc Marten, Jason Bentley, Jun, Marvski and Miles Om Tacket. The best way to gauge the club current is to scour shop counters for flyers. Try the fashion shops along Melrose Avenue, and definitely check **Beat Non Stop** dance music record shop (7262 Melrose Avenue, at Poinsettia Place, Hollywood; 1-323 930 2121) for tips on where to go. The free *LA Weekly* newspaper is the superior source of up-to-date club listings, while on the newsstands, *URB* ($3.50) – a one-time smudgy local 'zine and now a slick national mag – drops a few hot hints.

Los Angeles is also the capital of West Coast hip-hop. New York may have given birth to the genre, but LA is the home of gangsta rap – despite the collapse of Death Row records, there's still plenty of it around. Mainstream hip-hop shows have stagnated as a result of borderline paranoia about wearing the latest fashions, but good underground hip-hop clubs can still be found, such as the **Breaks** and **Chocolate Bar**. Venues change so frequently that you'll have to stop in at the city's premier hip-hop record store **Fat Beats** (*see page 160* **Shops & Services**) to find out what's happening where.

Across a cultural chasm worthy of Southern California's geology is the current craze for swing dancing. In part a reaction against gawk-stadium Hollywood clubs, the recent phenomenon of young people dressing in period formal wear and going out for a little swing is a perfect example of how a Los Angeles dance trend can be resourceful and vibrant. The **Derby** nightclub in Los Feliz is the top swingin' place.

If you're not passionate about either pure hip-hop or swing, some of the best nights out happen in bars with live DJs, such as the **Burgundy Room** and the **Room** (*see chapter* **Bars**); these create a club atmosphere even without a real dancefloor. And no list of LA dancefloors can ignore the **Conga Room** (*see page 213* **Music**), more Latin than Julius Caesar.

The club scene picks up in summer, when the infectious sunshine makes party vibes undeniable. Lubricants of all kinds work better in the heat, while there's nothing like a trip to the beach at dawn for coming down after a night out. Summer rave events are often held in the mountains and desert: be warned that heat and sandstorms make water and a scarf or face mask essential. The caves at **Big Bear** (*see page 238* **Trips Out of Town**) are a popular locale for summer solstice raves. Keep an eye out for flyers: **Moonshine** is the big promoter, and fairly reliable.

PRACTICAL INFORMATION

In work-obsessed Los Angeles, clubbing begins a couple of hours earlier than the past-midnight norm of other cities. But an early start need not mean an early night – plan your club-going strategically and you can see the evening through till dawn. The biggest problem for clubbers is the lack of useful public transport (and don't bet that the problematic Metro is going to help much). You have to either bring along a teetotaller to drive, or budget in cab fares that can dwarf the admission prices of the clubs themselves.

Few clubs have tough door policies or feel stiflingly exclusive once you're inside. Which is not to say that it's not a fashion-conscious scene – even the most loose-limbed LA clubbers are trying to cultivate a look and 'overdressed' is a word rarely used in the clubland vocabulary. (Still, do remember to wear sensible shoes.)

You have to be 21 (or over) to drink in California; clubs will 'card' punters (ask to see photo ID) at the door and issue over-21s with a stamp or wrist band, which will allow them to get served at the bar. Some places don't admit under-21s at all, and very few dance clubs accept credit cards.

As is usual in club culture, people of different ethnic groups and sexual preferences get along pretty well in LA clubs. For more gay-oriented nightlife, *see chapter* **Gay & Lesbian**.

Viper the *Room*

merchandise available inside

t-shirts, baby t's, hats,

knit caps, zippos, keychains

ring the bell

Where Johnny Depp hangs out (see p217).

Arena

6655 Santa Monica Boulevard, at Las Palmas Avenue, Hollywood (1-323 462 0714). Bus 4, 420/US 101, exit Santa Monica Boulevard west. **Open** 9pm-4am Thur-Sun. **Admission** $8-$10. **Map 5 A2**
Thursday and Friday are prime nights – this former icehouse packs them in by the thousands for floor-filling house, techno and disco. But don't worry about the crowds – at 22,000sq ft (2,050sq m), the club has room to spare. Getting in can require an hour in an immigration-length queue, but the chatty, happy, cha-cha darlings that compose Arena's core crowd are more than content to swap lipstick and hair gel application tips to pass the time. On Saturdays, the club takes on a distinctly Latin vibe, as live bands take over and the ostensibly 'family' night ends at 2am. Under-18s must be accompanied by an adult.

Bud Brothers' Monday Social

Louis XIV restaurant, 606 N La Brea Avenue, between Clinton Street & Melrose Avenue, Hollywood (1-323 934 5102). Bus 10, 11, 212/I-10, exit La Brea Avenue. **Open** 10pm-2am Mon. **Admission** 21s and over only; $5. **Map 4 C2**
Patterned after London's famous Heavenly Social, the Bud Brothers' Monday gathering is a Big Beat affair of hip-house,

funk and dub. Previous guests include the likes of Dub Pistols and Fatboy Slim. Worth checking early, around 10pm (free admission before 10.30pm). The restaurant location means no real club vibe, but its saving graces are its two floors and fresh-air front patio.

Cherry

Upstairs at the Love Lounge, 657 N Robertson Boulevard, between Melrose Avenue & Santa Monica Boulevard, West Hollywood (1-213 896 9099). Bus 4, 10, 11, 220, DASH Hollywood/I-10 exit Robertson Boulevard north. **Open** 10pm-2.30am Fri. **Admission** 21s and over only; $10. **Map 4 A2**
One of LA's longest-running serial clubs, operating beneath an alternative-new-wave-glam-punk banner, Cherry is heavy on sweaty bodies singing along to floor-filling tunes from the not-too-distant past. Regular theme nights such as Warhol's Factory give the go-go dancers a reason to climb atop their pedestals, while the inevitable rock star sighting is eagerly awaited by those who never manage to make it down from the balcony.

Circus

For listings, see above **Arena**. *Information 1-323 462 1291.* **Open** 8pm-2am Tue, Thur-Sat. **Admission** 21s and over only; $3-$15 (sometimes free before 10pm). **Map 5 A2**
This long-running disco's outdoor patio provides a cooling break from the latest house and techno in its two rooms. On Tuesdays, gay boys get their own night (including a drag show at 11.30pm), and on Thursdays the popular Paradise 24 lets an attractive straight crowd get its groove on to hip-hop and R&B. The nice dress code is strictly enforced. *Valet parking $3.*

Club Los Globos

3040 W Sunset Boulevard, at Descanso Drive, Silver Lake (1-323 663 6517). Bus 1, 2, 3, 4, 201/US 101, exit Silver Lake Boulevard north. **Open** 8pm-2am daily. **Admission** $10. **Map 6 B3**
The dazzling neon exterior is indicative of the sheen of joy flying off the fun-loving, slightly older, Spanish-speaking crowd. Salsa and merengue are the orders of the night, as live bands alternate with DJs. If you don't have a partner to show you how, watching and nursing a cerveza is indeed the next best thing.

Coven 13

El Rey Theatre, 5515 Wilshire Boulevard, at Burnside Avenue, Miracle Mile. Bus 20, 21, 22, 320/I-10, exit Fairfax Avenue north. **Open** 10pm-2am every other Sun. **Admission** 18s and over only; $10. **Map 4 C3**
This is LA's premier goth club, which means honest-to-gosh vampires, dominatrixes in latex and the dedicated undead in black Victorian dress reeling beneath the mammoth chandeliers and red velvet curtains. A large hall with an equivalent dancefloor provides plenty of room for capes to sweep.

Crush Bar

1743 N Cahuenga Boulevard, at Hollywood Boulevard, Hollywood (1-323 461 9017). Bus 163, 180, 181, 212/US 101, exit Cahuenga Boulevard south. **Open** 9pm-2am Fri, Sat. **Admission** 21s and over only; $8-$10. **Map 5 B1**
Setting out its stall with a white-on-black Hollywood-hero mural on its outside walls, the Crush Bar is not the youngest or the hippest Hollywood club, but it still makes a bid for being one of the most fun. Fridays and Saturdays present vintage Motown; Sunday is reggae night.

The Derby

4500 Los Feliz Boulevard, at Hillhurst Avenue, Los Feliz (1-323 663 8979). Bus 180, 181/US 101, exit Sunset Boulevard east. **Open** 4pm-2am daily.

*You'll feel in the **Pink** at Santa Monica's fave nightspot.*

Admission 21s and over only; $5 Mon, Tue, Thur, Sun; $7 Wed, Fri, Sat. **Credit** AmEx, MC, V. **Map 6 A1**
In a city smitten with swing dancing, sharp-dressed youth in the know can count on the Derby for floor-filling live music most nights of the week. Novices are welcome, and can join in a free swing lesson (8-9pm on Wednesdays and Sundays). Intermediate/advanced lessons are on Tuesdays. The Derby's circular bar in the middle of the ballroom with its 30ft (9m) high domed ceiling is the spot to be if you just want to watch. Dress nice or be sent packing.
Parking $3.50.

Florentine Gardens

5951 Hollywood Boulevard, between Bronson Avenue & N Gower Street, Hollywood (1-323 464 0706). Bus 1, 180, 181, 217, 429/US 101, exit Hollywood Boulevard west. **Open** 9pm-2am Thur, Sun; **Admission** 18s and over only; $8 Thur, Sun; $12 Fri, Sat. **Map 5 B1**
Where many hardened clubbers got their start, this cavernous danceteria is consistently packed with stylish kids (many of them Latino) who welcome the mix of funk, hip-hop, disco and techno. While the volume of the crowd transforms the free buffet into a mess-hall chow line, the eagerness of the tireless youth infuses the atmosphere with energy long after the most carefully constructed hairdo has wilted. Expect to queue to get in, and dress to impress to make sure that you do.

The Garage

4519 Santa Monica Boulevard, at Virgil Avenue, Silver Lake (1-323 683 3447/662 6802). Bus 4, 26, 304/US 101, exit Santa Monica Boulevard east. **Open** 5pm-3am Mon-Sun. **Admission** 21s and over only; $3-$8.
Map 6 A3
The formerly low-key Garage was recently renovated, expanded and emblazoned with hell-spawned firepaint (which stayed for a couple of weeks until complaining neighbours got it painted black). Call ahead to find out what's on offer: possibilities range from a grrrl-band agit-fest to a strictly dancehall knees-up to the weekly Cadillac Club (where the music is loud and grinding and tattoos and nasty

looks rule). Super-hip gay gals and their pals come for Meow Mix West (on Fridays). Don't forget Club Sucker, the Sunday afternoon punk-and-beerathon that has no real closing time, hosted by cross-dressing beauty Vaginal Creme Davis.

Goldfingers

6423 Yucca Street, between Wilcox Avenue & Cahuenga Boulevard, Hollywood (1-323 962 2913). Bus 1, 180, 210, 212/US 101, exit Sunset Boulevard west.
Admission 21s and over only; $5. **Map 5 A1**
For those who have tired of lolling around their space-age bachelor pads, Switched On (call for which night it's on) is the place for Moog grooves, bossa nova, Latin jazz, spy soundtracks, Italian softcore, 1960s pop chanteuses and modern experimentalists, all within the plush environs of Goldfinger's velvet walls. On Saturdays, Revolver proffers DJ Coyote Shivers giving up the best of the 1970s and 1980s as go-go dancers the Golden Pussycats do their thang. Not a great area of Hollywood, so keep your wits about you.

The Palace

For listings, see p209 **Music. Open** 9pm-3am Fri, Sat.
Admission 18s and over only; $10-$12. **Map 5 B1**
Located across the street from the landmark Capitol Records building, this cavernous blue edifice can – and does – hold a couple of thousand youngsters from all over the metropolitan area who file in as the rock crowd is leaving the gig just finished. With a 20,000-watt (translation: really loud) sound system at full power and a laser show, the Palace is anything but intimate. An upstairs balcony provides a refuge from smoking and the odd grope. Music is provided by radio station DJs, so the fare is predictably commercial club cuts, new-wave classics and alternative floor-fillers.

The Pink

2810 Main Street, between Ashland & Pier Avenues, Santa Monica (1-310 392 1077). Bus 33, 333, Santa Monica 1, 2, 10/I-10, exit Lincoln Boulevard south.
Open 10pm-2am Wed-Sun. **Admission** 21s and over only; $5-$10. **Map 2 A4**
A small Westside club with exposed brick walls and hard-

wood floors, home to an intimate, underground group of clubbers. Bump! on Wednesdays is LA's only speed garage night, and both Thursdays and Sundays feature drum 'n' bass. Cult DJ Jason Bentley – host of KCRW's night-time music show Metropolitan – dispenses justice on Thursdays, with name DJs such as Jun in the house at other times.

Rudolfo's

2500 Riverside Drive, at Fletcher Drive, Silver Lake (1-323 669 1226). Bus 93, 96, 201, 603/US 101, exit Silver Lake Boulevard east. **Open** 9pm-2am Sat, Sun (9pm-4am Dragstrip 66). **Admission** 21s and over only; $10; $15 Dragstrip 66. **Map 6 C2**
Featuring live bands and DJs, large patio and blasting sound system, this Silver Lake Mexican restaurant plays host to a slew of different clubs on different nights. But it earns its true notoriety when the seven-year-old Dragstrip 66 night (1-323 969 2596) goes off: a gender-bending, glamour-lovers crowd dances through themed nights such as 'Jesus, Mary – You're a Superstar'. The first and last Saturdays of the month offer Salsa Con Clase, a gay and lesbian salsa night.

Salsa Sundays

The Boathouse, 301 Santa Monica Pier, at Colorado Avenue, Santa Monica (1-310 393 6475). Bus 20, 33, Santa Monica 1, 7/I-10, exit Fourth/Fifth Streets north. **Open** 11am-2am daily. **Admission** under-21s only with adult; $5. **Map 2 A2/3**
This weekly club is a godsend for salsa devotees of all degrees, even novices. Instructor Albert Torres offers an afternoon lesson from 2-3pm, and then around 5pm the seasoned salsa dancers show up: the women in mini-skirts and heels, the men wearing loafers with slick bottoms. All ages welcome; plenty of spicy dancefloor fun to be had.

The Viper Room

8852 Sunset Boulevard, at Larrabee Street, West Hollywood (1-310 358 1880). Bus 2, 3, 105, 302, 429, DASH B/I-10, exit La Cienega Boulevard north. **Open** 9pm-2am Tue, Thur-Sat. **Admission** 21s and over only; $10-$15. **Map 4 A1**

The teeth-gnashing wait and surly doormen set the scene for this Johnny Depp-owned club, which will always be most famous for hosting River Phoenix's death. It's an uninviting, low-ceilinged sweatbox that specialises in funk and disco favourites while packing in Valley Girls and the guys who love them. Tuesday night is DJ Carbo's Atmosphere, a drum 'n' bass club that regularly grants guest slots to some of the genre's best DJs. There is also a whimsical and varied selection of live talent: if you can stand the collagen-enhanced crowd, this can be a wonderfully intimate spot to witness jam sessions by big-name artists.
Website: www.viperroom.com

The West End

1301 Fifth Street, at Arizona Avenue, Santa Monica (1-213 656 3905). Bus 4, 304, Santa Monica 1, 2, 3, 8/I-10, exit Fourth/Fifth Street north. **Open** 9pm-2am daily. **Admission** 21s and over only; $7. **Map 2 A2**
If you've spent the day on the Westside at the beach, and brought a change of clothes, this nearby club is a worthwhile bet. Rotating themed nights include reggae (Wed, Thur) and disco (Fri). Saturdays start at 4pm, when you can relive the 1980s all the way till 2am.

The World

7070 Hollywood Boulevard, at N Sycamore Avenue, Hollywood (1-323 467 7070). Bus 1, 180, 181, 212/US 101, exit Highland Avenue south. **Open** 10pm-3am Wed-Sat. **Admission** 18s and over only, except Wed; $7-$15. **Map 5 A1**
Once you realise that the World hosts clubs formerly held in a shopping mall, you'll understand the scented, weekend collegiate crowd. The most musically progressive night is Wednesday (all ages), when rave devotees revel in the light and sound of the large main room. Gothic-tinged Thursdays is the night for the club Perversion, where the black-clad go to see the more-goofy-than-titillating bondage show (real, nonetheless) and dance to industrial and techno in the aptly named, ambience-heavy Velvet Lounge.

Strip clubs

While New York's strippers have felt the chill wind of Mayor Guiliani's crackdown on sleaze, forcing many clubs to close their doors, Los Angeles still has plenty of flesh on display. Enthusiastic patrons such as Quentin Tarantino have made strip joints fashionable as hangouts for Hollywood players, male and female alike; in their wake have come hustling, networking execs, excited more by the whiff of a deal than the nudity on offer.

Crazy Girls (1433 N La Brea Avenue, at Sunset Boulevard, Hollywood; 1-323 969 0055) was used as a Pulp Fiction location and its VIP room, the Valentino Lounge, has hosted such eminent oglers as (if you believe every rumour you read) Julia Roberts, Geena Davis, Mick Jagger, Leonardo DiCaprio, Keanu Reeves, Nicolas Cage, Kevin Spacey and the entire cast of *Friends*. You'll find private table dancing, pool tables and giant-screen televised sports.

Other clubs' come-ons range from lingerie wrestling at **Hollywood Tropicana** (1250 N Western Avenue, at La Mirada Avenue, Hollywood; 1-323 464 1653) to the private rooms at **Paris House** (7527 Santa Monica Boulevard, between Gardner & Sierra Bonita Streets, West Hollywood; 1-323 876 0033), where the model of your choice will pose for you.

Two clubs where women and couples can feel welcome are neighbourhood joint **Cheetah's** (4600 Hollywood Boulevard, at Rodney Drive, Los Feliz; 1-323 660 6733) and the **Body Shop** (8250 Sunset Boulevard, at Harper Avenue, Hollywood; 1-323 656 1401), a venerable showgirl palace that stays open until 4am on Friday and Saturday.

Most clubs have newspaper ads redeemable for discounted or free admission, and some have free lunch buffets. To find out which porn star is performing where, check the listings hidden discreetly at the back of the *LA Times* sports pages.

Comedy clubs

Los Angeles is the commercial proving ground for aspiring US comedians. As such, it is a seething marketplace where the insatiable entertainment industry searches for the next megastar comedian. It's this make-or-break atmosphere that makes comedy clubs laugh-tastic funny farms or laugh-tastrophe torture. Perhaps surprisingly, the hunger for success pushes most comics towards innovation: even proven comics work relentlessly in LA, refining their 'quality minutes' and hoping for that career-making television or film deal.

In addition to the numerous touring comics who swing though LA, big names such as Jerry Seinfeld and Robin Williams flex their new material in surprise appearances around town. Many TV comedy writers use the clubs to stay sharp, and there are always countless newcomers waiting for their chance and working the various open-mike shows around town. Many clubs that used to feature only stand-up are now broadening their offerings to include sketch and improv comedy. While the number of venues may have decreased in the 1990s, there has been an overall increase in the quality of the comedy. Check the comedy section of the *LA Weekly* for up-to-date listings.

For a free night out with guaranteed star content, join the audience for the taping of a television sitcom; *see page 183* **Film**.

Aaah! Cappella

5907 Lankershim Boulevard, between Oxnard Avenue & Tiara Street, North Hollywood (1-818 509 6738). Bus 30, 31, 40, 42, 434, 439, DASH A, exit Burbank Boulevard east. **Open** 6pm-6am. **Admission** $5. **No credit cards.**
This 'theatrical café' is a second home for the House Full of Honkeys troupe and is part of the 'NoHo' (North Hollywood) bohemian coffeehouse scene, newly arisen amid much renovation of the neighbourhood.

Acme Comedy Theater

135 N La Brea Avenue, between Beverly Boulevard & First Street, Hollywood (1-323 525 0202). Bus 14, 212/ I-10, exit La Brea Avenue north. **Shows** 8pm, 10.30pm Fri, Sat; 7.30pm Sun. **Admission** $8-$14. **Credit** AmEx, MC, V. **Map 4 C2/3**
On a very happening thoroughfare (plenty of great bars and restaurants within laughing distance), this brand new theatre has three in-house performing sketch companies that provide a consistently good comedy product. The theatre is home to the Acme Players, known for their Acme Schmacme sketch comedy, and masters of improvisation House Full of Honkeys. Booking advisable.
Valet parking $2.75.

The Comedy Store

8433 Sunset Boulevard, at La Cienega Boulevard, West Hollywood (1-323 656 6225). Bus 2, 3, 429/I-10, exit La Cienega Boulevard north. **Open** 7.30pm-2am daily; show times vary. **Admission** $5-$15; 2-drink minimum. **Credit** AmEx, MC, V. **Map 4 A/B1**
Owned by Mitzi Shore, mom of Pauly Shore (current king of the adolescent B-movie wave), this warhorse of a comedy club, in the heart of Sunset Strip, has three rooms whose offerings run from A-list stand-up talent such as Roseanne

and Richard Pryor to sketch and comedy fledglings. It has been the birthplace of such megastars as Robin Williams, David Letterman and Sam Kinison, among others. Regular stand-up showcases include the Clean Comedy Show and the Gay and Lesbian Show.
Parking $6.

Groundling Theater

7307 Melrose Avenue, at Poinsettia Place, Hollywood (1-323 934 9700). Bus 2, 3, 429/I-10, exit Fairfax Avenue north. **Shows** 8pm Thur; 8pm, 10pm Fri, Sat; 7.30pm Sun. **Admission** $10-$17.50. **Credit** AmEx, MC, V. **Map 4 C2**
Located on hip-and-happening Melrose Avenue, this sketch and improv company is a hot ticket. The Groundlings have been around for over 20 years and still manage to produce sketch comedy that hits the mark with stunning consistency. Their ranks have spawned top talents such as Julia Sweeney, Jon Lovitz and Paul Reubens (aka Pee Wee Herman). On their improv jam night Cookin' with Gas (8pm Thur), you might find any number of celebrity guests riffing with the regulars. Booking advisable.
Valet parking at Tommy Tang's, 7473 Melrose Avenue, $3.50.

The Ice House

24 N Mentor Avenue, at Colorado Boulevard, Pasadena (1-818 577 1894). Bus 181, 188, 256, 401/I-110 to Arroyo Parkway, exit Colorado Boulevard east. **Shows** 8.30pm Tue-Thur; 8.30pm, 10.30pm Fri; 7pm, 9pm, 11pm Sat; 8pm Sun. **Admission** $8.50-$12.50; 2-drink minimum. **Credit** AmEx, MC, V.
One of the oldest comedy venues in the Los Angeles area, this Pasadena club has two rooms; the Ice House (stand-up) and the Ice House Annex (sketch). Talent ranges from the ridiculous to the sublime; usually, the sublime is to be found in the stand-up room.

The Improvisation

8162 Melrose Avenue, between Kilkea Drive & La Jolla Avenue, West Hollywood (1-323 651 2583). Bus 10, 11, DASH Fairfax/I-10, exit La Cienega Boulevard north. **Shows** 8pm Mon-Thur, Sun; 8pm, 10pm Fri; 8.30pm, 10.30pm Sat. **Admission** $8-$11. **Credit** AmEx, MC, V. **Map 4 B2**
Celebrity haunt and industry watering hole, the Improv is one of the highest rungs on the Hollywood comedy ladder. Deals – as well as drinks – are made at the bar nightly. Booking recommended.
Valet parking $3.50.

LA Connection

13442 Ventura Boulevard, between Woodman & Coldwater Canyon Avenues, Sherman Oaks (1-818 784 1868). Bus 424, 522, DASH Sherman Oaks/US 101, exit Coldwater Canyon Avenue south. **Shows** 9pm Thur; 8pm, 9pm, 10.30pm Fri; 7.30pm, 9pm, 10.30pm Sat; 3.30pm (improv for kids), 7pm, 8pm, 9pm Sun. **Admission** $7-$12. **Credit** MC, V.
The long-running LA Connection is a company of comics known for their live dubbing of B-movies. They offer numerous improv and sketch shows, which are funny but pretty predictable. Book in advance.

The Laugh Factory

8001 Sunset Boulevard, at Crescent Heights Boulevard, West Hollywood (1-323 656 1336). Bus 26, 163, 212, 217/I-10, exit Fairfax Avenue north. **Shows** 8pm Mon-Thur, Sun; 7.30pm, 10pm Fri, Sat. **Admission** $8-$10; 2-drink minimum. **Credit** MC, V. **Map 4 B1**
Another premier stand-up club with plenty of industry connections and big-time celebrity surprise appearances. Many comics who appear on the *Tonight Show* perform here.
Parking $3.

*Top talent and famous faces appear at the **Laugh Factory**.*

LunaPark

665 N Robertson Boulevard, at Santa Monica Boulevard, West Hollywood (1-310 652 0611). Bus 4, 10, 220, West Hollywood A, B, N/I-10, exit Robertson Boulevard north. **Open** *restaurant* 6.30-11pm Tue-Thur, Sun; 6.30pm-midnight Fri, Sat; *club* 6.30pm-2am daily; shows vary. **Admission** $5-$12. **Credit** AmEx, MC, V. **Map 4 A2**
LunaPark, with its two intimate stages, now features alternative comedy five nights a week, as well as showcasing live music. Acts usually perform here when they're hoping to generate some industry buzz. *See also p211* **Music**.

TheatreSports

1713 N Cahuenga Boulevard, at Hollywood Boulevard, Hollywood (1-323 469 9689). Bus 163, 180, 181, 212/ US 101, exit Cahuenga Boulevard south. **Shows** 8pm Mon, Thur; box office opens 7.30pm. **Admission** $8-$10. **No credit cards. Map 5 A/B1**
This critically acclaimed company is 100% improv. Running for the past ten years in infamous B-movie director Ed Wood's old theatre in the heart of Hollywood, they offer unique improv formats and consistent, dangerous fun. *Parking $3.*

Cabaret & cigar bars

LA has a smaller cabaret scene than New York or Las Vegas, but old-school swank and class can still be found. The cigar craze, meanwhile, is on the wane, but still has its followers. Stogie nirvana can be found at the **Grand Havana** in Beverly Hills (1-310 247 2900), but unless you're tight with Jack (Nicholson) or Arnold (Schwarzenegger), you'll need a miracle to get in – and at $2,000 for a locker in the humidor, who really cares?

Bloom's General Store

716 Traction Avenue, at Hewitt Street, Downtown (1-213 687 6571). Bus 16, DASH A, Montebello 14/ I-110, exit Fourth Street east. **Open** 8am-11pm Mon-Thur, Sun; 8am-11.30pm Fri, Sat. **No credit cards.**

Quite possibly the coolest place in LA to fire up a stogie, with over three dozen brands of hand-wrapped cigars.

The Gardenia Club

7066 Santa Monica Boulevard, at La Brea Avenue, Hollywood (1-323 467 7444). Bus 4, 212, West Hollywood A, B/I-10, exit La Brea Avenue north. **Open** *dinner* from 7pm, *show* 9pm, daily. **Admission** 21s and over only; $10; 2-drink minimum. **Credit** AmEx, MC, V. **Map 4 C1**
You're as likely to hear a Broadway veteran singing Cole Porter and Jerome Kern as you are to catch a Hollywood actress tackling Brian Wilson and Tom Waits. A no-frills, comfortable room and decent Italian food.

Masquers Cabaret & Dinner Theater

8334 W Third Street, between Kings Road & Orlando Avenue, West Hollywood (1-323 653 4848). Bus 14, 16, 105/I-10, exit La Cienega Boulevard north. **Open** *dinner* from 6pm, *show* 7.30pm, daily. **Credit** MC, V. **Map 4 B3**
With Moroccan and Italian food on the table, loud art on the walls and a mirror ball spinning overhead, the entertainment here ranges from improvised lounge acts to musical comedy to stand-up. All ages welcome.

San Gennaro Cigar Lounge

9543 Culver Boulevard, between Hughes Avenue & Robertson Boulevard, Culver City (1-310 836 0400). Bus 220, Commuter Express 438, Culver City 1, 4, 5/I-10, exit Robertson Boulevard south. **Open** 11am-10pm Mon-Thur; 11am-11pm Fri; 4-11pm, *show* 8.45pm, Sat; 4-10pm Sun. **Admission** $10; 2-drink minimum; free with dinner. **Credit** AmEx, MC, V.
Ol' Blue Eyes lives at this weekly tribute to Frank Sinatra (with other Brat Pack crooners tacked on).

The Wine Merchant

9713 Little Santa Monica Boulevard, at Roxbury Drive, Beverly Hills (1-310 278 0347). Bus 4, 20, 21, 22, 27/ I-405, exit Wilshire Boulevard east. **Open** 4pm-2am Mon-Fri; 6pm-2am Sat. **Credit** AmEx, MC, V. **Map 3 B2**
A sartorial wine bar, where people come to schmooze, booze and cruise (and smoke some rather fine cigars). Check out the Raj room for live music. Multiple screen coverage of your favourite sports events.

Sport & Fitness

Forget Scientology – the biggest religion in town is the cult of health, combining LA's worship of youth with Californian faith in self-improvement.

Not satisfied with keeping their lungs pure of cigarette smoke (the exhaust fumes coughed out by their cars are, of course, another matter), many Angelenos pursue fitness with the dedication of monks and the consumerist avidity of, well, Americans. Sports gadgets, clothing and fads are snapped up enthusiastically; supposedly fitness-enhancing diets are fretted over endlessly; gyms are popular pick-up joints; and it often seems that LA's schools prize athletes far above academics. If it raises a sweat, you can do it here, and get plenty of kudos for it.

The great outdoors

Bracketed by the San Gabriel Mountains and the Pacific Ocean, LA's natural habitat provides the opportunity for everything from rock climbing to wind skating, cycling to snowboarding. In spite of this, LA is the capital of indoor exercise: the city where people drive to the aerobics or step class. But you can do that anywhere. Few places can rival LA's incredible outdoor resources.

Aviation

Although introductory flights are mainly promotional ploys by small flying schools to get you to join, they're also a great chance to fly small aircraft without any previous experience.

At Santa Monica Airport, try **American Flyers** (1-310 390 2099; $99 for one hour in the air) or **Justice Aviation Services** (1-310 313 6792; introductory flights $35-$45). At Van Nuys Airport in the San Fernando Valley, the **Van Nuys Flight Centre** (1-818 994 7300) offers introductory flights for $49-$85.

Air Combat USA

230 N Dale Place, at Artesia Boulevard, Fullerton, Orange County (1-800 522-7590). Bus Orange County Transit 25/I-5, exit Artesia Boulevard east. **Open** 7am-6pm daily. **Credit** AmEx, MC, V.
This is *not* a flight simulator. Air Combat allows you to take control of an SF-260 Nato attack fighter and engage in a real-life dogfight. The price varies from $795 to $1,395 and includes a video of your flight. You leave from Fullerton Municipal Airport (about an hour's drive from LA) and all dogfights take place over the channel between Catalina Island and the mainland.

Beach volleyball: the quintessential Southern California sport.

Orbic Helicopters
16700 Roscoe Boulevard, between Balboa Boulevard & Woodley Avenue, Van Nuys (1-818 988 6532). Bus 152, 236, 418, Commuter Express 573, 574/I-405, exit Roscoe Boulevard west. **Open** 8am-6pm daily. **Credit** MC, V.
Operating out of Van Nuys Airport, demo flights cost $70-$90 for 25 minutes; tours are $85-$140.

Beach volleyball

In this mecca for volleyball, the best courts are on **Manhattan Beach** and **Santa Monica Beach**, just south of the pier. **Will Rogers State Beach** has courts south of the Santa Monica Canyon, near the parking lot, and **Manhattan Beach** hosts an annual Volleyball Open. A good resource is the **Volleyball Organization in Los Angeles** (VOILA), 8424A Santa Monica Boulevard, West Hollywood; contact Lance on 1-213 656 4319.

Cycling & mountain biking

It's easy to bike long distances in Los Angeles, so take the necessary precautions: plenty of water and some sunscreen. Riding off-road isn't actually legal, but there haven't been any efforts to stop the hundreds of cyclists that weave through the **Santa Monica Mountains**, home to the most popular and accessible MTBing areas: numerous fire trails jut off Mulholland Boulevard from Beverly Hills to Topanga and Malibu. You may have to squeeze under a gate or two, but keep pedalling until you reach the peaks. **Topanga State Park** (20825 Entrada Road, off Topanga Canyon Boulevard, Topanga; 1-310 455 2465) and **Malibu Creek State Park** (1925 Las Virgenes Road, off Malibu Canyon Road, Calabasas; 1-818 880 0350/ranger office 1-818 880 0367) may seem a little out of the way, but they're well worth it.

You can get a map of **Santa Monica** with marked bike trails from the Visitor's Information Center just north of Santa Monica Pier. South of LA, **Torrance** has an easy scenic ride that starts at Del Cerro Park and ends at Crenshaw Boulevard in the Palos Verdes Estates; you can ride there and back in less than three hours.

Oceanfront stalls (there are many in Venice) rent beach bikes, usually with one gear and pedal brakes, so for anything more serious, visit a proper bicycle shop.

Bicycle Ambulance
1423 Sixth Street, between Broadway & Santa Monica Boulevard, Santa Monica (1-310 395 5026). Bus 4, 304, Santa Monica 1, 7, 10/I-10, exit Fourth-Fifth Street north. **Open** 9am-6pm daily. **Credit** AmEx, MC, V. **Map 2 A2**
Mountain bikes cost $15 a day; 21-speeds $20 a day.

Spokes 'n' Stuff
7614 Santa Monica Boulevard, at Spaulding Avenue, West Hollywood (1-213 650 1076). Bus 4, DASH West Hollywood/I-10, exit Fairfax Avenue north. **Open** 10.30am-6pm Thur-Sun. **Credit** AmEx, Disc, MC, V. **Map 4 C1**

Mountain bikes cost $22 a day, suspension $10 a day extra, road bikes $14-$30 a day. There's a huge selection.
Branches: 175 Admiralty Way, at Via Marina, Marina del Rey (1-310 306 3332); Loews Hotel, 1700 Ocean Avenue, between Colorado Avenue & Pico Boulevard, Santa Monica (1-310 395 4748).

Bike paths
All bike paths except MTB routes are paved.
Griffith Park Over 14 miles (22km) of bike trails; can be hilly. Contact Woody's Bicycle World (3157 Los Feliz Boulevard, Griffith Park; 1-323 661 6665) for information about the park and rentals.
Kenneth Hill Bikeway This five-mile (8km) path in Pasadena starts at Arroyo Boulevard and heads to Arroyo Seco and the Rose Bowl.
South Bay Bicycle Trail Extends 22 miles (35km) from Will Rogers State Beach south to Torrance.
Sepulveda Basin Recreation Area 17015 Burbank Boulevard, at Woodley Avenue, Encino (1-818 893 8448). Flat bicycle paths for nine miles (14km). Best in winter.

Fishing

Free public fishing is popular at the piers of many local beaches: try **Santa Monica Pier** (the nearest), **Seal Beach**, **Redondo Beach** or **Manhattan Beach**. For freshwater fishing, try the public park system's **Echo Park Lake** (1-213 250 3578) and **Lincoln Park Lake** in Lincoln Heights (1-213 237 1726). A much bigger lake is **Castaic Lake** (*see page 223*). Fishing parties – fishing trips in someone else's boat – are a good way to get out and do some deep-sea fishing at a spot where the fish are biting.

Redondo Sport Fishing
233 N Harbor Drive, at Herondo Street, Redondo Beach (1-213 772 2064/1-310 372 2111). Bus 130, 439/I-405, exit Artesia Boulevard west. **Open** 5am-8pm daily. **Credit** Disc, MC, V.
The overnight trip ($70-$100 per person) leaves at 11pm; the ¾-day trip ($31 per person) leaves at 6am.

Vermont Fishing Tackle Company
10522 S Vermont Avenue, at 106th Street, Midtown (1-213 757 0277). Bus 119, 204, 354/I-110, exit Century Boulevard west. **Open** 7am-7pm Mon-Sat; 7am-1pm Sun. **Credit** AmEx, MC, V.
Come here for live worms, live crickets, live water dogs, night-crawlers, catfish bait, frozen bait and fishing equipment.

Hang-gliding

Windsports International
16145 Victory Boulevard, between Havenhurst & Woodley Avenues, Van Nuys (1-818 988 0111). Bus 164, 236/I-405, exit Victory Boulevard west. **Open** 10am-6pm Tue-Fri; 9am-noon Sat. **Credit** MC, V.
Locations vary, but you'll always launch from sloping hills where the wind turbulence is more predictable, not from cliffs. An introductory lesson costs $120.

Horse riding

While horse riding in LA has its aristocratic aspects (Brentwood girls and their polo ponies), it also taps into the Old West archetype of the cowboy. Rent-a-horse options are plentiful in these stables on the northern edge of Griffith Park, and at

Catch dinner for free off Santa Monica Pier. See page 221.

Sunset Ranch in the Hollywood Hills (*see page 63* Sightseeing):

Circle K Riding Stables
910 S Mariposa Street, at Riverside Drive, Burbank (1-818 843 9890). Bus 152/I-5, exit Alameda Avenue west. **Open** 7.30am-7pm Mon-Fri; 7.30am-6pm Sat, Sun. **Rates** $15 first hour; $10 each additional hour; $10 refundable deposit. **No credit cards.**

Los Angeles Equestrian Center
480 Riverside Drive, at Main Street, Burbank (office 1-818 840 9066/stables 1-818 840 8401). Bus 152/I-5, exit Alameda Avenue west. **Open** 8am-5pm daily. **Rates** *horses* $15 1 hour; $24 1½ hours; $28 2 hours; $15 refundable deposit; no under-12s. **No credit cards.**
A public stables located on the northern edge of Griffith Park, built for the 1984 Olympics, LAEC rents horses for trail rides and also provides a map of 43 miles (69km) of bridle paths within the park.

Rock climbing

One of the best natural climbing surfaces is at the southernmost end of Point Dume at **Zuma Beach** (*see page 52* Sightseeing). Indoor walls, such as this one in West LA, are also very popular:

Rocreation
11866 La Grange Avenue, at Bundy Drive, West LA (1-310 207 7199). Bus Santa Monica 9, 10, 14/I-10, exit Bundy Drive north. **Open** 11am-10pm Mon, Wed; 6am-10pm Tue, Thur; 11am-8pm Fri; 9am-7pm Sat, Sun. **Credit** MC, V. **Rates** $15 a day plus $5 gear hire; classes with gear $35-$40.

Rollerhockey

Pick-up games often take place at the beach parking lot just north of **Ocean Park**, in south Santa Monica, and at **West Hollywood Park and Recreation Center** (647 N San Vicente Boulevard; 1-213 848 6534).

Venice Roller Works
7 Westminster Avenue, at Speedway, Venice (1-310 450 0669). Bus Santa Monica 2/I-10, exit Lincoln Boulevard south. **Open** 10am-6pm Mon-Fri; 9am-6.30pm Sat, Sun. **Credit** AmEx, Disc, MC, V. **Map 2 A5**
This is the place to rent skates, pads and helmet ($10), sticks ($15) and balls ($2).

Scuba diving

The best places to dive are off **Leo Carillo State Beach**, **Laguna Beach**, **Redondo Beach** and **Palos Verdes**, but if you're really serious, head to **Catalina Island** (*see page 237* **Trips Out of Town**). Most of LA's coastline consists of miles of sloping sand, but Catalina has rocky shores with kelp beds, fish and even shipwrecks to explore.

Just Add Water Sports
1803 Lincoln Boulevard, suite A, at Michigan Avenue, Santa Monica (1-310 581 2717). Bus Santa Monica 3, 7/I-10, exit Lincoln Boulevard south. **Open** 10am-7pm Mon-Fri; 9am-5pm Sat, Sun. **Credit** MC, V. **Map 2 A/B3**
The PADI (Professional Association of Diving Instructors) certification course takes place over two weekends and includes two beach dives and one boat dive.

Splash/Dive
2490 Lincoln Boulevard, between Venice & Washington Boulevards, Venice (1-310 306 6733). Bus Santa Monica 3, 7, 8/I-10, exit Lincoln Boulevard south. **Open** 10am-6pm Mon-Sat; 11am-5pm Sun. **Credit** AmEx, MC, V. **Map 2 B5**
As well as offering gear rental (to certified divers only), Splash runs a two-week certification course costing $295 ($320 if you have your own gear).

Skateboarding & rollerblading

Los Angeles has a vibrant street skating culture, with pro teams such as Hook-Ups, Woodstock, Girl and Chocolate (Girl's predominantly Latino brother company). The scene is documented irreverently in the Larry Flynt-owned Hollywood magazine *Big Brother* ($3.99). Small, street-style public parks in Temecula and Huntington Beach have regular quality skate sessions and skaters rehearse tricks near the basketball courts at Venice Beach. Large-scale skate parks are also making a comeback: at the end of 1998, shoe manufacturer Vans is opening what is billed as 'the Disneyland of all skate parks' in a new $165 million mall, the Block, in Orange County. The indoor/outdoor park will have birch ramps, waxy ledges, a street course and a 70-foot (21-metre) wide replica of the legendary Upland Pipeline combi pool that was bulldozed a decade ago.

Rollerblading (inline skating) is everywhere. The best and safest places to skate are **Ocean Front Walk** in Venice Beach and **Griffith Park**.

The Skate Lab Skate Park

4246 Valley Fair Street, off Capitol Street, Simi Valley (1-805 578 0040). US 118, exit Stearns Street south. **Open** times vary; call for details. **Admission** $5 Mon-Thur; $7 Fri-Sun; $3 day membership. **Credit** MC, V.
Travelling skaters should definitely check out this new, inexpensive, uncrowded park about a 50-minute drive from LA. Owned by Dodger pitcher Scott Radinsky, it's an awesome place, complete with half-pipe and numerous smaller ramps and obstacles. Under-18s require a parent's signature on a release form; over-18s must bring photo ID.
Website: www.skatelab.com

ZJ Boarding House

2619 Main Street, at Ocean Park Boulevard, Santa Monica (1-310 392 5646). Bus 33, Santa Monica 1, 2, 8, 10/I-10, exit Lincoln Boulevard south. **Open** 9am-8pm Mon-Sat; 9am-6pm Sun. **Credit** AmEx, Disc, MC, V.
Map 2 A3/4
Top-of-the-line skateboards and accessories for rent. Also snowboards ($25 a day), boots ($10), boot-and-board package ($30), surfboards ($25 a day, $15 a half-day) and wetsuits ($10 a day, $5 a half-day).

Skiing & snowboarding

See page 248 **Trips Out of Town**.

Skydiving

Perris Valley Skydiving School

2091 Goetz Road, Perris, Riverside County (1-800 832 8818). I-215, exit D south-east (one-way). **Open** 9am-7pm daily. **Credit** AmEx, Disc, MC, V.
A two-hour drive south-east of LA. Dives cost from $175.

California City Skydiving Center

6401 Shepard Place, California City (1-800 258 6744). Hwy 14, exit California City Boulevard east. **Open** 8am-4.30pm Mon-Thur; 8am-sunset Fri-Sun; call for reservations. **Credit** AmEx, MC, V.
A 90-minute drive north of LA. Costs range from $159-$279.

Swimming

If you want a change from the saltwater bodysurfing of the beach, there are a number of placid freshwater alternatives. At **Echo Park Lake**

Recreation Center (1632 Bellevue Avenue, at Glendale Boulevard; 1-213 250 3578) there is an outdoor swimming pool at the lake and an indoor pool just down the street at the recreation centre. The lake itself is for fishing, not swimming, though you can rent a paddle boat to explore its cool, lotus-filled environs.

Castaic Lake (1-805 257 4050), less than an hour outside of LA (head north on the I-5), is one of SoCal's nicest lakes. The cordoned-off swimming area is relatively small, but all power boats are confined to the upper lake, preserving the calm. Six dollars admits a car (and as many people, frisbees and picnic items as you can pack inside) to the lake all day.

The city's **YMCAs** (*see page 227*) also have swimming pools.

Watercraft

Watercraft fall into two categories: motorised (such as jet skis) and manual (such as sea kayaks). It's all about how much you want to pay, how much you want to exert yourself and how you want to experience the water.

Action Water Sports

4144 Lincoln Boulevard, between Maxella Avenue & Washington Boulevard, Marina del Rey (1-310 306 9539). Bus Santa Monica 3, 7, 8/I-10, exit Lincoln Boulevard south. **Open** 10am-6pm Mon-Sat; 11am-5pm Sun. **Credit** AmEx, MC, V.
Surf-style kayaks cost from $35 a day to rent. Jet skis are $70-$90 for 90 minutes.

Malibu Ocean Sports

22935 Pacific Coast Highway, at Malibu Pier, Malibu (surf shop 1-310 456 6302/kayak centre 1-310 456 8213). Bus 434/I-10, exit PCH north. **Open** 10am-6pm daily. **Credit** AmEx, Disc, MC, V.
Kayak rentals are $49 a person; 'moonlight paddles' $44.

Marina Boat Rentals

Fisherman's Village, 13719 Fiji Way, Marina del Rey (1-310 574 2822). Bus 220/I-10, exit Lincoln Boulevard south. **Open** 11am-5pm Mon-Fri; 10am-6pm Sat, Sun. **Credit** AmEx, MC, V.
Wave runners ($65 per hour); kayaks ($10 for a single, $15 double); electric boats ($45 per hour).

Nature Tours

1666 Euclid Street, at Colorado Avenue, Santa Monica (1-310 453 8754). Bus Santa Monica 9, 11/I-10, exit Lincoln Boulevard south. **Open** 8am-6pm daily.
No credit cards. Map 2 B2/3
You can rent wave runners and jet skis ($85-$90 per hour; $200 cash deposit) and also take tours.

Wind skating

WindSkate

Beach parking lots at Ocean Park & Santa Monica (1-310 453 4808). Call for an appointment.
Jamie Budget doesn't have a store but relies on demonstrations near Santa Monica Beach to attract custom. If you see someone clutching a hand-held sail device that propels them on their skateboard or rollerblades, it's probably a WindSkate. The sails cost $7 an hour or $25 a day.

Participation sports

Baseball batting cages

For those looking for the thrill of swinging a base-ball bat at an oncoming ball made of catgut and horsehide, there are a number of batting cages with automated pitching machines that throw at various speeds. Bats and helmets are provided.

Batting Practice

620 E Colorado Street, at Glendale Avenue, Glendale (1-818 243 2363). Bus 90, 91, 183/US 134, exit Glendale Avenue south. **Open** 11.30am-10pm Mon-Fri; 9am-10pm Sat; 9am-8.30pm Sun. **Rates** $7.50 per 15 mins; $19.50 per hour. **No credit cards.**
Open since 1965, with each pitching machine named after a classic Dodgers pitcher (Koufax, Sutton, Drysdale et al).

The Batcade

220 N Victory Boulevard, between Magnolia Boulevard & Olive Avenue, Burbank (1-818 842 6455). Bus 96, 152, 183/US 134, exit Alameda Avenue north. **Open** 10am-10pm Mon-Fri; 10am-midnight Sat, Sun. **Rates** $7 per 15 mins; $22 per hour. **Credit** AmEx, MC, V.
A new, hi-tech place, with a fierce machine that pitches at 90mph (144kph).

Bowling

There are plenty of places to bowl in the Los Angeles area; for details, call the **Southern California Bowling Proprietors Association** on 1-818 972 1112.

Strike one: **Batting Practice** *in Glendale.*

Bay Shore Bowl

234 Pico Boulevard, between Fourth & Main Streets, Santa Monica (1-310 399 7731). Bus 20, 33, 434, Santa Monica 1, 7, 8/I-10, exit Fourth Street south. **Open** 9am-midnight Mon-Thur, Sun; 9am-1am Fri, Sat. **Rates** $3.50 per person; $2.50 non-refundable shoe deposit. **Credit** AmEx, MC, V. **Map 2 A3**
This 24-lane alley includes the swanky Red Carpet Lounge, home to twin bartenders the Trimbel sisters (*see* **Red Carpet Lounge** *p147* **Bars**).

Hollywood Star Lanes

5227 Santa Monica Boulevard, between Hobart Boulevard & Kingsley Drive, Hollywood (1-323 665 4111). Bus 4/US 101, exit Santa Monica Boulevard east. **Open** 24 hours daily. **Rates** $3 per person (includes shoe rental). **No credit cards. Map 5 C2**
This is the place where the Coen brothers filmed *The Big Lebowski*. It's a hotspot for swinging singles, with a cocktail lounge and a coffeeshop.

Golf

The superstar popularity of Tiger Woods has expanded interest in golf among all age and ethnic groups across the US, and Los Angeles is no excep-tion. With its ideal weather conditions and numer-ous public courses, this is the perfect city for the novice or pro to get in a round; an LA reservation card (available from any public course), allows you to book in advance. The rise of female pro Se Ri Pak mirrors the popularity of golf among LA's one million Koreans, and a number of multi-tiered driving ranges in Koreatown can be found through the **Korean American Pro Golf Association** (1-562 802 0307).

Griffith Park Golf Courses

4730 Crystal Springs Drive, Griffith Park (course 1-323 663 2555/shop 1-323 664 2255). Bus 96/I-5, exit Crystal Springs Drive north. **Open** 6am-6pm daily.
There are two 18-hole championship courses and two nine-hole courses within Griffith Park. You can rent equipment at the pro shop. A round costs $17 weekdays, $22 weekends. Carts are $20.

Los Feliz Golf Course

3207 Los Feliz Boulevard, between the I-5 & Garden Avenue, Los Feliz (1-323 661 2355). Bus 180, 181/ I-5, exit Los Feliz Boulevard east. **Open** 7am-6pm or sunset daily.
A public nine-hole, par three course, meaning you only need your wedge and putter, leaving your other hand free to carry a six-pack. The LA River is one of the course boundaries. It costs only $4.50 to play a round and tee time reservations are not necessary. There's an Eatz coffeeshop on site.

Rancho Park Golf Course

10460 W Pico Boulevard, between Motor & Patricia Avenues, Rancho Park (1-310 838 7373). Bus Culver City 3, Commuter Express 431, Santa Monica 7, 13/ I-10, exit Overland Avenue north. **Open** 6am-6.30pm daily. **Map 3 B4**
Rancho Park (18-hole, par 71) claims to have more traffic than any other course in the world, which means that a) it's one of the nicest courses in LA and b) it's one of the hardest to get on. It costs $20-$25 to play.

Sepulveda Golf Complex

Balboa & Encino courses: 16821 Burbank Boulevard, at Balboa Boulevard, Encino (1-818 995 1170). Bus 154,

236, 573, Commuter Express 574/US 101, exit Balboa Boulevard south.
Woodley Lake course: 6331 Woodley Avenue, at Victory Boulevard, Van Nuys (1-818 780 6886). Bus 164, 236/ I-405, exit Burbank Boulevard west.
Both **Open** *6.30am-7pm daily.*
Balboa is an 18-hole, par 70 course, and both the Encino and Woodley courses are 18-hole, par 72. A round costs $17 during the week and $22 at weekends. Equipment and golf carts are available.

Ice hockey & ice skating

Ice hockey does exist under the sun. In fact, bizarrely, this traditionally winter sport is very popular in LA – more proof (if any were needed) that Angelenos love to defy nature. The local pro team, the **LA Kings**, has a loyal following and the strong non-LA-native population, including many displaced East Coasters, means there are plenty of opportunities to get in on a game. Regular ice skating sessions also exist.

Culver City Ice Arena
4545 Sepulveda Boulevard, at Braddock Drive, Culver City (1-310 398 5719). Bus Culver City 6/I-405, exit Sawtelle Boulevard south. **Open** *times vary; call for details.* **Credit** MC, V.
From 12.30-5pm Mon-Fri, it costs $8 to skate ($2 skate rental). There are pick-up games on Tuesdays, Thursdays and Fridays ($13).

Pool & billiards

You'll find a pool table in most bars and bowling alleys. But if you want the freedom to play as long as you like, try one of these:

Gotham Hall
1431 Third Street Promenade, between Broadway & Santa Monica Boulevard, Santa Monica (1-310 394 8865). Bus 4, 304, Santa Monica 1, 2, 3, 8/I-10, exit Fourth Street north. **Open** *4pm-2am Mon-Fri; 3pm-2am Sat, Sun.* **Rates** $7-$14 per hour. **Credit** AmEx, Disc, MC, V. **Map 2 A2**
A very swanky establishment in Santa Monica's popular, pedestrian-only shopping area. Dress up and bring a cigar.

Hollywood Billiards
5750 Hollywood Boulevard, between Van Ness Avenue & N Wilton Place, Hollywood (1-323 465 0115). Bus 1, 4/US 101, exit Hollywood Boulevard east. **Open** 11am-3am Mon-Thur; 11am-6am Fri; 1pm-6am Sat; 1pm-3am Sun. **Rates** $6 per hour for two players; *after 6pm* $11 per hour. **Credit** AmEx, Disc, MC, V. **Map 5 B1**
A new location for Hollywood Billiards: the original one burned down. It has a nice interior and a relaxed atmosphere. Dress presentably.

Yankee Doodles
1410 Third Street Promenade, between Broadway & Santa Monica Boulevard, Santa Monica (1-310 394 4632). Bus 4, 304, Santa Monica 1, 2, 3, 8/I-10, exit Fourth Street north. **Open** 11am-2am daily.
Rates $6-$12 per hour. **Credit** AmEx, MC, V.
Map 2 A2
Sports bar Yankee's has 30 pool tables, four foosball tables, a free-throw and football toss. There are also 42 monitors and eight big-screen TVs showing satellite sports all day. What more could a sports fan want?

Rollerskating

What was a disco-era leisure novelty has evolved and now thrives at LA's coolest roller rinks.

Moonlight Rollerway
5110 San Fernando Road, between Broadway & Glendale Avenues, Glendale (1-626 241 3630). Bus 94/US 134, exit San Fernando Road south. **Open** 1.30-4pm, 8.30-10.30pm, Mon; 1.30-4pm, 8-10.30pm, Tue, Wed; 1.30-4pm Thur; 1.30-4pm, 7.30-11pm, Fri; 7.30-11pm Sat.
Admission $4.25-$6; $2 skate rental. **No credit cards**.
Home to rollerdancing since the 1950s, Monday nights here (adults only) feature a young, hip, professional crowd. It's also the base of an organist who is one of the premier composers of roller rink music on the Rinx record label.

World On Wheels
Midtown Shopping Center, 4645½ Venice Boulevard, at San Vincente Boulevard, Midtown (1-213 933 3333). Bus 33/I-10, exit Fairfax Avenue. **Open** call for times.
Admission $4-$8 (includes skates). **No credit cards**.
Map 5 A5
A live DJ and full bar. The music is usually funk and oldies, except on Friday, which is gospel night.

Tennis & racquetball

You can find tennis and racquetball courts at most gyms and recreation centres throughout LA; book a couple of days in advance. **Griffith Park** also has tennis courts ($6 per hour) at two sites – 12 lit ones at Griffith/Riverside (1-323 661 5318) and 12 unlit ones at Griffith/Vermont Canyon (1-323 664 3521). On weekdays before 6pm, they're available on a first come, first served basis; after 4pm you can book if you have a registration card (open to non-residents).

Marina Tennis Center
13199 Mindanao Way, at Glencoe Avenue, Marina del Rey (1-310 822 2255). Bus 108, 220, Commuter Express 437/Hwy 90, exit Mindanao Way north. **Open** 8am-10pm Mon-Fri; 8am-6pm Sat, Sun. **Courts** $12-$14 per hour. **No credit cards**.

Rustic Canyon Recreation Center
601 Latimer Road, between Brooktree & Hiltree Roads, Santa Monica (1-310 454 5734). Bus 2, 576, Commuter Express 430, Santa Monica 9/I-405, exit Sunset Boulevard west. **Open** 9am-9.30pm Mon-Thur; 9am-5.30pm Fri; 9am-5pm Sat; 10am-5pm Sun.
No credit cards.

The Tennis Place
5880 W Third Street, at Cochran Avenue, Mid Wilshire (1-323 936 9900). Bus 16, DASH Fairfax/I-10, exit La Brea Avenue north. **Open** 7am-11pm daily.
Courts $13-$15 per hour. **Credit** MC, V.
Map 5 A4

Fitness
Circuit sculpting

Dove's Bodies
4010 Colfax Avenue, at Ventura Boulevard, Studio City (1-818 980 7866). Bus 424, 522/US 101, exit Laurel Canyon Boulevard south. **Open** call for times.
An inspired, customised yet ever-evolving workout class that will melt fat, firm, tone and define.

Dance classes & Pilates

Classes vary, so call for details of times and prices.

Arthur Murray Studio

262 N Beverly Drive, between Dayton Way & Wilshire Boulevard, Beverly Hills (1-310 274 8867). Bus 4, 20, 21, 22, 27, DASH Beverly Hills/I-10, exit Robertson Boulevard north. **Credit** AmEx, MC, V. **Map 3 C2**
A conservative dance studio that will teach you just about any step from ballroom to swing. However, the studio will want you to sign up for a whole course and it can get costly. Group classes are 10am-2pm Sat, so the best times for individual instruction are 1-10pm weekdays.

Delane Vaughn's Jazz Class

Alley Kat Studios, 1455 Gordon Street, at Sunset Boulevard, Hollywood (1-213 462 1755). Bus 2, 3, 210, 212/US 101, exit Vine Street south. **No credit cards. Map 5 B2**
The most inventive dance class in LA. Just listen to Delane's funky music selections and imitate his jaguar-like moves. Classes are usually held 6-7.30pm Wed and 10.30am-noon Sat.

Lichine Ballet Academy

405 N Foothill Road, between Burton Way & Civic Center Drive, Beverly Hills (1-310 276 5202). Bus 4, 14, 27, 576/I-10, exit Robertson Boulevard north. **No credit cards. Map 3 C2**
Darling, old-fashioned, one-room dance studio in Beverly Hills offering Russian ballet to all ages and levels.

Live Art Studios

1100 S Beverly Drive, suite 20, between Olympic & Pico Boulevards, Beverly Hills (1-310 277 9536). Bus 3, Santa Monica 5, 7/I-10, exit Robertson Boulevard north. **Map 3 C3**

Angels, towers, erotica (exercises), transformers, magic circles and wands (equipment) make up Pilates, a meditative, low-impact form of exercise designed to lengthen as much as strengthen. It was invented in the late 1920s and has been practised for years by dancers. Siri Dharma Galliano's clients at Live Art have included Glenn Close, Dennis Quaid and Jessica Lange. Call for an appointment.

Gyms

Gyms have sprouted in LA faster than Starbucks and Blockbuster combined; the following are open to non-members. YMCAs (*see below*) often have gyms. For gay-oriented gyms, *see page 188* **Gay & Lesbian**.

Family Fitness Center

9911 Pico Boulevard, floor A, between Roxbury Drive & Century Park East, Century City (1-310 553 7600). Bus Santa Monica 7, 13/I-405, exit Santa Monica Boulevard east. **Open** 24 hours Mon-Thur; 5am-11pm Fri; 6am-8pm Sat; 7am-8pm Sun. **Map 3 B/C 3/4**
Weights, aerobics and even cardio-kickboxing. For non-members, admission costs $10 a day.
Branches: 1500 Rosecrans Avenue, between Aviation & Sepulveda Boulevards, Manhattan Beach (1-310 536 9300); 465 N Halstead Street, at Rosemead Avenue, Pasadena (1-818 351 2222).

Gold's Gym

360 Hampton Drive, at Rose Avenue, Venice (1-310 392 6004). Bus 33, 436, Santa Monica 1, 2/I-10, exit Lincoln Boulevard south. **Open** 4am-midnight Mon-Fri; 5am-midnight Sat, Sun. **Credit** AmEx, Disc, MC, V. **Map 2 A4**

There she blows!

Whale watching provides California's most extraordinary wildlife experience, and if you're in the area at the right time it's not to be missed. The annual season off Southern California's coastline is in winter (from December to March), following the migratory habits of the grey and Wright whales, the two most commonly seen species. In the Santa Barbara area (north of LA), whale watching reaches its peak in summer. In recent years, a group of 800 humpback whales has been summering off Santa Barbara, and blue whales are known to show there as well. For an idea of how impressive these acquatic behemoths are, consider that a blue whale's *tongue* is a large as an African elephant, while the smaller humpbacks can measure up to 50 feet (15 metres) and weigh 100 tons. The whale-watching boats get surprisingly close, so that the power and size of these beasts are stunningly apparent.

Most marinas have numerous boats offering whale-watching trips and most operate on a 'sightings guaranteed' basis: if you don't see any whales, your money is refunded. Try these:

Catalina Cruises

320 Goldenshore Boulevard, at I-710, Long Beach (1-800 228 2546). Metro Transit Mall/bus Long Beach Transit Roundabout C/I-405, exit I-710 south. **Cost** $15; $10 3-11s. **Credit** AmEx, MC, V.

Sea Landing

Santa Barbara Harbor, off Harbor Way, Santa Barbara (1-805 963 3564).US 101, exit Cabrillo Way west. **Trips** Feb-Apr 9am, noon, 3pm; *July-Sept* 8am-5pm. **Cost** $24-$65; $14-$35 5-12s. **Credit** Disc, MC, V.
Captain Fred Benko and the 88ft (27m) luxury boat *Condor* (with a restaurant and full bar) bring you to the humpback whales feeding all summer (until mid-September) off Santa Barbara. Expeditions are guided by naturalists from the Santa Barbara Museum of Natural History, and include a stop at the Painted Cave, the world's largest underground sea cave.
Website: www.condorcruises.com

22nd Street Landing

141 W 22nd Street, between Via Cabrillo Marina & Outer Street, San Pedro (1-310 832 8304). Bus 446/ I-110, exit Gaffey Street south. **Cost** $14. **Credit** MC, V.
Trips run from January to March from 10am-1pm weekdays and 11.30am-2pm weekends.

Golf driving ranges are all the rage, especially in Koreatown.

'The mecca of bodybuilding' is how this truly impressive Temple of the Bod bills itself. Pay $15 a day or $50 a week. *Website: www.goldsgymla.com*
Branch: 1016 Cole Avenue, at Santa Monica Boulevard, Hollywood (1-323 462 7012).

Hollywood Gym & Fitness Center
1551 N La Brea Avenue, between Hawthorn Avenue & Sunset Boulevard, Hollywood (1-323 845 1420). Bus 107, 212/US 101, exit Highland Avenue south. **Open** 24 hours daily. **Credit** AmEx, MC, V. **Map 5 A1/2**
Yoga, Nautilus, free weights, aerobics, sauna and chiropractic facility. A day pass is $10; kickboxing is $15 a class.

Marina Athletic Club
12980 Culver Boulevard, between Lincoln Boulevard & Hwy 90, Marina del Rey (1-310 301 2582). Bus 220, Santa Monica 3/Hwy 90, exit Mindanao Way. **Open** 5am-midnight Mon-Fri; 5.30am-10pm Sat, Sun. **Credit** AmEx, DC, MC, V.
Lap pool, track, spinning cycles, volleyball/basketball gym, step aerobics, yoga, Jacuzzi – all within a cool, industrial-style hangar. A day pass costs $10.

YMCAs
For details of other locations, call 1-800 872 9622.

Hollywood Wilshire YMCA
1553 N Schrader Boulevard, between Sunset Avenue & Selma Avenue, Hollywood (1-323 467 4161). Bus 2, 3/ US 101, exit Sunset Boulevard west. **Open** 6am-10pm Mon-Fri; 8am-6pm Sat; 8am-4pm Sun. **Credit** Disc, MC, V. **Map 5 A1/2**
Facilities include racquetball and handball courts, free weights, Nautilus machines, running and rowing machines, boxing, aerobics, yoga, lap pool, spa and two basketball courts. Non-members pay $10 a day.

Santa Monica Family YMCA
1332 Sixth Street, between Santa Monica Boulevard & Arizona Avenue, Santa Monica (1-310 393 2721). Bus 4, 304, Santa Monica 1, 7, 10/I-10, exit Fifth Street north. **Open** 6am-10pm Mon-Fri; 7am-7pm Sat; 11am-7pm Sun. **Credit** MC, V. **Map 2 A2**

You'll find racquetball and handball courts, free weights, boxing, aerobics, a lap pool, spa, pick-up basketball and volleyball – and a running track on the roof. Non-members pay $10 a day.

Stuart M Ketchum Downtown YMCA
401 S Hope Street, at Fourth Street, Downtown (1-213 624 2348). Bus Commuter Express 423, 430, 437/I-110, exit Ninth Street east. **Open** 5.30am-9.30pm Mon-Fri; 8am-4.30pm Sat; 9am-3.30pm Sun. **Credit** MC, V. **Map 7 B2**
An indoor lap pool, running track, squash, racquetball and tennis courts. Non-members pay $10-$15 a day.

Yoga
Currently something of an obsession, particularly among professional women in their thirties and forties. Their role model may be Madonna, a recent devotee; her song *Shanti/Ashtangi* on the 1998 album *Ray of Light* is based on a Sanskrit chant she uses in yoga.

Govinda's Yoga Studio
3765 Watseka Avenue, suite C, at Venice Boulevard, Culver City (1-310 815 0105). Bus 33, Santa Monica 12/ I-10, exit Robertson Boulevard south. **No credit cards.**
At Govinda's, all postures and breathing exercises are taught in accordance with the method of BKS Iyengar, the pre-eminent yoga teacher in the world. His scientific approach to hatha yoga instruction is particularly relevant to Western culture, in that weak parts of the body are strengthened and stiff areas are made more flexible. There are two to four classes a day.

BKS Iyengar Yoga Institute of LA
8233 W Third Street, between La Jolla & Orlando Avenues, West Hollywood (1-323 653 0357). Bus 16, DASH Fairfax/I-10, exit Fairfax Avenue north. **No credit cards. Map 4 B3**
Start your class with an incantation and ease into Iyengar, which involves various props including ropes, tables and walls. A type of meditation in action.

Yoga Center West

1535 S Robertson Boulevard, at Cashio Street, Midtown (1-310 552 4647). Bus 220/I-10, exit Robertson Boulevard north. **Open** 10am-8pm daily. **Credit** MC, V. **Map 4 A4**

Classes in Kundalini yoga and stress reduction for all levels, from beginners to teachers-in-training. Choose from about 35 classes a week; prices range from $8-$14.

Yoga Works

1426 Montana Avenue, between 14th & 15th Streets, Santa Monica (1-310 393 5150). Bus 3, Santa Monica 3/ I-10, exit Lincoln Boulevard north. **Open** 6.30am-7.15pm (last class) Mon-Fri; 7.30am-5.30pm Sat; 8am-6.30pm Sun. **Credit** AmEx, MC, V. **Map 2 B1**

Astanga and Iyengar yoga are taught here. There's another branch in Santa Monica, at 2215 Main Street.

Spectator sports

There are very few days each year when there isn't at least one professional sporting event happening in LA. As one of the two largest sports markets in the US, LA features an abundance of athletic franchises, although there are some oddities: there is no longer an American football team in town (both the Rams and the Raiders have left) but there are three pro basketball teams (Lakers, Clippers and Sparks).

LA has twice hosted the Olympics (1932 and 1984) and once the World Cup Final (1994, at the Rose Bowl in Pasadena), but its trend of consistently superb home teams has wavered of late. Major league baseball's Dodgers have undergone a complete overhaul under new owner Rupert Murdoch, as the decades-old policy of building the team from within has been axed in favour of rash trades and managerial firings. In NBA basketball, the Lakers, featuring superstar Shaquile O'Neal and hot prospect Kobe Bryant, cruised into the 1998 playoffs only to fall hard in the first round. Nevertheless, the Lakers remain superior to the Clippers' brand of hapless hoops.

LA's sports map is due for a big change soon, as the Lakers and ice hockey's Kings abandon the Great Western Forum in Inglewood to join the Clippers in the glitzy Staples Center in Downtown; currently under construction, it is due to open in October 1999.

Finally, the local pro soccer team, the Galaxy, continues to draw some of the biggest crowds in town to the Rose Bowl in Pasadena, including a large Salvadoran turnout to see their native star player Cienfuegos.

INFORMATION & TICKETS

The sports section of the *LA Times* is one of the better parts of the paper; the Calendar lists the team fixtures and broadcast schedules for the day. There are magazines and papers for every sport: *ESPN Magazine* ($3.99) and *Sports Illustrated* ($3.50) provide well-written and fairly comprehensive general coverage of US sports.

The best place to go for tickets are the teams' box offices. Ticket agencies charge booking fees, but sometimes it's the only way to get a ticket (look in the *Yellow Pages* under 'Ticket'). A riskier approach is to buy tickets from unauthorised touts (scalpers) who wait outside the venue before the event; generally, the closer to the starting time, the cheaper such tickets become. For Dodgers games, scalpers can be found just off Sunset Boulevard at the Elysian Fields entrance to Chavez Ravine.

American football

The only options are **UCLA** (tickets 1-310 825 2101) and **USC** (tickets 1-213 740 4672), both strong college teams. The season runs from September to the end of January.

UCLA Bruins

Rose Bowl, 1001 Rose Bowl Drive, at Arroyo Boulevard, Pasadena (1-818 577 3100). Bus 177/Hwy 134, exit Orange Grove Boulevard north.

USC Trojans

Los Angeles Memorial Coliseum, 3911 S Figueroa Street, at Martin Luther King Jr Boulevard, Downtown (1-213 747 7111). Bus 40, 42/I-110, exit Martin Luther King Jr Boulevard west.

Baseball

Settling in LA after leaving their original home in Brooklyn 35 years ago, the **LA Dodgers** (1-213 224 1500) couldn't quite capitalise on the five consecutive Rookie of the Year winners it fielded to start the 1990s, and by midway through the 1998 season the new Fox Sports ownership had changed the roster dramatically, trading away marquee players like Mike Piazza and Hideo Nomo – much to the fans' disgruntlement. One mainstay at the ballpark is organist Nancy Bea Hefley, whose musical selection adds an old-school flavour to the spectacle. It's been ten years since the Dodgers won the World Series, and the next few years will be a rebuilding process. Dodgers Stadium in lovely Chavez Ravine is a must if only for its spectacular site and famous 'Dodger dogs'.

The **California Angels** (1-714 937 7200) play in Anaheim in Orange County; they are contenders for the American League West division title, and their Disney-renovated ballpark (renamed Edison Field) has a classic look (discounting the foam-core rock formations in centrefield). Among the Angels to watch for are superb hitters Jim Edmonds and Darin Erstad.

The baseball season runs from April to October.

Dodgers Stadium

1000 Elysian Park, at Stadium Way, Echo Park (1-213 224 1400). Bus 1, 2, 3, 4/I-110, exit Dodger Stadium north. **Open** 8.30am-5.30pm Mon-Sat & days of games. **Tickets** $6-$11. **Credit** MC, V.

Making waves

Be warned – learning to surf is difficult. It can take weeks just to learn to sit on the board properly, let alone negotiate the white-wash. Windsurfing is even harder. Most novices opt for the easier-to-learn alternatives: boogie-boards (aka bodyboards), bodysurfing and skimboarding. If you're learning to surf, choose a wide-open beach break such as **Zuma Beach** (1-310 457 9891); **Will Rogers State Beach** (1-310 451 2906) – the surfing is best where Sunset Boulevard meets the Pacific Coast Highway; **Santa Monica Beach** (1-310 458 8311); or El Porto, at **Manhattan Beach**.

Excellent beach breaks for intermediate surfers can be found at **Manhattan, Hermosa, Redondo** and **Huntington Beaches**. Only experienced surfers should test their skill at the competitive, surfers-only point breaks, such as **Topanga State Beach**, near the intersection of PCH and Topanga Canyon Road; **Surfrider Beach** (one of the most famous surf breaks in the world), by PCH and Cross Creek Road, just north of Malibu Pier; and the **Wedge**, a very dangerous break located at the end of Balboa and Ocean Boulevards at the top of the Balboa Peninsula in Orange County.

If you surf between October and May, you'll need a wetsuit; try **ZJ Boardinghouse**, which also provides a daily surf report, and **Malibu Ocean Sports** (for both, *see page 223*). For recorded **surf conditions**, call 1-900 844 9283 or check with the **Department of Beaches & Harbors** (1-310 305 9503) for the beach you're interested in.

Paskowitz Surfing Camp San Onofre
164 W Avenida Ramona, San Clemente (1-714 361 9283/booking 1-714 350 5808/fax 1-714 361 9211).
This outfit has been on the waves for 25 years, offering lessons with professional surfers. The seven-day surfing safari ($980) lets skilled surfers and beginners work on technique, relax by a campfire and sleep under the stars. The trip includes three meals a day, camping equipment and warm showers. Classes run from early June to mid-September; call to enroll.

ET Surfboards
904 Aviation Boulevard, between Ocean Drive & Pacific Coast Highway, Hermosa Beach (1-310 379 7660). Bus 225, 232/I-405, exit Hwy 91 (Artesia Boulevard) west. **Open** 10am-8pm Mon-Fri; 10am-7pm Sat; 10am-6pm Sun. **Credit** AmEx, MC, V.
All types of boards in stock, including surfboards (rental $15 a day) and snowboards ($30 a day).

Edison Field

2000 Gene Autry Way, between Katella & Orangewood Avenues, Anaheim, Orange County (1-714 940 2000/ ticket information 1-714 634 2000). Bus Orange County Transit 49, 50/I-5, exit Katella Avenue east. **Open** 8.30am-5pm Mon-Fri & days of games. **Tickets** $5-$14.50. **Credit** AmEx, Disc, MC, V.

Basketball

The two men's teams are the terminally hip **Lakers** (1-310 419 3131), who play at the Great Western Forum and whose all-star supporters are led by Jack Nicholson, and the **Clippers** (1-213 748 8000), NBA's perennial losers, who play at the LA Sports Arena. The NBA season runs from October to April.

Come summertime at the Forum it's the girls' game, as the **Sparks** (1-310 412 5000) are led by Lisa Leslie towards the WNBA title.

Great Western Forum

3900 Manchester Boulevard, at Prairie Avenue, Inglewood (1-310 673 1300). Bus 115, 211, 315, 442/ I-405, exit Manchester Boulevard east. **Tickets** $21-$110.

LA Sports Arena

3939 S Figueroa Street, at Martin Luther King Jr Boulevard, Exposition Park, Downtown (1-213 748 6131). Bus 81, 102, 200, 442, 444/I-110, exit Exposition Boulevard west. **Open** box office 10am-6pm Mon-Fri & days of games. **Tickets** $10-$275.

Horse racing

There are three tracks in the LA area, as well as at La Jolla, a couple of hours down the coast. They all feature flat racing and are closed for part of the year. Call for post times.

Hollywood Park Race Track & Casino

1050 S Prairie Avenue, between 90th Street & Century Boulevard, Inglewood (1-310 419 1500). Bus 115, 211, 315, 442/I-405, exit Manchester Boulevard east. **Admission** $6.

Los Alamitos Race Course

4961 Katella Avenue, at Walker Street, Los Alamitos, Orange County (1-714 995 1234). Bus Orange County Transit 50/I-5, exit Katella Avenue west. **Admission** $3.

Santa Anita Park

285 W Huntington Drive, between Baldwin & Santa Anita Avenues, Arcadia (1-626 574 7223). Bus 79, 188, 268, Foothill Transit 184/I-210, exit Baldwin Avenue south. **Admission** $4.
Apparently, the stables here were used to intern Japanese-Americans after the attack on Pearl Harbour.

Ice hockey

The **LA Kings'** (1-310 673 6003) former star Dave Taylor is now the team's general manager, and he's brought in high-scoring centre Jozef Stumpel as the Kings again are contenders in the National Hockey League. The **Mighty Ducks** (1-714 704 2700), another Disney-owned franchise, play in Anaheim. The Long Beach **Ice Dogs** (1-562 423 3647) are one of the top teams in the second-tier International Hockey League. The NHL season runs from late November to late March.

Motor racing

The main event is the Indy car **Long Beach Grand Prix**, which takes place on a street circuit in Long Beach every April (*see page 91* **Los Angeles by Season**). **California Speedway** in Fontana (tickets 1-909 428 9300), 90 minutes from LA, is the focal point for motor sports in the Southland, and between April and September there's moto-cross every Friday at the **Orange County Fairgrounds** (1-714 708 3247).

Soccer

Although you wouldn't guess it by the minimal coverage of soccer on network TV and the sports pages of the *LA Times*, Los Angeles is arguably the mecca for soccer in the United States, due in no small part to its significant and soccer-crazed Latin population (most of whom weren't too bothered by the fact that the US lost all three of its matches in the 1998 World Cup Finals).

Soccer is one of the most popular sports in the US at high school and university level, and the three-year-old Major Soccer League is attempting to make a go of it professionally. Upwards of 30,000 enthusiastic fans are drawn to the Rose Bowl in Pasadena to see the Galaxy play. Around town you'll see all ethnicities wearing the gold and green Galaxy shirts. The thriving Latin 'futbol' culture provides a base for the million or so expat Europeans living in LA to get their fix, while a surprising number of Americans who have grown up with the sport remain hopelessly devoted.

There exists a huge number of amateur teams and leagues, often organised by native country, which can be seen in action evenings and weekends at high schools, sports grounds and public parks. Numerous bars and cafés around town show overseas matches on satellite TV; check the sports section of the Spanish newspaper *La Opinion* for Spanish-speaking coverage. If you want to watch English Premier League footie, plenty of bars, particularly in Santa Monica, broadcast games; try the **Cock & Bull** pub (2947 Lincoln Boulevard, at Pier Avenue; 1-310 399 9696).

The Los Angeles Galaxy

The Rose Bowl, 1001 Rose Bowl Drive, at Arroyo Boulevard, Pasadena (1-626 577 3100). Bus 177/ Hwy 134, exit Orange Grove Boulevard north. **Tickets** $10-$30.
Heading into World Cup '98, the Galaxy was an undefeated juggernaut that benefited greatly from the league's practice of assigning star players to it in an attempt to make LA's fertile soccer market the cornerstone of the league. Fan favourites include Mexican goalkeeper Jorge Campos and Cobi Jones, the dreadlocked winger who also plays for the US national side.

Theatre & Dance

The movies pay better, but LA's actors, directors and designers know that theatre is where the art is. And the city has become a world-leading laboratory for adventurous dance.

Theatre

All the world's a stage – except in LA, where it's a silver screen. But although Hollywood is obsessed by celluloid, theatre is an integral part of that obsession. Many original works are performed on stage here before they make their way to TVs or cinemas around the world. Up-and-coming actors do live theatre in order to be seen by movie agents, while established stars tread the boards for a fix of 'experimental' work after their latest blockbuster. But there are also many thespians who perform every night simply for the love of real theatre. It is these actors, producers and directors who bring world-class shows to LA and have contributed to a very healthy theatre industry.

Unlike New York, which is limited by space, Los Angeles has room for a huge variety of venues: from picnicking outdoors with Shakespeare in a rustic canyon, to watching a Broadway musical in a lavish art deco movie palace, to seeing a movie star in a tiny 99-seat black box.

The best way to discover what's on is to pick up a copy of the *LA Times* or *LA Weekly*. For tickets and general information for most theatres, call **Tickets LA** (1-800 660 8587), **Telecharge** (1-800 233 3123) or **Ticketmaster** (1-323 480 3232).

Major venues

Henry Fonda Theater
6126 Hollywood Boulevard, at Gower Street, Hollywood (1-323 468 1770). Bus 1, 180, 181, 212, 217/US 101, exit Hollywood Boulevard west. **Credit** AmEx, MC, V.
Map 5 B1
Even though it's just down the street from the classy Pantages, the Henry Fonda suffers because those few blocks take it into a more depressed neighbourhood. Though often dark, it houses touring shows such as *And the World Goes Round*, *The Kathy and Mo Show* and the gay musical *Party*.
Parking $6.

James Doolittle Theater
1615 N Vine Street, at Hollywood Boulevard & Vine Street, Hollywood (1-323 462 6666). Bus 1, 180, 181, 212, Community Connection 208/US 101, exit Vine Street south. **Credit** AmEx, MC, V.
Map 5 B1

Over 70 years old – it got a facelift a few years ago – this vast theatre has housed such productions as *Angels in America* and *Smokey Joe's Café*. At intermission, you can go outside and look down at the stars beneath your feet on the Hollywood Walk of Fame.

John Anson Ford Amphitheatre
For listings, see p208 **Music**.
This intimate amphitheatre is just up the street from the more famous Hollywood Bowl and has been a landmark since the 1930s. A wonderful outdoor venue to see any show, it's part of LA County Regional Park and so the stage is set against a rustic backdrop of chaparral and cypresses. From June to September it's hom Pe to Summer Nights at the Ford, when you can see and hear world music and dance, classical music, jazz, blues and theatre shows.
Parking $8.

Music Center of Los Angeles
For listings, see **Dorothy Chandler Pavilion** *p205* **Music.**
The Music Center is LA's foremost performing arts centre, housing the Dorothy Chandler Pavilion, the Ahmanson Theater and the Mark Taper Forum. The Ahmanson seats nearly 2,000 but there's not a bad chair in the house for huge Broadway musicals like *Chicago*, *Phantom of the Opera* and *Rent*. The smaller Mark Taper Forum has 760 seats surrounding a thrust stage, so even if you're stuck in the back row you won't miss such plays as Moises Kaufman's *Gross Indecency: The Three Trials of Oscar Wilde*, David Hare's *Skylight* and Patrick Marber's *Dealer's Choice*.
Parking evenings & weekends $7; weekdays $12.50 per 20 mins ($15 dollar maximum); valet parking $17. Park at the DMV across the street for $5.

Pantages Theater
For listings, see p209 **Music**.
Though the Metro Rail construction has upset many businesses along Hollywood Boulevard, the Pantages is not one of them. Built in 1929, its rich art deco style will have you staring in awe at its ceiling and at intermission you'll have to tear yourself away from the beautiful lobby with twin sweeping staircases. The 1950s saw it host the Academy Awards and the 1960s transformed it from a movie palace to a regular theatre. Legend has it that the ghost of eccentric millionaire Howard Hughes still roams the Pantages; he owned it for a few years in the early 1950s.
Parking $6.

Shubert Theatre
2020 Avenue of Stars, at Constellation Boulevard, Century City (1-800 477 7400). Bus 22, 27, 28, 316, 328, Santa Monica 5/I-405, exit Santa Monica Boulevard east. **Credit** AmEx, DC, Disc, MC, V. **Map 3 B3**

The Shubert vies with the Ahmanson for the larger touring productions. Long-running shows have included *Beauty and the Beast*, *Sunset Boulevard* and the Korean opera *The Last Empress*. Plenty of underground parking below. *Parking $5.*

Smaller theatres

Coronet Theater
366 N La Cienega Boulevard, at Melrose Avenue, West Hollywood (1-310 657 7377). Bus 10, 11, 105, 576/I-10, exit La Cienega Boulevard north. **Credit** AmEx, MC, V. **Map 4 B2**
Monday nights are when the stars come out. This 272-seater fills up quickly as actors such as Gwyneth Paltrow, Lou Diamond Phillips, Frank Lagella, Carol Burnett, Leonard Nimoy and Lily Tomlin read scripts at 'PKE' – the Playwrights' Kitchen Ensemble. Many of these scripts have gone on to TV and film. It's free and there's always a buzz each week, so get there early.

Geffen Playhouse
10886 Le Conte Avenue, at Tiverton Avenue, Westwood (1-310 208 6500/box office 1-310 208 5454). Bus 2, 302, Santa Monica 8, Culver City 6, Commuter Express 573, 576/I-405, exit Wilshire Boulevard east. **Credit** AmEx, MC, V.
Lately, the Geffen has brought great productions to Los Angeles, such as Terence McNally's *Love! Valour! Compassion!*, Martin McDonagh's *The Cripple of Inishmaan* and works by David Mamet, John Patrick Shanley and Doug Wright. It's a beautiful little theatre with a gorgeous outdoor patio to while away the intermission. *Parking $2.*

Pasadena Playhouse
39 S El Molino Avenue, between Colorado Boulevard & Green Street, Pasadena (1-626 356 7529). Bus 180, 181, 188, 256, 401, 402, Foothill Transit 187/I-110 to Arroyo Parkway, exit Colorado Boulevard east. **Credit** AmEx, MC, V.
A Pasadena landmark, the Playhouse opened in 1924, fell on hard times in the 1970s, was restored and now stages many premières and productions, some of which have moved on to Broadway. It has a cute outdoor patio, similar to the Geffen's, and a good restaurant next door. *Parking $4.*

Will Geer Theatricum Botanicum
1419 N Topanga Canyon Boulevard, at Cheney Drive, Topanga (1-310 455 3723). Bus 434/I-10, exit PCH north. **Tickets** $12-$17 adults; $10-$12 students, seniors. **No credit cards.**
Bring a picnic: the Botanicum is an outdoor venue in the late Will Geer's backyard. Better known as Grandpa on *The Waltons*, Geer founded the theatre as a haven for blacklisted actors, artists and musicians in the 1950s. Although the company concentrates on Shakespeare, it has also produced such plays as *The Crucible* and *Lettice and Lovage*.

99-seat theatres

Under the 99-Seat Equity Waiver Agreement, theatres with fewer than 100 seats don't have to pay Equity (actors' union) wages. Therefore some of the bigger names in Los Angeles TV and film (who don't need the money) hone their skills in them and fringe productions (which don't have it) flourish.

In addition to the theatres listed below, the area known as Theater Row, in a run-down Hollywood neighbourhood, has several small spaces often used for short one-off runs (which can be very hit-and-miss). Look out for shows at the **Complex** (6476 Santa Monica Boulevard; 1-800 980 5438), the **Attic Theatre Centre** (65622 Santa Monica Boulevard; 1-323 469 3786) and the **Hudson** (6539 Santa Monica Boulevard; 1-323 856 4249). The Hudson is a group of four 99-seat theatres, all producing very different works: the Main Stage is primarily conventional theatre; the Hudson Avenue is more eclectic; the Hudson Backstage presents works in progress; and the Hudson Guild presents classical pieces.

Actors' Gang Theatre
6209 Santa Monica Boulevard, at El Centro Avenue, Hollywood (1-323 465 0566). Bus 4, 210, 310, 304, 420, 426/US 101, exit Vine Street south. **Credit** AmEx, Disc, MC, V. **Map 5 B2**
Now in its 17th year, the Actors' Gang has become something of a Los Angeles institution under (former) artistic director Tim Robbins. It's known for its workshop productions and daring adaptations of classic plays such as *Woyzeck* and Oscar Wilde's *Salomé*. The company won five Drama-Logue Awards last year for *Bat Boy – The Musical*.

Highways Performance Space
1651 18th Street, at Olympic Boulevard, Santa Monica (1-310 453 1755). Bus Santa Monica 8, 9/I-10, exit Cloverfield Avenue north. **Credit** (advance only) AmEx, MC, V. **Map 2 B3**
From Latina comics to sculptural theatre, the Highways Performance Space leads the way in experimental works in dance, spoken-word and theatre productions.

Met Theatre
1089 N Oxford Avenue, at Santa Monica Boulevard, Hollywood (1-323 957 1741). Bus 4, 175, 207, 304, 357, 420/I-10, exit Western Avenue north. **Credit** MC, V. **Map 5 C2**
Founded by actors Amy Madigan, Ed Harris, Holly Hunter and Beth Henley, this company hosts actor/director/writer workshops, out of which came Susan Emshwiller's *Brush Strokes*, a compilation of six short plays inspired by the paintings of Edward Hopper. *Parking $3.*

A Noise Within
234 S Brand Boulevard, at Colorado Street, Glendale (1-818 546 1924). Bus 92, 93, 183, 410, Glendale Transit B/Hwy 134, exit Central Avenue south. **Credit** AmEx, MC, V.
Known for its Shakespeare productions, this young theatre is one of the few in the US to have a resident acting company on rotating repertory. It offers student outreach programmes, Conservatory Classes and an annual Summer with Shakespeare programme for teenagers. *Free parking.*

Odyssey Theatre Ensemble
2055 S Sepulveda Boulevard, between Olympic & Santa Monica Boulevards, West LA (1-310 477 2055). Bus Culver City 6, Commuter Express 574/I-405, exit Santa Monica Boulevard east. **Credit** AmEx, MC, V. **Map 3 A5**
Nearly 30 years of productions have made this one of the most successful small theatres in LA. With its three under-100-seat houses, the Odyssey has been experimental and innovative in both the classical and original works it puts on. Past productions include Miller's *All My Sons*, Odets's *Awake and Sing* and Mamet's *Speed the Plow*. *Parking $2.50.*

Tiffany Theater

8532 Sunset Boulevard, at La Cienega Boulevard, West Hollywood (1-310 289 2999). Bus 2, 3, 302, 429/I-10, exit La Cienega Boulevard north. **Credit** AmEx, MC, V. **Map 4 A1**

Housing two 99-seat theatres, the Tiffany has had a variety of quality drama on its bill, though it now concentrates on lighter fare such as Brit comedian Eddie Izzard and Preston Whitmore's one-man shows.

Parking $3.

Also recommended

Matrix Theater *7657 Melrose Avenue, between Spaulding & Stanley Avenues, West Hollywood (1-323 852 1445)*; **Canon Theatre** *205 N Canon Drive, at Wilshire Boulevard, Beverly Hills (1-310 859 2830)*; **Coast Playhouse** *8325 Santa Monica Boulevard, between Kings Road & Sweetzer Avenue, West Hollywood (1-213 650 8509)*; **Falcon Theatre** *4252 Riverside Drive, Burbank (1-818 955 8004)*; **Santa Monica Playhouse** *1211 Fourth Street, at Arizona Avenue, Santa Monica (1-310 394 9779)*.

Outside LA

For those who are prepared to travel to see a show, beyond Los Angeles lie several legendary Tony Award-winning theatres:

La Jolla Playhouse *Mandell Weiss Center for the Performing Arts, University of California San Diego, at Revelle Campus & La Jolla Village Drives, La Jolla (1-619 550 1010)*; **Laguna Playhouse** *606 Laguna Canyon Road, Laguna Beach (1-714 497 2787)*; **Old Globe Theatre** *Laurel Street & Sixth Avenue, Balboa Park, San Diego (1-619 239 2255)*; **South Coast Repertory** *655 Town Center Drive, between Anton & Sunflower Avenues, Costa Mesa (1-714 708 5555)*.

Dance

Los Angeles has a bad reputation as a dance town, but it's undeserved and it's changing. The land that spawned the Hollywood musical and the MTV video has long been a haven for tap and jazz dancers. Moreover, every dance craze this century, from merengue to macarena, got its first toe-hold in Los Angeles.

This is also the city that gave birth to a significant branch of American modern dance led by Ruth St Denis and Ted Shawn. These legendary innovators, who elevated vaudeville to high art by choreographing ersatz versions of Asian dance forms, established their Denishawn school in the Hollywood Hills in the early 1900s. Martha Graham passed through its portals, as did film choreographer Jack Cole. But that was then. Except for Lester Horton (Alvin Ailey's first mentor) and Bella Lewitzky (another of Horton's protégés, now an octogenarian), subsequent generations of art dancers seem to have passed LA by. Until recently, that is. Over the past decade, three new brands of concert dance have begun to blossom in Los Angeles.

Dance companies representing non-Euro-American cultures are flourishing in LA. The city

Hang on – it's the **Diavolo Dance Theatre**.

boasts dance companies representing India (both south and north), Iran, Native America (the famous American Indian Dance Theatre is based here), Mexico, Cambodia and West Africa: all directed by first-rank artists and boasting excellent casts.

You can attend a show by one of these companies virtually any week. For listings, check the Calendar section of the *LA Times*, the *LA Weekly* or (if you're really serious about dance) *LA Dance and Fitness Magazine* ($3.95), which carries extensive performance listings as well as ads for classes at local studios. In the summer, best bets are the free performances at the **Watercourt at California Plaza** (*see page 234*) and reasonably priced offerings at the **John Anson Ford Amphitheatre** (*see page 231*).

'Hyper-dance' is the name given by Lewis Segal, the *LA Times*'s smart dance critic, to the city's newest style. Resembling dancing as demolition derby, this new genre looks like a descendant of a 1980s mosh pit. But it also bears a similarity to the 'Popaction' choreography of New Yorker Elizabeth Streb, who almost certainly got there first. Some hyper-dance practitioners, such as Mehmet Sander, prefer a violent edge, with muscular bodies falling hard on one another or pounding noisily against tilted ramps and walls. Others, such as Jacques Heim and his Diavolo Dance Theatre, strive for a sense of wonder. (Heim has said that he is trying to recreate in his work the love and intensity he felt after the 1994 Northridge earthquake.) This type of dancing is likely to turn up at

Highways (*see page 232*) or visual art spaces such as the **Geffen Contemporary** (*see page 196* **Museums & Galleries**).

The most recent sign of dynamic change in LA-area dance has come from the most unexpected of places: the universities. Stuck in a rut for decades, the academies are renewing themselves as safe havens for choreographers and forward-looking artists, mostly of a 'postmodern' (or, in British terms, 'new dance') bent. The best explanation for this change is the dramatic downturn in federal funding for the arts in the US, thanks in large part to North Carolina senator Jesse Helms, who has branded art he doesn't like 'obscene'.

In this new, unfriendly climate, artists are streaming out of New York to look for new ways to support themselves. The 1990s have seen Tim Miller, a gay choreographer and performance artist, developing an alliance with Cal State LA; hyper-dancer Heim turning up at UCLA along with movement portraitist Victoria Marks (whose works appear regularly on Britain television) and dance-theatre artist David Rousseve; Boston's Susan Rose taking up residence at the University of California at Riverside; and New York dancer-choreographer Douglas Neilsen accepting a job at Cal Arts. The work of these artists can be seen in a number of venues and occasionally as part of the Friday night performance series at the **Getty Center** (*see page 199* **Museums & Galleries**).

Los Angeles doesn't have a resident top-flight ballet company, though most major troupes, with their famous names and proven pedigrees, make stops somewhere in the Southland, whether in the prime civic venues or the new regional theatres currently sprouting in the area.

Major venues

The **Dorothy Chandler Pavilion** at the Music Center in Downtown (*see page 205* **Music**) is the place to catch touring ballet companies, including American Ballet Theater and San Francisco Ballet. Many theatre venues also often put on dance performances.

Harriet & Charles Luckman Fine Arts Complex at Cal State LA

For listings, see p206 **Music**.
A state-of-the art theatre that presents local artists, national touring companies and performers from around the world.

UCLA Center for the Performing Arts

405 Hilgard Avenue, at Sunset Boulevard, Westwood (1-310 825 2101). Bus 2, 21, 429, 561, 576/I-405, exit Sunset Boulevard east. **Credit** AmEx, MC, V.
The Center hosts many out-of-town performers. During term time, watch out for the artists-in-residence programme, which includes free lectures, masterclasses and open rehearsals. **Royce Hall**, one of the two main venues on the campus (the other is **Schoenberg Hall**), has been lavishly restored after damage incurred in the 1994 earthquake.

Regional venues

Cerritos Center for the Performing Arts

12700 Centre Court Drive, at Bloomfield Avenue, Cerrito (1-562 916 8500). Bus 130, Norwalk Transit 3/Hwy 91, exit Bloomfield Avenue south. **Credit** AmEx, Disc, MC, V.
Ballet and big-ticket performances.
Free parking.

Irvine Barclay Theater

4242 Campus Drive, at Bridge Drive, Irvine, Orange County (1-949 849 4646). Bus Orange County Transit 65, 74, 76, 175, 382/I-405, exit Jamboree Road west. **Credit** AmEx, MC, V.
Larger-scale national touring companies appear here, including Mark Morris and Pilobolus.
Parking $3.

Orange County Performing Arts Center

600 Town Center Drive, between Bristol Street & Sunflower Avenue, Costa Mesa, Orange County (1-714 556 2787). Bus Orange County Transit 53, 55, 57, 59, 74/I-405, exit Bristol Street north. **Credit** AmEx, MC, V.
A wide-ranging programme includes touring ballet companies and Broadway musicals.
Parking $6.

Summer presentations

Watercourt at California Plaz

350 S Grand Avenue, at W Third Street, Downtown (1-213 687 2000/events line 1-213 687 2159). Metro Civic Center/Tom Bradley or Pershing Square/bus 30, 31, 40, 42, 436, 445, 466, DASH A, D/I-110, exit Fourth Street east. **Map 7 B2**
Like the **John Anson Ford Amphitheatre** (*see p231*), this is a perfect place to see dance performances in the open air. A water fountain serves as a backdrop and some performers dally directly into the water pond. The season runs from June through October, and shows are free.

Dance-theatre artist **David Rousseve**.

Trips Out of Town

Trips Out of Town

You'd be mad to miss the other worlds that lie within a day's drive of LA: alpine lakes and mountains, strange deserts, surreal Las Vegas – not to mention Mexico.

Even Lotus Land can get wearying. When you've overdosed on LA's traffic jams and concrete, you can do what Angelenos have always done: retreat to the relatively unspoiled natural environments and interesting cities just a few hours away. This being California, there is, of course, an abundance of choice: arid and semi-arid, high and low deserts to the east; alpine vistas, mountain lakes and skiing in the nearby San Gabriel mountains; quaint, ocean-fresh coastal towns on Catalina Island; and Las Vegas, San Diego and the Mexican border just (by US standards) a shortish drive away.

This is the land of the automobile, so the easiest – sometimes the only – way to get to the places listed below is by car. On some trips, such as those up US 101 towards San Francisco or through the Mojave desert, the drive itself is the experience. All the destinations described involve a drive of an hour and a half upwards.

It is also possible to travel by plane, train and bus to larger destinations such as Palm Springs, Santa Barbara, Las Vegas and San Diego. Check the ads in the 'Travel & Adventure' section of *LA Weekly* for bargain fares or consult a travel agent. Call **Amtrak** for information on trains, which you catch at **Union Station**, while **Greyhound** long-distance buses depart from a Downtown terminus (*for both, see page 254* **Directory**). For car rental, useful organisations and tips on driving, *see page 255* **Directory**.

General information

LA's bookshops (*see p154* **Shops & Services**) have shelves of travel guides to Southern California. Sunday's *LA Times* has a travel section that includes a Weekend Escape feature.
California Trade & Commerce Agency Division Office of Tourism
801 K Street, suite 1600, Sacramento, CA 95814 (1-916 322 3424).

Accommodation

California Association of Bed & Breakfast Inns (CABBI)
2715 Porter Street, Soquel, CA 95073 (1-408 464 8159).
California Hotel & Motel Association
PO Box 160405, Sacramento, CA 95816 (1-916 444 5780).

Camping & outdoors

California Department of Parks & Recreation
PO Box 94296-0001, Sacramento, CA 94296 (1-916 653 6995). Website: www.cal-parks.ca.gov

California Department of Fish & Game
1416 Ninth Street, 12th floor, Sacramento, CA 95814 (1-916 653 7664).
State Park campground reservations
1-800 444 7275. Website: www.park-net.com
US Forest Service
630 Sansome Street, San Francisco, CA 94111 (1-415 705 2874/camping reservations 1-800 283 2267).

Mountains

You've no doubt heard the claim that in Los Angeles you can ski in the morning and surf in the evening. Well, at the right time of year, and if you are prepared to get up early enough, you can get to **Big Bear** or **Lake Arrowhead** for the snow and back to the coast for the waves in one day. These resorts are under two hours away from LA in the San Bernardino Mountains north-east of the city, a drive that takes you east on the I-10 through Downtown and various uninteresting suburbs until you get to the other side of San Bernardino. There you are engulfed by looming mountains and transported into a winding drive up slopes that go from arid and brush-covered to alpine.

Though close to each other, the two resorts are different in character. Lake Arrowhead is prettier, affluent and more artsy, while the focus at Big Bear is on mountain sports.

Lake Arrowhead

At an altitude of 5,000 feet (1,500 metres) – 1,000 feet (300 metres) higher than the peak of Scotland's Ben Nevis – Lake Arrowhead is another world: an artificial lake in an alpine setting of pine and oak forests and crystal-clear air, with the neo-Bavarian **Arrowhead Village** and various smaller tourist and residential communities tucked discreetly away in the woods. Snow-covered in winter and desert-hot in the summer, it is, like many such delightful places, overrun with tourists (best to go off-season or on a weekday).

This being the States, however, and not Bavaria, the tourists can't let go of the internal combustion engine; the lake is speedboat heaven and so not too good for swimming. You can swim – if you want to join loud, white America at play – at the nearby, smaller **Lake Gregory**.

Catalina Island

It's hard to imagine anywhere in Southern California where the golf cart could replace the automobile as the preferred mode of street transport, but this is the case on Catalina. *The Prisoner* would have felt at home on this small, impossibly cute island, about 20 miles (32 kilometres) from San Pedro, with its clean beaches and clear water, undulating pastures, natural bay and twee town named Avalon – almost all of which is owned by the Santa Catalina Island Company (1-310 510 2000), which maintains strict limits on cars and growth.

In the early part of this century, Catalina was an offshore playground for movie stars. In 1919, it was purchased by William Wrigley Jr – heir to the chewing gum fortune – who built the impressive art deco Avalon Theater and Casino, now the **Santa Catalina Island Museum** (1 Casino Way, Avalon; 1-310 510 2414), dedicated to the island's history. A herd of buffalo (aka American bison) were brought to the island in 1924 for the filming of Zane Grey's *The Vanishing American*. They are now the main attraction on Catalina, some 86 per cent of which is a nature reserve.

As well as buffalo, there are pigs, goats, deer, native ground squirrels, quail, foxes, rattlesnakes, the reinstated bald eagle, swordfish, tuna and numerous other species of flora and fauna. You can examine cacti, succulents and local plants at the **Wrigley Memorial and Botanical Garden** (1400 Avalon Canyon Road; 1-310 510 2288), check out fine Arabian horses at **El Rancho Escondido** (1-310 510 2288) or kayak, snorkel, jet-ski, scuba dive or fish at **Two Harbors**, a resort village on the north-west of the island, and at some of the other beaches. The island's climate and topography are similar to

that of LA – but the air is much fresher.

Shopping, restaurants, hotels and other tourist attractions are mainly to be found in the picture-postcard, white stucco, bayside town of **Avalon**. With a population of about 3,000 (jumping in summer to 6,000 in the week and 10,000 at weekends), it is the largest residential community on Catalina.

You can tour the island on foot, by sightseeing bus or rented bicycle, horse or golf cart. To hike, you need a permit, available free of charge from the Catalina Island Conservancy (125 Claressa Avenue, Avalon; 1-310 510 2595).

Getting there

By boat: Catalina Express (1-310 519 1212) runs a regular, one-hour, $36 round-trip service from Long Beach and San Pedro Harbors, while Sail Catalina (1-310 510 0607) offers a 75-minute trip on a catamaran from Huntington Harbor ($48.50 round trip). Catalina Cruises (1-800 228 2546) offers a two-hour leisure cruise from Long Beach Harbor ($25 round trip). Catalina Flyer (1-714 673 5245) is a 75-minute catamaran service from Newport Beach ($36 round trip).

By air: Island Express (1-310 510 2525) offers a 15-minute helicopter flight from San Pedro and Long Beach Harbors ($121 round trip). Super Shuttle (1-310 782 6600) and Best Shuttle (1-310 670 7080) run airport shuttle services from all LA airports to Catalina Island sea and air terminals.

Where to stay

You can camp on Catalina, though you must get a permit and book in advance. For the Hermit Gulch Campground in Avalon Canyon, call 1-310 510 8368; for other sites, contact Catalina Island Camping, PO Box 5044, Two Harbors, Catalina Island, CA 90704 (1-310 510 0303). For hotels, contact the Chamber of Commerce.

Tourist information

Catalina Island Chamber of Commerce & Visitors Bureau
1 Green Pleasure Pier, Avalon, Catalina Island,
CA 90704 (1-310 510 1520/fax 1-310 510 7606).
Website: *www.catalina.com*

More pleasant is the hiking and fishing, or you could walk the three-mile (five-kilometre) circumference of the lake and tackle the gym apparatus en route. In winter, the focus is on cross-country skiing and skating – there's a big ice rink in Blue Jay village. The restaurant food is nothing to write home about; your best bet is to buy picnic supplies at **Jensen's Market** in Blue Jay Village, halfway round the lake from Arrowhead Village.

Getting there

By car: Take the I-10 east to the I-215 (heading east), then take Hwy 30 east for one mile (1½km) to Hwy 18 (Waterman Avenue exit). Follow Hwy 18 up the mountain and take the Lake Arrowhead turn-off.
By train: Mountain Area Regional Rapid Transit Authority

(MARTA) offers daily round trips through Arrowhead and San Bernardino (1-909 584 1111) for $7.50.

Where to stay

There are numerous inns, hostelries and camping sites to choose from in Arrowhead. For details, contact the Lake Arrowhead Community Chamber of Commerce.

Tourist information

Crestline/Lake Gregory Chamber of Commerce
23840 Lake Drive (inside Vineyard Bank), Crestline,
CA 92325 (1-909 338 2706/fax 1-909 338 5022).
Lake Arrowhead Community Chamber of Commerce
PO Box 219, Lake Arrowhead, CA 92352 (above Subway restaurant) (accommodation 1-800 337 3716/1-909 337 3715/marketing & tourism 1-909 336 1547/fax 1-909 336 1548).

Ski in winter and mountain bike in summer at **Big Bear**.

Big Bear

Under snow, Big Bear is very inviting. In high summer, it is less so – an exposed, windy and downmarket version of Arrowhead. But it has a large lake and offers some of the best downhill and cross-country skiing in the region – for more information, *see page 248* **Skiing & snowboarding**. During summer, the mountains become the site for downhill mountain bike races, hiking and horse riding, while the lake is used for windsurfing, sailboarding, water-skiing, jet-skiing and fishing. At the solstice, it's a prime spot for outdoor raves (*see page 214* **Nightlife**).

Getting there

By car: Go east on the I-10 to join Hwy 30 in Redlands. Follow Hwy 30 to Hwy 330, then join Hwy 18, heading west. Turn right across the dam to Big Bear Lake.
By air: Big Bear Shuttle (1-909 585 5514) offers a door-to-door air service to Ontario and LAX airports and also a van service that can carry bikes, skis and snowboards ($70).
By train: As for Arrowhead; *see above*.
By van: $80 from Ontario airport; $110 from LAX.

Where to stay

Apples Bed & Breakfast Inn
42430 Moonridge Road, Big Bear Lake, CA 92315 (1-909 866 0903). **Rooms** $145-$185.

Truffles Bed & Breakfast
43591 Bow Canyon Road, Big Bear Lake, CA 92315 (1-909 585 2772). **Rooms** $115-$150.

Moonridge Manor Bed & Breakfast
43803 Yosemite Drive, Big Bear Lake, CA 92315 (1-909 585 0457). **Rooms** $70-$175.
Website: www.moonridge.com

Windy Point Inn
39015 N Shore Drive, Fannskin, CA 92333 (1-909 866 2746). **Rooms** $125-$245.
There are also several campsites in Big Bear; for more information, contact the Big Bear Lake Resort Association.

Tourist information

Big Bear Lake Resort Association
630 Bartlett Road, Big Bear, CA 92315 (1-909 866 7000). Website: www.bigbearinfo.com

Idyllwild

If you want alpine without the skiing, an alternative destination is **Idyllwild**, a pleasant, artsy community at the crest of the San Jacinto Mountains above Palm Springs. For information on getting there via the Palm Springs Aerial Tramway, *see page 239* **Palm Springs**. Alternatively, come off the I-10 at the junction with Highway 243 and follow it south.

Deserts

Las Vegas and Palm Springs may seem like they are here to stay; but yank their water supply and they would dematerialise, becoming once more part of the arid, bone-bare landscape that is the Mojave desert. This forbidding dry moat encircles most of Los Angeles, extending east to the state border. It is magnificent, humbling, weird – and not to be missed.

The desert consists of mile upon mile of subtly hued, near-naked mountain ridges and plains, dotted with the vestiges of human habitation: dead mining towns, abandoned gas stations and diners on the old Route 66; shiny new towns with their surreal golf courses and swimming pools; and the ubiquitous US military, with its vast, sinister bases. The wilderness is inhabited by strange creatures of both the four- and the two-footed variety: coyotes and roadrunners, gun-toting rednecks and UFO believers. Don't expect fusion cuisine and gay rights once you cross the San Bernardino Mountains; the desert is another world.

Climate

In the Los Angeles basin it is easy to forget that you're on the same latitude as North Africa. The cold Pacific acts as a giant air-conditioner for the coast, but inland, during summer, is like the Sahara, with temperatures regularly topping 110°F (43°C). In winter, after dark, it can plummet below freezing. The best time to visit the desert is during temperate February and March, when most years it bursts briefly – but spectacularly – into spring bloom.

Desert safety

Sunstroke and heat exhaustion are the two dangers to watch for in the desert. If you're visiting in the hot season – April to October – wear a hat, plenty of sunscreen and cover up. Hike early in the morning or late in the day; don't even think of going out at noon – and never go hiking alone. Take plenty of water: a half-pint of Evian isn't going to cut it for a day out in Joshua Tree in July. A gallon a day per person is the recommended intake. In summer, high winds blow at 30-40mph (50-65kph), so lip salve is essential.

Make sure your vehicle is up to the trip, too. If it starts to overheat, turn the air-conditioning off, open the windows and turn the heating full on to let heat escape from the engine. If you park for any length of time, leave a window ajar.

Suggested itinerary

Palm Springs and Las Vegas are destinations in themselves but they are also in the midst of striking desertscapes. One way to enjoy them is to take a three-day (or more) road trip taking in Palm Springs, Joshua Tree National Park, Anza-Borrego Desert State Park, East Mojave National Preserve, Las Vegas, Death Valley National Park and the Ridgecrest/Edwards Air Force Base area.

The following is one of many possible routes: head east on the I-10 to Palm Springs, Anza-Borrego and environs. From Palm Springs, take Highway 62 north and east to Joshua Tree and Twentynine Palms. Then follow Highway 247 to Barstow and head east through the East Mojave National Preserve; either via the I-15, which continues to Las Vegas, or via the I-40 or the remaining stretch of Route 66 (from Ludlow to Essex) to the more southerly town of Needles (from there, take US 95 north to Las Vegas). From Vegas, take Highway 160 to Pahrump, then Highway 372 and Highway 178 into Death Valley. Drive through Death Valley and take Highway 178 south to the US 395. Join Highway 14 and head south, taking in the Mojave/Ridgecrest area and drop back down into LA.

Palm Springs

The I-10 freeway to Palm Springs heads east through sprawling San Bernardino and Riverside Counties, passing near the city of Fontana (site of the world's largest truckstop). Development finally peters out at the Banning Pass, which cuts through the sparse San Jacinto Mountains. From there, the hills are covered in whirring wind farms. This eloquent, Christo-like composition of man and nature is followed by the surreal green carpet in a parched desert valley that is Palm Springs. Take Highway 111 into the town itself.

Sheltered from the smog and haze of the LA basin by the bulk of Mount San Jacinto, this affluent, amply irrigated and manicured desert town is

the home of retired movie stars and amateur golfers. It has been enjoying a comeback in recent years, thanks to a revival of interest in the modernist architecture and lounge-lizard lifestyle that flourished in its post-war heyday. While the city has tried hard to demolish this legacy in favour of bland, sub-Santa Barbara Spanish-styling, many gems still exist: the Jetson-style Tramway Gas Station on Highway 111 as you enter the city, the Aerial Tramway Valley Station and Mountain Station (immortalised in Hitchcock's *North by Northwest*) and Bob Hope's spectacular home, as well as some retro (albeit down at heel) hotels.

Beyond poolside living and golf, Palm Springs offers touristy shops and restaurants on **Palm Canyon Drive**, and some great scenic spots. Take the **Palm Springs Aerial Tramway** (1-760 325 1391; $17; $11 children; open 10am-8pm Mon-Fri; 8am-8pm Sat, Sun) to the crest of San Jacinto for a total change of ecosystem. From this alpine spot you can walk a mile to **Idyllwild**, a mountain retreat housing a small artsy community and school. **Agua Caliente Indian Reservation** has lush hiking trails through three canyons; call the Tribes Administration (600 E Tahquitz Canyon Way; 1-760 325 3400) for more information. Don't miss the 3,000 varieties of desert plants at the eccentric **Moorten Botanical Garden** (1701 S Palm Canyon Drive; 1-760 327 6555).

Getting there

By car: Take the I-10 east all the way to Palm Springs: 103 miles (165km); about 2 hours.

By air: From LAX on American Eagle (1-800 433 7300; $88-$482 round trip), Sky West (1-800 453 9417; $95-$260 round trip) or United Express (1-800 241 6522; $117-$245 round trip); about 50 mins.

By bus: Greyhound operates ten buses a day. Cost: $29 round trip; 2½-4 hours.

Where to stay

There are many lodgings in Palm Springs, but recommended are: **L'Horizon** (1050 E Palm Canyon Drive; 1-760 323 1858), **San Marino** (225 W Baristo Road; 1-760 325 6902) and, if you want a good laugh, the 'clothing optional' **Terra Cotta Inn** (2388 E Racquet Club Road; 1-760 322 6059). If you want to mingle with LA's young and stylish in surroundings with a more foreign flavour, try the Greco-Moorish **Korakia Pensione** (257 S Patencio Road, Palm Springs, CA 92262; 1-760 864 6411). It's very popular, so book ahead.

Tourist information

Palm Springs Visitor Information Center
2781 N Palm Canyon Drive, CA 92262 (1-800 347 7746/1-760 778 8418).
Website: www.palm-springs.org

Anza-Borrego Desert State Park

The drive to Anza-Borrego from Palm Springs takes you south, past the San Jacinto Mountains and through the new, bland desert cities of Cathedral City and Rancho Mirage – all the rage with retirees – and the ancient **Living Desert** (1-760 346 5694), a 1,200-acre (490-hectare) wildlife

Spas & hot springs

You won't have fully experienced the laid-back West Coast lifestyle until you have soaked in a hot tub. Native Americans in this region knew that the secret of life lay in the therapeutic mineral waters that bubble up from the ground all over California – and so do some of their successors. Wallow in warm waters or hot mud, in natural surroundings, enclosed spas or redwood tubs; the sophistication scale extends in both directions. For transport and driving directions, contact the individual resorts.

Greater Los Angeles

Glen Ivy Hot Springs Spa

25000 Glen Ivy Road, at Temescal Canyon Road, Corona, CA 91719 (1-909 277 3529/1-800 454 8772). I-15 south, exit Temescal Canyon Road west. **Open** 10am-6pm daily. **Rates** $19.50 Mon-Thur; $25 Fri-Sun. **Credit** AmEx, MC, V.
Otherwise known as Club Mud, this spa in nearby Riverside County is a fave with those who want to wallow in the ooze but on a budget. For a mere $19.50 (weekdays), you can enjoy day-long use of the mineral sulphur baths (don't worry, the rotten egg smell soon disappears) and a good lathering in soft red clay.
Website: www.glenivy.com

Between LA & San Francisco

Sycamore Mineral Springs Resort

1215 Avila Beach Drive, at US 101, San Luis Obispo, CA 93405 (1-800 234 5831/1-805 595 7302). US 101, exit Avila Beach Drive west. **Open** *spa* 24 hours daily; *restaurants* 7.30am-9pm Mon-Thur, Sun; 7.30am-10pm Fri, Sat. **Massages** $40-$85. **Rooms** $109-$265. **Credit** AmEx, Disc, MC, V.

It's worth driving the 200 miles (320km) north to San Luis Obispo (make it a stop on your coastal trip to San Francisco) to soak in a secluded open-air redwood tub under a tree. Twenty such spas dot the sycamore- and oak-lined hillside at this 100-year-old resort; the balcony of each bedroom in the hotel also has a private tub, if you choose to stay overnight.
Website: www.sycamoresprings.com

Tassajara Buddhist Meditation Center

Tassajara Springs, Carmel Valley, CA 93924 (booking: day 1-408 659 2229/overnight 1-415 431 3771). Hwy 1, then east on Hwy 16. **Prices** call for details.
Between 1 May and Labor Day, members of the public have access to this wooded mountainside retreat with two spring-fed pools, south-east of Monterey. Book in advance and check your brakes; the road is steep.

Desert

Deep Creek Hot Springs

Hesperia, CA.
Getting there: Take the Hesperia exit off the I-15 between LA and Barstow, then follow Hesperia's Main Street until it veers right, when you make a smooth left turn. Continue until you come to a left turn with a 15mph sign; take that, then the first right. Follow signs for Bowen Ranch, where the parking attendant will give you a hiking map.
There is no phone and no good road to Deep Creek; instead, you will have a 45-minute drive over increasingly bad roads until you park your car at Bowen's Ranch, and then a steep 2½-mile (4-km) hike. But the soak is that much sweeter when you finally arrive at the river at the base of the dramatic San Bernardino Forest Canyon, with its 'clothing optional' hot spring pools at different levels on the rock face. The best time to visit is in the week (weekends can be hectic) in late spring after the rains, when the river is high and the weather mild.

Two Bunch Palms

67425 Two Bunch Palms Trail, Desert Hot Springs, CA 92240 (1-800 472 4334/1-760 329 8791). I-10, exit Palm Drive north. **Suites/villas** $175-$570. **'Relaxation services'** $50-$200. **Credit** AmEx, MC, V.
The soak of choice for celebs; this is where Tim Robbins took a mud bath in *The Player* (*see* photo). He could have chosen a herbal or salt steam, or a lounge in the steamy spa swimming pool, an oasis in this desert paradise of bungalows and palm trees. If you can't afford the rates at Two Bunch Palms, then try one of the many other hotels or motels in Desert Hot Springs, Palm Springs' neighbour; many of them have Jacuzzis or swimming pools that use natural mineral waters.
Website: www.twobunchpalms.com

and botanical park in Palm Desert, a couple of miles south of Highway 111.

Anza-Borrego (1-760 767 5311; website: www.anzaborrego.statepark.org) is a huge, 600,000-acre (243,000-hectare) state park 100 miles (160 kilometres) south-east of LA. It has everything: mountains, palm-lined canyons, ancient fossils, scrubby, sandy wastes and a few oases. You can hike, mountain bike, camp rough or in one of two campgrounds or stay in a motel in the small town of **Borrego Springs** (which has one of the few roundabouts in the US). There is a visitor centre two miles west of the town on Palm Canyon Drive (1-760 767 4205; open daily Oct-May, weekends and holidays only June-Sept). The spring wild-flowers peak in February or March (if there's been enough winter rain), covering the desert in sunflowers, June primroses and other exotica.

Joshua Tree National Park

To the north of Palm Springs, the desert valley gives way to massive granite monoliths, scrub and, as far as the eye can see, strange, jagged trees with spiky blooms. These are Joshua trees, actually a form of cactus, of which thousands grow in the astonishing Joshua Tree National Park (enter from the north via Highway 62 and Twentynine Palms or from the south via the I-10). Admission is $10 per vehicle; there are two visitors' centres, one at each entrance (the main one is at 74485 National Park Drive in Twentynine Palms; 1-760 367 7511; website: www.nps.gov/jotr).

As well as Joshua trees and other desert flora and fauna, the area has spectacular rock formations that are very popular with climbers. Wildlife tends to be shy and nocturnal; early morning and evening are the best times to see coyotes or road-runners. It is rumoured that Byrds musician Gram Parsons is buried somewhere in the park. Twentynine Palms itself is a small, uninteresting town that services a Marine base in the flat desert north of Joshua Tree. The 29 palms, and more, grow thanks to a real oasis (now full of ducks).

Where to stay

There are nine campgrounds in the park (but only two with water) and plenty of motels in Twentynine Palms. Try the delightful, quirky **Twentynine Palms Inn** (73950 Inn Avenue; 1-760 367 3505; website: www.29palmsinn.com). It is a last staging post before the empty expanses of the East Mojave; it has been in the same family for four generations and present owner Jane Smith is a mine of local lore.

Weird and wonderful Joshua trees.

Also recommended is **Homestead Inn** (74153 Two Mile Road; 1-760 367 0030; website: www.desertgold.com). This B&B owes its charms to its owner, the incorrigible Jerri Hagman, who has given every room in her ranch house its own 'personality', cooks up a breakfast worthy of *The Famous Five* and even provides cassette tapes with directions to local sights.

East Mojave National Preserve

*Unmissable: the **Mad Greek** diner in Baker.*

En route to Las Vegas you will drive for several hours through the unrelieved reddish-brown plains and hills of the high desert. Signs of life are few – the uninteresting desert town of **Barstow** is the biggest staging post. More fun is tiny **Baker**, which boasts the tallest thermometer in the world and the eccentric delights of the **Mad Greek** diner, and is the northern gateway to the East Mojave National Preserve. Home to two campgrounds, plenty of Joshua trees, sand dunes, the abandoned Spanish-style **Kelso** train depot and the former health resort of Soda Springs at **Zzyzx** (run by early radio evangelist Curtis Howe Springer), the preserve is criss-crossed with roads (many unpaved). Just outside its boundaries is the tiny railroad settlement of Nipton, where the delightful, four-room **Hotel Nipton** (1-760 856 2335) offers spectacular views across the Ivanpah Valley.

For more information, contact the **Desert Information Center** (72157 Baker Boulevard; 1-760 733 4040), beneath the thermometer in Baker.

Las Vegas

The cluster of casinos at the state border is a brief desert bloom that signals your arrival in the gambling state of Nevada. When you finally enter the Las Vegas Valley, the city emerges from the nothingness like Shangri-La dipped in neon.

You've arrived in the capital of kitsch: several mind-blowing miles of neon extravaganzas, over-the-top fantasy hotels, magic shows, sex shows, free drinks and all-you-can-eat buffets, all enticing you to part with your cash. It's horrendous and fabulous at the same time. Find a hotel, drop everything and join the party. The gambling never stops

Las Vegas: *home of casinos and kitsch.*

– which is exciting at night, depressing by day – and nor will you, until the adrenaline rush is over and you want to pass out or get out.

To get the biggest thrill out of Vegas, try to arrive at night and head straight for **Las Vegas Boulevard** (aka the **Strip**). Most of the action in Vegas takes place in the new themed casino-hotels that line the four-mile (6.5-kilometre) length of the Strip, and on **Fremont Street** in downtown.

For the full story, you'll need the *Time Out Guide to Las Vegas*.

The Strip

Apart from their deluxe suites and private gaming rooms, hotel rooms and casinos are pretty generic. The difference is in the theming, the betting odds and stakes and the quality of the cheap food. So pick one, stay there and visit the rest.

Casinos in Vegas change faster than the seasons: by the time you read this, another kitsch colossus will have appeared. But the following essential establishments should be still standing. All major credit cards are accepted.

Caesars Palace

3570 Las Vegas Boulevard S, at W Flamingo Road, Las Vegas, NV 89109 (reservations 1-800 634 6001/1-702 731 7110/fax 1-702 731 6636). **Rooms** $99-$299. **Suites** $450-$750.

How can you not love a place where, at one time, you could literally ask the waitress to peel you a grape? Caesars is the archetypal Vegas casino – low ceilings hung with crystal prisms and staff clad in Roman costume. Make sure you check out the outsize version of Michelangelo's *David* – this one, unlike the original, is uncircumcised – and the surreal Caesars Forum Shops, a huge, enclosed, Rome-themed shopping mall complete with trompe l'oeil sky and programmed lighting that simulates a transition from dawn to dusk. *Website: www.caesars.com*

The Mirage

3400 Las Vegas Boulevard S, between W Flamingo & Spring Mountain Roads, Las Vegas, NV 89109 (reservations 1-800 627 6667/1-702 791 7111/fax 1-702 791 7414). **Rooms** $79-$399. **Suites** $225-$900.

Created by local casino tycoon Steve Wynn, this was the first of the massive themed casinos, opened in 1989. It draws the crowds with its elaborate Polynesian theming, an erupting volcano on the street and its hugely successful – not to mention expensive – show by bizarre illusionists Siegfried and Roy and their white tigers. *Website: www.themirage.com*

New York-New York

3790 Las Vegas Boulevard S, at W Tropicana Avenue, Las Vegas, NV 89109 (reservations 1-800 675 3267/ front desk 1-702 740 6969/fax 1-702 740 6700). **Rooms** $89-$129. **Suites** $200-$500.

Opened in 1997, this $460 million resort is Vegas theming at its most extreme, with a one-third real-size New York skyline rising out of the desert, complete with Empire State building, Chrysler building and Statue of Liberty. Above them all, the Manhattan Express rollercoaster twists, turns and rolls, with a 144ft (44m) dive past the valet entrance. *Website: www.nynyhotelcasino.com*

Other casinos

Next door to the Mirage, and also owned by Steve Wynn, is **Treasure Island** (3300 Las Vegas Boulevard S; reservations 1-800 944 7444; website: www.treasureislandlasvegas. com), which offers the best spectacle in town, Buccaneer Bay. For no expense you can join thousands of other pedestrians to watch pirates and the British navy duke it out amid much pyrotechnic cannonballing until a full-scale frigate disappears underwater.

At **Excalibur** (3850 Las Vegas Boulevard S; reservations 1-800 937 7777; website: www.excalibucasino.com), Wagner meets King Arthur and a flaming dragon in a confused medieval-themed cartoon castle. Inside it is light and bright, and the ceilings are higher than in some of the other casinos – they sometimes make you feel a bit claustrophobic.

The gargantuan **MGM Grand** (3799 Las Vegas Boulevard S; reservations 1-800 929 1111; website: www. mgmgrand.com), the largest hotel in the world with more than 5,000 rooms, is in the process of scrapping its not-so-great theme park and building yet more rooms. A 70ft (21m) high bronze lion presides over the entrance.

Familes should check out **Circus Circus** (2880 Las Vegas Boulevard S; reservations 1-800 634 3450; website: www.circuscircus.com), where acrobats turn somersaults above the slot machines. The same company owns the **Monte Carlo** (3770 Las Vegas Boulevard S; reservations 1-800 311 8999): it looks upmarket with its majestic fountains and crystal chandeliers, but the atmosphere is bright and casual and the gambling cheaper than at other places. Definitely upmarket is the recently remodelled and very opulent **Desert Inn** (3145 Las Vegas Boulevard S; reservations 1-800 634 6906), famous for its 18-hole golf course and former owner-occupier reclusive billionaire Howard Hughes.

For Egyptian theming and a better-than-average buffet, head for the **Luxor** (3900 Las Vegas Boulevard S; reservations 1-800 288 1000; website: www.luxor.com), a 30-storey, sleek black glass pyramid at the south end of the Strip which has recently been upgraded with 2,000 new rooms and a dramatic exterior lighting system.

Towering over the Strip at its northern end is the retro sci-fi tower of the **Stratosphere** (2000 Las Vegas Boulevard S;

reservations 1-800 998 6934; website: www.stratlv.com).
There, the term 'high roller' might be applied to the hair-raising, open-air rollercoaster that zooms around the 'pod' at the top of the tower, 1,150ft (350m) above the Strip. Even more terrifying is the Big Shot, a ride that propels you 160ft (50m) into the air at 45mph (72kph) – as if gambling wasn't exciting enough. Visit the tower; forget the mediocre hotel.

New casinos

At the time of writing, the newest kid on the block was the $1.8 billion, 3,000-room **Bellagio** (3600 Las Vegas Boulevard S; reservations 1-888 987 6667; website: www.bellagiolas vegas.com), the latest extravaganza by Steve Wynn. It replaces the famous Dunes hotel, whose dynamiting Wynn turned into a publicity stunt, is modelled on an Italian village surrounding a 12-acre (5ha) artificial lake and takes Vegas to a new level of refinement with its collection of paintings by Monet, Picasso and others. Go there at night to see the truly amazing fountain display. Other new casinos expected to open by 2000 include **Paris**, inspired by – guess where? – Paris, complete with a mini-Eiffel Tower; the gargantuan **Venetian**, which sits on the site of the Sands, the Rat Pack's favourite casino, and features bridges, canals, gondoliers and 6,000 suites; and '**Project Paradise**', offering a tropical playland with a surfing beach.

Fremont Street

If you're starting to get annoyed that your gambling dollars are funding all these extravagant spectacles, take yourself to **El Cortez** (600 Fremont Street; 1-800 634 6703/1-702 385 5200). The nicotine-stained walls, smoke-filled, jammed gaming room and sour, ageing cocktail waitresses are a welcome relief after all the razzmatazz of the Strip. It also has the 'loosest' slots in Vegas and single-deck and $2 blackjack tables. El Cortez is one of the few remaining outposts of seediness on Fremont Street – formerly Vegas's tawdry 'Glitter Gulch', now the **Fremont Street Experience** (though El Cortez keeps its distance on an unimproved stretch of Fremont Street). Four street blocks have been enclosed in a huge barrel vault holding thousands of lightbulbs, which provide stunning, computer-programmed light and sound shows, on the hour. Don't miss it.

You can play high-stakes poker at **Binion's Horseshoe** (128 Fremont Street; 1-800 237 6537/1-702 382 1600; website: www.horse shoe.com), host of the annual World Series of Poker, and have a good meal at the **Golden Nugget** (129 Fremont Street; 1-702 385 7111), also owned by Wynn and the snazziest casino-hotel on Fremont.

Off-Strip

Join locals at the popular **Rio** (3700 W Flamingo Road; 1-888 746 7482/1-702 252 7777; website: www. playrio.com) for gaudy Latin-American theming, waitresses in teeny thongs and the best casino food in Vegas, or mingle with Angeleno media and movie folk at the **Hard Rock Hotel** (4455 Paradise Road; 1-800 473 7625/1-702 693 5000; website: www.hardrock.com). With 1950s Miami styling and only 340 rooms, this is a somewhat precious homage to the glamorous, adults-only Vegas of old.

Sightseeing

Also of interest is the very kitsch **Liberace Museum** (1775 E Tropicana Avenue; 1-702 798 5595). Here, Mr Showmanship's toys are divided up by category: massive costumes suitable for Ruritanian monarchs in one wing, be-rhinestoned pianos and Rolls-Royces in another, and everywhere photos of the relentlessly grinning tinkler.

From the ridiculous to the sublime: just 30 miles (50 kilometres) from Las Vegas is the extraordinary **Hoover Dam**, the engineering marvel that made Vegas possible. Head south on US 93 to reach this monument to FDR's Depression-era public works programme. A monolith of concrete and art deco styling, it is 726 feet (221 metres) high and 660 feet (201 metres) across at the base, in a stunning Lake Mead setting – marred only by a veritable forest of pylons and power lines above it.

Getting there

By car: Take the I-10 east to the I-15 north until you reach Las Vegas: 286 miles (458km); 5-6 hours.
By air: From LAX on American Eagle (1-800 433 7300; $108-$398 round trip), Southwest (1-800 435 9792; $76-$160 round trip), United Express (1-800 241 6522; $76-$200 round trip) or America West (1-800 235 9292; $84-$350 round trip); about 1 hour 15 mins.
By train: Currently no trains run to Las Vegas, but Amtrak will resume a daily service in February 1999 (leaving LA at 9am); about 5½ hours.
By bus: 19 Greyhound buses a day. Fare: $60 round trip.

Where to stay

The casino-hotels above tend to fall into the medium to expensive range (though they all offer massive off-peak discounts, usually Mon-Thur, Sun). There are numerous cheaper lodgings. Contact the visitor centre for comprehensive hotel listings and the latest discount information.

Tourist information

Las Vegas Convention & Visitors Authority
3150 Paradise Road, Las Vegas, NV 89109 (1-702 892 0711).
Website: www.lasvegas24hours.com

Death Valley National Park

A land of desolate plains and mountain ranges, punctuated here and there by pitstops offering little more than gas and junk food: this barren other-worldliness is the essence of Death Valley, one of the hottest places in the world. Its stillness belies a varied terrain riddled with diverse plant and animal life, whose beauty lies in the subtle colours and geological formations of the undulating rock, dunes and dry, salt lake bed – at 282 feet (86 metres) below sea level, it's the lowest point in the western hemisphere. Despite killer temperatures of 120°F (49°C) during the summer, and little water, humans have tried to inhabit Death Valley, leaving such landmarks as **Scotty's Castle**, a 1920s Spanish-Moorish mansion, and the **Harmony Borax Works** ruins. There are many dramatic vistas, but if you've seen Antonioni's

Out of this world: **Death Valley**.

Heading north

The drive from Los Angeles to San Francisco along the Pacific Coast Highway (Highway 1) is one of the great American road trips: at some point, you'll press the pedal to the metal and realise that hitherto you had experienced only a pale imitation of happiness.

But every now and then you'll need to get out of the car, and there are plenty of great places to stop. This trip takes you on Highway 1 and US 101 through the **Central Coast**, the coastal region that stretches from the northern end of Malibu for about 400 miles (640km) to just south of Santa Cruz, through terrain that goes from the sunny white beaches of the Santa Barbara coastline in the south through the rugged, misty mountain ranges of Big Sur. You can do it in two days, or more, depending on how long you choose to rest.

The PCH starts in Santa Monica and wends its way through the hilly coastline of Malibu and to the agricultural flatlands of the small towns of Oxnard and Ventura. They serve as a jumping-off point for the **Channel Islands National Park**, a wildlife sanctuary on an archipelago of five islands: take a boat or plane from Oxnard's Channel Islands Harbor or Ventura Harbor (contact the Ventura Visitors & Convention Bureau; 1-805 648 2075; website: www.ventura-usa.com).

After Ventura, it's well worth taking a detour inland on Highway 33 to idyllic **Ojai**, a small community in a semi-arid valley of oaks and orange groves nestled at the foot of the imposing Topa Topa Mountains. (Ojai is a destination in itself, and if you go direct from LA, try to enter from the east – on Highway 150 – for a staggering drive through mountains into the seemingly hidden valley.)

The town is charming, a combination of left-over hippiedom and a provincial arts community that has spawned such treats as the annual and much respected **Ojai Music Festival** in early summer, and **Barts Books** (302 W Matillija Road; 1-805 646 3755) – an open-air, second-hand bookshop with bookshelves on the exterior walls. For more information on the town, contact the Ojai Valley Chamber of Commerce (150 W Ojai, Ojai, CA 93023; 1-805 646 8126).

After Ojai, you can head west along Highway 150 and rejoin US 101 for a pleasant drive through the sparkling, south-facing mountainous coastline leading into Montecito and Santa Barbara.

sexy film *Zabriskie Point*, you won't want to miss that spot. Park admission is $10 per vehicle.

Getting there

Death Valley has several approach roads, leading from US 395 on the California side and US 95 from Nevada. The California approaches are probably the most breaktakingly scenic, particularly Hwy 190.

Where to stay

There are several **campgrounds** (you can book at the Furnace Creek and Texas Spring group campgrounds on 1-800 365 2267; website: www.nps.gov/deva), and three lodgings: the ultra-posh **Furnace Creek Inn**, the rustic-style **Furnace Creek Ranch** (both on 1-800 236 7916/1-760 786 2345; website: www.furnacecreek.com) and inexpensive **Stovepipe Wells Village** (1-760 786 2387). They're less crowded out of season – summer, for obvious reasons.

Tourist information

Death Valley Visitors Center
Death Valley National Park, Hwy 190, at Furnace Creek, Death Valley, CA 92328 (1-760 786 2331).

Mojave & Ridgecrest

Moving south on Highway 178 and then Highway 14 towards Los Angeles from Death Valley, you'll descend through the Mojave/Ridgecrest area; from red-brown desert into flat, whitish salt lakes, largely occupied by military bases. See the erosion-carved formations in **Red Rock Canyon State Park**, made famous in *Jurassic Park*, and Trona Pinnacles, also a popular movie location.

Just before you enter Lancaster on the edge of the LA region, stop at the famous **Edwards Air Force Base**, home of *The Right Stuff* and occasional site of space shuttle landings. There is a museum on the base, open five days a week, which has planes and memorabilia from over 50 years of flight testing. Once a year, usually in October, there is an open day when the public can see a display of the latest USAF technology in action (1-805 277 1110 for details).

Santa Barbara

Santa Barbara is California's Riviera. Ninety miles (145 kilometres) north of LA, next to the sparkling ocean (marred only by offshore oil rigs) in a fertile valley hugged by the lush Santa Ynez Mountains, Santa Barbara is the seaside getaway of choice for affluent Angelenos. They inhabit the hillside community of **Montecito** and have brought gentrification and exclusiveness to a town that also has great surf and a laid-back beach community.

It was once home to the Spanish, who left a firm imprint in the shape of **Mission Santa Barbara** (*see page 246* **On a mission**) and some of the best mission-style architecture in this region. There's only one tall edifice, the El Encanto Hotel; the rest are white-stucco, red-tiled buildings. There are also some historic adobe structures.

Park in any of the municipal car parks (first 90 minutes free) and take a walk through the 12 blocks of downtown up busy **State Street**, lined with cafés and pleasant, useless shops, from Gutierrez Street to Victoria Street and back down Anacapa Street, to see some stunning Spanish-style architecture and plazas. The Moorish **Santa Barbara Courthouse** is a marvel. Drive the official Scenic Route for a climb through the surrounding hill communities, a stop at the mission, and, from Alameda Padre Serra Road, a spectacular view over town and ocean. The **Botanical Gardens** and **Hot and Cold Springs Trails** are among many natural standouts.

Being a celeb city, Santa Barbara has many restaurants on a par with those of LA. However, the unmissable, totally affordable gourmet experience is to be had at **La Super Rica Taqueria** (622 Milpas Street, 1-805 963 4940), where, for under $10, you can eat some of the best Mexican food this side of Oaxaca. Great coffee can be had at the **Santa Barbara Roasting Company** (1-800 321 5282/ 1-805 962 0320) at the south end of State Street.

Getting there

By car: For the scenic route, head north on Hwy 1 (Pacific Coast Highway) and join the US 101, which goes direct to Santa Barbara: 96 miles (110km); about 2 hours.
By air: From LAX on American Eagle (1-800 433 7300; $88-$284 round trip), Sky West (1-800 453 9417; $88-$218 round trip) or United Express (1-800 241 6522; $88-$207 round trip); about 40 mins.
By train: Amtrak (1-800 872 7245) schedules eight trains a day. Fare: $32-$48 round trip; 2½-3 hours.
By bus: Greyhound (1-800 231 2222) has 11 buses daily for a 2-4-hour journey. Fare: $24 round trip.

Where to stay

If you can afford it, stay at the luxurious **Biltmore Hotel** in Montecito (1260 Channel Drive, Santa Barbara, CA 93108; reservations 1-800 332 3442). Otherwise, there are numerous B&Bs, including the **Cheshire Cat** (36 W Valerio Street, Santa Barbara, CA 93101; 1-805 569 1610; website: www. cheshirecat.com). **Sycamore Cottage** (646 N Hope Avenue, Santa Barbara, CA 93110; 1-805 687 7055), run by Saral, a massage therapist and minister, and David, a screenwriter, is a secluded, woodsy retreat with only one (large) room.

Tourist information

Santa Barbara Visitor Information Center
1 Garden Street, Santa Barbara, CA 93101
(1-805 965 3021).
Santa Barbara Chamber of Commerce
12 E Carrillo, Santa Barbara, CA 93101
(1-805 965 3023).

The wild coast

After Santa Barbara you'll be back on US 101 for a 30-mile (48-kilometre) coastal stretch until you turn inland to the curious Danish-American town of **Solvang**, with preserved Nordic architecture alongside the **Mission Santa Ines**. The road then passes, to the west, the flower fields of **Lompoc**, which burst into radiant bloom in June and July, on the way towards **San Luis Obispo**.

The must-see in this mission town, fittingly, is a Madonna – but a secular one: the unbelievable **Madonna Inn** (100 Madonna Road, off the US 101, San Luis Obispo, CA 93405; reservations 1-800 543 9666; website: www.madonnainn.com). Created and decorated by road builder Alex Madonna and his wife Phyllis, the Madonna Inn leaves all other themed and kitsch environments at the starting block. The hotel's 110 rooms are all different; elaborate fantasies based on a palette of blue, green and, predominantly, pink, pink, pink. Also in San Luis Obispo are the **Sycamore Hot Springs** (*see page 240* **Spas & hot springs**).

After San Luis Obispo, you can rejoin the coastal Highway 1, passing charming **Cambria** in a wooded valley, until you enter the open, rolling hills of **San Simeon**. There, set back from the sea, is the extraordinary and completely over-the-top **Hearst Castle**. Designed by celebrated California architect Julia Morgan for newspaper tycoon William Randolph Hearst, the Castle is a monument to Hearst's excess (and the model for Xanadu in *Citizen Kane*). It can be visited only by guided tour – make sure to get on one that includes the swimming pools. For more information, contact Hearst San Simeon State Historical Monument, 750 Hearst Castle Road, San Simeon, CA 93452 (reservations 1-800 444 4445; website: www.hearstcastle.org).

*Take a guided tour of **Hearst Castle**.*

On a mission

'With the best theological intentions in the world,' argues late LA historian Carey McWilliams in his seminal book *Southern California: An Island on the Land*, 'the Franciscan padres eliminated Indians with the effectiveness of Nazis operating concentration camps.' During the Spanish conquest of California, the Spanish missionary monks, led by Father Junipero Serra, founded a string of 21 missions from San Diego in the south to Sonoma, about 40 miles north of San Francisco. The first, San Diego de Alcala in Mission Valley in San Diego was established in 1769; the last, San Francisco Solano, in 1823; and by 1848 the mission system had come to an end.

The aim behind the missions was to convert the tribal peoples and establish self-sustaining communities. They succeeded in creating productive, wealthy farms and a reputation for hospitality for all who passed by. Meanwhile, the forced Native American converts died in thousands from a combination of depression, disease and malnutrition.

In the late nineteenth century, the Californian missions were reinvented as an icon of tradition, solid values and romance. For the zealous Spanish padres had also left a legacy of mission architecture: white, sometimes Moorish buildings with bougainvillea-shaded quadrangles and simple, solid interiors with hand-crafted furniture. The defunct missions began to stand for a simple elegance and serenity, something seen as missing, then as now, in California's secular culture. This revised image spawned mission-style architecture and décor, a popular and influential branch of Californian design.

It is possible to tour the missions, many of which have been renovated or reconstructed and now function as Catholic parishes. The 21 missions are all located near US 101, which loosely follows the old El Camino Real ('royal road'), named in honour of the Spanish monarchy that financed the colonising expeditions. (The stretch of the 101 from San Diego to Los Angeles is now the I-5.)

In San Diego you can see the first mission to be founded, **San Diego de Alcala** (10818 San Diego Mission Road; 1-619 281 8449), and – a few miles north, just east of Oceanside on Highway 76 – the 18th, **San Luis Rey de Francia** (4050 Mission Avenue, San Luis Rey; 1-760 757 3651). The remains of **San Juan Capistrano** (1-949 248 2049), in the shape of a cross, lie at Camino Capistrano in San Juan

Capistrano, about 40 miles (64 kilometres) south of Long Beach. Every year, on 19 March, this mission celebrates the return of the cliff swallows from Argentina.

In LA County itself you can visit **San Gabriel** (428 S Mission Drive, San Gabriel; 1-626 457 3035), formerly one of the wealthiest missions, with a copper baptismal font from King Carlos III of Spain and priceless altar statues. **San Fernando Rey de España** (15151 San Fernando Mission Boulevard, Mission Hills; 1-818 361 0186), in the north-west of the Los Angeles urban area, is the largest free-standing adobe structure in California. Just north of LA, in Ventura, is **San Buenaventura** (225 E Main Street; 1-805 643 4318).

If you tour the Central Coast (*see page 244* **Heading north**), you can visit **Santa Barbara** (2201 Laguna Street, Santa Barbara; 1-805 682 4713), **Santa Ines** (1760 Mission Drive, Solvang; 1-805 688 4815) and **La Purisima Conceptión** (2295 Purisima Road, Lompoc; 1-805 733 3713), the most completely reconstructed mission in the state.

San Luis de Obispo de Tolosa, whose chapel was built of logs, is further north in San Luis Obispo (751 Palm Street; 1-805 543 6850); further north still is **San Miguel Archangel** (775 Mission Street, San Miguel; 1-805 467 3256); then **San Antonio de Padua** (Mission Creek Road, Jolon; 1-408 385 4478), followed by **Nuestra Señora de la Soledad** (36641 Fort Romie Road, Soledad; 1-408 678 2586). The Moorish **San Carlos Borromeo de Carmelo** is at 3080 Rio Road in Carmel (1-408 624 3600) and the last in the Central Coast region is **San Juan Bautista** (Second and Mariposa Streets, San Juan Bautista; 1-408 623 4528).

Santa Barbara mission.

The peaceful coastal path on the **Monterey Peninsula**.

After San Simeon, the road hugs the coast, passing along the cliffs of the Santa Lucia range: you'll see stunning vistas of forested headlands and huge kelp beds in the water, and, from one of many stopping points, you can watch for seals and sea otters. You then reach the **Julia Pfeiffer Burns State Park**, where an 80-foot (24-metre) waterfall drops on to the beach, in spectacular Big Sur.

Sometimes compared to the Scottish highlands, **Big Sur** is a stunning stretch of coastline, with fog-swathed redwood forests and winding cliffs that drop sharply down to chilly beaches. A mecca for well-to-do New Agers who flock to the Esalen Institute educational centre and spa, it is also home to the Henry Miller Library. If you can afford it, stay at the **Post Ranch Inn** for hippy luxury (Highway 1, PO Box 219, Big Sur, CA 93920; reservations 1-800 527 2200; website: www.postranchinn.com); if not, try **Ripplewood Inn** (Highway 1, Big Sur, CA 93920; 1-831 667 2242). For more information, call Pfeiffer Big Sur State Park (1-831 667 2315).

After this, you'll be on the road to **Carmel** – a well-preserved, pretty town most famous for its one-time mayor, Clint Eastwood – and then the **Monterey Peninsula**, a scenic, 17-mile (27km) coastal drive on a toll road that passes through the famous Pebble Beach Golf Course.

Monterey, site of John Steinbeck's *Cannery Row*, used to be a large fishing port. These days, the fish are confined to the **Monterey Bay Aquarium** (886 Cannery Row; 1-831 648 4888; website: www.mbayaq.org), which claims the world's largest plate glass windows in its million-gallon tank. Steinbeck is remembered in the Spirit of Monterey Wax Museum on **Cannery Row**, itself metamorphosed into a shopping mall with piscine-themed restaurants.

From here it is another 100 miles (160 kilometres) or so, via the surfing town of **Santa Cruz**, to

San Francisco and its environs; that's most definitely another story, covered in the *Time Out San Francisco Guide*.

Returning to LA

Route 5

The fastest route from San Francisco back to LA is along the inland I-5. This whips you through California's central valley, mile upon mile of fruit-growing and cattle-rearing plains. The cattle farms, where miserably thin cows are jammed together in arid, open fields, are not a pretty sight – nor smell. The fruit farms, acres of uniform orchards worked by Mexican immigrants, dotted with small, dusty towns, offer an insight into the underbelly of the California dream.

Route 99

Alternatively, you can deviate from the I-5 on to the more inland Hwy 99, which stretches for some 500 miles (800km) from Red Bluff in Northern California to just south of **Bakersfield** – centre of the agricultural industry and California's country music capital – just over 100 miles (160km) north of LA. From here, rejoin the I-5 to Los Angeles. Hwy 99 takes you through the irredeemably awful **Fresno**, which appears to have only chain stores and fast-food restaurants (though residents say its thrift stores are a great source of 1950s and 1960s tat). Fresno is a necessary staging post on the way to the Sierra Nevada Mountains further east, where you will find more natural wonders in the shape of **Yosemite**, **Kings Canyon** and **Sequoia National Parks** and **Mammoth Lakes** ski area.

Heading south

San Diego

San Diego is wholesome America by the sea. Two facts: the Republican Party's annual convention was held here in 1996, and the city has the largest US Navy base on the West Coast. This should give you some idea of its character. But it's a pleasant place to visit and worth a day's sightseeing – or even two, if you want to take in its abundance of

Skiing & snowboarding

It's easy to go skiing or snowboarding from Los Angeles: there are numerous resorts within a day's – or less – drive. The ski season varies greatly: from December through April in LA-area mountains and November through June for the Sierra Nevada. If you're driving, you'll need to hire tyre chains for many mountain routes.

If you want to rent gear in LA before you hit the slopes, try **Val Surf & Sport, Sports Chalet** (for both, *see page 173* **Shops & Services**) or **REI** in Carson (405 W Torrance Boulevard, at the I-110; 1-310 538 2429).

San Gabriel Mountains

These resorts are the closest to LA; they can be the least exciting in a drought year, but offer the best bargain going in a good snow season.

Mount Baldy Ski Area
1-909-982-0800. From the I-10, take the Mountain Avenue exit in Upland and head 16 miles (26km) north to where the road becomes Mount Baldy Road; continue to the end. **Open** 8am-4.30pm Mon-Fri; 7.30am-4.30pm Sat, Sun. **Lift pass** day $40; $25 children; *half-day* $25; $15 children. **Hire** skis $17; snowboard & boots $27.
Mount Baldy (officially known as Mount San Antonio), the highest peak in the San Gabriel Mountains, has the steepest and hardest runs of the LA-area resorts. Intermediate and advanced skiers will love the rugged terrain on this 10,064ft (3,068m) mountain.

Mount Pinos
Ranger station 1-805-245-3731. From the I-5, take the Frazier Park exit, head west on Frazier Mountain Park Road, then Cuddly Valley Road past Lake of the Woods about 9 miles (14km).
This 2,000-acre (810-hectare) cross-country ski area in the Los Padres National Forest gets about 6ft (1.8m) of snow between mid-December and mid-April. It's an ideal family spot for cross-country skiing, snowshoeing or sledding. Hire options are limited, so rent in LA before you go – or try Frazier Ski & Pack (1-805 245 0408).

Mount Waterman
1-626 440 1041. From the I-210, take Hwy 2 north for 34 miles (55km). **Lift pass** day $25; $12 children. **Hire** skis $15; snowboard $25.
Mount Waterman is the oldest ski resort in Southern

California and among the closest to Downtown LA. Its 8,030ft (2,448m) peak is good for intermediate and advanced skiers, with a few runs that qualify as black diamond.

New Mountain High Resort
1-760-249-5808. From the I-15, take Hwy 138 west to Hwy 2 and go 3 miles (5km) past Wrightwood. **Lift pass** day $39; free under-10s with paying adult.
Mountain High near Wrightwood was the first resort in Southern California to offer snowboarding. It's good for intermediates and beginners, with special 'night' skiing from 3.30-10pm daily.

Snowcrest Snow Park at Kratka Ridge
1-626 440 9749/1-626 792 6906. From the I-210, take Hwy 2 north for 36 miles (58km). **Lift pass** day $15 Mon-Thur; $25 Fri-Sun; $10 children (1 free with paying adult). **Hire** skis $15; snowboard $27.
Snowcrest is a small (58-acre/23-hectare) resort popular with snowboarders. The best part: it's cheap and it's near LA.

San Bernardino Mountains

These resorts are further away – about 100 miles (160 kilometres) north-east of LA – but can be counted on to deliver good winter weather. All are off the I-10 along Highway 18 between Lake Arrowhead and Big Bear Lake. For accommodation details, call the Big Bear Lake Resort Association at 1-909 866 7000.

Bear Mountain Ski Resort
1-909 585 2519. **Lift pass** day $42; $10 children. **Hire** *skis or snowboard* $28.
The largest and most popular resort in Big Bear, Bear Mountain is also the highest in the San Bernardinos at 8,805ft (2,684m). Half the runs are intermediate, with the rest split between beginners and advanced skiers. **Website:** *www.bearmtn.com*

Snow Summit Mountain Resort
1-909 866 5766. **Lift pass** day $32; $10 children.
This 230-acre (93-hectare) resort in Big Bear Lake is good for families and all-level skiers, has 12 lifts and offers night skiing at weekends and holidays.

Snow Valley
1-909 867 2751. **Lift pass** day $34; $9 children.
Also good for families, Snow Valley, near Arrowhead Lake, has fine beginner and intermediate runs. It has 12 lifts and night skiing on Fridays, Saturdays and holidays.

---

cultural institutions and historical districts. Its beaches and animal attractions also make it a great place for children. The climate is wonderful: like Los Angeles, but cooler and less smoggy, with sea breezes blowing in to its stunning bayside location. It's also a mere 25 miles (40 kilometres) from gutsy – and unmissable —**Tijuana** on the Mexican border (*see page 251*).

The second largest city in California, with a population of about two million, San Diego's

economy was built on the defence industry; the losses resulting from defence cuts are now being recouped through its growing tourist, biomedical, telecommunications and high-tech industries – it's sometimes referred to as Silicon Valley South. You can still get a sense of the might of the US Navy if you drive across the two-mile long Coronado Bay Bridge (which swoops over the harbour from downtown to the 'island' of **Coronado** – actually a peninsula): it yields a dra-

There's downhill and cross-country skiing at **Yosemite National Park**.

Nearby is Big Air Winter Park (1-909 867 2338), a 40-acre (16-hectare) park for snowboarding, skiing and tubing.

Further north

The heart of California's best ski country and scenery lies in the incomparable Sierra Nevada, about 400 miles (640 kilometres) north of LA.

Lake Tahoe

Squaw Valley 1-530 583 6985. **Lift pass** $49; $24 13-15s; $5 under-12s; *Heavenly 1-702 586 7000.*
Lift pass $52; $38 teens; $24 under-12s.
This famed resort area straddling California and Nevada has no less than 14 alpine resorts and nine cross-country resorts. The 4,000-acre (1,620-hectare) Squaw Valley, which hosted the 1960 Winter Olympics, is very popular, though Heavenly's runs have the best views of the lake. And when you tire of the slopes, you can always hit the light-years-from-Vegas casinos on the Nevada side.

Mammoth Mountain & June Mountain

Mammoth: 1-888 462 6668/1-760 934 0745.
Lift pass *day* $49; $37 teens; $25 children, seniors.
Website: www.mammoth-mtn.com
June: 1-760 648 7733. **Lift pass** *day* $40; $30 teens; $20 children, seniors.
Website: www.junemountain.com
Mammoth Mountain in the eastern Sierra lives up to its name: it's huge, with 150 trails and varied terrain leading to stunning rock formations such as the Minarets. Nearby June Mountain offers a more intimate ski experience. There are also three cross-country resorts at Mammoth: Tamarack Lodge (1-760 934 2442), Rock Creek Lodge (1-760 935 4170) and Sierra Meadows Ranch (1-760 934 6161). For information on accommodation, call 1-888 466 2666.

Yosemite

Information 1-209 372 1000;
reservations 1-209 252 4848.
Lift pass *day* $22-$28; $13 children.
Winter at Yosemite National Park is Ansel Adams country at its best. Badger Pass is a small but scenic downhill ski area, good for beginners and intermediates, while cross-country skiing offers a great opportunity to explore Yosemite at your leisure.
A beginner's package, including park entry fees, costs $40.
Website: www.yosemitepark.com

matic view of the cruisers, aircraft carriers, destroyers and other vessels anchored in the bay.

Coronado is also home to the historic Victorian **Hotel del Coronado** – scene of shenanigans in *Some Like It Hot* and now a resort complex that specialises in organising family reunions (1500 Orange Avenue, San Diego, CA 92118; reservations 1-800 468 3533).

If you stay out of the poorer, rougher neighbourhoods that occupy the fringes and lie to the south, the San Diego you will see is thoroughly spruce and well organised. It consists of distinct neighbourhoods loosely knitted together by freeways. Although, as is usual in Southern California, the car is the most efficient way to take it all in, you can also get around the metropolitan area on **San Diego Transit Corporation** buses or use the **San Diego Trolley** between downtown and Old Town to the north or Tijuana to the south.

The heart of the city is downtown, a combination of sparkling high-rise business district and commercial core. Head for **Horton Plaza**, a complex of shops and restaurants on six lavishly decorated open-air levels: this vibrant, highly coloured collage of buildings, conceived by Los Angeles architect Jon Jerde, is a forerunner of his more recent themed mall, CityWalk at Universal Studios. Next to Horton Plaza is the historic, 16-block **Gaslamp Quarter**, a nineteenth-century district now transformed into San Diego's hottest place for shopping and eating. At present the emphasis is on Italian cuisine – there are numerous good restaurants.

Also in downtown, by the waterfront, is the maritime-themed **Seaport Village**. You can stay – or just have afternoon tea – at the grand **US Grant Hotel** (326 Broadway, San Diego, CA 92101; 1-800 237 5029 from California/1-800 237 5029 from elsewhere; website: www.grandheritage.com) on the corner of Fourth Avenue and Broadway.

From downtown head north-east to the expansive **Balboa Park**. Stimulated by the 1915 and 1936 International Expositions, Balboa Park is a monument to the improving zeal of the WASP. Encompassing 1,200 acres (490 hectares) of landscaped gardens and cultural monuments, it houses three theatres and 13 museums covering the fine arts and sciences, among them the **Reuben H Fleet Science Center** (1-619 238 1233; website: www.rhfleet.org), the ornate 200-foot (60-metre) high **California Tower** and the **Old Globe Theatre** (1-619 231 1941/tickets 1-619 239 2255), the West Coast's oldest residential theatre – San Diego is a West Coast theatrical hub.

Other attractions in Balboa Park include the famous **San Diego Zoo** (2920 Zoo Drive; 1-619 234 3153). Here, wild environments are simulated in contrived climate zones, such as Gorilla Tropics, Tiger River and the Polar Bear Plunge. You can see animals in a more natural habitat in the zoo's **Wild Animal Park** (15500 San Pasqual Valley Road), a preserve 30 miles (48 kilometres) north of downtown (get a pass and directions from the zoo).

More animals, this time of the trick-playing, marine variety, can be seen at **Sea World Adventure Park** (1720 S Shores Drive; 1-619 226 3901; website: www.seaworld.com). Sea World is part of **Mission Bay Park**, a vast aquatic resort that encompasses 17 miles (27 kilometres) of glistening beaches, with all the usual watersports. It is also home to **Belmont Park**, which features the Plunge – reportedly the largest indoor swimming pool in Southern California – and the Giant Dipper, a restored, 1925 wooden rollercoaster.

San Diego offers a dose of its pre-Anglo history in the form of **Point Loma**, west of downtown, and **Mission Valley** and **Old Town**, north of the same. From the Cabrillo National Monument at the southern tip of Point Loma, you get a panoramic view of San Diego as seen by Portuguese explorer Juan Rodriguez Cabrillo when he 'discovered' the West Coast in 1542. The Mission San Diego de Alcalla that founded San Diego moved from here in 1774, but some of San Diego's remaining Spanish settlement has been preserved in the six-block **Old Town State Historic Park**; the subsequent transition to US rule is recorded in the adjacent **Heritage Park**.

Get a taste of 1950s and 1960s San Diego in the Fifth Avenue business district of the **Hillcrest** neighbourhood; there's a bevy of vintage cafés and shops, as well as the very popular, 1950s-themed **Corvette Diner Bar & Grill** (3946 Fifth Avenue; 1-619 542 1001), where you can view a high-sheen 1954 Corvette and eat some classic diner food.

Last but not least, San Diego is a mecca for sports. Specialities include great surfing at **Ocean Beach** and sports fishing at **Point Loma**. You can watch horse racing at the **Del Mar Thoroughbred Club** (Jimmy Durante Boulevard, at Via de la Valle; 1-619 755 1141) in the emerging Del Mar suburb in north San Diego, polo at the **San Diego Polo Club** (14555 El Camino Real; 1-619 481 9217) and football at the **Jack Murphy Stadium** (9449 Friars Road; 1-619 280 2121), site of the Super Bowl in 1997.

Getting there

By car: From downtown LA, take the I-5 south. From west LA, take the I-405 south and then join the I-5. The built-up LA region seems to go on and on – as far as San Clemente. After this you'll be driving through rolling hills and inaccessible shoreline, much of which is taken up by the Camp Pendleton Marine base.

Watch for people running across the freeway (there are road signs to warn you of the danger spots): this area is notorious for illegal immigrants trying to do a runner from boats that have sailed from Mexico. From LA, the trip takes about 2½ hours.

By air: From LAX on American Eagle (1-800 433 7300; $88-$330 round trip), Sky West (1-800 453 9417; $100-$165 round trip) or United Express (1-800 241 6522; $88-$578 round trip); about 50 mins.

By train: Amtrak operates ten trains per day, sometimes more. Fare: $46 round trip; about 2 hours 40 mins.

By bus: Greyhound has 31 buses a day. Fare: $22 round trip; 2-3 hours.

Hotel Coronado, *San Diego. See page 249.*

Where to stay

There is a huge choice of accommodation in San Diego; call **San Diego Hotel Reservations** (1-800 728 3227; website: ww.savecash.com) for information and reservations.

Tourist information

Conventions & Visitor's Bureau
International Visitor Information Center
11 Horton Plaza, at First Avenue & F Street, San Diego, CA 92101 (1-619 236 1212).
Website: www.sandiego.org
Balboa Park Visitors Center
House of Hospitality, 1549 El Prado, San Diego, CA 92101 (1-619 239 0512).
The Transit Store
102 Broadway, San Diego, CA (1-619 234 1060).
Public transport information, plus tokens, passes ($5-$15), timetables, maps and brochures. Alternatively, for bus route info call 1-619 233 3004; for trolley info 1-619 231 8549.

Get a taste of Mexico in **Tijuana**.

Tijuana

After squeaky-clean San Diego, Tijuana smacks you in the face like a strong Margarita. It's loud, it's messy, it's gaudy – and it's great. On the one hand, it's a busy business city of almost two million inhabitants; on the other, it remains true to its origins as a high-kicking border town. Noisy American students descending on the Avenida Revolución for weekend drinking binges (alcohol is not sold to under-21s in California) are the most recent incarnation of northerners escaping to Tijuana for drink, gambling and cheap sex, as they have since the time of prohibition.

The city is also a first, intoxicating taste of the vibrant yet impoverished land of Baja California and Mexico. Although Tijuana feels very different from the US, it is an easy place to visit. You can stay there without a visa for up to 72 hours, but take your passport – you will need it to get back into the US once again. You can use dollars in Tijuana, which will go a long way. And while speaking Spanish is obviously an asset, you can also get by with English.

Local spectacles include bullfighting, which takes place from May to September at the **El Toreo de Tijuana** (Boulevard Agua Caliente, at Avenue Cuauhtémoc; 01152-66 86 15 10), dog racing which takes place at the famous **Agua Caliente Racetrack** (Boulevard Agua Caliente, at Avenida Salinas; 01152-66 81 78 11) and jai alai (a fast game involving throwing and catching a ball in a long wicker basket) at the **Jai Alai Palace** (Avenue Revolución, at Seventh Street; 01152-66 85 36 87).

Otherwise, the main attraction for the day visitor is the tourist-oriented **Avenida Revolución**, a pulsating strip of vividly decorated discos, bars, restaurants, shops and street vendors selling everything from religious kitsch, leather goods and Mexican pottery to cheap cigarettes. Buy the Mexican-made US brands to avoid trouble with Customs; you can also buy alcohol (the best

bargains are the Mexican tequilas, brandies and beers) and pharmaceutical drugs (this is where prescription drug-addicted Americans come to stock up on products they can't get over the counter at home).

If you want to go where the Mexicans go, head to the newer **Zona Rio** district east of Avenida Revolución. There, at the bars on the old-style **Plaza Fiesta**, you can eat tapas with the locals. Or go to **Señor Frogs** in the Pueblo Amigo shopping centre by the border: a bar that's very popular after Sunday bullfights. For good Mexican food, try **Guadalajara Grill** (19 Avenida Diego Rivera) or **La Casa del Mole** (near the Lucerna Hotel on Paseo de los Heroes). For excellent seafood, Tijuana's speciality, try **El Faro de Mazatlan** (9542 Sanchez Taboada Boulevard).

Getting there

By car: Take the I-5 or I-805 south from San Diego for 25 miles (40km) until you reach the San Ysidro International Border. There you can park for a minimal fee at one of the many border parking lots and walk, bus or taxi the short distance into Tijuana. You could drive in, but most US rental cars are not insured for Mexico and the traffic is chaotic. Remember that in Mexico it is illegal to turn right on red.
By bus: Take the San Ysidro South Line trolley (1-619 233 3004) from downtown San Diego, destination San Ysidro. It runs every 15 mins from 5am-midnight and all night Sat; $4 round trip.

Getting back

Retrace your steps (look for 'To USA' signs) until you get to US Customs. Be prepared to wait up to 15 mins if you are on foot, up to an hour in a car. Unless you are a Mexican trying to make a break for the border, the Customs officials will probably give you no trouble. You can bring in $400-worth of incidental purchases, including no more than one litre of alcohol, 200 cigarettes and 100 cigars.

Where to stay

Try **La Villa de Zaragoza** (1120 Avenida Madeo, between Calles 7 & 8, Zona Centro; 01152-66 85 18 32/37) or the **Hacienda del Rio** (10606 Sanchez Taboada Boulevard; 01152-66 84 86 44).

Tourist information

There are two information centres at the border and one in downtown, at 8206 Avenida Revolución, at Calle 1 (01152-66 88 16 85/88 05 55). Or call 01152-66 84 05 37/38.

Directory

Directory

For abbreviations *see page vi* **About the Guide**.

Getting Around

Given the sheer size and sprawl of LA, it's hardly surprising that Angelenos have a special relationship with the car. Driving is the quickest and easiest way to get around the city and, once you get the hang of the freeway system, it can actually be fun.

But if you don't have access to a car, it doesn't mean that you're condemned to staying within walking distance of your hotel. Los Angeles has a very efficient bus system that goes just about everywhere, as well as a number of infant Metro (subway train) lines that are slowly gaining in popularity as they start to extend across the city. Because of the distances involved, if you're using public transport to get around, plan ahead and always allow plenty of time for your journey.

To & from LAX

Los Angeles International Airport (LAX)
1-310 646 5252.
LAX is situated on the Westside and has eight terminals; flights from Europe usually arrive at the Tom Bradley International Terminal. A touch-screen booth in the terminal provides free printouts on transport from the airport; the same information (for LAX and a host of other US airports) can be found on website **www.quickaid.com**.

By shuttle

A fleet of shuttles flits between LAX and every neighbourhood in LA, 24 hours a day. Most will drop you at your hotel; fares start at $15. You pick them up immediately outside the arrival terminals: the

shuttle dispatchers will tell you which one to take.

If you're flying out of LAX, the following companies will pick you up and take you there. Book 24 hours in advance.

SuperShuttle *1-323 775 6600/ 1-310 782 6600.*
Californian Dream Airport Shuttle *1-800 503 7326.*
Shuttle 2000 *1-800 977 7872.*

By taxi

Taxis can be found immediately outside the arrivals terminals. If you're staying on the Westside, a taxi will cost around $20 plus tip. If you're heading to Hollywood or beyond, it'll be at least $40 and a tip. There's a flat rate of $24 between LAX and Downtown.

By bus

There's a free shuttle from LAX to the nearby MTA bus terminal at Vicksburg Avenue and 96th Street. From there, buses go all over the city. If you're arriving at night, it's safer to hop on a shuttle rather than the bus.

To & from Burbank

Burbank-Glendale-Pasadena Airport
2627 Hollywood Way, Burbank (1-818 840 8847).
If you're flying from a US airport, you may land in Burbank rather than LAX. It's served by shuttles and taxis like LAX and several car hire agencies have offices there. A free shuttle bus will take you to the MTA bus stop at Hollywood Way and Thornton Avenue in Burbank.

Airlines

For more airlines, consult the *Yellow Pages*.

Major international
Air New Zealand *1-800 262 1234.*
American Airlines *domestic 1-800 433 7300; international 1-800 433 7300.*
British Airways *1-800 247 9297.*
Continental Airlines *domestic 1-800 525 0280; international 1-800 231 0856.*
Delta Air Lines *1-800 221 1212.*
Lufthansa *1-800 645 3880.*
Northwest Airlines *domestic 1-800 225 2525; international 1-800 447 4747.*
Swissair *1-800 221 4750.*
TWA *domestic 1-800 221 2000; international 1-800 892 4141.*
USAir *1-800 428 4322.*
United Airlines *1-800 241 6522.*
Virgin Atlantic Airways *1-800 862 8621.*

Airlines flying to Burbank
American and **United** (*see above*) also fly to Burbank.
Alaska *1-800 426 0333.*
America West *1-800 247 5692.*
SkyWest *1-800 453 9417.*
Southwest *1-800 435 9792.*

Public transport

Information services

LA's public transport system is run by the **Metropolitan Transportation Authority** (MTA). Its telephone information operators will plan your journey for you, including connections, if you tell them where you are and where you want to go, as well as giving information on bus and Metro train timetables, fares and passes. Expect to wait on hold for a while, though. For a copy of the MTA's *Self-Guided Tours*, write to: Metro, 425 Main Street, LA, CA 90013-1393.

MTA information lines *1-800 266 6883/1-213 626 4455*.
MTA information centres *515 S Flower Street, at Fifth Street, Downtown.* Open *7.30am-3.30pm Mon-Fri.* Map 7 B3
6249 Hollywood Boulevard, at Vine Street, Hollywood. Open *10am-6pm Mon-Fri.* Map 5 B1
Website: www.mta.net

Buses

The main mode of public transport in Los Angeles is thousands of **MTA** buses, painted white with orange-and-red trim and often covered in garish advertising, not to mention graffiti. They cover over 200 routes throughout LA.

The **DASH** (Downtown Area Short Hop) A, B, C, D and E are express shuttles, running every 15-45 minutes, which service Downtown and most of its important sites and landmarks, including the Garment District, Convention Center, MOCA, City Hall, USC, Union Station, Little Tokyo, Exposition Park and the Music Center. DASH also provides express services to other areas, including Beverly Hills, Venice, Hollywood, West Hollywood, Pacific Palisades, Crenshaw and Van Nuys/Studio City, for only 25¢ a ride.

Municipal bus services include **Santa Monica City Bus Lines**, aka 'The Big Blue Bus' (50¢ fare), which serves Santa Monica, Malibu and Venice; **West Hollywood Cityline** (50¢), a shuttle service covering 18 locations in West Hollywood; **Commuter Express** ($1.10-$2.70), essentially a commuter bus service from Downtown LA to, among other destinations, Glendale, Encino, Westwood, Brentwood, Culver City and the San Fernando Valley; **Foothill Transit** (90¢-$2.75), primarily serving the San Gabriel and Pomona Valleys; and **Culver CityBus** (60¢), covering Culver City, Venice, Mar Vista, LAX and Westwood/UCLA.

On busy lines, buses run every 5-10 minutes during peak hours; at night, it's every half hour or so. On the main crosstown routes the service is 24 hour, but there's only one bus an hour after 11pm. The buses stick to their schedules, more or less.

Buses also provide an insight into a different side of LA. Most people only take the bus if they haven't got a car and consequently they're mainly used by the poor, the old and recent immigrants. They are safe, however.

Commuter Express *1-800 266 6883*.
Culver CityBus *1-310 253 6500*.
DASH information *1-213 580 5444*.
Foothill Transit *1-626 967 3147*.
Santa Monica City Bus Lines *1-310-451 5444*.
West Hollywood Cityline *1-800 447 2189*.

FARES & BUS STOPS

One trip on an MTA bus costs $1.35; children under five travel free. You'll need the exact fare and the machines on the buses take notes. If you plan to change buses, ask the driver for a 'transfer' (25¢), a ticket that you can use on a subsequent journey that day.

The MTA bus stop sign is a big orange 'M' on a white rectangle. In Santa Monica, it's a blue triangle on a light pole marked 'Big Blue Bus'.

If you're going to use the buses a lot, you can buy tokens from supermarkets and local stores. A bag of ten costs $9 and it's one token per journey. Or you can get a monthly pass for $49. You can use the same tokens on the Metro system.

OUTSIDE LA

For long-distance buses, head to the main **Greyhound** terminal; there's no booking, so it's first come, first served for seats. It's in a distinctly dodgy area, but the terminal itself is safe.

Greyhound terminal *1716 E Seventh Street, between S Alameda & Decatur Streets, Downtown (1-800 231 2222/1-213 629 8400).* **Open** *24 hours daily.*

Trains

The concept of the **Metro** subway train system is a new one for LA and public awareness of the three lines – Red, Blue and Green – is still fairly low. As a result, the trains are rarely crowded, but then they only cover certain areas of the city. The MTA is opening new stations as fast as they can be built, so by the time you read this there will probably have been a couple of additions to the network.

One trip costs $1.35 and transfers (between lines and between buses and trains) are available. Trains run 4.45am-11.30pm daily. For a **map** of the Metro system, *see p285.*

Metro Red Line

A genuine underground subway, this is the newest line: it opened in 1993 and starts at Union Station in Downtown and runs to Wilshire Boulevard and Western Avenue. By 2001, the line is scheduled to go as far as Hollywood.

Metro Blue Line

Starting at the Red Line station at Seventh Street and Figueroa Street in Downtown, the Blue Line heads south, above ground, through South Central, before ending up in Long Beach. This is one of the most popular routes, and the view along the way offers a glimpse of a part of LA not usually seen by visitors.

Metro Green Line

This overground route links the area around LAX (though there's no station at the airport itself) with South Central and then Norwalk to the east. You probably won't need to use this particular route.

OUTSIDE LA

Union Station is the place to go for any train heading out of Los Angeles. The **Metrolink** suburban lines cover Orange County, Riverside County and San Bernardino County. All other US destinations are served by **Amtrak** trains.

Union Station *800 N Alameda Street, between Cesar E Chavez Avenue & US 101, Downtown (1-213 683 6987/Metrolink 1-808 5465/Amtrak 1-800 872 7245).* **Map 7 C1**

Taxis & limos

Because of LA's size, taxis are not a cheap way of getting around. The basic fare is $1.90 and then $1.60 per additional mile. They take credit cards. You can't hail cabs on the street, although there are taxi ranks in certain areas. Bars, restaurants and supermarkets will often call a cab for you. The following companies all offer a 24-hour service:

Checker Cab *1-800 300 5007.*
Independent Taxi *1-800 521 8294.*
Yellow Cab *1-800 200 6693.*

The limo is the quintessential LA form of transport; you'll see more here than just about anywhere else in the world. The cost of hiring a limo starts at around $40 an hour and the driver will expect a decent tip.

A1-West Coast Limousine Service *1-310 671 8720.*
Gold Coach Limo *1-800 546 6232.*
The Ultimate Limousine *1-800 710 1498.*

Driving

Driving in LA presents its own unique challenges. At first sight, the five-lane freeways seem like racetracks, with cars jockeying for position by overtaking on both sides and weaving in and out of lanes. But, intimidating as it may seem, LA is far less terrifying for drivers than London, Paris or New York .You'll quickly get used to it; and when it's late at night and the freeways are less crowded, driving can be a positive pleasure.

Freeways are referred to by their numbers – the 10, 110, 405 and so on – and often by names as well. The I-10 (I stands for Interstate) west of Downtown, for example, is known as the Santa Monica Freeway. Any road apart from a freeway is known as a surface street.

On the freeways there is a speed limit of 65mph (104kph),

but you'll see many cars going much faster. Don't expect people to indicate when they change lanes: locals will often simply point out of the window to the space they want, or not bother to give any indication at all. The outside lanes are the fast lanes (though it's normal to overtake on the inside): it's best to stay in the middle ones until you need to exit.

When you merge on to a freeway from a surface street, it's important to accelerate to freeway speed; similarly, be prepared to brake sharply when exiting. Exits are marked by the name of the surface street you join; remember that you may be exiting off either side of the freeway.

Always plan your route before you leave: the freeway system does not take you directly from A to B and it moves swiftly, so you must know your freeway entrance and exit and the direction you are going (north, south, east or west) before you start. Otherwise, you can easily find yourself being sucked off at the wrong exit and getting lost in an unknown area.

Cars carrying two or three people (depending on the signs) can often use car-pool lanes. This is not a members-only scheme: if you fit the criterion, you can use the lane (but make sure you get out of it well before your exit). Anti-social drivers who use the lane without the requisite passengers risk a fine of more than $250.

On surface streets, driving is much the same as in any US city. You can turn right on a red light if your way is clear and the speed limit is 35mph (56kph); though, again, it's often flouted. At four-way crossings, 'courtesy driving' is expected: cars cross in the order that they arrive at the junction. Note that California law requires everyone in a car to wear a seatbelt.

For more on Los Angeles's unique automobile culture, *see chapter* **Car City**. For an overview of LA's freeway system, *see Map 1 at the back of the guide*; for a list of freeway names and numbers, *see page 42* **Sightseeing**.

Car rental

To rent a car in the States – it will almost always be an automatic – you'll need a credit card and a driver's licence. Most companies won't rent to anyone under 25 (or, if they do, will add on a hefty surcharge). There are dozens of car rental companies in LA and it pays to shop around. The national companies, which tend to offer the best deals and the most reliable vehicles, all have free 1-800 numbers; many companies require you to book on these rather than at the local office.

Rates seesaw wildly, depending on demand; it can be a good idea to make a reservation weeks in advance (possible, now that 1-800 numbers are accessible from abroad). You can put a hold on a car without committing yourself (and if they run out of a car in that class, they will upgrade you – a frequent and pleasurable occurrence). As a rule, you will not be allowed to take a rental car into Mexico.

Remember that the price quoted will *not* include sales tax or any form of insurance, but also that you may qualify for a discount: AAA members usually do, and you may be able to wangle a corporate deal if you show your business card.

Insurance will almost double your bill, but it is essential – and you are unlikely to be covered by your domestic policy. You will be offered both liability insurance (for damage you cause to other cars and their occupants) and a collision damage waiver (CDW), both around the $9-a-day mark. We recommend you take both –

Directory

even though it will make the insurance as costly as the rental itself. Unlike other states, the baseline fee gives you no cover at all in California.

Bearing all this in mind, it is probably worth considering fly-drive deals, renting via your home travel agent or getting quotes from a local branch of an international company.

The LAPD suggests you keep the rental lease agreement with you at all times in case your car gets towed or stolen (most people stick it in the glove compartment; bad idea).

Car rental companies

Alamo *1-800 327 9633.*
Avis *1-800 331 1212.*
Budget *1-800 527 0700.*
Dollar *1-800 421 6878.*
Enterprise *1-800 325 8007.*
Hertz *1-800 654 3131.*
National *1-800 328 4567.*
Thrifty *1-800 367 2277.*
Rent-A-Wreck (second-hand cars) *1-800 535 1391.*

Parking

Parking in popular areas can be frustrating and sometimes impossible. If you see numerous spaces in busy areas, beware: parking restrictions vary enormously from area to area and street to street, and the signs detailing them are far from straightforward.

You must park in the same direction that the traffic is going. Don't block driveways or fire hydrants and pay particular attention to kerb markings: if they're red, don't park there or you could get towed. Then go and look at all the signs on your side of the block – they will tell you the local parking laws. Most streets have street-cleaning days when parking is illegal, while after 6pm and at weekends many allow parking for residents'-permit holders only. West Hollywood is probably the most heavily 'permitted' and difficult place to park.

All parking tickets accrued while in a rented vehicle are your responsibility. And don't think the car hire company will never track you down once you're back home. They always do. Even worse, fines double if not paid within 30 days.

If you do get towed, call the nearest police precinct (in the front of the phone book in the City Government listings) to find out which impound lot the car has ended up in – there are ten in the LA area. To reclaim your car, you'll need your rental papers, your passport or international driving licence and a wad of cash to pay for the parking ticket, the cost of towing ($70) and a day's storage (usually $12). You'll also need to know the car's licence plate number.

Fortunately, parking meters and free or cheap car parks are plentiful. Most parking meters take quarters (25¢), dimes (10¢) and nickels (5¢). Many car parks allow two hours' free parking before 6pm. Car parks for major shopping complexes are free or cheaper if you validate your ticket at the checkout (don't feel you have to buy anything to have your ticket validated). Here are some useful car parks:

Beverly Hills

241 N Canon Drive, between Clifton & Dayton Ways **Map 3 C2**; *461 N Bedford Drive, at Little Santa Monica Boulevard* **Map 3 B2**; *440 N Camden Drive, at Little Santa Monica Boulevard* **Map 3 B2**; *438 N Beverly Drive, at Little Santa Monica Boulevard* **Map 3 C2**; *Beverly Center, at La Cienega and Beverly Boulevards* **Map 4 B3**; *Beverly Connection, directly opposite Beverly Center* **Map 4 B3**.

Santa Monica

Public parking structures stand virtually side by side on Second and Fourth Streets, between Broadway & Wilshire Boulevard. **Map 2 A2**

West Hollywood

Sunset Boulevard, between Crescent Heights Boulevard & Laurel Avenue **Map 4 B1**; *8383 Santa Monica Boulevard, at Kings Road* **Map 4 B1**; *8700 block of Melrose Avenue, at Robertson Boulevard* **Map 4 A2**.

Roadside assistance

If you break down or have an accident in a rental car, call the rental company immediately,

and be sure to get the other party's driving licence number, address and insurance details.

Should you lock yourself out of your car, rental companies will sometimes assist you, sometimes not. It might be worth borrowing a slim jim from a garage and trying to do it yourself. Failing that, call a locksmith on 1-800 300 6807.

There are about 4,500 yellow public call boxes, at quarter-mile intervals, on the sides of all the major freeways in LA County, from where you can call emergency roadside service 24 hours a day from either the AAA (*see below*), the California Highway Patrol (CHP) or the Metropolitan Freeway Service Patrol (MFSP). In 1999, 500 more call boxes will be added to regular LA County roads.

If you have car trouble and must pull to the side of a freeway, Caltrans and the police advise that you get to the side of the road or the hard shoulder as soon as possible, all the while signalling appropriately. But most important: don't panic. And never attempt to cross the lanes of freeway traffic.

American Automobile Club Emergency Roadside Service

1-800 222 4357.
There are 4,000 call boxes at the sides of freeways to call for help (as well as the yellow public boxes; *see above*).

Freeway Service Patrol

FSP sends out roving tow trucks during the rush hours (6-10am and 3-7pm Mon-Fri) and offers continuous service in Downtown LA (6am-7pm daily). The FSP will change a flat tyre, jump-start your car, refill your radiator, put a gallon of fuel in your gas tank and tow you to designated 'drop' locations. The service is, mercifully, free.

Driving information

American Automobile Association

Automobile Club of Southern California, 2601 S Figueroa Street, at W Adams Boulevard, Downtown, Los Angeles, CA 90007 (1-213 741 3686).
Open 9am-5pm Mon-Fri.

The 'Triple A' provides excellent maps, guidebooks (with restaurant and accommodation listings) and campground guides – and they won't cost you a penny if you're a member or belong to an affiliated club, such as the British AA. Some hotels offer dicsounts to members.
Website: www.aaa-calif.com

CalTrans Highway Information Network
1-800 427 7623/1-916 445 1534.
Recorded information on road conditions of all major California state highways; the website below gives up-to-the-minute freeway conditions. Or call the Department of Transportation: CalTrans LA (District 7) on 1-213 897 3656.
Website: www.scubed.com/caltrans/la/

Radio stations
KNX (1070 AM) offers up-to-date traffic reports every six minutes (reports are suspended when a sporting event is being broadcast).

KFWB (980 AM) provides reports every ten minutes, 24 hours a day, seven days a week.

Motorbike rental
If you want to cruise the streets on a Harley, try **Eagle Rider Motorcycle Rental** on 1-310 320 3456 (20917 Western Avenue, at Torrance Boulevard, South Bay; open 9am-5pm daily). You have to be over 21 and have a credit card and motorbike licence.

Cycling
You can cycle the bike paths that head down the coast from Santa Monica or mountain bike in Griffith Park and Topanga Canyon, but

otherwise the volume of traffic and distances involved make cycling difficult in LA; except on the boardwalk in Venice, which is infested by beach cruisers. For other bike paths and rentals, *see page 221* **Sport & Fitness**.

Walking
Perversely, certain sections of LA are best covered on foot, notably Downtown, central Hollywood, West Hollywood, Pasadena Old Town and the Santa Monica and Venice beachfronts. Jaywalking – crossing the street anywhere except at a designated pedestrian crossing – can get you a $100 ticket. Seriously.

Directory A-Z

Attitude & attire
Most people you come across in Los Angeles will be perfectly, almost surreally, polite and even chatty (unless they're in their cars, of course, where they suffer from the usual pumped-up motormania). Be polite in return and communication is unlikely to be a problem.

However, it is not how you drive or talk, but how you look that counts – and you definitely don't want to look like a tourist if you can help it – which means no fanny packs (bumbags), sandals with black or white socks and nothing with the word 'California' on it. Angelenos tend to dress with a deceptive, and usually expensive, casualness – for men, an open-necked, button-down shirt (Armani, though), blue jeans (French, of course), tennis shoes (imported from Spain), sunglasses ($500 and up). Women in LA have it a bit better (or worse, depending on your perspective): almost without exception they dress better than the men.

If you want to dress to impress, remember that beige, cream, black, taupe, olive, grey and pale peach are considered the 'power' colours, whereas Hawaiian shirts or any sign of gold or white will peg you as a tourist as quickly as a camera around your neck.

Consulates
For problems with passports and other emergencies, call your consulate office. Only the countries listed below have offices in LA; nationals of other countries should call their consulate in Washington. To find the number, call directory assistance for Washington on 1-202 555 1212.

Australia *1-213 469 4300.*
Canada *1-213 346 2700.*
European Commission *1-800 852 0262.*
France *1-310 235 3200.*
Germany *1-213 930 2703.*
Italy *1-310 820 0622.*
The Netherlands *1-310 268 1598.*
New Zealand *1-310 207 1605.*
Republic of Ireland *in San Francisco; 1-415 392 4214.*
Spain *1-213 938 0158.*

United Kingdom *1-310 477 3322/ 24-hour emergency number 1-213 856 3755.*

Consumer advice
Department of Consumer Affairs
Consumer Information Hotline 1-800 344 9940/deaf callers 1-916 322 1700.
Investigates complaints and gives information/referrals for over 42 state agencies on what actions and rights are available to consumers.

Better Business Bureau
1-714 527 0680.
Good for filing complaints against businesses. Also provides information on reliable businesses in your area.

Disabled
Since 1982, California's strict state building codes have ensured easy and equal disabled access to all city facilities, businesses, parking lots, restaurants, hotels and other public places; conse-quently, newer facilities will be more accommodating than older ones, which, in many cases, comply with the barest requirements of the codes.

To locate areas with handicapped facilities or access, look for the blue-and-white handicapped symbol of a wheelchair.

The MTA has special reduced fares and 'lift' buses with fixed times and schedules. For more public transport information, phone its **Disabled Riders Information** line on 1-800 621 7828.

Dial-A-Ride
1-800 431 7882.
Refers mobility-impaired people and senior citizens to door-to-door transportation services.

Mayor's Office for Handicapped People
1-213 485 6334.
Information, resources and employment referral. Also has an old copy of the out-of-print *Around Town With Ease* booklet: if you ask, they will photocopy relevant sections and send them to you.

Society for the Advancement of Travel for the Handicapped
1-212 447 7284/fax 1-212 725 8253.
Offers advice and referrals for disabled travellers planning trips to all parts of the US.

Electricity

Rather than the standard 220-240V, 50-cycle AC used in Europe, US voltage is 110-120V, 60-cycle AC. Except for dual-voltage shavers with flat-pin plugs, you will need to run any appliances you bring with you via an adaptor, available at airport shops.

Health & medical

It is rumoured that if you don't have medical insurance, some of LA's hospitals – and emergency rooms, in particular – will turn you away. This is, in fact, illegal. ERs are not allowed to refuse you if your injury is an emergency (though they will still do all they can to make you pay up).

Taking out medical cover is nevertheless imperative,

preferably with a large company that will pay upfront rather than reimburse you later. Treatment for a broken finger, for example, might set you back $5,000; a leg, $25,000. A visit to an emergency room to treat an allergic reaction can cost as much as $1,000.

If your medical problem is not an emergency and you do not have health insurance, try the **LA Free Clinic** (*see below* **Dentists**), but don't expect an immediate appointment.

Abortion & contraception

Family Planning Associates Medical Group
12304 Santa Monica Boulevard, between Bundy Drive & Centinela Avenue, West LA (1-310 820 8084). Bus 4, Santa Monica 1, 10, 14/I-405, exit Santa Monica Boulevard west. **Open** 8am-4.30pm Mon-Fri; 8am-2pm Sat.
6000 San Vicente Boulevard, at Fairfax Avenue & Olympic Boulevard, West Hollywood (1-323 937 1390). Bus 27, 28, 217/I-10, exit Fairfax Avenue north. **Open** 8am-4.30pm Mon-Fri; 8am-2pm Sat. **Map 4 B3**

AIDS & HIV

See also below **Helplines** *and page 188* **Gay & Lesbian**.

AIDS Clinic for Women
3860 W Martin Luther King Jr Boulevard, between Marlton Avenue & Buckingham Road, Crenshaw (1-323 295 6571). **Open** 8am-4.30pm Mon-Fri.

AIDS Healthcare Foundation Clinic
W Hollywood Cedars-Sinai Medical Office Towers, 8631 W Third Street, suite 740E, between N La Cienega & N Robertson Boulevards, West Hollywood (1-310 657 9353). **Open** 8.30am-5pm Mon-Fri. **Map 4 A3**
HIV/AIDS medical provider offering care regardless of your ability to pay.

AIDS Project Los Angeles
1313 N Vine Street, at Fountain Avenue, Hollywood (1-323 993 1600/24-hour hotline in English 1-800 922 2437/24-hour multilingual hotline 1-800 922 2438). **Open** 9am-5pm Mon-Fri. **Map 5 B2**

An outreach organisation for people with AIDS/HIV.

Jeffrey Goodman Special Care Clinic
1625 Schrader Boulevard, at Hollywood Boulevard, Hollywood (1-323 993 7500). **Open** 9.30am-8pm Mon-Fri; 9.30am-1.30pm Sat. **Map 5 A1**
Free anonymous AIDS testing.

Southern California HIV/AIDS Hotline
1-800 590 2437.
Information and support, including referrals to reputable test centres.

Dentists

LA Dental Society
1-213 380 7669.
Referrals to approved practices.

Western LA Dental Society
1-310 641 5561.
A phone referral service that provides locations and phone numbers of dentists who keep emergency hours.

LA Free Clinic
8405 Beverly Boulevard, at Orlando Avenue, West Hollywood (1-323 653 1990). Bus 14/I-10, exit La Cienega Boulevard north. **Open** 9am-7.45pm Mon-Thur; 9am-4.45pm Fri. **Map 4 B2**
Call first to book an appointment.

Hospitals

These hospitals all have emergency rooms, open 24 hours daily:

Cedars-Sinai Medical Center
8700 Beverly Boulevard, at George Burns Road, West Hollywood (1-310 855 2000). Bus 14, 16, 27, 83, 40/I-10, exit La Cienega Boulevard north. **Map 4 A3**
Cedars-Sinai is the hospital of the rich and famous and therefore may cost a lot. It is, however, conveniently located for West Hollywood and Beverly Hills.

Century City Hospital
2080 Century Park E, between Constellation & Olympic Boulevards, Century City (1-310 553 6211). Bus 28, 328, 573, Commuter Express 534, Culver CityBus 3/I-405, exit Santa Monica Boulevard east. **Map 3 B3**

Children's Hospital of Los Angeles
4650 W Sunset Boulevard, at Vermont Avenue, Los Feliz (1-213

Emergencies

Police, fire, ambulance
911 (free from payphones).
Open 24 hours daily.

American Red Cross
1-213 739 5200.
Open 24 hours daily.
Disaster information. For advice on
what to do in a earthquake, *see p21*
Geography & Climate.

Child Abuse Hotline
1-800 540 4000 (free).
Open 9am-5pm Mon-Fri.

Coastguard
1-310 215 2112.
Open 24 hours daily.
Search and rescue emergencies.

HIV/AIDS
See opposite Health & medical.

LA County Department of Mental Health
1-800 854 7771.
Open 24 hours daily.
Information and referral for
psychiatric emergencies.

LA Suicide Prevention Hotline
1-213 381 5111.
Open 24 hours daily.

Poison Information Center
1-800 876 4766.
Open 24 hours daily.

Pregnancy Hotline
1-800 743 7348.
Open noon-4pm Tue-Fri.
See opposite Health & medical.

---

*660 2450). Bus 2, 3, 204/US 101,
exit Vermont Avenue north.*
Map 6 A2

St John's Hospital & Health Center
*1328 22nd Street, at Santa Monica
Boulevard, Santa Monica (1-310 829
5511). Bus 4, Santa Monica 1/I-10,
exit 26th Street north.* **Map 2 B/C2**

St Joseph's Medical Center
*501 S Buena Vista Street, at
Alameda Avenue, Burbank (1-818
843 5111). Bus 96, 152/Hwy 134,
exit Buena Vista Street north.*

Helplines

AIDS & HIV

CDC National HIV & AIDS Hotline
1-800 342 2437. **Open** 24 hours
daily.

Alcohol abuse

Alcoholics Anonymous
1-323 936 4343. **Open** 24 hours
daily.

Rape & assault

LA Commission on Assaults Against Women Rape Hotline
*Central LA 1-213 626 3393;
LA County 1-310 392 8381.*
Open 24 hours daily.
If you need another woman to talk to
or to take you to hospital or to court.

East Los Angeles Rape & Battery Hotline
1-800 585 6231. **Open** 24 hours
daily.

YWCA-Greater LA Sexual Assault Crisis Program
1-310 764 1403. **Open** 24 hours
daily.

Major crime

Federal Bureau of Investigation
1-310 477 6565.

US Service – LA Bureau
1-213 894 4830.

Immigration & Customs

Before you even hit the ground,
your flight attendant will give
you two forms to fill out: one for
immigration, one for Customs.
When you land, expect the
Customs/ immigration process
to take about an hour. Customs
officials are a charmless bunch,
so smiling a lot and looking cute
won't get you through any
faster. And if they decide you
might outstay your tourist visa,
they'll ask some fairly personal
questions about why, where and
with whom you're staying.
Don't take offence, just accept
your entry permit and move on.

Current US Customs
regulations allow foreign
visitors to import the following,
duty-free: 200 cigarettes or 50
cigars (not Cuban; over-18s
only) or 2kg of smoking
tobacco; one litre of wine or
spirits (over-21s only); and up

to $100 in gifts ($400 for
returning Americans). You can
take up to $10,000 in cash,
travellers' cheques or endorsed
bank drafts in or out of the
country tax-free, and goods
worth up to $1,000 (you pay a
flat tax rate of ten per cent on
any excess).

For more info, contact the
US Customs Service at LAX
on 1-310 215 2414.

Insurance

Baggage, trip-cancellation and
medical insurance should be
taken care of before you leave
home. The US is renowned for
its superb healthcare facilities;
the catch is that the cost is likely
to put you back in hospital.
Most medical centres require
details of your insurance company and policy number before
you get treatment (unless it's an
emergency; *see opposite* **Health
& medical**).

Left luggage

Los Angeles International
Airport (LAX) has storage lockers, but Union Station doesn't.
If you wish to store something
for more than a week or so, call
Public Storage on 1-800 447
8673 for your nearest location.
The company has storage
facilities all over LA. Minimum
charges are for one month.

Directory

Legal problems

Los Angeles is a sue-happy city and however frivolous or unlikely you may think it, being sued is common. If you bump into someone's car at 15mph, they may try to sue you for thousands of dollars. If in doubt, consult an attorney: there are hundreds listed in the *Yellow Pages*.

If you think you have a claim against someone else, also consult an attorney. Although legal fees are high, most attorneys will work for a percentage of any settlement – usually one-third. If you are arrested and held in custody, call your insurer's emergency number for legal advice. Uninsured Brits can call the UK consulate's 24-hour emergency number (*see page 257*).

Libraries

Central Library

630 W Fifth Street, between Grand Avenue & Flower Street, Downtown (general information 1-213 228 7000/ business 1-213 228 7100). Bus 16, 18, 78, 79, 96, Foothill 492, DASH E/I-110 north, exit Sixth Street east. **Open** 10am-5.30pm Mon, Thur-Sat; noon-8pm Tue, Wed; 1-5pm Sun. **Map 7 B3**
The most comprehensive library in the city, with excellent facilities and a very knowledgeable reference staff.

LA County Law Library

301 W First Street, at Broadway, Downtown (1-213 629 3531). Bus 4, 96, 420, 424/US 101, exit Broadway south. **Open** 8.30am-10pm Mon-Thur; 8.30am-6pm Fri; 9am-5pm Sat.
Map 7 B2
The third largest in the US.

Southwestern University Law Library

3050 Wilshire Boulevard, between Shatto Place & Westmoreland Avenue, Midtown (1-213 738 5771). Bus 20, 21, 22/I-10, exit Vermont Avenue north. **Open** 8am-midnight Mon-Thur; 8am-9pm Fri; 9am-9pm Sat; 10am-9pm Sun.
Map 6 A5
This revitalised art deco structure, which used to be the historic Bullocks Wilshire department store, is a good place to do law research.

Liquor laws

Bars, dance clubs, restaurants, liquor stores and supermarkets that sell liquor can do so between 6am and 2am only. Strip or burlesque clubs are not allowed to serve alcohol at all. Twenty-one is the legal age for the purchase and consumption of alcoholic beverages. Picture ID, whether a state or foreign driver's licence or a passport, is strictly required for all patrons who wish to imbibe.

Lost property

Los Angeles is not the world's most honest city, but if you really think an honest soul may have handed in your beloved lost property, the best place is the local police department (listed at the front of the phone book under 'City Government'). If you've lost something at LAX, first try your airline, then the general lost-property number (1-310 417 0440).

Money

As they say in Los Angeles: 'Cash talks; bullshit walks.'

Currency

The US dollar ($) is divisible into 100 cents (¢). Coin denominations run from the copper penny (1¢, with a relief of Abraham Lincoln); the silver nickel (5¢, Thomas Jefferson); dime (10¢, Franklin Delano Roosevelt); quarter (25¢, George Washington); and the less common half-dollar (50¢, John F Kennedy). Notes ('greenbacks'), all the same size, come in $1 (George Washington); $5 (Abraham Lincoln); $10 (Alexander Hamilton); $20 (Andrew Jackson); $50 (Ulysses S Grant); and $100 (Benjamin Franklin) denominations. Should you find yourself with the Susan B Anthony silver $1 coin or the Thomas Jefferson $2 bill, don't spend them; they are collectors' items reflecting the US resistance to change.

The design of the $100 bill has recently been altered; the old design is still in circulation and is still valid. The new ones still have a picture of Ben Franklin (but now apparently on steroids). Be warned that there are a lot of counterfeit $50 and $100 bills around, and some small shops will not accept them; they also tend not to carry much change for fear of robbery.

Travellers' cheques & bureaux de change

Obtain travellers' cheques – in US dollars and from a well-known company – before your trip. Almost all shops, restaurants and so on will accept them with a passport or other identification, save for the occasional establishment that requires a minimum purchase. If you need to buy travellers' cheques while in Los Angeles, many commercial banks sell them for face value plus one to three per cent.

Most currency exchange can be taken care of at LAX, where both **Lenlyn Limited** (7.30am-11.45pm daily; 1-310 417 0366) and **Traveler's Exchange** (6.30am-11pm daily; 1-310 649 1656) have offices in terminals two and five and in the Tom Bradley International Terminal.

If you need money wired to you, then **American Express MoneyGram** (1-800 926 9400 for locations) or **Western Union** (1-800 325 6000) can receive funds from anywhere in the world, although their high commission (usually around ten per cent) underscores their 'emergency only' status. The centrally located AmEx offices offer this facility.

American Express Travel Services

327 N Beverly Drive, between Brighton & Dayton Ways, Beverly Hills (1-310 274 8277/lost or stolen travellers' cheques 1-800 221 7282).

Bus 4, 20, 27, DASH Beverly Hills/ I-10, exit Robertson Boulevard north.
Open 10am-6pm Mon-Fri, 10am-3pm Sat. **Map 3 C2**
Branch: *8493 W Third Street, at La Cienega Boulevard, West Hollywood (1-310 659 1682).* **Map 4 A/B3**

Associated Foreign Exchange
433 N Beverly Drive, between Brighton Way & Little Santa Monica Boulevard, Beverly Hills (1-310 274 7610). Bus 4, 20, 21, 22, 320/I-10, exit Robertson Boulevard north.
Open 9am-5pm Mon-Fri; 10am-3pm Sat. **Map 3 C2**

Thomas Cook Foreign Exchange Service
452 N Bedford Drive, between Brighton Way & Little Santa Monica Boulevard, Beverly Hills (all branches 1-800 287 7362/lost or stolen travellers' cheques 1-800 223 7373).
Open 9am-5pm Mon-Fri.
Map 3 B2
Branches: *735 S Figueroa Street, between Seventh & Eighth Streets, Downtown* **Map 7 A3**; *8901 Santa Monica Boulevard, at San Vicente Boulevard, West Hollywood* **Map 4 A2**; *401 Wilshire Boulevard, at Fourth Street, Santa Monica* **Map 2 A2**.

ATMs

Automated Teller Machines (ATMs) are as numerous as cars in LA, found in and outside banks, in some of the bigger shopping malls and in stores such as 7-Eleven.

There are many different card networks, including Star and Interlink, but the main ones are **Cirrus** (1-800 424 7787 for locations) and **Plus** (1-800 843 7587). Banks worldwide link into these two systems; if you have the appropriate symbol on your cash card you will be able to get money out using your usual PIN, though you might incur a $1.50-$2 charge.

Most ATMs will also dispense cash advances from **MasterCard** and **Visa** and some will also take **American Express**. There is an interest charge for cash advances on credit or charge cards and sometimes a 'handling' charge, too.

Maximum withdrawal ranges from $200 to $300 a day.

Try to get to an ATM before the sun goes down, and in somebody else's company, as robbing ATM customers at gun-point is a popular sport in LA – though it doesn't happen so very often. Beggars will hang out by them as well, for maximum guilt factor.

Banks

Most major banks can raise cash on a credit card. They also offer usually competitive currency exchange rates, along with international banking services, including cable transfers, foreign drafts on overseas banks and import/export financing.

Bank of America *1-800 388 2265.*
Home Savings of America *1-800 933 3000.*
Great Western *1-800 492 7587.*
Wells Fargo *1-800 869 3557.*
The above all have numerous locations all over the city.
Open 10am-4.30pm Mon-Thur; 9am or 10am-6pm Fri; 9am or 10am-2pm or 3pm Sat.

Credit cards

Don't even think of coming to LA without at least one major credit card. The two accepted just about everywhere in the US are **MasterCard** (1-800 826 2181) and **Visa** (1-800 336 8472). **American Express** (1-800 528 4800) is also a prominent card, although some establishments will not accept them because of the high costs that AmEx charge them.

Other, less common, credit cards are: **Discover** (1-800 347 2683), **Carte Blanche** (1-800 234 6377), **JCB** (1-800 366 4522) and **Diner's Club** (1-800 234 6377), which are more likely to be accepted at higher-end places.

Lost or stolen cards
American Express *1-800 992 3404.*
Diner's Club *1-800 234 6377.*
Discover *1-800 347 2683.*
MasterCard/Visa *1-800 556 5678.*

Although many establishments – such as city, state or government agencies, museums and coffeeshops – open at 8am or 9am, the magic hour is 10am: most places open their doors at this time. Many office-type places close at 5pm, while shops usually stay open until 6pm or later. Many shops and museums will have one or two days during the week when they are open until 8pm or 9pm; and many stay open on Sunday from noon-5pm or later.

Postal services

Post offices are generally open 9am-5pm Mon-Fri, but often have last collections at 6pm. Many are open on Saturdays from 9am-1pm or 2pm. They offer a notoriously slow and peevish service: 'going postal' is now a common term for going nuts, after a series of murderous rampages by postal workers against colleagues.

Out of hours, you can often use stamp-vending machines and scales in post office lobbies. For general postal information and locations, check the front of any *Pacific Bell LA Metropolitan* phone book or dial 1-800 275 8777.

US mailboxes are red, white and blue, with the US Mail's bald eagle logo printed clearly on the front and side. Pull the handle down and put your post (no packages) in the slot. Collection times are listed inside the mailbox slot. Post offices in the central areas of Los Angeles include:

Beverly Hills
325 N Maple Drive, at W Third Street, Beverly Hills.
Open 8.30am-5pm Mon-Fri.
Map 3 C2

Downtown
760 N Main Street, at Cesar E Chavez Avenue, Downtown.
Open 8am-7pm Mon-Fri; 8am-4pm Sat. **Map 7 C1**

Directory

Studying in LA

Just as remarkable as Tinseltown are LA's numerous colleges and universities offering world-class instruction, both public (that is, state-funded) and private. This distinction is rarely noticeable in the quality of instruction, and only in tuition costs if you're a legal resident of California (residents pay considerably lower fees at public schools than non-residents). However, California's enduring fiscal crisis has left public institutions (such as UCLA) short on facility and equipment upgrades and with a high student-to-instructor ratio.

If you want to study in LA, expect to pay $10,000-$25,000 (including tuition and basic living expenses) for a year of full-time study. Financial aid for foreign students – usually in the form of scholarships or 'work-study' (working for the school) – varies among institutions, so investigate the options early with their Financial Aid Officers to learn how to qualify. Scholarships are usually scarce and competition is always fierce.

FILM SCHOOL

Let's face it: there's no better place to study the technical, creative, commercial and critical aspects of the movies than Los Angeles. There's the US's first film school, **USC**'s School of Cinema-TV (1-213 740 2235), whose generous alumni, among them George Lucas, have helped keep the equipment state-of-the-art and the teaching supreme. **UCLA**'s Department of Theater, Film and Television (1-310 825 5761) also has some of the best directing and producing courses in the country

as well as a first-rate critical studies division. The **American Film Institute** (2021 N Western Avenue, LA, CA 90027; 1-323 856 7600; *see p180* **Film**), the **Art Center College of Design** (*see below*) and the burgeoning graduate programme at **Chapman University**'s School of Film and Television (333 N Glassell Avenue, Orange, CA 92866; 1-714 997 6765) are also smart choices for prospective film students.

LA is also well endowed with libraries and research facilities for the student of film. UCLA's **Archive Research and Study Center** (1-310 206 5388) and USC's **Warner Brothers Archives** (1-213 748 7747) can prove important resources for serious film scholars, but a more beautiful facility and holder of many rare, film-related materials is the **Margaret Herrick Library** at the Academy of Motion Picture Arts and Sciences (333 S La Cienega Boulevard, Beverly Hills; 1-310 247 3000). It also has a phone reference service (1-310 247 3020), where operators research the answer to your most vexing movie trivia question. The **Museum of Television & Radio** (465 N Beverly Drive, Beverly Hills; *see p196* **Museums & Galleries**) has a large collection of TV shows and news footage on video that you can view. The **Central Library** (1-213 228 7000) also holds films and recordings in its vast data banks. **Southwestern University** now has its law library in an art deco landmark, the former Bullocks Wilshire department store (for both libraries, *see p260*).

Santa Monica

1248 Fifth Street, at Arizona Avenue, Santa Monica. **Open** 9am-6pm Mon-Fri; 9am-1pm Sat. **Map 2 A2**

West Hollywood

1125 N Fairfax Avenue, at Santa Monica Boulevard, West Hollywood. **Open** 8.30am-5pm daily. **Map 4 B1**

Poste restante

No fixed abode? Have your post sent to: General Delivery, [your name], Los Angeles, CA 90086-9999, USA. You can pick it up at the main Downtown post office: take ID with you.

Private mail services

Mail Boxes Etc

(1-800 789 4623). **Open** 9am-6.30pm Mon-Fri; 10am-5pm Sat. **Credit** AmEx, Disc, MC, V. One of the numerous mail receiving and forwarding services in the city, with 90 locations in LA. It also offers shipping and business services.

Public toilets/ restrooms

There is a dearth of public toilets in LA. Big shopping malls have them, as do cinema complexes. Santa Monica and

Venice beaches have plenty, though they're functional at best, squalid at worst. You may find yourself having to buy a coffee or a drink simply to use a restroom.

Religion

Whether established religion or cult, if it exists, then it's here. Recruiting can take place in the unlikeliest settings, so beware of eager young things with invitations to 'special guest events': many cults are more interested in your wallet than

Where to study

Art Center College of Design

1700 Lida Street, at Linda Vista Avenue, Pasadena, CA 91103 (1-626 396 2200/admissions 1-626 396 2373/fax 1-626 795 0578).
The private and very stylish Art Center focuses on art and commercial and industrial design. It also has a site in La Tour-de-Peilz, Switzerland.

California Institute of Technology

1201 E California Boulevard, at Hill Avenue, Pasadena, CA 91125 (1-626 395 6811/admissions 1-626 395 6341/fax 1-626 683 3026).
This private college (known as CalTech) counts more than 20 Nobel laureates among its alumni and past and present faculty. This is where the local news turns for information on California earthquake activity.

Loyola Marymount University

7101 W 80th Street, between McConnell Avenue & Fordham Road, LA, CA 90045 (1-310 338 2700/ admissions 1-310 338 2750/fax 1-323 338 2797).
Founded by Jesuits, this private school is primarily an undergraduate institution but also offers advanced degrees in law, education and business administration. Its library holds extensive materials on early LA.

Occidental College

1600 Campus Road, at Alumni Avenue, LA, CA 90041 (1-213 259 2500/admissions 1-213 259 2700/ fax 1-323 341 4875).
You get a glimpse of 'Oxy' on *Beverly Hills 90210* whenever those perky TV teens hang out at 'California University'. It is also a fine liberal arts college, small, (about 1,600 students), private and conservative, with a large number of students from ethnic minorities.

Santa Monica College

1900 Pico Boulevard, between 16th & 20th Streets, Santa Monica, CA 90405 (1-310 450 5150/admissions 1-310 452 9381/fax 1-310 399 1730). **Map 2 B3**
A community college (state-funded and providing students with the first two years of the four-year

bachelor's degree), SMC ranks first among 107 California community colleges in the number of transfers to the esteemed University of California system. Its large enrolment includes over 2,000 students from 99 countries. The college radio station, KCRW, is the leading public radio station in Southern California.

Southern California Institute of Architecture

5454 Beethoven Street, at Jefferson Boulevard, LA, CA 90066 (1-310 574 1123/admissions 1-310 574 3625/fax 1-310 574 3801).
'SCI-Arc' may look like a modest warehouse from the outside, but it has been one of the leading architecture schools in the country since its establishment in 1972. Urban theorist Mike Davis (author of bestseller *City of Quartz*) is among this private school's distinguished faculty. It also has a terrific public lecture series.

University of California – Los Angeles

405 Hilgard Avenue, at Sunset Boulevard, LA, CA 90095 (1-310 825 4321/admissions 1-310 825 3101/ fax 1-310 206 1206).
Located in Westwood, across the street from the mansions of Bel Air, UCLA is a public research university highly regarded for its undergraduate and graduate courses in the liberal and fine arts, as well as the sciences (biology is the most popular major) and professional programmes. It has one of the largest library collections in the world and consistently fields championship sports teams.

University of Southern California

University Park, bounded by Figueroa Street, Exposition & Jefferson Boulevards, Vermont Avenue, LA, CA 90089 (1-213 740 2311/admissions 1-213 740 8899/fax 1-213 740 6364).
USC is the largest private, non-denominational university on the West Coast. Undergrads live amid a huge fraternity 'scene' where sports matter almost more than life itself (OJ went here). USC's best known undergrad fields are in journalism, business, theatre, architecture and communications. Also celebrated is the School of Cinema-TV's film production course.

your spiritual well-being. For more on religion in LA, *see page 14* **Let's get spiritual**.

Places of worship

Aatzei Chaim Synagogue

8018 W Third Street, between Laurel & Edinburgh Avenues, West Hollywood (1-323 852 9104).
Map 4 B3

All Saints Episcopal Church

504 N Camden Drive, at Santa Monica Boulevard, Beverly Hills (1-310 275 0123).
Map 3 B2

Beverly Hills Presbyterian Church

505 N Rodeo Drive, at Santa Monica Boulevard, Beverly Hills (1-310 271 5194).
Map 3 B/C2

Buddhist Universal Association

2007 Wilshire Boulevard, at S Alvarado Street, Westlake (1-310 484 6500).
Map 6 B5

Congregation Beth Israel Synagogue

8056 Beverly Boulevard, at Crescent Heights Boulevard, West Hollywood (1-323 651 4022).
Map 4 B2

First Baptist Church of Hollywood

6682 Selma Avenue, at Las Palmas Avenue, Hollywood (1-323 464 7343).
Map 5 A1

First Southern Baptist Church of Hollywood

1528 N Wilton Place, at Sunset Boulevard, Hollywood (1-323 466 9631).
Map 5 B2

Hope Lutheran Church of Hollywood

6720 Melrose Avenue, at Mansfield Avenue, Hollywood (1-323 938 9135). **Map 5 A3**

Islamic Cultural Centre

434 S Vermont Avenue, between Fourth & Fifth Streets, Midtown (1-213 382 9200).
Map 6 A5

St Mary of the Angels Anglican Church

4510 Finley Avenue, between Hillhurst Avenue and Rodney Drive, Los Feliz (1-323 660 2700).
Map 6 A2

St Monica's Roman Catholic Church

725 California Avenue, at Lincoln Boulevard, Santa Monica (1-310 393 9287). **Map 2 A/B2**

Westwood United Methodist Church

10497 Wilshire Boulevard, at Warner Avenue, Westwood (1-310 474 4511). **Map 3 A3**

Safety

Unlikely as it may sound, the city that invented the terms 'car-jacking' and 'drive-by shooting' is actually a safer place for visitors than, say, Florida. As in any big city, don't fumble with your wallet or a map in public, always plan where you're going, avoid walking alone at night, keep your car doors locked while driving, avoid parking in questionable areas (if in doubt, use valet parking when you can) and always lock your car.

As a pedestrian, walk with brisk confidence and people will most likely stay out of your way. As a motorist, avoid coming off the freeway in unfamiliar areas, never cut anyone off in traffic or yell epithets at other drivers, never drive too slowly or too quickly (65mph/104kph is a good median speed) and always take a map with you. If you can afford it, rent a mobile phone.

A few areas that you should be careful about travelling to or through after dark include: parts of Silver Lake; Hollywood (especially Hollywood Boulevard); Koreatown; Compton; South Central; Inglewood; East LA; Echo Park; Downtown and Venice.

Smoking

California has some of the most stringent anti-smoking laws in the world; as of 1 January 1998, it became the first state in the US to effect a ban on smoking in all enclosed public areas.

This includes not only obvious places like shops, restaurants, cinemas, theatres, libraries, museums and art galleries, but also waiting areas and ticket lines for trains and cruise ships, airports, bus depots, city buses, elevators, public toilets and bathhouses, and also 35,000 bars and casinos across the state. Most hotels also prohibit smoking, except in designated rooms.

There are a few exceptions to this edict: the statute does not apply to casinos on Native American land, establishments that are owner-operated or have no employees, tobacco retailers or (bizarrely) establishments 'that are not enclosed by four walls or a ceiling'.

Those who ignore the ban can be fined up to $100 for a first offence, $200 for a second and $500 for a third. *See also page 16* **Mind if I smoke?**.

Telephones

The local Pacific Bell *Yellow Pages'* Customer Guide is a valuable resource that gives essential emergency numbers, instructions on how to use public phones and information on call rates. Voicemail is inescapable in LA; note that the 'pound' key is marked **#** and the 'star' key *****.

Emergency Dial **911** for police, fire or medical emergency services.
Operator Dial **0**.
International operator Dial **00**.
Directory enquiries: local
For enquiries about numbers within your area code district, dial **411**.
Directory enquiries: national
Dial **1** + **area code** + **555 1212** (if you don't know the area code, dial the operator).
Toll-free numbers These are prefaced by 1-800, 1-888 or 1-877. For help on these numbers, dial **1-800 555 1212**.

AREA CODES

These are being altered as we go to press; phone numbers in this guide all have the new codes. If the number you dial doesn't get you through, try these alternative codes:

For 213, try 323 and vice versa; likewise:
310 – 562
408 – 831
619 – 760
818 – 626

The districts covered by some of the most common codes are (roughly):

213 Downtown
310 Santa Monica, West LA
323 Beverly Hills, Culver City, Hollywood, Inglewood, parts of Pasadena, parts of West Hollywood
562 Long Beach
626 Glendale, Monterey Park, parts of Pasadena
818 parts of San Fernando Valley

Tips on tipping

Bartender 10%-15% (50¢ minimum)
Chambermaid 50¢-$1 per night
Doorman $1-$2 (more for special services)
Cloakroom attendant $1 per item
Valet parking attendant $1-$2
Hairdresser/barber 15%-20%
Porters $1-$4 for unloading, $1 per bag (including supermarket bag packers if they help you to your car)
Taxi driver 15%
Waiter 15% (20% for superb service, or if the place is very fancy and expensive or if you're drunk). Some of the snazzier establishments will include the tip in the final tally anyway.

Long distance codes

Las Vegas **702**
Orange County **714**
Santa Barbara **805**
San Diego **619**
San Francisco **415**

How to dial

Direct dial calls

If you're calling a number with the same area code as the phone you're calling from, dial the (seven-digit) number *without* the area code. If you're calling a diff.rent area code, dial **1** + three-digit **area code** + seven-digit **number**.

International calls

Dial **011** followed by the country code (UK **44**; New Zealand **64**; Australia **61**; Germany **49**; Japan **81** – see the phone book for others). If you need operator assistance with international calls, dial **00**.

Collect calls

Also known as reverse charge calls; dial **0** + **area code** + **number**.

Hotel & public phones

On a hotel phone, you may have to dial a **0** or **9** to get a line before dialling the number (hotels put dialling and billing instructions on the phone). You will also pay a surcharge: ask how much, as often using a phonecard, credit card or payphone will work out cheaper, especially on long-distance/international calls Smaller hotels and motels often will not allow you to call long-distance unless you call collect or use a credit card.

Public payphones are plentiful in LA. Although they vary in appearance, they don't in practice: pick up the receiver, listen for a dialling tone and feed it change. Operator and directory calls are free. Local calls cost 35¢, with the cost increasing with the distance (a recorded voice will tell you to feed in more quarters). Make sure you have plenty of change as payphones only take nickels, dimes and quarters.

It's nigh on impossible to make international calls this way, but you can usually use your **MasterCard** with **AT&T**

Tourist information

Los Angeles Convention & Visitors Bureau

685 S Figueroa Street, between Seventh Street & Wilshire Boulevard, Downtown (1-213 689 8822). Metro Seventh Street/Metro Center/bus 26, 60, 427, 434, 460, Commuter Express 437, 448, Foothill Transit 495, DASH A/I-110, exit Ninth Street east. **Open** 8am-5pm Mon-Fri; 8.30am-5pm Sat. **Map 7 A3**
Branch: *The Janes House, 6541 Hollywood Boulevard, at Hudson Avenue, Hollywood (1-213 624 7300). Bus 1, 180, 210, 212/ US 101, exit Hollywood Boulevard west.* **Open** 9am-5pm Mon-Sat. **Map 5 A1**
The Janes House, built in 1903, is the last survivor of the Victorian houses that once lined Hollywood Boulevard.

Los Angeles Area Chamber of Commerce

350 S Bixel Street, LA, CA 90017 (1-213 580 7500/fax 1-213 580 7511). **Open** 8.30am-5pm Mon-Fri. **Map 7 A2**
Similar to the Visitors Bureau, providing a wide range of information and referral services.

(1-800 225 5288) or **MCI** (1-800 950 5555) or buy pre-paid **phonecards** ($4-$50) from large stores like Thrifty and Payless Drug, which give you a fixed amount of time anywhere in the US – or less time internationally.

Message service

American Answering Service

(1-310 478 0604). **Open** 24 hours daily. **Credit** MC, V.
Live and voicemail answering service, with private, local and 1-800 numbers.

Mobile phones

Shared Technology Cellular

(1-800 933 3836). **Open** 24 hours daily. **Credit** AmEx, DC, Disc, MC, V.
Daily, weekly and monthly cellular phone rentals available. The phones themselves are free; you pay for the air time ($1.95 per metered minute, including domestic long distance calls and calls outside your own area code).

Time & dates

California operates on **Pacific Standard Time**, which is eight hours behind Greenwich Mean Time (London), three hours behind Eastern Standard Time (New York), one hour behind Mountain Time (Denver), and two hours behind Central Time (Chicago).

Clocks go forward by an hour on the last Sunday in April, and back again on the last Sunday in October. Many outdoor establishments, such as beaches, gardens, driving tours and museums, change their hours accordingly.

In the US, dates are written in the order of month, day, year; therefore 2.5.99 is the fifth of February 1999, not the second of May.

Visas

Under the Visa Waiver Scheme, citizens of Japan, the UK and all other West European countries (except Ireland, Portugal, Greece and the Vatican City) do not need a visa for stays of less than 90 days for business or pleasure, as long as they have a passport that is valid for the full 90-day period and a return or onward journey ticket (an open standby ticket is acceptable). Some restrictions apply: if you have previously been turned down for a visa, for example.

For British citizens, the US embassy in London provides a reasonably comprehensive (though expensive) recorded message for all general visa enquiries (0898 200290).

Canadians and Mexicans do not need visas, but they may be

Directory

LA's best websites

@LA
www.at-la.com

Boulevards Guide
www.losangeles.com

LA Source
http://members.tripod.com/~rshurtz/la.html

Begin your surf-ploration with these vast compendia of links, which will connect you to a bewildering variety of LA-related sites. Useful stuff includes arts and entertainment listings and reviews, weather forecasts, surf conditions, maps, route-finding services, public transport information, sports listings, accommodation and restaurant listings and reviews, job vacancies, local government and residents' associations.

If you've got a few hours to kill, try the live(ish) relays from video cameras dotted around LA, photo galleries, virtual tours, lonely hearts, actors' castings, an independent filmmakers' organisation, science and technology sites, lawyer jokes, blonde jokes and pictures of Southern California from space. @LA wins the oddity prize with its exhaustive links to police 'Most Wanted' websites, complete with mugshots of fugitive murderers and armed robbers next to cute cartoons of felons behind bars.

Digital City Los Angeles
http://losangeles.digitalcity.com

Log on to the 'Citywise' section, where 'Best of LA' contains Angelenos' own choices for their favourite bar, burrito, snogging place, frozen yogurt and much much more. Irate quote from the driving shortcuts bulletin board: 'People need to quit experimenting with cigars while driving.'

Monk
www.monk.com

This underground 'zine specialises in ground-up travel guides to the streets of America's cities. Log on for their long, hilarious essays on driving through LA.

Newspapers
www.latimes.com
www.laweekly.com
www.newtimesla.com

The sites of the *LA Times*, the *LA Weekly* and the weekly *New Times Los Angeles* (*see also chapter* **Media**).

California: Culture's Edge
www.californiasedge.com

The LA Convention & Visitors Bureau's contribution to rainbow culture. It suggests itineraries for those interested in the culture, history (and, where appropriate, cuisine) of different ethnic groups, gay and lesbian communities and science. *See also p35* **The multicultural tourist**.

Surflink
www.surflink.com

Info on the day's surfing conditions, with online video images.

Wild Southern California
www.csulb.edu/~persepha/wildLA.html

As in 'wildlife'. An enthusiast's site about LA's natural environment, with photos, links and all your earth-science questions answered.

Hollywood gossip sites
www.aint-it-cool-news.com
www.mrcranky.com
www.ZENtertainment

Three of the hottest websites for insiders' Hollywood scuttlebutt and pre-reviews of upcoming movies. These cyber-scourges are web nerds tapping into a network of Hollywood moles who report what the major studios might not want you to hear.

Cybersleaze
www.cybersleaze.com

Hollywood wouldn't be Hollywood without juicy gossip: this is as shameless as they come. Daily(ish) reports.

The Grim Society
http://felix.scvnet.com:80/~highlite/grim

'Dedicated to the least savory aspects' of local history and lore.

Los Angeles: Past, Present & Future
www.usc.edu/isd/archives/la

A database of information on LA history and culture, plus links to other relevant sites.

City of Los Angeles
www.ci.la.ca.us

The City of Los Angeles government home page: everything from 'AIDS Walk Los Angeles' to 'Economic & Demographic Info' via the intriguing 'Hazardous Brush Clearance'.

Also recommended

Find news and works from LA's emerging artists at **www.knowtribe.com**, while *City Walls LA: A Graffiti Guide to LA* is at **www.graffiti.org**. An East LA street murals guide is at **http://latino.sscnet.ucla.edu/murals/index1.html** and 'adult' entertainment listings are at **http://paranoia.com/faq/los angeles.text**. Find famous overdose sites, musical anecdotes and other rock 'n' roll Babylonia at **http://net101.com/rockn**.

---

asked for proof of their citizenship. All other travellers, including those from Australia and New Zealand, must have a visa; contact your nearest US embassy or consulate for more information, and allow plenty of time for your application.

Weather

See chapter **Geography & Climate**.

Working

Officially, in order to work in the United States, you need to be a US citizen or hold a Green Card or work visa. Labour laws are strict and any company hiring illegal aliens faces substantial fines. Many occupations are indeed restrictive but restaurants and the garment industry, for example, still employ undocumented workers: garment manufacturing would collapse without them. There are also many self-employed people in creative fields getting by ingeniously and illegally.

If you wish to consult an immigration attorney, however, Ralph Ehrenpreis (1801 Century Park E, suite 450, Century City, LA 90067; 1-310 553 6600; **Map 3 B3**) is a specialist.

Further Reading

Non-fiction

Richard Alleman *The Movielover's Guide to Hollywood.* Famous sites and tales.
Alternative Press of America *Inside the LA Riots.* Compendium of opinions on the 1992 riots.
Kenneth Anger *Hollywood Babylon.* The dark side of the Tinseltown myth.
Reyner Banham *Los Angeles: The Architecture of Four Ecologies.* Architectural history and paean to life in the fast lanes.
Leon Bing *Do or Die.* History of LA gang culture.
Lou Cannon *Official Negligence.* A *Washington Post* journalist's attempt at a definitive analysis of the causes of the LA riots.
Al Clark *Raymond Chandler in Hollywood.* Biography of the author who made 'noir' and 'LA' synonymous.
Carolyn Cole & Kathy Kobayashi *Shades of LA: Pictures from Ethnic Family Albums.* Beautifully rendered scrapbook of the ethnic family in LA.
John & LaRess Caughey (editors) *Los Angeles: Biography of a City.* Anthology of essays on the city.
Mike Davis *City of Quartz.* Exhilarating Marxist critique of LA's city 'planning'. *Ecology of Fear.* More apocalyptic LA-bashing by Davis, this time focusing on LA's precarious ecology. Entertaining paranoia.
David Gebhard & Robert Winter *Los Angeles – An Architectural Guide.* Walking tour through some well-known (and not so well-known) architectural landmarks.
William A Gordon (editor) *The Ultimate Hollywood Tour Guide.* A walking/driving tour of Hollywood past.
Steve Harvey *The Best of Only in LA.* Collection of absurdities from popular *LA Times* columnist.
Barney Hoskyns *Waiting for the Sun: Strange Days, Weird Scenes, and the Sound of LA.* The music scene in LA from the 1960s to now.
Norman Klein *The History of Forgetting.* Part factual, part fictional analysis of LA's myth creation by eccentric cultural critic.
Anthony R Lovett & Matt Maranian *LA Bizarro.* Hilarious, off-the-wall guide to 'the obscure, the absurd and the perverse in LA'.
Charles Moore, Peter Becker & Regina Campbell *The City Observed: Los Angeles, A Guide to its Architecture & Landscapes.* Geographical and architectural study.
Carey McWilliams *Southern California: An Island on the Land.* A history of LA's sinfulness and its

scandals – yeah! *North From Mexico: The Spanish-Speaking People of Los Angeles.* Pioneering celebration of the Mexican heritage in the Southwest (written in 1948).
Leonard Michaels, David Reid, Raquel Scher (editors) *West of the West.* Superb collection of essays on LA and California by Joan Didion, Rudyard Kipling, Amy Tan, MFK Fisher, Jack Kerouac, Aldous Huxley, Octavio Paz et al.
Marry Ovnick *LA: At the End of the Rainbow.* Analysis of LA's social history through its houses.
Dian Phillips *Los Angeles: A Guide to Contemporary Architecture.* Compact, useful guide in Ellipsis's popular series.
David Reid (editor) *Sex, Death & God in LA.* Wonderful, navel-gazing essays from writers such as Eve Babitz, Ruben Martinez, Mike Davis and David Thomson.
Brian Roberts & Richard Schwadel *LA Shortcuts: A Guidebook for Those Who Hate to Wait.* Exactly what it sounds like.
Luis J Rodriguez *Always Running.* Autobiography of a Latino gang member.
Richard Romo *East Los Angeles.* A fascinating, scholarly history of the Barrio from the turn of the century to the Depression.
Sanyika Shakur *Monster: Autobiography of an LA Gang Member.* A look inside the LA gangs by one who lived to tell the tale.
Tim Street-Porter *The Los Angeles House.* Astute, fascinating history of LA residential architecture.
Stuart Swezey (editor) *Amok Journal: A Compendium of Psycho-Psychological Investigations.* From LA's Amok bookstore comes an anthology of the macabre and grotesque. Not for the squeamish.
Paul Theroux *Translating LA.* Around the neighbourhoods with the great traveller.
Jeffery Toobin *The Run of His Life: The People v OJ Simpson.* Solid overview of the Trial of the Century.
Alexander Vertikoff & Robin Winter *Hidden LA.* Discover LA's lesser-known landmarks, from the International Banana Museum to the Tower of Wooden Pallets.
Roger Waldinger & Mehdi Bozorgmehr (editors) *Ethnic Los Angeles.* Academic essays on LA's ethnic geography: interesting for social and political scientists.
Michael Webb *Architecture and Design LA.* Slim but comprehensive guide to the city's architectural highlights.
Zagat Survey. Useful annual restaurant guide.

Fiction

T Coraghessan Boyle *The Tortilla Curtain.* Post-Proposition-187 drama about prejudice, immigration and cultural barriers.
Charles Bukowski *Hollywood.* The legendarily drunk poet's musings on making a movie in Tinseltown.
James M Cain *Double Indemnity, Mildred Pierce.* Classic '30s/'40s noir.
Raymond Chandler *The Big Sleep, The Long Goodbye.* Philip Marlowe in *the* classic hard-boiled detective novels.
Bret Easton Ellis *Less Than Zero.* 1980s coke-spoon-chic novel about being young and fast on both coasts.
James Ellroy *The Black Dahlia, The Big Nowhere, LA Confidential, White Jazz.* Ellroy's LA Quartet is a masterpiece of contemporary noir, while the black and utterly compelling *My Dark Places* recounts his search for his mother's killer.
John Fante *Ask the Dust.* Depression-era Los Angeles as seen by an Italian emigré.
David Fine (editor) *Los Angeles in Fiction.* Anthology: includes Walter Mosely, Norman Mailer, Hysaye Yamamoto, Thomas Pynchon, James M Cain and Oscar Zeta Acosta.
F Scott Fitzgerald *The Pat Hobby Stories.* Short stories about living and working in Hollywood from a Great American Writer who died there.
Dennis Hensley *Misadventures in the 213.* A laugh-out-loud romp through gay Hollywood.
Elmore Leonard *Get Shorty.* Miami loan shark turns movie producer in gutsy thriller.
John Miller (editor) *Los Angeles Stories.* Fiction and essays by Henry Miller, F Scott Fitzgerald, Raymond Chandler, et al.
Walter Mosely *The Easy Rawlins Mystery Series.* The heir apparent to Philip Marlowe, Mosely's Easy Rawlins is an African-American PI in post-war LA.
Budd Schulberg *What Makes Sammy Run?* Furious attack on the studio system by one of its employees.
University of California Press *California Fiction Series.* Reissues of novels that explore the culture and history of California include *Fat City* by Leonard Gardner, *Golden Days* by Carolyn See and *Continental Drift* by James Houston.
Bruce Wagner *I'm Losing You.* Biting Hollywood satire.
Nathaniel West *The Day of the Locust.* Classic, apocalyptic raspberry blown at the movie industry.
Evelyn Waugh *The Loved One.* Hilarious and accurate satire on the American way of death.

Index

Advertisers' Index

Please refer to the relevant sections for addresses/telephone numbers

Section sponsored by
AT&T

Maps

California has over
5000 ways to
get in touch
with yourself,

and **one way**
to get in touch with the world.

1 800 225-5288

Want to visit home while you're visiting here?
I 800 CALL ATT® connects you fast and clear within
the U.S. or to anywhere in the world. You can use
your AT&T Calling Card or any of these credit cards.
And send out some good vibes.

It's all within your reach.

Metro Rail

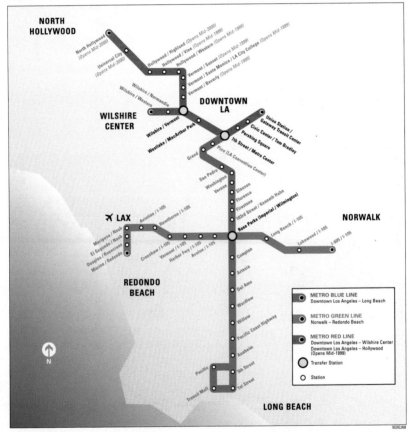

NORTH HOLLYWOOD

North Hollywood (Opens Mid-2000)

Universal City (Opens Mid-2000)

Hollywood / Highland (Opens Mid-2000)
Hollywood / Vine (Opens Mid-1999)
Hollywood / Western (Opens Mid-1999)

Vermont / Sunset (Opens Mid-1999)
Vermont / Santa Monica / LA City College (Opens Mid-1999)
Vermont / Beverly (Opens Mid-1999)

Wilshire / Normandie
Wilshire / Western

WILSHIRE CENTER

Wilshire / Vermont

Westlake / MacArthur Park

DOWNTOWN LA

Union Station / Gateway Transit Center
Civic Center / Tom Bradley
Pershing Square
7th Street / Metro Center

Grand
Pico (LA Convention Center)

San Pedro
Washington
Vernon
Slauson
Florence
Firestone
103rd Street / Kenneth Hahn

✈ **LAX**

Aviation / I-105
Hawthorne / I-105

Rosa Parks (Imperial / Wilmington)

Long Beach / I-105

Lakewood / I-105

I-605 / I-105

NORWALK

Mariposa / Nash
El Segundo / Nash
Douglas / Rosecrans
Marine / Redondo

Crenshaw / I-105
Vermont / I-105
Harbor Fwy / I-105
Avalon / I-105

Compton

REDONDO BEACH

Artesia

Del Amo

Wardlow

Willow

Pacific Coast Highway

Anaheim

Pacific

5th Street

Transit Mall

1st Street

LONG BEACH

↑ N

METRO BLUE LINE
Downtown Los Angeles – Long Beach

METRO GREEN LINE
Norwalk – Redondo Beach

METRO RED LINE
Downtown Los Angeles – Wilshire Center
Downtown Los Angeles – Hollywood
(Opens Mid-1999)

◯ Transfer Station

○ Station

9028ZJMB

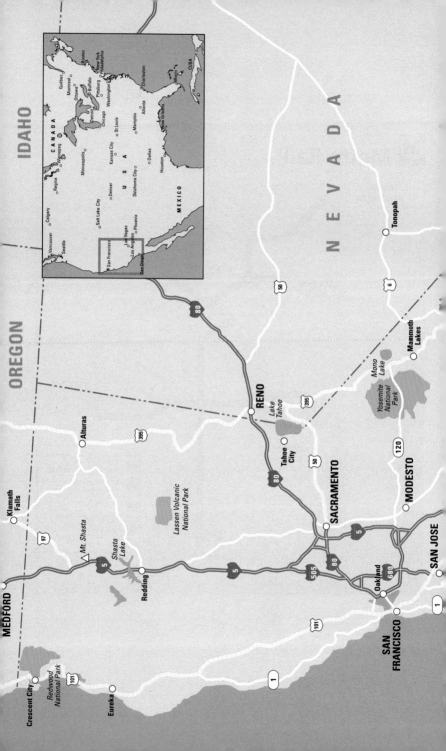

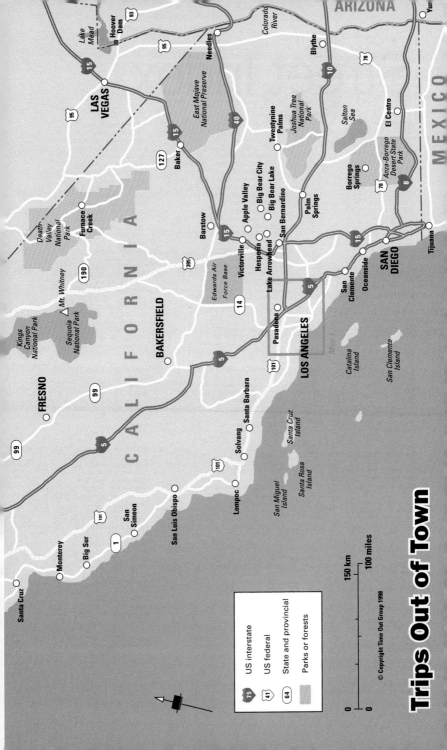

Trips Out of Town

75	US interstate
41	US federal
64	State and provincial
	Parks or forests

© Copyright Time Out Group 1998

150 km

100 miles

Street Index